ANNALS

OF

POLITICS AND CULTURE

(1492–1899)

BY

G. P. GOOCH, M.A.

WITH AN INTRODUCTORY NOTE BY LORD ACTON

BURT FRANKLIN
NEW YORK

Published by LENOX HILL Pub. & Dist. Co. (Burt Franklin)
235 East 44th St., New York, N.Y. 10017
Originally Published: 1905
Reprinted: 1971
Printed in the U.S.A.

S.B.N.: 8337-13809
Library of Congress Card Catalog No.: 79-170959
Burt Franklin: Research and Source Works Series 805
Selected Essays in History, Economics & Social Science 291

PREFACE.

THE present work was undertaken at the suggestion of Lord Acton, in the belief that it might be useful, not only for students but for the general reader, to possess a concise summary of modern times, embracing the life of mankind in its entire range of thought and action. No presentation of history can be adequate which neglects the growth of the religious consciousness, of literature, of the moral and physical sciences, of art, of scholarship, of social life. Numerous handbooks deal with politics alone, and a few with what the Germans call 'Kultur-Geschichte'; but no systematic attempt has hitherto been made either in English or in other languages to combine them. The plan of the book which, not less than the idea, represents a new departure, may be briefly explained. The left-hand page deals with Politics, the right-hand page with what I have termed, for the sake of brevity, Culture. The Politics and Culture of each year are, as nearly as possible, level, in order that the reader may see at a glance what was taking place in the chief departments of thought and action at any given moment. It will also be noticed that each paragraph is numbered. By this means the student is enabled to trace through the centuries the growth of a country, a literature, a science, or an art. If, for instance, we wish to discover the main outlines of the history of Poland, or Italian Literature, or Geology, or the Jesuits, we turn to the index and find under these names the paragraph numbers of the entries relating to them. In this way what may be called a system of double entry is obtained: in the first place, we find the context of an event, and, secondly, we are enabled to discover in what relation the special link that we are holding stands to the rest of the chain.

It need scarcely be said that such a survey aims only at the inclusion of what are commonly regarded as the most notable events. Every handbook is written from some standpoint, its plan being governed by the desire to supply the needs of those by whom it will probably be used. In the present instance more space is devoted to England than to France; to West than to East Europe; to North America than to South America; to India than to China; to South Africa than to Morocco.

A work covering such a large field would properly require a committee of specialists; and the present writer would send out his book with far greater hesitation were it not for the ready response with which his requests for the revision of certain parts of the work have been met. To Lord Acton is due, as I have already said, both the idea and the form of the work; and he has also found time to read the greater part of the proofs and to write an Introductory Note. To him belongs the greater part of whatever value the book may be held to possess. Mr Archbold, one of the sub-editors of the *Dictionary of National Biography,* and author of *The Dissolution of the Somersetshire Monasteries,* has kindly revised the greater number of the pages relating to the 16th century. The paragraphs dealing with Philology and Scholarship have been revised by Professor Sir Richard Jebb, M.P.; Italian, Spanish, and Portuguese literature by Dr Garnett; Dutch, Danish, and Scandinavian literature by Mr Edmund Gosse; Education by Mr J. B. Mullinger, author of the *History of the University of Cambridge*; Physics and Astronomy by Mr Arthur Berry, Fellow of King's College, Cambridge, and author of *A History of Astronomy*; Mathematics by Mr Rouse Ball, author of numerous works on the history of Mathematics, and by Mr Sedgwick, Senior Wrangler in 1894; the Biological Sciences by Mr W. M. Fletcher, Fellow of Trinity College, Cambridge; Chemistry by Mr J. E. Purvis, assistant to Professor Liveing in the University of Cambridge; Geology by Mr Thomas, assistant to Professor Sollas in the University of Oxford; the Painting of the 16th century by Mr Roger Fry, author of a Study of *Giovanni Bellini*; Law by Mr Reddaway, Fellow of King's College, Cambridge, author of *The Monroe Doctrine*; Music by Mr H. W. Richards, Mus.Bac. To all of these, and to other friends, I am indebted for valuable suggestions and corrections; but the responsibility for the errors, which are probably only too numerous, is mine alone. I shall be sincerely grateful to all those who are good enough to inform me of any mistakes or omissions which they may happen to detect.

I have added a selected list of guides to the various subjects dealt with in the book. Numberless Bibliographies exist; but some are useless for the general reader by their very completeness, some again are too elementary to be of value to any but beginners, while others are rendered worthless for advanced students by omitting works written in foreign languages. The present attempt includes only the most important and reliable guides in English, French, German, Italian and Spanish. References to less familiar languages would, I believe, be of little use. The Bibliography has been rendered less imperfect by the kindness of Dr Ward, Master of Peterhouse, whose profound acquaintance with foreign scholarship requires no testimony.

Mrs Marian Marshall has been good enough to assist in preparing the Index for the press.

G. P. G.

January, 1901.

In the present reprint a few mistakes have been corrected, but no complete revision of the book has been attempted.

G. P. G.

South Villa,
Campden Hill Road, W.
October, 1905.

INTRODUCTORY NOTE.

WHOEVER desires to understand modern times, the prize of all History, and to trace the causes that made the present world, knows the need of a plain guide to facts and books, as a deliverance from abridgments, and an aid to fuller information. The present volume has been written by a man of rare ability and attainment, surrounded and supported by auxiliary experts.

Mr Gooch gives first of all the external course of public events which are the essential basis of History. But a man ignorant of the *Advancement of Learning*, the *Principia*, or the *Analogy*, would possess little of that which makes such studies interesting and valuable for the formation of the mind; and many of our most instructive historians, Whewell, Max Müller, Lightfoot, Rashdall, Leslie Stephen, are not concerned, directly, with politics.

It would be an arbitrary and unscientific definition which should exclude them and the topics on which they write from their proper position; for History embraces ideas as much as events, and derives its best virtue from regions beyond the sphere of State.

No previous writer has grasped this fundamental truth with deeper conviction and understanding than Mr Gooch. Viewing Modern History as a whole, he does justice to its several elements, to thought as well as action, to the mass of influences which constitute opinion and govern the life of nations and the progress of civilization.

ACTON.

January, 1901.

CHRONOLOGICAL TABLES.

POLITICS

1. **England.** Perkin Warbeck of Tournai, acclaimed Duke of York by Desmond and Kildare 1491, is invited to the Court of France. [1492

Henry VII. undertakes an expedition to France (for which money is raised by Benevolences) to punish Charles VIII. for his marriage with Anne of Brittany and the union of the last great independent fief with the French crown. On commencing the siege of Boulogne, however, he is bought off, and returns after signing the Peace of Étaples, by which Warbeck is expelled from France.

2. **Spain.** The 11 years' war caused by the refusal of tribute by the Moors ends with the capture of Granada, chiefly owing to the divisions among the Moorish chiefs. The termination of the struggle of 800 years is celebrated throughout Christendom. The Moors are allowed to retain their religion; but large numbers cross to the African coast and take to piracy.

3. **Italy.** The political balance established by Lorenzo de Medici is ended by his death. Exasperated by the misrule of Ferdinand, King of Naples, a number of nobles appeal to France to interpose.

Roderick Borgia becomes Pope Alexander VI.

---

4. **England.** On leaving France, Warbeck goes to Flanders, where Margaret, Duchess of Burgundy, receives him as her nephew. Henry breaks off commercial relations, thereby alienating English merchants, and the Yorkists regain hope from the King's unpopularity. [1493

5. **France.** Charles makes peace with Spain by the Treaty of Barcelona, restoring Roussillon and Cerdagne, and, by the Treaty of Senlis, with Maximilian, the new Emperor.

6. **Spain.** Being invited to confirm the claim of Spain to Columbus' discoveries, the Pope issues a Bull, granting to Spain everything not possessed by a Christian prince 100 leagues west of the Azores, and the discoveries to the east of that line to Portugal. On the protest of the latter, the line is moved 270 leagues further west.

CULTURE

1. **Spanish Ch.** Three months after the fall of Granada, the Jews, at the instance of Torquemada, are offered the alternatives of conversion or exile, and about 150,000 leave the country for different parts of Europe and the Ottoman Empire. [1492

2. **Spanish Lit.** Lebrija, the father of Spanish Humanism and the tutor of Isabella, publishes his Arte de la Lingua Castellana and his Spanish-Latin Dictionary ; Encina writes his first Eclogues ; and Peter Martyr of Anghiera, an Italian pupil of Pomponius Laetus, receives a post at Court, whence he maintains a correspondence with the leaders of politics and letters for 30 years.

3. **Geography.** After various attempts of the Portuguese to reach India by the West, Columbus, a native of Genoa, influenced by his voyages with Prince Henry's captains, by his correspondence with Toscanelli of Florence and by his friendship with Martin Behaim, the Nuremberg cartographer, leaves Spain with three vessels, under the patronage of Ferdinand and Isabella, to find a western route to India and Japan, and discovers the Bahamas, Cuba and Hayti (Oct.). Thinking he has reached India, he names the islands the West Indies.

---

4. **Eng. Lit.** Wynkyn de Worde of Lorraine, an apprentice of Caxton and his successor at the printing-office at Westminster, enters on a course of rapid publication. In the next seven years, 100 works issue from his press, some merely reprints of Caxton. At the same moment appears the first work of Pynson, a Norman, the successor to the business of Machlinia and Lettou, a printer less prolific but more scholarly than Wynkyn de Worde. [1493

---

7. **Italy.** Lodovico Sforza, desiring to supplant his nephew in the duchy of Milan, and fearing intervention from Naples and Florence, invites Charles of France to assert his right to Naples.

8. **America.** Columbus returns to found the Spanish Empire, bringing 17 vessels and 1,500 persons. He explores the Lesser Antilles, Jamaica and the southern coast of Cuba; founds Isabella and San Domingo in Hayti, and remains Governor till 1500.

---

9. **England.** Poynings becomes Deputy for Ireland, and, on account of the reception of the Pretenders, announces that the [1494
Irish Parliament may meet only when sanctioned by the King, that English laws are binding on Ireland, and that the Acts of the Irish Parliament must be revised by the King and Privy Council. By these Acts, known collectively as Poynings' Law, Ireland becomes for the first time directly subject to England.

10. **Italy.** The death of Ferdinand of Naples, of an illegitimate branch of the house of Aragon (Jan.), determines Charles VIII. to advance his claims derived from the house of Anjou, despite the Pope's recognition of Alfonso II., the son of the late King. He crosses the Alps (Sep.), recognises Sforza as Duke of Milan, and advances on Florence, where the republican party, owing to the weakness of Piero de Medici and the influence of Savonarola, regains strength and expels its rulers. At this moment, Pisa throws off the Florentine yoke. After an agreement by which the King receives a large sum of money and is recognised as the protector of the liberties of Florence, Charles marches towards Rome. The Pope, finding resistance impossible, dismisses the Neapolitan troops and opens the gates (Dec.).

11. **Spain.** Ferdinand and Isabella retain the vacant Mastership of the Military Order of Alcantara (as they had done in a similar case in 1487 and do again in 1499), thereby greatly contributing to the power, wealth and prestige of the crown.

---

12. **England.** Stanley is executed for complicity with Warbeck, despite the aid he had rendered to Henry at Bosworth. Warbeck [1495
shortly after is repulsed in a descent on Kent, is rebuffed in Ireland and passes on to Scotland, where James IV. recognises his claim. In face of this danger, Henry causes a statute to be enacted by which no subject obeying the *de facto* King can at any subsequent time be reached by a charge of Treason.

Judges are empowered to initiate proceedings, on the information of any individual, and to award punishment. The statute is used to exact fines, and Empson and Dudley are made judges in order to apply it.

13. **Germany.** The Estates at the Diet of Worms, taking advantage of Maximilian's necessities, attempt a reorganisation of the Empire by abolishing the right of private war, creating an Imperial Chamber, or

5. **Eng. Ch.** The Pope grants bulls for the suppression of two monasteries, in each of which there are only three monks. [1494

6. **Scotch Ch.** Thirty 'Wycliffites' are arrested for extreme anti-hierarchical teachings, but released with a warning, the only persecution between 1433 and 1528.

7. **German Ch.** Brandt's Narrenschiff (Ship of Fools), one of the earliest monuments of modern German prose, enjoys a European circulation (Latin trans. 1497), owing to its satire and didactic tone. The work is discussed in the sermons of Geiler of Kaisersberg, his fellow Alsatian, and contributes to the revival of popular preaching.

8. **Italian Ch.** Savonarola's influence in Florence, steadily growing since his Lent sermons in the Cathedral, 1491, and the death of Lorenzo, now reaches its highest point. Prior of San Marco since 1491, Vicar-General of the Dominicans of Tuscany since 1493, and, since the arrival of Charles VIII., director of the policy of the city and founder of its new Constitution, Savonarola now carries out his schemes for moral reform. His influence is maintained by his sermons, by his claim to receive direct communications from God (some of which he publishes in his Compendium Revelationum), by his attack on the Paganism of the Renaissance in his Triumphus Crucis, etc., and by his commentaries.

9. **Philosophy.** With the expulsion of the Medici from Florence, the Platonic Academy is for a time broken up, and Averroistic Aristotelianism again becomes dominant in Italy, through the activity of the Paduan school, Pomponazzi, Nifo and Achillini. The Neapolitan Academy, founded 1471, becomes the most influential of Renaissance circles, in part owing to the influence of Pontano.

10. **Philology.** An edition of Musaeus appears, the first work issued from the Venetian press of Aldus, who follows it with editions of Aristotle and Aristophanes, in which he receives aid from Marcus Musurus and other Cretans.

11. **Education.** Aberdeen University is founded.

12. **Deaths.** Pico, Politian.

---

13. **Spanish Ch.** Ximenes (chosen as her confessor by Isabella, 1492, and Provincial of the Franciscans, 1494), becomes Archbishop of Toledo and Chancellor of Castile, and obtains a unique position in Church and State. [1495

14. **Portuguese Ch.** The Jews are expelled from Portugal by the King, in order to induce the Spanish sovereigns to give him their eldest daughter.

15. **Philosophy.** Reuchlin's de Verbo Mirifico introduces the work of his friend Pico into Germany. The ideas are expanded in his Ars Cabbalistica, and inspire Agrippa's Occult Philosophy, 1510.

Court of Appeal at a fixed place, of which the President alone is to be chosen by the Emperor, and by the imposition of the Common Penny, collected by the Diet.

14. **Italy.** In return for trifling concessions, the Pope receives the obedience of France, and Charles withdraws, taking with him Caesar Borgia, who escapes. Alfonso II. abdicates in favour of his son Ferdinand, who is, however, deserted, and flies, Charles entering Naples unopposed. Maximilian, Ferdinand, the Pope, Sforza, and Venice form a Holy League (March) for the expulsion of the French, Maximilian being alarmed at French preponderance in Europe, Ferdinand fearing for Sicily, Sforza disquieted by the claim to Milan of the Duke of Orleans, derived through the Visconti. After three months in Naples, Charles marches northward (May), defeats the Venetian troops at Fornovo (July), and leaves Italy (Nov.), the Duke of Orleans remaining behind. Ferdinand, who has already returned to Naples, brings the French occupation to an end with Spanish arms (Nov.). (Their last stronghold capitulates, Aug. 1496.) The League is broken up by Sforza, who accepts French overtures for peace. The expedition, though in itself a failure, forms a turning-point in history, revealing the weakness of Italy, introducing into European politics the notion of the balance of power, and familiarising France with the ideas and products of the Renaissance.

---

15. **England.** Warbeck and James invade England; but the expedition is little more than a raid. In view of the insecurity at home, Henry makes the Intercursus Magnus with Philip of Burgundy, by which the latter throws over Warbeck, and the commercial privileges between England and Flanders are restored, violations and disagreements, however, shortly ensuing. [1496

16. **Spain.** Philip, son of Maximilian, marries Joanna, daughter of Ferdinand and Isabella, who, by the death of her only brother (1498), becomes heiress of the Spanish empire.

---

17. **England.** Henry's demand for a subsidy to resist a Scotch invasion is resisted by the Cornishmen, who march on London, but are overpowered at Blackheath (June). Warbeck lands in Cornwall (Sep.), and is joined by 6,000 men, whom he deserts at Taunton, on the approach of the King's troops. The army melts away and Warbeck is captured. [1497

18. **Italy.** On the departure of Charles from Italy, the Pope attacks the barons who had sided with him (above all the Orsini), calls the Spaniards under Gonsalvo de Cordova to his aid, and expels the French from Ostia.

---

16. **Italian Lit.** Boiardo's Orlando Innamorato, the first Italian romantic epic, the fame of which is soon dimmed by Ariosto's treatment of the theme and by Berni's *rifacimento* of the poem itself, 1541.
17. **Art.** The equestrian statue of Bartolommeo Colleoni, designed by Verrocchio, is completed (Venice).
18. **Social.** Columbus sends home for sale as slaves 500 prisoners, who are released and sent back by Isabella.

[1496

19. **Eng. Ch.** Colet returns from his studies in Italy and France, and begins to lecture at Oxford on the Epistles of St Paul, thereby aiding the movement towards classical study initiated by Selling, Linacre, Grocyn and Vitelli, and revolutionising the theological curriculum by introducing the study of the books of the Greek Testament in their historic setting.
20. **Dutch Lit.** The Chamber of Eglantine is founded in Amsterdam, the most famous of the Chambers of Rhetoric, i. e. dramatic and literary societies.
21. **Art.** Michelangelo comes to reside in Rome, executes the Pietà (St Peter's), and on the accession of Julius II. is commissioned to design his tomb, of which only the Moses (Rome) and two Slaves (Paris) are completed.

Veit Stoss, the wood-carver, settles in Nuremberg, and, with Adam Krafft and Peter Vischer, workers in stone and bronze, and Dürer, renders the city for a generation the centre of German art.
22. **Social.** As a concession to the growing power of the nobility in Poland, the King allows the Diet to bind the peasantry to the soil.

[1497

23. **Geography.** John Cabot, a Genoese resident in Bristol, receives a patent from Henry VII. to discover and occupy lands across the Atlantic, and, with two vessels, reaches the American coast, probably at Newfoundland or Labrador, for the first time (June).
24. **Education.** The convent of St Rhadegund in Cambridge, containing two nuns, is suppressed, and its funds devoted to the foundation of Jesus College.

Celtes, after wandering in Italy and Germany, settles at Vienna and founds the Danube Literary Society for the spread of Classical culture, introduced by Peter Luder and Agricola. Humanism is in the same year introduced at Tübingen by Bebel, and at Erfurt in the circle that Mutianus Rufus gathers round him, Hutten, Eoban Hess, Crotus Rubianus and Busch.

---

19. **France.** Charles VIII., the last of the direct line of the Valois, is succeeded by his cousin, the Duke of Orleans, Louis XII., whose friendship is at once sought and won by Venice and the Pope. In August, Louis makes peace with Spain by the treaty of Marcoussis, which finally destroys the Holy League, and in which the partition of Naples is discussed. [1498

20. **England.** Warbeck attempts to escape, but is captured and removed to the Tower, where Warwick, son of Clarence, is kept a prisoner.

---

21. **England.** Warbeck and Warwick plan a flight, and, on its discovery, are executed, Henry seizing the opportunity of destroying the last of the Yorkist stock. [1499

22. **Italy.** Louis enters Italy to enforce his claims on Milan, whence he expels Sforza (Oct.), who flies to Switzerland. Venice joins in the war, and extends her territory beyond the Adda.

Stirred up by Sforza, the Sultan attacks Venice, who is defeated at Sapienza, and, after a three years' war, loses what remains of her Levantine empire.

23. **Switzerland.** The Swiss Confederation resist Maximilian's attempt to enforce old claims, and by the war with the Suabian League that follows, gain independence in all but name. The Confederation is now joined by Basle and Schaffhausen, and (1513) Appenzell, thus reaching the number of 13, at which it remains till Napoleon.

24. **Asia.** After a period of anarchy, Ismail wins the throne of Persia and founds the Sufi dynasty (so called from the School to which his family has belonged for generations), which lasts till 1736.

---

25. **Germany.** The Diet at Ausburg proceeds with the reorganisation of the Empire by establishing a Council of Regency, composed of representatives from the three Colleges of Electors, princes and towns. To facilitate administration, Germany is divided into six circles or provinces. [1500

26. **Italy.** Sforza recaptures Milan, but is again expelled by the French and imprisoned in France.

Taking advantage of the fall of Sforza, the Pope undertakes the conquest of the Romagna. Caesar Borgia captures Imola and Forli, and, after securing the goodwill of Venice, Rimini and Pesaro.

Louis resolves to conquer Naples, but, on the opposition of Ferdinand, submits by the Treaty of Granada to a compromise, by which France is to have the kingship and the northern provinces and Spain the southern.

27. **America.** Cabral, a Portuguese, is carried by a storm to Brazil, which he declares an appanage for Portugal. Vespucci is sent out to erect a fort, and trade begins, though the settlement is for a time neglected.

---

25. **French Ch.** Louis XII. re-establishes the Pragmatic Sanction of 1438, by which the election of Bishops was given to the Chapters. [1498

26. **Italian Ch.** The Florentine magistrates, emboldened by his excommunication, 1497, and terrified by the threat of an Interdict on the city, forbid Savonarola to preach. The spell is broken by his refusal of a challenge to ordeal (April), and, next day, San Marco is attacked and its Prior imprisoned. Six weeks later Savonarola dies a victim to his opposition to the Pope's schemes, and to the reaction produced by his strictness.

27. **Eng. Lit.** Erasmus comes to reside at Oxford, attracted by the fame of its Greek school, and forms intimate friendships with Colet and with More, (now living in London,) their fellow-work introducing the ideas of the Renaissance and preparing the way for far-reaching religious changes.

28. **German Lit.** Reuchlin's Henno, in the style of Terence, creates the Latin drama in Germany.

29. **Geography.** Columbus starts on his third voyage, discovers Trinidad, and sails along the Southern mainland.

Vasco da Gama sails round the Cape of Good Hope (discovered by Diaz 1486) and lands at Calicut, substituting Portuguese commercial supremacy for that of the Italian cities.

30. **Education.** Hegius dies, and the school at Deventer, founded by the Brethren of the Common Life, loses its influence, its traditions, however, being continued by the writings of Wimpheling and by the schools of Elsass.

---

31. **Art.** Bramante leaves Milan on the fall of Sforza, and settles at Rome, where he perfects the classic style in his palaces and in his additions to the Vatican. [1499

Leonardo finishes the 'Last Supper' (Milan).

32. **Geography.** Pinçon sails along the coast of Brazil (already surveyed by Vespucci, if the reputed voyage of 1497 was really undertaken), and takes possession in the name of Spain, though without making a settlement.

33. **Deaths.** Ficino, Torquemada.

---

34. **Bohemian Ch.** The Pope sends inquisitors to cope with the Bohemian Brothers, who deny the Real Presence and refuse oaths, and who exercise commanding influence, in part owing to the preaching of Lucas of Prague. [1500

35. **Literature.** The first edition of Erasmus' collection of Adages.

36. **Philology.** Aldus founds an Academy at Venice, for the study and publication of the Greek classics. By the efforts of its members, 1000 volumes a month are sometimes issued, mainly in the italic type, borrowed from the handwriting of Musurus, and in small size.

37. **Geography.** Cortereal, a Portuguese, sails along the coast of Labrador and discovers the entrance to Hudson Strait.

---

28. **England.** Arthur, Prince of Wales, marries Catherine of Aragon, after long negociations, but dies 1502, when Catherine, again after long negociations, is contracted to Prince Henry. [1501
29. **Spain.** A revolt of the Moors is provoked by the efforts of Ximenes and Talavera to effect their conversion, but is suppressed, the Moors being offered the alternative of exile or baptism.
30. **Italy.** The Pope confirms the secret treaty of Louis and Ferdinand, and decrees the deposition of the King of Naples. After a slight resistance Frederick withdraws, and the allies enter Naples (Aug.).

---

31. **Scotland.** Margaret, eldest daughter of Henry VII. of England, marries James IV. [1502
32. **Italy.** France and Spain begin to quarrel over the division of Naples.
Caesar Borgia seizes Urbino, breaks up a conspiracy of barons, reduces Sinigaglia and Perugia, and destroys the Orsini.

---

33. **Italy.** Gonsalvo de Cordova defeats the French, enters Naples (May), and, by a victory on the Garigliano and the consequent surrender of Gaeta, expels them from the country. [1503
Alexander VI. dies (Aug.), several of Caesar Borgia's conquests are reoccupied by their late possessors, and, shortly after the election of Julius II., Caesar himself is imprisoned for refusing to surrender the fortresses he still holds in the Romagna to the Pope.
34. **Asia.** To strengthen the settlements planted by Cabral and Vasco da Gama (in a second voyage, 1502), three squadrons (one under Albuquerque), are sent out, and a fort is built at Cochin, the commander of which, Pacheco, defeats an army sent by the ruler of Calicut.

---

35. **France.** Louis is induced by his wife to ally with Maximilian and Philip in the Treaties of Blois, promising his daughter to Charles, the son of Philip, with the reversion of Burgundy, Brittany, and Milan (the investiture of which he receives from the Emperor, 1505), and undertaking to join in seizing the mainland territories of Venice and to attack the Pope. [1504
36. **Germany.** Maximilian defeats the Count Palatine in the war of the Bavarian Succession, and annexes part of his territory.
37. **Italy.** Aragon annexes Naples, which is ruled by Gonsalvo de Cordova till 1507, and afterwards by a Viceroy.

38. **Church Hist.** Erasmus' Enchiridion Militis Christiani attacks the confusion of scholasticism and ceremonies with piety, and reflects the general spirit of Colet's teaching. [1501

39. **Scotch Lit.** Gawain Douglas' Palace of Honour, the principal poem of its author and the first purely allegorical romance produced in Scotland.

---

40. **Eng. Lit.** The Nut-Brown Maid first printed. [1502

41. **Portuguese Lit.** Gil Vicente's first drama (in Castilian), influenced by the plays of Encina. Ribeiro's Eclogues now appear and found the pastoral school.

42. **Education.** Wittenberg University.

43. **Art.** Michel Colombe, trained in the Burgundian school, makes the tomb of the Duke of Brittany.

44. **Science.** Leonardo da Vinci serves under Caesar Borgia as an Engineer, devoting himself not only to Mechanics, but to Optics, Chemistry, Astronomy and Geology.

---

45. **Eng. Ch.** The Lady Margaret, mother of Henry VII., endows Professors of Divinity at both Universities, on the advice of Fisher, her confessor, who becomes the first occupant of the chair at Cambridge. [1503

46. **Scotch Lit.** Dunbar celebrates the marriage of the King in his Thistle and the Rose.

47. **Art.** Leonardo commences the portrait of Mona Lisa (Paris).

48. **Social.** Portugal transports African slaves to America.

---

49. **Eng. Ch.** Colet becomes Dean of St Paul's and exerts a wide influence by his sermons. [1504

50. **Italian Lit.** Sannazzaro's pastoral romance, Arcadia, modelled on Boccaccio's Ameto, introduces into prose the reforms effected by Lorenzo and his circle in verse.

51. **Art.** Leonardo and Michelangelo design cartoons for the Hall of Council at Florence for the Battle of the Standard.

Raphael leaves Perugia for Florence, where he works with Fra Bartolommeo, and developes a style independent of Perugino.

Giorgione's Madonna at Castelfranco, the first great work of the new style at Venice, as Bellini's altar-piece at S. Zacharia, 1505, may be regarded as the last great work of the old.

Michelangelo completes his David.

Cranach is attached to the person of the Elector of Saxony and executes portraits, among them, later, those of the Reformers.

38. **Savoy.** Charles III. becomes Duke of Savoy (1504–1553), and, while attempting to avoid participating in European wars, engages in frequent struggles with Geneva and Vaud.

---

39. **France.** Ferdinand, weakened by the death of Isabella and the claim of Philip to Castile, persuades Louis to throw over the Treaty of Blois and to give him his niece, transferring with her the French claims on Naples. [1505

40. **Italy.** The plan of partition being laid aside owing to changes in the relations of France and Spain, the Pope hastens to get what he can, and Venice restores all her conquests in the Romagna except Rimini and Faenza, the retention of which, however, the Pope refuses to guarantee.

41. **Poland.** By the Constitution called Nihil Novi the Diet agree to make unanimity essential for all changes; the whole legislative power in consequence passes to the nobility, the Crown becoming, under Sigismund I. and II. (1506–72) steadily weaker. The rule of the oligarchy and the wars with Turkey and Russia reduce Poland to impotence.

42. **Russia.** Ivan III. dies, after a reign of forty-three years, having founded the Autocracy, expelled the Tartars of the Golden Horde, extended the frontier on the North and West, reduced the great semi-independent municipalities, established relations with the Western powers, and married a princess of the house of the Palaeologi.

43. **Asia.** A force is sent out to Cochin under Almeida, who receives the title of Viceroy, to secure Portuguese commerce.

44. **Africa.** The East African Empire of Portugal is begun by the occupation of the coast from the Zambesi to Delagoa Bay, and the foundation of forts at Sofala and Mozambique (1507), but never extends far inland.

---

45. **England.** The Archduke Philip is wrecked on the English coast on his way to Spain, and is forced by Henry to surrender the Earl of Suffolk, nephew of Edward IV. (who remains in prison till 1513, when he is executed), and to introduce changes in the Intercursus Magnus, a final settlement being reached 1507. [1506

46. **Spain.** Philip and Joanna go to Spain to compel Ferdinand to surrender the regency of Castile. The nobles joining Philip, Ferdinand retires to Aragon; but Philip dies, Joanna becomes insane, and Ferdinand is invited to return.

47. **Italy.** Julius marches without warning against Perugia and Bologna, both of which surrender without a struggle.

48. **Netherlands.** The Regency is entrusted to the youthful Charles' aunt, Margaret of Austria.

---

52. **Social.** Henry places Gilds and Companies under the direct supervision of the State. The Gild system declines, its place being gradually taken by the 'domestic system.'
53. **Death.** Isabella.

---

54. **German Ch.** Luther joins the Augustinians at Erfurt (the strictest Order owing to the revival effected by Proles and Staupitz, the Visitors), and, on the advice of the latter Visitor, studies Augustine. [1505
55. **Church Hist.** Erasmus commences his work as a biblical critic by editing Valla's Annotations on the New Testament.
56. **Italian Lit.** Bembo's Asolani, or disquisitions on Love, become a model of style.
57. **Education.** The Lady Margaret founds Christ's College and Saint John's College at Cambridge (1509).
58. **History.** Wimpheling's Epitome Rerum Germanicarum, the first history of Germany from original sources, a study patronised by Maximilian, and cultivated by Peutinger and Aventin at Augsburg, Pirkheimer at Nuremberg, and Stabius, Cuspinian and Celtes at Vienna.
59. **Social.** Henry grants a more complete constitution to the Merchants' Adventurers (an offshoot from the Mercers' Co., c. 1400), assigns Calais as their head-quarters, and reduces the entrance fee.

---

60. **Eng. Lit.** Hawes' Pastime of Pleasure (printed 1517), an elaborate allegory in the style of Lydgate, &c. [1506
61. **Art.** Julius II. lays the foundation-stone of a new Cathedral of St Peter, designed by Bramante in the form of a Greek cross, for which Raphael, Bramante's successor, substitutes a Latin cross.

Dürer visits Italy, meeting Bellini, Raphael and others.

The Laocoon is discovered.

62. **Philology.** Reuchlin's Hebrew Grammar and Dictionary, the earliest composed by a Christian, renders the study of Jewish literature less uncommon.
63. **Education.** Joachim of Brandenburg founds a University at Frankfort on the Oder, chiefly for the study of Roman law, which now finds its way into German codes.
64. **Death.** Columbus.

---

49. **Germany.** The Imperial Chamber is re-established; but the Diet accepts the principle of taxation by separate states. [1507

Maximilian obtains men and money for an expedition to receive the imperial crown and assert his rights in the Milanese. The scheme of Cardinal d'Amboise, to call a council and get himself substituted for Julius, turns Maximilian's thoughts towards becoming Pope himself.

50. **Italy.** The democratic party in Genoa, long under the suzerainty of France, revolts against the nobles and sets up a Doge. Louis enters Italy with a large army, retakes the city and abolishes its privileges.

---

51. **Germany.** Maximilian assumes the title of Emperor Elect at Trent, thereby asserting that the German King, by his election, becomes Emperor without further confirmation. The title is henceforward recognised by the Popes. [1508

52. **Italy.** Maximilian invades Venice, but is repeatedly beaten and forced to make a three years' truce, Venice retaining her conquests. Her success precipitates the formation of a league against her, sketched some months previously (Feb.), and finally signed at Cambrai (Dec.) by D'Amboise for Louis and Margaret of Austria for her father Maximilian. The Emperor and the Pope are to regain the towns claimed by them, France to round off the Milanese, the King of Aragon to have the cities on the Neapolitan coast taken by Venice in the war (1495), Hungary to receive Dalmatia, Savoy Cyprus, the Duke of Ferrara and Marquis of Mantua to recover their losses.

The Pope's nephew is adopted by the childless Guidobaldo of Urbino as his heir, the Duchy remaining in the Rovere family till 1626.

---

53. **England.** Henry VII. dies, and his son marries Catherine of Aragon. [1509

54. **Italy.** Though the real author of the League of Cambrai, the Pope only enters it when he finds France is in earnest (March), rejects the offer of Venice to restore Faenza and Rimini, the cities long claimed by him, and excommunicates her. The French now advance and win a battle at Agnadello, the allies seize what they desire, and the Pope replies to her demand for peace with impossible terms. Venice soon regains Padua from Maximilian, who retires from Italy (Oct.); but loses her fleet (Dec.), and agrees to the Pope's terms, ceding Faenza, Rimini, and Ravenna.

Pisa finally becomes subject to Florence.

55. **Africa.** After four years of fighting in North Africa, the Spaniards, under Ximenes, take Oran, whence they push on to Tripoli (1510), and compel Algiers and Tunis to pay tribute.

56. **Asia.** Almeida defeats the fleet of the Mohammedan princes of North-West India. He is succeeded by Albuquerque, who transfers the capital to Goa, which he captures 1510, conquers Malacca 1511, and plants Portuguese rule in the Malay Peninsula and in the Spice Islands,

65. **Geography.** Waldseemüller, a professor of Geography in Lorraine, publishes a letter of Amerigo Vespucci, containing an account of his travels, and proposes that the new Continent should be named after him. [1507

66. **Art.** Giorgione and Titian, fellow-pupils of Bellini, are commissioned to fresco the Pindaco dei Tedesci at Venice.

67. **Death.** Caesar Borgia.

---

68. **German Ch.** Luther is appointed, by Staupitz' influence, Professor of Theology at Wittenberg. [1508

69. **Italian Lit.** Bibbiena's Calandra founds Italian Comedy.

70. **Spanish Lit.** Amadis de Gaula, a Spanish version of the Portuguese work of Lobeira, revives interest in the poems of Chivalry, in part through the French translation of Herberay.

71. **Education.** Ximenes founds the University of Alcala, which becomes the centre of exegetical, as Salamanca is of dogmatic theology.

72. **Art.** Michelangelo begins to fresco the roof of the Sistine chapel.

Raphael is invited by the Pope to reside in Rome, and is set to fresco the rooms and colonnades of the Vatican.

Titian's Tribute Money (Dresden).

---

73. **German Ch.** Pfefferkorn, an apostate Jew of Cologne, with the aid of Ortwin Gratius and Hoogstraten, obtains an order from Maximilian to the Jews to surrender their books. The Archbishop of Mainz urges consultation with Hebrew scholars, and Pfefferkorn suggests Reuchlin, who, however, declares boldly against persecution. Though condemned by Paris and other Universities, Reuchlin is acquitted by the Bishop of Speyer, deputed by the Pope to try the case, and by a Commission at Rome, and wins the sympathies of the Humanists and the general public of Germany. [1509

74. **Eng. Lit.** The Paston Letters end (1422—1509).

75. **Art.** Andrea del Sarto's frescoes in the cloister of the Annunziata, Florence.

---

conciliating his native subjects by his just and tolerant administration. His attempt to seize Aden, the key to the trade of the Red Sea, fails 1513.

---

57. **Italy.** Venice receives absolution, and promises free navigation in the Gulf of Venice for the subjects of the Papal States. The Council of Ten, however, secretly execute a protest against the validity of the pact as obtained by violence, and the war leaves a deep hostility to the Papacy. [1510

58. **France.** The Pope, having obtained his own object by the war, sets himself to form a league against France, and declares war against Louis' ally, Ferrara. Louis replies by summoning to Tours a synod of French Bishops, who condemn the conduct of the Pope and recommend the assembling of a General Council to inquire into it.

---

59. **Italy.** The Pope fails to take Ferrara, and the French shortly after capture Bologna. French and Spanish Cardinals now summon a General Council to meet at Pisa, to which Julius retorts by convoking a Council at the Lateran. The Papacy, Ferdinand and Venice undertake the recovery of Bologna and the defence of the Church (Oct.), and a month later Henry VIII. enters European politics by joining the League. Meanwhile the Council meets at Pisa (Sep.), but is soon transferred to Milan, owing to the attitude of Florence, the withdrawal into French territory proving a mere move in the game of politics. [1511

60. **America.** Diego Velasquez conquers Cuba.

---

61. **England.** An expedition is sent to cooperate with Spain against the south-west of France, but the troops mutiny and Ferdinand fails to support them. [1512

62. **Italy.** The Spanish and Papal troops are out-manœuvred by the French under Gaston de Foix, who wins a victory, but loses his own life near Ravenna (April). The Council at Milan decrees the suspension of the Pope, who replies in the first session of the Lateran Council (May), by declaring its adherents schismatics. The League is joined by Maximilian, and the French evacuate Milan and retire beyond the Alps, even Genoa shaking off their yoke. The Council withdraws to Lyons, and the Pope recovers Bologna. The victorious allies meet at the Congress of Mantua (Aug.), and agree to concede Parma and Piacenza to the Pope, to restore Milan to the son of Lodovico Sforza, and to win back Florence for the Medici. Maximilian now recognises the Council of Lateran.

On the expulsion of the French, the Medici capture Florence with a Spanish army. The republican changes of 1494 are swept away, and the republican chiefs are banished.

63. **Spain.** Ferdinand seizes Navarre, south of the Pyrenees, from the House of D'Albret, which obtained the crown by a marriage with the Queen, Catherine de Foix, 1484.

76. **Italian Lit.** Ariosto's Orlando Furioso. [1510
77. **Art.** Titian's Sacred and Profane Love (Villa Borghese, Rome).
78. **Social.** Las Casas is ordained a priest and begins his lifelong crusade on behalf of the native races in the Spanish colonies, in which he receives support from Ximenes, Ferdinand, Vittoria and Soto, but is bitterly opposed by a large party led by Sepulveda and Oviedo.
79. **Education.** Colet, having come into a large fortune on the death of his father, founds St Paul's School, and appoints Lily, who has learned Greek in Rhodes, headmaster. The statutes lay stress on classical study and on the formation of character, and concede to the Trustees the power of making unlimited changes. The school-books are composed by Colet, with the aid of Lily and Erasmus.
80. **Death.** Botticelli.

---

81. **Eng. Ch.** Some 'Lollards' are burned, and several persons are forced by the Bishops to do penance. [1511
82. **German Ch.** Luther is sent to Rome on the business of his order, and is much influenced by his visit.
Maximilian employs Wimpheling to draw up a programme of reform for the Council at Pisa.
83. **French Lit.** Gringoire's satirical farce, Le Prince des Sots, is followed by the decline of the mediaeval theatre.
84. **Literature.** Erasmus' Praise of Folly, composed while staying with More, satirising pilgrimages, indulgences, prayers to the Virgin, scholasticism, and attacking the attitude of Kings and Popes in regard to war, forms an important link in the chain of events which leads to the Reformation.
85. **Education.** Erasmus takes up his residence in Cambridge as Lady Margaret Professor and lecturer in Greek.
86. **Death.** Comines.

---

87. **Eng. Ch.** Convocation is summoned to deal with heresy, and a contest takes place between Bishop Fitzjames, the leader of the extreme party, and Colet, whose opening sermon severely censures the clergy. [1512
88. **French Ch.** Lefèvre, already famous as a philosopher, publishes a commentary on, and translation of, St Paul's Epistles, affirming the exclusive authority of the Bible, and attacking Transubstantiation, clerical celibacy, Latin prayers, etc.
89. **German Ch.** On his return from Rome, Luther lectures on the Epistle to the Romans, and developes his theory of Justification.
90. **Art.** Raphael's fresco of Galatea (Villa Farnesina, Rome).
91. **Education.** Brasenose, Oxford, is founded, the statutes of which urge the study of the old Scholastic curriculum.

---

64. **Germany.** To the circles of 1500 are added four, each with a Governor. A short-lived Aulic Council is instituted under the control of the Emperor, to which part of the work of the Imperial Chamber is diverted.

[1513

65. **France.** Henry plans a league for the partition of France, in which Maximilian and Ferdinand join at the Treaty of Mechlin (April). To break up the confederacy, Louis sends a force to recover the Milanese, which is routed by the Swiss mercenaries of Sforza (June). Henry now crosses to Calais, is joined by Maximilian and besieges Terouenne, the chief fortress on the Netherlands frontier. The relieving army flies without a blow at the Battle of Spurs, and Terouenne and Tournai surrender. Meanwhile the Swiss overrun Franche-Comté, but are bribed to retire, and France issues unscathed from her campaigns.

66. **Scotland.** James IV. takes advantage of the absence of Henry to invade England, but is routed and slain at Flodden by the Earl of Surrey, the greater part of the Scotch nobility falling with him. His heir, James V., is still a child.

[1514

67. **England.** An Arsenal is constructed at Deptford, and Trinity House is instituted to protect English shipping.

68. **Scotland.** The country is split into factions, Margaret marrying Angus and desiring an English alliance, Archbishop Beaton demanding the regency of Albany, long resident in France.

69. **France.** Ferdinand, not desiring to weaken France too much, makes peace with Louis and persuades Maximilian to do the same. Deserted by his allies, Henry resolves on a close alliance with France, and marries his sister to the King.

70. **Hungary.** The Diet enacts Verböczy's *Decretum tripartitum Juris*, which increases the privileges of the nobility and establishes the independence of the King in regard to Pope, Emperor and clergy.

71. **Turkey.** Selim I. defeats the Persians at Tauris and Aleppo.

[1515

72. **England.** Wolsey, who has risen into prominence by his organisation of the campaigns of 1512–13 and already holds the See of York, becomes Chancellor and Cardinal, and in 1517 Legate, and adds Durham and the Abbey of St Albans *in commendam*, and Bath, Worcester, and Hereford in farm.

73. **Scotland.** Albany, nephew of James III., reaches Scotland, assumes the Regency, and suppresses the Queen's faction, but by his partiality for France drives Margaret and the nobles into the arms of England.

92. **Eng. Ch.** Benefit of clergy in cases of murder and robbery is limited to the higher orders of the Church. This attack being resented by the clergy, the King has the case argued in his presence, and Standish, a Franciscan, denies the validity of decretals in England unless legally ratified, and is supported by Henry. [1513

93. **Italian Ch.** The Lateran Council condemns the assertion that the soul is mortal or one in all men, without, however, imposing penalties.

94. **Scotch Lit.** Gawain Douglas' translation of the Aeneid.

95. **Politics.** Macchiavelli, suspected of treason, leaves Florence and composes The Prince, which he dedicates to Lorenzo de Medici, in hope of employment. Though not published till 1532, it circulates freely in MS., and in a plagiarism by Agostino Nifo. In 1516 Macchiavelli developes and qualifies its positions in lectures on the first decade of Livy.

96. **Art.** Holbein settles in Basle and begins his career as a painter, gradually passing from fresco and religious subjects to portraiture.

97. **Geography.** Vasco Nuñez de Balboa sets out from Antigua in search of the Pacific, of which he is told by an Indian chief, and which he sights from Darien.

Ponce de Leon discovers Florida.

98. **Education.** The new Pope, Leo X., appoints Bembo and Sadoleto his secretaries. He restores and extends the Gymnasium, founded by Eugenius IV. and robbed by Julius, and invites Lascaris to teach Greek, aided by his pupil Musurus, who establishes a Greek printing-press. A sculpture gallery is now formed at the Vatican, and Raphael prepares a scheme for the excavation and maintenance of the antiquities of the city.

---

99. **Spanish Ch.** The Complutensian Polyglot, planned by Ximenes and executed by Zuniga, Nebrija, and by Greek and Jewish converts. [1514

100. **Art.** Correggio discovers and applies full chiaroscuro.

101. **Social.** Eck defends Usury, the Lateran Council at the same moment allowing the Montes Pietatis to charge moderate interest.

102. **Philology.** Budaeus' De Asse opens the French or second period of classical studies.

103. **Death.** Bramante.

---

104. **Italian Lit.** Trissino's Sophonisba, the first blank verse in modern literature, is imitated by Rucellai, Alamanni, Aretino, Cinthio, etc. [1515

105. **German Lit.** Eulenspiegel, a coarse but humorous satire, perhaps by Murner, rivals the Narrenschiff in popularity.

106. **Literature.** In imitation of a volume published by Reuchlin, Mutianus Rufus and his friends compose Epistolae obscurorum Virorum (second series, 1517, by Hutten), supposed to be received by Ortwin Gratius, in which the ignorance of the Orders is ridiculed. The work, representing the open breach between the Humanists and

74. **France.** Immediately on his accession, Francis sets out to conquer the Milanese, and defeats the Swiss in the decisive battle of Marignano, shattering the military supremacy of the Swiss mercenaries, expelling Sforza, and forcing the Pope to enter into an alliance and to restore the cities he had taken from the Milanese and from the Duchy of Ferrara.

[1516

75. **Italy.** Maximilian descends on Milan with Swiss troops, paid by England, but retreats without striking a blow, though the expedition prevents Francis from attacking Naples. Francis secures the alliance of Charles, the young King of Spain, and shortly after makes peace with Maximilian.

76. **Switzerland.** Francis makes peace with Switzerland, which undertakes to furnish mercenaries.

77. **Hungary.** Louis II., King of Bohemia, becomes King of Hungary, and the faction fights of the great and small nobility prepare the way for the Turkish invasion. Ferdinand, grandson of the Emperor, marries Louis' sister.

78. **Montenegro.** The Prince resigns and the Vladikas, or Prince Bishops, begin to rule.

79. **Turkey.** Selim invades and conquers Syria as a step to the conquest of Egypt.

[1517

80. **Scotland.** Albany returns and makes a treaty of mutual defence, hinting at a marriage between the young King and a daughter of Francis. On the Regent's departure, faction fights break out between the Hamiltons and the Douglases.

81. **Italy.** Maximilian makes peace with Venice and restores Verona, thus terminating the wars that had grown out of the League of Cambrai, from which Venice emerges with undiminished territory, though with her military power broken.

82. **Turkey.** Selim conquers Egypt, beheads the Mameluke Sultan, takes Mecca and Medinah, and revives the Caliphate, or headship of the Mahommedan world, which had been practically extinct since 1258.

83. **Africa.** Barbarossa, a Lesbian pirate, takes Algiers and defeats the Spanish fleet, but is slain by a new Spanish expedition, and succeeded by his brother, the more famous Barbarossa, the founder of the Barbary Corsairs, who becomes the vassal of the Sultan, by whom he is recognised as ruler of Algiers.

84. **Asia.** The Portuguese establish a factory at Colombo, and gradually gain control of Ceylon.

---

the old learning, enjoys immense popularity, but is disapproved by Erasmus.

107. **Art.** Henry VII.'s chapel is completed, and about the same time the last great examples of Perpendicular, such as Magdalen Tower, the churches of Bristol, Coventry, Boston, Windsor Chapel, the central tower at Canterbury, King's College Chapel, are finished. Torrigiano's work on Henry VII.'s tomb introduces Renaissance influences in sculpture. Raphael's 'Sistine' Madonna (Dresden).

108. **Law.** Zasius' Commentaries on Roman law.

109. **Deaths.** Albuquerque, Aldus.

---

110. **French Ch.** Francis and Leo arrange a Concordat, by which the annates are restored to the Pope, appointments of [1516
Bishops and Abbots are transferred to the King, though requiring papal approval, appeals to Rome are restricted, and excommunications, bulls, etc., must receive the sanction of the Crown. The Parliament and University of Paris and the Chapters in vain protest.

111. **German Ch.** Luther meets with Tauler's sermons and a mystical work which he publishes with the title German Theology.

112. **Church Hist.** Erasmus' Novum Instrumentum compiled from late MS. Erasmus' edition of Jerome.

113. **Philosophy.** Pomponazzi, an Aristotelian, contends that immortality cannot be proved by reason.

114. **Politics.** More's Utopia (in Latin) attacks the social and political evils of England, and outlines an ideal Commonwealth, free from wars of aggression, class legislation, ecclesiastical hierarchy, and persecution.

115. **Education.** Fox, Bishop of Winchester, founds Corpus College, Oxford, and endows lecturers on Greek, Latin and Divinity, the latter to discard the scholastics in favour of the original texts.

116. **Geography.** Peter Martyr's Decades describes the discoveries in the New World.

117. **Death.** Giovanni Bellini.

---

118. **Eng. Ch.** A Protestant party forms around Bilney, Barnes and Stafford at Cambridge. [1517

119. **Italian Ch.** The Lateran Council is closed, the Pope declaring that schism has been destroyed and all necessary reforms accomplished.

120. **German Ch.** Tetzel, the agent of Albert, Archbishop of Mainz and Magdeburg (to whom Leo had granted the power to sell indulgences to pay the annates of his See), arrives at Juterböck, but is forbidden by the Elector of Saxony to enter his dominions. Luther nails 95 theses to the door of the Castle Church, describing Indulgences as a scholastic innovation. The theses are attacked by Tetzel himself, Hoogstraten, Prierias and Eck.

121. **German Lit.** The Theuerdank, in part composed by Maximilian, the last German Epic of Chivalry.

122. **Spanish Lit.** The plays of Torres Naharros, the father of Spanish Comedy.

85. **England.** Wolsey negociates the Treaty of London, by which France buys back Tournay, and the dauphin is betrothed to the princess Mary. The league is joined by the Pope, the Emperor, and the King of Spain, thus realising for the moment Wolsey's dream of a universal peace. [1518

More at last yields to the King's entreaties and becomes a Privy Councillor.

86. **Sweden.** Christian II., of Denmark, invades Sweden to attack Sten Sture, the leader of the nobles, and carries away hostages, among them Gustavus Vasa, son of a senator.

---

87. **Germany.** Maximilian dies, and, after a protracted struggle, in which Henry VIII. intervenes as a candidate, and in which the Pope favours Francis, Charles is supported by Frederick of Saxony, and is finally elected unanimously. [1519

At his coronation, Charles grants a Capitulation, undertaking to make no treaty nor declare war without the consent of the Estates, to put none to the ban without trial, to introduce no foreign troops, to reside principally in Germany, and to restore the Council of Regency.

Ulric of Wurtemberg, put to the ban of the Empire for quarrels with his nobility, etc., is ejected by the Suabian League, his duchy being administered by the Emperor.

88. **America.** Cortez leaves Cuba for Mexico, destroys his fleet on disembarking, and enters the capital after overcoming great obstacles. He is expelled with much loss, 1520, but re-enters the city 1521.

89. **Africa.** The family of the Sherifs founds the Moorish empire of Morocco.

---

90. **England.** The struggle for the Empire causes strained relations between Francis and Charles, both of whom in consequence desire the English alliance. On his way from Spain, Charles visits Henry (May), who at once crosses to Calais and meets Francis at the Field of the Cloth of Gold (June), returning to a second interview with the Emperor, with whom he makes a treaty (July). [1520

91. **Spain.** Exasperated by Charles' Flemish counsellors, especially Chièvres, by his neglect of Spanish customs, by his election as Emperor and his rapid departure, leaving another foreigner, Adrian of Utrecht, as regent in Castile, the Spaniards, led by Padilla and Bishop Acuña, revolt in Toledo and Castile. The rebels petition the Emperor for reforms, but are weakened by the defection of the nobility and crushed at Villalar, 1521. On the arrival of Charles, 1522, the towns, prosperous in their silk and cloth trade, are robbed of their liberties and begin to decline.

92. **Sweden.** Christian again invades Sweden, defeats Sten Sture, is recognised King and grants an amnesty, but massacres many of the nobility, including Eric Vasa, in the Blood Bath of Stockholm.

123. **Education.** The Collége des Trois Langues at Louvain.

124. **Social.** A Commission is appointed to report on Enclosures, now becoming frequent in England, despite the Acts of 1490 and 1516.

Charles grants a monopoly of importing slaves into Spanish America.

125. **Death.** Ximenes.

---

126. **German Ch.** Luther dedicates an amplification of his theses to the Pope, and meets Cajetan, the Papal Legate, at Ausburg (Oct.). Miltitz is sent as special envoy to the Elector of Saxony, carrying the Golden Rose for presentation if Frederick yields. [1518

Melanchthon, a relative and pupil of Reuchlin, becomes Professor of Greek at Wittenberg, connects the new movement with Humanism, and himself becomes a theologian.

127. **Swedish Ch.** Two Swedes return from Wittenberg and introduce Protestantism, which spreads in the towns.

128. **Church Hist.** Julius Exclusus, a satire on the Pope.

129. **Science.** Linacre founds the Royal College of Physicians.

---

130. **German Ch.** Luther meets Miltitz (Jan.), and writes respectfully to the Pope. In a disputation with Eck, at Leipsig (June), he discovers his kinship with Huss, and is forced to criticise the Council of Constance, his new position winning him sympathy from Pirkheimer, Crotus Rubianus, Eoban Hess, Justus Jonas, Hutten, and Sickingen, from Oecolampadius, and from the Bohemian Brethren. His advances to Reuchlin are met with hostility, and to Erasmus with evasions. [1519

131. **Art.** Titian's Assumption of the Virgin (Venice).

132. **Education.** Street fights take place at Oxford, and the 'Trojans' are rebuked by the King and More.

133. **Geography.** Magellan, a Portuguese in the service of Spain, sails round Cape Horn and is killed on the Philippines, 1521, his ship, however, completing the circuit of the world, 1522.

134. **Death.** Leonardo da Vinci.

---

135. **Eng. Ch.** Wolsey burns Luther's works at Paul's Cross, where Fisher delivers a violent sermon. The Cambridge Protestants in consequence meet secretly at the White Horse Inn, where they are joined by Coverdale and Latimer, the Inn being nicknamed Germany, and its frequenters Germans. [1520

136. **French Ch.** Briçonnet, Bishop of Meaux, a follower of Lefèvre and friend of Farel and Roussel, attracts a semi-protestant circle round him, and gains the patronage of the King's sister, Margaret of Navarre.

137. **German Ch.** Luther's To the Christian Nobility of the German Nation, pleads for a free Council, urges the princes and nobility to nationalise the Church, and combats ordinances not to be found in the N. T. His Babylonish Captivity rejects all the Sacraments of the

Gustavus Vasa, who has escaped from captivity, 1519, persuades Lubeck, the chief of the Hansa Towns, to aid in raising Sweden against Christian, gradually undermines Christian's authority, and is recognised as Regent by part of the nobility.

93. **Turkey.** Soliman the Magnificent begins his reign, the most glorious chapter of Ottoman history in the arts both of war and peace, in part owing to the Grand Vizier Ibrahim (executed 1536).

[1521

94. **England.** The Duke of Buckingham, son of the antagonist of Richard III., is executed on a charge of treason, his death closing the list of the powerful nobles.

95. **Scotland.** Albany returns, and Angus is forced to retire.

96. **France.** Charles V. allies with the Pope to expel the French from Italy (May), and Wolsey, after failing to avert the war by a Conference at Calais (Aug.), joins the Emperor (Nov.). Meanwhile the French are expelled from Milan, where Sforza is restored, and France itself is invaded. Parma and Piacenza are annexed to the Papacy.

97. **Germany.** The Diet of Worms reconstitutes the Imperial Chamber and revives the Council of Regency, which lasts for three years.

The Emperor resigns his hereditary dominions in Germany, except the Netherlands, to his brother Ferdinand.

98. **Portugal.** With the accession of John III. (1521–1557), the decline of Portugal commences, N. Africa being abandoned, except Ceuta, and African slaves being imported to till the soil.

99. **Switzerland.** Zwingli obtains the abolition of the Reislaufen, or mercenaries, in Zurich.

100. **Turkey.** With the excuse of avenging an insult to the Turkish envoy, Soliman captures Belgrade, and frightens Venice into paying tribute for Zante and Cyprus.

101. **America.** Ponce de Leon returns to Florida and founds a settlement which ends in disaster, owing to the climate and the hostility of the natives.

[1522

102. **Scotland.** Albany retires, but French influence remains supreme.

103. **France.** England declares war against France, but the invasion leads to no result save that Francis allies with Scotland.

104. **Germany.** The Knights, or lesser German nobility, under Hutten and Sickingen, attack the Elector of Trier, but obtain little support, owing to Luther's disapproval of violent measures.

105. **Turkey.** After a heroic defence of five months, the Knights of St John in Rhodes, a number of them English, are forced to surrender, but receive Malta from the Emperor, 1530. The victory leaves the Turks supreme in the Eastern Mediterranean.

106. **Asia.** The Portuguese settle at Macao (near Hong-Kong).

Church except Baptism and the Lord's Supper, and demands the cup for the laity. His Freedom of a Christian Man maintains the priesthood of every believer. Eck now circulates the Pope's Bull of Excommunication (brought by Miltitz, 1518), which Luther publicly burns. A new war of pamphlets is waged by Luther and Hutten on one side, and by Murner and Emser on the other.

138. **Italian Ch.** Sadoleto, Contarini, Giberto, Caraffa, Gaetano da Thiene, the poet Flaminio, Carnesecchi, etc., some of them accepting the Lutheran theory of Justification, begin to meet, and, in 1523, give the Society the name of the Oratory of Divine Love.

139. **Art.** Correggio begins his 10 years' labour on the frescoes of the domes of San Giovanni and the Cathedral at Parma.

140. **Death.** Raphael.

---

141. **Eng. Ch.** Henry replies to Luther's Babylonish Captivity in his Seven Sacraments, for which he receives the title of Defender of the Faith. Luther retorts, attributing the work to Lee, and is attacked by More and Fisher. [1521

142. **French Ch.** The Sorbonne condemns the Colloquies of Erasmus, and 100 propositions from Luther's writings.

143. **German Ch.** Aleander, the Papal legate at the Diet of Worms, fails to induce the Emperor to enforce the bull without hearing Luther (Ap.), who refuses to retract anything but what is proved unscriptural. Charles allows him to return, but puts him to the ban of the Empire (May). Luther hides in the Wartburg, where he translates the Bible. At Wittenberg his work is carried on by Melanchthon and Carlstadt, and by the newcomers, Bugenhagen and Justus Jonas. Melanchthon lays the foundations of Lutheran theology in his Loci Communes.

144. **Spanish Ch.** A number of Spanish Bishops visit Worms to complain of the entry of Lutheran doctrines into Spain.

145. **Scotch Lit.** Major, Principal of Glasgow, and, later, of St Andrew's (where Knox and Buchanan are among his pupils), writes his History of Scotland.

146. **Social.** The manufacture of silk is introduced into France.

---

147. **French Ch.** Lefèvre's Commentary on the Gospels. [1522

148. **German Ch.** Mystical Anabaptism appears in Zwickau, whence it is expelled by the magistrates, Münzer roaming over Germany, Storch, Stübner and Cellarius visiting Wittenberg. Melanchthon being too undecided to preserve order, Luther returns to Wittenberg (March), and persuades the Anabaptists to leave the city. He now publishes his translation of the N. T., the first rendering from the original into German prose, of which it is the first important monument.

Murner, the Franciscan, attacks the extravagances of the Reformation in his Great Lutheran Fool.

149. **Swiss Ch.** Zwingli, pastor at Zurich, attacks fasting, clerical celibacy, etc., and urges the substitution of the Bible for the Church. His example is followed by his old teacher Wyttenbach, and by Pellicanus and Oecolampadius at Basle.

107. **England.** Requiring money for the French war, Henry summons a Parliament (the only one 1516–28), which, however, refuses Wolsey's enormous demand of £800,000. [1523

108. **Scotland.** Henry's offer of alliance is rejected, and Surrey ravages the Border.

109. **France.** Owing to the loss of his position as Constable and the Queen dowager's lawsuit to obtain his estates, Bourbon, the most powerful of French nobles, joins the league of Charles, Henry, and most of the Italian powers. The invasion, despite the attack of Picardy by England, of Guienne by Spain and of Champagne by the Emperor, results in failure.

110. **Germany.** The Knights' War is terminated by the capture of Sickingen's castle and the death of its owner, quickly followed by that of Hutten.

111. **Spain.** Charles refuses to receive petitions for redress before the grant of supplies, thus reducing the Castilian Cortes to impotence.

112. **Denmark.** Christian II. is expelled by his subjects, aided by Lubeck, his uncle Frederick of Schleswig Holstein succeeding to the throne.

113. **Sweden.** On the flight of Christian from Denmark, the garrison in Stockholm surrenders, the long war of sieges comes to an end, and Gustavus Vasa becomes King of Sweden, the throne being declared hereditary in his family, 1544. Gustavus founds Swedish commerce by abolishing the Hanseatic monopoly, re-organises the finances, developes the internal resources of the country and creates a standing army.

---

114. **Scotland.** Albany, who had returned, 1523, finally retires, and an English party begins to form. Beaton is imprisoned, the Queen is joined by Arran, and the young king is proclaimed. [1524

115. **France.** The French invade Italy, but are repulsed and lose the Chevalier Bayard. Bourbon advances from Lombardy to the siege of Marseilles, but is forced to return, Francis following him, capturing Milan, laying siege to Pavia, and drawing the Pope to his side.

116. **Sweden.** By the Treaty of Malmo the independence of Sweden (except the southern provinces), is recognised by the King of Denmark, the Union of Calmar, 1397, thus coming to an end.

---

117. **France.** The French troops, weakened by the despatch of a large force against Naples, are routed near Pavia by Pescara, Launoy and Bourbon (Feb.), Francis being carried captive to Spain and forced to resign Milan and Genoa. The battle terminates the first war, 1522–6, and marks the supremacy of the Spanish infantry, who for the first time use muskets. [1525

118. **England.** On the news of Pavia, Wolsey desires to restore the balance of power by allying with France. Henry, however, determines to invade France, and Wolsey is compelled to ask for an Amicable Loan, which meets such wide-spread resistance that the invasion is given up and a treaty negociated.

150. **Bohemian Ch.** The Bohemian Catechism, probably by Lucas of Prague, who is strongly influenced by a visit to the Waldensians.
151. **Eng. Lit.** Skelton attacks Wolsey in Why come ye not to Court?
152. **Italian Lit.** Sannazzaro's De Partu Virginis, a model of Latin style and a blend of Christian and classical ideas.
153. **Death.** Reuchlin.

---

154. **German Ch.** Carlstadt and Münzer become more and more Anabaptist, and retire to small parishes, whence they foment the Revolution by word and pen. [1523
155. **Spanish Ch.** Juan d' Avila, 'the Apostle of Andalusia,' is persecuted as a Lutheran.
156. **Netherlands Ch.** Flemish Protestantism, which has centred in Augustinian monasteries, now begins the translation of Luther's writings and the composition of original works, and loses its first martyrs.
157. **Swiss Ch.** Zwingli draws up 67 articles and holds two public disputations, after which the clergy marry, the monasteries are dissolved, 1524, Mass is discontinued, and a theological college is instituted.
158. **Eng. Lit.** Lord Berners' translation of Froissart.
159. **Art.** Titian's Bacchus and Ariadne (London) first renders movement.
160. **Social.** Fitzherbert's Husbandry, the first agricultural handbook since that of Walter of Henley (c. 1250).

---

161. **German Ch.** Many Humanists who had joined the Protestants in their attack on the clergy, without sharing their religious ideas, sever their connection with Luther, the signal being given by Erasmus' book on Free Will, to which Luther replies, 1525. [1524

Luther and Walther collect and compose the first German hymn-book.
162. **Italian Ch.** Gaetano da Thiene, with the aid of Caraffa, founds the Theatine Order to educate the secular priesthood, to preach and to visit.
163. **French Lit.** Gryphius begins to print at Lyons, with the aid of Dolet.

---

164. **Scotch Ch.** Parliament forbids the import of Luther's books; but propagandism is at this moment begun by Patrick Hamilton. [1525
165. **French Ch.** Owing to the increasing antagonism aroused by the works of Lefèvre and his followers, the Dowager Louise, left supreme by the captivity of the King, and influenced by Cardinal Duprat, breaks up

119. **Germany.** The revolt of the peasants, the greatest of a large number in the last half century, due to poverty, to feudal oppression, and to the teachings of Münzer, Carlstadt and their followers, and in a less degree to the principles of the Reformation, spreads from south to central Germany. Their grievances are formulated in the Twelve Articles, supported from Scripture, in which they claim the right of each parish to choose its minister, the right to hunt and fish, the reduction of tithes, the abolition of clerical jurisdiction, etc. They destroy castles and convents, are denounced by Luther, and defeated in a series of battles. Münzer is captured and executed, and the revolt pitilessly stamped out (May).

The Catholic Electors form the League of Dessau.

Albert of Brandenburg, Grand Master since 1511 of the Teutonic Knights, accepts the Reformation, surrenders the lands of his Order to the King of Poland, from whom he receives them back as a fief, takes the title of Duke of Prussia, and establishes Protestantism.

---

120. **France.** By the Treaty of Madrid (Jan.), Francis is re- [1526
leased on promising to yield the Duchy of Burgundy and his claims in Italy, Flanders, and Artois, and leaving two sons as hostages. Once free, however, the King, with the Pope's approval, repudiates the compact, and joins with England, the Pope, Venice, and Milan in the League of Cognac (May), to compel the Emperor to restore the royal hostages and make Sforza independent in Milan. The second war of Francis and Charles commences with the capture of Milan by Bourbon (July), the arrival of German reinforcements under Frondsberg, and his advance on Rome.

121. **Germany.** To be ready for resistance to the victorious Emperor, Philip of Hesse joins with John, Elector of Saxony, the princes of Brunswick-Lüneburg, Anhalt, Mecklenburg and the city of Magdeburg, in the League of Torgau (March). In face of this confederacy, and of the alliance of the Pope with Francis, the Diet at Spire (June) practically drops the Edict of Worms by leaving its execution to the conscience of individual rulers, until a General Council.

122. **Hungary.** King Louis and 20,000 are slain at Mohacz (Aug.) by the Turks, who occupy Buda. Ferdinand, brother-in-law of the late King, and Zapolya, a prominent noble and the candidate of the Porte, are chosen King by rival factions. Bohemia passes to Ferdinand, who declares it a hereditary possession, 1547.

123. **Russia.** After 20 years' war, peace is made with Poland, by the mediation of the Western powers, Russia retaining Smolensk, her chief conquest. The remnants of the Tartar hordes are now expelled.

124. **Turkey.** The fleets of the Sultan destroy the Arab Corsairs of the Red Sea, and extend his authority over Arabia, his influence being felt in India, whence embassies are sent.

125. **Asia.** Baber, a descendant of Tamerlane (after seizing, 1504, and ruling the kingdom of Cabul), enters India, defeats the Mohammedan King of Delhi at Panipat, and a Hindu confederacy, 1527, and founds

the circle at Meaux (where Briçonnet submits), and burns a number of Protestants, the leaders, however, being saved by Margaret. With the return of the King, the persecution is arrested.

166. **German Ch.** Luther marries Catherine Bora, once a nun, to the vexation of most of the Reformers.

The purely commemorative view of Holy Communion now explained in Zwingli's True and False Religion is accepted by Oecolampadius, and in part by Bucer and Capito, and begins to spread over South Germany.

167. **Education.** Wolsey creates Cardinal College, Oxford, on the site of St Frideswide's Monastery, with its endowments, and those of other monastic houses, summons several of its first teachers from Cambridge, and founds a Grammar School at Ipswich, specially for classical studies, to feed his college. On his fall, Ipswich is confiscated and Cardinal College re-christened and re-endowed as Christ Church, 1546.

---

168. **Eng. Ch.** After great difficulties, Tyndale's translation of the N. T. appears at Worms, and quickly circulates in England, [1526 but is burnt at Paul's Cross and charged with wilful mistranslations by Tunstall, Lee, and More. The work gives a new stimulus to English Protestantism, of which Latimer now becomes leader.

169. **German Ch.** Luther composes a German service, and organises the systematic visitation of parishes.

170. **Polish Ch.** Despite the efforts of the King and the Church, Protestantism gains a hold through books, through the education of youths at Wittenberg, and through commerce with German towns, and loses its earliest martyrs.

171. **Philosophy.** Vittoria becomes Professor of Theology at Salamanca, and substitutes the study of Aquinas for that of Peter the Lombard. The study of Thomism revives, and is spread by the alumni of Salamanca, Melchior Cano, De Soto, and Carranza.

172. **Spanish Lit.** Acting on a suggestion of the Venetian ambassador, Boscan begins to imitate Italian forms and initiates a literary revolution.

173. **Portuguese Lit.** About the same time Sa de Miranda returns from Italy and founds the classic school in Portugal.

174. **Art.** Holbein pays a visit to England, bringing a letter from Erasmus to More by whom he is introduced at Court. Except for visits to Basle, he remains in England as Court painter till his death.

175. **Social.** While resident at the court of Henry VIII., Vives composes his De Subventione Pauperum, the principles of which are widely applied, are approved by the Sorbonne, 1531, despite the opposition of the Mendicant Orders, and initiates the modern treatment of poverty.

---

the Moghul Empire, leaving at his death, 1530, the whole of the Punjab to his son, Hamayun.

---

126. **England.** Henry's secret negociations with Clement concerning a divorce (first clearly referred to 1525), miscarrying owing to the Pope's captivity and their discovery by the Queen, the King tells his wife that his conscience compels their separation, and imposes silence on her. Wolsey informs More and Fisher that the King's scruples have been raised by the Bishop of Tarbes in negociating for the hand of his daughter, and forbids them to see the Queen. [1527

127. **Italy.** The German troops mutiny for pay, and are led by Bourbon to Rome, which is given over to the most terrible pillage it has ever experienced (May). The Pope, who has taken refuge in the Castle of St Angelo, is compelled to come to terms with the Emperor, and the Papal States are dismembered by the princes and cities of North Italy.

On the news of the sack, a French army enters Italy, captures Genoa and marches on Naples, whither the Emperor's army is transported from Rome. Naples is saved by a pestilence and by the entry of Doria (who has been blockading the city on behalf of France) into the service of Charles, on account of an insult by Francis to Genoa, his native town.

The Medici are expelled a second time from Florence.

128. **Sweden.** Needing money, Gustavus, by threats of resignation, induces the Diet of Westeras to give him the disposal of Church property, and to institute religious liberty.

129. **America.** Pizarro, after numerous rebuffs, resolves, with a handful of followers, to go forward, and finds traces of a great civilisation. He therefore procures patents from Spain, and starts from Panama, 1531, conquers Peru without difficulty, enters Cuzco, 1534, and founds Lima, the capital of Spanish Peru.

---

130. **England.** Gardiner and Fox are sent to Rome to urge the Pope to appoint a decretal Commission. Clement, not daring to insult the Emperor, the nephew of Catherine, refuses, and sends Campeggio to join Wolsey, with a verbal promise to confirm their arrangements. It is now found that Julius had given a Brief, preserved in Spain, even more definite than the dispensation. Henry vainly urges the Pope to declare this a forgery. During this delay, Wolsey consults the Bishops, who declare the case doubtful, and urge him to consult the Universities. [1528

131. **Scotland.** The King escapes from Angus, becomes master of his kingdom, and makes peace with Henry.

132. **Germany.** Philip of Hesse, suspecting a conspiracy among the Catholic princes, pays Pack, an official of the Duke of Saxony, to produce documents proving its existence. On the strength of Pack's revelations, Philip prepares for war, but desists on finding that the documents are forged.

176. **Scotch Ch.** Hamilton writes his Commonplaces, and lectures at St Andrews, where he converts Alesius. He is arrested and burnt, 1528. [1527

177. **French Ch.** Margaret of Angoulême marries Henry of Navarre, gathers round her at Nérac Marot, Desperiers, etc., and holds Lutheran services in the Castle.

178. **German Ch.** Philip of Hesse founds a University at Marburg, much visited by English, and where Busch and Lambert of Avignon teach.

179. **Italian Ch.** The sack of Rome, which may be said to terminate the Italian renaissance, breaks up the Oratory of Divine Love, some of its members becoming strongly ultramontane, the more moderate settling in Venice. At the same moment, Renée, daughter of Louis XII., marries the Duke of Ferrara, and makes her court the centre of Protestant influences in Italy.

180. **Swiss Ch.** Zwingli's Elenchus contra Catabaptistas records the first Baptist Confession, adherents of which are drowned at Zurich. Berne, Basle, Schaffhausen and St Gall become Protestant.

181. **Asiatic Ch.** Chaitanya, a Brahman reformer of Vishnuism, dies, and about the same time Vallabha-Swami preaches a sensuous Vishnuism, and Nanak Shah founds the community of the Sikhs in the Punjab.

182. **Art.** Sansovino becomes official architect of Venice.

183. **Science.** Paracelsus lectures on Medicine at Basle, and founds the modern science by applying his knowledge of chemistry.

184. **History.** Macchiavelli's History of Florence traces the operation of political forces.

185. **Death.** Macchiavelli.

---

186. **Eng. Ch.** Fish's Supplication of Beggars, attacking the avarice of the clergy, the belief in purgatory, etc., is answered by More in his Supplication of Souls, and by Fisher. [1528

Tyndal's Obedience of a Christian Man and how Christian Rulers ought to govern, defends Protestants from the charge of being bad subjects, and attacks the clergy and the Papal system. The book falls under the notice of the King.

187. **German Ch.** Schwenkfeld breaks with the Lutherans, from whom he differs on baptism, justification, the Lord's Supper and Church organisation, and settles in South Germany, where he founds a sect and composes his polemical and mystical works.

188. **Italian Ch.** The order of the Capucins is founded, as a branch of the Observants (from 1619 self-governing) and is patronised by Caterina Cibo and Vittoria Colonna.

189. **Spanish Lit.** Juan de Valdez' Dialogo de Mercurio y Caron, the chief prose work of the reign, discusses the political and religious problems of the time.

190. **Italian Lit.** Castiglione's Courtier, a manual of polite conduct, inspired by the Court of Urbino.

133. **Italy.** The last French attack is made on Naples by Lautrec, who is routed at Aversa (Aug.) The French at the same time are expelled from Genoa by Doria, who gives the Republic a new Constitution with a Doge, chosen for two years.

---

134. **England.** On the meeting of the Court (May), the Queen appeals to Rome, and Fisher declares for the legality of the marriage. Campeggio adjourns the Court, the Pope having revoked the cause according to secret agreement. On the failure of his policy, Wolsey is deprived of the seal (Oct.), and his possessions are adjudged to the King, More succeeding him as Chancellor. Cranmer recommends that the Universities should be consulted, and that the case should be dealt with by an English Court. [1529

The Seven Years' Parliament meets, the members of which are chiefly lawyers and country gentlemen, in some cases owing their election to the influence of the Crown.

135. **France.** A final French expedition to Italy is defeated, and the second war between Francis and Charles terminated by the Peace of Cambrai (Aug.) Francis receives back his sons, renounces his claims on Italy, Flanders and Artois, and pays a large indemnity.

136. **Germany.** By the Treaty of Barcelona, Charles promises to leave Milan to Sforza for life, to restore the Medici to Florence and to extirpate heresy, Clement undertaking to crown Charles, and to invest him with the kingdom of Naples.

The majority of the Diet at Spire (March), desiring to annul the Edict of 1526, the Evangelical princes draw up a formal protest, signed by John of Saxony, Hesse, Brandenburg, Brunswick, Anhalt and 14 cities, thus earning the name of Protestants.

137. **Switzerland.** In consequence of a League formed by Zurich with Constance 1527 and joined by other cities as they become Protestant, the Catholic States ally with Austria. War is averted through the intervention of neutral states, the Austrian alliance is broken off and each district is left free to settle its own religion.

138. **Turkey.** The Turks advance on Vienna, and after three weeks' siege withdraw with great loss.

---

139. **England.** Wolsey is restored to partial favour (Feb.), which he loses on the discovery of negociations with Francis. He is arrested (Nov.), and dies of fright. [1530

The King consults the Universities (Feb.), which return an evasive reply. Parliament urges the Pope, to whom Cranmer has forwarded the opinions of the foreign Universities, to nullify the marriage, warning him that other arrangements may be made. The Pope deprecates the threat, and Henry issues a Proclamation forbidding transactions with Rome and the introduction of Bulls.

140. **Italy.** Charles is crowned Emperor by the Pope at Bologna. The Hapsburg hegemony in the peninsula is confirmed and the

191. **Literature.** Erasmus satirises the slavish adherence of Humanists like Longolius of Padua to the vocabulary of Cicero in his Ciceronianus, to which Julius Scaliger and Dolet reply.

192. **Education.** Melanchthon propounds his educational reforms.

193. **Death.** Dürer.

---

194. **French Ch.** Despite the efforts of Margaret of Navarre, Berquin, the friend and translator of the German reformers, is burned. The execution leads to a reaction in the mind of the King. [1529

195. **German Ch.** Philip of Hesse, desiring Protestant unity and sympathising with the views of the Swiss reformers, invites Luther, Melanchthon and Justus Jonas from Wittenberg, Zwingli and Oecolampadius from Switzerland, Bucer, Hedio, Osiander and Brenz from South Germany to Marburg to discuss the theory of the Sacrament. Luther and Zwingli, having already disputed for three years, fail to find a compromise, Luther's deep consciousness of sin rendering a merely commemorative act inadequate for his spiritual needs. The Conference marks the definite severance of the churches.

Luther's Larger and Smaller Catechism.

196. **Spanish Lit.** Guevara's Dial of Princes, a didactic novel with Marcus Aurelius for its hero, creates the style afterwards practised by Lyly, Gongora and Marini. (Translated by Lord Berners, 1531.)

197. **Education.** Influenced by Margaret, Budaeus, and the Du Bellays, Francis founds the Collége de France for Greek and Hebrew, continuing the work of Lascaris and carrying out a plan suggested by Erasmus. Owing to the hostility of the party of Beda, and to the changeableness of the King, the college for some years maintains a precarious life. Additional chairs are gradually endowed.

198. **Philology.** Budaeus' Commentarii Linguae Graecae.

Robert Stephanus succeeds to his father's printing business at Paris (established about 1502), issues a vast number of works in Greek, Latin and Hebrew, including many of his own editions, and is appointed printer to the King, 1539, but is driven by the Sorbonne to remove to Geneva, 1551.

---

199. **Eng. Ch.** Parliament reduces the Probate charged in Church Courts, and forbids the procuring of licenses from Rome for pluralities, the latter Statute striking the first blow against the Papal power. [1530

200. **German Ch.** Melanchthon represents Lutheranism at the Diet of Augsburg, Luther staying within reach at Coburg. Though admitting the practical identity of doctrine, anxious for a restoration of episcopal authority, and ready to accept the Mass with explanations, Melanchthon's Confession is rejected by the Diet. He now draws up an Apology for the Confession, based on the Articles of the Marburg Conference, the Schwabach and Torgau Articles. Zwingli sends a Confession; and Bucer and Capito, in a first attempt at an Eirenicon, present the Confessio Tetrapolitana, on behalf of four cities of South Germany. The alliance of Spain and the Papacy commences, Venice alone standing outside their influence.

Alexander de Medici is restored by Spanish troops to Florence, which yields after a long siege, the last relics of the communal *régime* being swept away.

141. **Switzerland.** Geneva becomes independent of the Duke of Savoy.

---

142. **England.** The clergy forfeit their possessions under Praemunire for recognising Wolsey as Legate, but are allowed to compound, on condition of recognising the King as supreme head of the Church of England. They introduce the qualification, 'so far as is allowed by the law of Christ.' [1531

Convocation urges the withdrawal of Annates from the Pope, adding that, if he retaliate, obedience should be withdrawn.

143. **Germany.** The Protestant League of Schmalkald is signed by John of Saxony, Hesse, Brunswick-Luneberg, Anhalt, and many towns, and is welcomed by France and Denmark.

144. **Switzerland.** The War of the Cantons breaks out and Zwingli is defeated and slain at Cappel. The Peace provides that each Canton should settle its own religious affairs; but a decided Catholic reaction sets in.

145. **America.** A rumour spreads that Brazil contains precious metals, the first royal governor is sent out, and the coast is divided into Captaincies. A steady flow of colonists takes place, the sugar-cane is introduced from Madeira, and negroes are imported from Guinea.

---

146. **England.** Convocation is forced to sign the Submission of the Clergy, in which it engages neither to meet nor to enact new Canons without the King's leave. On this More resigns the Chancellorship. [1532

147. **Scotland.** James V. founds the College of Justice, modelled on the Parliament of Paris, for civil actions.

148. **Germany.** Owing to the advance of the Turks into Austria, the Emperor agrees with the Schmalkaldic allies to the Peace of Nuremberg, by which toleration is guaranteed till a General Council.

149. **Italy.** Don Pedro de Toledo commences his Viceroyalty, during which he creates modern Naples, introduces law and order, and fortifies the country.

---

150. **England.** The King secretly marries Anne (Jan.), and, on hearing of the Pope's forthcoming decision, induces Parliament to forbid Appeals to Rome. He forces Convocation to condemn Catherine's marriage (March), and licenses Cranmer to hold a Court, which pronounces the marriage void (May). He ratifies the Act of Annates, passed 1532, and appeals to a General Council. [1533

Recess of the Diet forbids Protestant teaching, and orders the restoration of Church property, but promises to urge the Pope to summon a Council.

201. **Philosophy.** Agrippa's De Vanitate Scientiarum et Artium.

202. **Art.** Quintin Matsys dies, and Italian influences become dominant in Flemish art with Mabuse and Van Orley, both of whom study in Italy.

---

203. **Eng. Ch.** The first collection of English hymns and carols. [1531

204. **Swiss Ch.** On the death of Zwingli, Bullinger succeeds to his position and in great measure to his influence.

205. **Church Hist.** Servetus' De Trinitatis Erroribus stimulates the growth of Unitarian ideas, already broached by Denck, Hetzer and Campanus and condemned by the Confession of Augsburg.

Cajetan maintains the doctrine of Papal infallibility.

206. **Education.** Elyot's 'Governor,' a treatise on education, urges gentleness and the study of individuality. Similar ideas are expressed about this time in the De Disciplinis of Vives.

207. **Art.** Primaticcio is appointed Court painter, and aids Rosso and Benvenuto Cellini in naturalising Italian styles in French art, the supremacy of the School of Tours now coming to an end.

---

208. **French Ch.** The Waldenses declare themselves Protestants. [1532

209. **Swiss Ch.** After six years' work in French Switzerland, Farel settles in Geneva and rapidly gains a foothold for Protestantism in the Great Council.

210. **French Lit.** Rabelais' Pantagruel and Gargantua (1535) sketch a scheme of education, recommending the study of the sciences and physical exercises, and satirising scholasticism.

211. **Art.** The Church of St Eustache, at Paris, is begun, marking the transition from Gothic to Italian, visible also in the Château of Blois, now rebuilt.

212. **Philology.** The Thesaurus Latinus of Stephanus.

213. **Law.** The Caroline Code, composed from Roman, German and Christian sources, to reform the criminal jurisprudence of Germany, is published by the Diet of Ratisbon.

214. **Social.** The first Bourse is instituted at Antwerp.

---

215. **Eng. Ch.** Fryth is burnt for rejecting Transubstantiation, though willing to leave it an open question. His death makes [1533 such a sensation that an Act is passed, forbidding Bishops to proceed *ex officio* against heretics.

216. **French Ch.** The influence of Protestantism at Court reaches its high-water-mark, owing to the death of Louise, the King's mother, and

The Nun of Kent is executed for attacking the religious changes and the divorce, Fisher and others being involved by misprision of treason.

151. **France.** To render the Council impossible, the Pope enters into close alliance with Francis, to whose son he marries his niece, Catherine de Medici.

152. **Hungary.** Ferdinand makes peace with the Turks, Solyman receiving the right to be consulted on any measures concerning Hungary.

153. **Denmark.** On the death of Frederick, the throne is disputed, his son Christian being resisted by the clergy as a Lutheran. Wullenweber, Burgomaster of Lubeck, interposes and schemes to recall Christian II.

154. **Turkey.** Barbarossa visits Constantinople and rebuilds the Turkish navy, of which he becomes Admiral.

The Turks enter on war against Persia, 1533—6, and annex part of Georgia.

---

155. **England.** Henry procures from Parliament acts, transferring the Annates of all benefices to the King, regulating the appointment of Bishops by a royal *congé d'élire*, abolishing Peter's Pence, transferring to the Archbishop the Pope's right to issue dispensations, and directing that appeals from the Archbishop's court should be heard by royal commissioners. [1534

The Act of Succession declares Mary illegitimate and Elizabeth heir to the crown. More and Fisher, though willing to recognise any succession appointed by Parliament, refuse to condemn Catherine's marriage, and are imprisoned. Parliament passes a new Treason act for denial of the King's titles.

156. **Ireland.** Kildare is summoned to England and dies in prison, on news of which the Fitzgeralds revolt and are suppressed, six of them being hanged at Tyburn, 1537, a boy of 12 alone surviving. The first great forfeitures are now carried out.

157. **Germany.** The Swabian League being dissolved, Philip of Hesse, with encouragement from Francis and the princes who wish to weaken the Austrian power, resolves to expel King Ferdinand from Wurtemberg and restore Duke Ulrich. Owing to the Emperor's absence and the Turkish attacks in the Mediterranean, Ferdinand, after a defeat at Laufen, accepts the Treaty of Cadan, but secures recognition as King of the Romans. Ulrich at once introduces the Reformation into Wurtemberg.

Lubeck, though failing to carry the other Hanse cities with her, presses on to the attack of Denmark.

---

to the influence of Margaret and Madame d'Étampes, the King's mistress. Calvin is rescued from punishment for an outspoken sermon to the Sorbonne, Beda, the leader of the obscurantists, is banished, and Du Bellay sent to negociate with the German Reformers.

217. **Italian Ch.** Juan Valdez, a Castilian, who has gone to Italy as an official, gathers round him at Naples a circle including Vittoria Colonna, Giulia Gonzaga, Caterina Cybo, Peter Martyr, Ochino, Marcantonio Flaminio, Caraccioli, in which reform and doctrinal changes are freely discussed.

218. **Hungarian Ch.** Though discouraged by both Kings, Lutheranism filters in through Saxony, and is spread by Devay and Honter.

219. **Education.** Smith becomes Professor of Greek at Cambridge, and does much to popularise its study, preparing the way for his successor, Cheke, 1540.

220. **Art.** Michelangelo begins his eight years' labour on the Last Judgment, in the Sistine Chapel.

221. **Social.** Leland is appointed King's antiquary, and starts on his six years' survey of the libraries of England.

222. **Death.** Ariosto.

---

223. **Eng. Ch.** Fourteen 'Anabaptists' are burnt. [1534

224. **French Ch.** A violent reaction against the toleration of Protestants sets in at Paris with the mutilation of a favourite Madonna and the posting of insulting placards about the city, Margaret being forced to declare herself a Catholic.

The translation of the Bible begun by Farel and continued by Olivétan, Calvin's uncle, is published.

Calvin, after receiving his education from Mathurin Cordier at Paris and learning Greek at Bourges from a Lutheran, leaves the Church.

225. **German Ch.** Owing to the Millenarian and Anabaptist teaching of Jan Matthys and Rothmann in Münster and to its recognition by the Council, refugees enter the city in great numbers. The more violent, under John of Leyden, establish 'The Kingdom of Sion,' a *régime* of communism, polygamy and religious terrorism.

226. **Swiss Ch.** The First Confession of Basle, by Oecolampadius and Myconius.

227. **Church Hist.** Loyola, and his fellow-students at Paris, Salmeron, Xavier, Bobadilla, Lainez, Peter Faber and Rodriguez, take an oath at Montmartre to evangelise Palestine, or, failing that, to put themselves at the Pope's orders.

228. **Art.** Michelangelo's Moses.

229. **Social.** English farmers are forbidden to own more than 2,000 sheep, but the attempt to check enclosures fails.

---

158. **England.** The Act of Supremacy proclaims Henry Supreme Head on Earth of the Church of England (Jan.). [1535
For refusing to recognise the title, the Prior and several members of the London Carthusians, imprisoned 1534, are executed, Fisher and More quickly sharing their fate. The new title is attacked by Pole in his De Unitate, for which he is made a Cardinal, and by Gardiner, now Bishop of Winchester, in his De Vera Obedientia. Henry nevertheless makes Thomas Cromwell his Vicar-General, suspending the jurisdiction of the Bishops till a Visitation of the monasteries is completed.

159. **France.** After several years of intrigue, Francis openly allies with Solyman, who grants Capitulations to French subjects which still remain in force.

160. **Denmark.** The Hansa forces are defeated both by land and sea, and at the Hanseatic Diet Wullenweber is bitterly attacked by members of the aristocratic and Catholic party, and shortly deposed and executed. The dominant party at once recognises Christian III. as King of Denmark.

161. **Italy.** Francesco Sforza dies, and the Emperor occupies the Milanese.

162. **Africa.** The Emperor, with a fleet under Doria, defeats Barbarossa and takes Tunis, sacks the city and restores the ruler exiled by Barbarossa as a vassal of Spain.

---

163. **England.** Henry becomes tired of Anne Boleyn and has her executed on a charge of infidelity. On the day after the [1536
execution he marries Jane Seymour, and obtains an Act of Parliament settling the succession on Jane's children, and declaring both Mary and Elizabeth illegitimate.

The King persuades Parliament (March) to dissolve all monastic houses with a revenue of less than £200 a year, amounting to 376, on the ground of evil conduct revealed in the reports (though Cromwell's agents had neither time nor wish to learn or state the truth, the crime of the monasteries consisting less in their conduct than in their close relations to the Papal system). The Court of Augmentations is instituted to conduct the dissolution, the members of the dissolved houses being given the choice of entering others or of receiving, in some cases, a small indemnity.

Annoyed by the religious innovations, by the violence of the dissolution, by the cessation of poor-relief, by Cromwell's monopoly of power, by the spread of enclosures, the northern counties break into a revolt under Aske, a lawyer. The Duke of Norfolk, who is sent to crush the 'Pilgrimage of Grace,' finds it too formidable to attack ; and Henry is obliged to issue an amnesty and to promise a Parliament at York.

230. **Eng. Ch.** Coverdale's translation of the Bible from Latin and German is encouraged by Cromwell and the King. [1535
231. **Irish Ch.** Brown becomes Archbishop of Dublin and the real ruler of the Irish Church for 20 years.
232. **French Ch.** Paris witnesses the first great *Auto-da-fé,* the introduction of strict censorship of the press, and the return of Beda. Duprat, however, dies, and is succeeded by the tolerant Dubourg, Francis returning to a policy of conciliation.
233. **German Ch.** Münster is captured by the Emperor and the Bishop, Protestantism being excluded from the city and the Protestant cause everywhere suffering from the supposed connection with its excesses.

The new edition of Melanchthon's Loci diverges from Luther in the treatment of Justification and the Real Presence, and gives rise to the school of Philippists.
234. **Bohemian Ch.** The First Bohemian Confession, probably by John Augusta, is composed and sent to King Ferdinand and to Luther.
235. **Italian Ch.** The new Pope, Paul III., creates the leaders of the reform party, Pole, Contarini, Sadolet, Caraffa, Cardinals (Erasmus refuses), and appoints a Commission on Church Reform, the report of which is drawn up chiefly by Contarini.
236. **Scotch Lit.** Lyndsay's Satire of the Three Estates criticises Church and State.
237. **Education.** Cromwell issues Injunctions, encouraging the New Learning and forbidding the study of Canon Law or Scholasticism. His visitors find the pages of Duns Scotus scattered about New College.

---

238. **Eng. Ch.** The King, with the aid of Cranmer and Fox, frames the Ten Articles, in part from the Confession of Augsburg, to secure uniformity. [1536
239. **French Ch.** Calvin's Institutes of the Christian Religion.
240. **German Ch.** The Wittenberg Concordia, composed by Melanchthon, is accepted by the Protestants of South Germany, chiefly owing to Bucer.
241. **Netherlands Ch.** The moderate anabaptists, under the lead of Menno, dissociate themselves from the extremists, of whom David Joris becomes the leader. About the same time, Families of Love are formed by Henry Nicholas.
242. **Portuguese Ch.** The Inquisition is introduced, deals principally with the descendants of the Jews converted 1492, and harasses Damian de Goes and other Humanists. (In 1557, it is made a department of State.)
243. **Danish Ch.** At the instance of the King, the Diet deposes the Bishops and secularises much ecclesiastical land.
244. **Swiss Ch.** Farel having, since his arrival in Geneva, 1534, persuaded the city to adopt Protestantism, induces his friend Calvin to

164. **Wales.** Wales is united to England in matters of law.
165. **Ireland.** The Irish Parliament registers the Act of Supremacy, dissolves Monasteries, and orders the adoption of the English language, dress and customs.
166. **France.** France conquers Savoy and Piedmont (Feb.), and repels Charles' invasion of Provence (July), and his attack on Marseilles (Sept.); the Turkish fleet meanwhile ravages the Italian coast.
167. **Germany.** The Schmalkaldic League receives as members the princes of Wurtemberg, Pomerania and Anhalt and several cities.
168. **Switzerland.** The Duke of Savoy attacks Geneva, but is defeated by the aid of Bern and forced to cede part of his territories.

[1537

169. **England.** The King, knowing that the Scotch are planning an invasion and that Pole is busy in Flanders, cancels his amnesty and executes the leaders of the recent insurrection. A Council of the North is appointed, the nobles being bribed into acquiescence by the grant of the greater monastic houses, which are dissolved in great numbers on charges of complicity in the insurrection or of evil living.
170. **Scotland.** Despite the efforts of Henry to secure his friendship, James enters into a close alliance with France by marrying a daughter of Francis.
171. **Germany.** The Princes of Brandenburg and Liegnitz form a treaty of mutual inheritance. The Duke of Liegnitz is compelled by Ferdinand, as King of Hungary, to revoke the treaty; but the revocation is never recognised by the Hohenzollerns.
172. **Italy.** Alessandro de Medici is murdered, and Cosimo, of a collateral branch of the Medici, succeeds, and crushes the conspiracy of Filippo Strozzi, the leader of the Republicans. He annexes Siena, 1555, and obtains the title of Grand Duke from the Pope, 1569, which the Emperor recognises 1576.

[1538

173. **England.** The destruction of the tomb of Becket at Canterbury impels the Pope to launch his excommunication of Henry, withheld since 1535 at the entreaty of Francis.

    The Marquis of Exeter, first cousin of the King, and several of the Poles are executed on a charge of conspiracy.
174. **Scotland.** On the death of his first wife, James marries Mary of Guise.
175. **France.** The third war (1536–8) between Francis and Charles is terminated by the 10 years' Truce of Nice, both retaining their conquests, the Duke of Savoy thus being excluded. The peace is seemingly confirmed by a personal interview at Aigues-Mortes.
176. **Germany.** The Vice-Chancellor Held, acting as the agent of Charles, unites Austria, Bavaria, Brunswick, and George of Saxony in the League of Nuremberg against the Schmalkaldic allies.

come to his aid. Calvin draws up a Catechism, which he imposes on every citizen, and creates a spiritual Consistory.

Bullinger, Myconius, and other Zwinglians draw up the First Helvetic Confession, in view of a General Council.

245. **Classics.** Dolet's Commentarii Linguae Latinae.

246. **Social.** The first comprehensive Poor Law forbids begging, and ordains the collection of alms for the impotent and the supply of work for others.

An attempt is made to free land from 'Uses.'

The manufacture of silk is commenced at Lyons by Italians, whom Francis induces to settle there.

247. **Death.** Erasmus.

---

248. **Eng. Ch.** The Institution of a Christian Man, a work slightly more conservative than the Ten Articles, is composed by a committee of lawyers and divines. [1537

249. **German Ch.** The Pope having invited Protestants to a General Council at Mantua, the Elector of Saxony orders the preparation of a Creed. Luther therefore draws up the strongly anti-Papal Schmalcald Articles, to which Melanchthon adds an appendix attacking the primacy of the Pope.

250. **Danish Ch.** To complete the organisation of the Lutheran Church, Bugenhagen is summoned to Copenhagen, draws up a constitution and form of worship, and reorganises the University, of which he becomes Rector and Professor of Theology.

251. **Science.** Tartaglia applies mathematics to military defence, and explains the curve of bullets, etc.

252. **Education.** The University is finally transferred from Lisbon to Coimbra, and enters on its golden age with Andrea Govea and Buchanan.

John Sturm begins to teach classics in Strassburg, his school soon containing 1000 boys.

253. **History.** Guicciardini loses influence, retires to his home, and composes his Florentine History and his Maxims.

---

254. **Eng. Ch.** Cromwell, as Vicar-General, issues Injunctions, e.g. that a Bible should be placed in every Church. Some Lutheran divines, however, invited to England by Cranmer, offend the King by criticising the English Church. From this moment a reaction in Henry's mind begins. [1538

255. **Scotch Ch.** Buchanan attacks the clergy in his Franciscanus.

256. **French Ch.** The persecution of Protestantism recommences.

257. **Swiss Ch.** Calvin is compelled to leave Geneva for Strassburg.

258. **French Lit.** Despériers, an imitator of Rabelais, mocks at all religions in his Cymbalum Mundi, which the Sorbonne burns.

259. **German Lit.** Kirchmayer's Pammachius, a Protestant picture of Anti-Christ and the typical drama of the Reformation.

177. **Spain.** The Nobles and Clergy are excluded from the Castilian Cortes, deputies of the cities alone being admitted.

178. **Hungary.** The rivals agree that Ferdinand shall rule Hungary on the death of Zapolya.

179. **Turkey.** Barbarossa takes Morea and part of the Archipelago from Venice.

---

180. **England.** Parliament declares the proclamations of the King as valid as its own Acts. It also presents to the King the property of the remaining monasteries, most of which he gives or sells to new families, a small part being devoted to the endowment of six new Bishoprics and the construction of ships and fortifications. The disappearance of the Abbots from the Upper House gives the secular peers a majority. [1539

181. **Scotland.** David Beaton succeeds his uncle as Archbishop of St Andrews, and becomes chief adviser to the King, supporting the anti-English policy to which James has pledged himself.

182. **Germany.** Duke George of Saxony, a vigorous opponent of the Reformation, dies and is succeeded by his brother Henry, who introduces Lutheranism. At the same moment, Joachim, Elector of Brandenburg, allows the adoption of Protestantism, the old faith now being represented in North Germany by Brunswick alone.

183. **America.** De Soto lands with a large army in Florida, and pushes North-West to the Mississippi, where the survivors of the expedition build boats and sail down to Mexico, 1543.

---

184. **England.** To pledge the King to a Protestant policy beyond power of drawing back, Cromwell persuades him to marry Anne of Cleves, of whom Holbein paints a too flattering portrait. Henry, however, becomes anxious for the friendship of the Emperor, divorces Anne and sacrifices Cromwell (condemned by a bill of attainder without being heard in his own defence,) to the nobles, of whom Norfolk, the uncle of the new Queen, Katherine Howard, exercises the chief power. [1540

185. **Netherlands.** Ghent, which has refused a subsidy, 1536, offers its allegiance to Francis, who informs the Emperor. All charters are therefore annulled, gild property is confiscated, the commercial prosperity of the city is crippled, and the way is prepared for the war of independence.

The Emperor makes René of Chalons Stadtholder in Holland, Zealand and Utrecht, thus introducing the family of Orange.

186. **Hungary.** Zapolya dies, but the treaty of 1538 is broken by the proclamation of his son as King and his recognition by the Sultan, who, however, in the following year carves out for himself a province with the capital at Buda, between Western or Austrian Hungary and Transylvania, and compels Ferdinand to pay tribute for the former.

260. **Politics.** Melanchthon's Ethicae Doctrinae Elementa contains the first Protestant statement of Natural Right.

261. **Philology.** Postel, after two journeys in the East, becomes the first Professor of Oriental Languages at the Collége de France.

---

262. **Eng. Ch.** The King persuades Convocation and Parliament to enact Six Articles, affirming transubstantiation, Communion in one kind, clerical celibacy, the perpetual obligation of vows of chastity, private masses and confession. Savage penalties are attached, but are not often applied. Latimer is driven from his see and Cranmer forced to dismiss his wife. [1539

The Great Bible, a revision of Tyndale's and Coverdale's, is printed by royal letters-patent.

263. **German Ch.** Philip of Hesse, desiring to take a second wife into his household, consults Luther, Melanchthon and Bucer, who reply that the practice is sanctioned by the O. T., and not forbidden by the N. T. The marriage and its sanction by the Protestant leaders form an effective weapon against the Lutheran cause.

264. **Swiss Ch.** Cardinal Sadoleto writes an open letter to the Genevese, urging them to return to the Church, and provokes a spirited reply from Calvin.

Calvin's first Commentary on the Epistle to the Romans.

---

265. **German Ch.** The Lutherans formally condemn the mystical Pantheists, Franck and Schwenkfeld. [1540

John Agricola leaves Wittenberg, after quarrelling with Luther and Melanchthon, on account of the stress they lay on the observance of the law.

Melanchthon revises the Confession of Augsburg, especially in regard to the Real Presence and Justification, the changes being adopted at the Conference of Worms. The Confessio Variata is signed by Calvin, and used at Regensburg, 1541, and elsewhere.

266. **Italian Ch.** An anonymous tract on the Benefits of Christ's Death, written from the standpoint of Luther's theory of Justification, finds an immense circulation, and powerfully contributes to the spread of Protestantism in Italy.

Steuco, Librarian of the Vatican, maintains, in his De Perenni Philosophia, that the Christian doctrines of the Trinity, Creation, Immortality prevailed in the earliest times and in all lands.

267. **Church Hist.** Loyola and his companions, adding to the vows of Poverty, Chastity and Obedience an oath of obedience to the Pope, are constituted the Society of Jesus by a Papal Bull, Loyola being chosen first General, 1541, and are urged to devote themselves to missionary and educational work in Europe.

268. **Art.** Tallis is appointed to the Chapel Royal, and begins his long series of compositions of Church Music, some of which are designed for

187. **America.** Cartier returns to the Saint Lawrence with five ships, and attempts to found a settlement.

Attracted by the stories of wealth collected by Narvaez (1528–36) and others, an expedition under Coronado is sent northwards from Mexico, but, after marching as far as Nebraska, returns without finding gold.

188. **Asia.** After 10 years of fighting, Hamayun is.driven out of India by Afghan settlers under Sher Shah who becomes Emperor of Delhi.

---

189. **England.** Margaret, Countess of Salisbury, daughter of Clarence, is executed on a charge of conspiracy, but in reality for being mother of Cardinal Pole. [1541

190. **Africa.** The Emperor fails in an attack on Algiers, his fleet being destroyed by a storm, and leaves the Mediterranean in the hands of the French and the Turks. A Spanish expedition to Jerba, 1560, is repulsed, and in 1574, with the withdrawal from Goletta, Spanish influence over Tunis comes to an end.

---

191. **Scotland.** After a period of uneasy peace, war breaks out again, and Norfolk ravages the border. A Scotch army enters Cumberland, but flies in panic to Solway Moss, where nearly all the troops are slain or captured. James V. dies a few days later, leaving the throne to his daughter Mary, now a week old. [1542

192. **Ireland.** Henry is acknowledged King of Ireland by a Parliament at Dublin, attended by native chiefs, to whom he gives English titles and abbey lands, the change of title (from that of Lord, granted to Henry II. by the Pope) serving to mark his independence of Rome.

193. **France.** Francis allies with Denmark and Sweden and commences his fourth war against Charles in the Netherlands, in Italy and on the Spanish frontier, owing to the investiture of Charles' son with Milan.

194. **Germany.** At the Diet of Spires, the Protestants contribute money for use against the Turks, in return for a five years' truce.

The Duke of Brunswick, refusing to obey the Recess of the Diet of Ratisbon, is expelled by the Schmalkaldic League, which establishes Protestantism in his dominions. Indignant at this treatment, the Elector of Brandenburg withdraws from the League and secretly joins the Emperor, his example being followed by Duke Maurice of Saxony, who covets the possessions of his Ernestine cousin.

195. **America.** Roberval arrives in Canada as Viceroy; but the colonists whom he brings are forced to return after two years, and the settlement of Canada is postponed for half a century.

---

use with the new Prayer-book. With Byrd, Orlando Gibbons, etc., he forms the so-called Sixth English School.

269. **Philology.** Scaliger's De Causis Linguae Latinae.

270. **Education.** The Regius Professorships of Divinity, Law, Physics, Hebrew and Greek are instituted at Oxford and Cambridge.

271. **Deaths.** Budaeus, Guicciardini, Vives.

---

272. **German Ch.** At the Diet of Ratisbon, the most important of several similar attempts at reunion, Melanchthon and Bucer meet Contarini, the Legate, who approximates to the Lutheran view of Justification, but cannot persuade the Pope to allow re-union on that basis, nor to accept his compromise in relation to the Papal Supremacy. Though re-union is not achieved, the Treaty of Nuremberg is confirmed and Protestants are allowed to enter the Imperial Chamber. [1541

273. **Swiss Ch.** Calvin returns to Geneva, on the invitation of the city, which now accepts his Ordonnances Ecclésiastiques, and restores the Consistory of pastors and lay elders. His opponents, the so-called Libertines, whom he attacks in a vigorous polemic, 1545, are one after another executed or banished.

Calvin's Tract on the Lord's Supper.

274. **Deaths.** Paracelsus, Pizarro.

---

275. **German Ch.** Luther provokes violent hostility by consecrating a Bishop. [1542

276. **Italian Ch.** The establishment of the Inquisition at Rome, on the advice and under the direction of Caraffa, initiates the crusade against Protestantism throughout Italy. Ochino, already charged with heresy, now declares his conversion and flees to Geneva, and the circle at Ferrara is scattered.

277. **Asiatic Ch.** Xavier's expedition to Goa initiates mission work in the East, he himself passing on to Japan, 1549. (Nagasaki becomes largely Christianised, 1573.)

278. **Church Hist.** Luther attacks the Jews in his Juden und ihre Lugen.

279. **Spanish Lit.** Montemayor's Diana naturalises the pastoral romance.

280. **Science.** Vesalius of Brussels founds modern Anatomy by his Fabrica Corporis Humani, in which he incorporates the researches of Mundino, Achillini, Berenger of Carpi, openly parts from Sylvius, his old Paris teacher, a follower of Galen, and introduces illustrations of his researches on human bodies.

281. **Art.** The Academia Vitruviana, which is now founded in Rome, marks, with the treatises of Palladio, the supremacy of classic models in architecture.

282. **Education.** Castellio, Rector of the college at Geneva, composes his Dialogues Sacrés, a favourite school-book of Latin for 200 years.

---

196. **England.** Henry marries Katherine Parr, with whom Protestant influences reappear at Court. [1543

197. **Wales.** The country is divided into counties, and the Court of the Welsh Marches is instituted.

198. **Scotland.** A Treaty for the marriage of Prince Edward with Mary, who is to be sent to England in 10 years, is negociated, but fails, owing to the hostility of Beaton, the Queen-mother and Bishop Hamilton, whose party the Regent Angus joins.

199. **France.** Francis defeats Charles at Landreçies, and, with the aid of the Turkish fleet, which now sails the Mediterranean unchallenged, captures Nice from Savoy. The Emperor, however, compels the Duke of Cleves to yield Gelderland.

200. **Germany.** The Archbishop of Cologne is deposed for admitting Protestantism, to which he has been drawn by Bucer, into his dominions.

---

201. **England.** Henry, having allied with Charles, 1543, invades Picardy and captures Boulogne, the expense being in part provided by debasing the coinage. At the same moment, Parliament declares that the King need not repay a loan which he has collected. [1544

202. **Scotland.** Hertford and Lisle invade Scotland, ravage the Lowlands and burn Edinburgh.

203. **Germany.** At the Diet of Spires, Charles, on promising a Council in Germany or a Diet to deal with religion, receives supplies against the French and Turks, invades Champagne and threatens Paris. The last war of Francis and Charles is, however, terminated by the peace of Crépi (Sept.), concluded without consulting England. Conquests on both sides since the truce of Nice, 1538, are restored; Francis surrenders his claims to Naples, Flanders, Artois, Gelderland, and Charles his claim to Burgundy, though retaining Milan as a fief for Philip. A marriage alliance is also discussed.

204. **Savoy.** The Peace of Crépi decrees the restoration of his estates to Charles of Savoy, which, however, is not carried out.

205. **Sweden.** On the attempt of Christian III. of Denmark to win the Emperor's aid against Sweden, Gustavus makes a close alliance with France, and enters into European politics.

206. **Hungary.** Solyman divides Hungary into 12 administrative districts.

---

207. **England.** A benevolence of 1/8 in the £ on land and 10*d.* in the £ on goods is levied to combat the French, who land on the Isle of Wight. [1545

208. **Scotland.** A division of the English army is defeated at Ancrum Moor, after which reinforcements are sent, and the ravages are recommenced.

209. **Italy.** The Pope creates the duchy of Parma and Piacenza for his son, Piero Farnese.

283. **Eng. Ch.** The Erudition of a Christian Man, issued by the King's orders, is substituted for the more Protestant Institution. [1543

284. **Spanish Ch.** The first Protestant is burned; Enzina is imprisoned for his translation of the New Testament; and Juan Diaz is murdered by his brother, 1546.

285. **Spanish Lit.** Garcilaso's poems carry on the tradition of Boscan.

286. **Philosophy.** Ramus' Animadversiones Aristotelicae is condemned by the Sorbonne and attacked by Schegk and others, but creates a school, influences Taurellus, Patrizzi, Bruno, Gassendi, the logicians of Port-Royal, and finds its way into most Protestant Universities in Germany, and into England and Scotland.

287. **Science.** Copernicus' De Revolutionibus Orbis Terrarum rejects Ptolemy's explanation of the movements of the planets by the theory of epicycles. The new teaching is tabulated and spread by Reinhold and Maestlin, but is combated by Maurolycus and Tycho Brahe, and remains little known till championed by Bruno, Campanella, Kepler and Galileo.

288. **Deaths.** Copernicus, Holbein.

---

289. **Eng. Ch.** Cranmer lays the foundation of the English Prayer-book by composing a Litany, prayers for the King and private devotions. [1544

290. **German Ch.** Luther makes a final attack on the sacramental theory of the Zuinglians.

291. **Church Hist.** In consequence of the Emperor's explicit utterances at the Diet of Spires, the Pope summons a Council to meet at Trent in 1545.

292. **French Lit.** Margaret of Navarre's Heptameron, aided by Despériers, on the model of Boccaccio.

Maurice Scéve's Délie creates the 'Lyons school,' inspired by Plato and Petrarch and developed by Louise Labé.

---

293. **Eng. Ch.** The dissolution of Chantries is decreed. [1545

294. **French Ch.** Francis almost exterminates the Vaudois.

295. **Spanish Ch.** St Peter of Alcantara's De Oratione et Meditatione initiates Catholic mysticism in Spain.

296. **Church Hist.** The long-promised Council is opened at Trent (Dec.). Cardinal Del Monte presides, and Charles sends Mendoza as his ambassador. Pacheco, Carranza and Soto represent Spain. No German prelates are present.

297. **Science.** Cardan's Ars Magna communicates Tartaglia's plan of solving cubic equations.

Paré's Manière de traitez les Plaies founds modern surgery by substituting ligature for cauterisation.

210. **Germany.** A truce is made with the Turks, and the Emperor, now everywhere at peace, becomes ready for the Council.

211. **Asia.** John de Castro is appointed Viceroy of Portuguese India, defeats a large Turkish fleet and the King of Gujarat in a pitched battle, and reforms the administration, dying 1548.

---

212. **England.** Henry arrests Norfolk and his son Surrey, the poet, for treason. [1546

213. **Scotland.** Wishart is arrested and burned by Beaton, partly for heresy and partly for joining in a plot to murder him. His death inflames the English party among the nobles, of whom Leslie and Kirkaldy of Grange, both in Henry's pay, murder the Cardinal at St Andrews.

214. **France.** Henry makes peace with France, in which Scotland is included, undertaking, on payment of a large sum, to restore Boulogne.

215. **Germany.** The death of Luther (Feb.) gives the signal for the civil war so long expected. John Frederick and Philip are put to the ban of the Empire (July). Duke Maurice of Saxony secretly joins the Emperor and occupies the Electorate, and Charles reduces the members of the League in South Germany.

216. **Turkey.** The Turks occupy Moldavia.

---

217. **England.** Surrey is executed (Norfolk being saved by the King's death), the conservative party being so weakened that [1547 Henry's plan of a balance in the Council is set aside and Hertford is made Protector with the title of Duke of Somerset. The newly-made treasons, and the Act giving legal force to Proclamations are repealed. Parliament vests in the King the endowments of all Chantries and religious societies dissolved by the Act of 1545, but only now executed.

218. **Scotland.** St Andrews being recaptured by a French fleet, Somerset determines to force on the marriage of Edward with Mary, and destroys the Scotch army at Musselburgh, where the English navy for the first time cooperates with the army, and at Pinkie Cleugh, and burns Holyrood and Leith.

219. **France.** The new King, Henry II., still further increases the royal power by appointing Intendants of Police and Justice, and instituting new tribunals overriding the Seignorial Courts.

220. **Germany.** The Emperor routs the Schmalkaldic allies at Muhlberg (April), John Frederick of Saxony is captured and his electorate and nearly all his dominions transferred to Maurice, only a few scattered territories in Thuringia being reserved for his sons. Philip of Hesse submits, the Duke of Brunswick is restored to his duchy, all North Germany except the city of Magdeburg is reduced, and Protestantism enters on its most critical period.

Ferdinand invades Bohemia, which refuses troops to the Emperor, makes it a hereditary possession, and curtails the privileges of the nation.

298. **Art.** Cellini sculptures Perseus (Florence).
299. **Education.** Henry VIII. refounds Wolsey's College as Christ Church.
300. **Social.** Silver mines are opened in Potosi, in Peru, the output from which largely decreases the value of money.

---

301. **French Ch.** Dolet, the printer of Lyons and the leading scholar and humanist of France, is burned at Paris for printing Protestant books and disbelieving in the immortality of the soul. [1546

The first edition of Stephanus' N. T., based on the Complutensian and on that of Erasmus.
302. **Church Hist.** The Council of Trent declares revelation continuous in the Church of which the Pope is the head, maintains the sole authority of the Vulgate, and forbids monks to preach without the Bishop's license except in churches of their own order.
303. **Science.** Agricola's De Re Metallica founds mineralogy, to which few additions are made for two centuries.
304. **Art.** Palissy makes a white enamel.

Lescot begins his 30 years' labours on the construction of the Louvre, Jean Goujon undertaking the sculptural decoration.

Michelangelo designs the dome of St Peter's.
305. **Education.** Trinity College, Cambridge, is founded by Henry VIII., by combining King's Hall and Michaelhouse and adding monastic lands. The first three Masters and many of the lecturers are drawn from St John's College.
306. **Death.** Luther.

---

307. **Eng. Ch.** Bonner and Tunstal are deprived, and Gardiner is imprisoned. A visitation is commenced, homilies and the Paraphrases of Erasmus are circulated, and the cup is given to the laity. [1547

Peter Martyr teaches theology at Oxford.
308. **Italian Ch.** An attempt to introduce the Spanish Inquisition into Naples fails.
309. **Church Hist.** Luther's theory of Justification is condemned, the doctrine of the sacraments is defined, and a compromise is reached in reference to episcopal residence, forbidding pluralism but safeguarding the Papal dispensing power. The Pope, relying on the support of France, revokes the Council to Bologna on the plea of the plague (March). Most of the Spanish Bishops, however, refuse to leave Trent, neither branch dares to continue work, and the Pope shortly postpones the Council indefinitely.
310. **Social.** The King confiscates the religious endowments of the English gilds, the influence of which henceforward steadily diminishes.
311. **Deaths.** Bembo, Vittoria Colonna, Sadoleto.

---

221. **Russia.** Ivan IV. is crowned, assumes the title of Tsar, takes Kazan (1548) and Astrakhan (1550) from the Mongols, thus extending Russia to the Caspian, strengthens the defences, reorganises the Church, introduces a printing-press and institutes schools.

---

222. **Germany.** At the Diet of Augsburg, the Emperor carries his proposals without opposition. The Imperial Chamber is reconstituted, the appointment of its members being vested in the Emperor; the Netherlands are formed into a Circle of the Empire; and a new military treasury is formed under the Emperor's control. [1548

223. **Scotland.** Mary is sent for protection to France.

224. **Italy.** Henry of France occupies the marquisate of Saluzzo.

225. **Asia.** Mendez Pinto establishes a factory in Japan and opens up the country to Portuguese settlers.

---

226. **England.** A rebellion, provoked by the innovations of the Council, and, above all, by the issue of the new Prayer-Book, breaks out in Devon and Cornwall, and is put down with difficulty by Russell with foreign mercenaries. Simultaneously, a rising takes place in Norfolk, provoked chiefly by enclosures, led by Ket, who establishes a camp on Mousehold Hill. Palings near Norwich are pulled down, but the revolt, despite the sympathy of the Protector, is suppressed by Dudley, Earl of Warwick. The failure of Somerset's foreign policy and his unpopularity in the country embolden the Council to depose him and to abolish the Protectorate, Warwick at once assuming a leading position. [1549

227. **America.** De Sousa arrives in Brazil with troops, officials and Jesuits and governs with remarkable ability, the natives being well treated and the Inquisition excluded.

---

228. **England.** Warwick makes peace with France, surrendering Boulogne, and with Scotland, prisoners being released on both sides. At this moment, Somerset regains some power in the Council. [1550

229. **Africa.** Fez is captured by the Sheriffs of Morocco.

230. **Germany.** The Emperor attempts to secure the succession of his son Philip to the Empire, but is resisted by his brother Ferdinand, King of the Romans, and by several German princes. At this moment, Maurice of Saxony, feeling that the Emperor has nothing more to give him, resolves to desert the Imperial cause, and refuses to appear at the Diet of Augsburg, ostensibly because Philip of Hesse is not released from imprisonment.

---

312. **Eng. Ch.** A new Communion Office is established by proclamation of the Council, images are removed, and preaching is forbidden. [1548

313. **German Ch.** Owing to his quarrel with the Pope, the Emperor asks the Diet to accept the Interim, conceding the cup and the marriage of the clergy. The Interim leads to a fierce strife between the Adiaphorists, chiefly Melanchthonians, who accept it, and the strict Lutherans, led by Flacius.

314. **Church Hist.** Loyola's Spiritual Exercises.

315. **Education.** The Elector of Saxony founds Jena University.

---

316. **Eng. Ch.** The Committee of Divines sitting at Windsor present their draft of a Prayer-Book, largely compiled from the Sarum Use and the Consultation of Archbishop Hermann, composed by Melanchthon and Bucer, 1543, with slight additions from Greek and Mozarabic rites. The Act of Uniformity establishes its use. [1549

Bucer becomes Regius Professor of Theology at Cambridge.

Ochino, a refugee, attacks the Papacy in his Tragedy.

Joan Bocher is burned for denying the divinity of Christ.

317. **German Ch.** Osiander attacks the Lutheran theory of Justification.

The Jesuits enter Ingoldstadt and spread over Germany.

Melanchthon composes the Little Interim for Saxony.

318. **Scotch Lit.** The Complaint of Scotland, an attack on English policy, the first important monument of modern Scotch prose.

319. **French Lit.** Du Bellay's Défense et Illustration de la Langue Française initiates the reform of the Pleiade, Ronsard, Jodelle, Belleau, Baïf, Daurat, Pontus de Tyard and Du Bellay. Their ideas, exemplified by Ronsard's Odes, 1550, dominate French literature until Malherbe.

320. **German Lit.** Dedekind's Grobianus, developed from Brandt.

321. **Death.** Margaret of Navarre.

---

322. **Eng. Ch.** Hooper refuses to wear episcopal vestures. [1550

Cranmer's True and Catholic Doctrine of the Sacrament.

Lasco, a Pole, receives the Church of the Augustinians for refugees, the congregation appointing its officers.

Henry Nicholas, a friend of David Joris, a mystical Pantheist, founds Families of Love among the Dutch refugees.

323. **Netherlands Ch.** The Emperor establishes the Inquisition.

324. **Eng. Lit.** Udall's Ralph Roister Doister founds English comedy.

325. **Death.** Alciati.

---

231. **England.** The King and Warwick attempt to forbid Mary to hear Mass, but yield before the displeasure of the Emperor. Warwick's growing unpopularity strengthens Somerset, but the King sides with Warwick and has his uncle arrested, and (1552) executed. [1551

232. **Germany.** Maurice, owing to the Emperor still refusing to release his father-in-law, Philip of Hesse, undertakes to force the acceptance of the Interim on Magdeburg, the head-quarters of opposition, as a pretext for collecting an army, and allies with the Protestant Princes.

233. **Turkey.** The Turks attack Malta, without success.

234. **Africa.** Tripoli is taken from the Knights of St John, by Dragut, once a lieutenant of Barbarossa.

---

235. **Germany.** The Protestant Princes persuade Henry II. to join them against the Emperor, promising him the rule of Metz, Toul, Verdun and Cambray as Imperial vicar. Maurice, having terminated the siege of Magdeburg, openly deserts the Emperor, seizes Augsburg, and only misses the capture of Charles at Innsbruck by a few hours. The Emperor therefore empowers Ferdinand to conclude peace at Passau. John Frederick of Saxony and Philip of Hesse are released (though the Electoral dignity is never restored to the Ernestine branch), the Lutherans are allowed free exercise of their religion and admitted into the Imperial Chamber, and a Diet is promised to effect a permanent settlement. [1552

236. **France.** Meanwhile the French overrun Lorraine and occupy Toul, Verdun, and Metz (April), the latter of which Charles attempts to retake (Oct.). He is, however, forced by the winter to withdraw, leaving the border fortresses in Henry's possession.

237. **Hungary.** The Turks take Temesvar.

---

238. **England.** Northumberland, observing that the King cannot live long, and, dreading the accession of Mary, induces him to set aside his father's Will, though sanctioned by Parliament, and to leave the crown to Jane Grey, a Protestant, the granddaughter of Mary, younger sister of Henry VIII., whom he marries to his son. The Council, at the entreaty of the dying King, signs the Will, and, on Edward's death, Lady Jane is proclaimed Queen (July). Owing, however, to the unpopularity of Northumberland, she is deserted by the troops, and Mary, who had fled to the Howards in Norfolk, is proclaimed Queen in London. Northumberland is executed and Gardiner becomes Chancellor, and shapes the Queen's policy till the arrival of Pole. The Parliament which now meets, though not disapproving the [1553

326. **German. Ch.** Major declares good works necessary to salvation, and is attacked by Amsdorf. [1551
327. **Italian Ch.** The Jesuits found the Collegio Romano.
328. **Church Hist.** The new Pope, Julius III., allows the Bishops to reassemble at Trent, but the Council, to which certain Protestant princes send ambassadors, is paralysed by the refusal of France to join, and, after defining the Eucharist, is suspended (1552), on pretext of danger from the army of Maurice of Saxony.
329. **German Lit.** Wickram's novels of bourgeois life.
330. **Science.** Gesner's Historia Animalium, the first original work on Zoology since Aristotle and Theophrastus.
331. **Social.** The English currency reaches its greatest debasement.
332. **Death.** Bucer.

---

333. **Eng. Ch.** The Prayer-Book is revised by Cranmer, Ridley, Cox, Taylor, on the lines of the Swiss reformers. [1552
334. **Scotch Ch.** Hoping to retain waverers in the Church, Archbishop Hamilton issues a Catechism omitting mention of the Papal supremacy.
335. **German Ch.** Westphal of Hamburg attacks Crypto-Calvinist notions of the Lord's Supper, held by Major and Peucer, Melanchthon's son-in-law.
336. **Swiss Ch.** Calvin replies to Bolsec's attack on Predestination.
337. **Russian Ch.** A few Bohemian Brothers enter the country; but neither Protestantism nor Roman Catholicism, which the Jesuit Possevin is sent to champion, gains any foothold.
338. **Scotch Lit.** Sir David Lyndsay's Monarchy, an historical and philosophical survey with a strong anti-Catholic bias.
339. **French Lit.** Jodelle's Cléopatre founds the classical drama, developed by Grévin, Garnier, Hardy, and Montchrétien, etc. In the same year Jodelle's La Rencontre, the first French comedy, is produced.
340. **Art.** Vignola builds the Villa di Papa Giulio outside Rome, and explains the 'Jesuit' style in his Trattato degli Ordini.
341. **Education.** Christ's Hospital and over 30 grammar schools are founded by the King, whose interest in education is aroused by Ridley.
342. **Death.** Xavier.

---

343. **Eng. Ch.** The Confession of Faith, drafted by Cranmer and Ridley, on the basis of the 13 Articles agreed on by Cranmer and the Lutheran divines, 1538, is ratified by Convocation, and published by the King's command in 42 Articles. [1553

On the accession of Mary, the imprisoned Bishops are restored, the foreign refugees leave the country, and the Reforming Bishops are committed to the Tower. The Commons repeal the religious legislation of Edward VI., but retain that of Henry VIII.

Queen's Church policy, petitions against the Spanish marriage now being negociated, and is in consequence dissolved.

239. **Germany.** Rendered reckless by his losses, the Emperor encourages Albert of Brandenburg (who refused to lay down his arms at Passau, but subsequently joined Charles) in his raids, thereby alienating both classes of his subjects, and driving Ferdinand to form a league to guarantee the execution of the provisions of Passau, and to oppose Philip's succession to the Imperial dignity. Maurice undertakes to reduce Albert, and routs him in a battle in which he loses his life. Albert, in consequence, recovers his position, but, after repeated defeats, retires to France and enters the service of Henry.

240. **Africa.** English trading ships visit the West African coast for the first time.

---

241. **England.** The opposition to the Spanish marriage culminates in a revolt, led by Wyatt, in Kent, and Suffolk, father of [1554
Lady Jane, in the Midlands, with a view to make Elizabeth Queen. Suffolk fails, but Wyatt reaches London, where he is defeated and captured. Lady Jane, her husband, and her father are executed, and Elizabeth imprisoned. Parliament consents to the Spanish match, and Philip comes to England and marries Mary (July). A new Parliament is summoned, which repeals all statutes against the Pope since 1529, on condition that the surrender of the abbey lands is not demanded. The Kingdom is received back into the jurisdiction of the Pope by Pole, who, though appointed Legate on Mary's accession, is only now allowed by the Emperor to enter the country.

242. **Scotland.** The Queen Mother, by the aid of France, obtains the regency from Arran, whose avarice and weakness have rendered him unpopular. She alienates the nobles, however, by filling offices with foreigners, garrisons Dunbar with French soldiers, and proposes to levy taxes for a standing army.

---

243. **England.** The Queen restores all Church property vested in the Crown, and a few monastic houses are in consequence re- [1555
founded.

244. **Germany.** The Diet promised at Passau meets at Augsburg, under the Emperor's plenipotentiary, Ferdinand, repeats the principle of Cujus Regio, Ejus Religio, laid down at Spires, 1526, and admits both parties in equal numbers to the Imperial Chamber. Secularisations of Church property before 1552 are confirmed, but Ferdinand and the Catholics insist on an Ecclesiastic Reservation, by which future converts to Lutheranism shall resign their offices and patronage. Against this the Lutherans issue a protest, which is incorporated in the Treaty. Though recognising no Protestants except Lutherans, and conceding no individual freedom of conscience, the Treaty forms the basis of religious and political life in Germany till the Thirty Years' War.

344. **Swiss Ch.** Servetus' Christianismi Restitutio, a scheme of Neo-Platonism, leads Calvin to obtain the author's prosecution at Lyons, and to send his letters and notes on the Institutes. On escaping from Lyons, Servetus is arrested in Geneva and burned. His punishment is censured by Castellio but applauded by Beza, Melanchthon, and Bullinger. Unitarianism, however, is taught in Geneva and Zurich by the Italian refugees, Gribaldo, Biandrata, Alciati, Gentile, Ochino, and carried to Poland and Transylvania.

345. **Church Hist.** Hosius' Confessio Fidei Catholicae, a popular symbol.

346. **Geography.** Furnished with plans by Cabot, Chancellor and Willoughby start on the North-East passage to China. Willoughby is lost, but Chancellor lands at Archangel, reaches Moscow, and opens up commerce, for which the Muscovy Company is chartered, 1554.

347. **Death.** Rabelais.

---

348. **Eng. Ch.** Mary enjoins clerical celibacy. Convocation elicits from Cranmer, Latimer, and Ridley that they reject Transubstantiation. [1554

349. **Church Hist.** Knox becomes minister of the English refugees at Frankfort, but is expelled on the arrival of Richard Cox and others, 1555, who desire the ritual of the Prayer-Book.

350. **Italian Lit.** Bandello's collection of Tales, a quarry for Shakespeare and other dramatists.

351. **Spanish Lit.** Lazarillo de Tormes, long ascribed to Mendoza, the first example of the picaresque novel.

352. **Art.** Antonio Moro, a Fleming, educated in Italy, settles in England as Court painter to Philip and Mary.

353. **Science.** Rondelet's Historia Piscium and Belon's De Aquatilibus found Ichthyology.

354. **Philosophy.** Cardan's De Varietate Rerum relates the psychic experiences of the author and his father.

355. **Death.** Cortes.

---

356. **Eng. Ch.** Strengthened by her husband, Mary appoints Gardiner (shortly replaced by Bonner), Tunstal, and 3 other Bishops to try heretics. Rogers (the Matthew of Matthew's Bible) suffers at Smithfield, Hooper at Gloucester, Rowland Taylor in Suffolk, and Ridley and Latimer at Oxford (Oct.). [1555

357. **French Ch.** An attempt by the Cardinal of Guise to revive persecution is frustrated by Parliament, and the first Protestant Church in Paris is instituted on a Presbyterian basis.

358. **German Ch.** Pfeffinger's De Libero Arbitrio, developing Melanchthon's Synergism, is opposed by Flacius and Amsdorf, who maintain that man can oppose but cannot facilitate the workings of Grace, the synergistic controversy lasting for twelve years.

In consequence of the failure of his schemes, the accession of the anti-Hapsburg Pope, Paul IV., and advancing age, the Emperor resigns the Netherlands and his Italian provinces to his son Philip.

245. **America.** Villegagnon, with the approval of Coligny, founds a Huguenot colony in Rio Bay, which is suppressed by the Portuguese, 1558.

---

246. **England.** Sir Henry Dudley, the cousin of Northumberland, and a number of young nobles plot to dethrone Mary and make Elizabeth Queen. The plan, however, is betrayed, and the conspirators are executed. [1556

247. **Germany.** The Emperor transfers the Spanish crown to his son, and his German possessions to his brother. He resigns the Empire, commending Ferdinand to the Electors, and retires to the monastery of San Juste, in Spain, though remaining busily occupied with politics till his death, 1558.

248. **Italy.** The new Pope, wishing to take advantage of Philip's youth, bribes Henry II. with the promise of Naples to send Guise into Italy to expel the Spaniards. Alva, the Governor of Naples, however, repels the invasion, but, from reverence for the Papacy, refrains from seizing Rome, and thus gives Guise time to raise new troops.

249. **Asia.** Bairam Khan and Akbar, the 14-year-old son of Hamaioun, defeat the Afghan dynasty at Panipat, and finally win India. Shortly after the battle, Hamaioun dies and is succeeded by Akbar, under the regency of Bairam Khan.

---

250. **England.** Sir Thomas Stafford, an exile at the Court of Paris, sails for England with two ships and seizes Scarborough castle. The people refuse to rise against the queen, and the rebels are executed. [1557

251. **Scotland.** The first Covenant is drawn up by Argyll and Morton, renouncing the 'Congregation of Satan,' and resolving on Protestant worship in private houses.

252. **Italy.** Guise again invades Italy, but Alva bribes Parma and Tuscany with lands and repels the French, the Spanish supremacy not being again challenged.

253. **France.** A Spanish army under the Duke of Savoy, who wishes to recover his Duchy, besieges St Quentin, and is routed by the relieving army (Aug.), before the English troops, which Mary sends to her husband, arrive. Philip, however, refuses to risk an advance on Paris.

254. **Asia.** The Portuguese, who have carried on trade with China since 1517 and established two factories, withdraw to Macao, near Canton, and are recognised as independent, 1587.

---

359. **Spanish Ch.** Peter of Alcantara, a Franciscan, the earliest of Spanish mystics, founds the congregation of the Barefooted Friars.

360. **Swiss Ch.** A final revolt of the Libertines in Geneva, under Ami Perrin, is suppressed.

361. **Polish Ch.** Calvinism having spread among the nobles and Lutheranism among the citizens, owing to the tolerance of the King, a Synod permits all to worship freely in their own houses.

362. **Polish Lit.** The first critical history of Poland is written by Cromer.

363. **History.** Busbequius is sent by Ferdinand to Constantinople, and describes the Ottoman Empire.

364. **Geography.** Eden's Decades of the New World, the first English account of recent discoveries.

---

365. **Eng. Ch.** Cranmer is induced to sign seven forms of recantation; but when brought to the stake at Oxford, he [1556 recants his recantations and stretches his right hand into the flames. Pole is consecrated Archbishop of Canterbury on the following day.

366. **Italian Ch.** Philip Neri commences meetings at his house in Rome, for reading and discussion. The members undertake evening preaching in the City churches, and are created the order of the Oratory, 1575.

367. **Church Hist.** Loyola dies, and is succeeded as General by Lainez, who perfects the organization of the Society and issues the Constitutions and the Declarations.

---

368. **Eng. Ch.** The Pope revokes Pole's legatine Commission and summons him to Rome to answer to a charge of heresy. [1557 Mary, however, declares that Pole shall remain legate, and the Pope gives way.

The persecution continues, and Pole undertakes a Visitation of the Universities.

369. **German Ch.** The Venetian ambassador reports that only a tenth part of the German nation remains Catholic.

Frederick III., the new Elector Palatine, introduces Calvinism, which remains the established religion.

370. **Hungarian Ch.** The majority of the Hungarian clergy formally adopt Calvinism at the Synod of Czenger, the Confession rejecting Lutheranism and Unitarianism.

371. **Church Hist.** The Pope imprisons Morone on a charge of favouring Lutheran opinions.

372. **Eng. Lit.** In Tottel's Miscellany, the first of English anthologies, appear the works of Wyatt and Surrey, who introduce the sonnet and blank verse from Italian Literature.

The Stationers' Company is incorporated.

373. **Science.** Record's Whetstone of Wit, the first English algebra, invents the sign =, etc., and explains how to extract a square root.

---

255. **England.** Guise, who has been recalled from Italy after the battle of St Quentin, storms Calais and the outlying post of Guisnes, and terminates the English occupation of 211 years. Though deeply chagrined by the loss of their last foothold in France, the English people trust the Queen too little to aid in the prosecution of the war. Mary dies (Nov.), and her sister Elizabeth retains the Council, to which she adds Sir William Cecil. [1558

256. **Scotland.** The Lords of the Congregation petition the Regent for concessions, but receive evasive replies. Their position, however, is greatly strengthened by the death of the English Queen and by the return of Knox from Geneva.

257. **France.** Egmont routs a detachment of the French army at Gravelines, aided by the English fleet (July).

Mary, Queen of Scots, marries Francis, the Dauphin, the King yielding to the pressure of the Guises. A secret treaty binds Mary to bring over her kingdom.

---

258. **England.** Philip offers marriage to Elizabeth (Jan.), but withdraws when Parliament meets and passes a new Act of Supremacy, imposing on officials or graduates an oath to acknowledge the Queen as Supreme Governor in all Spiritual things as Temporal, and restoring the election of Bishops by *congé d'élire.* [1559

259. **Scotland.** The Regent forbids preaching, summons the disobedient clergy to Perth, and outlaws them for not appearing. Knox denounces 'idolatry,' and the churches and monasteries are sacked. Both parties advance to Perth, but a compromise is made reserving the controversies for Parliament. The rebels offer to marry Arran's son, a Protestant, to Elizabeth, to counterbalance the union of France and Scotland. Elizabeth refuses, but sends money.

260. **France.** At the Treaty of Cateau-Cambresis, between France and Spain (April), Savoy and Piedmont are returned to the Duke of Savoy. Both sides restore their conquests, though the French keep Saluzzo, one of the gates of Italy, and Calais, and Philip marries the daughter of Henry II. The Treaty closes the 40 years' war, and leaves Spain supreme in Italy.

On the accession of Francis II., power passes to his wife's uncles, the Guises, who are opposed by the Bourbons and Coligny.

261. **Italy.** The Pope deposes his nephews, whom he had raised to power on account of their support in his anti-Spanish policy.

262. **Netherlands.** Margaret, sister of Philip, becomes Regent, and Granvelle her chief adviser. The States refuse supplies till the 4,000 troops left by Philip are removed.

263. **Turkey.** Turkey, the ally of France, is not included in the Treaty of Cateau-Cambresis, and Philip attacks Algiers.

---

374. **Eng. Ch.** The persecution is ended by the simultaneous death of the Queen and Pole, about 300 persons having suffered, chiefly in Bonner's Diocese of London, and in Canterbury and Norwich. [1558

Aconcio, an Italian refugee, introduces Unitarianism into England, and writes his 'Stratagems of Satan.'

375. **Church Hist.** The Bull Cum ex Apostolatus Officio declares that heretical kings and bishops are *ipso facto* deposed, and incur sentence of death, and that the Pope judges all and can be judged by none.

376. **Politics.** Poynet, the dispossessed Bishop of Winchester, in his Political Power, and Goodman, the colleague of Knox at Geneva, in his How Superior Powers should be Obeyed, maintain the right and duty of the people, by the Law of Nature and of God, to resist and depose ungodly rulers. Knox more directly attacks two reigning Queens in his Blast of the Trumpet against the monstrous Regiment of Women.

377. **Geography.** Zeno of Venice publishes a map of the northern seas.

378. **Social.** Tobacco is brought to Spain, whence it is sent to Paris by Nicot, the French ambassador.

379. **Death.** J. C. Scaliger.

---

380. **Eng. Ch.** The Act of Uniformity, exacting a fine for absence from church and restoring the second Prayer-Book of Edward VI., with a few alterations, is passed after vigorous opposition in the Lords, and without consent of Convocation. All the Bishops, except Kitchin of Llandaff, and about 200 clergy are deprived. Parker becomes Primate, and Commissioners are sent through the country with Injunctions dealing with images, celibacy, and ceremonial. [1559

381. **French Ch.** The first Protestant Synod is held, under the presidency of Morel, and adopts a Confession, composed by Calvin, and a Presbyterian organisation.

382. **German Ch.** Flacius edits a Church History, the Magdeburg Centuries, the first historical defence of Protestantism.

Brenz defends Luther's theory of ubiquity against Melanchthon.

383. **Italian Ch.** The Index compiled from the lists made at Louvain and by the Spanish Inquisition is issued at Rome. A revised edition is published by the Council of Trent, 1564, including a department 'donec corrigatur.' A Congregation of the Index is instituted, 1571.

384. **Spanish Ch.** Autos-da-fé are held at Valladolid and Seville, by which Lutheranism is almost eradicated. Carranza, Archbishop of Toledo, is imprisoned (for 17 years) for his theory of Justification, and the Illuminati are persecuted.

385. **Church Hist.** Joasaph, Patriarch of Constantinople, makes enquiries about Protestantism, but leaves unanswered a letter of Melanchthon, enclosing the Confession of Augsburg.

386. **French Lit.** Amyot translates Plutarch.

---

264. **Scotland.** At Cecil's entreaty, the Queen sends troops and a fleet to Scotland. The joint forces besiege the French in Leith, which surrenders after the death of the Regent, who has been deserted by nearly all her counsellors, including Maitland. By a treaty at Edinburgh, France ceases to govern Scotland, and acknowledges Elizabeth's title, though Francis refuses to ratify this stipulation, and the government is vested in 12 nobles till Mary's return. [1560

265. **France.** A conspiracy to rescue the King from the Guises at Amboise fails, but frightens them into promoting L'Hôpital, who grants liberty of private worship to Huguenots. The Guises, however, imprison Condé; but their plans are frustrated by the King's death and the regency of Catherine de Medici, who favours Coligny and the Politiques.

266. **Netherlands.** After a delay of thrice the stipulated period, the Spanish troops are recalled. The Council of State, including Orange and Egmont, is rendered powerless by the secret council of Granvelle, Berlaymont, and Viglius. Further discontent is aroused by the creation of 14 bishoprics and 3 archbishoprics.

267. **Asia.** Akbar quells a revolt of Bairam Khan and assumes power, and builds up an Empire from his new capital at Agra, conquering the Rajput kingdoms, Lower Bengal, Orissa, Gujerat, Kashmir, Kandahar, and Scinde, but failing to subdue the south. He divides the Empire into Provinces with Viceroys, abolishes the non-Mussulman poll-tax, and creates justice and police. His finance minister, Todar Mall, makes the first land survey, and imposes a land-tax.

---

268. **England.** Lady Catherine Grey, sister of Lady Jane, marries Hertford, son of the Protector Somerset, without the Queen's consent, and is thrown into the Tower. [1561

269. **Scotland.** Mary arrives in Scotland by sea, Elizabeth refusing her a passage through England unless she renounces her claim to the English crown. She acknowledges the new Calvinistic establishment, but retains the Mass for her own use, and accepts her half-brother Murray and Maitland as ministers.

The first Book of Discipline is rejected by Parliament.

270. **France.** The States-General meet at Orleans, and L'Hôpital appeals to all parties to support the throne and cease their bitter struggles. The Edict of Orleans attacks a number of legal and other abuses; the Parliament of Paris, however, refuses to register it. Feeling grows more and more embittered, and L'Hôpital and the Queen Regent therefore summon men of moderate opinions from the Parliaments and the Privy Council to an assembly at St Germains.

271. **Poland.** Livonia, which threw off allegiance to the Teutonic knights, 1521, in fear of Russian aggression, surrenders itself to Poland, which retains it, despite the attacks of Sweden and Russia. The Grand Master keeps part of the province as Duke of Courland, under the suzerainty of Poland.

---

387. **Eng. Ch.** The 'Breeches,' or Geneva, Bible, with Calvinistic annotations, remains the most popular edition till 1611. [1560

388. **Scotch Ch.** At the request of Parliament, Knox and five other ministers draw up a Confession, which is approved. The authority of the Pope is rejected, the mass is abolished, and all laws against Protestantism are repealed. The first General Assembly meets (Dec.), and approves the First Book of Discipline (compiled by the authors of the Confession), adopting in part the system of Geneva.

389. **German Ch.** Flacius declares that original sin is not accidental but substantial, and is accused of Manichaeism.

390. **Asiatic Ch.** Akbar, with the aid of his minister, Abul-Fazl, constructs an eclectic Mohammedanism, and grants religious liberty throughout India.

391. **Science.** Battista Porta's Magia Naturalis discusses the structure of the eye, and invents the Camera obscura. He also founds the Academia Secretorum Naturae at Naples, the first scientific society.

Eustachius describes the tube running between the mouth and the ear.

392. **Art.** Tintoretto begins to fresco the Scuola di San Rocco, Venice.

Germain Pilon's Three Graces (Louvre).

Jean Goujon's Diana and a Stag (Louvre).

393. **Philology.** Sigonius begins to study Roman law and customs.

394. **Deaths.** Doria, Lasco, Melanchthon.

---

395. **Eng. Ch.** The Queen is dissuaded by Cecil from issuing an ordinance against the marriage of the clergy, but forbids members of colleges or cathedral churches to marry or to retain their wives. [1561

396. **French Ch.** At a Conference at Poissy (Aug.), Beza confesses his dissent from ten of the Articles of Augsburg, including that relating to the Real Presence.

Marlorat's N. T. Expositio, a popular Calvinist commentary.

397. **German Ch.** The Protestant Princes adopt the revised Confession of Augsburg of 1540, and the Apologia of the earlier edition.

398. **Netherlands Ch.** The Belgic Confession is drawn up by Guido de Bres, a Calvinist. The Genevese Church system is introduced, 1563.

399. **Literature.** J. C. Scaliger's Poetics, the first modern work of literary criticism and analysis.

400. **Education.** The Merchant Taylors' School in London is founded.

401. **Social.** Sandwich is licensed to receive 400 Flemish refugees as clothworkers. Colchester, Norwich, and other towns quickly follow suit.

402. **Death.** Schwenckfeld.

---

272. **England.** The Oath of Supremacy is imposed on the members of the House of Commons, Catholics being thus excluded. [1562

273. **Ireland.** After a visit to London, on the invitation of the Queen, Shane O'Neill rebels a second time, and, after five years' struggle, is murdered.

274. **France.** The Edict of January, promulgated by the Assembly of St Germains, formally authorises Protestantism, though enjoining respect for the ancient worship. To oppose the policy of toleration, a league is formed by the Guises and Montmorency, which the King of Navarre is persuaded to join. The massacre by the followers of the Duke of Guise of a congregation at worship in Vassy leads to the first of the long series of religious wars. The Huguenots receive aid from the German Princes, and the Catholics obtain support from Spain and Switzerland. The Huguenots prove successful at the outset, and the King of Navarre is killed, his son of ten, Henry, becoming head of the Bourbons. Condé and Montmorency, the rival commanders, are taken prisoners at Dreux (Nov.), Coligny becoming leader of the Huguenots.

The Huguenots obtain the aid of Elizabeth by offering her Havre, which she hopes to exchange for Calais.

275. **Austria.** Maximilian is elected King of the Romans.

276. **America.** Ribault establishes a colony of Huguenots in Florida, at the instance of Coligny, and leaves a number of settlers, who volunteer to hold the country for the King of France till Ribault returns with recruits and supplies.

---

277. **England.** Arthur and Edmond Pole, the last of the Yorkists, are convicted of treason and imprisoned till their death. [1563

278. **France.** The murder of the Duke of Guise (Feb.), when advancing against Orleans, terminates the war, though Coligny is anxious for its continuance. The peace made at Amboise (March) tolerates the Reformed faith where established before the war (except in Paris), and a town in every district is selected for Huguenot worship. War is declared against England, and Havre is recaptured. Three years of peace ensue, the Edict of Amboise, however, only being executed where the Huguenots are strong.

279. **Germany.** The claims of the Elector of Brandenburg and his heirs to the succession of the Duchy of Prussia are recognised by the King of Poland.

280. **Africa.** A Spanish fleet is destroyed by a storm, but Oran is successfully defended against the Turks.

---

281. **England.** Elizabeth is compelled to make peace with France, without recovering Calais. [1564

282. **Austria.** On the death of Ferdinand, the Imperial title, with Austria, Bohemia and Hungary, passes to Maximilian II., the remaining provinces being divided among his two younger sons.

403. **Eng. Ch.** Jewel's Apology for the Church of England.

404. **German Ch.** Chemnitz criticises Catholic theology in his Examen Consilii Tridentini. [1562

The Elector Palatine, Frederick III., the first Calvinist prince in Germany, orders Ursinus and Olevianus to compose the Heidelberg Catechism, the most popular of Calvinistic symbols.

405. **Spanish Ch.** Theresa founds a convent of barefooted Carmelites in her birthplace, Avila. She is aided by John of the Cross, who extends the reform to the male Carmelites.

406. **Church Hist.** The Council of Trent meets for the third time, under the presidency of Hosius and four other legates. The concession of the cup to the laity, demanded by Germany and France, is defeated by Lainez and the Spaniards. The Cardinal of Lorraine arrives with the French bishops (Sept.), and takes the anti-papal side in the discussion of the divine origin of Episcopacy.

407. **Art.** Paul Veronese's 'Marriage of Cana' (Louvre).

408. **Social.** John Hawkins makes the first English slave-trading expedition from Guinea to the Spanish Indies.

409. **Death.** Laelius Socinus.

---

410. **Eng. Ch.** The 42 Articles are reduced to 39, accepted by Convocation, and ratified by the Queen with a few alterations. [1563

Foxe's Book of Martyrs.

411. **Church Hist.** The Emperor is won over to terminating the Council by the Pope's promise of the cup to the laity. Reforms are rapidly resolved on in reference to clerical seminaries, the discipline of Cardinals and bishops and the visitation of chapters, and the theory of purgatory, indulgences and the invocation of saints is defined.

412. **Eng. Lit.** Sackville's Induction to the Mirror for Magistrates.

413. **Art.** Philip commissions Herrera to build the Escurial.

414. **Social.** The Statute of Apprentices empowers Justices of the Peace to periodically settle the rate of wages. The number of apprentices is laid down in relation to the number of journeymen and the status of the master.

---

415. **Church Hist.** The Pope confirms the acts of the recent Council, the disciplinary decrees being accepted by several German princes, Italy, Poland, Portugal, and the Spanish Empire, and rejected by Hungary and France, though certain of the reforms are quietly adopted. [1564

The Professio Fidei Tridentinae defines the theory of the Sacraments, Purgatory and Indulgences.

416. **German Ch.** Asked by the new Emperor for his opinion on the decrees, Cassander recommends the permission of the cup to the laity and of marriage of the clergy.

417. **Bohemian Ch.** Owing to the concession by the Pope of the cup to the laity, the Utraquists become merged in the Catholic Church.

283. **Netherlands.** On the demand of the Nationalists and of the Regent, Granvelle is recalled. Philip, however, refuses to change his policy, and enforces still more strictly the edicts against heresy.

284. **Asia.** The Philippines are occupied by the Spaniards, and Manila is built.

---

285. **Scotland.** After contemplating various foreign matches and rejecting Elizabeth's offer of Leicester, Mary marries her cousin, Darnley, a Catholic. Regarding this as a defiance, Elizabeth urges the Scottish malcontents, led by Murray, to a revolt, which is easily crushed, and in consequence is disowned by Elizabeth. [1565

286. **France.** Catherine meets Alva at Bayonne, but refuses to change her system of compromise.

287. **Switzerland.** The Catholic cantons ally with the Pope, Spain and Savoy, though without taking overt action.

288. **Netherlands.** The nobles despatch Egmont to Philip to demand concessions. The King makes some vague promises, and loads the ambassador with gifts and honours.

289. **Turkey.** The Knights of St John in Malta, under Lavalette, sustain a siege by the Turks, and, after three months, are relieved by Spanish troops from Sicily.

290. **America.** Menendez is sent by Philip, who fears the loss of his Mexican fleets, to Florida to destroy the Huguenot colony.

---

291. **England.** The Commons resolve to petition the Queen to marry, but are ordered to leave the matter alone. Paul Wentworth asks if such a command is not contrary to their privileges. [1566

292. **Scotland.** Darnley and the Protestant nobles murder Rizzio, the unofficial Foreign Secretary of the Queen.

293. **Germany.** The Elector Palatine successfully defends his adoption of Calvinism before the Diet of Augsburg.

294. **Netherlands.** St Aldegonde, Brederode and William's brother, Louis of Nassau, form a league, in which a number of Catholics join, called the Compromise, to resist the Inquisition, and present a request to the Regent. Berlaymont urges her not to fear the 'beggars' (a name that the nationalists at once adopt), and the Regent signs a Moderation, making trifling concessions. She refuses to follow the advice of Orange in the Council and to summon the States-General, till, frightened by an attack on the churches, she issues the Accord, abolishing the Inquisition and granting an amnesty, secretly protesting to Philip that it is obtained by force. Acting on orders from Spain, she captures several towns, and re-establishes the Inquisition, William withdrawing from the country.

295. **Turkey.** The Turks capture Chios, the last Genoese possession in the Levant. The decline of the Ottoman Power, however, begins with the death of Solyman, and the Janissaries become an hereditary caste.

At the same time the Bohemian Brothers, under the leadership of Blahoslav, obtain toleration from the Emperor.

418. **Swiss Ch.** Beza succeeds to Calvin's position as the head of the Calvinist Churches.

419. **Art.** Delorme designs the Tuileries for Catherine de Medici.

420. **Social.** Wierus, a pupil of Agrippa, attacks the belief in witchcraft, which is defended about this time by Bodin, Erastus and Delrio.

421. **Deaths.** Calvin, Lainez, Michelangelo, Vesalius.

---

422. **French Ch.** The first contest takes place between the University of Paris, represented by Pasquier, and the Jesuit college, founded by the Bishop of Clermont. [1565

423. **Spanish Ch.** Francis Borgia, Viceroy of Catalonia, becomes General of the Jesuits, and greatly extends the Order in Spain.

424. **Polish Ch.** The Unitarians are excluded from the synods of the Reformed Church.

425. **Italian Lit.** Cinthio's Hecatomithi, a collection of tales.

426. **Art.** Palestrina's Missa Papae Marcelli rescues music from the suspicions of the Counter-Reformation.

427. **Philosophy.** Telesio's De Rerum Natura, a system of mystical pantheism, influenced by Paracelsus and Cardan.

428. **Death.** Gesner.

---

429. **Eng. Ch.** Parker's Advertisements (issued without the imprimatur of the Queen), supplement the Injunctions of 1559 and declare the minimum of ritual. The appended declaration of conformity is refused by about 40 London clergy, who are suspended or deprived. The malcontents begin to organise meetings, but their separation from the Church is condemned by Knox, Beza, and Bullinger. [1566

430. **Swiss Ch.** Bullinger's Confessio Helvetica Posterior, blending Calvinism with Zwinglianism, gradually wins recognition throughout Switzerland.

431. **Church Hist.** The Catechismus Romanus, planned by the Council of Trent and based on its decrees, becomes the favourite manual of teachers, though disapproved by the Jesuits. The Catechismus Parvus of Canisius is also widely adopted.

432. **French Lit.** Henry Stephanus replies to the criticisms of Herodotus in his Apologie pour Herodote, in which he attacks the morals and credulity of the Roman clergy.

433. **Art.** Colins completes the reliefs on the tomb of Maximilian I. at Innsbruck.

434. **History.** Bodin's Methodus ad Historiarum Cognitionem discusses the laws of progress and causation.

435. **Social.** The Royal Exchange is founded by Gresham.

436. **Death.** Las Casas.

---

296. **Scotland.** Darnley is murdered by Bothwell (Feb.), who traps the nobles into signing a bond at Ainslie's Tavern, declaring his innocence and urging the Queen to marry him. The marriage takes place (May), but her subjects rise against her and capture her at Carberry Hill. She is imprisoned on Loch Leven, and is forced to abdicate in favour of her infant son, who is placed in Protestant hands, and for whom Murray becomes Regent. [1567

297. **France.** The Huguenots plan to seize the King at Meaux, but the Court escapes to Paris, which Condé besieges, and a drawn battle is fought at St Denis.

298. **Netherlands.** Philip sends Alva to aid Margaret, who shortly retires. Egmont and Horn are arrested, and the Council of Disorders (the 'Council of Blood') is instituted.

299. **Asia.** Nobunaga becomes supreme in Japan, deposes the Shogun, centralises the government, encourages Christian missions, and maintains peace.

---

300. **Scotland.** Mary escapes (May), is defeated by Murray at Langside, and flies to England, demanding an army to replace her. Elizabeth appoints Commissioners, who pronounce the Casket Letters produced by Murray authentic. Though refusing to recognise her deposition, the Queen detains Mary in England. [1568

301. **France.** The Treaty of Longjumeau confirms the settlement of Amboise. The Pope, however, releases the Queen from her obligations. Cardinal Guise returns. L'Hôpital is dismissed, the reformed service is forbidden, Condé and Coligny leave Paris, and war again breaks out.

302. **Spain.** Owing to the enforcement of the laws against Moorish customs and language, the Moors revolt, but are crushed by Don John, the half-brother of Philip.

303. **Netherlands.** William formally joins the Reformed Church, and collects an army, part of which defeats the Spaniards at Heiligerlee. Alva executes Egmont and Horn, and defeats Louis at Jemmingen.

---

304. **England.** The northern nobles conspire to marry Norfolk to Mary Stuart. Norfolk is imprisoned on suspicion, and Northumberland and Westmoreland openly revolt (Nov.), but flee before the army sent against them. [1569

305. **France.** The Huguenots are routed and Condé slain at Jarnac (March). Coligny becomes leader, but is defeated at Montcontour (Oct.).

306. **Netherlands.** Alva's financial policy ruins manufactures and commerce.

307. **Poland.** Sigismund II. unites Lithuania (loosely connected since 1386) to Poland by the Treaty of Lublin.

---

437. **Eng. Ch.** The Queen orders the Ecclesiastical Commissioners to break up the Nonconformist congregations in London. [1567
100 sectaries are seized at Plumber's Hall, London, which had been hired under pretence of a wedding, and imprisoned. A centre of propaganda, however, is instituted at Wandsworth; but separation from the Church rarely occurs outside the London district.

438. **Scotch Ch.** Lay patronage is adopted.

439. **Italian Ch.** Carnesecchi is surrendered by the Duke of Tuscany and burnt at Rome, Paleario suffering, 1568. Their deaths mark the close of the Protestant movement in Italy.

440. **Netherlands Ch.** Baius, Professor of Theology at Louvain, who has been condemned by the Sorbonne, 1560, is censured by the Pope, at the instance of the Franciscans, for his teaching in regard to Predestination and Grace. He submits, but his ideas remain in circulation and are appropriated by Jansen in the succeeding generation.

441. **Education.** Rugby School is founded by Laurence Sheriff.

---

442. **Eng. Ch.** The 'Bishops' Bible,' revised by Parker and his suffragans, is authorised, and forms the base of the translation of 1611. [1568

William Allen, sometime Fellow of Oriel, founds a college in the University of Douai for English Catholics, especially for those desiring to work for the conversion of England. Similar institutions are created at Rome and Valladolid.

443. **Netherlands Ch.** Marnix de Ste Aldegonde composes the Wilhelmuslied, which takes its place as a national anthem.

444. **Bohemian Ch.** Blahoslav translates the Bible, adds commentaries, and composes hymns, his writings exercising a profound influence over the Bohemian Brethren.

445. **Polish Ch.** The Unitarians of Transylvania separate from the Protestants.

446. **Church Hist.** Pius V. issues the Breviarium Romanum, revised by order of the Council of Trent.

447. **Philosophy.** Soto's De Justitia et Jure, the first ethical work of the century, attempts to combine the conceptions of Roman and Canon Law.

448. **Economics.** Bodin explains the revolution in prices, returning to the public revenues, in the République.

449. **Death.** Ascham.

---

450. **Netherlands Ch.** Marnix' Beehive violently satirises the Catholic Church. [1569

451. **Science.** Mercator's hydrographical Chart introduces the new projection by crossing parallels and meridians at right angles. His atlas appears 1598.

452. **Philosophy.** Montaigne translates the Theologia Naturalis of Raymond de Sebonde into French, and composes an Apology for the author.

---

308. **England.** The Pope excommunicates Elizabeth and absolves her subjects from their allegiance. The bull is affixed to the door of the Bishop of London's house. [1570

309. **Scotland.** Murray is murdered by the Hamiltons. Mary's supporters again come forward and resist the new Regent, Lennox, and confusion ensues till Morton obtains the regency, 1572.

310. **France.** The success of the Catholic arms leads to a reaction against the Guises and the Spanish party, and to the Treaty of St Germain (Aug.), which grants religious freedom to the Huguenots. The young King, Charles IX., assumes power, and deserts the religious system of the Counter-Reformation, offering his brother Anjou to Elizabeth and welcoming Louis of Nassau at Court. Margaret, the sister of the King, is betrothed to Henry of Navarre, and Coligny's influence becomes supreme.

311. **Sweden.** Denmark recognises the independence of Sweden, confirming the treaty of Brömsebro (1541), at the peace of Stettin, and Sweden surrenders her claim to Norway.

312. **Turkey.** Cyprus, bequeathed to Venice by Caterina Cornaro, 1489, is attacked by the Turks, and the chief towns are taken and destroyed.

313. **Africa.** The Turks capture Tunis from Spain.

---

314. **England.** Strickland is excluded from the House of Commons by the Queen for proposing to amend the Prayer-book. To avoid a quarrel, Elizabeth allows him to return, the question of the Prayer-book being dropped. [1571

An Italian banker, resident in England, Ridolfi, informs Alva that the peers desire him to send a Spanish army of 6,000 soldiers, murder the Queen and set Mary and Norfolk, who has been released from the Tower, on the throne. The scheme, which is approved by Philip, is discovered by Burleigh, diplomatic relations with Spain are broken off (till 1578), and Norfolk is imprisoned. Parliament declares traitors all who introduce Bulls, who are reconciled to Rome or reconcile others.

315. **Turkey.** The Pope arranges a Holy League with Spain and Venice against the Turks, whose fleet is destroyed at Lepanto by Don John (Oct.). The victory is rendered useless by the jealousies of the Powers.

316. **Hungary.** The Zapolya dynasty in Transylvania ends, and Stephen Bathory is elected.

---

317. **England.** The Queen executes Norfolk, but refuses the demand of Parliament for the death of Mary Stuart. In her anxiety to find support against Spain, she resumes negociations for a French marriage, this time with Alençon, Anjou's brother, a youth 21 years younger than herself, and makes a defensive alliance with France at Blois. [1572

453. **Eng. Ch.** Cartwright is deprived of the Lady Margaret Professorship for Puritanism, largely owing to Whitgift, Master of Trinity. [1570

454. **German Ch.** Fischart, a Calvinist, begins his career of Protestant champion, translates Dutch and Huguenot polemics, and attacks the Jesuits.

The introduction of presbyteries into the Palatinate is attacked by Erastus, a professor at Heidelberg, who contends for state control.

455. **Polish Ch.** By the consensus of Sendomir, on the lines of Melanchthon's later ideas, the Calvinists, Lutherans and Bohemian Brothers are united. At the same moment, the Jesuits enter the kingdom.

456. **Church Hist.** Pius V. issues the Missale Romanum, ordered by the Council of Trent.

457. **Science.** Ortelius' (of Antwerp) Theatrum Orbis Terrarum, the first modern atlas.

458. **Art.** Palladio's Treatise on Architecture.

459. **Education.** Ascham's Schoolmaster recommends, for the learning of Latin, the study of a model book in preference to a long preliminary course of grammar.

In consequence of the support given to Cartwright by the younger Masters of Arts, the Elizabethan Statutes are enacted, vesting the administration of the University in the Caput or Heads of Houses.

---

460. **Eng. Ch.** Subscription to the XXXIX Articles is enforced by Parliament on the clergy, and the Canon Law compiled under Henry and Edward finally disappears. [1571

461. **Philosophy.** Patrizzi's Dissertationes Peripateticae strongly attacks Aristotle, and urges the recognition of the Platonists by the Church.

462. **Politics.** Gentillet's Anti-Machiavel, the first important attack from the Protestant side.

463. **Education.** Harrow School is founded by John Lyon.

464. **Geography.** Jenkinson carries a letter from Elizabeth to the Shah of Persia, travelling through Russia and Bokhara.

465. **Law.** Plowden's Reports.

466. **Death.** Cellini.

---

467. **Eng. Ch.** Cartwright and his followers draw up the First and Second Admonition to Parliament, denouncing Anglican ceremonial, above all the use of vestments. Whitgift replies, and a long controversy begins. [1572

Sanders attacks the English Reformation in his De Visibili Monarchia.

318. **France.** Catherine plots with Anjou to murder Coligny, who is wounded but not killed. At this moment, Henry of Navarre's marriage with the King's sister brings many Huguenots unarmed to Paris, and the King is persuaded by his mother and the Guises to order a massacre, which begins with the murder of Coligny on St Bartholomew's Day (Aug. 24), and is repeated in the provinces. The news of the massacre, in which many thousands lose their lives, is warmly welcomed by Philip and the Pope, who strikes a medal in honour of the event. A few Protestants find refuge at the Court of Renée of Ferrara, at Montargis. Henry of Navarre is spared on condition that he attends Mass.

319. **Netherlands.** The Dutch exiles and refugees, known as 'sea beggars,' capture Brill, and hold it in the name of Orange. Troops sent by Alva to recapture it are repulsed, and the foundations of an independent Netherlands are laid. Holland, Zealand, Friesland and Utrecht acknowledge William of Orange as Stadtholder. The Flemish towns, however, in part owing to the massacre of St Bartholomew, return to their allegiance.

320. **Poland.** Sigismund, the last of the Jagellons, who have reigned since 1386, dies, and the Estates declare the Crown elective. An Austrian Archduke claims the throne, which, however, is secured for the Duke of Anjou by the French ambassador.

---

321. **Scotland.** Elizabeth sends aid to the party of the young King, and captures Edinburgh, in which Maitland and Kirkaldy, [1573 who joined Mary's party after her flight, have held out. Maitland dies, and Mary's party ceases to exist.

322. **Ireland.** The revolt of the Desmonds and the nobles of Munster, led by James Fitzmaurice, 1569—73, in part owing to the threat of Plantations, is crushed.

323. **France.** Peace is made with the Huguenots, partly owing to the growth of the party of the Politiques, led by the Montpensiers. Protestant worship is permitted in four towns.

324. **Netherlands.** Haarlem is taken, but Alkmaar holds out, and Alva's petition for his recall is granted. English aid is for the first time secretly sent.

325. **Poland.** Anjou becomes King of Poland, promising not to marry nor make war without consent of Parliament, and recognising the right of the nobles to resist him if he breaks the pact.

326. **Turkey.** Cyprus is surrendered by Venice to the Porte after three years' war, and a large indemnity is paid.

---

327. **Netherlands.** Requesens succeeds Alva and defeats and kills Louis of Nassau at Mooker Heath. Leyden, however, is [1574 gallantly defended, and is relieved by cutting the dykes and flooding the country (Oct.). The Constitution of Holland is drawn up, and William becomes Commander-in-Chief and Dictator.

468. **Scotch Ch.** Morton appoints the so-called Tulchan Bishops, who pass on their fees to the nobles, perform no duties, and are subject to the General Assembly.

469. **German Ch.** Weigel, a mystical Saxon pastor, is denounced as a heretic.

470. **Spanish Ch.** Luis de Leon is imprisoned for his views on biblical criticism.

471. **Eng. Lit.** Parker founds the Society of Antiquaries, for the study and preservation of manuscripts. The Society is dissolved by James I, but is revived 1717.

472. **Portuguese Lit.** The Lusiads of Camoens, who has resided in the East 16 years, describes the heroic age of Portuguese conquest in the East, and becomes the national epic.

473. **Science.** Bombelli improves the notation of algebra.

474. **Philology.** Stephanus' Thesaurus Linguae Graecae.

475. **History.** Buchanan's Detection relates the life of Mary Stuart.

476. **Social.** Justices of the Peace are empowered to assess for the relief of the poor, to house them, and to appoint overseers.

477. **Deaths.** Knox, Goujon, Ramus.

---

478. **Eng. Ch.** In consequence of Cartwright's attack, the Queen appoints Commissioners to compel suspected clergy to approve the Articles and Prayer-book and sign a recantation. [1573

479. **Church Hist.** Crusius and Andreae, Professors at Tübingen, open negotiations for union with the Greek Church, which are terminated by the condemnation of the Confession of Augsburg.

480. **Italian Lit.** Tasso's Aminta founds Italian pastoral drama.

481. **Philosophy.** Taurellus attacks the philosophy of Aristotle.

482. **Politics.** The anonymous De Jure Magistratuum reveals the more extreme ideas adopted by the Huguenots in consequence of the massacre of St Bartholomew.

483. **Agriculture.** Tusser's 500 points of Husbandry strongly recommends the enclosing of land and convertible husbandry.

484. **Death.** L'Hôpital.

---

485. **Eng. Ch.** Cartwright translates Travers' Presbyterian Doctrina Ecclesiae. [1574

486. **German Ch.** The Elector of Saxony banishes the Crypto-Calvinists.

487. **Asiatic Ch.** Tulsi Das' Wanderings of Rama.

488. **Art.** The Gate of Honour at Caius College, Cambridge, the first completely classical design in England. Longleat, erected about the same time, shows that the 'Elizabethan' style of Penshurst, Haddon and Knowle is yielding to Italian influences.

328. **Poland.** Henry secretly leaves Poland on the death of his brother, and Stephen Bathory, of Transylvania, who has married a Jagellon, succeeds. He repels the attacks of Ivan the Terrible, organises the Cossacks, and, though probably a Protestant, allows a free hand to the Jesuits.

329. **Turkey.** John the Terrible, prince of Moldavia, attacks the Turks and is killed. His army is annihilated and the country devastated.

330. **Africa.** The Portuguese, under Paulo Diaz, colonise Angola and found the city of San Paulo.

---

331. **England.** Elizabeth visits Leicester at Kenilworth. [1575

332. **France.** On the arrival of the new King, the strife of parties recommences, Alençon, Condé and Henry of Navarre join the Politiques, and John Casimir, brother of the Elector Palatine, advances with troops. The alliance is broken up by promising further concessions to the Huguenots and the summoning of the States-General, and by giving the duchy of Anjou to Alençon.

333. **Netherlands.** The states of Holland and Zealand are united, and the crown is offered to and refused by Elizabeth.

---

334. **England.** Peter Wentworth attacks the Queen's interference with free debate, and is committed to the Tower by the Commons. [1576

335. **France.** By the truce of Monsieur (May), Huguenot worship is allowed, except in Paris. This leniency leads to the formation of a League by Guise, which undertakes to obey the King if he obeys the Estates. The States-General, however, which meet at Blois (Dec.), despite the efforts of the Politiques, Bodin and Basmaison, attack the Huguenots.

336. **Netherlands.** Requesens dies, and the unpaid troops mutiny and sack Antwerp ('The Spanish Fury') and other cities. These outrages induce the provinces to unite in the Pacification of Ghent (Nov.), by which they recognise Philip, but agree to expel the troops, secure toleration and convene a federal assembly. The Archduke Matthias is invited to be Governor.

337. **Austria.** The new Emperor, Rudolf II., devotes himself chiefly to astrology and alchemy, and by his patronage of the Jesuits initiates the Catholic reaction in Austria.

338. **Asia.** The head Lama of the chief monastery of Lhassa is made Grand Lama of Tibet.

---

339. **England.** Drake sets out in the Pelican to attack Spanish shipping and treasure in the Pacific, and returns home viâ the Cape of Good Hope, 1580, being the first commander to make the circuit of the world. [1577

Miniature painting in England begins with Hilliard and the Olivers.

489. **Politics.** Hotman's Franco-Gallia argues, on historical grounds, in favour of the rights of the people in the election and deposition of Kings. The Réveille-Matin des Français, however, fiercely denouncing the royal house and authorising regicide, is disowned by the Huguenots.

490. **Social.** Reginald Scot explains the cultivation of hops.

[1575

491. **Eng. Ch.** Dutch Anabaptists are burned in Smithfield.

492. **Bohemian Ch.** The Second Bohemian Confession, based on the Augsburg and the First Bohemian Confession, is drawn up by Lutherans, Calvinists, Utraquists, and Bohemian Brethren.

493. **Science.** An observatory is constructed for Tycho Brahe by the King of Denmark.

494. **Economics.** Calvin's Letter on Usury hastens the reaction against mediaeval economic conceptions.

495. **Education.** Leyden University is founded to commemorate the siege.

496. **Philology.** Lipsius' edition of Tacitus.

497. **Deaths.** Bullinger, Parker.

[1576

498. **Eng. Ch.** Elizabeth orders the suppression of the Prophesyings, or meetings of clergy and laity for theological discussion, begun about 1571. Archbishop Grindal, however, who favours them as a training-ground for preachers, refuses.

499. **German Ch.** The Torgau Book, a Confession of 12 Articles, is drawn up by Andreae, Chemnitz and other Lutherans, and is submitted to all Lutheran princes for revision.

500. **Italian Ch.** Archbishop Borromeo combats the plague in Milan.

501. **Eng. Lit.** Gascoyne's Steel Glass, a social satire.

502. **German Lit.** Frischlin's Rebecca, based on the classical comedy.

503. **Politics.** La Boétie's Contre-Un, written about 1548, from the standpoint of extreme individualism.

504. **Education.** Duke Julius of Brunswick founds Helmstadt University.

505. **Geography.** Frobisher's first voyage, the earliest exploration of the North-West, sights part of Labrador and Frobisher's Strait.

506. **Deaths.** Cardan, Titian.

[1577

507. **Eng. Ch.** Grindal reproves the Queen for her overbearing interference in Church matters, and is suspended. The Prophesyings are suppressed by the Bishops, though most of them believe in their utility. Despite his suspension, the Archbishop is allowed to continue his visitation and to consecrate Bishops.

340. **France.** The Huguenots take up arms; but the war is quickly ended by the treaty of Bergerac, which cedes a town in each district, nine strongholds, and seats in certain provincial Parliaments. Worship is allowed to continue where held at the time of the treaty. France enjoys comparative peace for seven years.

341. **Netherlands.** The new Viceroy, Don John, finds himself compelled to grant the Perpetual Edict, and to confirm the Pacification of Ghent and promise the removal of the troops, with which he hopes to invade England. William suspects Don John's good faith, and refuses to recognise the Edict.

342. **Austria.** The Hungarian Serbs receive districts from the Emperor as military colonists. In 1606 they are definitely merged in the Austrian dominions.

343. **Africa.** The first English Ambassador is sent to Morocco, with which the Barbary Merchants, incorporated 1585, trade.

---

344. **England.** Elizabeth abrogates the special privileges of the Hansards in retaliation for their expulsion of the Merchant Adventurers from Hamburg. [1578

345. **Netherlands.** Don John defeats Matthias at Gemblours (Jan.), but is not supported by Philip, who disapproves his scheme of invading England and marrying Mary Stuart, and orders Antonio Perez to murder Escovedo, his agent in Madrid. Don John dies broken-hearted, and is succeeded by Alexander Farnese of Parma.

Holland adopts the Excise.

346. **Sweden.** John III., son of Gustavus, secretly becomes a Catholic, owing to his Catholic wife, and to the Jesuit, Possevino, and perhaps to the prospect of the Polish throne.

347. **Africa.** A defeated usurper of Morocco appeals to Sebastian, King of Portugal, who invades Morocco and is slain at Alkazar, his army being annihilated.

About the same time Portuguese and Christian influence at the mouth of the Congo come to an end.

348. **Portugal.** Cardinal Henry, aged 67, becomes King.

349. **America.** Gilbert's attempt to settle in North America fails.

---

350. **England.** The Duke of Anjou visits Elizabeth, and a treaty of marriage is signed. The project is strongly attacked by Sir Philip Sidney, who has to retire from Court, and by Stubbe, who loses his right hand. [1579

The Eastland Company is chartered to trade with the Baltic states.

351. **Scotland.** Esmé Stuart, a Catholic cousin of the King, arrives in Scotland, and wins his favour.

352. **Ireland.** The Desmond revolt breaks out again, Sir James Fitzmaurice being joined by mercenaries, sent by the Pope under Stukely and Saunders, at Smerwick, which is stormed by Lord Grey, the Deputy, who massacres the prisoners. In consequence, the Earl of Desmond himself takes the lead, the rebellion continuing till his death, 1583,

Cuthbert Mayne suffers, under the Act of 1571, for maintaining that Catholics should assist a foreign force to reduce England to the obedience of the Pope.

508. **German Ch.** Andreae, Chemnitz, Chytraeus and others compose the Formula of Concord, on the basis of the Torgau Book, approving a modified form of Brenz' theory of ubiquity, and entirely rejecting synergism.

509. **Church Hist.** Medina, a Dominican, founds Probabilism, authorising conduct allowed by a single doctor, which, though attacked by Bellarmine, is elaborated by Toletus, Suarez, and many others.

510. **Scotch Lit.** 'The Admirable' Crichton leaves Scotland for France and Italy, where he distinguishes himself in a series of scholastic discussions.

511. **French Lit.** D'Aubigné begins his Tragiques, an invective against Catholics.

512. **Politics.** Bodin's La République, the first modern discussion of the principles and forms of Government.

513. **Law.** Cujas' Commentaries on Roman Law are collected.

---

514. **Scotch Ch.** The Second Book of Discipline, embodying the ideas of Melville, and adopted by the General Assembly, transfers authority and discipline to the Kirk Session, the Presbytery, the Provincial Synod, and the General Assembly. The Presbytery, consisting of the ministers of the district and an elder from each congregation, controls the Kirk Session, examines candidates, ordains and deposes ministers, and becomes the mainspring of the system. [1578

515. **Church Hist.** The English college is moved from Douai to Rheims, owing to the hostility of the Calvinists of the Low Countries to partisans of Spain. (The college is restored to Douai, 1593.)

516. **French Lit.** Du Bartas' La Semaine, a didactic poem on the Creation, the first French Christian epic. In its translation by Sylvester, it becomes very popular in England.

517. **Polish Lit.** Kochanowski writes the Despatch of the Greek Ambassadors, the first regular Polish drama, and his Lamentations, the first Polish lyrical poetry.

518. **Death.** Sachs.

---

519. **Polish Ch.** Faustus Socinus settles in Poland, where he attempts to unite the Anti-Trinitarians. [1579

520. **Swiss Ch.** Carlo Borromeo founds the Collegium Helveticum at Milan for missionaries to Switzerland.

521. **Eng. Lit.** Spenser's Shepherd's Calendar.

Lyly's Euphues, a fantasy dealing with education, written in a style modelled on Guevara's Mirror for Princes, influences English literature for half a century. With Greene and Lodge, Lyly founds the novel of manners.

North's translation of Plutarch's Lives.

leaving Munster a desert. The confiscations are granted to 'Undertakers,' such as Raleigh and Hatton.

353. **Germany.** Albert of Bavaria is succeeded by William, a devoted adherent of the Jesuits, who makes the country the head-quarters of the Catholic reaction.

354. **Netherlands.** Owing to the religious differences between the northern and southern provinces, which Parma fosters, William finds it impossible to maintain the Pacification of Ghent, and founds the Dutch Republic by the Union of Utrecht (Holland, Zealand, Utrecht, Gelderland, Friesland, Groningen, Overyssel), Philip's authority being nominally retained.

---

355. **England.** Campion and Parsons lead a Jesuit mission to the conversion of England, and explain that nobody need act on the Bull of Disposition till opportunity arises. [1580

The first royal Proclamation is issued against the growth of London.

356. **Scotland.** Mary Stuart informs Philip that she places herself in his hands.

357. **France.** An insult to the wife of Henry of Navarre leads to a short war. The Huguenots are worsted; and the Peace of Fleix renews the terms of Bergerac. Guise now allies with Spain.

358. **Netherlands.** Philip issues a Ban against William, who replies in an Apology, defending his past conduct and present attitude.

359. **Portugal.** On the death of King Henry, Philip, as grandson of Emmanuel the Fortunate, enters Portugal and quickly defeats by land and sea the rival candidate, Antonio, an illegitimate. Though promising to respect all privileges, he excludes Dutch vessels from Lisbon, increases the royal domains, and depresses the nobility. By the conquest of Portugal, Spain thus doubles her colonial empire.

360. **Asia.** Yermak, a Cossack in the service of the Stroganoff family, enters Siberia; hunters and traders follow, and garrisons are established. Within 80 years, Russia reaches the Pacific.

---

361. **England.** Regarding the Jesuits and the seminary priests as conspirators against the Crown, Parliament enacts the Recusancy Laws, imposing fines and imprisonment for hearing mass and for absence from Church. Campion is arrested and executed; other priests are tortured, and Parsons escapes abroad. [1581

Elizabeth pushes on negociations for the Anjou marriage, and Anjou arrives at Court for a visit of three months.

The Turkey or Levant Company receives a Charter, Aleppo being chosen as its chief mart.

362. **Netherlands.** After urgent pressure from William, the Northern Provinces formally renounce their allegiance to Philip, and are per-

522. **French Lit.** Larivey's works, based on Plautus and Terence and the Italian comedy.

Henry Stephanus protests against the predominance of Italian fashions in his Précellence de la Langue Française.

523. **Politics.** The Vindiciae Gallicae, by Languet and Duplessis-Mornay, a philosophical defence of the right of the people to maintain their liberties and religion against a ruler.

Buchanan, tutor to James VI., in his De Jure Regni, inculcates obedience to a good ruler, even if an usurper, and resistance to a bad ruler. The work is burned, 1584, and attacked by Blackwood and Barclay.

Paruta's Perfezione Politica eulogises the Venetian constitution as combining monarchy, aristocracy and democracy.

524. **Death.** Hosius.

---

525. **Scotch Ch.** The Second Book of Discipline is presented to Parliament; but episcopacy is maintained. [1580

526. **German Ch.** Andreae adds a conciliatory Praefatio to the Formula Concordiae, which is now published, and is adopted by most Lutheran churches, with the Liber Concordiae, containing the Augsburg Confession and Apology, Luther's Catechism, and the Schmalkald Articles of 1537. Many Melanchthonians, on the other hand, join the Calvinists, who increase largely in the Palatinate, Nassau, Anhalt, Bremen, Hesse and Brandenburg.

527. **Eng. Lit.** Gabriel Harvey attempts to naturalise classical metres, especially hexameters, and infects Spenser and his circle.

Sidney's Arcadia, a romance suggested by Euphues.

528. **French Lit.** Montaigne's Essais, Livres 1, 2.

Garnier's Les Juives.

529. **Netherlands Lit.** The Elzevirs establish their press at Amsterdam.

530. **Spanish Lit.** Herrera's Annotations on Garcilaso de la Vega.

531. **Science.** Palissy asserts that fossil-shells were real sea-shells left by the ocean, and belonged to marine animals that had lived where they were found.

532. **History.** Zurita completes his Annals of Aragon.

533. **Death.** Camoens.

---

534. **Scotch Ch.** The Second Scotch Confession, fiercely anti-papal, is drawn up by Craig, subscribed by the King and the Assembly, and frequently confirmed. [1581

535. **Italian Ch.** Bellarmine's De Controversiis Christianae Fidei.

536. **Eng. Lit.** Sidney's Defence of Poesy, in answer to Gosson's School of Abuse.

537. **Italian Lit.** Tasso's Gerusalemme Liberata.

538. **Spanish Lit.** Cervantes' first work, Galatea, a pastoral novel.

539. **Philosophy.** Sanchez, a Portuguese, living at Toulouse, declares certainty impossible in his Quod nihil scitur.

suaded by William to offer the sovereignty to Anjou, who accepts it, and attacks Parma.

363. **Portugal.** Antonio of Portugal obtains the promise of aid from Catherine de Medici.

[1582

364. **England.** Anjou leaves England, the matrimonial negotiations never being resumed.

365. **Scotland.** In the Raid of Ruthven, the King is snatched by the Protestant and English party from Esmè Stuart, whose plans for the association of Mary with her son and the restoration of Catholicism are upset.

366. **Netherlands.** The Prince of Orange narrowly escapes assassination.

367. **Germany.** The Catholic princes refuse to admit to their College the deputy of the Bishopric of Magdeburg, held by the Protestant Joachim Frederick of Brandenburg, on the ground that he is not lawful Bishop. The Catholics in the College of Cities at the same time unsuccessfully attempt to exclude the deputies of the city of Aachen, which has recently become Protestant.

368. **Portugal.** A French fleet of 60 ships is defeated at Terceira, in the Azores, and Antonio escapes to England.

369. **Asia.** Nobunaga dies, and his general Hideyoshi becomes supreme in Japan.

370. **Africa.** A number of Rouen merchants, expelled from Guinea by the Portuguese, form a Company and fortify the island of St Louis, Senegal.

[1583

371. **England.** Throgmorton is arrested and reveals under torture the intended invasion of England by Guise's army.

372. **Scotland.** The King escapes from Gowrie's hands, the Raid of Ruthven is declared treason, the chief Protestant lords are banished, and Esmè Stuart is recalled.

373. **Germany.** The Archbishop of Cologne, Gebhard Truchsess, marries, announces his conversion to Calvinism and resolves to retain his see, contrary to the Treaty of Augsburg and to the precedent set by his predecessor, Hermann von Wied. He is excommunicated and driven from his see, the Lutherans refusing to aid a Calvinist, the Catholics thus saving their majority in the Electoral College.

374. **Netherlands.** Anjou determines to carve out a principality for himself in the Southern provinces, and seizes a number of towns, the resistance in Antwerp giving rise to the so-called French Fury. On the failure of his plot he retires to France. Parma takes advantage of the quarrels of his enemies, and conquers several towns.

375. **America.** Gilbert lands in Newfoundland, and takes possession in the Queen's name, but is drowned on his way home.

---

540. **Education.** Mulcaster's Positions urge exercise, adaptation to the learner, postponement of foreign languages, the education of girls, and the training of teachers.

541. **Death.** Languet.

---

542. **Eng. Ch.** Browne, a pupil of Cartwright, is expelled from the ministry and crosses to Holland, where he pleads for the separation of Church and State, and liberty for individuals, however few, to form an independent congregation. His follower, Barrow, however, recommends friendly intercourse between congregations. [1582

Beza presents the Codex Bezae to Cambridge University.

Gregory Martin translates the Bible (the Douai Version).

543. **Russian Ch.** The Metropolitan of Moscow is made a Patriarch, and the Russian Church becomes autocephalous.

544. **Church Hist.** Gregory XIII. revises the Corpus Juris Canonici.

Beza's first edition of the N.T., based on Stephanus.

545. **Asiatic Ch.** Ricci, a Jesuit, settles in China, maintains that Confucianism is related to Christianity, permits ancestor-worship, and wins many converts.

546. **Eng. Lit.** Watson's Century of Love, a collection of Sonnets.

547. **Italian Lit.** The Accademia della Crusca is founded at Florence to reform the language.

548. **Science.** The Julian Calendar is reformed by Clavius, Lilio and Ciacconius, and promulgated by the Pope, but is not adopted in Protestant countries.

549. **History.** Buchanan's History of Scotland.

550. **Geography.** Hakluyt's Collection of Voyages.

551. **Education.** Edinburgh University is founded.

552. **Deaths.** Alva, Buchanan, St Theresa.

---

553. **Eng. Ch.** On the death of Archbishop Grindal, the Queen appoints Whitgift, who orders the clergy to subscribe a recognition of the Queen's ecclesiastical supremacy, and the Prayer-book and Articles. To crush opposition, Elizabeth creates the Court of High Commission, consisting of Bishops and Privy Councillors. [1583

554. **Spanish Lit.** Luis de Leon's Los Nombres de Cristo, mystical prose dialogues.

555. **Science.** Galileo discovers the principle of the pendulum from observation of a lamp hanging in the Cathedral at Pisa.

Caesalpinus classifies plants by their flowers and seeds.

556. **Philosophy.** Bruno visits England, and explains his physical views in the Cena delle Ceneri, and his metaphysical in Della Causa, Principio ed Uno.

557. **History.** Scaliger's De Emendatione Temporum first compares and criticises the sources of ancient history.

558. **Politics.** Sir Thomas Smith's Commonwealth of England first describes the machinery of English government, and discusses sovereignty in the spirit of Bodin.

559. **Death.** Maldonatus.

---

376. **England.** Mendoza, the Spanish Ambassador, is expelled, on the instigation of Leicester, and an Association is formed to defend the Queen, and, in the event of her murder, to execute the person for whose sake the crime is committed. [1584

Leicester's Commonwealth, an anonymous lampoon, fiercely attacks the Earl.

377. **France.** Anjou, the only remaining brother of the childless King, dies, and Henry of Navarre becomes heir to the throne. In consequence, the Guises form a league to exclude Protestants from the succession, with the aid of Spain.

378. **Spain.** Philip imprisons Perez for the murder of Escovedo, for misrepresenting Don John, and for tampering with State Papers.

379. **Netherlands.** William is murdered in the seventh attempt made on his life and encouraged by Philip, and is succeeded by his son Maurice, with Barneveldt as chief counsellor.

380. **Russia.** Ivan the Terrible is succeeded by his son Feodor, who is entirely subject to the influence of his brother-in-law, Boris Godounoff.

381. **America.** Raleigh, to whom the patent of his half-brother, Gilbert, is transferred, sends an expedition to ascertain whether North America is suitable for colonisation. A favourable report is brought back.

382. **Africa.** A Turkish fleet attempts to wrest the Zanzibar coast from Portugal, but is routed.

---

383. **England.** The Association is confirmed by Parliament, which banishes Jesuits and seminary priests. [1585

384. **Scotland.** James makes a league with England, and disowns his mother's cause. Arran falls, and the banished lords return.

385. **France.** In the Treaty of Joinville (Jan.), Spain and the Guises agree to support the candidature of Cardinal Bourbon, the uncle of Henry, Philip to receive Navarre and Béarn. Paris is divided into districts, the representatives of which form 'Les Seize.' The King is forced to sign the Treaty of Nemours, recalling all edicts of toleration. The Pope excommunicates Henry of Navarre, and a desultory war breaks out.

386. **Italy.** Sixtus V. becomes Pope, and divides the government among 15 congregations of Cardinals, whom he limits to 70, suppresses brigandage, fosters agriculture and industries, and builds a new aqueduct and churches.

387. **Netherlands.** Parma captures Brussels and Antwerp, and Elizabeth, though declining the sovereignty of the Netherlands, sends troops under Leicester.

388. **America.** Drake plunders Vigo and attacks St Domingo.

Raleigh sends colonists to Roanoke Island, who are, however, brought home by Drake, 1586. A second expedition in 1587 fares no better.

---

560. **Eng. Ch.** Whitgift is forced by Leicester, Burleigh and Walsingham to hold a conference at Lambeth with Puritan divines, which effects nothing. Burleigh proposes his chaplain Travers, Cartwright's chief follower, for the mastership of the Temple, but withdraws him, on the opposition of Whitgift, in favour of Hooker. The Puritans offer petitions to the Commons, some of which are adopted, but are rejected by the Lords. [1584

561. **Art.** Lodovico Caracci, with two cousins, begins to fresco at Bologna, and founds the Eclectic school, among their pupils being Guido Reni and Domenichino. The school is attacked by the realist Caravaggio, whose work is continued by Ribera.

562. **Philosophy.** Sir William Temple introduces the logic of Ramus into England.

563. **Education.** Emmanuel College, Cambridge, is founded by Sir Walter Mildmay, and becomes, under its first master, Chaderton, a stronghold of Puritanism. Hooker, Cotton, Harvard and others who afterwards emigrate to New England are among the early members of the college.

564. **History.** Knox's History of the Reformation in Scotland.

565. **Social.** A public bank is instituted at Venice.

Scott's Discovery of Witchcraft vigorously attacks the superstition.

566. **Death.** Borromeo.

---

567. **Eng. Ch.** To strengthen the position of the Bishops and to stem the growth of Puritanism, Whitgift composes disciplinary Canons, supplementing those of 1576 and 1583, but relaxes subscription for all but those entering the ministry. [1585

568. **Scotch Ch.** The King's supremacy in matters ecclesiastical is affirmed, bishops are allowed to hold synods, and presbyteries are deprived of jurisdiction. This attack on Presbyterianism is vehemently denounced by Melville and the exiled ministers.

569. **Italian Lit.** Guarini's Pastor Fido, modelled on Tasso's Aminta, is acted.

570. **Science.** Stevinus of Bruges, the founder of Statics, discovers the law of equilibrium on the inclined plane, and measures the pressure of fluids.

571. **Geography.** John Davis visits West Greenland, discovers Davis Strait, and penetrates further west than any of his predecessors.

572. **Education.** On the report of a commission appointed by Aquaviva, the Ratio Studiorum of the Jesuits is published. Revised in 1599, it remains in use in Jesuit schools till 1832. The method includes training colleges for teachers, constant inspection of schools, the use of Latin, short hours, repetition of lessons, mutual criticism and emulation among the pupils, and physical exercise.

573. **Deaths.** Muretus, Ronsard, Sigonius.

---

389. **England.** Babington, Ballard and other Catholics, plot to murder the Queen, but are detected and executed by Walsingham, who maintains Mary's complicity. She is condemned to death, and Parliament urges the Queen to execute the sentence. [1586

390. **Holland.** Leicester is offered and accepts the government, is censured by the Queen and returns to England. Many, however, remain, and in the battle of Zutphen Sir Philip Sidney is slain.

391. **Switzerland.** Pfyffer forms the Golden or Borromean League between the seven Catholic Cantons. The Jesuits enter the country.

392. **Poland.** The Ultramontane, Sigismund III., son of the King of Sweden and a Jagellon Princess, succeeds Stephen Bathory.

393. **Asia.** Abbas the Great, of Persia, begins his reign of 42 years, during which he developes the material resources of the country, extends his rule along the Persian Gulf and Afghan frontier, recovers territory from the Turks, and maintains religious toleration.

---

394. **England.** Elizabeth signs Mary's death warrant, which is carried out (Feb.), but fines and disgraces Secretary Davison. [1587 The Pope proclaims a crusade against England, and Mary's death precipitates the Spanish invasion ; but the fleet, when about to start, is attacked by Drake in Cadiz harbour, and crippled.

395. **France.** Henry of Navarre defeats the King's forces at Coutras ; but Guise defeats and expels his German allies.

396. **Holland.** Leicester returns and attempts to raise the siege of Sluys, but quarrels with the Dutch and is recalled.

---

397. **England.** Peter Wentworth is committed to the Tower for questions to the Speaker touching the liberties of the House. [1588

The Armada, under Medina Sidonia, enters the Channel, where it is harassed by the English (whose ships, though smaller, are more numerous and possess better artillery), under Howard of Effingham, Frobisher and Drake, and is defeated off Gravelines (Aug.). A storm rises during the battle and sweeps the remnants of the fleet past the coast of Flanders, where Parma's army is waiting to be convoyed to England, and round the north of Scotland, only 54 out of 120 ships returning to Spain.

398. **France.** Guise enters Paris, and barricades are erected round the Louvre. The King flies to Blois, where he is forced to concede Guise's demands and to assemble the States-General (Oct.), which insists on the removal of the King's favourites, and suggests the surrender of the crown to Guise. Henry assassinates Guise (Dec.), and imprisons the Cardinal of Bourbon.

399. **Spain.** Perez escapes to Aragon, but the Inquisition, hearing of his attacks on Philip's religion, removes him, and Aragon rises in revolt.

574. **Eng. Ch.** Whitgift is admitted to the Council. [1586

575. **French Ch.** The Feuillants, a reformed branch of the Cistercians, with exceedingly severe rules, are founded.

576. **German Ch.** Crell becomes Chancellor of the new Elector of Saxony, and the second period of crypto-Calvinism begins, extending till the death of the Elector and the strictly Lutheran Articles of Visitation of 1592.

577. **Eng. Lit.** Shakespere leaves Stratford for London, and becomes an actor in the Lord Chamberlain's Company.

Camden's Britannia.

578. **Italian Lit.** Chiabrera's Lyrics.

579. **Social.** Drake brings tobacco and potatoes to England from Virginia.

580. **Economics.** The Pope forbids Usury in the bull Detestabilis. It is defended, however, by the Canonists Navarrus and Scaccia.

581. **Politics.** Dorleans and other French preachers defend the League in their sermons, and warn the King that orthodoxy is a higher duty than loyalty.

---

582. **Eng. Ch.** On the failure of an attempt to legalise the Book of Discipline, several hundred clergy subscribe it as binding on them, and the more extreme commence a violent pamphlet war. [1587

583. **Eng. Lit.** Marlowe's Faust, and Tamburlaine, closely followed by the Jew of Malta and Edward II., found English drama, aided by the works of the 'University Wits,' Lyly, Peele, Greene, Kyd, Lodge, Nash.

584. **German Lit.** English actors perform English plays at the Courts of Hesse and Brunswick, and influence the works of Duke Julius and Jacob Ayrer.

585. **Numismatics.** Agustino's Dialogo de Medallas y Inscriciones founds numismatics.

586. **Death.** Foxe.

---

587. **Eng. Ch.** The Martin Marprelate pamphlets appear, chiefly composed by Penry, Udal, Throgmorton and Fenner, and printed from a movable press, which is at length captured at Manchester. Udal is condemned under the libel law of 1581, and thrown into prison, where he dies, 1593. At Whitgift's suggestion, Cooper, Bishop of Winchester, replies to the attacks on the Church and clergy. [1588

Penry attacks the Welsh clergy, and commences a Puritan movement in Wales.

Gerard arrives in England and works under Garnet, till he is captured, 1594.

588. **Italian Ch.** The first volume appears of Baronius' Annales Ecclesiastici, which, despite its author's ignorance of Greek, becomes the official ultramontane text-book of Church History.

400. **Denmark.** Christian IV. becomes King, and encourages the industry and commerce of Norway.
401. **Africa.** The first English Guinea Company is chartered to trade with West Africa, but no settlement is formed.

[1589

402. **England.** An expedition sails under Drake to assist Antonio of Portugal, and seizes much booty.
403. **France.** Catherine dies (Jan.). Mayenne declares war on the King, who is thus thrown into the arms of the Huguenots. Henry of Navarre professes his loyalty to the crown, and extorts toleration. Many moderate Catholics rally round the throne, the Swiss and Germans cross the borders, and the King marches on Paris, but is murdered by Jacques Clément at St Cloud. Henry of Navarre at once assumes the royal title, which is also claimed by the Duke of Lorraine, Cardinal Bourbon, and Philip.
404. **Switzerland.** The Duke of Savoy attacks Geneva, which is deserted by Bern, the struggle lasting till the Peace of Vervins, 1598.

[1590

405. **France.** The Cardinal of Bourbon is proclaimed Charles X., and Mayenne, with a large army of mercenaries, is defeated at Ivry (March). Henry lays siege to Paris, but is compelled to retire by the advance of Parma from the Low Countries (Sept.). The Cardinal of Bourbon dies.
406. **Holland.** While Parma is away, Maurice of Nassau captures Breda.
407. **Africa.** The Emperor of Morocco annexes Timbuctoo and the Upper Niger.

[1591

408. **England.** Eleven judges protest against illegal commitments by the Council.
409. **France.** Henry captures several towns, lays siege to Rouen, and receives reinforcements from Germany and England, Mayenne being aided by Spanish and Italian troops. Navarre, Foix and Albret are annexed to the French Crown.
410. **Spain.** A royal army enters Aragon, and the defenders of Perez are ruthlessly punished. Philip fills the Cortes with nominees, leaving it only the right to petition, and appoints the judges.
411. **Russia.** Demetrius, son of Ivan the Terrible by his seventh wife, dies, perhaps killed by Boris, who aspires to the Tsardom.
412. **Asia.** Lancaster undertakes the first English voyage to the East Indies.

---

589. **Church Hist.** Molina, a Portuguese Jesuit, writes a semi-Pelagian treatise on Grace, which is approved by Aquaviva, but attacked by the Dominicans and Augustinians. The case is transferred to Rome, 1597, and a Congregation is appointed.

590. **Politics.** Boucher attacks the King in his De justa Abdicatione Henrici.

591. **Geography.** Davis undertakes a third voyage, and reaches 72° 12′.

592. **Deaths.** Paul Veronese, Weigel.

[1589

593. **Eng. Ch.** Bancroft maintains the Divine Right and Apostolical Succession of Bishops in a sermon that may be regarded as the first manifesto of the High Church or Anglo-Catholic party.

Bacon's Advertisement touching Controversies of the Church of England impartially points out the faults of Puritan and Anglican.

594. **Netherlands Ch.** Arminius, minister at Amsterdam, is invited to confute Cornheert, Coolhaes and other sub-lapsarians, but ends by adopting their position.

595. **Science.** Galileo disproves Aristotle's law that the pace of falling bodies varies with their weight.

596. **Education.** The Academy of Kiev, the first educational institution in Russia.

597. **Social.** The spinning-wheel is used at Cambridge.

[1590

598. **Eng. Ch.** Cartwright is summoned before the High Commission, refuses to recant, and, with six other clergy, is imprisoned.

599. **Eng. Lit.** Spenser's Fairy Queen, Books 1—3.

600. **Art.** Giovanni of Bologna's equestrian statue of Cosmo I., and his Mercury (Florence).

601. **Philosophy.** Campanella's De Sensu Rerum, a system based on Telesio, but more idealistic and theosophical.

602. **Deaths.** Cujas, Palissy, Paré, Sixtus V., Walsingham.

[1591

603. **Eng. Lit.** Sidney's Astrophel and Stella is followed by the sonnets of Daniel, Barnabe Barnes, Giles Fletcher, Lodge, Drayton, Spenser, and Sir John Davies. The fashion lasts for six years.

Shakespere's first play, Love's Labour's Lost, reveals Lyly's influence.

604. **Science.** Vieta's In Artem analyticam Isagoge improves algebraic notation.

605. **Education.** Queen Elizabeth founds Trinity College, Dublin.

606. **Death.** John of the Cross.

---

413. **France.** Parma again enters France, and relieves Rouen (Apr.). Henry profits by the reaction caused by Philip's plan of placing his daughter on the throne. Périgord and Béarn are annexed to France. [1592

414. **Spain.** Drake sacks Corunna, but fails to take Lisbon.

415. **Netherlands.** Parma dies on his return from Rouen, having completely reduced the southern provinces, now known as the Spanish Netherlands, of which the Archduke Ernest becomes Governor.

416. **Sweden.** Sigismund of Poland becomes King of Sweden, but is resisted by his Protestant uncle Charles of Sodermannland.

417. **Asia.** As a stepping-stone to China, Hideyoshi invades Korea, which obtains aid from its suzerain.

418. **Africa.** To confirm their menaced authority, the Portuguese build a fort at Mombasa, which becomes the capital of the northern settlements.

---

419. **England.** The Speaker, in answer to his request for liberty of speech, is told that it is granted, 'but not to speak everyone what he listeth—their privilege was to say Aye or No.' [1593

420. **France.** The States-General meet at Paris to choose a King, and suggest that Henry should turn Catholic. Henry therefore attends mass in St Denis, and is joined by the nationalist Leaguers.

421. **Holland.** The States-General are organised by Barneveldt.

422. **Russia.** Boris Godounoff forbids peasants to leave the service of their masters.

423. **Turkey.** Michael the Brave buys the throne of Wallachia, and at once revolts and wins independence.

---

424. **England.** An anonymous treatise on the succession declares the Infanta of Spain, as descendant of John of Gaunt, heir to the throne. [1594

425. **Ireland.** Hugh O'Neill, Earl of Tyrone, heads a rising in Ulster and appeals to Spain for help, which is promised, but does not arrive.

426. **France.** Henry is crowned at Chartres and enters Paris, where he is warmly received. Most of the nobles are won over by separate negotiations, and Laon, the last stronghold of the League in the north east, is taken after a long siege. The Spanish army withdraws to the Netherlands, and Normandy submits. The King sends D'Ossat and Duperron to Rome to discuss with the Pope the removal of the excommunication.

---

607. **Scotch Ch.** The Presbyterian system is fully established by the Scotch Parliament, which ratifies the Second Book of Discipline. Episcopacy, though not abolished, possesses no jurisdiction. [1592

608. **German Ch.** Hunnius and other Lutherans draw up Four Articles of Visitation with a view to suppress crypto-Calvinism in Saxony.

609. **Swiss Ch.** Francis de Sales, Bishop of Geneva, begins to preach in Chalais.

610. **Church Hist.** The revision of the Vulgate, ordered by the Council of Trent and published 1589, is revised, owing to the criticisms of Bellarmine, the final revision appearing 1593.

611. **Spanish Lit.** Lope de Vega's dramas begin to be acted at Madrid.

612. **Science.** Galileo's Scienza Mechanica explains the raising of weights.

613. **History.** Mariana's History of Spain till 1516.

614. **Archaeology.** The remains of Pompeii are discovered.

615. **Death.** Montaigne.

---

616. **Eng. Ch.** Parliament banishes all above 16 who refuse to attend Church. A large number of Catholics and Puritans leave the country. The Brownist leaders, Barrow, Penry and Greenwood, are executed under the libel law of 1581. [1593

Bancroft's Dangerous Positions maintains that Puritan teachings involve a danger to society.

617. **Asiatic Ch.** The first Christians are executed in Japan.

618. **French Lit.** The Satire Menippée, composed by Pithou, Rapin, Passerat, Gillot, satirises the extreme members of the League.

619. **Philology.** Scaliger's departure for Leyden ushers in the third or Dutch period of classical learning, of Grotius, Heinsius, Gronovius, Gerard and Isaac Vossius, Cluverius, Meursius, Graevius.

620. **Archaeology.** Bosio begins to explore the Roman Catacombs.

621. **Death.** Marlowe.

---

622. **Eng. Ch.** Hooker's Ecclesiastical Polity, Books 1—4, defends the Anglican Via Media against Rome and Geneva, and maintains that the external ordering of the Church is a matter of expediency. [1594

623. **French Ch.** Pithou's Libertés de l'Église Gallicane first fully states Erastian Gallicanism. The Pope is declared to be without power in temporal, and bound by the old French Councils in spiritual, matters.

624. **Eng. Lit.** Shakespere composes most of his Sonnets.

Nash's Jack Wilton introduces the novel of adventure.

625. **Literature.** Casaubon and Scaliger begin to correspond.

626. **Politics.** Hooker declares the primitive condition of men to have been one of war, and government to have originated by a contract.

627. **Deaths.** Palestrina, Tintoretto.

---

427. **Ireland.** Sir John Norris is sent to subdue the revolt of Tyrone, but fails. [1595

428. **France.** Henry formally declares war against Spain, which captures a number of towns on the N.E. frontier. At the most critical moment he is absolved by the Pope, and agrees to restore Catholic property and worship in his hereditary dominions, and to accept certain of the articles of the Council of Trent.

429. **Netherlands.** The Age of the Archdukes begins with the appointment of Albert of Austria, the husband of Philip's daughter Isabella, to the position of Governor.

430. **America.** Raleigh visits Guiana in search of El Dorado, and sails up the Orinoco.

431. **Asia.** The Dutch establish their first Factory in the East in Java.

---

432. **England.** An offensive and defensive coalition is formed by France and England against Spain, to which the Dutch, who are thus recognised as an independent State, shortly accede. [1596

Essex, Raleigh and Howard of Effingham lead an expedition, in which the Dutch join, against Spain. The Spanish fleet is destroyed in Cadiz harbour, and the city is sacked.

433. **France.** Mayenne submits to Henry, and Épernon is deserted in Provence. Mercoeur alone holds out in Brittany. The Archduke Albert, however, takes Calais.

Henry convokes an Assembly of Notables at Rouen, and lays before them his scheme of reforms. He permits the establishment of a Council of Finance, which, however, only exists for three months.

434. **Netherlands.** Philip repudiates debts contracted by Spanish troops and officials.

---

435. **England.** The privileges of the Hanse merchants are withdrawn. [1597

436. **France.** The Spaniards seize Amiens, but Henry retakes it. Negotiations begin under the Pope's mediation. Mercoeur, the last French noble in arms against the King, yields.

437. **Netherlands.** Maurice and Vere rout the Spaniards at Turnhout.

---

438. **France.** The war with Spain is terminated by the Treaty of Vervins, by which France regains her losses, and Philip resigns his claim to the French throne. [1598

439. **Spain.** Philip II. is succeeded by his son, Philip III., who is guided by Lerma.

440. **Germany.** The Gera Bond is made by which the younger branch of the Hohenzollerns is to possess Culmbach; if either branch fails, the

628. **Eng. Ch.** Barret attacks the authority and doctrine of the German and Swiss Protestants, and founds the Anglo-Catholic movement at Cambridge. In reply, Whitaker draws up the strictly Calvinist Lambeth Articles, which are adopted, with slight modifications, by Whitgift and several other bishops. [1595

Bound's True Doctrine of the Sabbath systematises and expounds the Puritan theory.

629. **French Ch.** The Jesuits refuse to recognise Henry as King, despite his conversion, and are attacked by Arnauld on behalf of the University of Paris. On an attempt by Chastel, a student of Clermont College, on the King's life, the Order is expelled.

630. **Polish Ch.** At the synod of Brzesc, the Polish Church attaches itself to the Western Church.

631. **Deaths.** Philip Neri, Tasso.

---

632. **Eng. Ch.** Peter Baro, Lady Margaret Professor at Cambridge, attacks the Lambeth Articles from an Anglo-Catholic standpoint, and is warmly supported by Overall and Andrewes. [1596

633. **French Ch.** Maldonatus' Commentaries on the New Testament.

Bodin leaves his Heptaplomeres in MS., a sceptical dialogue on religions, published 1847.

634. **German Ch.** The Archduke Ferdinand in Styria, and Maximilian in Bavaria, stamp out Protestantism.

635. **Eng. Lit.** Ben Jonson's Every Man in his Humour.

636. **Science.** Rheticus' Opus Palatinum, a computation of pure trigonometrical tables. Pitiscus supplies the addition formulae, 1599.

637. **Education.** Lectures begin at Gresham College, London.

638. **Geography.** Barents, the pilot of a Dutch expedition, discovers Spitzbergen, and sails round the N.W. of Nova Zembla.

639. **Deaths.** Bodin, Drake.

---

640. **Eng. Lit.** Bacon's first ten Essays.

Bodley bequeathes his library to Oxford University. [1597

---

641. **French Ch.** Desiring to ward off political danger, Henry issues the Edict of Nantes, by which the Huguenots obtain toleration and the right of worship wherever it has been celebrated within two years, admission to schools and colleges and eligibility to office. They must, however, pay tithes, renounce all dealings with foreign powers, and dissolve their provincial assemblies. The Edict is violently opposed by the Pope and Parliament, by which it is not registered till 1599. The clause concerning admission to office remains a dead letter. [1598

Du Plessis-Mornay's L'Institution de l'Eucharistie.

other is to inherit the Electorship and the Margravate until they can be again divided.

Catholicism is restored in Aachen by military force.

441. **Italy.** Ferrara is annexed by the Pope, on the death of Alfonso II., the last of the Este. Modena passes to an illegitimate member of the family.

442. **Russia.** Feodore dies, and the house of Rurik comes to an end. Boris succeeds, and forces the head of the Romanoffs, who are related to the house of Rurik by marriage, to become a monk.

443. **Asia.** The War of China and Japan ends. Hideyoshi dies, and his general, Jeyasu Tokugawa, restores the Shogunate, which remains in his family till 1868. Korea does not recover from the struggle for several generations.

---

444. **Ireland.** Essex is sent to cope with Tyrone's rebellion, which has grown into a national movement. He fails, returns without permission, and is imprisoned. [1599

445. **France.** Gabrielle d'Estrées dies.

Sully becomes superintendent of the finances, pays off the debt and accumulates a reserve, reduces the Taille, recovers part of the royal domain, revives agriculture, constructs roads and canals, and reorganises the artillery and ambulance departments of the army. He also abolishes sinecure offices, and makes seats in the Parliament hereditary on payment of an annual tax. The King supports Sully in his reforms, but devotes his chief attention to manufactures and commerce.

446. **Spain.** An Armada for the invasion of England is equipped at Lisbon, but on sailing is scattered by a storm.

447. **Hungary.** Michael the Brave, of Wallachia, defeats Andrew Bathory, a tool of the Sultan, and conquers Transylvania, with the Emperor's approval.

---

448. **France.** Henry obtains the sanction of the Pope for his divorce from Margaret of Valois, and marries Mary de Medici, who brings him male heirs. [1600

Henry declares war on the Duke of Savoy, who has annexed Saluzzo, 1588, and refuses to surrender it.

449. **Netherlands.** Negotiations begun by the Archduke fail, and Maurice enters Flanders and besieges Nieuport. The Archduke with a relieving army is utterly routed; but Maurice, too weak to conquer Flanders, returns to Holland.

450. **Asia.** In consequence of the raising of the price of pepper by the Dutch, an Association of London merchants for trading with the East Indies is formed, with 125 shareholders and £70,000 capital. The first

642. **Spanish Ch.** Paramo's History and Methods of the Inquisition.
643. **Netherlands Ch.** St Aldegonde's Différends de la Religion Chrétienne.
644. **Eng. Lit.** Stow's Survey of London.
645. **Spanish Lit.** Lope de Vega's Arcadia, a pastoral novel.
646. **Philosophy.** Du Vair's Philosophie Morale des Stoïciens.
647. **Education.** Henry IV. reorganises the University of Paris, and attempts to encourage the direct study of the classics, the Bible and the natural sciences.
648. **Geography.** Lindschoten publishes his voyages and maps of the East, from which the Dutch and English obtain their first reliable information.
649. **Deaths.** St Aldegonde, Burleigh, Stephanus.

---

650. **Asiatic Ch.** At the Synod of Diamper, convened by the Archbishop of Goa, the Syrians or Nestorian Christians are compelled to join the Roman Church. [1599
651. **Spanish Lit.** Lope de Vega's San Isidoro, a poem in honour of Madrid's patron saint.

Guzman d'Alfarache, a picaresque novel.
652. **Science.** Aldovrandus' Encyclopaedia of Natural History.

Wright's Errors in Navigation Detected explains the theory of meridional parts.
653. **Politics.** Mariana's De Rege discusses the origin and limits of royal power, with illustrations from contemporary France, from an extreme Ultramontane standpoint.

King James' Basilican Doron, composed for his son Henry, condemns Presbyterianism as a foe to royal power.
654. **Philology.** Scaliger's De Europaeorum Linguis Diatriba, the first classification of languages.
655. **Education.** The Collegium Mauritianum is instituted at the Court of Kassel, the chief of the Ritter-Academien for the education of the nobility.
656. **Death.** Spenser.

---

657. **Scotch Ch.** James appoints three new Bishops, who, however, are not recognised by the Church. [1600
658. **French Ch.** The King arranges and is present at a Conference at Fontainebleau, to discuss Du Plessis-Mornay's work on the Eucharist. Mornay's accuracy of quotation is successfully impeached by Duperron, and French Protestantism loses prestige.
659. **Italian Ch.** After seven years' imprisonment by the Inquisition, Bruno is burned in Rome for maintaining the plurality of inhabited worlds, having recanted his other heresies.
660. **Eng. Lit.** England's Helicon, a collection of fugitive verse by Sidney, Raleigh, Greene, Lodge.
661. **Science.** Gilbert's De Magnete, the first considerable work in English science since Roger Bacon.

Kircher invents the Magic Lantern.

voyage of the East India Company, commanded by Lancaster, is made 1601, and a factory is established at Bantam.

451. **Hungary.** Michael the Brave conquers Moldavia, and for a moment unites all Roumanian lands. Hungary, however, throws off his yoke, and Michael is killed, 1601.

[1601

452. **England.** Essex, who has been deprived by the Queen of the monopoly of sweet wines on which he depends and who, though liberated, is forbidden to come to Court, attempts to force the Queen to change her ministers. He is arrested, accused of plotting with the Scotch King, prosecuted by Coke and Bacon, and executed.

To pay for the conquest of Ireland, the Queen summons Parliament, which grants supplies, but compels Elizabeth to promise to revoke all burdensome monopolies.

453. **Ireland.** A Spanish fleet and a small army land at Kinsale, but are defeated and compelled to withdraw.

454. **Savoy.** Peace is made at Lyons, Savoy retaining Saluzzo, and ceding Valromey, Gex, Bresse and Bugey, which connect France and Switzerland.

455. **Russia.** The false Demetrius, perhaps a *protégé* of the Jesuits, appears in Poland, and is acknowledged by the King.

[1602

456. **England.** Elizabeth attempts to revive the coalition of 1596, and proposes to Henry an offensive alliance against Spain. The offer is rejected, renewed after the conspiracy of Biron, and again rejected.

457. **France.** Biron's plot with Spain and Savoy and Bouillon, the Huguenot leader, for the dismemberment of France, is discovered, and Biron is executed.

458. **Switzerland.** The Duke of Savoy's attempt to seize Geneva (the 'Escalade') fails.

459. **Asia.** The Dutch Companies are amalgamated into a national East India Company, which ejects the Portuguese from the Moluccas, and monopolises the spice-trade.

[1603

460. **England.** Elizabeth indicates her preference for the King of Scots, though the legal heir is William Seymour, representative of the Suffolk line. On the death of the Queen, James succeeds without opposition, retains Robert Cecil as Secretary of State, and makes peace with Spain. The Main Plot, perhaps to put Arabella Stuart, a descendant of Margaret Tudor, on the throne, is discovered, and Raleigh is imprisoned.

662. **Art.** Eurydice, the libretto by Rinuccini, the music by Peri, is performed at the marriage of Henry IV. and Mary de Medici, and founds the opera, which is developed by Monteverde.

The first Oratorio, composed by Cavaliere, is performed in the Oratory at Rome.

663. **Law.** Coke's Reports.

664. **Philology.** Casaubon's Commentaries on Athenaeus.

665. **Agriculture.** Olivier de Serre's Théâtre de l'Agriculture, based on 30 years' experience, aids the revival of agriculture.

666. **Death.** Hooker.

---

667. **Philosophy.** Charron's De la Sagesse, the first modern attempt at a system of ethics without theology, deeply influenced by his friend and master Montaigne. [1601

668. **Philology.** Gruter, with the aid of Scaliger, edits a Corpus Inscriptionum Antiquarum Orbis Romani.

669. **Social.** The Poor Law assumes the form which it substantially retains till 1834. The administrators are empowered to provide work for the able, relief for the impotent, and punishment for the idle, and children are to be trained to work.

670. **Death.** Tycho Brahe.

---

671. **French Ch.** Francis de Sales preaches the Lent course of sermons in the Louvre, and becomes Archbishop of Geneva. [1602

672. **Bohemian Ch.** The Emperor revives the edicts of persecution against Protestants.

673. **Church Hist.** Cyril Lucar, a Cretan, becomes Patriarch of Alexandria. Having visited Wittenberg and Geneva, he attempts to introduce Calvinism into the Eastern Church, sends students to Protestant Universities, and corresponds with Abbot, Utenbogaert, and other Protestants.

674. **Eng. Lit.** Shakespere's Hamlet.

675. **Art.** Guido Reni settles in Rome, and paints, among other works, the Aurora in the Rospigliosi palace.

---

676. **Eng. Ch.** The new King is greeted with the Millenary and other petitions from the various parties in the Church, and promises a conference for their discussion. [1603

677. **French Ch.** Despite the opposition of the Parliament and University of Paris, the Jesuits are re-admitted. They receive the royal Château at La Flêche for a seminary, and Coton becomes the King's Confessor.

678. **Polish Ch.** Socinus rallies the Unitarian parties to his own views at the synod of Racau.

679. **Eng. Lit.** Florio's translation of Montaigne.

461. **Ireland.** Tyrone submits to Mountjoy, the country being more thoroughly reduced than at any previous time.

462. **Germany.** The Anspach line of Hohenzollerns dies out and the Elector of Brandenburg grants their possessions to his brothers. He gives Jägerndorf, in Silesia, bought by George of Anspach in 1524, to his second son, from whom it is confiscated by the Emperor, 1623.

[1604

463. **England.** James' first Parliament meets, vindicates its claims to the control of its own elections and the freedom of its members from arrest, and resists the King's proposal for a union with Scotland.

Despite Sully's mission to London, peace is made with Spain, James promising not to support the Dutch, nor trade in the Indies.

464. **Netherlands.** Spinola takes Ostend, after three and a half years' siege.

465. **Sweden.** Sigismund is deposed and succeeded by Charles IX.

466. **Russia.** Demetrius invades Russia, but is twice defeated by Boris.

467. **Hungary.** The Hungarians join Stephen Bocskai, who invades Hungary and is proclaimed King of Hungary and Transylvania, 1605. He obtains from the Emperor constitutional government and toleration.

468. **America.** Henry IV. sends De Monts to colonise Acadia. Port Royal (the present Annapolis) is founded, and Champlain explores the coasts.

[1605

469. **England.** In consequence of the banishment of priests from London, 1604, Catesby and some friends resolve to blow up King and Parliament, and send for Guy Fawkes from Flanders to execute the scheme. Gunpowder Plot, however, is revealed by one of the conspirators, on the eve of the meeting of Parliament, Nov. 5.

470. **Russia.** Boris dies, and Demetrius is killed in a revolution in Moscow. A relative of the house of Rurik becomes Tsar, on making cessions of territory to Sweden, and receiving the aid of a Swedish army. A second Demetrius is brought forward by the Poles.

471. **America.** Possession is formally taken of Barbadoes, the first English colony, which is not settled till 1624.

472. **Asia.** Akbar is succeeded by Jehangir, under whom the Moghul Empire is weakened by the revolts of his sons and the loss of Kandahar.

---

680. **Science.** Cesi founds the Academia dei Lincei in Rome. Fabricius of Acquapendente discovers valves in the veins.

681. **Politics.** Althusius' Politica recommends a republican government, in which the chief magistrate is aided and controlled by Ephors, and the representatives are chosen only among the wealthy. His teaching is developed by his follower Boxhorn.

682. **Deaths.** Cartwright, Gilbert, Vieta.

---

683. **Eng. Ch.** A Conference is held at Hampton Court, represented by Whitgift, Bancroft, Bilson and others on the Anglican side, and Reynolds, Chaderton and others on the Puritan. The King rejects every demand of the Puritans, except that for the revision of the Bible. [1604

Convocation composes some new canons, and orders the clergy to subscribe the ecclesiastical supremacy of the Crown, the Prayer-book, and the Articles. The Canons, though not enforced by law, lead to the ejection of a number of clergy.

684. **German Ch.** Paraeus, Professor at Heidelberg, which has succeeded to Geneva as the chief School of Calvinism, issues an Irenicum, which is attacked by Hutter and other Lutherans.

685. **Netherlands Ch.** Arminius is appointed Professor of Theology at Leyden, and commences his struggle with Gomarus, his colleague.

686. **Science.** Kepler's Optics explain the structure of the eye, and the formation of images on the retina.

687. **History.** De Thou's History of his Times.

688. **Social.** Elizabeth's mild statute against witchcraft is superseded by a severe Act, under which hundreds are executed.

689. **Deaths.** Faustus Socinus, Whitgift.

---

690. **Scotch Ch.** James banishes a number of Presbyterian ministers, alienates Church property and restores the Bishops, and is recognised as supreme in temporal and spiritual matters. [1605

691. **German Ch.** Johann Arndt's Wahres Christenthum (and Paradies-gärtlein), based on the teaching of Weigel and other mystics, initiates a reaction against dogmatism and founds Pietism in Germany.

692. **Polish Ch.** The Racovian Catechism, compiled by Socinus, Crell and others, becomes the recognised creed of the Unitarians.

693. **Eng. Lit.** Ben Jonson writes Volpone, and begins to compose masques, or plays for the Court, adapted to scenery and music, which remain popular till the Civil War.

694. **French Lit.** Vauquelin de la Fresnaye's L'Art Poétique, the *résumé* and last product of the Pleïade movement. Malherbe now settles at Court, and his verses develope the classical style.

695. **Spanish Lit.** Cervantes' Don Quixote, Part I.

696. **Philosophy.** Bacon's Advancement of Learning, a survey of the condition and needs of the sciences, introductory to a reconstruction of human knowledge.

697. **Death.** Beza.

---

473. **England.** Bates, a merchant, challenges the King's right to levy a duty on currants; but the Court of Exchequer decides that the King may levy impositions by his own authority. [1606

474. **Italy.** The claim of Venice, whose attitude is largely determined and defended by Sarpi, to exercise criminal jurisdiction over priests is met by an interdict, the last issued by the Roman Church, on which the Republic banishes the Orders. France arranges a compromise, the prisoners being tried by an Ecclesiastical Court, while the Jesuits remain in banishment till 1651.

475. **America.** Largely in consequence of the satisfactory reports brought back by Gosnold, 1602, and Weymouth, 1605, Virginia is divided between the London and Plymouth Companies.

476. **Asia.** The fifth Governor of the Sikhs dies, and the Governorship becomes hereditary. The sect is transformed into an army, and begins a Holy War against the Moghul Emperors.

---

477. **England.** Parliament refusing to concede free-trade and to recognise the Scotch, the King obtains a decision from the judges, by a test case (the Post-Nati), that Scottish subjects born after his accession are legally naturalised. [1607

478. **Ireland.** Tyrone and Tyrconnel, finding resistance hopeless, flee to Spain; James confiscates a large part of Ulster, which is colonised by English and Scotch settlers.

479. **Holland.** Heemskerk destroys the Spanish fleet at Gibraltar, and Spinola's troops mutiny for want of pay.

480. **Spain.** Owing to Spanish repudiations, the Bank of Genoa fails.

481. **America.** A settlement is made by the Plymouth Company in North Virginia; but many of the colonists die and the rest return, 1608.

At the same time a settlement is made at Jamestown, in Southern Virginia, by John Smith.

---

482. **Germany.** In consequence of the annexation of the strongly Protestant Donauwörth, on account of a riot, by Maximilian of Bavaria, acting on the order of the Aulic Council, the Protestants at the Diet of Ratisbon deny the right of the majority to bind the minority, and a Protestant Union, from which, however, Lutherans stand aloof, is formed. [1608

483. **Austria.** The Archdukes, exasperated by the conduct of Rudolf, compel him to name his brother Matthias Governor of Austria, Hungary and Moravia, and to promise him the succession in Bohemia.

698. **Eng. Ch.** Though James informs the Pope that he will acknowledge him as the first Bishop and President of the Church, [1606 if he will renounce the claim to depose sovereigns, Garnet, arrested for complicity in Gunpowder Plot, equivocates. An oath of allegiance is imposed on Catholics, and is condemned by the Pope, attacked by Bellarmine, Barclay, Suarez, Becanus and Scioppius, and defended by the King himself, Andrewes and others, the controversy lasting for 10 years.

The King requests convocation to draw up a number of canons on civil government. The articles irritate the King by inculcating obedience to the *de facto* ruler, and are neither ratified nor published.

Field's Book of the Church.

699. **Hungarian Ch.** Bocskay obtains perfect equality for Protestants.

700. **Dutch Ch.** Teellinck, 'the reformed Kempis,' after a visit to England and acquaintance with the Puritans, begins his mystical yet orthodox teaching at Leyden.

701. **Polish Lit.** The Macaronic Period, dominated by the Jesuits, begins and continues for a century and a half.

702. **History.** Scaliger's Thesaurus Temporum contains every chronological relic in Greek and Latin, and reconstructs the Chronicon of Eusebius.

703. **Geography.** Torres, a Spaniard, sails between New Guinea and Australia.

704. **Death.** Lipsius.

---

705. **Church Hist.** The Pope dismisses the Congregation De Auxiliis without pronouncing a decision, and imposes silence on [1607 the disputants.

706. **Eng. Lit.** Hall's Mundus Alter et Idem, a philosophical romance, revives the style of More, and is followed by Bacon's New Atlantis and Godwin's Man in the Moon.

707. **Literature.** Scioppius, the gladiator of the Jesuits, attacks Scaliger in his Scaliger Hypobolimaeus, in which he ridicules his claim to descent from the Scala family of Verona.

708. **Art.** The Friedrichsbau is added to the Schloss at Heidelberg, with very rich ornamentation.

709. **Education.** The Lutherans leave Marburg and institute a rival University at Giessen, also in Hesse.

710. **Death.** Baronius.

---

711. **Eng. Ch.** The Separatist congregation meeting in Brewster's house at Scrooby, Northamptonshire, emigrates to Holland. [1608

712. **French Ch.** Francis de Sales' Introduction to a Devout Life, followed by his Spiritual Letters.

713. **Eng. Lit.** Beaumont and Fletcher's first play, Philaster.

714. **French Lit.** Regnier's Satires.

715. **American Lit.** Captain John Smith's True Relation of Virginia.

716. **Science.** Hans Lippersheim invents the telescope, and Joannides or Galileo invents the microscope.

484. **America.** Champlain founds Quebec, and begins the struggle with the Iroquois.

---

485. **Germany.** A Catholic League is formed by Maximilian, of which Philip III. becomes Protector. [1609

The Duke of Cleves and Jülich dies, and the succession is claimed by the Elector of Brandenburg, the son of the Duke of Neuburg, both Lutherans, and six others. Fearing, however, the presence of a heretic ruler near the Netherlands, the Emperor claims the provinces, in consequence of which the rivals join hands and annex the country.

486. **Spain.** The Moors and the Moriscoes, numbering about 500,000, are expelled by Lerma, to the irreparable damage of agriculture and industry.

487. **Bohemia.** Zerotin and the Protestants of Bohemia compel the Emperor to issue his Majestätsbrief granting toleration to the Protestants.

488. **Holland.** Owing to the mediation of President Jeannin and others, a truce of 12 years is made with Spain and guaranteed by France and the Emperor. Spain, however, refuses to recognise the independence of the Netherlands, and the States refuse to pledge themselves to tolerate Catholics.

The Bank of Amsterdam is instituted and largely contributes to the prosperity of the country.

489. **Russia.** The Poles invade Russia, proclaim the son of their King Tsar, and take Moscow.

490. **America.** Paraguay, occupied by Spain since 1586, is handed over to the Jesuits, who establish a theocracy based on communism.

491. **West Indies.** The Bermudas are taken by the Virginia Co., and a colony is planted in 1612.

---

492. **England.** To gain money, James agrees to abandon certain feudal dues and part of the Impositions, and to declare that all further levy of such duties without Parliamentary consent is illegal, in return for a grant of £200,000 a year. [1610

The absolutist teaching of Dr Cowell, Professor of Civil Law at Cambridge, in his Interpreter, is brought before Parliament by Coke, and receives a censure in which the King joins.

493. **Germany.** The Archduke Leopold seizes Jülich, but is expelled by a force of English, Dutch and Germans.

494. **France.** Henry allies with the Protestant Union, and prepares to intervene in Germany. At this time, he is said by Sully to have elaborated a plan of international federation or Christian Republic, and a rearrangement of the map of Europe to secure peace and to resist Hapsburg encroachments. On the eve of setting out, he is murdered

717. **Art.** After seven years' study in Italy, Rubens settles in Antwerp and becomes Court-Painter to the Archduke Albert.

---

718. **Eng. Ch.** Jacob, an Independent, writes An Humble Supplication for Toleration. [1609

719. **French Ch.** Angélique Arnauld, who has been made Abbess of Port-Royal at 10, is awakened (at 17) by an itinerant preacher and begins the reform of the monastery (Journée du Guichet), in which she is aided by Francis de Sales and Madame Chantal.

720. **Eng. Lit.** Shakespere's Sonnets are published without his sanction.

721. **Italian Lit.** The Ambrosian Library at Milan is founded by Cardinal Frederick Borromeo.

722. **Science.** Jansen, a Dutch spectacle-maker, and Galileo construct telescopes. The latter applies it to astronomy, and discovers irregularities in the surface of the moon, four satellites of Jupiter, the phases of Venus (both of which confirm his belief in the Copernican system), and the sun-spots, from the observation of which he learns that the sun revolves on its own axis in 28 days.

Kepler discovers that Mars does not revolve as Tycho's observations led him to expect, and proves in his Astronomia Nova that it moves not in a circle but in an ellipse. His Second Law explains that the planets move quickest when near the sun, so that a line from the sun to a planet moves over equal areas in equal times.

723. **Law.** Grotius' Mare Liberum declares that, by the law of nature, the sea cannot be monopolised by any single country.

724. **Deaths.** Arminius, Caravaggio, Scaliger.

---

725. **Eng. Ch.** Abbot, the opponent of Laud at Oxford, becomes Archbishop of Canterbury. [1610

726. **Scotch Ch.** The titular Bishops are consecrated in England and receive full authority from the General Assembly, the Scotch Parliament ratifying all that has been done. Courts of High Commission are instituted at Glasgow and St Andrews.

727. **French Ch.** Francis de Sales and Madame Chantal found the female Order of the Visitation, modelled on the Ursulines, which rapidly spreads beyond Savoy, and is approved by the Pope, 1618.

728. **German Ch.** Gerhard's Loci Theologici, a Lutheran text-book.

729. **Dutch Ch.** On the death of Arminius, Episcopius, Utenbogaert and Vorstius compose a Remonstrance, of five Articles, declaring that predestination is conditional. The Gomarists reply in a Counter-Remonstrance.

730. **Church Hist.** Bellarmine maintains the infallibility and universal monarchy of the Pope, relying, in part, on the Isidorian Decretals.

731. **Eng. Lit.** Donne's Anatomy of the World, followed by his Satires, founds the so-called Metaphysical School.

732. **French Lit.** D'Urfé's Astrée introduces the pastoral novel.

Mme de Rambouillet begins to gather a literary circle round her, which dominates French taste for a generation.

by Ravaillac (May). Mary de Medici and her favourite Concini throw themselves into the arms of Spain and the Jesuits, and Sully retires from office.

495. **Italy.** Henry of France concludes the Treaty of Brusol with Savoy for the liberation of Lombardy; but the execution of the scheme is prevented by the murder of the King.

[1611

496. **England.** The marriage of the Princess Elizabeth with the young Elector Palatine is discussed.

Owing to the Commons' attack on the High Commission and Royal Proclamations, James dissolves Parliament before the Great Contract is finally arranged. The King raises money by instituting the order of Baronets.

Arabella Stuart is imprisoned for marrying William Seymour, a descendant of Mary, sister of Henry VIII.

497. **Germany.** The Duchy of Prussia passes to the Elector of Brandenburg, though remaining subject to the suzerainty of Poland.

John George becomes Elector of Saxony and leader of the Lutheran party.

498. **Bohemia.** Rudolf, who has tried to evade his promises of 1609, is deposed by the Bohemians, and the Crown is transferred to Matthias.

499. **Sweden.** Gustavus Adolphus becomes King and Oxenstiern his Chancellor.

500. **Asia.** The Dutch receive permission to trade with Japan.

[1612

501. **England.** Cecil dies, and the Treasury is put in Commission. James resolves to become his own Secretary; but Carr, afterwards Earl of Somerset, becomes the King's favourite.

Prince Henry dies, at 19, under suspicion of poison.

502. **Germany.** The Protestant Union allies with the Elector Palatine.

503. **Austria.** Matthias becomes Emperor.

504. **Italy.** On the death of the Duke of Mantua and Montferrat, Charles Emanuel of Savoy claims Montferrat for a granddaughter, but is expelled by France and Spain. Spain orders him to disband his

733. **Science.** Harriott, Fabricius and Scheiner discover sunspots.

734. **Politics.** The Sorbonne renews the decree of the Council of Constance against tyrannicide, and condemns Mariana. Aquaviva, the Jesuit General, disclaims the tenet on behalf of the Order.

735. **Geography.** Hudson, a marine in the Dutch service, discovers Hudson's Bay, but is turned adrift in an open boat by mutineers.

736. **History.** Sarpi's History of Ecclesiastical Benefices.

737. **Death.** Ricci.

---

738. **Eng. Ch.** The revision of the Bible, commenced 1607 by [1611
47 divines, including Andrewes, Overall, Miles Smith, Reynolds, Saravia, Chaderton, on the basis of the Bishops' Bible, becomes the Authorised Version.

The General or Arminian Baptists draw up their first Confession.

739. **French Ch.** A third attack on the Jesuits by the University of Paris is made by Richer, the Syndic. The Order is compelled to disown regicide and anti-Gallican tenets, and is forbidden to teach. In defending the Gallican position, however, and in the De Ecclesiastica et Politica Potestate, which he composes by request, Richer lays himself open to the attacks of Duperron, is deserted by Parliament in its fear of a breach with Rome, and deposed from his post of Syndic.

A branch of the congregation of the Oratory is founded by Bérulle in order to raise the secular clergy by study and personal influence. On Bérulle's death, Charles de Condren becomes General.

740. **American Ch.** The Jesuits found a mission in Canada.

741. **Spanish Lit.** Gongora developes 'Culteranismo,' introduced into Spain by Carrillo. Despite the attacks of Lope, euphuism influences Spanish literature for a century.

742. **Dutch Lit.** Brederoo's Roderick and Alphonsus initiates modern Dutch Comedy.

743. **Death.** Perez.

---

744. **Eng. Ch.** Legatt and Wightman, Unitarians, are burned. [1612

Smith and Helwisse, seceders from the Congregationalists, return from Amsterdam, where they have been influenced by the Mennonites, and found a Baptist Church in London.

Sir Henry Savile's edition of Chrysostom.

745. **German Ch.** Böhme's Aurora, a system of theosophic pantheism, owes much to Paracelsus, Schwenkfeld, and Weigel.

746. **Dutch Ch.** At the instigation of Abbot, King James obtains the dismissal of Vorstius, Professor of Theology at Leyden.

747. **Church Hist.** The Monita Secreta Societatis Jesu, professing to be derived from private instructions from Aquaviva to probationers, are published.

748. **Dutch Lit.** Vondel's first Biblical play, Het Pascha.

749. **Italian Lit.** The Accademia della Crusca issues its Dictionary.

troops ; but he appeals to the Italian States to expel the stranger, and, though impotent, is hailed as the liberator of Italy.

505. **Asia.** The English settle at Surat, near Bombay, and Sir Thomas Roe, Ambassador to Jehangir, obtains privileges for them.

---

506. **England.** Princess Elizabeth marries Frederick, Elector Palatine. [1613

Bacon becomes Attorney-General, and wins the confidence of the King, being made Chancellor 1617.

Gondomar, the Spanish Ambassador, arrives and gains immense influence over the King.

507. **Germany.** The Protestant Union allies with the Dutch Provinces.

The Diet, the last before the war, refuses to aid the Emperor against the Turks, desiring to discuss religious questions alone.

508. **Hungary.** Bethlen-Gabor, a Protestant, establishes himself in Transylvania, where he reigns till 1629.

509. **Russia.** The Troitza Monastery holds out against the Poles, Moscow is retaken, and the Poles expelled.

Michael, son of Philaret, Patriarch of Moscow, becomes Tsar and founder of the house of Romanoff.

---

510. **England.** The Second, or Addled Parliament, summoned on the advice of the so-called Undertakers, meets, but is dissolved for refusing supplies till it has discussed the King's impositions. [1614

Peacham, a country Rector, is arrested and tortured for an attack on the King, found among his papers.

Gondomar proposes to James a Spanish marriage.

511. **France.** The first of a new series of Civil Wars breaks out under Condé, who aspires to the Regency, and obtains a promise to summon the States-General. At their meeting, in which Richelieu speaks on behalf of the clergy, the Tiers État attacks the Taille and the Paulette, urges the abolition of pensions, and demands a declaration that no power can depose the King. The Estates are dissolved before the answers to the Cahiers are given, and do not meet again till 1789.

512. **Germany.** The danger of war incurred by Neuburg's conversion to Catholicism and his appeal to the Catholic League is removed by the Convention of Xanten, which confirms the partition of the duchies with Brandenburg.

513. **America.** The United New Netherland Company is established in Holland, and receives territory at the mouth of the Hudson.

---

750. **Art.** Rubens' Descent from the Cross (Antwerp).
751. **Education.** By the aid of the Prince of Anhalt-Köthen, Ratke sets up a school at Köthen, where he carries out his principles of following nature, mastering one thing at a time, studying the mother tongue, eliminating the practice of learning by heart.

---

752. **Eng. Ch.** At the dictation of King James, Lady Essex is declared by a Commission of Bishops, including Andrewes, to be divorced from her husband. Immediately after, she marries Carr. Abbot, who refuses to share in the judgment, forfeits the King's favour. The moral prestige of the Church is greatly diminished by this episode. [1613
753. **Eng. Lit.** Drayton's Polyolbion, a poetical description of England.

Browne's Britannia's Pastorals, with Giles and Phineas Fletcher and Wither, carry on the Spenserian tradition.
754. **Philology.** Erpenius' Arabic Grammar.
755. **Economics.** Serra's Causes of Wealth asserts the superiority of manufactures over agriculture as a source of national wealth and the importance of a large supply of gold and silver.
756. **Social.** The New River, engineered by Sir Hugh Myddelton, enters London.
757. **Death.** Regnier.

---

758. **Eng. Ch.** Busher, a Baptist, writes a Plea for Liberty of Conscience. [1614
759. **German Ch.** A book entitled Generalreformation der ganzen Welt describes the Rosicrucians, for whom a Confession is drawn up 1615, and of whom an Order is founded. The movement springs from the desire of Andreae, a Lutheran pastor, for a religious revival, but quickly breaks up into many branches and becomes connected with alchemy and Cabbalism.

Sigismund, Elector of Brandenburg, issues a Calvinistic Confession, but makes no attempt to enforce it.
760. **Asiatic Ch.** Jeyasu orders the exile of missionaries and the recantation of native converts. A terrible persecution begins, and after twenty years not a Christian is known to exist in Japan, though a few continue secret adherents.
761. **Eng. Lit.** Overbury's Characters.
762. **Science.** Napier invents Logarithms and explains their construction, 1619. The tables are constructed by his friend Briggs, 1617.
763. **Philosophy.** With the death of Cremonini, the Aristotelians in Italy come to an end.
764. **History.** Raleigh's History of the World.

At the wish of James I., Casaubon criticises Baronius, admitting his sincerity, but exposing his ignorance of Greek and Hebrew and his employment of a large quantity of apocryphal material.
765. **Geography.** John Smith explores the coast of Northern Virginia, and publishes a description with a map.

Pietro della Valle starts on a journey in Syria, Persia and India.

---

514. **England.** Somerset and his wife (the Countess of Essex) are accused and found guilty of poisoning Sir Thomas Overbury. The King spares their lives, but banishes them from Court, where Somerset's place is taken by George Villiers. [1615

515. **France.** The Second Civil War breaks out, Condé allying with Bouillon and the Huguenots. The government, unable to resist, makes peace.

Louis marries Anne, daughter of Philip III., who resigns her claims to the Spanish throne, Philip's son at the same time marrying Louis' sister. The Queen-Mother's policy of union with Spain is thus completed.

516. **America.** Champlain undertakes an expedition to Lake Huron.

517. **Asia.** The English defeat a superior Portuguese fleet off the Bombay coast at Swally.

---

518. **England.** An action is brought against Bishop Neile, to whom the King has granted a living in commendam; but James orders the judges not to give sentence till they have consulted with him. Against this Chief Justice Coke protests and is in consequence dismissed. He is succeeded by Sir Henry Montague, a thorough-going supporter of the King. Henceforth the prerogative is safe from attack in the courts of law. [1616

519. **France.** Condé is arrested, and Richelieu becomes Secretary of State.

520. **America.** The cultivation of tobacco is introduced into Virginia.

521. **Asia.** The Manchoo Tartars invade China, conquer the province of Lao-Tung, 1619, and proclaim their independence, 1620.

---

522. **England.** Raleigh, who has been liberated by Buckingham, 1616, sails for Guiana, in search of a gold mine, promising the King not to molest the dominions of Spain. [1617

Negotiations for a Spanish match are formally opened, but are dropped, 1618, on the demand for privileges for English Catholics.

523. **France.** Concini, whom Louis has long wished to overthrow, is murdered, and Luynes, the King's favourite, takes his place, the Queen-Mother joining the opposition.

Béarn is united to the crown, and the restoration of Catholicism and Church property is decreed.

524. **Bohemia.** The Bohemian Estates are bribed by promises and threats to recognise Ferdinand of Styria, cousin of Matthias, the prospective heir to the Empire, as heir to the throne.

766. **Irish Ch.** The first Convocation of the Protestant clergy adopts a strictly Calvinistic Confession, drawn up by Ussher. [1615
767. **German Ch.** Pareus, Professor of Theology at Heidelberg, where liberalism has been encouraged by Frederick IV., 1592–1610, issues an Irenicon.
768. **Spanish Lit.** Cervantes' Don Quixote, Part II.
769. **Science.** Kepler's Nova Stereometria Doliorum investigates the area of surfaces, the capacity of casks, and conic sections, by infinitesimals.
770. **Economics.** Montchrétien, the dramatist, dedicates his Traité de l'Économie Politique to the King and the Queen-Mother, suggested by visits to England and the Netherlands. The work recommends the mercantilist principles on which Richelieu and Colbert later act.
771. **Philosophy.** Vanini's De Admirandis Naturae Arcanis, a system of naturalistic pantheism, is condemned by the Inquisition.
772. **Death.** Pasquier.

---

773. **Eng. Ch.** De Dominis, late Archbishop of Spalatro, professes himself an Anglican and settles in England, where he is presented with several benefices. [1616

Henry Jacob returns from Leyden and collects the scattered Brownists or Independents surviving from 1593 into a congregation at Southwark.
774. **French Ch.** Francis de Sales' work On the Love of God.
775. **Science.** Galileo is threatened with punishment unless he undertakes not to teach the Copernican system in future.

The views of Copernicus are condemned, having hitherto escaped owing to the preface of Osiander declaring them hypothetical.
776. **Art.** Bernini's Apollo and Daphne (Rome), his first work.
777. **Geography.** After several voyages, Baffin discovers and describes Baffin's Bay.
778. **Deaths.** Cervantes, Shakespere.

---

779. **Church Hist.** Cornelius a Lapide's Commentaries begin to appear. [1617

De Dominis' De Republica Ecclesiastica maintains that the Bishops, not the Pope, are head of the Church.
780. **Scotch Lit.** Drummond's Forth Feasting, a complimentary address to James on his return to Scotland.
781. **German Lit.** Die Fruchtbringende Gesellschaft of Weimar, modelled on the Italian societies, renders the formation of literary circles in Germany fashionable.
782. **Philosophy.** A collected edition of Fludd's works is published, dealing with medicine, occultism, and Rosicrucianism.
783. **Politics.** Suarez' De Legibus ac Deo Legislatore declares all power from God, rejects the theory of the Divine right of Kings, and authorises

525. **Sweden.** By the treaty of Stolbovo, Gustavus obtains Ingermannland and Karelia, and recovers the former rights of Sweden in Livonia. Novgorod and other Swedish conquests in Russia are given up.
526. **Africa.** The Dutch buy the island of Goree from its native rulers.

---

527. **England.** Raleigh attacks the Spaniards, fails to find gold, and returns to England empty-handed. He is executed on the original charge of treason, but in reality to humour Spain. [1618
528. **Germany.** Albert II., Duke of Prussia, dies childless, and his dominions are joined to the electorate of Brandenburg, though remaining under Polish suzerainty.
529. **Bohemia.** Indignant at the anti-national and anti-Protestant policy of the government, the Bohemian nobles, led by Count Thurn, revolt, and hurl the two regents from a window of the palace at Prague, by this act commencing the Thirty Years' War. Ferdinand despatches troops to subdue the rebels, to whose assistance Mansfeld is sent by the Protestant Union.
530. **Spain.** Lerma, who has alienated the Austrian Hapsburgs by his French proclivities, is dismissed, and Spain prepares to co-operate in the war.
531. **Italy.** Bedmar, the Spanish ambassador at Venice, concerts with the Governors of Milan and Naples a land and sea attack on the Republic, which, however, is quickly discovered.
532. **Asia.** The Dutch found Batavia in Java.
533. **Africa.** A British company is chartered to trade with West Africa, and establishes forts on the Gambia and the Gold Coast.

---

534. **England.** Cranfield reduces the finances to order. [1619
535. **Bohemia.** On the death of Matthias, the Bohemians depose Ferdinand, who becomes Emperor two days later, and elect Frederick the Elector Palatine. Maximilian of Bavaria and the League declare for Ferdinand. At this moment Bethlen-Gabor declares war and besieges Vienna, but is forced to retreat. James I. refuses to support the aggression of his son-in-law, but sends Doncaster to offer the mediation of England, which is rejected.
536. **Holland.** Maurice seizes the opportunity presented by the defeat of the Arminians to execute Barneveldt on a charge of treason, and to imprison Grotius and others in the castle of Louvestein.
537. **America.** The first Colonial Parliament for South Virginia meets at Jamestown.

Negro slaves are brought to Virginia.

---

their deposition either by the Church or by the people where the contract, from which they derive their power, is broken.

784. **Deaths.** Suarez, De Thou.

---

785. **Eng. Ch.** Selden is forced by the High Commission to recant his utterances on the secular origin of tithes. [1618

The King enjoins certain amusements for Sunday afternoon in a Book of Sports, which many clergy refuse to countenance.

786. **Scotch Ch.** At the General Assembly at Perth, kneeling at Communion, observance of Holy Days, private Communion and Baptism in case of sickness, and episcopal confirmation are enjoined. A new liturgy is composed by the Bishops and authorised by the King, but is not introduced.

787. **French Ch.** The Benedictines of St Maur settle in Paris, receive St Germain des Près, and under D'Achéry, their first librarian, commence their historical studies.

Vincent de Paul founds the order of Sisters of Mercy for the care of the sick.

Cameron, a Scotchman, becomes Professor of Theology at Saumur, where he teaches a modified Calvinism (described by opponents as semi-Pelagianism), and forms a school.

788. **Spanish Ch.** St John of the Cross' Spiritual Works.

789. **Dutch Ch.** A Synod is held at Dort, at which Deodatus, Scultetus, Breitinger, Hall, Davenant, Hales are present, to close the Arminian controversy. Despite the defence of Episcopius, the Arminians are banished, and the Belgic Confession of 1561 (revised) and the Heidelberg Catechism are confirmed. The five articles of the Remonstrance are rejected, and five Calvinistic canons adopted. Calvinistic Scholasticism is further elaborated by Gomar, Voetius, and Hoornbeck.

790. **Church Hist.** A Conference for the reunion of Catholics and Protestants is held at Prague.

791. **Death.** Duperron.

---

792. **French Ch.** Vanini is burnt at Toulouse as an 'atheist.' [1619

793. **Church Hist.** Scioppius' Classicum Belli Sacri summons the Catholic Princes of the Empire to the annihilation of heretics.

794. **Eng. Lit.** Ben Jonson visits Drummond at Hawthornden.

795. **Science.** In his lectures at St Bartholomew's Hospital, Harvey reveals his discovery of the circulation of the blood, in which he has been aided by the works of his master, Fabricius, Servetus, Columbus, Caesalpinus, and Sarpi.

Kepler's Harmonia Mundi states his Third Law, that the squares of the periodic times (revolutions round the sun) of the planets are proportional to the cubes of their distances from the sun.

Decimal notation for fractions is used by Briggs and Napier.

796. **History.** Sarpi's History of the Council of Trent, based largely on the information supplied by eye-witnesses, is pseudonymously published in England, and fiercely attacked by ultramontane writers.

---

538. **England.** Owing to rumours of a Spanish attack on the Palatinate, James, who is willing to aid his son-in-law in self-defence, allows volunteers under Vere to garrison the fortresses. [1620

539. **France.** The discontented nobles join Mary in an attack on Luynes; but Richelieu negotiates peace, and the King and his mother are reconciled. Louis enters Béarn and roughly enforces the proclamation of 1617.

540. **Bohemia.** Frederick is crushed by Tilly and the army of the League at the battle on the White Hill, outside Prague, and expelled from Bohemia, and the Protestant Union is dissolved. The leaders of the Bohemian revolt are executed, the Protestant clergy are expelled, the Jesuits return and Prague University is merged in a Jesuit College, Protestant children are forbidden to inherit land, the towns are deprived of their charters, the national language is neglected, trade and population decline. Finally, in 1627, the Protestants are expelled.

541. **Germany.** A Spanish army invades the Lower Palatinate and a Bavarian army the Upper.

542. **Italy.** Protestants are massacred in the Valtelline (a subject land of the Protestant Grisons League), and an independent republic is proclaimed, and supported by Spanish and Austrian troops.

543. **America.** A hundred of Robinson's congregation at Leyden cross the Atlantic in the Mayflower, draw up a Compact of Government, and land at Plymouth.

---

544. **England.** Parliament meets and attacks monopolies, which are withdrawn by the King. Sir Giles Mompesson, one of the holders, leaves the country. [1621

The Commons impeach and disgrace the Chancellor for accepting sums of money before giving judgment. Bacon admits the charge, but denies that his decision was thereby influenced. He is degraded and fined, and Williams, Dean of Westminster, succeeds him.

The King informs Parliament that he is sending Digby to Vienna to ask Ferdinand to restore the Palatinate, which, however, is now secretly conferred on Maximilian. Parliament declares that if diplomacy fails, it will defend Frederick, and petitions the King to marry his son to a Protestant. The King rebukes the Commons for their interference.

545. **France.** Scared by events in Béarn and Germany, the Huguenots rebel under Rohan and Soubise. To reassure the moderates, the King confirms the Edict of Nantes, and sends Luynes and Lesdiguières, the latter a Huguenot, to quell the revolt.

546. **Holland.** The 12 years' truce comes to an end.

547. **Netherlands.** The Archduke dies, and the direct government of the Netherlands is resumed by Spain.

548. **America.** Alexander, the Scotch poet, obtains a patent for Acadia, described as Nova Scotia; but an attempt at settlement fails.

---

797. **French Ch.** The Decrees of Dort are accepted by the French Protestants at the Synod of Alais. [1620

798. **Science.** Drebbel constructs a thermometer, employing spirits of wine. Galileo has previously filled the bulb with air.

Bacon suggests that heat may be a movement.

799. **Art.** Rubens is invited to Paris by the Queen-Mother to paint pictures for her palace of the Luxembourg, now in the Louvre.

800. **Philosophy.** Bacon's Novum Organum points out the species and causes of error, and declares experience the starting-point and induction the true method of knowledge. Of a third part, a series of Natural Histories, only fragments are written. A fourth part is designed to supply a knowledge of the forms underlying phenomena.

Campanella's De Sensu Rerum, a system of occultist pantheism, deeply influenced by the study of Telesio.

801. **Philology.** Salmasius issues Casaubon's Commentary on the Augustan History with additional notes.

802. **Death.** Stevinus.

---

803. **Eng. Lit.** Robert Burton, of Christ Church, Oxford, (writing as Democritus Junior) publishes his Anatomy of Melancholy, which he largely alters and increases in subsequent editions. [1621

John Barclay's Latin romance, Argenis, of which an English version quickly appears.

804. **Dutch Lit.** Constantine Huyghens' Batava Tempe, a poem in praise of the Hague, the most elegant Dutch poem up to this time written.

805. **Science.** Snell (a Dutchman) discovers the law of refraction of light, and calculates the index of refraction for water and other substances.

806. **Art.** Inigo Jones designs a magnificent palace at Whitehall in the style of Palladio, of which only the Banqueting Hall is carried out.

807. **Economics.** Mun's Discourse of Trade from England to the East Indies, and England's Treasure by Foreign Trade, first clearly state the theory of the balance of trade, and recommend the attraction of money from abroad. The export of money is permitted where the re-export of the foreign wares that it procures will bring back more than the original price of purchase. The 'Mercantilist' theory remains virtually uncontested till the close of the century.

808. **Death.** Bellarmine.

---

549. **England.** Parliament is dissolved, its protest being torn from the Journals by the King, and Coke, Pym, and Selden are imprisoned. [1622

Porter is sent to Madrid to arrange a visit from Prince Charles, and to demand Spanish aid for Frederick.

Knight's sermons before Oxford University on the right of resistance to rulers, based on Paraeus' Commentary on Romans, is burnt, and the doctrine is condemned by the University.

550. **Germany.** Bethlen-Gabor makes peace with the Emperor, and Tilly defeats the Margrave of Baden and Christian of Brunswick. Despite the aid sent by James I., the Palatinate is conquered.

551. **Spain.** Olivarez becomes chief minister.

552. **America.** Gorges and Mason obtain a grant of Maine.

553. **Asia.** English rivalry with Portugal in the East ends with the taking of Ormuz.

---

554. **England.** Charles and Buckingham visit Madrid to woo the Infanta, but are informed that she will only be sent to England when religious liberty has been given to the Catholics. The scheme is in the highest degree unpopular with the Spaniards, and after wearisome negotiations they leave Spain, in a rage. The failure of the match is hailed by England with enthusiasm. [1623

555. **France.** The Huguenots are forced to accept the Treaty of Montpellier, which forbids political gatherings and leaves them La Rochelle and Montauban.

556. **Germany.** Frederick is put to the ban of the Empire, and his Electoral dignity and the Upper Palatinate are given to Maximilian of Bavaria, the Catholics thereby obtaining a majority in the Electoral Diet.

John George of Brandenburg is banned by the Empire, and Jägerndorf is confiscated by the Emperor.

557. **Italy.** Venice and Savoy ally to wrest the Valtelline from the Hapsburgs; but the troops of the Pope occupy the valley.

Urban VIII. becomes Pope and, fearing the Hapsburg supremacy, leans to France.

558. **Asia.** The English traders at Amboyna are massacred by the Dutch on the charge of conspiring to surprise the garrison.

559. **West Indies.** English and French settlements are made in St Kitts, and the other Leeward Islands are colonised from thence.

---

809. **Eng. Ch.** Laud holds a Conference with Fisher, a Jesuit [1622
who has converted Buckingham's mother.

De Dominis, hearing that the Pope is willing to welcome him, renounces his Anglicanism and returns to Rome.

810. **Church Hist.** The Congregation De Propaganda Fide, planned by Gregory XIII., is instituted by Gregory XV. The decrees of the Propaganda are declared to have the force of apostolical constitutions. A College for the education of missionaries is instituted, 1627.

811. **Eng. Lit.** Butter, a London stationer, publishes the Weekly News.

812. **French Lit.** Sorel's Histoire Comique de Francion founds the novel of bourgeois manners.

813. **Italian Lit.** Tassoni's Secchia Rapita (the Rape of the Bucket) perfects the Comic Epic.

Campanella's Sonnets are printed in Germany by his disciple, Tobias Adami.

814. **Science.** Asellius discovers the tubes that carry nourishment to the blood, and names them lacteals.

815. **History.** Bacon's Life of Henry VII.

816. **Deaths.** Melville, Francis de Sales.

---

817. **Eng. Ch.** The King allows a Catholic Bishop in Partibus [1623
in England, a victory for the Seculars over the Jesuits, who fear a diminution of their authority.

818. **French Ch.** Père Garasse's Doctrine Curieuse des Beaux Esprits attacks the creed and conduct of the Libertins.

819. **German Ch.** Glassius' Philologia Sacra, a Lutheran classic, gives an impetus to exegetical work, which is continued by Walther, Calov and Pfeiffer.

820. **Church Hist.** Uriel Acosta, a Portuguese Jew resident in Amsterdam, attacks Judaism, is banned by the Synagogue, and commits suicide, 1647.

821. **Asiatic Ch.** The Pope authorises the Malabar Rites, i.e., the accommodations practised by Nobili and other Jesuits.

822. **Eng. Lit.** The First Folio of Shakespere, nominally collected by his fellow-actors, Heming and Condell, really by Jaggard and a syndicate of publishers, contains all the published plays except Pericles, and classifies them as Histories, Comedies, Tragedies.

Webster's Duchess of Malfi.

823. **Italian Lit.** Marini's Adone, a descriptive poem in the style of Gongora, becomes a model for a century.

824. **French Lit.** Chapelain writes an elaborate Introduction to a French translation of Marini's Adone.

825. **Art.** Velasquez is invited by Olivarez to settle in Madrid, where he is shortly appointed Court-Painter.

826. **Politics.** Campanella's Civitas Solis, a communistic Utopia in the style of Plato and More.

827. **Philology.** The elder Buxtorf's Hebrew Grammar commences the seventy years' labour at Semitic languages of father and son.

828. **Death.** Sarpi.

---

560. **England.** The fourth and last Parliament of James is summoned and votes supplies for the recovery of the Palatinate, which Charles and Buckingham persuade the King to undertake. Believing that the Treasurer, Cranfield, is opposed to a war, the Commons, encouraged by Charles and Buckingham, impeach him for malversation. Believing, too, that the King wishes a war in Germany, and themselves desiring a war at sea, the Commons appropriate part of their grant to refit the navy, in addition to supplying Mansfeld with 12,000 men. Parliament is prorogued and a marriage treaty made with France, by which, despite the promise made to the Commons, liberty is granted to the English Catholics. [1624

Monopolies are finally declared illegal.

561. **France.** Richelieu, who has received a Cardinal's hat, 1623, becomes supreme. The Council consists henceforward rather of lawyers than of nobles and clergy.

562. **Italy.** Richelieu allies with Venice and Savoy, and Swiss and French troops expel Spain from the Valtelline.

563. **Sweden.** Gustavus Adolphus makes proposals to England in regard to intervention in the war.

564. **America.** A Dutch West India Company is formed to drive the Portuguese out of South America. For some years plundering expeditions are made, with little attempt at trade or colonisation.

---

565. **England.** Mansfeld's troops reach Holland without money or provisions, and three-fourths of them soon die. Disgusted with the mismanagement of the war, the new Parliament refuses to grant a large sum for the war except to counsellors in whom it has confidence, and is in consequence dissolved. A fleet sent by the King to Cadiz to intercept the Spanish treasure-ships returns without striking a blow. [1625

566. **France.** A new revolt breaks out under Soubise and Rohan, owing to the erection of a fort near La Rochelle, but is ended by the defeat of the Huguenot fleet.

567. **Germany.** Tilly and Wallenstein enter Saxony, and the Danish period of the war begins, Christian IV. being Duke of Holstein and head of the Lower Saxon Circle.

568. **Netherlands.** Spinola retakes Breda (captured by Maurice 1598), after 11 months' siege.

569. **America.** Corten a merchant of Flemish descent, plants a colony in Barbadoes.

---

829. **Eng. Ch.** Montagu, an Anglican rector, replies to a Catholic attack on Calvinism in his New Gag for an old Goose, recognising the Roman Church as part of the true Church, and authorising confession, belief in the Real Presence, and similar doctrines. [1624

830. **French Ch.** Vincent de Paul founds the Lazarists or Priests of the Mission for evangelical and charitable work in the rural districts.

831. **German Lit.** Opitz' Buch von der deutschen Poeterey insists on beauty of form, purifies German style, and founds the first Silesian School.

832. **Science.** Van Helmont introduces the term Gas.

833. **Philosophy.** Lord Herbert's De Veritate introduces Deism into England, and maintains that we have five 'common notions,' namely that God exists, that He should be worshipped, that virtue is a means of worship, that repentance is necessary, and that rewards and punishments will follow this life.

834. **Philology.** Gerard Vossius' De Historicis Graecis.

835. **Deaths.** Böhme, Mariana.

---

836. **Eng. Ch.** In consequence of Abbot's censure on Montagu's distinction between Puritan and Anglican principles, Montagu writes Appello Caesarem, for which Parliament impeaches him. Owing in part to Laud, now rising in influence, the King replies by making Montagu his chaplain, and shortly after Bishop of Chichester. [1625

Nicholas Ferrar withdraws from the world and settles with his family at Little Gidding in Huntingdonshire, where he spends his time and devotion in parish work. The community is twice visited by the King, but is broken up by the civil wars.

Laud draws up a list of Orthodox and Puritan clergy.

837. **Church Hist.** At the request of Lutheran friends, Metrophanes, a disciple of Cyril Lucar, draws up a Confession strongly attacking Romanism, but silent in regard to Protestantism.

838. **Eng. Lit.** Howell's Letters begin.

839. **French Lit.** Balzac's Letters and Voiture's Letters and Vers de Société improve French prose by their dignity and correctness.

840. **Dutch Lit.** Vondel defends the memory of Barneveldt in his tragedy of Palamedes, which is bitterly attacked by Cats and other Calvinists.

Cats' Marriage, and Emblems of Fancy and Love, remain universal favourites for two centuries.

841. **Science.** De Dominis attempts to explain the rainbow.

842. **Law.** Grotius' De Jure Belli et Pacis, based on Oldendorp, Hemming, Winkler, Vittoria, Ayala, Gentilis, and in part suggested by the Thirty Years' War and by the Dutch East India Company, gives a great impetus to the discussion of international law by appealing to natural law as springing from the social nature of man.

843. **Geography.** Purchas his Pilgrims.

844. **Deaths.** Marini, Maurice of Nassau.

---

570. **England.** Charles' second Parliament meets, the King having chosen the more independent members sheriffs for the year. The Commons, however, find a leader in Eliot, who impeaches Buckingham on the charge of lending ships to the French King to suppress the Huguenots. The King dissolves Parliament without a grant of supplies, and orders a forced loan. [1626

571. **France.** The Huguenots are accorded the terms of 1623; but Richelieu resolves to break their political power, and interrupts his war with Spain in Italy by the treaty of Mouzon, without knowledge of his allies. The Valtelline remains subject to the Grisons, though Catholic worship is guaranteed.

The nobility and courtiers revolt against the Cardinal and win the king's brother to a scheme to depose him and murder Richelieu. The plot is discovered, and its authors punished with death or exile.

Brittany petitions against the rule of descendants of its ancient dukes, and prays for the destruction of its fortresses.

572. **Germany.** Tilly routs the Danes at Lutter, and Wallenstein, who raises an army and takes the field for the Emperor, defeats Mansfeld at the bridge of Dessau. Mansfeld and Christian of Brunswick die shortly after.

573. **Italy.** The Duchy of Urbino is bequeathed to the Pope by the last of the Rovere, who dies childless.

574. **America.** The Dutch settlement of New Amsterdam is made on Manhattan Island.

---

575. **England.** Discontent is caused by the practice of billeting and the exaction of forced loans, for refusing which five knights are imprisoned on a royal warrant. The King's prerogative is at the same time magnified by Sibthorp and Mainwaring. [1627

576. **France.** The Huguenots once more revolt and the siege of La Rochelle commences. An expedition under Buckingham fails to relieve the city.

577. **Germany.** Wallenstein expels the Danes from Silesia, and overruns Holstein, Schleswig and Jutland.

578. **Italy.** The Gonzaga line dies out at Mantua, and Nevers, a French Prince, succeeds. The Emperor, however, claims Mantua as feudal suzerain.

579. **America.** The Guiana Company is chartered; but colonisation does not extend.

580. **West Indies.** Lord Carlisle obtains the grant of the Caribbean Islands.

---

581. **England.** Charles summons his third Parliament, desiring money for a second expedition to La Rochelle. Wentworth attacks the government, but retires from the struggle when the King refuses his recommendations, and becomes President of the Council of [1628

845. **Irish Ch.** A Presbyterian Church is established in Ulster. [1626
846. **French Ch.** A work of Sanctarel, reviving the contention of the power of the Pope to depose a King, is disowned by the court Jesuits and burnt.
847. **American Lit.** Sandys' verse translation of Ovid's Metamorphoses, the first purely literary work undertaken in English America.
848. **Science.** Desargues lectures on projective geometry, the new method, however, being shortly displaced by the analytical method of Descartes.

A Jardin des Plantes, for students of medicine and the culture of medicinal herbs, is instituted at Paris.
849. **Law.** Spelman's Glossary of Law terms.
850. **Deaths.** Andrewes, Bacon.

---

851. **Eng. Ch.** Cosin composes Devotions, of a pronounced Anglican type, for the ladies of the Court. [1627
852. **Dutch Ch.** Grotius' De Veritate Religionis Christianae combats the spirit of the French sceptics and attempts to rise above the differences between the Churches.
853. **Church Hist.** The Bull In Caena Domini excommunicates heretics and schismatics and their defenders, the owners of heretical books, and all who appeal from a Papal decree to a future General Council. Clerics cannot be taxed or punished without Papal permission.
854. **Eng. Lit.** Bacon's New Atlantis.
855. **Spanish Lit.** Quevedo's Visions found 'Conceptismo,' or pedantry of the idea, a companion and a contrast to the Culteranismo of Gongora.

Tirso's earliest plays carry on the work of Lope, with an added strength and realism.

Mendoza's Guerra de Granada.
856. **Art.** Vouet, after 14 years' residence in Italy, is summoned to the French Court, and revives French painting.

Schütz' Daphne, the first German opera, introduces Italian reforms into German music.
857. **History.** Petavius' Doctrina Temporum attacks the chronology of Scaliger.

---

858. **Eng. Ch.** The King issues a declaration, composed by Laud, forbidding public discussion of predestination and other disputed doctrines. At the same moment Laud is made Bishop of London, and Mainwaring, lately censured by the Commons for his views of the prerogative, receives promotion. [1628

By the King's order, Laud edits Andrewes' sermons.
859. **French Ch.** Daillé's L'Usage des Pères maintains that the Fathers are of little assistance in the disputes of the day. His work is used by Hales and Chillingworth.

the North. Eliot, Coke, and Selden carry the Petition of Right, forbidding martial law, enforced billeting, forced loans or taxes without Parliamentary grant, and imprisonment without cause shown.

Buckingham is murdered at Portsmouth when about to embark on a second expedition to La Rochelle.

582. **France.** La Rochelle is starved into surrender and dismantled, and the political power of the Huguenots is broken.

583. **Germany.** Wallenstein attacks the Hanse Towns, but fails to take Stralsund. Gustavus turns from his Polish war to the aid of Denmark.

584. **Holland.** The Dutch capture the Spanish silver fleet.

[1629

585. **England.** Eliot introduces resolutions declaring enemies of the kingdom those who introduce innovation in religion and those who recommend or pay tonnage and poundage without Parliamentary grant. The Speaker, who has orders to adjourn the House, is held down while the resolutions are read. Parliament is dissolved, Eliot is sent to the Tower. Personal Government commences, supported by Wentworth, Laud and Weston. France renounces her support of the English Catholics, and England her support of the Huguenots.

586. **France.** The Huguenots rise for the last time under Rohan and receive subsidies from Spain, but are quickly reduced.

587. **Germany.** Tilly and the Catholic League refusing to grant Wallenstein's plea for aid, Christian invades Germany, but is defeated by Wallenstein and forced to conclude peace at Lubeck. He receives back his conquered territories, but withdraws from German politics. The Dukes of Mecklenburg are put to the ban, and Wallenstein is invested with their lands.

The Edict of Restitution restores property secularised since 1552. The refusal to recognise the Calvinists alienates Saxony and Brandenburg.

588. **Italy.** The War of the Mantuan succession breaks out. Spain besieges Casale, which is relieved by France.

589. **America.** The King grants a charter to the Massachusetts Bay Company and Mason receives New Hampshire.

Quebec is captured by England.

[1630

590. **England.** Peace is made with Spain.

591. **France.** Angered by Richelieu's anti-Spanish policy, the Queen-mother heads a plot to overthrow his authority, but fails at the Day of Dupes, and flies to Brussels. The Duke of Orleans takes refuge in Lorraine, and Marillac, one of the Queen-mother's tools, is executed.

592. **Germany.** The Catholic princes meet at Ratisbon and press for the resignation of Wallenstein. The demand being supported by Father Joseph, whom Richelieu sends to sow discord between the princes and

860. **German Ch.** Drechsel's Meditations supply devotional literature for educated Catholics.

861. **Literature.** Cyril Lucar, patriarch of Constantinople, presents the Codex Alexandrinus to Charles I.

862. **Science.** Harvey publishes his De Motu Cordis et Sanguinis, the tenets of which are accepted by Descartes, Hobbes and other thinkers, but cost the author his practice, and lead him into controversy with Riolan, Professor of Anatomy at Paris.

Castelli, a pupil of Galileo, founds hydraulics by his Misura dell' Acque Correnti.

Kepler's Rudolphine Tables are published, based on Tycho Brahe's observations.

863. **Art.** The Arundel marbles reach England.

Shah Jehan builds the Taj Mahal at Agra.

864. **History.** Blondel's False Decretals attack the Pseudo-Isidore.

865. **Law.** Coke's Institutes, a Commentary on Littleton.

866. **Geography.** Dutch expeditions reach Western Australia.

867. **Death.** Malherbe.

---

868. **Eng. Ch.** The King issues Instructions, composed by Laud, forbidding Puritan 'lecturers' and the employment of chaplains, except by noblemen, and attacking non-resident Bishops. [1629

869. **Irish Ch.** Bedell becomes Bishop of Kilmore, and helps to reform the Irish Church.

870. **Church Hist.** Cyril Lucar, Patriarch of Constantinople, writes a Calvinistic Confession in Latin, which he hopes may be adopted by and reform the Greek Church.

871. **Spanish Lit.** The plays of Alarcon, the most polished of Spanish dramatists, are collected.

872. **Philosophy.** Descartes settles in Holland, only thrice re-visiting France. Mersenne, his old schoolfellow, becomes his literary representative in Paris. Descartes also corresponds with Elizabeth, daughter of the Elector Palatine.

873. **Philology.** Salmasius' Commentary on Solinus.

874. **Deaths.** Bérulle, Buxtorf (senior), Bethlen Gabor.

---

875. **Eng. Ch.** Dr Leighton is imprisoned by the Star Chamber for an attack on episcopacy. [1630

George Herbert becomes Rector of Bemerton.

876. **Church Hist.** Dury, chaplain to the English merchants at Elbing, begins to travel over Europe with a view to reunion.

877. **Danish Lit.** Arrebo's Hexameron, modelled on Du Bartas, founds modern Danish literature.

878. **American Lit.** Winthrop begins to keep a Journal.

the Emperor, Ferdinand, who wishes to secure his son's election as King of the Romans, gives way. Tilly assumes the command of Wallenstein's army, and the Emperor once more becomes overshadowed by the League. At the same moment, Gustavus crosses to Germany, and is joined by Bernard of Weimar and other petty princes.

593. **Italy.** Richelieu leads an expedition to Italy, reduces Pinerolo, and occupies Saluzzo.

594. **America.** Fifteen vessels, bearing over 1,000 colonists, including Winthrop, the governor, reach Massachusetts, and found Boston and other towns. In the next decade they are joined by 20,000 immigrants.

595. **West Indies.** The Buccaneers (adventurers of all countries) settle in Tortuga, off Hispaniola, and prey on Spanish commerce throughout the century.

---

596. **Italy.** By the Treaty of Cherasco, the Emperor recognises Nevers as Duke of Mantua, allows Savoy to obtain part of the Duchy of Montferrat, and withdraws the Imperial troops from Italy, leaving the reward of the Mantuan war to France, which again obtains a footing in Italy. [1631

By a secret agreement with the Duke of Savoy, Richelieu obtains the fortress of Pinerolo, which dominates Savoy, and Victor Amadeus marries a sister of the King of France.

597. **Germany.** Gustavus concludes a subsidy treaty with France, and attempts to win over Saxony and Brandenburg He succeeds with the latter, but too late to relieve Magdeburg, which, after a long siege, is stormed and sacked by Tilly. The Emperor orders an attack on Saxony, which is thus forced to ally with Gustavus. The two powers rout Tilly at Leipsig, and Gustavus occupies the Rhine principalities. At the Emperor's urgent entreaty, Wallenstein undertakes to collect an army, but he insists on complete control. At this moment, he begins to secretly negotiate with the Swedes.

598. **Holland.** A Spanish fleet sent against the Dutch privateers is destroyed.

---

599. **England.** The Treaty of St Germain between France and England cedes New France, Acadia and Canada to France. [1632

600. **France.** Montmorency, governor of Languedoc, receives Gaston of Orleans in his province and heads a rebellion against Richelieu, by whom it is quickly suppressed. Gaston is pardoned, but Montmorency, the last of the famous family, is executed.

601. **Germany.** Gustavus advances on Bavaria, defeats and kills Tilly, who attempts to bar the passage of the Lech, and enters Munich. Hoping to create a principality for himself, and perhaps even to become King of Hungary, Wallenstein attempts to detach Saxony from the

879. **Philosophy.** Ames' De Conscientia, inspired by the works of his Cambridge master, Perkins, developes Protestant casuistry in England.
880. **Philology.** Laud founds a Professorship of Arabic at Oxford, and sends Pococke, the first Professor, to the East to gather manuscripts.
881. **Social.** The Earl of Bedford and others undertake to drain the Cambridgeshire marshes, the work being directed by Sir Cornelius Vermuyden.
882. **Deaths.** D'Aubigné, Harvey, Kepler.

---

883. **French Ch.** Amyraut, Professor of Theology at Saumur, is ordered by the Protestant synod to inform the King of the infringements of the Edict of Nantes, and enforces his right to address the King standing, like the Catholic deputies. [1631
884. **German Ch.** An attempt to unite Lutherans and Calvinists is made at Leipsig by Hesse, Brandenburg and Saxony.
885. **Church Hist.** A women's Order, founded by Mary Ward, on the model of the Jesuits, is dissolved by the Pope on account of its lax discipline.
886. **French Lit.** Renaudot founds the Gazette de France, which becomes the organ of the Government, and which he edits for more than 20 years.
887. **Art.** Rembrandt's Lesson in Anatomy. (The Hague.)
888. **Education.** Comenius' Janua Quatuor Linguarum Reserata explains his system of learning Latin, Italian, French and German, but overestimates the acquisitive power of the mind.
889. **Social.** Spee attacks the belief in witchcraft, which is defended by Carpzov and others.
890. **Death.** Richer.

---

891. **Eng. Lit.** Falkland takes up his residence at Great Tew, near Oxford, and gathers round him a circle, including Hales, Chillingworth, Hammond, Morley, Sheldon, Clarendon, Selden, Carew, Suckling, Davenant, Waller. [1632
892. **French Lit.** Gomberville's Polexandre (a work of 6,000 pages) founds the school of Romans de longue Haleine, continued by Calprenède's Cassandra and Mlle Scudéry's Ibrahim and Grand Cyrus. This genre forms a transition from the romances of chivalry to the novel of society, and dominates French literature till Boileau.
893. **Art.** Van Dyck, a favourite pupil of Rubens, settles in England on Charles' invitation as Court painter.

Swedes. Gustavus, however, joins the Elector and defeats Wallenstein at Lutzen, where the Swedish King loses his life.

602. **Holland.** The Dutch take Maestricht, and Spain negotiates for peace.

603. **Sweden.** Christina, the daughter of Gustavus, succeeds to the throne under the regency of Oxenstiern.

604. **America.** Maryland, the northern part of South Virginia, is colonised by Lord Baltimore, a Catholic, who is allowed to tax and legislate only with the consent of the adult males, at first directly, later by representatives.

605. **West Indies.** English Colonies are planted in Antigua and Montserrat.

---

606. **England.** The City of London's property in Ulster is confiscated on a charge of mismanagement, and alleged encroachments on the royal forests are recovered. [1633

607. **Scotland.** Charles entrusts the selection of the Lords of the Articles to the Bishops.

608. **Ireland.** Wentworth lands in Ireland as Lord Deputy, and summons a Parliament, equally balanced between the two Churches, from which he obtains a grant rendering him independent. He reforms the civil service and the army, introduces flax, and raises Ireland to unprecedented material prosperity.

609. **Germany.** Wallenstein's negotiations with Saxony for a general peace, on the basis of a revocation of the Edict of Restitution, are disallowed at Vienna. He thereupon expels the Swedes from Silesia, but is checked by Bernard of Weimar's capture of Ratisbon.

Oxenstiern persuades several of the South German states to join Sweden in the Convention of Heilbronn.

610. **Netherlands.** The Infanta Isabella dies, and after the failure of a revolt, the Spanish provinces are governed directly from Spain. The States-General do not meet again till 1790.

---

611. **England.** The King, on the advice of Attorney-General Noy, persuades London and other port towns to furnish ships, on the pretext of defence against piracy. [1634

Prynne's ears are cut off for indirectly attacking the Queen in his Histriomastix.

612. **France.** Richelieu centralises the administration of the country by appointing Intendants.

613. **Germany.** The Emperor deserts Wallenstein, who is declared a traitor and assassinated. His army passes to the Emperor's son,

894. **Archaeology.** Bosio publishes the result of many years' explorations in the Catacombs in his Roma Sotteranea.

895. **Science.** Galileo's Systems of the World (a dialogue between a doubter, a Ptolemaic, and a Copernican) is licensed at Florence and Rome, but examined by the Inquisition, which summons him to Rome (1633), compels him to recant his Copernican utterances, and confines him to his home.

896. **Politics.** Lebret's La Souveraineté du Roy openly reçommends absolutism.

897. **Education.** Gustavus Adolphus founds an University at Dorpat.

898. **Death.** Eliot.

---

899. **Eng. Ch.** Laud becomes Archbishop of Canterbury, republishes the Instructions of 1629 and the Book of Sports, moves the Communion table to the chancel and increases ritual. His efforts are assisted by Wren of Norwich and other Bishops in their visitations. [1633

The Baptist Community is divided into Particular and General.

900. **Scotch Ch.** Charles visits Edinburgh with Laud to be crowned, and orders the Scotch Bishops to prepare a Liturgy.

901. **American Ch.** Cotton and Hooker arrive in Massachusetts and obtain almost absolute power in temporal and spiritual matters.

902. **Church Hist.** Scioppius' Anatomia Societatis Jesu reveals certain of the secrets of the Order.

903. **Eng. Lit.** Herbert's The Temple initiates the 'Metaphysical School' (based largely on Donne), which is developed by Quarles, Crashaw, and Vaughan.

Massinger's New Way to Pay Old Debts. With Ford and Shirley Massinger forms the third generation of English dramatists.

904. **Spanish Lit.** The first collection is made of Calderon's plays.

905. **Philosophy.** La Mothe le Vayer's Dialogues of Orasius Tubero develope the scepticism of Montaigne and Charron. His Virtue of the Heathen attacks the Jansenist contention that the virtues of the heathen were vices.

906. **Philology.** The second Elzevir edition of the N.T. (called the Textus Receptus), based on the text of Stephanus and Beza.

Morin's De Sinceritate Hebraei Graecique Textus compares and criticises the texts.

907. **Social.** The Lancashire witches are tried.

908. **Death.** George Herbert.

---

909. **Eng. Ch.** Father Davenport, chaplain to the Queen, declares that the 39 Articles are not contrary to Roman doctrine. [1634

Father Leander, an English Benedictine, and Panzani, an Oratorian, are sent by the Pope, with the sanction of the King, to investigate the position of the English Catholics and the English Church. Their report is favourable; but the idea of reunion falls through, owing to the opposition of the Jesuits and the Puritans.

Ferdinand, who is joined by Spanish troops from Italy, advances to the relief of Bavaria, and routs Bernard of Weimar and Horn at Nördlingen. The whole of South Germany is saved for the Church and Empire. At this point France succeeds Sweden as protector of the Protestants, and a French army enters the Palatinate.

614. **West Indies.** The Dutch take the island of Curaçoa, which becomes the headquarters of contraband trade with the Spanish mainland.

---

615. **England.** The King extends his demand for ship-money to the inland counties, thus creating a fleet independent of the mercantile marine. [1635

616. **Ireland.** Wentworth claims for the King the province of Connaught, and invites settlers from England.

617. **France.** Richelieu declares war against Spain, which attacks the Elector of Treves. At the same moment he renews the alliance with Sweden and makes the League of Rivoli with the Dutch, Savoy, Mantua and Parma.

618. **Italy.** Rohan occupies the Grisons.

619. **Germany.** Saxony withdraws from the war by the Treaty of Prague, which is accepted by Brandenburg and most Lutheran States. The Emperor limits the Edict of Restitution to 1627, and cedes Lusatia to Saxony as a fief of Bohemia. The war at this point ceases to be religious and becomes a struggle of French and Swedes against the Hapsburgs for territory.

620. **America.** Discontented with the system of government in Massachusetts, a number of settlers migrate to the Connecticut Valley, obtained by Lord Brooke and Lord Saye and Sele, in whose honour the fort of Saybrook is erected.

621. **West Indies.** The French occupy Martinique and Guadeloupe.

622. **Asia.** The Dutch occupy Formosa.

---

623. **France.** Spanish and Austrian invasions are repulsed; but no decisive battle occurs. [1636

624. **Holland.** The Dutch recapture Breda, the last stronghold held by Spain.

625. **Germany.** Oxenstiern retires to Sweden, but Baner defeats an army of Imperialists and Saxons at Wittstock.

---

910. **French Ch.** Amyrault's La Prédestination, supporting the theory of universal atonement, is defended by Daillé and Blondel, and attacked by Pierre Dumoulin, Spanheim and Rivet. A schism in the Protestant Church is, however, avoided.

Urbain Grandier is burnt for sorcery by Richelieu.

911. **Eng. Lit.** Milton's Comus is acted at Ludlow Castle.

912. **Philosophy.** Sanderson's Cases of Conscience.

913. **African Ch.** The Jesuit mission in Abyssinia, which has obtained considerable influence, collapses and is never renewed.

914. **Death.** Coke.

---

915. **Eng. Ch.** To prevent the emigration of Puritan ministers, an ordinance forbids any to leave the country but soldiers, sailors, or merchants. Many, nevertheless, escape to America. [1635

Laud begins his Visitation.

916. **Scotch Ch.** Diocesan Courts are established.

917. **French Ch.** Petrus Aurelius (probably St Cyran) defends the Gallican view of the rights of bishops against the Jesuits.

918. **French Lit.** A society of literary men, meeting weekly at the house of Conrart since 1629 for discussion and criticism of each other's works, is transformed by Richelieu, who is connected with the group through Chapelain, into the Académie Française. Conrart becomes its first secretary, and, on Chapelain's persuasion, the Academy resolves to compile a Dictionary.

919. **Science.** Cavalieri invents the principle of indivisibles, and applies it to the quadrature of curves and surfaces and the determination of volumes. The method replaces that of exhaustions, and is employed for half a century, when it is superseded by the integral calculus.

920. **Law.** Selden replies to Grotius' plea for an open sea in his Mare Clausum.

921. **Deaths.** Champlain, Lope de Vega.

---

922. **Eng. Ch.** Hales' Tract on Schism pleads for the toleration of theological differences, and founds English latitudinarianism. [1636

923. **French Ch.** St Cyran, the life-long friend of Jansen, becomes director of Port Royal and introduces Jansenism, i.e. ultra-Augustinianism, into France.

924. **American Ch.** In consequence of his separatist opinions, his attack on the Charter, and his opposition to oaths, Roger Williams is banished from Massachusetts and founds the town of Providence, on land which he buys from the Indians. Absolute religious liberty and complete separation of Church and State are here first carried out. He becomes a Baptist (1638), but renounces his re-baptism and becomes a 'Seeker.'

925. **French Lit.** Corneille's Le Cid, suggested by a play of De Castro, is referred by Richelieu to a committee of the Academy, which reports adversely to it. Henceforward the Academy ceases to issue reports.

626. **England.** The Judges are consulted by the King in reference to ship-money, and 10 out of 12 report that the King may enforce it if the kingdom appears to be in danger. Hampden determines to reassert the validity of the Petition of Right, and refuses 20/- levied for ship-money. Of the 12 judges, five pronounce for him and seven against. The levy is continued, but the arguments of Hampden's counsel are widely circulated. [1637

Prynne, Bastwick and Burton are heavily punished for attacks on episcopacy, and Bishop Williams is disgraced.

627. **France.** Artois is conquered (1637–40).

A revolt of the Croquants in Guienne leads to the abolition of the privileges of the Province. The same fate befalls Normandy, 1639.

628. **Italy.** Rohan is forced to retire from the Grisons.

629. **America.** The Pequods are exterminated by Mason, after five years of incursions.

Maurice of Nassau becomes Governor-General of the Dutch possessions in South America, suppresses piracy, builds forts, and developes trade. He fails, however, to conciliate the natives.

630. **Africa.** Maurice of Nassau despatches a force which captures Elmina and expels the Portuguese from the Gold Coast.

French traders from Dieppe found the Fort of St Louis, at the mouth of the Senegal.

---

631. **Scotland.** The Tables draw up a Covenant, the subscribers of which pledge themselves to remove the recent innovations. Hamilton is sent to revoke the Prayer-book and sanction the Covenant. The General Assembly is dissolved by Hamilton, but continues its session, and, under the leadership of Alexander Henderson, abolishes Episcopacy and restores the Presbyterian system. [1638

632. **France.** The birth of an heir destroys the hope of the Duke of Orleans.

633. **Germany.** Bernard of Weimar seizes Breisach, the chief fortress of Elsass. At the same moment, Turenne defeats the Duke of Lorraine, and the French fleet is victorious in the Mediterranean.

634. **America.** The heads of the Connecticut settlements, aided by Hooker, draw up the Fundamental Orders, perhaps the first written constitution, resembling that of Massachusetts, though establishing no religious qualification.

Davenport, a minister silenced by Laud, and Eaton, a parishioner, found a settlement in New Haven, in the government of which only Church members share.

Rhode Island is bought from the Indians and colonised by refugees from Massachusetts.

Swedes and Finns found a fort on the Delaware and call their settlement New Sweden. The colony is annexed to New Netherlands, 1655.

635. **Africa.** France takes Réunion, called Isle de Bourbon.

---

926. **Education.** A college is founded by Harvard, a minister of Charlestown, but remains for a time a seminary for clergy.

Laud's Statutes transfer the government of Oxford University to the Heads of Houses.

---

927. **Scotch Ch.** The use of the new liturgy in St Giles' Church, Edinburgh, leads to a riot and to the formation of a Committee called the Tables. [1637

928. **Eng. Ch.** Chillingworth replies to Knott, a Jesuit, in his Religion of Protestants a Safe Way of Salvation, discussing fully the meaning of Protestantism and enforcing its logical corollary of Toleration.

929. **American Ch.** Mrs Hutchinson introduces mystical antinomianism into Massachusetts, and receives sympathy from Vane, at this time Governor. She is expelled by his successor, Winthrop, and is welcomed by Roger Williams to Providence.

930. **Eng. Lit.** Milton's Lycidas.

931. **Philosophy.** Descartes discusses the grounds of certainty in his Discours sur la Méthode pour bien conduire la Raison et chercher la Vérité dans les Sciences. His ideas are spread by Clerselier, Mersenne, Rohault, Régis and the Logic of Port Royal in France, and by Geulincx, Renery and Le Roi in the Netherlands. Voetius, Huet and others attack the new philosophy as tending to atheism.

932. **Science.** In an appendix to his Discours, Descartes publishes his Géometrie, which by the adoption of the analytical method ushers in the period of modern mathematics. Fermat independently reaches similar principles.

In a second appendix, La Dioptrique, Descartes states the law of refraction, taken from Snell.

In a third appendix, Les Météores, Descartes partially explains the rainbow, though ignorant of the unequal refrangibility of different rays.

933. **Death.** Ben Jonson.

---

934. **Eng. Ch.** Joseph Mede's Clavis Apocalyptica extracts an elaborate Millenarianism from the Prophets. [1638

935. **French Ch.** St Cyran is imprisoned by Richelieu, who dislikes him for refusing his offers and for aiding Jansen in his attack on the Protestant alliance. While at Vincennes, St Cyran obtains influence over Arnauld, Lancelot, Singlin, and De Sacy, and sends Lemaître to represent him at Port Royal.

The brothers Dupuy compile Preuves des Libertés de l'Église Gallicane, at the instance of Richelieu. A reply by 'Optatus Gallus' is burnt.

936. **Polish Ch.** The school of Racov is closed by the Jesuits.

937. **Church Hist.** Cyril Lucar is murdered by the Sultan, at the instigation of his opponents, and his teaching is anathematised by a Council at Constantinople.

938. **Eng. Lit.** Milton sets out on his Italian journey.

939. **Science.** Horrocks applies the elliptical theory to the moon.

Galileo's Mathematical Discourses and Demonstrations, the first dynamical investigations of the laws of falling bodies.

940. **Deaths.** Jansen, Father Joseph.

---

636. **Scotland.** Charles marches north to punish the Scots for the refusal of the General Assembly to dissolve, but is confronted by an army under Leslie, supported by French money, before which his own troops melt away. The First Bishops' War is concluded by the Treaty of Berwick, by which the Scotch army is to be disbanded and Parliaments are to be regularly summoned. Parliament meets at Edinburgh; but the King orders its adjournment and prepares for a new attack. [1639

637. **England.** Wentworth is made Earl of Strafford, becomes the King's chief adviser, and advises the summoning of a Parliament.

638. **Germany.** On the death of Bernard of Weimar, his army passes with Elsass, his latest conquest, to France.

639. **Holland.** Spain's last Armada, under Oquendo, is annihilated in the Channel by Tromp, the English fleet remaining neutral.

640. **Savoy.** Victor Amadeus I. dies, and his wife, Maria Christina, assumes the regency, with French support. Her brothers-in-law, desiring a share of power, ally with Spain and seize Turin with Spanish troops. A French army comes to the rescue (1640), and recaptures Turin. In 1642, the regency question is compromised, and the civil war ends.

641. **Asia.** The English East India Company buys land on which it builds Madras, its first territorial possession in India.

---

642. **England.** A Parliament meets, but is dissolved after three weeks for opposing the Scotch war. The King marches to meet the Scots, who defeat part of his army at Newburn-on-Tyne, on which a truce is made at Ripon. Charles calls a Council of Peers to York, who urge him to summon another Parliament. The Long Parliament meets (Nov.), impeaches Laud and Strafford, releases and compensates the political prisoners, and nullifies the recent canons. The King yields everything to gain money with which to pay the Scots. [1640

643. **Germany.** The Great Elector succeeds to Brandenburg, and makes a truce with Sweden.

644. **Spain.** Exasperated by Olivarez' attempts to crush its ancient liberties, Catalonia revolts, allies with France, and remains partially independent for 16 years.

645. **Portugal.** The Portuguese, encouraged by the Catalonian revolt, proclaim John of Braganza John IV. An alliance is made with France; and the new King is recognised by the colonies, though Spain retains Ceuta and Tetuan.

646. **West Indies.** The manufacture of sugar is introduced into Barbados from Brazil, and becomes the staple industry of the West Indies.

647. **Asia.** The Dutch destroy Malacca, the Portuguese rival of Batavia.

---

941. **Eng. Ch.** Wroth, Erbery, and Cradock, Welsh clergymen, are deprived of their livings, set up Independent Churches, and organise Welsh Nonconformity. [1639

942. **Scotch Ch.** The General Assembly passes the 'Barrier Act,' forbidding changes in the laws of the Church till ratified by provincial Synods and Presbyteries.

943. **American Lit.** The first Printing-Press is established.

944. **Science.** Horrocks first observes the transit of Venus.

945. **History.** Ussher's Antiquitates Ecclesiae Britannicae.

Spelman's Councils, Laws and Constitutions of the English Church.

946. **Philology.** John Buxtorf's Lexicon chaldaeum, rabbinicum, talmudicum.

947. **Geography.** Father Cristoval de Acuña ascends the Amazon and writes the first adequate description of it.

948. **Death.** Campanella.

---

949. **Eng. Ch.** Henderson, Baillie and Gillespie arrive in London and exert great influence by their preaching. [1640

Convocation continues to sit after the dissolution of the Short Parliament and makes Canons, among them a new oath for the clergy, accepting the government of the Church by Bishops, 'et cetera.' This becomes the object of violent criticism, and Lambeth Palace is attacked.

At the meeting of the Long Parliament, a Committee for Religion is instituted. A sub-committee is formed, under the presidency of White, to deal with 'scandalous ministers.' A selection of cases that come before it is published as 'The First Century of Scandalous Ministers,' and many deprivations are made.

Millenarian doctrines begin to appear, and are attacked by Bishop Hall.

950. **Eng. Lit.** Isaac Walton's Life of Donne.

951. **Netherlands Ch.** Jansen's Augustinus is published posthumously, and, despite the Pope's command to avoid discussion, circulates widely.

952. **Art.** Poussin becomes First Painter in Ordinary to the King of France, and produces the Labours of Hercules, the Last Supper, the Triumph of Truth (Paris).

953. **History.** Selden's De Jure Naturali juxta Hebraeos, with his Uxor Hebraica, aids Pococke and Lightfoot to reconstruct Jewish life.

954. **Politics.** Selden maintains that Natural Law was supernaturally revealed to the first human beings and handed down to us.

Campanella's De Monarchia Hispanica claims universal dominion for Spain.

955. **Education.** Dr Busby becomes Headmaster of Westminster School, and occupies the post for fifty-five years.

956. **Death.** Rubens.

---

648. **England.** A triennial Act is passed, by which Parliament is to meet every three years, and to sit not less than 50 days. [1641 Strafford's impeachment is turned into an attainder when it is found that he is not reached by the statute of Edward III., and the Lords pass the bill on Pym's discovery of the plot of the Queen to bring up the army from the North and of the King to seize the Tower. Charles is frightened into signing the death-warrant, and agrees that the Parliament shall not be adjourned or dissolved without its own consent. Parliament abolishes the Star Chamber and High Commission Courts, and declares ship-money and distraint of knighthood illegal. Charles goes to Scotland, professedly to assent in person to the abolition of Episcopacy, but, in the belief of the Commons, to raise an army, and attempts to arrest Argyle and Hamilton. The Grand Remonstrance, nevertheless, claiming ministerial responsibility, only obtains a majority of 11, and a protest is drawn up by the minority. The King thus finds a party created for him, led by Falkland and Hyde. Twelve Bishops, who have been mobbed and have signed a protest against all done in their absence, are impeached.

649. **Ireland.** Fearing a fresh influx of colonists and renewed persecution, the native Irish massacre some thousands of English and Scotch in Ulster.

650. **France.** The King demands the registration of Royal Edicts by the Parliament of Paris without discussion.

651. **Italy.** Urban VIII.'s relatives, the Barberini, quarrel with the Farnesi, and the Pope is induced to claim the duchy of Castro. Parma is joined by Venice, Tuscany and Modena; but Castro is conquered by Urban's successor, Innocent X.

652. **Holland.** Princess Mary of England marries William, the eldest son of Frederick Henry.

653. **America.** The Body of Liberties, the first New England code of laws, is drawn up by Massachusetts.

---

654. **England.** The King, believing that the leaders of the Opposition invited the Scots to invade England in 1640, impeaches Pym, Hampden, Holles, Hazlerigg and Strode (Jan. 3), and [1642 comes to the House with 500 armed men to seize them (Jan. 4). The five members escape to the city, and the King leaves London (Jan. 10), the Queen going to Holland to raise money. Parliament fails to obtain the control of the militia, and Hotham refuses to allow the King to enter Hull to obtain arms (April). From this point both sides begin to raise forces, and the King's party leaves Westminster. Nineteen Propositions sent by the Commons are rejected by the King (June). Negociations cease, and Essex is appointed Commander, money being raised by tonnage and poundage, and by a tax on property and income. The King raises his standard at Nottingham (Aug. 22), and receives the support of the greater part of the north-west of the kingdom. An indecisive battle is fought at Edgehill (Oct.), after which

957. **Eng. Ch.** The Commons despatch Commissioners to destroy relics of idolatry in the churches. Hall's Remonstrance in favour [1641 of Episcopacy is answered by five Presbyterian divines (Smectymnuus), and Ussher, Falkland, Jeremy Taylor, and Milton join in the controversy.

The Commons pass the Root and Branch Bill for the abolition of episcopacy, and for the transference of the jurisdiction to committees of laymen in each diocese.

958. **French Ch.** De Marca's Concordia Sacerdotii et Imperii, propounding a moderate Gallicanism, is censured at Rome.

959. **German Ch.** The Weimar or Ernestine Exposition, inspired by Ernest of Saxe-Gotha, and composed by Gerhard, aids in the evangelical revival.

960. **Science.** Théophraste Renaudot announces his intention to render medical aid without payment, and is violently attacked by Guy Patin and the Faculty of Medicine, and in 1644 is forbidden to practise.

961. **Philosophy.** Descartes' Meditationes reply to criticisms of the Discours sur la Méthode by Hobbes, Arnauld, and Gassendi.

962. **Art.** Dobson becomes the first English Court painter.

963. **Politics.** Harry Marten, in conversation with Clarendon, gives utterance to the first republican sentiments recorded in England.

964. **History.** Naudé maintains that the De Imitatione Christi was written by Thomas à Kempis. The Benedictines of St Maur, on the other hand, ascribe it to Gersen, a Benedictine.

965. **Deaths.** Sully, Vandyck.

---

966. **Eng. Ch.** The Root and Branch Bill is revived and carried owing to the departure of most of the royalist members [1642 from Westminster, and, after 4 months' delay, is adopted by the Lords. Its provisions, however, are not to come into operation for a year, presumably to give time for an accommodation with the King.

A Committee for Plundered Ministers is appointed to provide for Puritan clergy ejected or plundered by the royal forces, and for their transference to vacant benefices. The work of sequestration is also carried on by local committees.

Ussher's edition of Ignatius declares nine epistles spurious and the other six partially interpolated.

Sir Thomas Brown's Religio Medici, a latitudinarian if not Unitarian confession.

967. **French Ch.** Olier founds the Seminary of St Sulpice, at Paris.

968. **Church Hist.** Grotius' Eirenicon, Via ad Pacem Ecclesiasticam earns for him the name of Grotius Papizans, and is hotly attacked by Rivetus and others.

969. **Eng. Lit.** Stage plays are forbidden by Parliament.

970. **French Lit.** Naudé becomes librarian to Mazarin and creates the Mazarin library.

the King pushes on to London; but, meeting the trained bands at Turnham Green, retires to Oxford for the winter.

655. **Ireland.** The Catholic nobles choose a Council, hold an Assembly at Kilkenny, and petition Charles for the redress of grievances.

656. **France.** Cinq-Mars, a favourite introduced by Richelieu, plots to supplant the Cardinal, who obtains evidence of his correspondence with Spain. Orleans betrays his associates, and Cinq-Mars and De Thou are executed. The Cardinal's death follows (Dec.).

Roussillon submits to France.

657. **Germany.** Torstenson defeats the Imperialists under Piccolomini at the second battle of Leipsig, and threatens the hereditary estates of the Emperor. These successes arouse the hostility of Denmark.

658. **Portugal.** The Spaniards invade Portugal, but are defeated at Montijo.

659. **America.** Maisonneuve takes possession of Montreal.

660. **Africa.** The French Compagnie de l'Orient is formed to colonise Madagascar.

---

661. **England.** The King plans that three armies, led by Hopton, Newcastle, and himself, shall converge on London. [1643
Hampden is slain at Chalgrove Field, Hopton defeats Waller at Roundway Down, Rupert storms Bristol, Newcastle defeats Fairfax in Yorkshire, and the King besieges Gloucester. The London trained bands under Essex march to its relief, the siege is raised, and the tide is turned. After a fierce but indecisive battle at Newbury, where Falkland is slain, Charles retires to Oxford for the winter. Meanwhile a better army is being formed by the Eastern Association, under the direction of Cromwell. The royalist successes, however, determine Pym to ask aid of the Scots, and the younger Vane is sent to Edinburgh. The Solemn League and Covenant is accepted by Parliament (Sept.), and imposed on the nation.

662. **Ireland.** Ormond is directed by the King to make peace (The Cessation) with the Catholics.

663. **France.** The King dies, but his widow, who becomes Regent, retains Mazarin, despite her Spanish predilections. The young nobles, nicknamed the Importants, are disappointed, and plot with Beaufort, a descendant of Henry IV., but are quickly suppressed. Beaufort is imprisoned, Mme de Chevreuse is exiled, and Mazarin's rule remains undisputed for five years.

Condé defeats the Spaniards at Rocroy, but the French are routed at Dutlingen by an Austro-Bavarian army.

664. **Germany.** Negociations begin in Münster-Osnabrück, but come to nothing, as the Emperor desires to retain Elsass.

665. **Denmark.** Torstenson marches rapidly north, conquers Holstein and Schleswig, and invades Jutland.

666. **America.** Roger Williams obtains a patent of Incorporation of Providence Plantations, permitting the settlements on Narragansett Bay to form a federation.

971. **Politics.** Bishop Bramhall attacks the prevalent exaltation of Nature over positive law, and points out the danger involved in the ideas of Parker and other Parliamentary writers.

972. **History.** Hooft publishes his History of the Dutch War of Independence.

973. **Geography.** Tasman is sent from Batavia by Van Diemen, Governor of the Dutch East India Company, and discovers Tasmania and New Zealand, which are not visited again till the time of Cook.

974. **Deaths.** Galileo, Guido Reni.

---

975. **Eng. Ch.** An Assembly of divines is summoned by Parliament to Westminster. Episcopalians are invited, but do not appear, and the Presbyterians possess a large majority. The first fifteen Articles are revised; but few alterations are made. On the arrival of the Scotch Commissioners the Covenant is laid before the Assembly and accepted. Many of the clergy, however, throughout the country reject it. [1643

Saltmarsh, Dell, and other 'Antinomians' make their appearance and cause the Westminster Assembly grave anxiety. Though sometimes called Anabaptists, few of them are members of the Baptist Churches.

976. **French Ch.** Arnauld's De la fréquente Communion, disapproving constant and unprepared communion, leads to the first Jesuit attack on Port Royal, but is approved by the Pope and Inquisition and brings many penitents to Port Royal.

A Bull is issued, condemning Jansenism, but is attacked by Arnauld, and is not recognised by the Sorbonne.

977. **Netherlands Ch.** Bolland, a Jesuit of Antwerp, commences a collection of the Acta Sanctorum, aided by Papebroch. (This work is still in progress.)

978. **Church Hist.** Mogilas' Orthodox Confession, attacking Catholics and the followers of Lucar, is approved by a synod at Jassy, and becomes the creed of the whole Eastern Church.

979. **Eng. Lit.** Birkenhead's newspaper, Mercurius Aulicus, and Needham's Mercurius Britannicus, champion respectively the royal and the Parliamentary cause.

980. **Science.** Torricelli finds that the changes of atmospheric pressure vary with its rarity, and invents the Barometer. The discovery is confirmed by Pascal's experiment on the Puy de Dôme, 1648.

981. **Art.** Teniers' Pilgrims. (National Gallery.)

982. **Philosophy.** Gassendi's Disquisitiones Anti-Cartesianae attacks Descartes' criterion of certainty.

983. **Politics.** Prynne's Sovereign Power of Parliament contends for constitutional monarchy.

984. **Law.** Conring's De Origine Juris Germanici founds the study of German law on a historical basis.

985. **History.** Mézerai's History of France.

For purposes of defence, Massachusetts, Connecticut, Plymouth and New Haven form a loose confederation.

Massachusetts omits the allegiance clause in the magistrates' oath, and politely refuses the offer of Parliament to pass any legislation required.

---

667. **England.** 20,000 Scots, under Leslie, enter England, and the control of the armies is entrusted to a Committee of both kingdoms. Rupert and Newcastle are routed by Leslie, Fairfax, Manchester (Lord Kimbolton), and Cromwell at Marston Moor (July). Waller's army, however, melts away, and Essex capitulates to Charles in Cornwall. A second battle at Newbury (Oct.) proves indecisive, owing to Manchester's and Waller's slackness in pursuit. Cromwell hereupon attacks Manchester, introduces a Self-denying Ordinance, excluding members of Parliament from command, and determines to organize a New Model Army. [1644

668. **Scotland.** Montrose takes arms for the King, raises Highland troops, and captures Perth.

669. **Germany.** Condé turns to aid Turenne against Austria and Bavaria, and wins the Rhineland by the battle of Freiburg.

670. **Sweden.** Christina begins to govern in person.

671. **America.** Maurice of Nassau is recalled from South America. In 1645, the Portuguese colonists in the Dutch captainships throw off the Dutch yoke, and by 1655 not an acre of ground remains in Dutch hands.

672. **Asia.** The Manchus are invited by the Emperor of China to aid in suppressing a rebellion, but seize Pekin, depose the last sovereign of the Ming dynasty, which has reigned since 1368, and establish that of the Manchus.

---

673. **England.** Negociations are opened with the King at Uxbridge, but broken off after three weeks, Charles refusing to establish Presbyterianism or to allow Parliament entire control of appointments. The Self-denying Ordinance is carried, Essex, Manchester, and Waller resign, and Fairfax becomes General of the New Model, the soldiers of which receive regular pay. Cromwell is exempted from the Ordinance and becomes Lieutenant-General. Fairfax and Cromwell defeat the King at Naseby, despite Prince Rupert's victorious attack on the left wing under Ireton (June). Letters shewing the King's persistent attempts to introduce a foreign army are taken and published. The war drags on until Fairfax forces Rupert to surrender in Bristol. Montrose, who has won several battles, is routed at Philiphaugh (Sept.). [1645

986. **Social.** Milton begins his series of tracts on marriage, suggested by his personal experience, and contends that incompatibility of temperament justifies divorce.

987. **Deaths.** Chillingworth, St Cyran, Episcopius, Pym.

---

988. **Eng. Church.** The Westminster Assembly agree to a Directory of Public Worship, differing but slightly from that of Cartwright and Travers. [1644

Whichcote becomes Provost of King's College, Cambridge, and by his sermons inaugurates the movement, neither Puritan nor Anglican, of the Cambridge Platonists, the chief of whom, except More, are members of Emmanuel College and influenced by Tuckney, first Tutor, later Master. In the same year John Smith becomes Fellow of Queens' and preaches his Discourses, and Cudworth becomes Master of Clare, and Regius Professor of Hebrew. Henry More's Philosophical Poems are published 1647.

The Baptists issue a Confession, exhibiting their doctrinal agreement with the Churches.

Hammond's Practical Catechism.

989. **French Ch.** Petavius' Dogmata Theologica.

990. **American Ch.** Roger Williams attacks the views of Cotton and the elders of Massachusetts, who distinguish between 'fundamentals' and 'circumstantials,' in his Bloody Tenet of Persecution, the first widely-read plea for complete religious freedom.

991. **Eng. Lit.** Some of his own tracts having been condemned by the licensers, Milton protests in his Areopagitica against subjection to Presbyterian belief and policy, and demands liberty for books no less than for men.

992. **Science.** Descartes' Principia Philosophica, dedicated to the Princess Elizabeth, daughter of James I., discusses the laws of motion, propounds the theory of vortices, and replies to the criticisms of the Meditations.

993. **Education.** Milton writes a Letter on Education, at the request of Hartlib, a disciple of Comenius, many of whose views Milton has reached independently.

994. **Philosophy.** Sir Kenelm Digby's treatises on Bodies, and on Man's Soul.

995. **Politics.** Rutherford's Lex Rex contends that kings are elective and can be deposed by the people, and that parliaments are equally subject to the popular will.

---

996. **Eng. Ch.** Laud is executed, the impeachment having been changed into an attainder. [1645

The Westminster Directory is imposed, and the use of the Prayer Book, in public or private, is forbidden under heavy penalties. The Directory is attacked by Jeremy Taylor, Sanderson, and Hammond, and its use is forbidden by the King. Five Independent Ministers, led by

674. **Ireland.** The King sends the Earl of Glamorgan, a Catholic, to Ireland, to raise men and money (Aug.). The Earl accepts the demand for the transference of the churches to the nobles and for clerical jurisdiction, on the promise of 10,000 men. A papal nuncio, Rinuccini, lands in Ireland and requires fresh concessions, to which Glamorgan also assents.

675. **Germany.** The Imperial force that has been sent to aid the Danes is pursued into Germany by Torstenson, and routed at Magdeburg (Jan.). Torstenson defeats another Imperial army at Jankau, in Bohemia (March), joins Rakoczy, prince of Transylvania, overruns Moravia, and advances on Vienna. He fails, however, to capture Brünn, retires to Bohemia, resigns, and is succeeded by Wrangel.

Turenne and Condé defeat the Imperialists at Nördlingen, but are forced to retire to the Rhine. Turenne captures Tréves and restores the Elector.

676. **Denmark.** Christian is forced to accept the Treaty of Bromsebro, ceding the islands of Gotland and Oesel, and commercial exemptions to Sweden.

677. **Turkey.** The Turks land in Crete and commence a war of conquest, which lasts 24 years.

678. **Russia.** Krijanitch, a Croatian Catholic, settles in Moscow, and champions the conception of Panslavism.

---

679. **England.** Charles' army in the west surrenders to Fairfax, [1646
most of the remaining fortresses fall, and the King surrenders to the Scots (May). He is taken to Newcastle, where he refuses to consent to the establishment of Presbyterianism in England, and is in consequence treated as a prisoner. He also rejects the demands of Parliament to surrender the militia for 20 years and support Presbyterianism. Shortly after, desiring to allow time for the opposition to Presbyterianism to grow, he offers to establish Presbyterianism for three years.

680. **Germany.** Turenne joins Wrangel, and devastates Bavaria.

681. **Hungary.** George Rakoczy's insurrection leads to the concessions of several political and religious privileges.

---

682. **England.** The Scots surrender the King to Parliament and [1647
retire, in return for the payment of their expenses. Charles is taken to Holmby House, Northamptonshire. The Presbyterian majority in Parliament accepts his proposal to establish Presbyterianism for three years as a basis for negociations, and at the same moment reduces

Goodwin, recently returned from Holland, appear in the Assembly, and join the Erastians, led by Selden, in opposition to the Presbyterians.

Lord Herbert's De Religione Gentilium first attempts a natural history of religion and discovers in all religions the ideas of a God, immortality and conscience.

997. **Polish Ch.** The colloquy of Thorn, from which Unitarians are excluded, discusses reunion, and is attended by the Lutherans, Calixtus, Calov, by the Moravian Comenius, and by Catholics, but serves only to widen the gulf.

998. **Asiatic Ch.** Owing to the attacks of the Capucins and Dominicans, Innocent X. condemns the Malabar Rites. Alexander VII., however, again authorises them, 1656.

999. **Eng. Lit.** Waller's Poems, among them his odes to Saccharissa.

1000. **Science.** Boyle, Hooke, Wilkins, Wallis, Petty, Seth Ward, and others begin to meet for weekly scientific discussions at Gresham College, London, and in Oxford.

1001. **Art.** Lesueur's Histoire de Saint Bruno (Louvre).

1002. **Philosophy.** Busenbaum and Spee, German Jesuits, publish the Medulla, a treatise on Casuistry, of which 45 editions appear in 25 years.

1003. **Philology.** Le Jay's Polyglot, to which Morin contributes the Samaritan Pentateuch.

1004. **Politics.** After the battle of Naseby Baxter visits the camp and witnesses the rapid growth of republican and revolutionary sentiments, fostered by Hugh Peters and other Independent chaplains. At this moment, Lilburne declares that sovereignty resides not in Parliament but in the people, and founds the Leveller movement in Southwark, whence it rapidly spreads to the army.

1005. **Deaths.** Grotius, Olivarez, Quevedo.

1006. **Eng. Ch.** Biddle, of Gloucester, attacks Trinitarianism, and translates the Racovian Catechism. After repeated imprisonments, he dies 1662, and his work is carried on by Firmin and other disciples. [1646

1007. **American Ch.** John Eliot begins his missionary labours in Massachusetts.

1008. **Eng. Lit.** Henry Vaughan, the Silurist, publishes his first poems. Sir Thomas Browne's Vulgar Errors.

1009. **Philosophy.** Escobar's Theologia Moralis, a treatise on Casuistry.

1010. **History.** Clarendon begins to write his History of the Rebellion.

1011. **Education.** The Schools at Port Royal are fully organised, and for twenty years remain the best in France. Lancelot compiles several text-books, and Arnauld and Nicole compose the Port Royal Logic.

1012. **Death.** Henderson.

1013. **Eng. Ch.** An election of elders under the new Presbyterian scheme takes place, and the Provincial Assembly of London meets. The system is also carried out in Lancashire, but never becomes widely adopted. [1647

the army, without paying arrears. The regiments, in consequence, choose Agitators, and refuse to disperse. The Presbyterians plan a Scotch invasion, and a royalist rising is reported to Cromwell, who orders Cornet Joyce to prevent the King from being seized (June). Joyce, fearing the approach of troops, takes Charles to Newmarket, and thence to Hampton Court. Parliament retorts by reorganising the trained bands ; whereupon the army marches on London, and 11 Presbyterian members fly abroad.

Meanwhile the officers try to reach an understanding with Charles, and Ireton offers the Heads of the Proposals, according to which Parliament is to control the army and navy for 10 years, and to appoint to great offices. Parliaments are to be biennial, and toleration is to be granted to all but Catholics. When the King rejects these terms, the Agitators draw up the Case of the Army and the Agreement of the People, demanding biennial Parliaments, freedom of religion and trade, and equality before the law, but only obtain the sanction of the Council of Officers for manhood suffrage, though this, too, is opposed by Cromwell and Ireton. The King becomes aware of his danger, and flies to the Isle of Wight, where he is detained in Carisbrook Castle (Nov.). He at once makes an arrangement with the Scots, promising three years' Presbyterianism in return for an army.

683. **Ireland.** Rinuccini fails to win Ireland, since Ormond prefers to hand over Dublin to the Parliamentary troops and leaves the country.

684. **Italy.** A revolt in Palermo against Spanish rule is suppressed, but leads to an outbreak in Naples, under Masaniello, against the taxation of food. After a dictatorship of a week, Masaniello is killed ; but the malcontents repulse a fleet sent under Don John, and proclaim a Republic. The nobility declare for Spain, and the rebels invite Henry of Guise, Duke of Lorraine, a representative of the Anjou claims, to become Doge. Guise, however, quarrels with the popular leader, Gennaro Annese, who joins Spain, and by whose help Don John recaptures the city.

685. **Holland.** Negociations for peace with Spain are opened, independently of France.

---

686. **England.** Parliament, finding that the King refuses its terms, declares that it will make no more proposals (Jan.). The resolution is approved by the officers, and the Levellers lose their influence in the army. The people, on the contrary, weary of the rule and expense of the army. Fairfax suppresses a revolt in Kent, and takes Colchester after a long siege. Cromwell suppresses a simultaneous insurrection in Wales, and, marching north, routs the Scots, who have invaded England, at Preston (Aug.). The army removes the King to Hurst Castle, and, when Parliament declares for a reconciliation with the King, sends Colonel Pride to exclude the royalist members from the House (Dec.). [1648

Jeremy Taylor's Liberty of Prophesying restates the positions of Chillingworth, excluding only the Anabaptists from toleration.

Jeremy Taylor's Dissuasive from Popery.

Baxter's Saints' Rest.

George Fox begins itinerant preaching, his doctrine of the Inner Light being in part derived from the Mennonite Baptists and from the Schwenkfeldians. He is joined by Dewsbury, Howgill, Burrough, and Margaret Fell, whom he marries.

On the fall of Oxford, Parliament appoints Commissioners for a Visitation. The University declares its abhorrence of the Solemn League and Covenant, and Sanderson, Hammond, and other Anglicans are expelled.

1014. **Scotch Ch.** The Westminster Confession is adopted without change by the General Assembly.

1015. **Eng. Lit.** Cowley's Mistress, a specimen of the Metaphysical School.

1016. **French Lit.** Vaugelas' Remarques control literary taste for sixty years.

Rotrou's Wenceslas.

1017. **Science.** Pecquet discovers that the lacteals empty themselves into a large tube, the thoracic duct, which carries the fluid into the principal veins. His discovery is confirmed by Rudbeck, 1649.

1018. **Philosophy.** Sanderson's De Obligatione Juramenti.

1019. **Politics.** Chemnitz' (Hippolytus a Lapide) De Ratione Status in Imperio declares that the Germanic Constitution is German and not Roman, and that absolutism has no place, and attacks Austria's hegemony.

1020. **Deaths.** Hooft, Torricelli.

1021. **Eng. Ch.** Parliament approves the Longer and Shorter Westminster Catechisms; the former composed chiefly by Tuckney, the latter probably in part by Wallis, the mathematician. The Shorter Catechism takes its place besides Luther's and that of Heidelberg, and is at once adopted in New England. [1648

Andrewes' Private Devotions are published.

Jeremy Taylor's Life of Christ.

1022. **Scotch Ch.** The Catechisms are adopted by the General Assembly, and are approved by Parliament, 1649.

1023. **German Ch.** The Treaty of Westphalia extends to the Calvinists the recognition confined by the Peace of Augsburg to the Lutherans.

Gerhard's first hymns contribute to the pietistic revival, and found German lyrical poetry.

1024. **Dutch Ch.** Coccejus' De Foedere et Testamentis Dei, a compromise between Calvinism and Arminianism, is attacked as Pelagian by Voetius and the rigid Calvinists.

687. **Germany.** The ravages of the Swedes in Bavaria and the victory of Condé at Lens precipitate the conclusion of the Treaty of Westphalia. In secular affairs a return is made to the conditions of 1618. The Electoral dignity and the Upper Palatinate are left with the Bavarian house, the Lower Palatinate being restored to the son of the Winter King, with a new (8th) Electorate. Brandenburg obtains part of further Pomerania, the Archbishoprics of Magdeburg and the bishoprics of Halberstadt and Minden. Questions of ownership of ecclesiastical estates are to be settled by the conditions of 1624. The Imperial Court is restored, its members being drawn equally from Protestants and Catholics. The princes are allowed to conclude alliances with each other and with foreign powers, if not directed against the Emperor and Empire.

688. **France.** On the news of the victory at Lens, the Queen-mother arrests Broussel, the leader of the opposition of the Parliament of Paris. Barricades are erected, De Retz, Coadjutor of the Archbishop of Paris, obtains the release of Brousset, and the Court is forced to accept certain of the demands of the Frondeurs.

France, which with Sweden becomes a guarantor of the Treaty of Westphalia, obtains the legal cession of Metz, Toul and Verdun, Breisach and most of Elsass, the overlordship of Pinerolo, and the right to garrison Philipsburg.

689. **Sweden.** Sweden obtains the greater part of Pomerania and the Bishoprics of Bremen and Verden as fiefs of the Empire.

690. **Switzerland.** Switzerland is declared independent of the Empire.

691. **Holland.** The Dutch are recognised as independent of Spain at the Treaty of Münster, and insist on the closing of the Scheldt.

[1649

692. **England.** The Commons declare that the people being the source of power, they, being chosen by them, are supreme. A Court for the trial of the King is constituted, but only half the appointed members are present. Charles refuses to plead and is condemned and executed (Jan. 30), his son taking the title of Charles II. The Commons abolish the Monarchy and the House of Lords, and appoint a Council of State of 41. The Levellers attack the Government, but are suppressed, and begin to plot with the Royalists.

693. **Ireland.** Cromwell crosses to Ireland, where Charles has been proclaimed, and storms Drogheda and Wexford.

694. **France.** The Court leaves Paris for St Germain, and the Frondeurs are joined by Conti, the Duc and Duchesse de Longueville, La Rochefoucauld, and Beaufort. Condé comes to the aid of the Court and captures the Fronde towns. The nobles retort by applying for aid to the Spanish Netherlands. President Molé, who desires a compromise, visits Ruel and concludes a treaty, which, however, is rejected by the nobles. A Spanish force enters Champagne, but Mazarin bribes Turenne's troops to desert their leader. The second Treaty of Ruel is made, and the Regent buys off the nobles with pensions and offices.

1025. **Bohemian Ch.** Comenius becomes chief Bishop of the Bohemian Brothers and revives the society.
1026. **Church Hist.** Innocent X. condemns the Peace of Westphalia, which is concluded without consulting him, and declares that it is not binding.
1027. **Eng. Lit.** Herrick's Hesperides.
1028. **Swedish Lit.** Stjernhjelm enters Christina's Court and founds Swedish poetry and drama. The Queen also receives visits from Salmasius, Grotius, Vossius, Naudé, Bochart, Huet, Descartes, and other distinguished foreigners.
1029. **Death.** Lord Herbert.

1030. **Eng. Ch.** Thorndike's Right of a Church in a Christian State. [1649
1031. **Scotch Ch.** Lay patronage is abolished.
1032. **French Ch.** Five propositions from the Augustinus are selected by certain doctors of the Sorbonne for disapproval, and 85 prelates urge the Pope to condemn them. A Committee decides against them, though without declaring that they are to be found in Jansen's book. The Jansenists admit the heretical character of the Propositions, but deny that they were held by Jansen. A new enquiry is therefore made by the Bishops, who report that they are in the book.
1033. **German Ch.** The mystical hymns of Spee are collected.
1034. **American Ch.** The Maryland Assembly passes a Toleration Act for all Christians, the Catholics fearing the increasing number of the Protestant immigrants.
1035. **Philosophy.** Gassendi's Syntagma Philosophicum Epicuri, following on his Life of Epicurus and his commentary on Diogenes Laertius, revives the study and system of Epicurus.
Bishop Hall's Practical Cases of Conscience.
1036. **Politics.** A fortnight after the King's death, Milton's Tenure of Kings and Magistrates appears, justifying the execution but not attacking monarchy. The Eikon Basilike, compiled by Gauden in part from the King's notes, quickly follows, and is answered in the Eikonoklastes of Milton, now Corresponding Secretary to the Government, in a fiercer tone both against the person of the King and the institution of monarchy.
1037. **History.** Lord Herbert of Cherbury's History of Henry VIII.
1038. **Social.** The Diggers begin to work at St George's Hill, Surrey, and on being prosecuted by the Government attack the institution of private property.
1039. **Agriculture.** Blith's treatise on Drainage.
1040. **Death.** Gerhard Vossius.

---

695. **Ireland.** Cromwell leaves Ireland, the conquest being carried on by Ireton and Ludlow till 1652, when a large part of Ulster, Munster, and Leinster is confiscated for the soldiers. [1650

696. **Scotland.** Montrose appears in arms for the King, but is betrayed and executed. Charles II. lands (June), signs the Covenant, and is welcomed by the whole nation. Fairfax refuses to lead an army to Scotland, and Cromwell, who takes his place, advances to Edinburgh. He is forced to retreat to Dunbar, where the Scots attack him and are utterly routed (Sept. 3). Edinburgh falls three months later.

697. **France.** Condé, who attempts to dominate the Court, is arrested with Conti and Longueville. Mme de Longueville (Condé's sister) wins back Turenne and makes a treaty with the Spanish Netherlands. Turenne is defeated; and Mazarin pacifies Guienne, where Condé's wife has raised a revolt, with the restoration of local privileges.

698. **Holland.** William II. and Mazarin agree to disown the Peace of Westphalia, to partition the Spanish Netherlands, and to restore the Stuarts to England; but the plot is foiled by the death of William.

699. **America.** The New Netherlands and the United Colonies establish a boundary between the Dutch and English settlements, Governor Stuyvesant having claimed as far as Cape Cod.

---

700. **England.** Charles is crowned at Scone by Argyll, collects an army, and marches across the border (Aug.), but is overtaken and routed by Cromwell at Worcester (Sept. 3). After many adventures, he escapes to France, and Argyll resumes friendly relations with Cromwell. [1651

The Council sends ambassadors to the Netherlands to suggest a close union; the provinces, however, with the exception of Holland, refuse to expel the Stuarts. In retaliation, the Navigation Act is passed, by which English vessels alone may import goods, excepting only the vessels of the country whence the goods come. This measure creates a commercial navy, and may be said to found England's commercial Empire.

701. **France.** Mazarin is forced to release Condé, whose insolence throws the Frondeurs into the arms of the Court. The King is declared of age, and Parliament declares Condé, who has raised a revolt in the south, guilty of treason.

702. **Poland.** The single veto is first used.

703. **Asia.** The Portuguese are expelled from Muscat.

704. **Africa.** St Helena is occupied by the English, and becomes a station of the East India Company.

1041. **Eng. Ch.** Jeremy Taylor's Holy Living and Holy Dying. [1650
Baxter contends for a modified predestination on the lines of Amyraut's teaching.

1042. **American Lit.** Anne Bradstreet's Poems.

1043. **Science.** Guericke of Magdeburg invents an air-pump by which vessels can be exhausted, and proves that the air presses equally in all directions. Boyle hears of the pump and makes one of a somewhat similar character.

Descartes' Les Passions de l'Ame calls attention to reflex action, and declares that the brain changes with the changing states of consciousness.

Glisson's Treatise on the Rickets.

1044. **Art.** Hobbema paints his first pictures, which, with the works of Ruysdael, found Dutch landscape.

1045. **History.** Ussher's Annales Veteris et Novi Testamenti.

Launoi attacks the legend of Pope Joan, which is defended by the Abbé Thiers.

1046. **Law.** Sir Matthew Hale's Analysis of the Civil Law presents a scheme of codification.

Zouch's Explicatio Juris inter Gentes, the first systematic work on international law produced in England.

1047. **Philology.** Cappel, Professor of Theology at Saumur, publishes his Critica Sacra, attacking the theory of inspiration of the Hebrew vowels, maintained by the elder Buxtorf.

1048. **Agriculture.** Hartlib describes the agricultural methods in use in Flanders, and Weston calls attention to the advantages of turnips.

1049. **Death.** Descartes.

1050. **Eng. Ch.** Sancroft's Fur Predestinatus attacks Justification by Faith from an Arminian standpoint. [1651

1051. **Asiatic Ch.** A body of Dominicans arrives in China and is greatly shocked at the attitude adopted by the Jesuits in regard to Chinese ceremonies and beliefs.

1052. **French Lit.** Furetiére's Roman Bourgeois, with Scarron's Roman Comique, introduces a reaction against the conventional Romans de longue Haleine.

1053. **Science.** Harvey's De Generatione Animalium founds embryology and suggests Epigenesis.

1054. **Politics.** Milton replies to Salmasius' attack on the execution of the King in his Defensio pro Populo Anglicano, in which he assumes a definitely republican position.

Hobbes returns to England, notifies his submission to the Council of State and publishes his Leviathan, a *résumé* of his previous works. He contends that the *de facto* sovereign, whether by contract or by conquest, has a right to absolute obedience in all matters of Church and State. This obedience alone has rescued society from its primitive anarchy, and can alone prevent its relapse.

1055. **Philosophy.** Hobbes separates theology from philosophy, but rejects the purely empirical methods of Bacon. He finds the origin of

705. **England.** The Commons propose to raise their numbers to 400, existing members retaining their seats, with power to veto the new members. [1652

War breaks out with the Dutch over the right of search, and Vane, the Secretary and organiser of the Navy, entrusts the fleet to Blake. After indecisive battles, Tromp defeats the English (Dec.).

706. **Holland.** A treaty is made with Denmark to close the Sound against English ships.

707. **France.** Turenne, who has rejoined the Court, forces his way to Paris and defeats Condé in the Faubourg St Antoine, but is compelled by the victories of Spain in the N.E. to withdraw. Condé, however, loses his influence, and the Court returns, sentences Condé to death and arrests Retz.

708. **Spain.** Don John, an illegitimate son of Philip IV., takes Barcelona, and ejects the French from Catalonia.

709. **Russia.** The Cossacks on the Dnieper take the oath of allegiance to the Tsar.

710. **America.** Maine is joined to Massachusetts.

711. **Africa.** Van Riebeck is sent by the Dutch East India Company to the Cape of Good Hope, to make a fort and a hospital for invalided soldiers and sailors, in consequence of the wreck of an East Indiaman in Table Bay. In 1657, several members of the Dutch garrison become farmers and begin the Boer settlement, which remains unmolested except by the Hottentots.

---

712. **England.** Despite an assurance that nothing will be done in a hurry (April 19), Parliament proceeds (April 20) to pass the Perpetuation Bill. Cromwell, spurred on by Harrison, arrives before the motion is put, and expels the members. The officers appoint a Council of State, which requests the Independent ministers to recommend candidates for a new Parliament. Of these the Council selects 139, who meet as the Little, or Barebones, Parliament (June). Alarmed by the attempt to carry out ambitious reforms, the more cautious declare the Parliament dissolved (Dec.). The Instrument of Government is drawn up, by which Cromwell becomes Lord Protector with a Council of 21 life members, whose concurrence is necessary for peace or war. Legislation is vested in a single house, which must meet once every third year for not less than five months, and in time of war. The Protector receives a fixed revenue and must ask Parliament if he needs more. [1653

Blake, Deane and Monk defeat Tromp and Ruyter off Beachy Head (March), and Monk again defeats Tromp off the Texel (Aug.). Negociations are opened, and Cromwell vainly presses for a complete union as the nucleus of a Protestant League.

713. **France.** The Fronde flickers out in the Provinces, and Condé and the Spaniards are repulsed by Turenne.

knowledge in sense-impressions, and defines the good as that which is desired by the individual and that which tends to self-preservation.

De Lugo's Responsa Moralia, a handbook which obtains great authority.

1056. **Eng. Ch.** Gataker's Commentary on the thoughts of Marcus Aurelius. [1652

1057. **Dutch Ch.** Lodensteyn, the leader of the Pietists, becomes pastor at Utrecht.

1058. **Russian Ch.** Nicon becomes Patriarch, and, secure in the support of the Tsar Alexis, introduces many small changes into the Church, allowing western music and art, reviving preaching and revising the Bible. The Raskolniks (Dissenters) leave the Church, owing to the liturgical changes. Nicon quarrels with the Tsar, 1658, and retires. A Council of the Eastern Patriarchs meets in Moscow and condemns him, and elects a new Patriarch, 1667.

1059. **Art.** Paul Potter's Bull (The Hague).

1060. **Philosophy.** Culverwell's Light of Nature declares the Jus Naturae a code antecedent to all human law, yet dependent on the Divine Will.

1061. **Politics.** Winstanley's Law of Freedom unfolds an elaborate system of communism, with the prohibition of buying and selling, the election of office-holders, equal salaries, technical instruction, civil marriage, and a priesthood to lecture on the day of rest.

1062. **Deaths.** Inigo Jones, Petavius, John Smith.

1063. **Eng. Ch.** A large section adopts Millenarian ideas, and James Naylor allows himself to be recognised in Bristol as the Messiah. Fifth Monarchy men, led by Feake and Rogers, also become definitely Antinomian, though Vane and Harrison stand aloof. [1653

Jeremy Taylor's course of Sermons for the Christian Year.

1064. **French Ch.** Innocent X. condemns five Propositions concerning Grace, professing to be drawn from the Augustinus, without declaring whether they are in Augustine or in Jansen.

1065. **German Ch.** The Great Elector confirms the declaration of Sigismund, granting toleration to Lutherans and Calvinists.

1066. **Dutch Ch.** Many Dutch Catholics accept Jansenism, denying that the condemned propositions are drawn from Jansen's work. The States-General declare against the Unitarians, many of whom in consequence become professing Arminians.

1067. **Asiatic Ch.** Syrian Christians renounce the Roman Church and enter into relations with the Jacobites.

1068. **Eng. Lit.** Isaac Walton's Complete Angler.

1069. **Scotch Lit.** Sir Thomas Urquhart's translation of Rabelais, the last monument of old Scotch prose.

1070. **Spanish Lit.** Gracian's Oráculo Manual, an anticipation of La Rochefoucauld.

714. **Germany.** The Great Elector issues a Constitution and suppresses his Diet.

715. **Holland.** De Witt is elected Pensionary of Holland, and becomes the ruler of the United Provinces for 20 years.

---

716. **England.** Cromwell terminates the war with the Dutch, the House of Orange being excluded from the Stadtholdership. [1654
He also decrees a union with Scotland and Ireland, and a reform of Chancery. On the meeting of the first Protectorate Parliament, elected on the lines of Vane's Reform Bill, an attack is made on the new government; but the Protector excludes about 100 members who refuse to promise not to attempt to alter the Constitution.

Cromwell offers his alliance to Spain, in return for freedom to trade in the West Indies and toleration for the English in Spanish territory. On Spain's refusal, he sends a fleet under Penn and Venables to attack the Spanish Indies.

Blake sails for the Mediterranean, obtains compensation from Tuscany and the Pope for injuries inflicted with their countenance on English merchants, and bombards Tunis for refusing a similar indemnity.

Cromwell forces Denmark to reopen the Sound and to pay damages. Whitelocke is sent to Sweden, and Christina proves friendly.

717. **Sweden.** Christina resigns the throne to her cousin, Charles X., and declares herself a Catholic.

718. **Switzerland.** Cromwell sends Dury and Pell to arrange a league with the Protestant Cantons.

---

719. **England.** The Protector, finding the members persist in criticising the Constitution, dissolves Parliament. Some refuse [1655
to pay taxes, on the ground that the Instrument has not been recognised by Parliament, and the judges who agree with them are ejected. A royalist plot breaks out in Wiltshire, and the republicans become increasingly active. Cromwell in consequence divides England into military districts under Major-Generals.

Blake destroys the Barbary fleet and releases the captives in Algiers.

Cromwell makes an alliance with France, Dunkirk to be taken by the joint armies and handed over to England, and religious freedom to be granted to Englishmen in France. At this moment the Duke of Savoy attacks the Vaudois, and Cromwell forces Mazarin to stop the persecution as the price of his alliance.

Penn and Venables are repulsed from San Domingo, but seize Jamaica, in which a number of settlers arrive from Barbados and St Kitts.

The Levellers plot with the Royalists, but nothing is done, both from want of money and from opposition to the royal veto and episcopacy. Sexby, the leader, is seized, 1658, and the Levellers disappear.

1071. **Swedish Lit.** Stjernhjelm's Hercules, a didactic allegory, improves the language.
1072. **Death.** Salmasius.

1073. **Eng. Ch.** Cromwell appoints Triers, among them Rouse and Peters, to provide a good Puritan clergy. [1654
1074. **French Ch.** Pascal, scared by a carriage accident, enters Port-Royal.
1075. **Church Hist.** Cromwell commissions Dury to work for re-union in Switzerland, Germany and Holland.
1076. **Eng. Lit.** Roger Boyle's Parthenissa imitates the French Romans de longue Haleine, at this time widely read in England.
1077. **American Lit.** Johnson's Wonder Working Providence of New England replies to the charges against the colonists and contends that the settlements were undertaken for religious purposes, and are sustained by miracles.
1078. **Dutch Lit.** Vondel's Lucifer, a drama in five acts.
1079. **Science.** Pascal and Fermat found the theory of probabilities.

Hobbes, who has spoken slightingly of the Universities and urged the State to teach obedience to itself and to prohibit the study of scholastic philosophy and the classics, is attacked by Ward, Professor of Astronomy at Oxford and by Wallis, Professor of Mathematics, who mercilessly expose his mathematics and science. The controversy with Wallis continues till 1678.

Glisson discovers the fibrous sheath of the liver known as 'Glisson's Capsules' and detects irritability.
1080. **Philosophy.** The controversy between Hobbes and Bishop Bramhall on the Freedom of the Will begins.
1081. **Politics.** Milton's Defensio Secunda attacks a reply to his Defensio Prima written by Peter Dumoulin, and edited by Morus, a Scot, and urges the Protector to associate the 'Commonwealths men' in the Government.

Conring's De Finibus Imperii Germanici discusses the relation of the Empire to the States.
1082. **Social.** Petty executes a survey of Irish land, rendered necessary by the changes of the last generation.
1083. **Deaths.** Gataker, Oxenstiern, Selden.

1084. **Eng. Ch.** Frightened by the rising in Wiltshire, the Protector forbids the private use of the services of the Church, the employment of Anglican clergy as chaplains or schoolmasters, and the practice of repeating prayers from memory. Gunning, however, continues to preach in London, and the Episcopal Church is upheld by Hammond, Sheldon, Sanderson and others. [1655

Cromwell is induced by Manasseh ben Israel of Amsterdam to consider the return of the Jews. The committee appointed failing to agree, Cromwell resolves to proceed alone, despite the attacks of Prynne and others. The Jews from this time gradually creep back.

720. **Sweden.** Charles X. invades Poland, whose King, Casimir, refuses to recognise him, and overruns the country almost without resistance. The Great Elector, hitherto neutral, prepares to bar his return, but is attacked and defeated.

721. **Switzerland.** An attempt to draft a new federal constitution fails, and the Catholic cantons renew the Borromean League. The first Vilmergen war breaks out, in which the Protestants are defeated, and after which the sovereign right of each state is affirmed.

722. **Asia.** The Emperor of China allows Russia to send a caravan yearly to Pekin. Russia also builds some forts on the south shore of the Amur, and moves steadily towards the East. The Chinese Government, finally, determines to hinder the advance, demolishes the forts, and forces Russia to sign the treaty of Nertchinsk (1689) (the first treaty concluded by China with an European power), promising not to meddle with the territory south of the Amur.

---

723. **England.** War is declared by Spain, and a second Parliament is summoned to grant money, about 100 members of which are, however, excluded. Part of the Spanish treasure-fleet is captured. [1656

Vane's Healing Question, written in response to the Protector's request for advice, advocates the calling of a Constituent Assembly.

724. **Portugal.** A fleet under Blake and Montague compels King John to ratify his treaty with England.

725. **Sweden.** The Great Elector is forced to make a treaty with Charles X., agreeing to hold the duchy of Prussia of Sweden (Jan.). The Poles rise and repulse the Swedes, and Charles obtains the alliance of the Elector by ceding part of Poland. With his aid, he defeats John Casimir in the three days' battle of Warsaw. To retain the alliance, Charles surrenders his suzerainty over the duchy of Prussia. The other nations are by this time alarmed, and Russia interrupts her conflict with Poland to ally with her against Sweden. The Emperor and the Danes at the same time declare against Sweden. Charles thereupon secures the help of Rakoksy of Transylvania, and attacks Russia in Lithuania. At this moment the Danes, with the Emperor and the Dutch, attack the Swedish coasts, and Charles returns.

726. **Turkey.** After a long period of misrule, Kiuprili, an Albanian, becomes Vizier, and reorganises the State and the Army. His son, Turkey's greatest statesman, succeeds him 1661, and for 15 years maintains his position as virtual Sultan. Though his administration is successful, his military career is a complete failure.

The Venetians destroy a Turkish fleet.

1085. **French Ch.** The Duc de Liancourt, a rich patron of Port-Royal, is refused absolution at St Sulpice unless he deserts the Jansenists. Arnauld writes two pamphlets, denying that the condemned propositions are in the Augustinus, and is in consequence expelled from the Sorbonne.

La Peyrére's Systema Theologicum, the first definitely rationalist work on creation, inspiration, miracles.

D'Achéry's Spicilegium (in which Mabillon shares), the first of a long series of works of erudition issuing from the Benedictines of St Maur.

1086. **German Ch.** Calov's Consensus of the Lutheran Faith attacks Calixtus' Syncretism, and is approved by Wittenberg and Leipsig. The symbol, however, is rejected at Jena by the pupils of Gerhard, and never becomes widely adopted. Calov commences his Loci Theologici, a summary of rigid Lutheran orthodoxy.

1087. **History.** Dugdale's Monasticon.

1088. **Philosophy.** Stanley's History of Philosophy.

1089. **Eng. Ch.** Muggleton and Reeve describe the revelations [1656 vouchsafed to them in the Divine Looking-glass, and proclaim themselves the two witnesses of the Apocalypse.

1090. **French Ch.** The Pope declares the condemned propositions to be in the Augustinus, and all ecclesiastics are ordered to accept this decision.

Pascal's (anonymous) Lettres Provinciales attack the Jesuits, 1—3 dealing with Grace and the condemnation of Arnauld, 4—16 attacking Jesuit casuistry. The last two letters return to the 5 Propositions and assert that the Pope is infallible in matters of faith alone. The work is answered by Père Daniel and others, but initiates a reaction in favour of Port-Royal which is increased by the effect of the Sainte Épine on Pascal's niece.

1091. **Dutch Ch.** Spinoza, after narrowly escaping assassination, is excommunicated by the Jews at Amsterdam.

1092. **American Ch.** The Quakers reach Massachusetts and are violently persecuted, a few being killed.

1093. **Eng. Lit.** Cowley's Pindaric Odes.

Waller's Ode to Cromwell.

1094. **French Lit.** Chapelain's Epic, La Pucelle, obtains a great though short-lived popularity.

1095. **Science.** Wallis' Arithmetica Infinitorum extends the methods of analysis of Descartes and Cavalieri.

1096. **Politics.** Harrington's Oceana, a system of aristocratic republicanism, strongly influenced by Venetian institutions, containing remarkable anticipations of modern reforms in regard to education, the franchise, and the ballot, imposing a limit on accumulation of land and filling the offices of state by rotation, appeals to the Protector to reorganise the government. Harrington's system is attacked by Baxter in his Holy Commonwealth on the ground that men are not wise or good enough to make it a success.

727. **England.** In return for a grant of money, Cromwell removes the Major-Generals. Parliament offers the Protector the title of King, and the power to appoint his successor, and draws up the Humble Petition and Advice, by which the members of the Council of State are nominated and removable by consent of Parliament, which is to consist of two Houses. The Protector accepts the new Constitution, but refuses the Kingship. Meanwhile Blake destroys a Spanish fleet off Teneriffe, but dies on his way home. [1657

728. **France.** Condé's success against Turenne encourages Spain, and the war revives. Cromwell sends 6,000 men to co-operate, and Mardyck is taken.

729. **Sweden.** The Great Elector joins Poland against Sweden, and receives Prussia free from Polish suzerainty. The Swedes are driven out of Poland, retaining only Polish Prussia. Charles, however, attacks Denmark, with which the Great Elector allies.

730. **Hungary.** George Rakoksy II., wishing to extend the power of Transylvania, allies with Sweden for the partition of Poland, and gains several victories. He is crushed, however, by Imperialist and Turkish armies and deposed, part of Transylvania passing under direct Turkish rule.

731. **Asia.** Aurungzebe deposes his father and becomes Emperor.

---

732. **England.** The Commons meet for their second session and restore the excluded members; but on attacking the Upper House, they are dissolved (Feb.). The Protector loses his favourite daughter (Aug.), and dies (Sept. 3), and is succeeded by his son Richard, whom he is said to have named on his death-bed. [1658

733. **France.** With the aid of the English troops, Turenne routs the Spaniards under Condé and Don John at the battle of the Dunes (June), and takes Dunkirk, which is retained by England.

734. **Germany.** Failing to secure the election of Louis as Emperor, Mazarin creates a Confederation of the Rhine, nominally to guarantee the Treaty of Westphalia.

735. **Sweden.** Charles crosses the frozen belt to Copenhagen, and compels Denmark to cede her East Sound provinces and to close the Baltic against the enemies of Sweden (Feb.). Charles concludes a truce with Russia, and again attacks Denmark, which receives aid from the Dutch and the Great Elector.

736. **Asia.** The Dutch take Jaffnapatam, the last important Portuguese port in Ceylon.

---

737. **England.** Richard is attacked by the officers, who demand that Fleetwood shall become their general and independent of the Protector. The latter demand is refused, and the army forces Richard to dissolve Parliament (April). A fortnight later, 42 members of the Rump, ejected in 1653, meet at Westminster and attempt to dictate to the officers. Richard abdicates (May), and Booth rises in [1659

1097. **History.** Fuller's Church History of Britain.
1098. **Deaths.** Calixtus, Gassendi, Ussher.

1099. **Eng. Ch.** The Whole Duty of Man (anonymous) is published with a preface by Hammond. [1657
1100. **French Ch.** De Marca draws up a formula of renunciation of the 5 Propositions, which the Pope approves. Arnauld again denies that the condemned tenets are in the Augustinus.
1101. **German Ch.** Angelus Silesius (Scheffler), a recent convert to Catholicism, publishes his Geistliche Seelenlust, a collection of mystical songs, influenced by his study of Behmen.

Schupp's Solomon, Friend in Need, and other didactic tracts, foster practical theology.

1102. **French Lit.** Ninon's Salon in Paris is frequented by the Libertins, St Evremond, Scarron, Gourville, Sarrasin, and later, by Lafare, Chaulieu and the habitués of the Temple.
1103. **Science.** The Academia del Cimento is founded at Florence, among its members being Torricelli and Castellio. The Society exists for 10 years.
1104. **Education.** Comenius' Orbis Sensualium Pictus, the child's first picture-book.

Cromwell founds a University at Durham for the northern counties. It is suppressed at the Restoration, but revived 1837.

1105. **Philology.** Brian Walton completes his Polyglot, in nine languages, aided by Pococke, Thorndike, Hyde, Hammond, Ussher, Lightfoot, and other scholars.
1106. **History.** Prynne's Abridgement of the Records of the Tower.
1107. **Deaths.** Carpzov, Harvey.

1108. **Eng. Ch.** The Savoy Declaration, the fundamental Congregational Confession, is drawn up by Goodwin, Owen, and Nye, and differs but slightly from the Westminster Confession. [1658
1109. **Science.** Pascal, following the work of Roberval, solves certain problems of the cycloid by the method of indivisibles. His work in this direction is continued by Wallis, 1659.

Sylvius becomes Professor of Medicine at Leyden and founds the iatro-chemical school, owing something to Paracelsus and Van Helmont. The teaching is imported into England by Thomas Willis.

Huyghens invents the cycloidal pendulum and applies the pendulum to clocks.

1110. **Philosophy.** Gassendi's Syntagma Philosophicum, less materialist than his criticisms on Descartes, presents a theory of ideas that almost anticipates Locke, and a system of Epicurean Ethics.
1111. **Philology.** Lightfoot's Horae Hebraicae.
1112. **Eng. Lit.** Sir T. Browne's Hydriotaphia advocates cremation.

1113. **Eng. Ch.** Pearson's Exposition of the Apostles' Creed. [1659

Stillingfleet, influenced by his training under the Cambridge

Cheshire for Charles II., but is defeated by Lambert (Aug.). The Rump is excluded from the House by Lambert (Oct.), but, after the failure of Ludlow's attempt to appoint Conservators of Liberty, is restored by the officers, who discover that they cannot obtain taxes (Dec.).

738. **France.** Mazarin negociates the Peace of the Pyrenees, by which Louis XIV. is to marry the Infanta, and France receives Roussillon, Artois and a number of fortresses on the N.E. frontier. Lorraine is to be conditionally restored to Charles, and the Governorship of Burgundy to Condé, and Portugal is not to be further assisted.

739. **Sweden.** The Great Elector drives the Swedes from the mainland. Holland, France and England ally to keep the Baltic open and force Charles X. to make peace.

---

740. **England.** Monk crosses the border, is joined by Fairfax at York, and enters London (Feb. 3). The City refuses to pay [1660 taxes without representation, and Monk declares for a free Parliament (Feb. 16). The Rump recalls the Presbyterians excluded by Pride, and Parliament votes its own dissolution and orders a new election. By the Declaration of Breda, Charles promises amnesty, toleration, payment of the soldiers' arrears, and confirmation of transfers of land (April 4). Parliament meets (April 25), and welcomes the Declaration, invites the King to return, and declares for the old Constitution. The King enters London (May 29). Hyde becomes supreme, and a return is tacitly made to the situation of August, 1641. A partial indemnity is granted, and 13 regicides, with Vane, are hanged. The army is paid, and, except for two regiments, disbanded, military tenures and feudal dues are abolished, and a revenue of £1,200,000, drawn from tonnage and poundage and excise is settled on the King.

Councils of Trade and Foreign Plantations are formed.

741. **France.** Louis marries the Infanta, who is compelled by the Spanish Court to renounce her claim to the Spanish throne, on condition of receiving a dowry, which is never paid.

742. **Sweden.** Charles dies, and the war is terminated by the treaty of Oliva between Sweden, Poland and Brandenburg, conquests being restored and Casimir renouncing his claims to the Swedish crown and to Esthonia and Livonia. The sovereignty of Russia is recognised by Sweden and Poland. Peace is renewed with Denmark, which surrenders the south of Scandinavia. The pacification of the north is completed by a treaty between Sweden and Russia, each restoring conquests, 1661. The Swedish estates confer almost unlimited power on the King.

743. **Denmark.** The clergy and citizens force the nobles to share in taxation, make the Crown hereditary, abrogate the privileges extorted from the infant King, and place the whole government under royal control.

744. **Turkey.** The Emperor sends Montecuculi to defend Transylvania, thus for the first time for 100 years becoming involved in war with the Porte.

Platonists, urges in his Irenicum a compromise between systems of Church government, none of which, in his opinion, can claim divine right.

More attacks Hobbes in his Immortality of the Soul.

Thorndike's Epilogue to the Tragedy of the Church of England emphasizes the need of return to the primitive Church.

1114. **French Ch.** A synod of the Protestant Church is held under the presidency of Daillé; the King, however, forbids further meetings.

1115. **French Lit.** Molière, who has settled in Paris and played before the Court 1658, produces his first masterpiece, Les Précieuses Ridicules, in part suggested by the affectations of the Rambouillet circle.

St Evremond is banished for his criticism on the Treaty of the Pyrenees, and settles in England.

1116. **German Lit.** Grimmelshausen's Simplicissimus.

1117. **Science.** Huyghens discovers that Saturn is surrounded by a ring.

1118. **Politics.** Various plans of government are suggested in England, Harrington's theories being discussed at the Rota Club and exciting special notice.

1119. **Eng. Ch.** Clarendon draws up a Declaration on behalf of the King making a number of concessions to nonconformists, which, however, are rejected by Parliament. (Oct.) [1660

Henry More's Mystery of Godliness, a system of mystical theosophy.

1120. **Scotch Ch.** Lay patronage is restored, the leading Covenanters are imprisoned, and Rutherford's Lex Rex and Guthrie's Causes of God's Wrath are called in.

1121. **Irish Ch.** The Irish Catholics are offered toleration if they will swear allegiance to the King and repudiate the Pope's claim to depose him. An address is drawn up by Carew and Walsh, and signed by 120 nobles, but is condemned by the Irish Bishops and the papal nuncio at Brussels.

1122. **Polish Ch.** Unitarians are expelled from Poland, and settle in large numbers in Holland.

1123. **Eng. Lit.** Pepys begins his Diary, which he keeps for 9 years.

1124. **German Lit.** Gryphius' Geliebte Dornrose.

1125. **Science.** The scientists (see 1645) again begin to meet at Gresham College, fulfilling the schemes of Bolton, 1616, Charles I., and more recently, of Evelyn, Cowley, and Petty for a college. Boyle, Wallis, Wren, Brouncker, and others, are incorporated as the Royal Society, 1662, and begin to publish Transactions, 1665. The Society is attacked by South, Gunning, and Stubbe, as hostile to religion and morality.

1126. **Philosophy.** Jeremy Taylor's Ductor Dubitantium, the most systematic English work on Casuistry.

1127. **Politics.** Milton's Ready Nay to establish a free Commonwealth recommends the election of a Grand Council, chosen for life.

1128. **Social.** Women appear on the stage, in part owing to the example of Mrs Betterton.

1129. **Deaths.** Hammond, Vincent de Paul, Velasquez.

---

745. **England.** A few Fifth Monarchy men, led by Venner, revolt in the City, but are easily suppressed, and political Millenarianism finally disappears. The incident, however, strengthens the reaction and allows the King to retain some regiments. A new Cavalier Parliament meets, declares war against the King to be unlawful, and passes the Corporation Act, by which all municipal officers must renounce the Covenant and receive the Sacrament according to Anglican rites. [1661

Charles announces his intended Portuguese marriage, to which he is encouraged by Louis. Charles promises to assist the Portuguese with troops and a fleet.

746. **Scotland.** The old form of government is restored, Argyle is executed, and the persecution of the Covenanters begins. Guthrie is executed, Rutherford escapes by death, Gillespie recants. Episcopacy is restored, and Sharp becomes Archbishop of St Andrews. A revolt is quelled at Ruthen Green.

747. **Ireland.** By the Act of Settlement, settlers during the Interregnum are confirmed in possession of their lands, and Catholics unconcerned in the rebellion of 1641 are restored. By the Act of Explanation, 1665, adventurers and soldiers surrender one-third of their lands.

748. **France.** Mazarin dies, and the King, aided by Le Tellier, Lionne and Louvois, who reorganises the army, personally assumes the government. Fouquet, the superintendent of the finances, is dismissed and succeeded by Colbert, who is recommended by Mazarin.

749. **Russia.** By the peace of Kardis, Russia ends the war with Sweden, and abandons all claims to Livonia.

750. **America.** Massachusetts draws up a Declaration of Rights, asserting its claim to defend itself against all who disturb the colony, and declares against the Navigation Act.

---

751. **England.** The sale of Dunkirk to France for £200,000 evokes angry remonstrances directed against Clarendon. [1662

752. **France.** The French Ambassador at Rome being maltreated by the Pope's Corsican guards, Louis sends troops to Rome and seizes Avignon, 1663, and the Pope is forced to send a legate to demand pardon. The King also refuses to lower his flag to England, and obtains ceremonial precedence for the French over the Spanish ambassador in London.

753. **Holland.** De Witt makes treaties with France and England, which promise aid if attacked.

754. **America.** Connecticut receives a liberal Charter.

755. **Asia.** Sivaji, chief of the Mahratta Confederacy of the Deccan, begins to fight with Aurungzebe, asserts his independence, 1664, and

1130. **Eng. Ch.** A conference to discuss the revision of the Prayer-book takes place at the Savoy Palace, the Anglicans led by Sheldon, Morley, Gunning, and Pearson, the Presbyterians by Baxter. The objections to the Prayer-book are not accepted, and the four months granted for the Conference elapse before the discussion is ended. The King orders Convocation to revise the Prayer-book. [1661

Beveridge's Private Thoughts on Religion.

1131. **Scotch Ch.** A packed Parliament passes an Oath of Allegiance to the king as supreme over all persons and in all causes, and Episcopacy is restored by proclamation.

1132. **French Ch.** The Declaration of 1656 is enforced, and four Bishops protest. The residents of Port-Royal refuse to declare that the Propositions are in Jansen and not in Augustine. The schools are therefore closed, and an interdict is laid on the abbey. Mère Angélique dies, and some of the inmates yield.

1133. **German Ch.** Grossgebauer's Alarm Cry demands an increase of preaching, and the concession of further privileges and power to the laity.

1134. **Church Hist.** At the instance of the King of Spain, Alexander VII. issues a Constitution, recommending the Immaculate Conception, which is hotly attacked by Launoy and others.

1135. **Eng. Lit.** Betterton joins Davenant's company at Lincoln's Inn Fields theatre.

1136. **French Lit.** Benserade begins to write ballets for the court. Pastoral poetry is initiated by Segrais, Fontenelle, and Mme. Deshouliéres.

1137. **German Lit.** Lohenstein's Cleopatra founds the Second Silesian school.

1138. **Science.** Malpighi discovers with the microscope the air-cells of the lungs, and shows that minute tubes, called capillaries, connect the arteries and the veins. He also discovers the vascular coils in the cortex of the kidney.

Boyle discovers his Law of Compressibility, i.e. that the volume of a gas decreases with the pressure.

Steno discovers Steno's conduit, and explains the saliva and investigates the muscles.

1139. **Philosophy.** Glanvil's Vanity of Dogmatising, partly influenced by Descartes, attacks the validity of the idea of Cause.

1140. **Philology.** Dalgarno's Ars Signorum suggests an universal language. Wilkins makes a similar attempt 1668.

Ludolf's Aethiopic Grammar and Lexicon.

1141. **Death.** Fuller.

1142. **Eng. Ch.** By the Act of Uniformity, clergy and schoolmasters, failing to use and assent to everything in the revised Prayer-book, to receive episcopal ordination, and to condemn the Covenant and resistance, by August 24, are ordered to resign. Several hundred Presbyterian ministers in consequence leave the Church. [1662

The Prayer-book, revised by Convocation and greatly aided by the collections of Cosin, is accepted by Parliament.

maintains it till his death, 1680. The Mahrattas gradually become the dominant power in the south, and encourage the small Mohamedan states in resistance to Aurungzebe's life-long purpose of subjugating the Deccan.

Catherine of Portugal brings Bombay as a dowry, which Charles sells to the East India Company. The seat of the Western Presidency is fixed there, 1687.

The Dutch take Cochin, the principal Portuguese station in South India, and the chief pepper ports on the Malabar coasts.

756. **Africa.** A new African company is formed, and contracts to supply slaves to the British West Indies.

Catherine of Braganza brings with her Tangier as a dowry.

---

757. **Ireland.** Irish ships are excluded from the benefit of the [1663
Navigation Laws.

758. **Germany.** The Diet of the Empire at Regensburg becomes permanent.

759. **Portugal.** Don John takes Evora; but Lisbon is saved by a victory at Almexial, in which the English auxiliaries share.

760. **Turkey.** The Turks seize the Upper Danube.

761. **America.** Rhode Island receives a Charter under which it lives till 1842.

The Colony of Carolina, south of Virginia, is founded by Clarendon, Monk, Shaftesbury, and other proprietaries.

Colbert incorporates a new Company to colonise Guiana, and unites it with the West Indies under a West India Company, 1665.

762. **West Indies.** Barbadoes passes to the English Crown.

---

763. **England.** The King persuades Parliament to repeal the [1664
Triennial Act of 1641; but the interval between Parliaments is limited to three years.

War with the Dutch breaks out, chiefly owing to friction in West Africa; ports are seized in the West Indies and Guinea.

764. **France.** Colbert establishes trading Companies for India and the Levant. His first tariff, unlike his second tariff, 1677, admits raw materials free. Colbert fails to build up manufactures for lack of markets, harasses agriculture by his changeable policy in regard to exportation, and cripples his trading Companies by a too strict monopoly. He neglects to remove the internal tolls on road and river.

Stillingfleet's Origines Sacrae declares primitive bishops no more than the equal of presbyters.

1143. **Scotch Ch.** Presbyterian assemblies are forbidden ; nobody may become a minister or schoolmaster without a bishop's license, nor may hold an office of public trust without abjuring the Covenant. 400 ministers refuse and are ejected.

1144. **Church Hist.** Antoinette Bourignon gathers round her a circle of believers in her revelations. She obtains great success in the Spanish Netherlands, where Poiret becomes her friend and interpreter.

1145. **American Ch.** Wigglesworth's poem on the Day of Doom depicts the damnation of unbaptised infants.

1146. **Eng. Lit.** Fuller's Worthies of England.

The Licensing Act revives many of the provisions of the Star Chamber Ordinances.

1147. **Art.** Le Brun, a pupil of Vouet and Poussin, becomes first painter to the King.

1148. **Philosophy.** Arnauld and Nicole compose the Cartesian Logique de Port-Royal, which is accepted by Bossuet and Fénelon, used in Holland, Germany, England and Italy, and remains the authorised text-book till Empiricism becomes dominant in the 18th century.

1149. **Economics.** Petty's Treatise on Taxes and Contributions allows the export of money, and declares that price depends on cost of production, and that division of labour tends to cheapness.

1150. **Death.** Pascal.

1151. **Eng. Ch.** The King's request for an Act allowing him to use the dispensing power is opposed by Clarendon and rejected [1663 by Parliament. The tolerant Archbishop Juxon is succeeded by Sheldon.

Convocation for the last time grants a subsidy.

1152. **Eng. Lit.** Butler satirises Puritanism in Hudibras.

L'Estrange is appointed licenser of the press, and issues The Intelligencer.

Dryden's The Wild Gallant originates the Restoration Comedy, developed by Etherege, Shadwell, Sedley, Mrs Behn, Wycherley.

1153. **French Lit.** The Académie des Inscriptions et Belles-Lettres is founded.

1154. **Science.** Newton discovers the Binomial Theorem.

Pascal's L'Équilibre des Liqueurs is published, proving that the pressure on a liquid is transmitted undiminished in all directions and acts with the same force on all equal surfaces in a direction at right angles to them.

1155. **Death.** Sanderson.

1156. **Eng. Ch.** The first Conventicle Act forbids nonconformist meetings of more than four besides the household under heavy [1664 penalties.

Tillotson becomes preacher at Lincoln's Inn, his Sermons being regarded as models for a century.

765. **Turkey.** Montecuculi, aided by French troops, routs the Turks at St Gothard. Owing, however, to Leopold's anxiety to terminate the war, a truce of 20 years is made, the continued quasi-independence of Transylvania being recognised.

766. **America.** Nicolls, one of the Commissioners sent to investigate complaints against Massachusetts, takes New Netherlands almost without a blow. Charles gives the territory to his brother; but the Duke grants the southern part to favourites, and names it New Jersey.

[1665

767. **England.** Parliament appropriates a large sum for the war, and the Duke of York wins a decisive victory off Southwold Bay (June). Charles employs the Bishop of Munster to attack the States on the flank.

768. **Ireland.** Irish cattle and dairy produce are excluded from England.

769. **Spain.** Louis offers to help to crush Portugal if Spain will declare his wife's renunciation invalid, or will cede Franche-Comté and part of the Netherlands. Philip refuses, and is routed by French and Portuguese troops at Villa Viciosa, which secures Portuguese independence and gives a final blow to Spain. Philip IV. dies, and is succeeded by his sickly son, Charles II. Maria Anna of Austria becomes Regent, but her subjection to her Jesuit confessor Nithard leads to the formation of a party under the late King's natural son, Don John, and the expulsion of Nithard, 1669.

770. **Austria.** The younger line of the Hapsburgs dies out, and Tyrol falls to the Emperor.

771. **America.** New Haven unites with Connecticut.

[1666

772. **England.** Louis, as an ally of Holland, declares war against England (Jan.), and drives off the Bishop of Munster. The Dutch, under Ruyter, defeat Monk and Rupert in a four days' battle off Dover (June), but are themselves worsted off the North Foreland (July).

Algernon Sydney and other exiles plot with Louis to raise a rebellion in England; but the plan fails, owing to the disapproval of De Witt.

Parliament appoints a Committee to inspect the accounts of naval and other officials.

1157. **Scotch Ch.** A Court of High Commission with unlimited powers is erected, on the advice of Sharp, Archbishop of St Andrews. A revolt breaks out, but is crushed at Pentland.

1158. **French Ch.** Nicole's Perpetuité de la Foi touchant l'Eucharistie contends that a belief in the Real Presence has always existed. The assertion is denied by Claude and other Protestants.

De Rancé begins to reform the abbey of La Trappe.

1159. **French Lit.** Molière's Tartuffe.

1160. **Science.** Willis' Anatome Cerebri first carefully investigates the brain.

1161. **Numismatics.** Spanheim's De Usu Numismatum.

1162. **Social.** Sir Matthew Hale condemns two women for witchcraft, and Sir Thomas Browne gives witness.

1163. **Death.** Amyraut.

1164. **Eng. Ch.** The Five Mile Act which Parliament bribes the King to accept, forbids those who refuse to swear to attempt no changes in Church or State to reside within five miles of a town or of their old ministry. [1665

1165. **French Ch.** Alexander VII. orders Jansenists to submit to the Bull of 1653, declaring the Propositions to be in the Augustinus in the sense condemned.

1166. **Eng. Lit.** Head's The English Rogue revives the picaresque novel.

1167. **French Lit.** La Rochefoucald issues his Maxims, which have been submitted to Mme. de Sablé.

The Journal des Savants, the first literary and scientific review, begins to appear weekly.

La Fontaine's Contes, followed by his Fables, 1668. The weekly dinners of La Fontaine, Boileau, Molière and Racine begin.

Bussy-Rabutin is exiled to his estates for exposing the morals of the Court in his Histoire Amoureuse des Gaules.

1168. **Art.** Perrault constructs the Colonnade of the Louvre.

1169. **Science.** Boyle proves that a candle cannot burn nor an animal breathe without air.

Hooke anticipates the undulatory theory of light.

1170. **Law.** Godefroy edits the Theodosian Code.

1171. **Philology.** Francis Junius edits the Codex Argenteus (Gothic Gospels).

1172. **Social.** The Plague breaks out in London and spreads to the Provinces.

1173. **Deaths.** Fermat, Poussin.

1174. **Eng. Ch.** Bunyan's Grace Abounding, his spiritual autobiography. [1666

1175. **French Ch.** The Huguenots begin to leave France in consequence of persecution.

1176. **Church Hist.** Sabbatai of Smyrna proclaims himself the Messiah and is widely recognised as such, but subsequently embraces Islam.

773. **Germany.** The Great Elector joins with Denmark to guarantee Dutch independence against France.

The Great Elector divides the Cleves-Julich inheritance with the Duke of Neuburg and receives Cleves.

774. **Hungary.** A conspiracy is formed against the Emperor's government by the nobles, who put forward the son of the late Rakoksy. Failing to secure external aid, the movement comes to nothing, and the leaders are seized and executed, 1670.

775. **West Indies.** Residents in the Bermudas move to the Bahamas, which are granted to the Proprietors of Carolina, 1670, and taken over by the English Government, 1717.

---

776. **England.** Louis secretly makes a treaty with Charles, by which he promises not to help the Dutch, in return for a free hand in the Spanish Netherlands. [1667

The Dutch are alarmed by the advance of the French, and open a conference at Breda. Charles disbands his fleet before the treaty is signed, and the Dutch in consequence sail up the Medway and burn English men-of-war. The Treaty is at once signed, England retaining Dutch North America, but surrendering her last spice islands and Surinam.

Meanwhile the Commons demand an inquiry into the expenditure of the money voted for the war. Clarendon protests, and the King seizes the opportunity of the Chancellor's unpopularity to dismiss him. The Commons impeach him; but, on a hint from the King, he withdraws to France. Charles calls to his counsels Buckingham and Arlington.

De Witt and Temple enter into unofficial discussions (Sept.), and the latter goes on a mission to the Hague (Dec.).

777. **France.** Louis, who on the death of Philip IV., 1665, claimed part of the Spanish Netherlands by the Law of Devolution (a feudal law by which property descends to the children of a first marriage), fails to obtain recognition of his claim. He therefore invades Flanders with Turenne, and takes a number of fortresses.

---

778. **France.** The French capture fortress after fortress, and Condé suddenly overruns Franche-Comté. England, Holland and Sweden therefore conclude the Triple Alliance, negociated by De Witt and Temple. A secret article binds England and Holland to reduce France, if she breaks her promises, to the position she occupied [1668

1177. **Eng. Lit.** The London Gazette begins to appear.

1178. **French Lit.** Boileau's Satires attack Chapelain, Ménage, Saint-Amant, and the authors of the Romans de longue Haleine, and respect only Corneille and the followers of Malherbe, Voiture and Racan.

1179. **Science.** Colbert founds the Académie des Sciences.

Newton uses the notation of Fluxions, and shews it in MS. to friends and pupils 1669. He measures the moon's orbit and discovers gravitation, of which he says nothing. He also discovers the dispersion and the compound nature of light, and explains the rainbow.

1180. **Art.** The Gobelin Tapestry Manufactory is instituted in Paris by Colbert.

1181. **Social.** The Great Fire of London burns for three days, destroying the city from the Tower to the Temple and from the Thames to Smithfield, St Paul's and many other churches being burnt. An elaborate plan of reconstruction is designed by Wren, but is not carried out.

Glanvil's Considerations concerning Witches (expanded into Sadducismus Triumphatus, 1681) declares the whole question of belief in the Supernatural at stake.

1182. **Death.** Franz Hals.

1183. **French Ch.** Paul Ferry, a Protestant minister at Metz, discusses reunion with Bossuet. [1667

1184. **Eng. Lit.** Milton's Paradise Lost, perhaps influenced by Vondel's Lucifer, Andreini's Adamo, and Du Bartas' La Semaine.

Dryden's Essay of Dramatic Poesy presents the first example of perfectly modern prose, and contains an eulogy of Shakespeare.

Dryden's Annus Mirabilis.

1185. **French Lit.** Racine, a pupil of Boileau, writes his first great drama, Andromache.

1186. **Science.** An Observatory is established at Paris, to which Cassini is appointed, and where Römer and Huyghens work.

1187. **Law.** Leibnitz' New Methods of Jurisprudence introduces the sanction of a future life, and discusses duties towards God.

Lamoignon compiles the Code Louis, a codification of French legislation. He is prevented from codifying the 285 Droits de Coutume.

1188. **Politics.** Puffendorf's De Statu Imperii Germanici attacks the Hapsburgs and the ecclesiastical princes, and proposes a Confederation, with a perpetual council for foreign affairs, a federal army, the secularisation of the ecclesiastical principalities, the abolition of convents, and the expulsion of the Jesuits.

1189. **Death.** Jeremy Taylor.

1190. **Eng. Ch.** Sir Matthew Hale, on behalf of the latitudinarian school of Wilkins and Stillingfleet drafts a bill for comprehension of all but Catholics and Socinians. The Commons, however, declare that no comprehension bill can be received. [1668

1191. **French Ch.** The Peace of Clement IX. permits the signature of

in 1659. Louis makes the Treaty of Aix-la-Chapelle with Spain, to which he restores Franche-Comté, but retains his conquests in the Spanish Netherlands. Louis has meanwhile secretly arranged with the Emperor to divide the Spanish inheritance, France to receive the Spanish Netherlands, Franche-Comté, Naples, and Sicily, the Emperor to obtain Spain and Spanish America.

779. **Portugal.** By the Treaty of Lisbon, Spain recognises the independence of Portugal.

780. **Switzerland.** The Defensionale, or common military organisation, devised 1647, is put in operation. This union, however, is rapidly broken up by French agents.

---

781. **England.** The Duke of York avows himself a Catholic, and the King secretly announces his own conversion to Arlington, Clifford and other Catholics, and considers how to restore Catholicism in England. [1669

The Committee appointed by Parliament to examine the public accounts secures the dismissal of the Treasurer of the Navy.

A 'Secretary at War' is appointed.

782. **Germany.** The Hanse Diet meets for the last time; henceforth, Lubeck, Hamburg and Bremen alone retain the name of Hanse Towns.

783. **Turkey.** The Turks capture Crete from the Venetians, after 20 years' war.

784. **America.** South Carolina is founded.

---

785. **England.** Charles drops his demand for toleration in return for a Parliamentary grant for eight years. [1670

Negociations are commenced with Louis, who sends Charles' sister Henrietta, Duchess of Orleans, to conclude an alliance. By the secret treaty of Dover, Charles promises to join in an attack on the Dutch and to support Louis' claim on Spain, if the King of Spain dies childless. In return, Louis promises troops and money for Charles' personal defence in case of need, and money during the war, in which a French fleet is to serve under an English admiral (June). Louise de Kérouaille is sent to keep Charles to his engagements. A promise to declare himself a Catholic at his convenience is confided only to Clifford and Arlington.

786. **France.** France allies with Bavaria, agreeing to act together in any partition of Spain or on the death of the Emperor.

The Duke of Lorraine is exiled for his negociations with the Dutch, and Lorraine is occupied by the French.

787. **America.** Sir Henry Morgan, the most famous of the Buccaneers,

the declaration of 1656, without asserting Jansen the author of the condemned propositions.

Mabillon collects and edits the Acta Sanctorum of his Order.

1192. **Eng. Lit.** Mrs Behn's Oronoko draws a picture of the happiness and virtue of the negro.

1193. **French Lit.** Racine's Comedy, Les Plaideurs.

1194. **Science.** Redi finds that maggots in meat are due not to spontaneous generation but to the eggs of flies.

1195. **Economics.** Child's Observations concerning Trade and Interest urge that a low rate of interest should be fixed, allows export of cash where necessary, and thinks the Navigation Act good politics rather than good economics.

1196. **Death.** Rembrandt.

1197. **Eng. Ch.** Gale's Court of the Gentiles attempts to establish that Greek philosophy is a distorted reproduction of the Bible. [1669

1198. **Austrian Ch.** Abraham a Santa Clara becomes Court-Preacher at Vienna, and by his witty and earnest sermons and books contributes to the religious revival.

1199. **Dutch Ch.** Labadie, a convert to Protestantism, refuses to sign the Confessio Belgica. He is deposed from his pastorate at Middelburg, and forms a new congregation at Amsterdam, with the aid of Anna Schurmann, based on Quietism and Communism. The community breaks up, 1725.

1200. **French Lit.** Mme. de Sévigné's daughter marries the Comte de Grignan and receives innumerable letters from her mother.

Bossuet begins his Oraisons funèbres.

1201. **Literature.** The letters of a Portuguese nun to a French officer appear in a French translation.

1202. **Science.** Malpighi studies silk-worms and other insects.

Swammerdam's History of Insects.

Bartholinus observes the division of a ray in Iceland spar.

Vauban writes La Conduite des Siéges.

1203. **Art.** The Académie Royale de Musique is instituted under Lully, a Florentine, who introduces the style of Carissimi, which lasts till Gluck.

1204. **History.** Anthony Wood's Antiquities of Oxford.

1205. **Deaths.** Coccejus, Escobar, Geulincx, Prynne.

1206. **Eng. Ch.** Jane Leade, with the aid of her master, Pordage, founds the Philadelphian Society. [1670

1207. **Scotch Ch.** Leighton, sometime Principal and Professor of Theology at Edinburgh, becomes Archbishop of Glasgow.

1208. **French Ch.** Pascal's Pensées, mutilated fragments of a great work on religion, appear posthumously.

1209. **Spanish Ch.** Maria d'Agreda's Mystica Ciudad de Dios.

1210. **Dutch Ch.** Spinoza's Tractatus Theologico-Politicus maintains that complete religious liberty is essential to the safety of a state,

attacks Panama and opens the way to the Pacific, where the Buccaneers cripple Spanish trade.

Charles grants a charter to Prince Rupert and 17 others as the Hudson Bay Company. They trade specially in furs.

788. **West Indies.** The Treaty of Madrid formally recognises the West Indian possessions of England.

---

789. **England.** To mislead his ministers, the King sends Buckingham to Paris to negociate a sham treaty, omitting mention of Charles' conversion, and representing all the money as a contribution to the war. [1671

790. **France.** Treaties of alliance or neutrality are made with several of the German States and with the Emperor. At the same moment, the death of Lionne, the Foreign Secretary, throws the power into the hands of Louvois, the Minister of War, an advocate of an aggressive policy.

791. **Holland.** A defensive treaty is made with Spain.

792. **Hungary.** A plan to eject the Germans is betrayed, and confiscations take place. Oppressive taxes are imposed, the Constitution is abolished, and Hungary becomes a province of Austria.

793. **West Indies.** The Government of the Leeward Islands is separated from Barbados and the Windward Islands.

The Danes settle in St Thomas.

794. **Africa.** France builds a fort at Whydah, in Dahomey, on the Gold Coast.

---

795. **England.** The King, in his need of money, refuses, probably on the suggestion of Clifford, to repay the principal of the Goldsmiths' loan, and reduces the interest from 12 p.c. to 6 p.c. (Jan.). [1672

796. **France.** Leibnitz recommends Louis to conquer Egypt and secure the monopoly of the Mediterranean trade.

797. **Holland.** The English fleet, without awaiting the declaration of war, attacks a Dutch merchant fleet (April); but the Duke of York is slightly worsted by Ruyter in Southwold Bay (June).

Louis, who declares war (April), crosses the Rhine and captures city after city almost without resistance. Though turned back by the cutting of the dykes, he rejects the favourable conditions offered by De Witt. The Stadtholderate is revived for William, now 22 years old, and the De Witts are murdered by the mob.

The rapid advance of the French induces the Great Elector to promise to aid the Dutch with 22,000 men, and the Emperor to ally with Brandenburg. The German armies, however, are kept at bay on the Rhine by Turenne.

denies that Moses wrote the Pentateuch, and declares that miracles do not happen.

1211. **Eng. Lit.** Dryden's Conquest of Granada, his masterpiece in the heroic style. The type is carried on by Crowne and Settle, and a little later, by Otway (Venice preserved), Lee, Congreve (Mourning Bride), Southerne and Rowe. Buckingham and others ridicule the extravagances of the heroic drama in The Rehearsal, 1671.

1212. **French Lit.** Molière's Le Bourgeois Gentilhomme.

1213. **Science.** The papers of Malpighi and Grew on vegetable anatomy are read before the Royal Society.

Mayow's experiments on respiration and combustion reveal the existence of two gases in the air, which he describes though does not name. His work is for the time superseded by Becher's theory of Phlogiston.

1214. **Politics.** The Fundamental Constitutions of Carolina are drawn up on the lines of a modified feudalism; but religious liberty is granted, probably at the instance of Locke.

1215. **Philosophy.** The Abbé Villars' Comte de Gabalis, a Rosicrucian romance.

1216. **Social.** Corn imported into England is charged 8*s.* a quarter between 53*s.* 4*d.* and 80*s.*, 16*s.* between 44*s.* and 53*s.* 4*d.*, and 21*s.* 9*d.* under 44*s.*

1217. **Eng. Ch.** Penn's Great Case of Liberty of Conscience.

1218. **French Ch.** Bossuet's conciliatory Exposition de la Foi [1671 Catholique becomes almost a symbolical book, converts Turenne and others, and is attacked by Jurieu.

Quesnel, a Jansenist Oratorian, publishes his Réflexions Morales sur le Nouveau Testament.

1219. **Bohemian Ch.** Comenius, the last Bishop of the Bohemian Brethren, dies.

1220. **Eng. Lit.** Milton's Paradise Regained, and Samson Agonistes.

1221. **French Lit.** Nicole's Essais de Morale.

1222. **Eng. Ch.** The King issues a Declaration of Indulgence, [1672 suspending penalties against Dissenters and Catholics.

1223. **French Ch.** Fléchier's funeral oration on Madame de Montausier.

1224. **Church Hist.** The last synod of the whole Greek Church is held at Jerusalem. The creed of Cyril Lucar is condemned, though his authorship is denied by Dositheus, and the Confession of Mogilas is adopted.

1225. **History.** Conring disproves the validity of the Charter of Lindau, the best piece of historical criticism before Mabillon.

1226. **Politics.** Puffendorf's De Jure Naturae et Gentium attempts to evolve a system of jurisprudence from the study of human nature. Law is derived from reason, the civil law and revelation; that is, there are three disciplines, natural law, civil law and moral theology. Natural law confines itself to regulating external acts. The state of nature was one of peace, but political institutions are necessary for progress.

798. **Sweden.** France allies with Sweden, which is anxious for money, and undertakes to make a diversion in Germany.

---

799. **England.** Rupert is defeated off the Texel, being deserted by the French fleet (Aug.). English opinion at this point begins to turn against France. [1673

Shaftesbury, who has recently learned of the secret treaty of Dover, turns against the Catholic party, supports the Test Act, which leads to the resignation of Clifford and the Duke of York, and is dismissed. The Cabal is broken up, and Osborne, later Earl of Danby, becomes chief minister.

The Duke of York marries Mary of Modena.

800. **France.** A secret Partition Treaty is signed at Vienna, by which the Emperor is to have Spain, the Indies and Milan, and Louis the Low Countries, Naples and Sicily (Jan.).

The Great Elector, wearied by his want of success, makes terms with France, and thus ends the first coalition. At the same time, Vauban reduces Maestricht. The war, however, now changes its character. The Emperor, Spain, Denmark, Saxony and Lorraine join in a new coalition against France. Montecuculi joins William, Bonn is captured, and the French are driven from the Rhine. The German Princes, except Bavaria, sever their connection with France.

The Parliament of Paris is forbidden to make remonstrances till the royal Edicts are registered.

The Man in the Iron Mask is imprisoned in the Bastille.

801. **America.** Frontenac reaches Quebec as Governor, builds Fort Frontenac at Ontario, and conciliates the Iroquois.

---

802. **England.** Charles is compelled by Parliament to make peace with the Dutch by the Treaty of London, the Dutch paying an indemnity and agreeing to salute the English flag (Feb.). Though remaining on friendly terms with Louis, the King offers his niece, Mary, to William, who refuses, expecting James to have a son. [1674

803. **France.** Sweden alone remains the ally of Louis, who, in consequence, attempts in vain to make peace with William. Franche-Comté is finally taken (May), and Condé fights a fierce but indecisive battle against the Dutch and Spanish at Seneff (Aug.) Turenne crosses the Rhine, defeats the Imperial troops and devastates the Palatinate.

804. **Holland.** The Stadtholderate is declared by the States-General hereditary in the Orange family.

805. **Poland.** Sobiesky, already distinguished for his victories over the Turks, becomes King of Poland.

International law is not restricted to Christian nations, since all nations form part of humanity.

1227. **Philosophy.** Cumberland's De Legibus Naturae attacks Hobbes, but renews Hobbes' attempt to find an independent morality. This he discovers in sociability, which leads him to propound the common good.

Glisson's De Substantia declares that substance consists of forces, self-sufficient and unrelated, and suggests the theory of monads to Leibnitz.

1228. **Social.** Colbert forbids processes for witchcraft.

1229. **Eng. Ch.** On the meeting of Parliament the King is compelled to recall his Declaration and to accept a Test Act against Catholics, by which all office-holders must deny transubstantiation and receive the sacrament according to Anglican rites. To further isolate them, the Commons pass a bill granting toleration to Dissenters, which is, however, thrown out in the Upper House by the Bishops. Many nonconformists take the test occasionally, and the practice of Occasional Conformity arises. [1673

Milton's Of true Religion, Heresy, Schism, advocates the exclusion of Catholics from toleration, as idolaters.

1230. **French Ch.** The efforts of the King to re-unite the Huguenots, who have steadily increased in prosperity and whose loyalty is now above suspicion, are rejected by a synod.

1231. **Science.** Huyghens works out the mathematical theory of the Pendulum.

1232. **Geography.** Jolliet and Marquette reach the Mississippi from Canada.

1233. **Death.** Molière.

1234. **French Ch.** Jurieu's Traité de la Dévotion. [1674

1235. **French Lit.** Boileau's Lutrin (the Lectern) satirises the ecclesiastical world in a mock heroic. His Art Poétique systematises and enforces the ideas of the Satires and influences French poetry till Victor Hugo. His principles are enforced by Bossu, Bouhours, Rapin, Fontenelle.

Moréri's Dictionnaire Historique.

1236. **Art.** Murillo completes a series of pictures for the Hospital de la Caridad in Seville.

1237. **Archaeology.** Spon of Lyons visits the Levant and Greece. His travels are printed 1676.

1238. **Philosophy.** Malebranche's Recherche de la Vérité applies Cartesianism to the philosophy of religion, declaring that the human mind immediately perceives God, and sees all things in Him. The work influences Fénelon, Père Lami, Boursier and others.

Knutzen publishes a letter denying God, devil and immortality.

1239. **Philology.** A series of Greek and Latin authors is edited for the use of the Dauphin (in usum Delphini) by Huet his preceptor, and Mme. Dacier.

1240. **Deaths.** Clarendon, Herrick, Labadie, Milton.

806. **England.** The formation of definite parties is hastened by Danby's Anglican policy. Danby introduces a bill compelling office-holders and Members of Parliament to take an oath to attempt no alteration in Church or State. The Bill is passed by the Lords, but Parliament is prorogued while the Commons are still discussing it. No money is granted, and Louis pays the King £100,000 a year. [1675

807. **France.** After brilliant campaigning in the Vosges, by which the Germans are forced to recross the Rhine, Turenne is killed (July). Montecuculi again crosses the river, but is driven back by Condé. After the campaign, both generals retire from military life. Créqui capitulates to the Duke of Lorraine with his whole army (Sept.).

808. **Sweden.** The Swedes, as the allies of France, at last attack Brandenburg, but are routed by the Great Elector at Fehrbellin and expelled from almost the whole of Pomerania (June). War also breaks out with Denmark.

809. **Germany.** The last Duke of Liegnitz dies, and the Emperor seizes Liegnitz, Brieg and Wohlau, and incorporates them with the kingdom of Bohemia. The Great Elector, relying on the treaty of 1537, protests.

810. **Hungary.** Exasperated by the tyranny of Lobkowitz, the minister of the Emperor Leopold, a new revolt breaks out under Tokoli, favoured by France, Poland, Transylvania and the Porte, and lasts four years.

811. **America.** New England engages in King Philip's war, which crushes the Indians but weakens the colonists.

---

812. **England.** Louis promises not to seize Dutch goods conveyed in English ships. [1676

813. **France.** Duquesne thrice defeats the Spanish and Dutch fleets, and Ruyter is killed. The first French successes on the sea, owing in large part to the reorganisation of the navy by Colbert, make a deep impression in Europe. But the Duke of Lorraine captures Philipsburg, and Louis, who desires peace, sends ambassadors to Nimwegen.

814. **Spain.** The Queen-Mother, whose policy has been guided by the exiled Nithard, is overthrown, and Don John, who is friendly to France, becomes supreme till the Peace of Nimwegen, 1678, when the Queen-Mother returns.

815. **Turkey.** The war with Poland ends, Turkey obtaining part of Podolia and of the Ukraine.

816. **America.** Owing to the misgovernment of the governor of Virginia, Berkeley, and the harassing regulations of the Navigation Act, Nathaniel Bacon takes advantage of the danger from the Indians to resist, intending to unite the colonies against the King's representatives. After a number of successes, Bacon dies, and the rebellion comes to an end.

Edmund Randolph is sent to Massachusetts by the King to complain of the breach of the Navigation laws and the purchase of Maine, but in reality to find a pretext for the revocation of the charter, Charles desiring to bring the colonies under his direct control.

1241. **German Ch.** Spinola, a Spanish Confessor of the Empress, undertakes, at the request of the Emperor, and with the secret encouragement of Innocent XI., a tour throughout Protestant Germany for the purpose of reunion. He offers a new council to fix the doctrine and constitution of the reunited Church, clerical marriage, and the recognition of Papal supremacy. The scheme is approved by the Catholic Duke of Hanover, Leibnitz, and Molanus, but receives little support. [1675

Spener, a Lutheran pastor in Frankfort, publishes his Pia Desideria, or Earnest Desires for a reform of the Evangelical Church, proposing private meetings for the study of the Bible, the greater participation of the laity in the government of the Church, the reorganisation of the theological training in the universities, and the laying of stress in sermons on the inner life. The meetings which Spener holds in his house (Collegia Pietatis) are widely adopted.

1242. **Italian Ch.** Molinos, a Spanish priest resident in Italy, declares in his Guido Spirituale that peace is to be found by contemplation, inward mortification, and frequent communion.

1243. **Swiss Ch.** Turretin and Heidegger compose the Consensus Helveticarum Ecclesiarum, the last strict Calvinist creed.

1244. **Science.** Leibnitz discovers the differential and integral calculus, and, next year, the infinitesimal calculus. Though in communication with Oldenburg, Secretary of the Royal Society, since 1670, he may not have known of Newton's discovery of Fluxions.

A Royal Observatory is instituted at Greenwich, and Flamsteed becomes the first Astronomer Royal.

1245. **Art.** The new cathedral of St Paul, London, is begun by Christopher Wren. Grinling Gibbons ornaments the Choir.

Purcell's Dido and Aeneas, the first English opera.

1246. **Death.** Lightfoot.

1247. **Eng. Ch.** Barclay's Apology for the Quakers. [1676

1248. **French Ch.** Pajon, Professor of Theology at Saumur, expresses ultra-Amyraldist views in conference with Claude, and is attacked by Jurieu and other Calvinists.

Louis institutes a fund for the conversion of Protestants.

1249. **Eng. Lit.** Etherege's Man of Mode, or Sir Fopling Flutter.

1250. **Science.** Ray edits Willoughby's Ornithology.

Römer measures the velocity of light by observation of Jupiter's moons, and estimates that the Sun's rays reach the earth in 11 minutes.

Wiseman, 'the father of English surgery,' publishes his Seven Chirurgical Treatises.

Sydenham's Observationes Medicae study epidemic diseases and treat small-pox by the cooling method, and ague by bark.

Mariotte independently discovers Boyle's law of atmospheric pressure.

1251. **Death.** Voetius.

---

817. **England.** On the meeting of Parliament, Shaftesbury and his friends question whether the prorogation of 15 months does not dissolve Parliament, and are sent to the Tower by the Lords. Louis now begins to intrigue with the leaders of the Opposition. [1677

The Commons vote a subsidy for the navy, and order it to be paid to their own receivers.

James' daughter, Mary, is married by the King and Danby, with the approval of both political parties, to William of Orange, who desires to draw England into the war.

818. **Scotland.** The Government sends a body of men, known as the Highland Host, to suppress the rebels in the West.

819. **France.** To force on a peace, Louis redoubles his efforts and wins successes in Flanders and Lorraine, and Créqui captures Freiburg. The Dutch republican party clamours for peace, and sends envoys to Nimwegen. William, however, regarding the war from an European rather than a nationalist standpoint, continues the campaign.

820. **Sweden.** The Great Elector captures Stettin, and the Danes take Gothland and Rügen.

---

821. **England.** The King's intention to go to war with France, for which Parliament votes money, yields to a secret alliance with Louis. Titus Oates announces a Popish plot to murder the King and land a French army for the support of the Duke of York (Aug.). Sir Edmund Berry Godfrey, the magistrate before whom Oates' depositions are taken, is found murdered near London, and a belief spreads that London is to be set on fire and Protestants massacred. Parliament reassembles, and the flame is fanned by Shaftesbury. A new Test Act is passed, excluding Catholics from both Houses of Parliament. Coleman, the secretary of the Duchess of York, is executed. The English ambassador in Paris reveals the secret treaty, and Parliament impeaches Danby. [1678

822. **France.** A treaty is signed at Nimwegen with Holland (Aug.). Four days later, William attacks the army of Luxemburg, but is repulsed. The French conquests are restored, and a commercial treaty is arranged.

Spain renounces Franche-Comté, and most of the barrier towns of the Netherlands to France (Sept.).

823. **Africa.** Goree is ceded by the Dutch to France. French influence becomes consolidated on the Senegal, and the Dutch are confined to the Gold Coast.

---

824. **England.** To save Danby, the King dissolves the Cavalier Parliament (Jan.). A new Parliament, however, proves more hostile than the old, and the King sends his brother out of the country. Danby, who is again impeached, produces a pardon from the King, which the Lords neglect, but drop proceedings on his being deprived of office and sent to the Tower. On the advice of Temple, the King appoints a Privy Council of 30, 15 being ministers, and the rest [1679

1252. **Eng. Ch.** The Baptists draw up a new Confession, a mere recension of the Westminster symbol. [1677

1253. **Dutch Ch.** Owing to the strife in Amsterdam of the Cocceians and Voetians, the magistrates are forced to interfere. The parties agree to have an equal number of preachers. Witsius, a Cocceian, attempts conciliation in his Economia Foederum.

1254. **Science.** Leeuwenhoek discovers animalcules in water and in animals.

1255. **Politics.** Spinoza's Tractatus Politicus arrives at the conclusions of Hobbes, though reserving liberty of thought.

1256. **Philosophy.** Spinoza's Ethics explain in mathematical form a system which starting from Descartes issues in Pantheism, phenomena being regarded as modes of the Absolute, or Substance.

1257. **Deaths.** Barrow, Harrington, Spinoza.

1258. **Eng. Ch.** Bunyan's Pilgrim's Progress, largely written in Bedford Gaol, 1660—72. [1678

Horneck, Smythies, Beveridge, and Bray found Religious Societies, or guilds for devotion and charity, which exert a wide influence for a generation.

South publishes a selection of his Sermons.

1259. **French Ch.** Bossuet begins his discussions with Claude before Mlle. de Duras, a niece of Turenne, who becomes a Catholic.

Simon, an Oratorian, publishes his Histoire Critique du Vieux Testament (1689, his Histoire Critique du N.T.) which rejects the Mosaic authorship of the Pentateuch, and is attacked by Bossuet and many others.

1260. **French Lit.** Mme. de la Fayette's Princesse de Cléves, the first French novel of character, a story of the court of Henry II.

1261. **Science.** Morison's Historia Plantarum classifies according to the fructifying organs and the fruit.

Huyghens proposes the undulatory theory of light.

1262. **Philosophy.** Cudworth's Intellectual System, the most considerable work of the Cambridge Platonists, defends idealism against Hobbes. (His Immutable Morality, published 1731, maintains the independence of Ethics.)

1263. **Philology.** Ducange's Glossarium Mediae et Infimae Latinitatis.

1264. **Geography.** La Salle sets out from Canada and explores the Great Lakes.

1265. **Eng. Ch.** Blount, the first English Deist since Herbert, publishes his Anima Mundi, a work on Immortality, and translates Philostratus' Life of Apollonius Tyanaeus. [1679

1266. **Scotch Ch.** The extremer sects, the Covenanters and Cameronians, make their appearance.

1267. **French Ch.** Port-Royal loses its protector with the death of Mme. de Longueville, and its numbers are reduced by royal command. Arnauld and Nicole leave the country.

influential men, with Shaftesbury as President. The scheme proves unworkable, and an inner council is formed in which Sunderland and Halifax exercise the chief influence. Parliament introduces a bill to exclude the Duke of York from the succession. Shaftesbury hints that Monmouth, believed by some to be legitimate, should be elected, and Parliament is in consequence dissolved, after passing the Habeas Corpus Act. A new House proves still more hostile, and is prorogued.

825. **Scotland.** Archbishop Sharp is murdered (May). Claverhouse is repulsed by an armed Conventicle, which he tries to disperse at Drumclog (June). The peasants declare against Prelacy and the succession of the Duke of York, but are suppressed by an army under Monmouth.

826. **Germany.** The Emperor, hampered by Créqui and the revolt in Hungary, comes to terms with France, which restores Philipsburg, but obtains Freiburg and a passage across the Rhine at Breisach. The Duchy of Lorraine remains in French hands.

827. **Sweden.** The Great Elector is forced by the Peace of St Germain to restore his conquests in Pomerania, in return for the reversion of East Friesland. Denmark and the Empire also make peace with Sweden.

828. **Hungary.** Tokoli concludes a truce with the Emperor.

[1680

829. **England.** During the prorogation, petitions are sent to the King, urging him to reassemble Parliament. Counter-petitions are sent by those who disapprove the Exclusion Bill. The two classes are named Petitioners and Abhorrers, soon replaced by Whigs and Tories. Shaftesbury indicts James as a recusant (June). Parliament meets (Oct.), and passes the Exclusion Bill, which is rejected in the Lords, owing to the argument of Halifax that James will probably not long outlive his brother, that his daughters are Protestant, and that the selection of Monmouth might lead to civil war. Lord Stafford, the last of the victims of the Popish plot, is executed (Dec.).

830. **France.** William's Principality of Orange is occupied, and the town dismantled.

831. **Germany.** The new Elector of Saxony, John George III., advocates the formation of a league of German Princes to counteract Louis XIV.

The Great Elector obtains the possessions of the Archbishop of Magdeburg.

[1681

832. **England.** The King dissolves Parliament, which refuses to vote supplies (Jan.), and summons another at Oxford, to avoid the London mob. The Whigs, fearing military intimidation, come

Huet's Demonstratio Evangelica declares Greek beliefs borrowed from the Jews.

1268. **Italian Ch.** Segneri's Sermons are collected and published.

1269. **Church Hist.** Innocent XI. condemns 65 probabilist propositions, extracted from Jesuit treatises on moral philosophy.

1270. **Swedish Lit.** Rudbeck's Atland identifies Sweden with Atlantis, the cradle of the human race.

1271. **History.** Bossuet's Histoire Universelle, written for his pupil the Dauphin, portrays the events of the ancient and early mediaeval world as the work of Providence leading mankind towards the Church.

Burnet's History of the Reformation.

1272. **Deaths.** Hobbes, De Retz, Vondel.

1273. **Eng. Ch.** Burnet's Sacred Theory of the Earth asserts that the early history of the Earth was a time of perpetual spring, and that the Flood was due to sin. [1680

1274. **French Ch.** La Salle founds the Frères des Écoles Chrétiennes for the education of poor children.

Thomassin's Dogmata Theologica, a philosophic study of Christian ideas.

1275. **German Ch.** Joachim Neander's Bundeslieder extends the Pietist movement.

1276. **Eng. Lit.** Bunyan's Life and Death of Mr Badman anticipates the realistic novel of Defoe.

1277. **Science.** Borelli's De Motu Animalium founds the iatro-physical school of medicine, explaining functions on physical and mechanical principles.

1278. **Art.** Lely dies, and Kneller becomes Court painter.

Scarlatti, a pupil of Carissimi, composes his first opera and improves counterpoint and scientific technique.

1279. **Philosophy.** Malebranche's Traité de la Nature et de la Grâce is attacked by Fénelon and Arnauld, at the wish of Bossuet, and placed on the Index as leading to the denial of freedom.

1280. **Politics.** Filmer's Patriarcha, written during the Civil War, grounds the absolute power of kings on the dominion granted directly by God to Adam and transmitted by him to the ruling sovereigns.

1281. **Social.** Dockwra institutes the penny post in London.

Dalgarno invents a hand-alphabet for the deaf and dumb.

1282. **Deaths.** Bernini, La Rochefoucauld, Sivaji, Swammerdam.

1283. **French Ch.** The persecution of Huguenots increases, conversions being heavily punished, mixed marriages forbidden, Huguenots excluded from offices and professions and doubly taxed, the churches in many cases destroyed, and emigration forbidden. Risings in the south are suppressed. Louvois quarters troops on Huguenot households till they abjure, thus commencing the Dragonnades. [1681

1284. **Eng. Lit.** Dryden attacks Shaftesbury in Absalom and Achitophel, followed by the Medal, 1682.

1285. **Politics.** Samuel Johnson, the chaplain of Earl Russell, asserts

armed and with armed followers. The King offers to accept the Regency of the Prince of Orange for his brother; but Shaftesbury insists on the recognition of Monmouth. Parliament is dissolved after a week's session, and public opinion, in fear of civil war, rallies to the King. In London, however, the Grand Jury of Middlesex throw out the bill for Shaftesbury's arrest for treason.

833. **France.** Desiring to make his eastern frontier impregnable, and to overawe the Rhine Electors, Louis appoints local courts, known as Chambers of Re-union, to decide on the extent of his treaty rights in Alsace, the three Bishoprics, and Franche-Comté. The Courts award to France the complete suzerainty of Alsace, and the free city of Strasburg is suddenly seized by Louvois (Sept.). On the same day, Casale, the Italian fortress, is seized by the Duke of Mantua. The duchy of Zweibrücken is also declared united to France.

834. **Sweden.** Charles XI., with the aid of the clergy and commons, expels the nobles from the lands alienated during his minority, reorganises the army and navy, and becomes an absolute monarch.

Sweden and Holland form a Convention to maintain the treaties of 1648 and 1678.

835. **Hungary.** The system of Lobkowitz is abandoned, natives are reinstated in offices, the arbitrary taxes are withdrawn, and liberty of conscience is granted. Tokoli suspects and rejects the concessions, and is nominated Prince of Hungary by the Sultan.

[1682

836. **England.** The King recalls James from Scotland; and Shaftesbury, who fails to induce Monmouth to take a decisive step, escapes to Holland (Oct.).

837. **Germany.** The League of Sweden and Holland is joined by the Emperor, Spain and a number of German princes.

838. **Russia.** The first war between Turkey and Russia ends, Russia securing part of the Ukraine and the Cossack territory.

839. **America.** Penn obtains Delaware Bay and the region behind, the King retaining the right to examine and annul the laws, though religious toleration is guaranteed. Pennsylvania is founded, and a constitution is drawn up by Penn.

La Salle descends the Mississippi to the sea, and takes possession of the country for Louis, under the title of Louisiana. The colony which he plants at the mouth ends in disaster.

840. **Africa.** The Great Elector founds a fort on the Gold Coast for trade; but the settlement only lasts 40 years. The Danes also settle on the Gold Coast.

---

the right of resistance in a work entitled Julian, to which Hickes replies in Jovian. Sherlock's Case of Resistance distinguishes between suffering tyranny and doing wrong at the king's bidding.

Nevile, the closest friend and disciple of Harrington, repeats his master's teaching in Plato Redivivus.

Sydney writes or perfects his Discourses on Government, published 1699.

1286. **Science.** Papin communicates to the Royal Society an account of his steam-engine.

1287. **History.** Mabillon's De Re Diplomatica founds historical criticism.

1288. **Law.** Stair's Institutions of the Law of Scotland.

1289. **Deaths.** Calderon, Conring, Nicon.

1290. **Eng. Ch.** Stillingfleet's Unreasonableness of Separation replies to Baxter and Owen, in a conciliatory manner. [1682

Bunyan's Holy War.

1291. **French Ch.** In consequence of the Pope's rejection of his claim to the Regale (the revenues and patronage of a vacant bishopric) where he does not already possess it, Louis summons a synod which approves the extension of the Regale and declares that the Papacy has power only in spiritual matters, that a General Council is superior to the Pope, that the Pope cannot alter the customs of the Gallican Church, and that Papal decrees are not binding till confirmed by the Church. An appeal to a future Council is excluded by Bossuet, who regards the declarations as inopportune. The subscribers of these Four Articles are refused confirmation by the Pope, and attacked by the Spaniards D'Aguirre, Gonzalez, Roccaberti, and other Ultramontanes, but defended by Bossuet.

Poiret's Économie Divine, a mystical system influenced by Mme Bourignon, attacks Cartesianism.

1292. **Church Hist.** Petrucci's Enigmi Disvelati, a work of Catholic mysticism, influenced by Molinos.

D'Aguirre makes the last important attempt to prove the Isidorian Decretals genuine.

1293. **Eng. Lit.** Dryden's Religio Laici.

Otway's Venice preserved.

1294. **Scotch Lit.** Sir George Mackenzie founds the Advocates' Library.

1295. **German Lit.** The Acta Eruditorum, founded by Leibnitz and Otto Mencke, begin to appear at Leipsic, modelled on the Journal des Savants.

1296. **Science.** Ray's Methodus Plantarum Nova divides flowering plants into monocotyledons and dicotyledons, but retains the division of plants into herbs, shrubs and trees.

1297. **Art.** Mansard builds Versailles, the Trianon and the Church of the Invalides.

1298. **Politics.** Petty's Political Arithmetic, the first attempt at comparative statistics.

1299. **Deaths.** Sir T. Browne, Murillo.

841. **England.** The King confiscates the charter of the City of London, and appoints the Lord Mayor and other offices. Provincial towns are treated in the same way by the Judges on circuit, and Tories are named members of the new corporations. [1683

Ferguson, Wildman, Rumbold, Walcot, and other old Commonwealthsmen resolve to attack the King and his brother at the Rye House, near Ware, on their return from Newmarket. The plot fails, the King returning a few days earlier than was expected, and several of the conspirators are taken and executed. A plan formed by Monmouth, Russell, Essex, Howard and other Whigs, designed to compel the summoning of another Parliament, is discovered. Essex commits suicide in prison, and Howard turns informer. Russell is executed, refusing to admit that resistance to the King is never lawful. Algernon Sidney is also executed, the want of a second witness being supplied by the production of a manuscript treatise, declaring the right of subjects to depose their King. Monmouth is sent into exile in Holland.

842. **France.** The French invade the Spanish Netherlands, besiege Luxemburg, and seize Trier, 1684. Lorraine is occupied permanently.

843. **Turkey.** In consequence of Turkish intervention in Hungary, a war breaks out with the Emperor. The Turks, with the aid of French officers, advance to the siege of Vienna, which is defended by Stahremberg, but are driven off by Sobieski, King of Poland, who marches to its relief with Charles of Lorraine, Louis of Baden, and Prince Eugene.

844. **Asia.** The Dutch are expelled from Formosa by Kang-He, Emperor of China, who also conquers Tibet.

---

845. **England.** The King is urged by Halifax to comply with the Triennial Act by calling a Parliament, but is dissuaded by Hyde, Earl of Rochester, President of the Council, and receives money from France. [1684

846. **France.** Luxemburg is besieged and taken, and a truce is made at Regensburg with Spain, the Empire and Holland, by which the Reunions and Luxemburg remain in French hands for 20 years.

Louis secretly marries Mme de Maintenon, his wife having died 1683.

847. **Italy.** Genoa is bombarded by Lavardin for preferring a Spanish to a French alliance.

848. **Turkey.** The Pope negotiates a Holy League against the Turks between the Emperor and Venice. Morosini invades and reduces the Peloponnesus, 1684–9, the Imperial armies, under the Duke of Lorraine, being swelled by volunteers from all countries except France, which subsidises the Sultan.

849. **America.** After a prolonged legal contest, the Massachusetts charter is annulled, and Andros, late governor of New York, assumes control.

850. **Africa.** England surrenders Tangier to Morocco, in consequence of repeated attacks by the Moors.

851. **Asia.** The East India Company builds Fort Marlborough in Sumatra.

1300. **French Ch.** Rancé, abbot of La Trappe, attacks learning [1683
in his Sainteté et Devoirs de la Vie Monastique. He is answered by Mabillon's Traité des Études Monastiques, and a controversy arises as to the relations of learning and piety.

The King ceases to enforce the teaching of the Four Articles in schools.

1301. **French Lit.** Fontenelle's Dialogues des Morts.

1302. **Italian Lit.** Filicaja writes a cycle of odes on the relief of Vienna.

1303. **Politics.** The University of Oxford burns the works of Buchanan, Milton, Hobbes, and Baxter, and declares its adhesion to the doctrines of non-resistance, which are at this time maintained by Mackenzie in his Jus Regium.

1304. **Geography.** Dampier commences his voyage round the world, sailing from South America to the Ladrones, and returning by the Philippines, Australia and the Cape of Good Hope. The account of his voyage appears 1697.

1305. **Deaths.** Colbert, Owen, Isaac Walton, Roger Williams.

1306. **American Ch.** Francis Makennie, an Irish Presbyterian [1684
minister, introduces Presbyterianism.

1307. **German Ch.** The Great Elector offers a refuge to the French Protestants.

1308. **Eng. Lit.** Locke is expelled from Christ Church by the Dean, Doctor Fell, for his connexion with Shaftesbury, and retires to Holland, where he makes the acquaintance of the Arminians, Limborch and Le Clerc.

1309. **French Lit.** Bayle begins his literary review, Nouvelles de la République des Lettres.

1310. **Literature.** The Turkish Spy, a criticism of western life and thought ostensibly by a Turkish envoy at Paris, is written by Paul Marana of Genoa, with additions probably by an Englishman.

1311. **Science.** Halley asks Newton to discover the orbit of a planet if the attraction is that of the inverse square. Newton replies that it would be an ellipse. Halley therefore persuades Newton to attack the whole problem of gravitation.

Leibnitz explains his Differential Calculus in the Acta Eruditorum, and the method is applied by James and John Bernoulli.

1312. **Geography.** Kämpfer accompanies an embassy to Persia, and visits the Persian Gulf, Java and Japan.

1313. **Death.** Corneille.

---

852. **England.** Charles dies, reconciled to the Roman Church (Feb.). James chooses as his ministers Rochester, Halifax, Sunderland and Godolphin, and summons Parliament, which proves strongly Tory, in part owing to the remodelling of Corporations, by which members are largely chosen. Monmouth, supported by a number of republicans, lands in the west (June), and enters Taunton with 5,000 men, but is routed at Sedgmoor by Kirk, captured and executed (July). Jeffreys is sent down to the west and holds the Bloody Assize, over 300 rebels being executed and over 800 transported to the West Indies as slaves. In gratitude for this achievement, James makes Jeffreys Lord Chancellor. The King appoints Catholics to posts in the army, and asks Parliament to repeal the Test Act, proroguing it when it remonstrates. Halifax is dismissed, and Sunderland becomes President of the Council. [1685

853. **Scotland.** In consequence of an enactment punishing with death anyone attending a conventicle, Argyle returns from his exile in Holland, and attempts to raise an insurrection, but is captured without a blow and executed.

854. **Germany.** Charles I., Elector Palatine, dies childless, and Louis claims part of the Lower Palatinate through the Elector's sister, the wife of his brother. The new Elector Palatine, a member of the house of Neuburg, rallies Germany to his side.

855. **Turkey.** Charles of Lorraine defeats the Turks and drives the Hungarians under Tokoli back into Transylvania.

856. **Greece.** The tribute of children for Janissaries ceases, and the Klefts, half patriots, half robbers, spring up.

857. **Asia.** A French embassy is sent to Siam.

---

858. **England.** The King brings the case of Hales, a Catholic officer, before a packed court, which declares that royal dispensations suspend the penalties of the law (June). The King appoints Massey, an avowed Catholic, Dean of Christchurch, and Parker Bishop of Oxford, and leaves Walker Master of University College, a recent convert, unmolested. Compton, Bishop of London, is ordered to suspend the Dean of Norwich for preaching against Romanism, but refuses, on which the King appoints an Ecclesiastical Commission Court under Jeffreys, which suspends Compton. Rochester, a devoted Tory, is dismissed for refusing to change his religion, and a camp of 13,000 men is formed at Hounslow. [1686

859. **Scotland.** James orders the Scotch Parliament to repeal anti-Catholic laws, and on its refusal dispenses with them by his own authority.

860. **Germany.** A league to guarantee the Treaties of 1648 and 1678 and the truce of Ratisbon, is concluded at Augsburg by the Emperor, Spain, Sweden, and a large number of German princes (July).

A compromise is made by the Great Elector and the Emperor,

1314. **Eng. Ch.** Bull's Defensio Fidei Nicaenae maintains, [1685
against Petavius, that the pre-Nicene thinkers were not Arian but essentially Athanasian. Bull is thanked by a synod of French Bishops over which Bossuet presides.

Spencer's De Legibus et Ritualibus Hebraeorum discusses the debt of the Jews to Egypt and other countries, and helps to found the study of comparative religion.

1315. **French Ch.** The General Assembly of the clergy urge strongly the revocation of the Edict of Nantes, and after much hesitation Louis complies, prohibits Protestant worship, exiles the ministers, and destroys the churches. The step irreparably weakens the country, many of the most thriving parts of the population, despite the prohibition of emigration, escaping to England, the Dutch Netherlands and Brandenburg. Under French pressure the Duke of Savoy recalls the concessions granted by his father to the Vaudois.

1316. **German Ch.** Pfeiffer's Pansophia Mosaica asserts that all the philosophy, science and law of the ancient world were derived from Moses.

1317. **Italian Ch.** Molinos and Petrucci are arrested at the instance of Louis XIV, spurred on by the Jesuits, examined by the Inquisition, and condemned to perpetual imprisonment. In 1687 the Pope approves the condemnation by the Inquisition.

1318. **Italian Lit.** Redi's Bacchus in Tuscany.

1319. **Science.** Cohorn's Treatise on Fortification.

1320. **Death.** Calov.

1321. **French Ch.** Mme Guyon publishes her Moyen Court [1686
pour l'Oraison, influenced by study of St Theresa and John of the Cross. With the aid of Lacombe, a Barnabite monk, she founds an institution for converts at Gex under the Bishop of Geneva. Lacombe is shortly removed and is followed by Mme Guyon.

Dupin's Ancient Discipline of the Church assumes an ultra-Gallican position, which he illustrates in his Bibliothèque des Auteurs Ecclésiastiques.

1322. **Dutch Ch.** Limborch's Theologia Christiana gives the fullest presentation of Arminianism since Episcopius.

Leclerc rejects the Mosaic authorship of the Pentateuch, and rationalises the story of Babel, Lot's wife, and the passage of the Red Sea.

1323. **Church Hist.** Bayle condemns the expulsion of the Huguenots in his Contrains les Entrer, the first systematic work of rationalist tendency.

1324. **Literature.** Mabillon describes his Italian journey in the Museum Italicum and the Iter Italicum.

Leclerc begins his literary review, La Bibliothèque Universelle.

1325. **Science.** Willoughby's and Ray's Historia Piscium constitute the first real advance since Rondelet. Their work is developed by Artedi and Linnaeus.

1326. **Philosophy.** Abercromby's Discourse of Wit anticipates Reid's doctrine of Common Sense.

Frederick William renouncing his claims on Jägerndorf and Liegnitz in return for the cession of the circle of Schwiebus, in Silesia. At the same moment, however, the Austrian ambassador makes a secret compact with the Elector's son, by which the latter pledges himself to restore the circle on his accession.

861. **Turkey.** Charles of Lorraine storms Buda, which the Turks have held since 1541 (Sept.).

[1687

862. **England.** The King issues a Declaration of Indulgence, suspending laws against Catholics and Dissenters, to whom, however, Halifax points out that such an indulgence, not being guaranteed by law, is of no value (April). A Catholic is nominated President of Magdalen College, Oxford, and the Fellows, who choose one of their own number, are ejected. Parliament is dissolved and the Corporations are remodelled.

863. **France.** Louis disputes with the Pope about the sanctuary which the French ambassador in Rome claims for his house.

864. **Germany.** The League of Augsburg is joined by Bavaria, Saxony, Savoy, and some of the Italian states, and receives the secret approval of the Pope.

865. **Austria.** The Emperor annexes the principalities of Liegnitz, Brieg, and Wohlau.

866. **Hungary.** Charles of Lorraine and Louis of Baden defeat the Turks at Mohacz and drive them out of Croatia and Transylvania. Tököli loses prestige, and Leopold suppresses the constitution.

867. **Asia.** The East India Company obtains independent jurisdiction and coinage, and power to build fortifications, levy customs, and enlist native militia.

868. **Africa.** Several hundred Huguenots settle at the Cape of Good Hope, but become quickly blended with the Dutch. Though their language completely disappears, their names survive in great numbers.

[1688

869. **England.** The King orders a second Declaration of Indulgence to be read in all churches. Archbishop Sancroft and six Bishops protest, and are tried in Westminster Hall for a seditious libel, but acquitted (June 30). Meanwhile the King has had a son, widely supposed to be supposititious (June 10), and, on the day of the acquittal, William of Orange is invited to defend English liberties. William accepts, and issues a Declaration, enumerating James's misdeeds and promising to abide by the decision of a free Parliament. James

1327. **Education.** Mme de Maintenon founds the Maison de Saint-Cyr for the daughters of the poor nobility.
1328. **Geography.** Chardin's Travels in Persia.
1329. **Deaths.** Condé, Pearson.

1330. **Scotch Ch.** James's Declaration of Indulgence suspends all penal laws, except as regards field-preaching, which, however, continues. [1687
1331. **French Ch.** Fontenelle's Histoire des Oracles attacks the priests and oracles of classical times and, indirectly, miracles.
1332. **Eng. Lit.** Dryden's Hind and Panther contrasts the Roman Church, which he has recently joined, with the Anglican. It is parodied by Montagu and Prior in the Country Mouse and City Mouse.
1333. **French Lit.** La Bruyère's Caractères.
1334. **Art.** The Parthenon is irretrievably damaged by the falling of a Venetian bomb into the powder stored within it.
1335. **Science.** Newton's Principia, dedicated to the Royal Society, shews that all the important characteristics of the motions of the solar system are explicable by three fundamental laws of motion and by the law of gravitation, namely, that every particle of matter attracts every other with a force varying directly as the mass of each, and inversely as the square of the distance between them. Hooke's claim to the discovery of the law of inverse squares is rejected by Newton. The theory is introduced into Cambridge by Clarke, Bentley, Whiston, into Oxford by Halley, into Edinburgh by Gregory. On the Continent Leibnitz, Huyghens, the Bernouillis cling to the vortex theory; and in France, despite Fontenelle, it is little known till Voltaire's return from England. It is introduced into Holland by 's Gravesande.

Newton states the three fundamental laws of motion. I. Every body continues in its state of rest or of uniform motion in a straight line except in so far as it be compelled by impressed force to change that state. II. The rate of change of momentum is proportional to the impressed force and takes place in the direction of the straight line in which the force acts. III. To every action there is an equal and opposite reaction.

Newton declares that the propagation of sound varies directly as the square root of the elastic force and inversely as the square root of the density of the medium.

Hans Sloane visits Jamaica, and lays the foundation of his botanical collections.
1336. **Philosophy.** Tschirnhausen's Medicina Mentis forms a transition between the systems of his friends Spinoza and Leibnitz.
1337. **Deaths.** Petty, La Salle, Steno.

1338. **Eng. Ch.** Cave's Scriptores Historiae Ecclesiasticae. [1688
1339. **Scotch Ch.** On the news of William's landing, Presbyterianism is quietly restored.
1340. **French Ch.** Mme Guyon is arrested, but liberated by the

abolishes the Ecclesiastical Commissioners, restores the City Charters and the ejected Fellows, and dismisses Sunderland and Petre, but refuses an offer of help from Louis, who transfers his army from the Netherlands frontier to the Palatinate and leaves William free to land in Torbay (Nov. 5). The North and the Midlands rise under Danby and Devonshire, and James is deserted by Churchill and by his daughter Anne. The King summons a Parliament, and proposes an accommodation with William, but resolves to leave the country. He is stopped by fishermen near Sheerness, and brought back to London, whence he is allowed to escape (Dec. 23). William consults the Lords, the members of Charles's Parliaments, and the City, and is advised to summon a Convention.

870. **France.** On the death of the Archbishop of Cologne, Louis supports a candidate who is opposed by the Emperor and the Pope (June). He declares war with Holland and the Empire, captures Philippsburg, overruns the Palatinate, and seizes Avignon from the Pope.

871. **Turkey.** The war against the Turks is resumed, and Belgrade is taken.

872. **America.** Andros is named Governor of the northern colonies, and revokes the charters of Connecticut and Rhode Island.

[1689

873. **England.** The Convention meets (Jan. 22), and the Commons resolve that James, having broken the original contract between King and People, and withdrawn from the kingdom, has abdicated the government and that the throne is thereby vacant. The Lords, after discussing a Regency, accept the resolution. A Declaration of Rights is prepared, and William and Mary are offered the Crown, and choose Danby, Halifax, Nottingham, Shrewsbury, and Godolphin for their ministers. The Convention Parliament embodies the Declaration of Rights in a Bill of Rights.

Owing to the mutiny of a regiment, a Bill is passed by which the troops cannot be paid without a special Act of Appropriation, and no soldier can be punished without the annual re-enactment of the Bill.

874. **Scotland.** Dundee rallies the Highland clans against the new sovereign, and defeats William's general at Killiecrankie, but is himself slain (July).

875. **Ireland.** James, with aid from France, against which William declares war, lands at Kinsale, finding an army prepared by Tyrconnel. The Scotch and English settlers take refuge in Enniskillen and Londonderry, which is relieved when reduced to extremities (July 30). The Irish army is defeated at Newtown Butler, near Enniskillen (Aug.). Meanwhile the Irish Parliament issues an Attainder, confiscating the land of about 2,000 of William's adherents (May).

876. **France.** Louvois orders the devastation of the Palatinate, which provokes a declaration of war from the Diet. Though ably served by Luxembourg, Boufflers and Catinat, the French armies are driven back.

influence of Mme de Maintenon, who invites her to her new foundation for girls at St Cyr and adopts her Torrents Spirituels as a handbook of devotion. At St Cyr she is brought into close relations with Fénelon.

Bossuet publishes his Histoire des Variations Protestantes, the most powerful Catholic attack of the century, distinguishes the tenets of the Albigenses from those of the Waldenses, and calls attention to the importance of Melanchthon.

1341. **French Lit.** Perrault, who had, in congratulating the King on his recovery from illness, declared the moderns superior in arts and letters to the ancients and had been attacked by Fontenelle, supports his contention in his Parallèle des Anciens et des Modernes. Boileau defends the ancients. Perrault and his adherents introduce the idea of progress into literary criticism.

1342. **German Lit.** Thomasius delivers the first lectures in German, and contributes to the first German review.

1343. **Literature.** Morhof's Polyhistor, a dictionary of authors.

1344. **Education.** Fénelon's Éducation des Filles, the first work on the subject, lays stress rather on character than on learning.

1345. **Deaths.** Bunyan, Cudworth, Du Cange, The Great Elector.

1346. **Eng. Ch.** A Toleration Act allows Dissenters to worship [1689
publicly on taking an oath, and permits Quakers to affirm, but excludes Catholics and Unitarians from its benefits. An attempt, however, made at the order of Parliament, by Burnet, Tenison, Stillingfleet, Tillotson, and Beveridge, to attract the Dissenters back to the Church by the alteration of the Prayer Book fails, owing to the opposition of Convocation.

Archbishop Sancroft, five Bishops, and about 400 clergy, including Ken, Hickes, Kettlewell, Leslie, and Jeremy Collier, refuse to take the oaths of supremacy and allegiance and are deprived, forming the Nonjurors, who are joined by laymen such as Nelson and Dodwell. Two bishops are consecrated 1694, and three others, 1713.

Locke's First Letter on Toleration advocates the exclusion of Catholics, as owing allegiance elsewhere, and of Atheists and Antinomians.

1347. **Scotch Ch.** The episcopal clergy are ejected, Presbyterianism is everywhere restored, and the Westminster Confession is reimposed. All acts in favour of episcopacy are rescinded; but, though Episcopacy is abolished, the Scotch Episcopate perpetuates itself.

1348. **American Ch.** Cotton Mather issues a collection of Memorable Providences relating to Witchcraft and Possession.

1349. **Danish Lit.** Kingo's Psalms.

1350. **Politics.** Locke publishes two Treatises on Civil Government, of which the first replies to Filmer's Patriarcha, and the second discusses the origin and end of government, and is designed to justify the Revolution of 1688 and 'establish the throne of our great restorer.' The contract theory, based on natural right, allows the formation of any government except Absolute Monarchy. Frequent revolutions are prevented by the inertia of mankind.

England and Holland join the League of Augsburg, and the Grand Alliance is formed.

877. **America.** Andros is imprisoned, William and Mary are proclaimed, and the old charters are resumed.

878. **Asia.** The Treaty of Nerchinsk excludes Russia from Amurland.

---

879. **England.** The Indemnity Bill is coupled with so many exceptions that the King dissolves the Convention Parliament [1690 and contemplates resignation. Halifax leaves the Government, and Danby becomes the leading minister. Parliament limits the grant of half the King's revenue to four years.

Admiral Tourville is sent to invade England, and meets the English and Dutch fleets off Beachy Head (June 30). By blundering or design, Admiral Herbert keeps his ships out of danger, the Dutch in consequence being defeated. Herbert is tried and acquitted, but dismissed from his post and replaced by Russell, brother of the victim of 1683. Tourville does not follow up his victory, and contents himself with burning Teignmouth.

880. **Ireland.** William crosses to Ireland, where Lauzun has arrived with French troops, and defeats James and Lauzun at the Battle of the Boyne (July), where Schomberg is killed. James escapes to France. William and Marlborough enter Dublin, but are prevented by Sarsfield from taking Limerick.

881. **Scotland.** The Lords of the Articles are abolished, and the process of defeudalisation begins.

882. **France.** Luxembourg defeats the Dutch under Prince Waldeck, at Fleurus, but is checked by the Elector of Brandenburg.

Louis restores Avignon to the Pope.

883. **Savoy.** Savoy joins the League of Augsburg, but is defeated by Catinat.

884. **Turkey.** The Prince of Transylvania dies, and Kiuprili nominates Tököli and sends an army which recovers Belgrade, Servia and Bulgaria, owing to the withdrawal of the Emperor's best troops for the French war.

885. **Asia.** A fort is founded by the East India Company at the mouth of the Ganges, which, by the purchase of three villages in 1700, becomes Calcutta.

---

886. **England.** Marlborough, jealous of William's Dutch generals, offers to James to move an address asking the King [1691 to expel the foreigners, and persuades Anne to join the opposition. For this treachery he is deprived of his offices.

The English Company, a rival to the East India Co., is established, and receives a charter, 1698.

887. **Ireland.** Ginkell, sent to Ireland with Mackay and Ruvigny, a French Protestant, destroys the Irish army at Aughrim, and takes Limerick. The soldiers and officers, among them Sarsfield, are allowed to enter the French service. The Irish Catholics are promised the

Halifax's Character of a Trimmer.

1351. **Law.** Domat's Lois Civiles founds law on ethical and religious principles.

1352. **History.** Pagi's Critica in Annales Baronii, the first searching examination of the entire work.

1353. **Social.** Export duties on corn are abolished in England, and a bounty of 5/- is given when the price is under 48/-. This measure greatly contributes to the revival of agriculture.

1354. **Deaths.** Christina of Sweden, Sydenham.

1355. **Eng. Ch.** Wallis' Doctrine of the Trinity is attacked by Sherlock and by South, who is censured by the University of Oxford for Tritheism. [1690

Bury's Naked Gospel, a Deistic work, is burnt.

1356. **Scotch Ch.** Lay patronage is abolished; the Act of Supremacy is rescinded; ejected ministers are restored, and a General Assembly meets.

1357. **French Ch.** The Pope condemns the theory of Philosophic Sin.

1358. **Eng. Lit.** Dunton's Athenian Gazette anticipates the Spectator.

1359. **French Lit.** Furetière's Dictionary of the French Language.

1360. **History.** Tillemont's Histoire des Empereurs des 6 premiers siècles.

1361. **Philosophy.** Locke's Essay on the Human Understanding attacks Descartes' conception of innate ideas, and derives knowledge from sensation and reflection. Philosophy must be approached by a study of the capacities of the human mind. The work gives a psychological direction to thought, and is attacked by Norris, Stillingfleet, bishop of Worcester, and Leibnitz in his Nouveaux Essais sur l'Entendement humain.

Huet's Faiblesse de l'Esprit humain declares the credibility of the axioms of reason to depend on revelation.

1362. **Economics.** Nicholas Barbon's Discourse of Trade asserts that value does not reside in things, but arises from their relation to human needs.

1363. **Death.** Teniers.

1364. **Eng. Ch.** Boyle founds a Lectureship in Apologetics, on which Bentley delivers the first course, inferring a First Cause from Newton's discoveries. [1691

1365. **Church Hist.** Gonzalez' Fundamenta Theologiae Moralis attacks Probabilism, which breaks into Equiprobabilism, Probabiliorism, and Tutiorism.

Leibnitz and Molanus, with the approval of the electress Sophia and the theologians of Helmstadt, negotiate for reunion with Bishop Burnet.

1366. **Eng. Lit.** Antony Wood's Athenae Oxonienses.

1367. **French Lit.** Racine's Athalie, his last and greatest work.

Perrault's Griseldis commences his fairy tales, in which he is followed by the Comtesse d'Aulnoy and Anthony Hamilton.

privileges they enjoyed under Charles II.; but the Parliament, representing the English colony alone, compels the King to revoke his concessions.

888. **Scotland.** Military execution is proclaimed against all who have not laid down their arms and taken the oath of allegiance by the last day of the year.

889. **France.** Louis advances in person to the North-east frontier, and takes Mons, which William is too weak to relieve. Catinat takes Nice. Louvois dies, and henceforth the King is served by men of slight ability.

890. **Turkey.** Louis of Baden meets and destroys a huge Turkish army at Szalankemen, where Kiuprili is killed. Transylvania is finally conquered, Tököli retiring and joining the Turkish ranks, and the Estates recognise the Habsburgs as princes, in return for a recognition of political and religious privileges.

---

891. **England.** James issues a long list of names to be excepted from his amnesty. Russell meets and destroys the French fleet, [1692
prepared for an invasion, at La Hogue. The French navy, perfected by Colbert and his son Seignelai, begins to decline.

To support the war Montagu borrows one million pounds, on which interest is steadily paid, and which may be regarded as the origin of the National Debt.

892. **Scotland.** The Macdonalds of Glencoe, having failed to swear allegiance to William by the given date, are treacherously massacred by order of Stair, who has obtained an ambiguous authorisation from the King. The indignation is so strong that Stair is dismissed.

893. **Ireland.** Catholics are forbidden to sit in Parliament, and severe laws deal with their worship, their property, and the education of their children.

894. **France.** Vauban takes Namur (June), which is defended by Cohorn, and Luxembourg wins an indecisive victory over William at Steinkirk (Aug.).

895. **Germany.** Ernest Augustus, Duke of Brunswick-Luneberg, obtains the Electoral title for Hanover, in return for a perpetual alliance with the Emperor.

896. **America.** Massachusetts receives a new Charter.

---

897. **England.** The King vetoes bills for Triennial Parliaments and for the exclusion of placemen from Parliament. [1693

Sunderland, who is allowed to return to Court, recommends the King to form a homogeneous Whig ministry.

The Smyrna merchant fleet is almost wholly destroyed by the French off Cape St Vincent.

A Land Tax, on a valuation carried out 1692, is imposed, beginning with 4/- in the pound.

898. **France.** Louis fails to take Liège and never appears in the field again. Catinat defeats the Duke of Savoy. Luxembourg defeats

1368. **Science.** Leibnitz' Protogaea, a geological work suggested by his mining duties in the Harz mountains.

1369. **Philosophy.** Norris' Ideal World introduces the ideas of Malebranche into England. His teaching is continued by Barthogge.

Geulinx declares extension and thought absolutely distinct, like two clocks at each instant adjusted by God.

1370. **Philology.** Bentley's Letter to Mill, in reference to an edition of Malalas, discusses metre and other subjects, and earns the praise of Spanheim and Graevius.

1371. **Economics.** North's Discourse of Trade maintains the unity of the world for trading purposes, declares human industry, not money, the source of wealth, and attacks restrictions on prices, interest, and the export of bullion.

1372. **Social.** Bekker and Thomasius attack the treatment of witches.

1373. **Deaths.** Baxter, Boyle, Fox, Pococke.

1374. **Eng. Lit.** Temple's Ancient and Modern Learning introduces the controversy into England, and selects for praise the Fables of Aesop and the Epistles of Phalaris. [1692

1375. **Italian Lit.** The Arcadian Academy is founded by Crescimbeni, Gravina, and Guidi.

1376. **Norwegian Lit.** Dass's Trumpet of Norway.

1377. **Science.** Newton's papers are burnt, a blow from which he never entirely recovers.

1378. **Education.** William and Mary College is founded in Virginia for the training of clergy.

1379. **Social.** Societies for Reformation of Manners are instituted.

A witchcraft frenzy breaks out at Salem.

On the news of the victory of La Hogue Queen Mary transforms the palace begun by Charles II. at Greenwich into a refuge for disabled sailors.

Lloyd's Coffee-house becomes an office for marine insurance.

1380. **Eng. Ch.** Leslie's Short and Easy Method with the Deists. [1693

1381. **French Ch.** Louis undertakes not to teach nor enforce the articles of 1682.

Godet, Bishop of Chartres, warns Mme de Maintenon against Mme Guyon, who is in consequence dismissed from St Cyr. She appeals to Bossuet, who reads her MS. commentary on the Apocalypse and is much shocked. Bossuet, Noailles and Tronson meet at Issy, and issue a condemnation of Mme Guyon's tenets, which, with a few changes, is signed by Fénelon. Mme Guyon promises not to write nor teach again, but breaks her promise, and is shut up in Vincennes.

1382. **Eng. Lit.** Hacket's Life of Bishop Williams.

1383. **Science.** Ray's Synopsis Animalium attempts a new classification.

Halley explains a method of ascertaining the distance of the Sun by observation of the transits of Venus.

William and the allies at Landen (July). The Palatinate is once more ravaged. Overtures for peace made by Louis are rejected.

Louis institutes the Order of St Louis.

899. **Sweden.** Charles XI. is declared absolute.

900. **America.** An expedition against Canada is arranged, but does not succeed.

---

901. **England.** Following the advice of Sunderland, the King dismisses his Tory ministers, except Godolphin and Danby, and fills their places with Whigs, his chief advisers, known as the Junto, being Somers, Admiral Russell, Montagu and Wharton. This step may be said to mark the origin of the Cabinet system, though the King regards the ministers as responsible to himself, not to Parliament. To guard against corruption and the abuse of patronage by the Ministry, a Bill is introduced forbidding members of Parliament to hold any office, but is defeated. The King, however, accepts a Triennial Act, limiting the duration of Parliament to three years. The death of Queen Mary from small-pox greatly weakens the King's position, and encourages negociations with James. [1694

On the suggestion of Paterson, a Scotch protégé of Montagu, who desires a safer place for the deposit of money than with the goldsmiths, the Bank of England is founded. A loan is made to the Government from the deposits on the promise of Parliament to pay interest. The shares are largely taken up by rich city Nonconformists.

902. **France.** An English expedition to Brest is defeated, owing to information secretly conveyed by Marlbororugh. The English fleet proceeds to bombard Havre, Dunkirk and other coast towns.

903. **Spain.** A French expedition against Spain achieves nothing decisive. Barcelona is saved by the English fleet.

904. **Germany.** Königsmarck, an officer of George of Hanover and a lover of his wife Sophia Dorothea, is murdered.

---

905. **England.** Danby, Duke of Leeds, is proved guilty of corruption in the granting of a new charter to the East India Company, and is forced to retire. An Act to restrain and punish bribery at elections is passed by Parliament. [1695

William revives the 'Board of Trade and Plantations,' the germ of the Colonial Office.

906. **Scotland.** A Company trading to Africa and the Indies is formed.

907. **France.** Luxembourg dies, and Villeroi, who succeeds him in command of the army in the Netherlands, bombards Brussels.

Namur, defended by Boufflers, surrenders to William and Cohorn, his first success in the war and the greatest triumph of his life (Aug.).

908. **Italy.** Casale is taken from the French by the Duke of Savoy.

909. **Turkey.** The Turks defeat the Venetians at sea, and rout part of the Imperial army.

1384. **Education.** Locke's Thoughts on Education declare that the study of individuality, the formation of character, and the acquisition of right methods of thought rather than the communication of knowledge are the objects to be pursued.

1385. **Law.** Leibnitz' Codex Juris Gentium Diplomaticus deserts Natural Law for Positive Law.

1386. **Politics.** Penn suggests the establishment of an European Diet.

[1694

1387. **Eng. Ch.** George Fox's Journal is published.

1388. **French Ch.** Mme Guyon is released. Fénelon issues an Explication des Maximes des Saints sur la Vie Intérieure, with the approval of Noailles and Tronson, but without the knowledge of Bossuet. At the same time Bossuet's Instruction sur l'Oraison appears, and displeases Fénelon.

1389. **French Lit.** St Simon begins notes for his Memoirs.

The Academy publishes its Dictionary.

1390. **Art.** Purcell's Te Deum and Jubilate.

1391. **Science.** Tournefort's Éléments de la Botanique adopt the flower or corolla as a basis of classification.

1392. **Education.** Mary Astell's Serious Proposal for a Woman's College is combatted by Burnet and others as too closely resembling a convent.

A University is founded at Halle.

1393. **Deaths.** Arnauld, Malpighi, Puffendorf.

[1695

1394. **Eng. Ch.** Locke's Reasonableness of Christianity incurs the charge of Socinianism.

Grabe deserts the Lutheran for the Anglican Church.

1395. **Scotch Ch.** The first Catholic Bishop is appointed, and the Roman Church in Scotland flourishes till 1745.

1396. **Eng. Lit.** The Licensing Act, imposed 1662, is allowed to lapse.

Congreve's Love for Love introduces the second period of the Restoration Comedy, developed by Vanbrugh and Farquhar.

1397. **Science.** Woodward founds a Geological Museum which he bequeaths to Cambridge, and publishes his Natural History of the Earth, in which he investigates fossils and the succession of strata.

1398. **Education.** Francke opens a School at Halle for poor children, the success of which leads to the creation of a number of other institutions, including a school for paying children, a training college for teachers, and a boarding-school for orphans. The classics are neglected, and all studies are subordinated to that of practical theology.

1399. **History.** Tanner's Notitia Monastica.

1400. **Deaths.** D'Herbelot, Halifax, Huyghens, La Fontaine, Purcell.

---

910. **England.** The King's proposal to give Bentinck, Earl of Portland, a large estate in Wales is resisted by the Commons and by public opinion. [1696

The Jacobites plan with Louis that Barclay should murder the King, and Berwick invade England. The plot is discovered, and a reaction in William's favour sets in. An association to support the war and to secure the succession of Anne in the event of his death is joined by most members of Parliament and by many thousands throughout the country.

Persons charged with treason are allowed to have a copy of the indictment and a list of the jury before the trial, witnesses are to be examined on oath, and two witnesses are necessary to the same or a similar overt act of treason.

Montagu, aided by Locke's pamphlets and by Newton, reforms the coinage and introduces milled edges.

911. **France.** Desiring to stop the drain of money and to have his hands free for eventualities in Spain, and failing to obtain peace by direct negociations, Louis resolves to break up the league, and detaches Savoy by the restitution of its territories with the addition of the fortresses of Pinerolo and Casale. The Duke's daughter is to marry Louis' grandson, the Duke of Burgundy.

912. **Russia.** Peter the Great conquers Azov.

913. **Montenegro.** The Prince-Bishops become hereditary, i.e. each Prince-Bishop nominates his nephew.

---

914. **England.** Fenwick, who has plotted the King's death, is executed. [1697

915. **France.** Weakened by the defection of Savoy, the allies accept the mediation of Sweden and open a conference at Ryswick. Louis recognises William as King of England and Anne as his heir, agrees to withhold assistance from his enemies, but refuses to expel James. The Dutch are to garrison the frontier towns of the Spanish Netherlands. All places won since 1678 by either side are restored. By the treaty with the Emperor, signed a month later, Louis retains Alsace and Strassburg, but surrenders Luxembourg, Freiburg, Breisach and Philippsburg, and withdraws from beyond the Rhine. Lorraine is restored to its duke, and the French claims in Cologne and the Palatinate are withdrawn.

916. **Poland.** Augustus the Strong, of Saxony, becomes a Catholic, and secures the Polish crown, defeating the French candidate, the Prince of Conti.

917. **Russia.** Peter sets out on a journey to the west, spending most of his time in studying the industries of Holland and England. He induces several hundred artisans to return with him.

918. **Turkey.** Prince Eugene takes command and routs the Turks at Zenta, failing, owing to floods, to follow up the victory.

1401. **Eng. Ch.** Toland's Christianity not Mysterious, professing to rest on Locke, founds the Deist movement in England, but is burnt by the hangman, and disowned by Locke. [1696

1402. **French Ch.** Quesnel's commentary is examined and disapproved by Bossuet; and Noailles, Archbishop of Paris, who sanctioned the edition of 1693, becomes further identified with Jansenism by refusing to publish Bossuet's attack on Quesnel.

1403. **Eng. Lit.** Baxter's autobiography is published.

1404. **French Lit.** Regnard's Le Joueur.

Muralt, a Swiss, visits and describes England, which also becomes known through the writings of the refugees, Rapin, Boyer, Desmaizeaux, and the works of Prévost.

1405. **Philology.** Hardouin declares most of the classics to be written by monks in the 13th century.

1406. **Economics.** In his Essay on the East India Trade Davenant contends for free exchange at home, but remains substantially a mercantilist.

1407. **Social.** John Bellers, a Quaker, urges the formation of Colleges of Industry, the members of which are to produce and consume in common.

The journeymen hatters, who have formed a permanent organisation or Trade Union, proclaim a strike.

1408. **Deaths.** Luxembourg, Mme de Sévigné, Sobieski.

1409. **Eng. Ch.** Speakers and writers against the divinity of Christ are declared outlaws. [1697

The Lord Mayor, after receiving the Sacrament, proceeds in state to the Congregational chapel, and renders Occasional Conformity fashionable.

Wilson becomes Bishop of the Isle of Man.

1410. **French Ch.** Fénelon appeals to Rome, and is banished to Cambrai by the king, who urges the Pope to condemn him. He is supported by the Jesuits, and the controversy reopens with Bossuet's Relation sur le Quiétisme, to which Fénelon replies.

Bayle's Dictionnaire Historique et Critique, based on that of Moreri, discusses religions from a purely sceptical standpoint.

1411. **German Ch.** Thomasius denies heresy to be a punishable offence and the right of a king to punish.

1412. **Eng. Lit.** Dryden's Alexander's Feast, perhaps modelled on Redi's Bacchus.

1413. **German Lit.** Wernicke's Epigrams attack the extravagances of Lohenstein, Hoffmannswaldau, and other members of the Second Silesian School.

1414. **Philosophy.** Shaftesbury's Inquiry concerning Virtue and Merit seeks a basis in the harmony of natural impulses.

1415. **Philology.** D'Herbelot's Bibliothèque Orientale.

Graevius, with the aid of Bentley, edits Callimachus, the first critical reconstruction of the fragments of an author.

919. **West Indies.** France gains the west of Hispaniola.

920. **Africa.** De Bruë is sent out as director of the Senegal Company, and lays the foundations of French West Africa.

---

921. **England.** The army is reduced to 10,000 and a few months later to 7,000, despite the opposition of the King. [1698

922. **Ireland.** To prevent the underselling of the English drapers in foreign markets, Parliament forbids the export of the Irish drapery, a new industry, practised in the North, expressly exempting, however, the frieze industry, long practised by the South. Molyneux' Case of Ireland being bound by Act of Parliament made in England, protests against this policy, but is burnt by the hangman. Many Presbyterians begin to emigrate to America.

923. **France.** Unable to secure approval for his own claims to the Spanish succession derived through his mother, eldest daughter of Philip III., and his wife, eldest daughter of Philip IV., and unwilling to see it fall to the Emperor, who claims through his mother and wife, younger daughters respectively of Philip III. and Philip IV., Louis XIV. accepts a partition proposed by England and the Dutch, giving the Milanese to the Archduke Charles, the Emperor's younger son by a second marriage, Naples and Sicily to France, and the rest to the son of the Elector of Bavaria, who has married the only daughter of the Emperor. The treaty is made without consulting Spain, and the King, to avoid partition, makes a will, declaring the Bavarian prince sole heir. This arrangement is accepted by the naval powers.

924. **Russia.** During Peter's absence, the Streltsi, or Russian guards, revolt. On his return they are dissolved and replaced by an army on an European pattern.

925. **Africa.** The Imam of Muscat establishes his authority at Mombasa, and Portuguese authority north of Cape Delgado disappears.

---

926. **England.** William is forced to dismiss his Dutch guards, and for a second time is tempted to abdicate. The Junto becomes so unpopular that Russell and Montagu resign, the King returning to a mixed ministry. [1699

927. **France.** The Bavarian prince dies (Jan.), and the claim of his father to stand in his place is resisted by France and England.

928. **Turkey.** By the Peace of Carlowitz, the King of Hungary obtains North Hungary, Transylvania, and the greater part of Slavonia and Croatia, Poland recovers Podolia, Russia keeps Azov, Venice retains the Morea, though restoring her conquests in North Greece, and Turkey obtains the Banate of Temesvar.

929. **Russia.** A Russian Ambassador is sent to the Hague.

930. **America.** The export of wool or woollens to Europe or to any other colony is forbidden.

1416. **Economics.** Boisguillebert's Détail de la France draws a gloomy picture. His theoretical works vigorously attack mercantilism.
1417. **Death.** Molinos.

1418. **Eng. Ch.** The Society for Promoting Christian Knowledge is founded. [1698
1419. **Scotch Ch.** Aikenhead is executed for blasphemy at Edinburgh.
1420. **French Ch.** Brousson, a Protestant preacher, is executed at Montpellier.
1421. **Eng. Lit.** Jeremy Collier, a Nonjuror, attacks the immorality of the drama in his Short View of the Stage, to which replies are attempted by Congreve and Dennis, but which proves the death-blow of the English drama.
1422. **Art.** The finest period begins of the work of Stradivarius, the last and greatest of the Cremona school of violin-makers.
1423. **Science.** Savery patents a pumping engine, which he recommends for clearing mines of water.
1424. **Politics.** Toland publishes the works of Sydney and Harrington, and contributes biographies. He also writes a life of Milton, and in his Anglia Libera declares on behalf of the old republican party that he is satisfied with the Revolution Settlement.
1425. **Law.** Daguesseau begins his Mercuriales, or addresses on the duties of magistrates.
1426. **Social.** Defoe's Essay on Projects recommends income-tax, the establishment of benefit societies, the higher education of women and other changes.
1427. **Deaths.** Frontenac, Redi, Tillemont.

1428. **French Ch.** The Pope condemns 23 articles of the Maximes des Saints, though not describing them as heretical, and Fénelon makes unreserved submission. [1699
1429. **French Lit.** Fénelon is exiled from the Court for writing Télémaque, in which he reflects on the king's government, and the book is suppressed.

The Duchesse du Maine settles at Sceaux, near Paris, and gathers round her a literary circle, including Mme de Staal, Fontenelle, Chaulieu, La Fare, and later, Voltaire.
1430. **Science.** Fontenelle becomes secretary to the Académie des Sciences, and commences the series of his Eloges.
1431. **Philology.** Bentley exhaustively exposes the Epistles of Phalaris, and closes the controversy begun by Sir William Temple and continued by Boyle and Atterbury.
1432. **History.** The Unparteiische Ketzergeschichte of Gottfried Arnold, a pietist and mystic, rescues heretics from misrepresentation and neglect,

Iberville and Bienville lead a French expedition to the mouth of the Mississippi, and found a settlement on one of the islands.

Gold is discovered in large quantities in Brazil, which has gradually become the most valuable of the Portuguese colonies.

---

931. **England.** The Commons attack the grants of Irish land made by the King to his favourites, and tack the Bill of Forfeitures to the grant of supplies. To avoid a rupture, the King dismisses Somers and recalls Godolphin and Rochester. [1700

932. **Scotland.** Colonising expeditions sent to Darien, 1698–9, suffer from the climate and want of food, and are expelled by the Spaniards, the blame of the disaster being thrown on William.

933. **Spain.** A Second Partition Treaty is arranged by Louis and William (March). The Archduke Charles is to have Spain, the Netherlands and the colonies, France to obtain the Sicilies and Lorraine, and the Duke of Lorraine to have Milan. The Emperor refuses his assent. The King of Spain makes a new will, owing to pressure from Harcourt, the French Ambassador and Cardinal Portacarrero, leaving his entire possessions to the Duke of Anjou, second son of the Dauphin, on condition that he renounces the French throne. Charles dies (Nov.), and the will is accepted by Louis. Philip marries a Savoy princess and enters Spain, and the Princesse des Ursins, who accompanies them, quickly gains unbounded influence over them.

934. **Sweden.** A league against Sweden is arranged by Patkul between Russia, which desires an outlet on the Baltic, Denmark, which desires to terminate the independence (guaranteed by Sweden) of the Duke of Holstein, and the Elector of Saxony, who, as King of Poland, is anxious to recover Livonia and Esthonia. The young King, Charles XII., forces Denmark to recognise the independence of the Duke of Holstein and to withdraw from the League, routs the Russians at Narva, and defeats a Saxon army in Livonia.

---

935. **England.** In consequence of the death of the Duke of Gloucester, an Act of Settlement gives the crown, on Anne's death, to Sophia, Electress of Hanover, granddaughter of James I. The future sovereign must belong to the Church of England, must not declare war on behalf of his Continental possessions, nor leave England without consent of Parliament. No royal pardon can protect from impeachment, and Judges can only be removed by an address from both Houses. [1701

The Tories impeach the leading Whigs, Somers, Orford (Russell), Portland (Bentinck), Halifax (Montagu), for their share in the Partition Treaties, but find the Lords hostile.

On the expulsion of the Dutch garrisons from the Barrier forts by the French, a petition is presented by five gentlemen of Kent, begging the Commons to support the King and to grant supplies. The Petitioners are arrested on the ground that the constituencies, having elected their members, have no right to interfere.

and censures Melanchthon for introducing Scholasticism into Protestant Christianity.

1433. **Geography.** De Lisle's Maps are published, aided by Cassini, who perfects the measurement of longitude.

1434. **Deaths.** Domat, Racine, Stillingfleet, Temple.

1435. **Eng. Ch.** A severe Act is passed against Catholics, forbidding a priest to exercise his functions, or a Catholic to hold, buy or inherit property, or to have his children educated abroad. [1700

1436. **French Ch.** Bossuet and Noailles preside over an Assembly of the French Church which condemns Probabilism and the Jesuit policy in regard to Chinese ceremonies.

1437. **German Ch.** The plan of the King of Prussia to unite his Calvinist and Lutheran subjects on an Anglican model is supported by his chaplain, Jablonski, Leibnitz and Archbishop Sharp. The liturgy is translated, and Dodwell urges the adoption of episcopacy in his Paraenesis to Foreigners. The negociations, however, are ended by the death of King Frederick, 1713.

1438. **Dutch Ch.** Van Espen's Jus Ecclesiasticum, an exposition of Gallican principles, is placed on the Index.

1439. **Church Hist.** Hyde's Religio Persarum, the first competent account of Zoroaster.

Eisenmenger attacks the Jews in his Entdecktes Judenthum.

1440. **Eng. Lit.** The Cottonian Library is presented to the nation.

1441. **Science.** An Academy of Science is founded in Berlin by the influence of Leibnitz, who is appointed its first president.

Sauveur measures and explains musical vibrations.

1442. **Education.** A college is founded at Newhaven, Connecticut, and called after Yale, who bequeathes his fortune and library to it.

1443. **Social.** Sewall's Selling of Joseph, the first American protest against slavery.

1444. **Deaths.** Dryden, De Rancé.

1445. **Eng. Ch.** Bray founds a mission branch of the Society for Promoting Christian Knowledge for America, which is chartered as the Society for the Propagation of the Gospel. [1701

Shower's Letter to a Convocation Man, urging the right of meeting and debate, is attacked by Wake, but supported by Atterbury, to whom Burnet, Kennett and Wake reply. Convocation is allowed to meet, but noisy disputes take place.

1446. **Church Hist.** Mechitar, an Armenian monk, who has become a Catholic, founds the order of the Mechitarists in Venice, where they print Armenian works.

William signs the Grand Alliance with the Dutch and the Emperor, to restore the Dutch control of the barrier fortresses, to secure the Milanese for the Emperor, and to prevent the union of France and Spain (Sept.). At the same moment, James II. dies, and his son is acknowledged King of England by Louis. William promptly dissolves Parliament and obtains a Whig majority.

936. **Italy.** Prince Eugene attacks the Milanese and defeats Villeroi.

937. **Germany.** The Elector of Brandenburg is authorised to call himself King of Prussia, on condition of joining the Emperor against France.

938. **Sweden.** Charles defeats the Saxons and Poles and takes Warsaw.

---

939. **England.** William dies from an accident, and Marlborough, Godolphin and Nottingham become the chief advisers of Anne. War is declared by the Grand Alliance. [1702

940. **Scotland.** In accordance with the wish of the late King, Commissioners meet to discuss terms of union between England and Scotland, but fail to agree on matters of trade.

941. **France.** Marlborough, who commands in the Netherlands, takes Liège and Spanish Guelderland. Spanish galleons are destroyed in Vigo Bay, and the French and Spanish fleets are defeated.

942. **Germany.** The Elector of Bavaria declares war against the Emperor.

943. **Holland.** The Stadtholderate lapses, and Heinsius becomes Grand Pensionary.

944. **Sweden.** Charles attacks Augustus and reduces the chief cities of Poland.

945. **West Indies.** Benbow is wounded by the French in the West Indies and disobeyed by his captains, who, however, are court-martialled.

---

946. **England.** A disputed election at Aylesbury produces a conflict between the Houses. [1703

947. **Scotland.** The Parliament resolves that the King of England may not declare war without its consent, and that it will name a successor from the family of Sophia, but not that member selected by England, unless satisfactory assurances are given in regard to religion and trade.

948. **France.** Marlborough takes Bonn and drives the French from the Electorate of Cologne.

Villars joins the Elector of Bavaria, and repulses two Austrian armies, Tallard at the same time recovering ground in Alsace. Savoy and Portugal, however, desert the French alliance, and the Protestants revolt in the Cevennes, under Chevalier.

949. **Russia.** Peter founds St Petersburg, and creates a navy.

950. **Sweden.** Charles continues to take towns in Poland and West Prussia. Patkul renews the Russian alliance, and a Russian army joins Augustus.

1447. **Eng. Lit.** Defoe defends King William in his poem, The True-born Englishman.

1448. **Economics.** The anonymous author of Considerations on the East India Trade first completely discards Mercantilist theories. No further progress is made in Economics until Hume.

1449. **Eng. Ch.** Defoe's Short Way with Dissenters satirises the sentiments of extreme High Churchmen. [1702

1450. **French Ch.** A Cas de Conscience, in which a cleric confesses on his death-bed that he has never believed the Church infallible in a question of fact, resuscitates the Jansenist Controversy. The attitude of 'respectful silence' is approved by 40 doctors of the Sorbonne.

1451. **Dutch Ch.** The apostolic vicar, Peter Kodde, Archbishop of Utrecht, declares for the Jansenists and is suspended by the Pope. The Chapter, however, refuses to recognise the Pope's nominees and is encouraged in its resistance by the States-General.

1452. **Russian Ch.** The Patriarchate of Moscow is abolished.

1453. **English Lit.** The Daily Courant, the first daily paper, is founded.

1454. **American Lit.** Cotton Mather's Magnalia, a history of religion in the American colonies.

1455. **Philosophy.** Bishop King's Origin of Evil attempts to reconcile divine goodness with omnipotence, and is answered by Bayle.

1456. **Social.** The Asiento Guinea Company is formed to transport negroes to Spanish America.

1457. **Death.** Hooke.

1458. **Eng. Ch.** A bill to prevent Occasional Conformity, recently practised by Abney, the Lord Mayor, and others, passes the Commons but is thrown out by the Lords, where the Whigs are in a majority and do not wish to alienate the Dissenters. [1703

Nelson's Fasts and Festivals of the Christian Church.

1459. **History.** Mabillon commences the Annals of the Benedictine Order (completed by Martène), and replies to Germon's sceptical attack on the De Re Diplomatica.

1460. **Philology.** Hickes' Grammar of the old Northern languages, Icelandic, Anglo-Saxon, Gothic.

1461. **Social.** By the Methuen Treaty, Portugal admits English manufactures, and England admits port wine at a lower duty than French wines. Port becomes the popular drink.

1462. **Deaths.** Pepys, St Évremond, Wallis.

---

951. **Hungary.** Rakoksy, son-in-law of Tököli, leads a revolt, aided by Louis XIV.

952. **Portugal.** The Methuen Treaty draws Portugal into a close alliance with England.

---

953. **England.** Nottingham is dismissed, and Harley and St John enter the Government, and aid in defeating the Occasional Conformity Bill. [1704

954. **Scotland.** In view of the danger abroad, the Queen assents to the Act of Security. England, however, retaliates by depriving Scotch residents of their rights under the Post-Nati decision until the English Settlement is adopted in Scotland.

955. **Germany.** Owing to danger to Vienna from the successes of the Elector of Bavaria, Marlborough leaves a small force in the Netherlands and marches to the Danube, drives back the Elector, joins Eugene, and defeats Tallard, Marsin and the Elector of Bavaria at Blenheim. Bavaria is overrun, French power in Germany is brought to an end, and the prestige of French arms is destroyed.

956. **Spain.** The Archduke Charles, with the consent of the allies, claims the throne of Spain, and is conveyed in the English fleet to Lisbon, the first foothold being won at Gibraltar by Admiral Rooke.

957. **Sweden.** Augustus is declared deposed, and Stanislas Leczynski elected King of Poland, by the will of Charles.

---

958. **Germany.** The Celle dominions fall to the Elector of Hanover. [1705

959. **France.** Owing to the opposition to the wishes of Marlborough and Joseph, the new Emperor, by Louis of Baden, the Allies give up their plan of invading France, and Marlborough returns to the Netherlands.

960. **Italy.** The Allies are beaten back by Vendôme.

961. **Spain.** Gibraltar is successfully defended against the French and Spanish, and Barcelona is captured by Lord Peterborough, on which Catalonia, Valencia and Aragon recognise Charles.

962. **Africa.** The Husseinite dynasty of Beys is founded in Tunis, in virtual independence of the Sultan.

---

963. **England.** The article of the Act of Settlement excluding placemen is modified, the holder of an office created before 1705 being henceforward allowed to retain it on re-election. [1706

964. **France.** Marlborough defeats Villeroy at Ramillies (May) and sweeps the French out of Flanders, where the Archduke Charles is proclaimed King. Louis' proposals for peace are rejected.

965. **Germany.** The Electors of Bavaria and Cologne are deprived of their dominions.

966. **Italy.** Eugene joins the Duke of Savoy, routs the French who are besieging Turin, and drives them out of Italy.

1463. **Eng. Ch.** Queen Anne surrenders the claim of the crown to first-fruits and tenths as a provision for the poorer clergy. [1704

Clarke's Being and Attributes of God attacks Hobbes from the standpoint of the ontological argument.

Swift's Tale of a Tub, a dialogue of Catholic, Calvinist and Lutheran, bitterly satirises the sectarian spirit.

Matthew Henry's Exposition of the Old and New Testament.

Toland's Letters to Serena (the Queen of Prussia) discuss the growth of belief in immortality.

1464. **Asiatic Ch.** Clement XI. sends a legate to report on the missions, and in consequence condemns several of the Malabar and Chinese Rites. Christian missions in the East are henceforth less successful.

1465. **Eng. Lit.** Defoe begins the Review, which appears till 1713, a political and miscellaneous journal entirely written by himself, under the patronage of Harley.

Swift's Battle of the Books, suggested by the discussion of ancient and modern learning.

1466. **French Lit.** The first European translation of the Arabian Nights is made by Galland.

1467. **American Lit.** The Boston Newsletter, the first American paper, is instituted.

1468. **Science.** Newton's Optics explain and defend the corpuscular or emission theory of light, and reject the wave theory, chiefly on account of its inability to explain the rectilinear path of rays.

1469. **History.** Clarendon's History of the Rebellion.

1470. **Social.** Beau Nash becomes Master of the Ceremonies at Bath.

1471. **Deaths.** Bossuet, Bourdaloue, Locke.

1472. **Eng. Ch.** The struggle between the Lower House of Convocation and the Bishops, creates a panic in the country, and both Houses declare that the Church is not in danger. [1705

1473. **French Ch.** At the demand of Louis XIV., Clement XI. issues the bull, Vineam Domini, reasserting the heretical character of Jansen's teaching, and thus destroys the Peace of Clement IX.

1474. **Science.** Halley conjectures that a comet seen 1682 was identical with comets seen 1456, 1531, 1607, and predicts its return in 1758.

Newcomen improves the steam-engine by forming a vacuum under the piston. A machine for the raising of water is set up at Wolverhampton 1711.

1475. **Art.** Vanbrugh designs Blenheim for the Duke of Marlborough.

1476. **Politics.** Thomasius' Fundamenta Juris Naturalis et Gentium distinguishes between law and ethics, the duty of the State being to secure happiness, not morality.

1477. **Education.** Moscow University is founded by Peter the Great.

1478. **Deaths.** James Bernouilli, Spener.

1479. **American Ch.** The first Presbytery is organised at Philadelphia. [1706

967. **Spain.** Philip, aided by a French fleet, in vain attempts to recapture Barcelona.

Ruvigny, Earl of Galway, occupies Madrid with English and Portuguese troops, and the Archduke Charles is proclaimed King. They withdraw on the news of the approach of reinforcements under Berwick, a son of James II.

968. **Sweden.** The Swedes rout a superior army of Saxons, Poles and Russians at Frauenstadt. Charles marches into Saxony and encamps at Altranstadt, near Leipsig, and compels Augustus to acknowledge Stanislas and to surrender Patkul, who is executed as a rebel.

---

969. **England.** The royal veto is for the last time exercised.

970. **Scotland.** Largely owing to Godolphin and Harley, and [1707 despite the opposition of Belhaven and Fletcher of Saltoun, the Union is accomplished. England pays £400,000 to cancel the Scotch debt and as indemnity for the Darien shareholders, and concedes free trade and commercial equality. Scotland retains her Church, her law and her fortresses, and sends 45 members to the Lower House and 16 to the Upper. No new Peers are to be created.

971. **France.** An attempt to take Toulon by a joint attack of Eugene on land and Sir Cloudesley Shovel by sea fails, Shovel being wrecked and drowned off the Scilly Isles on his return.

972. **Spain.** Ruvigny is routed at Almanza by Berwick, and Catalonia alone holds out for Charles.

973. **Germany.** Prussia obtains Neuchâtel by inheritance.

974. **Sweden.** Louis and Marlborough urge Charles to intervene in the war; but he refuses, and leaves Altranstadt.

975. **Hungary.** Rakoksy declares the deposition of the Hapsburgs.

976. **Asia.** Aurungzebe dies, and the Moghul dynasty rapidly decays. The Peshwa of the Mahrattas builds up a confederacy at Poona.

Russia takes Kamskatka.

---

977. **England.** The Whigs expel St John and Harley, the [1708 latter of whom has been intriguing against them with the aid of his cousin, Mrs Masham, who displaces the Duchess of Marlborough in the confidence of the Queen. Somers and Walpole join the Ministry.

The Old and New East India Companies are united.

Stanhope and Leake capture Sardinia and Minorca.

978. **Scotland.** The Pretender sets out on an invasion with a French fleet, which is put to flight by Byng at the mouth of the Forth.

979. **France.** Vendôme and Burgundy are routed at Oudenarde by Eugene and Marlborough (July), Lille is taken from Boufflers after a long siege, and the whole of Flanders submits.

980. **Italy.** The Emperor takes the Duchy of Mantua.

981. **Sweden.** Charles sets out for Moscow, but turns south owing to a promise of help by Mazeppa. On reaching the Ukraine he finds Mazeppa is powerless.

1480. **Eng. Lit.** Defoe's Apparition of Mrs Veal.

1481. **Philology.** Schultens' Use of Arabic in the Interpretation of Scripture shows the comparative value of the Semitic tongues.

1482. **Education.** The first Real-Schule is founded at Halle by Christoph Semler, a follower of Francke, for instruction in mathematics and applied science. The curriculum is extended by J. J. Hecker.

1483. **Art.** Schlüter designs the Arsenal at Berlin and the Palace at Charlottenburg.

1484. **Deaths.** Bayle, Evelyn.

1485. **Eng. Ch.** Watts' hymns largely supersede the compositions of Tate and Brady, Sternhold and Hopkins. [1707

1486. **German Ch.** Hollaz' Examen Theologicum, the last great dogmatic work of orthodox Lutheranism.

Thomasius leaves the Pietist movement.

1487. **Church Hist.** Clement XI. excommunicates Joseph I. for his dealings with Parma and Piacenza, over which the Pope claims suzerainty. The Emperor, however, resists, and the Pope yields.

1488. **Science.** Stahl's Theoria Medica Vera declares that while animals are merely machines, man possesses an Anima, which performs the ordinary functions of animal life, and which attempts by illnesses to rid itself of morbid influences.

1489. **Philology.** Mill's New Testament, based on Walton's Polyglot, notes 30,000 various readings.

1490. **Economics.** Vauban's Dîme Royale attacks exemptions and pleads for a uniform land and income tax. The book is burnt by order of the King.

1491. **Deaths.** Filicaja, Mabillon, Vauban.

1492. **Scotch Ch.** Simson begins to teach Arianism. [1708

1493. **French Ch.** Saurin's Sermons are collected, and are widely read by Protestants.

1494. **French Lit.** Lesage's Turcaret, a comic drama, influenced by Spanish models.

1495. **Italian Lit.** Gravina's Della Ragion Poetica contends that the idea of a literary work is more important than its form.

1496. **Science.** Boerhave's Institutiones Medicae trace disease to the vitiation of the fluids of the body, and develope the doctrines of inflammation, obstruction and plethora.

1497. **History.** Bingham's Antiquities of the Christian Church.

1498. **Geography.** Jesuit missionaries survey China, and make an accurate map.

1499. **Philology.** Montfauçon's Paléographie Grecque applies Mabillon's method to Greek.

1500. **Deaths.** Beveridge, Tournefort.

---

982. **England.** Sacheverell preaches before the Lord Mayor (Nov.), reflecting on the Revolution, decrying the toleration of Dissenters, and denouncing the Ministers as traitors to the Church, and is impeached. [1709

Marlborough begs to be made Captain-General for life, but is refused.

983. **France.** Louis undertakes that his grandson shall surrender Spain, but refuses to promise to aid in his expulsion. When the allies insist on the latter point, he appeals to the nation. A new army is formed, and Marlborough and Eugene, who defeat Villars at Malplaquet, lose more heavily than the French.

984. **Sweden.** Charles is crushed by Peter at Pultowa, and takes refuge at Bender. Poland and Denmark renew their alliance with Russia, which completes the conquest of Esthonia and Livonia, and Augustus recovers the crown of Poland.

985. **Asia.** Russian prisoners are first sent to Siberia.

---

986. **England.** At Sacheverell's trial, the Whigs make a declaration of Revolution principles, and Sacheverell replies in a speech composed by Bishop Atterbury. The popularity of the Doctor increases, and Dissenters' chapels are attacked. The sentence of the Lords, ordering the sermon to be burnt and silencing Sacheverell for three years, is regarded as a Whig defeat, and encourages the Queen to dismiss her ministers and to recall Harley and St John. The new Parliament proves strongly Tory, and the new ministers open secret negotiations with France, on the basis of leaving Spain to Philip. [1710

Swift joins the Tories.

987. **France.** A Congress opens at Gertruydenburg, but fails owing to Louis' refusal to aid in expelling his grandson. Meanwhile the frontier fortresses are taken by the allies.

988. **Spain.** Charles is reinforced by English troops under Stanhope and Austrian troops under Staremberg, takes the offensive and enters Madrid, but is quickly forced to evacuate it. Vendôme enters Spain and defeats Stanhope at Brihuega and Staremberg at Villa Viciosa.

989. **Russia.** Charles XII. persuades the Sultan to declare war against Russia.

990. **America.** An English fleet sent to take Quebec fails, but captures Port Royal and changes its name to Annapolis.

---

991. **England.** The Whig Peers vote for the Occasional Conformity Bill, in order to secure the support of Nottingham for the war; and Harley creates 12 peers. Meanwhile Harley has secretly sent Gautier and the poet Prior to France, and signs preliminaries of peace. [1711

To exclude the Whigs, who are mostly traders, the Government imposes a qualification of £600 a year in land for county members and £200 a year in land for borough members.

1501. **French Ch.** Port-Royal des Champs, dissolved by the Pope, 1708, is demolished and its members dispersed. The corpses are disinterred, and the Church demolished. Archbishop Noailles deserts the Jansenist cause. [1709

1502. **Eng. Lit.** Pope's and Ambrose Philips' Pastorals.

Steele's Tatler, a literary periodical to which Addison contributes.

Rowe publishes the first critical edition of Shakespeare.

Prior's poems.

The first Copyright Act is passed.

1503. **Science.** Berkeley's New Theory of Vision asserts that the eye only conveys sensations of colour, and that perceptions of form, and distance are gathered by touch.

1504. **History.** Strype's Annals of the Reformation.

1505. **Death.** Bull.

1506. **Dutch Ch.** Gichtel, a mystical German ascetic resident in Amsterdam, dies, leaving a small band of Gichtelians or Angelic Brethren. [1710

1507. **Eng. Lit.** Swift's Journal to Stella begins (1710—14).

Swift, Prior and other Tory writers edit the Examiner.

Bentley's struggle with the Fellows of Trinity College, Cambridge, of which he is Master, begins.

1508. **French Lit.** Madame de Lambert commences her Salon, which is frequented by Fontenelle, Abbé St Pierre, D'Argenson, Montesquieu, Marivaux.

Ramsay visits Fénelon, becomes a Catholic, remains with him till his death, and writes his life.

1509. **Art.** Handel arrives in London and produces his opera Rinaldo, 1711.

Böttiger manufactures hard porcelain and becomes director of a factory at Meissen near Dresden.

1510. **Philosophy.** Leibnitz publishes his Théodicée, an attack on Bayle suggested by discussions with the Electress of Hanover and Sophia Charlotte, Queen of Prussia.

Berkeley's Principles of Human Knowledge develope the theories of Malebranche.

Vico's De Italorum Sapientia explains his doctrine of metaphysical points or centres of force, which is afterwards adopted by Boscovitch.

1511. **Agriculture.** Enclosures for tillage become frequent, in part owing to the bounty on export.

1512. **Social.** Fénelon's Mémoire sur la Situation déplorable de la France en 1710 denounces the power of the King, and his Examen de Conscience sur les Devoirs de la Royauté, composed for his pupil the Duke of Burgundy, recommends the summoning of the States-General.

1513. **Eng. Ch.** Whiston, who has been deprived of his post at Cambridge, 1708, pleads in his Primitive Christianity Revived for the addition of the Apostolic Constitutions and Clementine Recog- [1711

Harley forms the South Sea Company, to which is promised the monopoly of trade with Spanish South America.

992. **France.** The Emperor dies childless, and the Archduke Charles, who is elected, recalls his troops. Marlborough is not supported from home, and, after breaking through Villars' lines at Bouchain, is recalled.

993. **Hungary.** The treaty of Szathmar ends the Rakoksy revolt. The Hapsburgs retain Transylvania and the crown of Hungary, and the Emperor promises to respect the Magyar liberties and Protestantism.

994. **Russia.** Peter advances south, but is not met by the allies he expects, and hastily makes peace. He restores Azov, destroys Russian fortresses in Turkey, and promises not to meddle with Poland.

Peter creates the Senate for judicial and administrative duties.

[1712

995. **France.** The diplomatists meet at Utrecht. Ormond receives orders forbidding him to fight, but directing him to conceal these orders from the Dutch. They are, however, communicated to the Dutch, who are defeated at Denain by Villars, and, thinking it impossible to carry on a war without England, withdraw.

The Duke of Burgundy, who has become heir by the death of the Dauphin, 1711, dies, followed by his eldest son. His second son, Louis, aged two, becomes heir.

996. **Switzerland.** The second Vilmergen (or Toggenburg) war breaks out, and the Protestant Cantons regain supremacy.

997. **Denmark.** The Danes take Schleswig from the Duke of Holstein-Gottorp, and conquer the Swedish duchies of Bremen and Verden.

[1713

998. **England.** The Tories, seeing the health of the Queen is failing, propose the succession of the Pretender; but his refusal to change his religion splits the party.

By the treaty of Utrecht, the Stuarts are excluded from France, the Protestant Succession guaranteed, and the possession of Gibraltar and Minorca confirmed. The Asiento allows the dispatch of one ship yearly to the Spanish Colonies, and transfers the monopoly of shipping slaves to Spanish America from France to England for 30 years.

999. **America.** Newfoundland, Nova Scotia, Acadia, and Hudson's Bay Territory are ceded by France to England. France retains the right of fishing on the east of Newfoundland.

1000. **Spain.** Philip renounces his claim to the French throne, but retains Spain and the Indies. The Catalans are deserted.

1001. **Netherlands.** The Spanish Netherlands are to be given to Austria; but the barrier fortresses are ceded to the Dutch, France regaining Lille and a few other towns.

1002. **Savoy.** The Duke of Savoy regains his territories and receives Sicily, with the title of King.

1003. **Germany.** Prussia receives from France Upper Guelderland, and the recognition of her possession of Neuchâtel.

nitions to the Canon. He leaves the Church of England and joins the General Baptists.

1514. **Scotch Ch.** Greenshields, an Episcopalian, uses the English Liturgy in Edinburgh and is condemned by the Court of Session; but the decision is reversed by the House of Lords.

1515. **Eng. Lit.** Pope's Essay on Criticism, an adaptation of the ideas of Boileau.

Steele and Addison edit the Spectator, to which Budgell contributes.

Swift's Conduct of the Allies attacks the war.

1516. **Art.** The Zwinger is built at Dresden by Pöppelmann in a style of exaggerated rococo.

1517. **French Lit.** Crébillon's Rhadamiste et Zénobie.

1518. **Philosophy.** Shaftesbury's Characteristics of Men and Manners, written from the standpoint of Deism, point out the excellence of virtue without regard to rewards and punishments. Ridicule is declared to be a test of truth.

1519. **Philology.** Bentley edits Horace.

1520. **Deaths.** Boileau, Ken.

1521. **Eng. Ch.** Clarke's Scripture Doctrine of the Trinity becomes the text-book of modern Arianism. [1712

1522. **Scotch Ch.** In opposition to the feeling of the Church, an Act restores the old rights of lay patronage, but is not recognised by strict Presbyterians, as violating the Act of Security.

1523. **Church Hist.** Mechitar's Order for uniting Armenians to the Roman Church and for the study of Armenian literature and history is confirmed by the Pope.

1524. **Eng. Lit.** Pope's Rape of the Lock, a mock heroic modelled on Boileau's Lutrin.

Arbuthnot's John Bull, a political satire, modelled on Swift.

A Newspaper Stamp Act is passed, and many journals are crushed.

Addison contributes his criticisms of Milton to the Spectator.

1525. **Art.** Crousaz' Traité du Beau, the first French discussion of aesthetics.

1526. **Philosophy.** Wolff begins the literary exposition of his system, an adaptation of Leibnitz' determinism and optimism, without the doctrine of monads.

1527. **Social.** The last execution for witchcraft in England takes place.

1528. **Death.** Cassini.

1529. **Eng. Ch.** Anthony Collins, the friend of Locke, publishes a Discourse on Freethinking, which is attacked by Bentley, Swift and many others. [1713

Gibson's Codex Juris Ecclesiastici Anglicani, a comprehensive study of the legal rights and duties of the English clergy, and of the constitution of the Church.

1530. **French Ch.** The Bull Unigenitus, procured by the King's Confessor, Le Tellier, condemns 101 propositions from Quesnel's Jan-

1004. **Austria.** The Emperor refuses to accept the Treaty, but is forced by Villars to come to terms.

The Emperor brings forward but does not publish the Pragmatic Sanction, fixing the succession, in default of male heirs, on his daughters.

1005. **Sweden.** The Swedes defeat the Danes, but are defeated by the Russians. Danes and Poles invade Pomerania, and Prussia occupies Stettin.

1006. **England.** Harley is driven from office (July 27). The Queen is taken ill; but Somerset and Argyle, suddenly appearing in the Council, secure the appointment of Shrewsbury as Treasurer in succession to Harley. The Queen dies (Aug. 7), and the Elector of Hanover is proclaimed George I., his mother, Sophia, having died a few weeks earlier. The King dismisses the Tories, and calls Townshend, Stanhope, and Walpole to office. Being unable to understand English, the King does not appear at meetings of the Cabinet. [1714

1007. **France.** The Duke of Berry dies, and Orleans, the King's nephew, becomes heir to the Regency. Louis confers the rank of princes of the royal blood on his two sons, Maine and Toulouse, declares them heirs, and makes a will appointing Maine guardian of the heir, and a Council of Regency of which Orleans is to be president.

1008. **Germany.** The Emperor makes peace with France at Rastadt, by which he receives as his share of the Spanish Empire Naples, the Milanese, Sardinia, Mantua and Breisach. The Electors of Bavaria and Cologne are restored, and the Electorate of Brandenburg is recognised. France restores all conquests east of the Rhine. The Emperor, however, does not recognise the Spanish King.

France makes a secret treaty with Bavaria, promising to support the Elector if he becomes a candidate for the Empire.

1009. **Spain.** Barcelona is stormed by Berwick, and Catalonia deprived of her privileges.

Philip marries Elizabeth Farnese, and Alberoni becomes chief minister. Mme des Ursins, the representative of French influence, is expelled.

1010. **Sweden.** Charles XII. returns from Turkey, and Prussia, Saxony, Denmark and Russia ally against him.

1011. **Africa.** Tripoli becomes independent of Constantinople.

1012. **England.** The new Parliament impeaches Bolingbroke, Ormond and Harley for secret negotiations with France previous to the peace. The two former flee to France, where Bolingbroke, who defends himself in his Letter to Wyndham, enters the service of the Pretender. Harley, who remains, is imprisoned for two years. [1715

The Riot Act is passed.

senist Reflexions. Noailles and others protest, and the Church is divided into Acceptants and Appellants.

Mme Jourdan, a Jansenist, institutes the Filles de Sainte-Marthe, established as a Congregation 1722, for the education of girls and the care of the sick.

1531. **French Lit.** Hamilton's Mémoires de Grammont.

Fénelon's Lettre à l'Académie Française approves the composition of a Dictionary, and discusses the duties of the Academy as arbiter of literary taste.

1532. **Science.** Roger Cotes edits a second edition of Newton's Principia, and maintains the doctrine of action at a distance.

1533. **Philosophy.** Collier's Non-Existence of an External World reaches Berkeley's position independently.

1534. **Politics.** The Abbé Saint Pierre explains a Projet pour la Paix Perpétuelle.

1535. **Philology.** Bentley infers a lost digamma from considerations of metre.

1536. **Law.** Gravina's Origines Juris Civilis.

1537. **Geography.** A Board of Longitude is created in England.

1538. **Death.** Shaftesbury.

1539. **Eng. Ch.** Bolingbroke introduces the Schism Act, aimed at Dissenting Academies, forbidding nonconformists to teach; but, owing to the death of the Queen almost immediately after, the Act is not enforced. [1714

1540. **Italian Lit.** Maffei's Merope imitates classical tragedy.

1541. **Spanish Lit.** The foundation of the Spanish Academy marks the epoch of the prevalence of French taste.

1542. **Philosophy.** Leibnitz' La Monadologie explains the world and human life by monads working according to a harmony pre-established by God.

1543. **History.** Helyot's Histoire des Ordres Monastiques.

1544. **Law.** Böhmer's Jus Ecclesiasticum Protestantium traces the modification of Canon Law by the Reformation, and developes Thomasius' territorial theory, according to which the prince possesses the highest ecclesiastical authority as sovereign ruler of the State, not as the chief member of the Church, as the 'episcopal' system of Carpzov maintained.

In 1719, Pfaff of Tübingen suggests the 'collegial' system, according to which the headship of the Church, jus circa sacra, belongs to the sovereign, while the matters pertaining to doctrine and worship belong to the whole body of Church members.

1545. **Death.** Magliabecchi.

1546. **French Ch.** Antoine Court becomes pastor at Nîmes and leader of French Protestantism till his death, 1760. He restores the synodal system, which has been upset since the Revocation, and discourages the 'inspirés' survivors of the Camisard wars. [1715

1013. **Scotland.** The Pretender orders Mar, his chief adherent in Scotland, to take the field. A drawn battle is fought at Sheriffmuir, but Mar allows Argyle to secure the advantages of a victory. On the same day Forster, a Northumberland gentleman who has declared for the Pretender and been joined by Lord Derwentwater and others, surrenders at Preston.

1014. **Netherlands.** The Barrier Treaty is arranged, the Emperor receiving the Spanish Netherlands and the Dutch garrisoning several fortresses.

1015. **France.** On the King's death his will is set aside and Orleans is appointed Regent by the Paris Parliament. Maine remains guardian of the King; but the Duke of Bourbon is appointed president of the Council of Regency. Seven Councils are created.

1016. **Germany.** The Danes sell the duchies of Bremen and Verden to Hanover, which undertakes to enter the war against Sweden.

1017. **Turkey.** The Turks expel the Venetians from the Morea.

1018. **England.** The Pretender appears in Scotland, but quickly returns to France. Despite the easy suppression of the rebellion, the Whigs pass a Septennial Act. [1716

The treaty of Hanover is made by Dubois, England promising to support Orleans in his claims to the throne, if the young King dies, the Regent in return promising to support the Hanoverian succession. The Dutch shortly join the alliance.

Walpole establishes a Sinking Fund.

1019. **Turkey.** Moldavia and Wallachia receive Phanariot governors.

The Turks are defeated at Peterwardein by Eugene, and Temesvar, the last Turkish possession in Hungary, falls.

1020. **England.** Goertz, the Swedish minister at the Hague, plots to aid the Pretender in an invasion of England; but his scheme is discovered through the Swedish ambassador in London. [1717

1021. **France.** Orleans makes a Convention with Russia and Prussia to maintain the treaties of 1713, his succession being guaranteed.

Law, a Scotch adventurer, persuades the Regent to transform his bank, established 1716, into a Government institution, and forms a Mississippi Company, to which the Regent grants Louisiana and the tobacco monopoly. The Company advances money to the Government, and its shares are eagerly bought. The opposition from the Parliament leads to the withdrawal of the right of protest. D'Aguesseau and Noailles are dismissed, the administrative Councils are suppressed, and Law is appointed minister of finance.

Fénelon's Traité de l'Existence de Dieu.

The Jansenists commence to publish the Nouvelles Ecclésiastiques, which appear regularly from 1729 and with brief intervals till 1803.

1547. **Italian Ch.** The Duke of Savoy, who has become King of Sicily without the sanction of the Pope, claims to exercise the 'spiritual rights of the Sicilian monarchy.' Clement thereupon proclaims an Interdict.

1548. **Eng. Lit.** Pope translates the Iliad.

1549. **French Lit.** Le Sage's Gil Blas, a tale of the times of Kings Philip III. and IV. of Spain, modelled on the Spanish picaresque novels.

1550. **Science.** Taylor's Methodus Incrementorum invents the calculus of finite differences, and proves the theorem that the functions of a single variable can be expanded in powers of it.

1551. **Philosophy.** Leibnitz repeats his criticisms of the Principia, outlined in the Acta Eruditorum 1689 and in the Théodicée, in a letter to the Princess of Wales, declaring that Newton's theories lead to a materialistic view of the universe, and repeating his own theory of pre-established harmony. Caroline gives the letter to Clarke, whose reply leads to a correspondence.

Anthony Collins' Inquiry into Human Liberty reaches determinist conclusions.

1552. **Philology.** Facciolati's Polyglot Lexicon.

1553. **History.** The Benedictines of St Maur commence the publication of the Gallia Christiana.

1554. **Deaths.** Burnet, Fénelon, Malebranche.

1555. **Eng. Ch.** Dr Williams founds the Williams Library. [1716

Arsenius, Metropolitan of Thebais, visits London, and the Non-jurors negotiate for reunion with the Greek Church. The Tsar favours the proposals and refers them to the Patriarchs, who refuse all concessions, 1721. After further correspondence, the Patriarchs send an ultimatum requiring acceptance of all the dogmas of the Eastern Church. Wake denounces the Non-jurors to the Patriarch of Jerusalem.

1556. **Science.** De Moivre's Doctrine of the Chances.

1557. **History.** Le Neve's Fasti Ecclesiae Anglicanae.

Hearne begins to edit the English Chronicles.

1558. **Deaths.** Leibnitz, Somers.

1559. **Eng. Ch.** In answer to some papers of Hickes accusing the English Church of schism, Hoadley, Bishop of Bangor, [1717 denies the necessity of communion with any church, and declares that sincerity is the only requirement of Christian profession. These views, repeated in a sermon On the Nature of Christ's Kingdom, in which Hoadley declares against tests of orthodoxy, are censured by Convocation, which is in consequence prorogued by the Government, and does not reassemble for business till 1852. Hoadley replies to the censure, and the Bangorian Controversy begins, in which Law and others take part.

1560. **French Ch.** Four Bishops appeal to a General Council and renounce the bull Unigenitus. They are joined by the Sorbonne,

1022. **Spain.** A Spanish army is sent to conquer Sardinia, professedly owing to the arrest of a Spanish subject in Italy.

1023. **Turkey.** Eugene annihilates the Turkish army at Belgrade and captures the town.

1024. **Russia.** An expedition against Khiva, sent out by Peter under Bekovitch, completely fails.

1025. **Spain.** A Spanish army seizes Sicily. The Emperor appeals to the Triple Alliance to aid him in upholding the articles of Utrecht, and Dubois frames a treaty by which the Emperor, who joins the Triple Alliance, resigns all claims on Spain, Philip renounces Austria's share, Savoy exchanges Sicily for Sardinia, and the succession to Parma and Tuscany is secured to the children of Philip's second marriage. These terms are declined by Spain, and the Spanish fleet is destroyed by Admiral Byng off Cape Passaro. Alberoni hereupon invites the Pretender to Spain, and prepares an expedition for him, and concerts with Goertz, Charles' chief adviser, for the reconciliation of Sweden and Russia. He also plots with the Duchess of Maine and other malcontents in France to depose Orleans and give the regency to Philip. [1718

1026. **Sweden.** Sweden and Russia agree to ally, Russia to aid Sweden to recover her German possessions, Sweden to cede part of Finland, Carelia, Esthonia, and Livonia, and both to expel George I. Charles XII., however, is killed at the siege of Friedrichshall, and the treaty is annulled. The nobles regain power, and the Diet revises the Constitution, and elects the late King's sister, Ulrica, who gives the government to her husband, Frederick of Hesse-Cassel.

1027. **Turkey.** By the peace of Passarowitz, Austria completes her possession of Hungary, gains Belgrade and a strip of Servia and Bosnia, the Banate of Temesvar and Little Wallachia; Venice retains Corfu and her conquests in Albania and Dalmatia; the Sultan keeps the Morea and Aegina, but promises to throw over Rakoksy.

1028. **America.** The French found New Orleans, and the Spaniards found Pensacola.

1029. **England.** Sunderland and Stanhope repeal the Occasional Conformity and Schism Acts. Fearing another wholesale creation of Peers by a Tory ministry, they introduce, but fail to carry, a Peerage Bill, forbidding the King to increase the existing number (178) of peerages by more than six, except for members of the Royal Family. [1719

1030. **Scotland.** Spaniards invade Scotland, and are joined by some Highlanders, but are defeated at Glenshiel.

1031. **Ireland.** A Declaratory Statute is passed that Ireland has been and is dependent on the crown, inseparably united, and King and Parliament may make binding laws.

Noailles and over twenty bishops. The Pope puts the Appellants to the ban, 1718.

Massillon's Petit Carême, a course of sermons preached before the King.

1561. **Church Hist.** Wake, sometime chaplain to the British Embassy to Paris, seizes the opportunity of the appeal of the four Bishops to discuss reunion with Dupin, who proceeds to report on the Articles in his Commonitorium. The scheme fails owing to the disfavour of Dubois and the Jesuits and the death of Dupin, 1719.

1562. **Art.** Watteau's Embarkation for the Isle of Venus, his diploma picture (Louvre).

1563. **Science.** Gravesande begins to lecture at Leyden on Newton's discoveries.

John Bernouilli perceives the universal applicability of the principle of virtual displacements to all cases of equilibrium.

1564. **Social.** After the rebuilding of the City of London and of St Paul's, most masonic lodges die out. The four which remain in London unite and renounce material masonry. A constitution is drawn up, 1721, lodges are formed in Paris, Berlin, and elsewhere, and the movement is condemned by the Pope, 1736.

1565. **Death.** Mme Guyon.

1566. **Eng. Ch.** Jeremy Collier reprints the first Prayer-Book of Edward VI. with additions from antiquity, and the so-called Usages, and leaves the Non-jurors. Both continue the succession of bishops. A further split occurs in reference to the question of lay baptism, 1733. The last regular bishop dies 1779, the last irregular, 1805. [1718

Toland's Nazarenus contrasts the positions of Jew, Gentile and Mahometan.

Clarke's Reformed Prayer-Book, an Arian liturgy.

1567. **French Ch.** Montfauçon edits Chrysostom.

1568. **Science.** Halley discovers that certain of the fixed stars have 'proper motions.'

1569. **Politics.** The Abbé Saint-Pierre's Discours sur la Polysynodie recommends the Regent Orleans' system of Councils, and attacks the memory and greatness of Louis XIV.

1570. **Geography.** D'Anville becomes Geographer to the King, and begins to construct his charts.

1571. **Deaths.** Baluze, Penn.

1572. **Eng. Ch.** A meeting, chiefly of Presbyterians, takes place at Salters Hall, to protest against the subscription of a belief in the Trinity by Nonconformist ministers. Pierce omits everything relating to the Trinity, but without attacking it. Though Calamy, Watts and Neal discountenance the movement, English Presbyterianism loses strength, and Unitarianism spreads. [1719

Waterland's Importance of the Doctrine of the Trinity replies to Clarke.

Col. Gardiner believes himself to have a vision of Christ.

1032. **Spain.** Alberoni's schemes fail, Görz is executed, Orleans detects and punishes his opponents. A French army under Berwick enters Spain, and the Emperor expels the Spaniards from Sicily. The allies compel Philip to dismiss Alberoni, and Spain sinks back into lethargy.

1033. **Sweden.** The Swedes make a treaty with Hanover, which retains Bremen and Verden, and pays one million thalers.

1034. **England.** A mania of speculation attacks the country, the shares in the South Sea Company being sold for £1,000, and creditors of the National Debt accepting shares in lieu of payment. A panic, however, sets in, and the shares fall to 135. [1720

1035. **France.** Law's reckless issue of notes (3 000 million francs), based on the land, raises prices and drives specie out of circulation. Holders of paper hasten to realise, the bank is forced to suspend payment, and Law is exiled.

1036. **Spain.** Philip accepts the terms of the Quadruple Alliance, the Emperor obtains Sicily, and Sardinia passes to Savoy, the Duke of which assumes the title of King of Sardinia.

1037. **Austria.** Having no sons, the Emperor publishes the Pragmatic Sanction, which is accepted by the different parts of the Empire and proclaimed irrevocable law, 1724.

1038. **Sweden.** After the long war, Denmark restores all conquests, and Sweden recognises the annexation of Schleswig. Prussia obtains Stettin and the adjacent district, thus reaching the Baltic, and pays two million thalers.

1039. **England.** Aislabie, Chancellor of the Exchequer, is sent to the Tower for his share in the frauds, Sunderland resigns, and Stanhope dies in a fit caused by a false accusation. Amidst the crash, Walpole, who has re-entered the government 1720, forms a ministry, including Townshend, Carteret and Pulteney, restores public credit, and becomes the first real Prime Minister, retaining his hold on Parliament in part through corruption. [1721

1040. **France.** Dubois obtains the Cardinalate, and wins the goodwill of Spain by betrothing Louis to the daughter of Philip. A defensive alliance between France, Spain and England is also arranged. The two former secretly agree to the first Pacte Famille.

1041. **Russia.** Peter issues an Ukase declaring the right of the sovereign to name his successor (repealed by Paul I.).

1573. **Irish Ch.** A Toleration Act is passed by the Irish Parliament.
1574. **Church Hist.** J. S. Assemanni, the Maronite librarian of the Vatican, publishes his Bibliotheca Orientalis, chiefly relating to the Nestorians and Monophysites. His work is aided and continued by his nephews.
1575. **Eng. Lit.** Defoe's Robinson Crusoe, suggested by the story of Alexander Selkirk.
1576. **Danish Lit.** Holberg's comic epic, Peder Paars.
1577. **Art.** The Abbé Dubos' Réflexions critiques sur la Poésie et la Peinture supply hints to Lessing.
1578. **Philology.** Montfauçon's Antiquité Expliquée.
1579. **History.** Le Long's Bibliothèque historique de la France, an account of books and manuscripts.
1580. **Deaths.** Addison, Flamsteed, Mme de Maintenon, Quesnel.

1581. **Scotch Ch.** Boston's Human Nature in its Fourfold Estate.
1582. **French Ch.** Dubois, who hopes for a Cardinal's hat, persuades Parliament to acknowledge the Bull Unigenitus, with express reservation of Gallican liberties, and begins to persecute the Appellants. [1720
1583. **German Ch.** The Irenicum of Pfaff of Tübingen is bitterly attacked by the strict Lutherans.
1584. **Eng. Lit.** The Cato Letters, by the Whig journalists Gordon and Trenchard, denounce the authors of the South Sea Bubble.
1585. **Science.** Fahrenheit employs mercury in a thermometer; Réaumur uses spirits of wine; and Celsius divides the scale into 100 degrees.
1586. **Philology.** Bentley's Proposals for printing the New Testament advocate the study of the oldest MSS., independently of the Textus Receptus.
1587. **History.** Père Anselme discusses the value of ancient records, and Pouilly and Beaufort criticise the authenticity of the early history of Rome, which is defended by Fréret.
1588. **Law.** Vico's De Uno Universi Juris Principio connects the philosophy of law with general philosophy, and applies the historical method.

1589. **Eng. Ch.** Waterland's Case of Arian Subscription Considered attacks Clarke's interpretation of the Articles. [1721
1590. **German Ch.** Brockes' Earthly Pleasure in God, a metrical work of optimistic deism.
1591. **Russian Ch.** In place of the Patriarchate of Moscow, the Holy Synod is appointed to rule the Church under the Tsar, who chooses its members, and may veto its decisions.
1592. **French Lit.** Montesquieu's Lettres Persanes trenchantly criticise political and ecclesiastical methods and ideas.

1042. **Sweden.** By the Treaty of Nystad, Sweden cedes to Russia Livonia and Esthonia and Ingermannland, Russia promising not to interfere with the internal affairs of Sweden and restoring Finland. The treaty confirms Russia's supremacy in the North.

1043. **Denmark.** Frederick founds a fort in Greenland and plants a colony. The Government reserves to itself the monopoly of trade.

1044. **Africa.** France occupies Mauritius, deserted by Holland 1712, and calls it Ile de France.

1045. **England.** Atterbury, Bishop of Rochester, is arrested for corresponding with the Pretender, and is banished 1723. [1722

1046. **Netherlands.** Desiring to revive Flemish commerce, but not daring to re-open the Scheldt, the Emperor forms an East India Company at Ostend, which is hotly opposed by England.

1047. **Russia.** Alexis is executed for his opposition to his father's policy.

Russia seizes Derbent and Baku on the Caspian.

1048. **England.** Bolingbroke is allowed to return, though he is not allowed to sit in the House of Lords. He begins to organise an opposition to Walpole, but never regains much political influence. [1723

1049. **France.** The King's minority ends, Dubois and Orleans die, and Bourbon, Condé's grandson, becomes chief minister. The real power, however, is exercised by the King's tutor, the Abbé Fleury, who continues Orleans' policy of friendliness to England.

1050. **Hungary.** By the Pragmatic Sanction, Hungary and Austria are declared inseparable under the same ruler, but Hungary is to remain independent and to be governed by her own laws.

1051. **England.** Carteret resigns his place in the ministry, disapproving of Walpole's alliance with France, and becomes Lord Lieutenant of Ireland. Newcastle and his brother, Henry Pelham, enter the Cabinet. [1724

1052. **Ireland.** To supply the want of copper coin, a patent is given to the King's mistress, who sells it to Wood, 1723. Though the coins are good, the Irish of both races strongly protest against the whole affair. Swift gives utterance to Irish sentiments in his Drapier's Letters, which denounce the job and plead for national self-government. Walpole withdraws the grant and compensates Wood.

1593. **American Lit.** Dummer's Defence of the New England Charters.
1594. **Politics.** Wolff's Politics derive Natural Right from the moral nature, and vindicate inborn rights for man.
1595. **History.** Vico attacks the credibility of early Roman History.
1596. **Social.** Inoculation for small-pox, introduced into England by Lady M. W. Montagu, wife of the English ambassador at Constantinople, is rendered fashionable by the Princess of Wales.
1597. **Deaths.** Huet, Watteau.

1598. **Eng. Ch.** Wollaston's Religion of Nature imitates Clarke and anticipates the Utilitarians. [1722
1599. **Bohemian Ch.** Zinzendorf collects the remnants of the Bohemian Brothers and forms the Moravian Brotherhood at Herrnhut.
1600. **Asiatic Ch.** The Christian Churches in China are destroyed.
1601. **Art.** Augustus founds a Picture Gallery at Dresden.
Farinelli makes his début.
Bach's Fugues.
1602. **Social.** Workhouses are erected in England.
1603. **Deaths.** Marlborough, Toland.

1604. **Dutch Ch.** The Utrecht Chapter elects an Archbishop who is consecrated by the Bishop of Babylon, and is defended by Van Espen, but is excommunicated by the Pope. Suffragan bishops of Harlem and Deventer are consecrated 1742 and 1752. [1723
1605. **French Lit.** Voltaire's Henriade.
1606. **Italian Lit.** Metastasio's Didone Abbandonata, an operatic libretto.
1607. **Philosophy.** Mandeville's Fable of the Bees, attacking the optimism of Shaftesbury (published 1705, expanded 1714, and 1723), is prosecuted by the Grand Jury of Middlesex, and is criticised by Law and Berkeley.
The King of Prussia banishes Wolff from Halle.
1608. **History.** Giannone's Civil History of Naples defends the civil power in its conflicts with the hierarchy.
Muratori collects the works of the historians of mediaeval Italy.
1609. **Deaths.** Leeuwenhoek, Wren.

1610. **Eng. Ch.** Anthony Collins' Grounds and Reasons of the Christian Religion maintains that the Old Testament prophecies on which Christianity rests were never literally fulfilled, and that Christianity is simply 'Mystical Judaism.' [1724
Hutchinson's Moses' Principia attacks Newton as the enemy of inspiration.

1053. **Spain.** Philip resigns the throne in a fit of religious mania, and perhaps also to be free for the French succession, but, on the death of his son, resumes his place owing to pressure from his wife.

1054. **France.** Louis suddenly dismisses the Infanta and marries Marie Leszczynski, the daughter of Stanislas, sometime King of Poland. [1725

1055. **Spain.** Angered by this insult, and spurred on by Ripperda, a Dutchman in the pay of Austria, Spain allies with the Emperor, who desires Spanish confirmation of the Pragmatic Sanction, by the Treaty of Vienna (April). Parma and Tuscany are to pass to Don Carlos, the Emperor to aid in the restoration of Gibraltar and Minorca, Philip to open Spanish ports to the Ostend Company and transfer the commercial privileges, hitherto enjoyed by England and the Dutch, to Germans. Ripperda also concludes a secret treaty by which the Emperor promises to aid Spain to forcibly recover Gibraltar, if necessary, and to support a Jacobite invasion of England. Marriages of the Emperor's daughters with Philip's sons are also discussed. Russia and several German states join.

1056. **England.** To counterbalance this confederacy, England allies with France and Prussia by the Treaty of Hanover (Sept.). The integrity of the contracting powers is guaranteed, the Prussian claims on Jülich are recognised, and the Ostend Company is to be abolished. Sweden, Denmark, and Holland shortly join the alliance.

Pulteney resigns his place in the Ministry.

1057. **Russia.** Peter the Great dies. His wife Catherine succeeds him, and rules with the aid of Menshikoff and Ostermann.

1058. **England.** Bolingbroke and Pulteney combine in opposition to Walpole, and found a weekly journal, the Craftsman, in which the Government is denounced as a despotism based on corruption. [1726

1059. **France.** Fleury procures the dismissal of Bourbon, and becomes first minister, and restores credit and economy.

1060. **Austria.** Seckendorf detaches Frederick William, King of Prussia, who repents of his alliances of 1725, and whose policy is now for some time dictated from Vienna through Grumkow. The friendliness of the Emperor to Spain, on the other hand, cools, Charles disliking the idea of a Spanish duchy in North Italy and a Spanish marriage.

1061. **Spain.** Ripperda falls, but his successor, Patiño, continues his policy. An English fleet blockades Porto Bello.

1062. **Russia.** A Treaty with Austria is arranged for 30 years, for common action against the Turks and for defence against other powers.

1611. **French Ch.** Bourbon forbids Protestant worship.
1612. **Polish Ch.** The Protestants who have attacked the Jesuit College are massacred at the 'Blood-bath of Thorn.'
1613. **German Lit.** The Patriot of Hamburg, by Brockes and Hagedorn, extends English influences. Gottsched becomes Professor at Leipsig and criticises the extravagances of Lohenstein and his school.
Gunther's Poems.
1614. **History.** Burnet's History of his Own Time.
1615. **Economics.** Possoschkoff recommends schemes of economic and social reform from a mercantilist standpoint, and supports the policy of the Tsar.
1616. **Death.** Harley.

[1725

1617. **Eng. Lit.** Allan Ramsay's Gentle Shepherd.
1618. **American Lit.** Ames' Astronomical Diary and Almanac introduces English literature, and is followed by Franklin's Poor Richard's Almanac, 1733.
1619. **Philosophy.** Hutcheson's Our Ideas of Beauty and Virtue defends Shaftesbury's Ethics against Mandeville, and maintains that we perceive Beauty by 'an internal sense' and independently of any advantage to be derived.
1620. **History.** Vico's Scienza Nuova declares that there is a special science of human history and traces the cycles of progress.
1621. **Geography.** Behring (a Dane) discovers Behring Straits.
1622. **Social.** Guy's Hospital is founded.

[1726

1623. **Eng. Ch.** Butler's 15 Sermons assert that man possesses rational benevolence as well as self-love, and that both are under the authority of conscience.
1624. **Eng. Lit.** Thomson's Seasons initiate a contest against the supremacy of town models.
Swift's Gulliver's Travels.
Theobald edits Shakespere.
Voltaire comes to reside in England for three years and studies English drama, Locke's philosophy and Newton's discoveries.
1625. **French Lit.** Mme de Tencin opens her Salon, which is frequented largely by the guests of Mme de Lambert.
1626. **Science.** Harrison invents a compensating balance for clocks.
1627. **History.** Mascou begins the first valuable History of Germany in the Middle Ages.

1063. **Ireland.** The Catholics are deprived of the franchise. [1727

1064. **Spain.** Spain besieges Gibraltar (Feb.), France standing aloof. The Emperor, losing his strongest ally by the death of Catherine of Russia, agrees with England and the Dutch to the Preliminaries of Paris, promising to suspend the Ostend Company, and resolving on a Congress.

1065. **Russia.** Menshikoff falls, and is exiled to Siberia.

1066. **England.** The publication of debates is declared a breach of privilege. [1728

1067. **Spain.** The Siege of Gibraltar is raised, and a convention with England is signed. The Emperor informs Spain that the marriages arranged in 1725 will not take place. A Congress meets at Soissons, without result.

1068. **Germany.** By the secret treaty of Berlin, between Frederick William and the Emperor, the former recognises the Pragmatic Sanction and promises his support to Charles' son-in-law as a candidate for the Empire, and Charles transfers his rights on Berg and Ravenstein.

1069. **Spain.** Seeing he can obtain nothing from the Emperor, and his claims on France being barred by the birth of an heir, Philip deserts the Austrian alliance and allies with France and England by the Treaty of Seville, which is shortly joined by the Dutch. Don Carlos is to succeed to Parma and Tuscany, which are to be occupied by troops, and the privileges to the Emperor's subjects granted by the Treaty of Vienna to be revoked. No mention is made of Gibraltar and Minorca. [1729

1070. **Italy.** The series of revolts in Corsica against Genoa begins, led by several able adventurers. For some years the island is given up to anarchy.

1071. **America.** The Charter being forfeited for misgovernment, the proprietors of Carolina sell their titles, and the colony becomes a royal government, and is divided into North and South.

1072. **Asia.** Nadir, a robber-chief, aids the deposed Shah of Persia, and defeats the Afghans. In 1732, he deposes the Shah on the ground of incompetence, and sets up his infant son.

1073. **England.** Townshend resigns, refusing to recognise Walpole as Prime Minister, and leaves political life. [1730

1074. **France.** The King holds a Lit de Justice to compel Parliament to register the Bull Unigenitus, and, on its refusal, issues an Edict declaring that it cannot meddle with politics.

1075. **Germany.** Hotham is sent to Berlin to arrange the double marriage desired by the Queen of Prussia, but is dismissed with insult. The Queen hereupon makes Frederick and Wilhelmina promise to hold to the English marriages ; but the King discovers what she has done, and Frederick is imprisoned at Küstrin.

1628. **Eng. Ch.** Woolston attacks the credibility of Miracles, and is answered by Sherlock's Trial of the Witnesses. [1727

Lardner's Credibility of Gospel History.

Walpole introduces the first annual bill of indemnity for neglect of the Test and Corporation Acts.

1629. **Church Hist.** Orsi attacks the Jesuits for allowing mental reservation. Zaccaria defends the Order, and is attacked by Patuzzi and Concina.

1630. **Eng. Lit.** Gay's Beggar's Opera.

Chambers' Cyclopaedia.

1631. **Science.** Stephen Hales' Statical Essays explain the nutrition of plants, and measure the flow of blood.

1632. **Agriculture.** Lawrence's Duty of a Steward reveals the plan of the large landowners to expropriate the yeomen or small farmers.

1633. **Deaths.** Francke, Newton.

1634. **Eng. Ch.** A Moravian Mission is planted in England. [1728

1635. **Death.** Thomasius.

1636. **Eng. Ch.** Law's Serious Call. [1729

Doddridge establishes a Presbyterian Academy at Market Harborough.

Middleton's Letter from Rome introduces the historic method into the deistic controversy, maintaining that the Roman Church adopted many Pagan ceremonies.

John Wesley and his friends begin to meet at Oxford.

Arminianism is spread in Wales by Jenkin Jones, and many adopt Arianism and Unitarianism.

1637. **American Ch.** Jonathan Edwards begins to preach.

Berkeley visits Rhode Island, hoping to Christianise Bermuda and the Indians by a missionary college.

1638. **Art.** Bach's St Matthew's Passion.

1639. **Science.** Gray finds that some bodies can, and others cannot, conduct electricity.

Bradley discovers the aberration of light.

1640. **Law.** D'Aguesseau begins to issue ordinances for the reform of French law, and plans its codification.

1641. **Deaths.** Clarke, Congreve, Menshikoff, Steele.

1642. **Eng. Ch.** Tindal's Christianity as old as the Creation declares that Christ merely confirmed the law revealed by the light of Nature. The book is vigorously attacked by Law. [1730

1643. **Scotch Ch.** Glas attacks the civil establishment of the Church, is deposed and forms the Glassite Sect, which is developed by his son-in-law Sandeman.

1644. **French Ch.** Antoine Court leaves France and founds a Huguenot seminary at Lausanne.

Adrienne Lecouvreur, the actress, is refused Christian burial.

1076. **Russia.** With Peter II., grandson of Peter the Great, the male line of the Romanoffs ends.

1077. **America.** Walpole allows Carolina and Georgia to export their rice and the West Indies their sugar in English ships, and repeals the duties on the importation of timber from the colonies.

1078. **Africa.** The Portuguese finally lose Mombasa.

1079. **France.** The Parliament of Paris declares the ministers of the Church accountable to itself, under the King, whereon Fleury exiles several of its members. [1731

1080. **Italy.** On the death of the Duke of Parma, the Emperor, indignant at the Treaty of Seville, seizes on his territory. France and England refuse to aid Spain in expelling him. Walpole, however, acting independently of France, forms the second treaty of Vienna with the Emperor, which is joined by Spain. England guarantees the Pragmatic Sanction, on condition Maria Theresa does not marry a Bourbon. Charles agrees to dissolve the Ostend Company, and allows Don Carlos to occupy Parma and Piacenza.

1081. **Poland.** Russia, Austria and Prussia propose, but do not agree, to oppose Stanislas and to settle the succession.

1082. **America.** English and Spaniards come into conflict in South America, the former feeding the one ship allowed to them by treaty from tenders kept beyond sight of land, the latter insisting on the right of search.

1083. **Germany.** The Pragmatic Sanction is accepted by the German Princes, except the Elector Palatine, Saxony and Bavaria. [1732

1084. **America.** To secure the western part of Carolina before it is claimed by France or Spain, Oglethorpe, Berkeley and others, as trustees for the crown for 21 years, found the colony of Georgia, chiefly as a refuge for persecuted Protestants and for criminals. Though the Charter forbids slavery, the colonists 'hire' slaves from Carolina.

1085. **England.** To suppress smuggling and frauds, Walpole proposes that tobacco shall be imported free of duty into supervised warehouses and sold at licensed shops, the duty being paid by the purchaser. Goods destined for re-exportation equally pay no duty. Walpole also abolishes the sinking-fund of 1716, and assures the Commons that he will be able to reduce the Land-Tax to one shilling in the £. Pulteney and Bolingbroke, however, persuade the country that the minister is imposing a general excise and raising the price of tobacco, and force Walpole to withdraw the scheme. Chesterfield and other disloyal members of the Government are in consequence dismissed. [1733

1086. **Italy.** Fleury allies with Spain and Sardinia by the League of Turin, by which Don Carlos is to renounce Parma and the succession to Tuscany to his younger brother, and to obtain Naples and Sicily.

1645. **Science.** De Moivre's theorems create (with Lambert) that part of trigonometry which deals with imaginary quantities.

1646. **Philology.** Vico (in the 2nd edition of the Scienza Nuova) declares the Homeric poems to be composed by different hands, and the Iliad to be the earlier.

1647. **History.** Rollin's Histoire Ancienne.

1648. **Agriculture.** Townshend begins the Norfolk or four-course system of husbandry, improves marling, and cultivates clover and turnips. Jethro Tull also experiments on his farm at Wallingford.

1649. **French Ch.** Miracles commence at the tomb of the Jansenist, Abbé Paris. At first approved by the Jansenist leaders, they soon degenerate, and the government closes the cemetery. [1731

1650. **German Ch.** 20,000 Protestants of the diocese of Salzburg are expelled by the Archbishop, and take refuge in Prussia, Holland and America.

Tersteegen's Spiritual Flower-Garden, a collection of pietist and mystical hymns.

1651. **Eng. Lit.** The Gentleman's Magazine is founded.

1652. **French Lit.** Marivaux' Marianne creates Marivaudage, or affectation posing as simplicity.

1653. **Dutch Lit.** Van Effen edits the Dutch Spectator.

1654. **Science.** Stahl's Observationes Chemicae introduces the first consistent theory of the composition of compounds and of chemical action, and declares that there are four elements, Water, Air, Earth, Phlogiston.

Hadley invents the quadrant for use at sea, which supersedes the astrolabe and the cross-staff. Dollond shortly invents the sextant.

1655. **Death.** Defoe.

1656. **Eng. Ch.** Berkeley attacks the Deists in Alciphron. [1732

1657. **Church Hist.** The Redemptionists are founded by Liguori, principally for missions to the rural poor.

1658. **Eng. Lit.** Pope's Essay on Man.

1659. **French Lit.** Voltaire's tragedy, Zaire.

1660. **German Lit.** The translation of Paradise Lost by Bodmer of Zürich is attacked by Gottsched, and leads to a controversy extending over 10 years between the Swiss and Saxon schools.

Haller's The Alps praises the beauty of nature.

1661. **Swedish Lit.** Dalin's Argus copies the Spectator.

1662. **Science.** Boerhaave's Elements of Chemistry founds organic chemistry, analysing the compounds of plants and animals.

1663. **History.** Maffei's Verona Illustrata.

1664. **Law.** J. J. Moser's Foundations of International Law, the first systematic work on positive international law.

1665. **Eng. Ch.** Hoadley's Plain Account of the Lord's Supper, describing the ceremony as purely memorial, is attacked in Waterland's Doctrine of the Eucharist. [1733

The King of Sardinia is to annex the Milanese, and Savoy is to be handed over to France.

France overruns Lorraine and the Milanese.

1087. **Spain.** A family compact is made by the Treaty of the Escurial, by which France and Spain agree that their forces shall act together, France promising the recovery of Gibraltar, Spain the withdrawal of her concessions to English trade. Walpole hears of the secret treaty through the King of Sardinia.

1088. **Poland.** Augustus dies, and the war party in France force the King and Fleury to promise support to Stanislas, who goes to Poland and is re-elected King by a majority of the nobles. Russia supports the son of Augustus, and the Emperor is won over by a promise of the young Augustus to recognise the Pragmatic Sanction. Stanislas is expelled by Russian and Saxon troops, French aid proves too small to be effective, and Augustus is acknowledged King by the Poles.

1089. **America.** By the Sugar Act, the colonies are forbidden to trade with the French islands and confined to the English West Indies.

1090. **France.** France and Sardinia conquer the Milanese and occupy Lorraine. [1734

1091. **Italy.** Don Carlos enters Naples, where he is welcomed. Tanucci becomes his chief minister, and reforms are introduced. The clergy are taxed, and feudalism is partially broken up.

1092. **Poland.** Danzig is taken by Russia, and Stanislas is forced to escape from Poland.

1093. **England.** Bolingbroke retires to France. [1735

1094. **Italy.** Don Carlos wins Sicily.

France deserts Spain and arranges preliminaries of peace with the Emperor. Stanislas is to renounce the Polish crown in favour of Augustus, and to receive in compensation Lorraine, which on his death is to pass to France. Francis of Lorraine is to receive Tuscany as indemnification on the death of the reigning Grand Duke. Don Carlos hands over Parma and Piacenza to the Emperor, and is recognised as King of Naples and Sicily. Other conquests are restored, and France guarantees the Pragmatic Sanction.

1095. **Africa.** Labourdonnais becomes Governor of Mauritius and Réunion under the French East India Company, and establishes the sugar industry in the islands.

1096. **Asia.** The war between Turkey and Nadir ends.

1097. **Scotland.** Porteous, captain of the Edinburgh City Guard, fires on the mob at the execution of Wilson, a smuggler, is sentenced to death, and reprieved. He is hung by the mob, and the riots in Edinburgh reveal the latent hostility felt by Scotland to the English crown. [1736

1098. **Spain.** The Preliminaries of Vienna are accepted by Spain.

1666. **Scotch Ch.** The restoration of lay-patronage is attacked by Ebenezer Erskine, who is suspended. He protests against the authority of the General Assembly, forms a new church, and is deposed.
1667. **Polish Ch.** Non-Catholics are excluded from office.
1668. **French Lit.** Gresset's Vert-Vert, the story of a parrot.
1669. **Art.** Rameau begins to compose operas and becomes recognised as Lulli's successor.
1670. **History.** Vaissette and Devic, Benedictines of St Maur, compile a Histoire de Languedoc. Others commence a Histoire littéraire de la France.
1671. **Law.** Proceedings in Court are to be in English.

1672. **German Ch.** Baumgarten becomes Professor of Theology at Halle and developes a Pelagian rationalism. About this time Pietism loses its influence in the Lutheran Church. [1734
1673. **French Lit.** Voltaire's Lettres sur les Anglais introduce the ideas of Locke and Newton, and direct attention to England.
1674. **Art.** The Dilettanti Society is formed to encourage art.
1675. **Philosophy.** Berkeley's Analyst declares that mathematics cannot justify its axioms any more than theology.
1676. **Education.** Mme de Lambert's Avis d'une Mère à sa Fille approves of the study of classics and Cartesianism by women.
1677. **History.** Montesquieu's Grandeur et Décadence des Romains.
1678. **Death.** Stahl.

1679. **Eng. Ch.** Scougal's Life of God in the Soul of Man. [1735
1680. **American Ch.** John Wesley goes to work in Georgia.
1681. **Science.** Linnaeus' Systema Naturae introduces a second or specific name for plants and animals, and proves the sex of plants, which he classifies according as the organs of reproduction are visible or not.

La Condamine is sent to South America and Maupertuis to Lapland to measure an arc of the meridian.
1682. **Economics.** Berkeley's Querist points out the true nature of money.
1683. **Law.** Heineccius declares Roman law inapplicable in Germany.
1684. **Death.** Peterborough.

1685. **Eng. Ch.** Butler's Analogy of Religion, Natural and Revealed, with the Constitution and Course of Nature contends that the difficulties of Christianity are no greater than those of natural religion, which his opponents, the Deists, recognise to proceed from God. [1736

Warburton's Alliance of Church and State contends for the necessity, both theoretical and practical, of an Establishment and a test law.

Walpole supports the Quakers in their protest against tithes, but is forced by the outcry to withdraw.
1686. **German Ch.** Wolff's Theologia Naturalis, distinguishing Veritas Aeterna and Veritates Contingentes, such as miracles, initiates the Aufklärung.

1099. **Italy.** Baron Neuhof, of Westphalia, becomes King Theodore I. of Corsica.

1100. **Turkey.** The Czarina Anne, desiring to recover Azov, declares war against Turkey, and seizes Azov. Russia's ally, Austria, sends an army under Seckendorf, a Protestant.

1101. **Asia.** The infant Shah dies, the Sufi dynasty ends, and Nadir becomes Shah of Persia.

1102. **England.** The King quarrels with the Prince of Wales, who retires to Leicester House and becomes the head of the opposition. Walpole's position is further weakened by the death of Queen Caroline. [1737

The Treaty of Vienna is ratified, and the war of the Polish Succession is closed.

1103. **Italy.** The Grand Duke of Tuscany dies, and is succeeded by the Duke of Lorraine.

1104. **France.** Stanislas succeeds to Lorraine and Bar.

The Corvée is established throughout France.

1105. **Turkey.** The Emperor's troops are repulsed, and Seckendorf is disgraced.

1106. **Russia.** Courland, which is legally under the overlordship of Poland, is obtained by the Empress Anne for Biron.

1107. **England.** The opposition is joined by Pitt and other young men indignant at the corruption of Walpole, who calls them the Boys. [1738

Captain Jenkins, who claims to have lost an ear in a scuffle with a Spanish coast-guard, is brought forward by the opposition, and a cry for war with Spain becomes general.

1108. **Austria.** The Treaty of Vienna is definitively signed.

1109. **Sweden.** The Hats, or the war-party, overthrow the Caps, the party of peace. Gyllenborg becomes chancellor, and the French alliance is renewed.

1110. **Turkey.** The new Austrian General, Königsegg, is driven back to Belgrade, and several fortresses are lost. Fleury offers mediation.

1111. **Asia.** Nadir Shah seizes the cities and territories of Kandahar and Cabul, the latter an outpost of the Moghul Empire.

1112. **England.** Walpole obtains an indemnity from Spain for actual damage to Englishmen in South America; but Spain threatens to cancel the monopoly. Walpole is forced to enter on war for the right of search. Porto Bello is captured by Vernon, and Anson attacks Peru in the course of his voyage round the world. [1739

1113. **France.** By a secret treaty with Austria, the House of Sulzbach is guaranteed provisional occupation of Jülich and Berg on the death of the Elector Palatine (Jan.). Three months later, France secretly

1687. **Science.** Euler founds analytical mechanics, retaining the old geometrical modes.

1688. **Art.** The exploration of Herculaneum, discovered 1711, is commenced.

1689. **Law.** Bynkershoek's De Foro Legatorum.

1690. **Social.** The English statutes against witchcraft are repealed, despite the protest of the Presbyterian ministers.

1691. **Deaths.** Eugene, Leclerc, Pergolesi.

1692. **Eng. Ch.** Cruden compiles a Concordance of the Bible.

1693. **Italian Ch.** St Paul of the Cross founds the Passionists. [1737

1694. **American Ch.** Arminianism and Socinianism begin to spread.

1695. **Eng. Lit.** The Lord Chamberlain undertakes the licensing of plays.

1696. **Science.** Réaumur's History of Insects.

1697. **Education.** Göttingen University is founded by the King of Hanover. Haller and Blumenbach teach science, Gesner and Heyne classics, Putter and Schlözer, history and politics.

1698. **Law.** J. J. Moser's German Law, a collection from treaties and other original sources of the rules of law at this time in force.

Bynkershoek's Quaestiones Juris Publicis discuss the positions of belligerent and neutral in sea warfare.

1699. **Eng. Ch.** Wesley returns from Georgia, falls under the influence of Peter Böhler, a Moravian, and is 'converted' on [1738 May 24. He visits Herrnhut and is much impressed with the life of the community.

Warburton's Divine Legation of Moses declares that Jewish society, having no doctrine of a future life, was supported by an extraordinary Providence.

1700. **American Ch.** Whitfield undertakes a mission in America.

1701. **Eng. Lit.** Johnson's London.

1702. **Science.** Voltaire introduces Newton's ideas into France; but the Cartesian Academy of Sciences declares that they revive scholastic notions of occult qualities.

Daniel Bernouilli asserts that gases are composed of molecules in constant motion, and anticipates the doctrine of Conservation of Energy.

1703. **Politics.** Bolingbroke's Patriot King urges that the monarch should stand outside and above party.

1704. **Social.** Kay's flying-shuttle enables weavers to produce double the quantity of calico.

1705. **Death.** Boerhaave.

1706. **Eng. Ch.** Wesley follows Whitfield's example of preaching in the open air, and finds himself excluded from the majority [1739 of pulpits.

Chubb's True Gospel of Jesus Christ explains Deism to the working-classes.

agrees with Prussia to allow the latter to share the duchies with Sulzbach. The two Powers agree to stand together in case of war.

1114. **Turkey.** The Turks rout the Austrians at Crocyka and threaten Belgrade. A treaty of Belgrade is therefore made by French influence. Austria cedes all territories gained by the Treaty of Passarowitz, but retains Temesvar, of which the fortresses are to be dismantled. Russia, being deserted by her ally, is forced to make peace, ceding all her conquests except Azov, which she is to dismantle, and promising not to maintain vessels on the Black Sea or the Sea of Azov.

1115. **Asia.** Nadir Shah of Persia invades India, sacks Delhi, and restores the dethroned Emperor.

Bassein, second in importance to Goa alone, and nearly all the Portuguese possessions on the North-west coast of India, are taken by the Mahrattas.

1116. **Austria.** On the death of the Emperor, the male line of the Hapsburgs becomes extinct (Oct.). Opposition to the succession of Maria Theresa is made by the Elector of Bavaria, husband of the second daughter of Joseph I. and claimant by the will of Ferdinand I., by Augustus of Saxony, through his wife, eldest daughter of Joseph I., and by Philip of Spain, as heir of the Spanish Hapsburgs. Russia, on the other hand, is neutral, and England and Holland friendly. [1740

1117. **Russia.** Anne, daughter of Peter the Great, dies, and Munnich, one of her German generals, sets aside her will, and deserts Austria for Prussia.

1118. **Germany.** Frederick the Great succeeds his father (May), and takes advantage of the contested succession to the Empire to seize Silesia (Dec.), basing his claim on the purchase of Jägerndorf, 1524, and the treaty of 1537 with the Duke of Liegnitz.

1119. **Asia.** On his return from India, Nadir Shah receives the submission of the Uzbek ruler of Balkh and Bokhara, and extends his dominions to the Oxus.

The capitulations granted to France by the Porte are collected and confirmed, and the Protectorate over the Syrian Pilgrims is explicitly stated.

1120. **Germany.** Frederick meets the Austrians at Mollwitz, where his cavalry is routed and he himself flies, the day, however, being retrieved by the infantry under Schwerin (April). [1741

Louis and Fleury are persuaded by Belleisle to attempt the partition of Austria, and agree by the secret Treaty of Nymphenburg to support the claims of the Elector of Bavaria to the Empire (May). Frederick, who fails to obtain the cession of Silesia from Maria Theresa, allies with France, promising to support Bavaria, Louis guaranteeing Lower Silesia. Saxony also joins France, on the promise of Upper Silesia and Moravia (July). George II. declares Hanover neutral, and promises his electoral vote to Bavaria. Belleisle crosses the Rhine, joins the Bavarian troops, and takes Linz, three days' march from Vienna (Sept.).

1707. **German Lit.** The Göttinger Gelehrte Anzeigen are commenced by Haller.
1708. **Russian Lit.** Lomonosof writes an ode on the taking of Khotin from the Turks.
1709. **Literature.** The President de Brosses visits Italy and describes its art and society, in letters to his friends in France.
1710. **Philosophy.** Hume's Treatise on Human Nature declares that only the particular exists; that the elements of all knowledge are simple perceptions, received passively; that the echo or survival of these forms impressions or ideas, association taking place according to likeness, contiguity and causal connection; that the ideas of a self or ego and of a cause are illusions; that the process of willing and acting is mechanical, being based chiefly on the pursuit of pleasure and the avoidance of pain.
1711. **History.** Blomefield's History of Norfolk.

1712. **Eng. Ch.** Wesley severs his connection with the Moravians. [1740

Challoner's Garden of the Soul, a Catholic manual.
1713. **Italian Ch.** Benedict XIV. becomes Pope and gathers round him Noris, Orsi, Saccarelli, and other scholars.
1714. **Asiatic Ch.** Wahab commences a Puritan movement in Persia, which rapidly spreads.
1715. **Church Hist.** Muratori discovers and publishes a fragmentary Latin Canon of the Christian Scriptures, dating from the second century.
1716. **Eng. Lit.** Richardson's Pamela commences the novel of sentiment.
1717. **German Lit.** Frederick the Great patronises Gottsched and Gellert; but the influence of the Gallic school begins to decline.
1718. **Art.** The French Salon begins to be held.
1719. **Science.** Lazzaro Moro explains the order of strata by the action of the sea, rivers, earthquakes, and volcanoes.
1720. **Law.** Wolff's Jus Naturae first completely separates the Law of Nations from the duties of individuals, basing the former on a presumed consent.
1721. **Politics.** Frederick the Great's Anti-Machiavel portrays the king as the 'premier domestique' of his people.
1722. **Geography.** Anson sails round the world in the Centurion.

1723. **Eng. Ch.** Wesley employs lay preachers and builds chapels for them. [1741

Whitfield returns from America, and engages in a controversy on predestination with Wesley.
1724. **American Ch.** The Moravians found Bethlehem and other colonies in Pennsylvania.
1725. **French Ch.** With the death of Montfauçon, the Benedictines of St Maur decline, their place in the van of scholarship being to some extent taken by the Académie des Inscriptions.

In face of this formidable alliance, Maria Theresa concedes to Hungary the right of arming and constitutional privileges; whereon the country rises in her favour and recognises her husband as joint ruler. She also concludes a secret treaty with Frederick at Klein Schellendorf, promising the cession of Lower Silesia (Oct.). At this moment, however, Prague is taken by the allies; a palace revolution substitutes Elizabeth, daughter of Peter the Great, who is inclined to a French alliance, for the Regent Anne; and Frederick breaks the convention, and sends Schwerin to invade Moravia.

1121. **Austria.** The Bohemian Aulic Chancery in Vienna, the last representative of Bohemian interests, is suppressed.

1122. **West Indies.** Vernon fails to take Carthagena and Santiago.

1123. **America.** A Russian expedition under Behring opens up a fur trade in Alaska.

[1742

1124. **England.** Walpole is defeated, and resigns, and Carteret and Newcastle take office.

1125. **Germany.** The Elector of Bavaria is chosen Emperor (Feb.), but Bavaria is overrun, the Austrian provinces are recovered, and Frederick's campaign in Moravia fails. He again negotiates, with English mediation; but Maria Theresa insists on his joining her to expel the French. He defeats her at Chotusitz (May), but accepts her request for peace. By the Treaty of Breslau he obtains almost all Silesia and the county of Glatz, takes over the debt on Silesia, and makes a defensive alliance with England. Saxony also deserts France by the Treaty of Dresden, but fails to obtain territory. France again wins Bavaria, but is driven out of Bohemia.

1126. **Italy.** Maria Theresa allies with Sardinia to keep a Spanish army out of Lombardy. Modena is captured, and an English fleet, anchored before Naples, compels Don Carlos to withdraw from the war. Sardinia and England, however, refuse to aid Maria Theresa in attempting to win back Naples and Sicily.

[1743

1127. **Ireland.** Charles Lucas demands Home Rule.

1128. **Germany.** Austria retakes Bavaria, which is ceded by a convention till a general treaty. The French give up Eger, their last Bohemian stronghold.

A mixed English and Hanoverian army that has entered the Netherlands is joined by Dutch troops, sent by the reviving Orange party. George II. arrives and defeats Noailles at Dettingen (June). The victory is not followed up, Carteret and Newcastle quarrel, and a proposed invasion of France fails.

1129. **Italy.** Savoy refuses to fight further without territorial concessions; but by English mediation, the Treaty of Worms is made, between England, Savoy and Austria (Sept.). Maria Theresa cedes

1726. **German Ch.** Ernest Augustus of Saxe-Weimar founds a mission to the Jews.

The Society of Alethophils is founded to spread the philosophy of Wolff, especially among the younger clergy. A large number accept the principles of the Aufklärung.

1727. **Italian Ch.** Benedict XIV., by a Concordat with Naples, allows the laity partial jurisdiction over the clergy.

1728. **Church Hist.** Benedict XIV. issues a Declaration to the bishops of Holland, allowing mixed marriages where the Protestant swears not to molest the Catholic in the exercise of religion, and promises to educate the children as Catholics. A similar brief is sent to Poland, 1748, and is extended to the whole Church, 1777.

The Pope forbids missionaries to take part in the slave trade.

1729. **Eng. Lit.** Garrick achieves his first great success in the part of Richard III.

1730. **Science.** Linnaeus plans a botanical garden at Upsala.

1731. **Politics.** Hume's Essays expose the notion of a historical contract, and adopt the principle of Utility.

1732. **Philosophy.** Brucker's Historia Philosophiae, the first systematic attempt at a history of thought.

1733. **Social.** The Highway Act imposes tolls, and English roads are greatly improved.

[1742

1734. **Eng. Ch.** Dodwell's Christianity not founded on Argument attacks both Deists and Christians for asserting the harmony of reason and revelation, and declares Rational Faith a contradiction in terms.

Edward Young's Night Thoughts on Life, Death and Immortality obtain immense success.

1735. **German Ch.** Frederick the Great grants equal rights to Catholics and Protestants in Prussia.

Bengel's Gnomon of the New Testament, a Lutheran Commentary, becomes classical.

At the Imperial election, gravamina against the Curia are discussed.

1736. **American Ch.** Muhlenberg, a pietist from Halle, becomes the leader of the Lutherans in Pennsylvania.

1737. **Eng. Lit.** Fielding's realistic novel, Joseph Andrews, commenced as a parody on Richardson's Pamela.

1738. **German Lit.** Elias Schlegel's work on Imitation discusses Aesthetics from the classical standpoint afterwards adopted by Lessing.

1739. **Science.** Maclaurin presents the first systematic account of Fluxions (which he regards as velocities), suggested by Berkeley's attack on the principles of the calculus in the Analyst.

1740. **Art.** Handel's Messiah.

1741. **Deaths.** Bentley, Massillon, Walpole.

[1743

1742. **Eng. Ch.** The Welsh Calvinistic Methodist body is founded by Whitfield and Howell Harris, once a churchman, who has been preaching in Wales for some years as a layman.

part of the Milanese to Savoy, and directs her troops to serve under the King of Sardinia. England promises subsidies; and secret articles provide for the expulsion of the Bourbons from Italy.

1130. **France.** Fleury dies, and the Belleisle party becomes supreme. To meet the Treaty of Worms, France and Spain make a new Pacte Famille at Fontainebleau, France promising to declare war against England and Sardinia, and to aid Spain to seize the Milanese and Parma, Gibraltar, Minorca and Georgia (Oct.).

1131. **Sweden.** After capitulating in the campaign of 1742, Sweden cedes South Finland to Russia by the Treaty of Abo, and the succession is guaranteed to the House of Holstein-Gottorp.

1132. **England.** Carteret is ejected by Newcastle, owing to his unpopular foreign policy. Henry Pelham, Newcastle's brother, becomes supreme. [1744

1133. **France.** An expedition to restore the Young Pretender is defeated by a storm. War is declared against England and Austria. Saxe captures several fortresses in the Netherlands. Charles of Lorraine crosses the Rhine with an Austrian army and overruns Alsace.

1134. **Germany.** Meanwhile Frederick forms the Union of Frankfort (May), joined by Charles of Bavaria, the Elector Palatine and the Landgrave of Hesse, to force Maria Theresa to restore Bavaria and make a general peace. As Maria Theresa hopes to recapture Silesia, Frederick renews his alliance with France, promising to conquer Bohemia for Charles of Bavaria, in return for the cession of part to him. He commences the second Silesian War by taking Prague. Charles of Lorraine is recalled from Alsace, and Saxony sends troops to aid Austria. Frederick falls back to Silesia. Bavaria, however, is meanwhile recaptured.

East Friesland passes by reversion to Prussia.

1135. **Russia.** Elizabeth's nephew and heir marries Catherine of Anhalt.

1136. **America.** The French take Annapolis.

1137. **Scotland.** The Young Pretender lands in Scotland (July), and marches to Edinburgh. Cope is defeated at Preston Pans (Sept.), and Charles crosses the Border and reaches Derby (Dec. 5), but turns back in fear. [1745

1138. **France.** Mme de Pompadour becomes supreme.

1139. **Germany.** The Emperor dies (Jan.), and the Austrians again overrun Bavaria and force the young Elector to renounce his claim and to promise to vote for Francis. France urges Augustus of Saxony to

1743. **Church Hist.** Swedenborg becomes convinced of his mission by revelations, retires from his post in a mining college, and composes his Arcana Celestia. His claims are little recognised in Sweden, but are introduced into Germany by Oetinger. No Swedenborgian Church is founded in England till towards the close of the century.

1744. **Literature.** Voltaire visits Frederick the Great, with whom he has been in correspondence for several years.

1745. **Science.** Haller begins to publish his anatomical drawings, and discovers the contraction of muscles.

Clairaut's Théorie de la Figure de la Terre measures the length of a meridian degree.

D'Alembert's Dynamique, developing the work of James and John Bernouilli and Taylor, states that forces equal to the product of the masses and their acceleration, but acting in a contrary direction, are in equilibrium with the impressed forces.

1746. **Education.** The Margrave of Bayreuth founds a University at Erlangen.

1747. **Death.** Bynkershoek.

1748. **Eng. Ch.** The first Methodist Conference is held at the [1744
Foundry Chapel, London, consisting of John and Charles Wesley, four clergy and four lay preachers. An outline of dogmatic teaching is drawn up, the Bishops are to be obeyed 'in all things indifferent,' the canons to be observed 'as far as can be done with a safe conscience,' and 'societies are to be formed wherever the preachers go.'

Annet replies to Sherlock's Trial of the Witnesses, and denies the resurrection of Christ.

1749. **Church Hist.** Amort's Demonstratio Catholica, an Irenicon to Protestants, attempts to prove the rationality of Roman practices.

1750. **Eng. Lit.** Akenside's Pleasures of Imagination.

1751. **Science.** Trembley investigates fresh-water Polyps.

1752. **Philosophy.** Berkeley's Siris commends the healing virtues of tar-water and passes on to reaffirm the unsubstantiality of material things, and to declare spirit their foundation.

1753. **History.** Muratori's Annals of Italy.

Hénault, President of the Parliament of Paris, compiles an Abrégé de l'Histoire de France.

1754. **Deaths.** Pope, Vico.

1755. **Eng. Ch.** Many of the Non-jurors are implicated in the [1745
Jacobite rebellion.

Hervey's Meditations and Contemplations popularise Wesley's theology, and obtain unrivalled popularity.

1756. **French Ch.** The persecution of Protestants recommences, and many ministers lose their lives.

1757. **Italian Ch.** Bianchi's Ecclesiastical Power, written from an extreme Ultramontane standpoint, becomes a text-book.

stand as Emperor; but Maria Theresa bribes him to renew the Austrian alliance and to promise to regain Silesia. Saxe defeats the Duke of Cumberland at Fontenoy (May). Charles of Lorraine invades Silesia and is routed by Frederick at Hohenfriedberg (June). George II. deserts Austria, and makes the Convention of Hanover with Frederick, promising to negotiate a peace with Austria (Aug.). Traun drives the French over the Rhine, and Francis is chosen Emperor at Frankfort (Sept.). Frederick repulses the Austrians at Soor, but sends his troops into winter quarters. Austria and Saxony determine to invade Silesia and Brandenburg; but Frederick hastily collects troops and, with the aid of Leopold of Dessau, defeats the Saxons at Kesselsdorf and enters Dresden (Dec.). By the Treaty of Dresden, Maria Theresa confirms and Augustus guarantees the cession of Silesia, and Frederick recognises the Emperor.

1140. **Italy.** Aided by France and Genoa, the Spaniards take Parma, Piacenza, and Milan (except the citadel). Charles Emmanuel of Sardinia feels hurt at the want of support, but rejects D'Argenson's plan of expelling the Hapsburgs from Italy.

1141. **America.** Colonial troops take Louisburg, on Cape Breton Island.

1142. **England.** Owing to the refusal of the King to employ Pitt, the Ministry resigns. Carteret fails to form a Ministry, and the Pelhams return to power with Pitt and Fox. [1746

1143. **Scotland.** The Pretender defeats Hawley at Falkirk (Jan.), but is defeated by Cumberland at Culloden (April). He evades capture by the devotion of Flora Macdonald and others, and escapes to France. The Highlanders are disarmed, and the hereditary jurisdiction of the chiefs is abolished.

1144. **Italy.** The Austrians and Sardinians expel the French and Spaniards from the greater part of Lombardy and Piedmont, and defeat them at Piacenza (June). The death of Philip causes the withdrawal of nearly all the Spanish troops. Genoa is therefore forced to surrender, and Sardinia takes Finale and Savona.

1145. **Netherlands.** Saxe takes Brussels and Antwerp, and defeats Charles of Lorraine and the Duke of Cumberland.

1146. **Austria.** Maria Theresa makes a defensive alliance with the Empress Elizabeth, secret articles providing for the restoration of Silesia.

1147. **Asia.** Labourdonnais takes Madras, but is hampered by Dupleix, Governor of Pondicherry. The English stir up the Nawab of the Carnatic to attack Madras; but Dupleix sends a small force, which routs a large Hindoo army at the battle of San Thomé.

1758. **French Lit.** Crébillon's (Fils) Le Sopha.

1759. **Art.** Hogarth's Mariage à la Mode.

Sans Souci is built for Frederick the Great.

1760. **Science.** The Leyden jar, which accumulates and preserves a store of electricity, is invented by Musschenbroek and Cunaeus. The discovery is made independently by Kleist, a Pomeranian clergyman.

Bonnet's Traité d'Insectologie minutely studies moss-grubs and records experiments on polyps and worms.

1761. **Philosophy.** Lamettrie's Histoire naturelle de l'Âme, followed by L'Homme Machine, leads to his expulsion from France. He takes refuge in Berlin, where he is joined by Cabanis and Destutt de Tracy. His work may be regarded as the first systematic presentation of the materialism which dominates French thinking till the appearance of Royer-Collard.

1762. **Education.** Van Swieten, a Dutch physician, settles in Vienna, and for 30 years directs education in the dominions of Maria Theresa.

1763. **Agriculture.** Bakewell, a Leicestershire farmer, begins to reform stock-breeding, and gradually doubles the weight of sheep.

1764. **Death.** Swift.

1765. **Eng. Ch.** Jones' Free and Candid Disquisitions on the [1746
Church of England, urging the abolition of subscription, are presented in manuscript to a Bishop to lay before Convocation. They are published 1749, and are defended by Clayton, Bishop of Clogher, and Blackburne, who becomes leader of the movement.

1766. **Scotch Ch.** In consequence of the rebellion, the Scotch episcopal clergy are bitterly persecuted for Jacobitism. Meetings of more than five besides the family are forbidden, and clergy are forbidden to act as private chaplains. Some resign their orders, others flee to America. The stringency of the persecution is not relaxed till the accession of George III.

1767. **Eng. Lit.** Collins' Odes.

1768. **French Lit.** Vauvenargues' Maximes et Pensées.

1769. **German Lit.** Gellert's Fables.

1770. **Science.** Guettard shows the distribution of rocks and minerals in France, points out the analogy of the disposition of mineral substances with those of England, and, later, discovers the volcanoes of Auvergne and lays the foundation of the theory of 'Vulcanism.'

Euler and Daniel Bernouilli discover the law of the Conservation of Areas.

1771. **Philosophy.** Condillac's Origine des Connaissances humaines follows Locke in deriving knowledge from sensation and reflection. His Traité des Sensations, 1754, derives the faculties themselves from sensation.

Diderot's Pensées Philosophiques criticise Pascal.

1772. **Law.** Cocceji undertakes a revision of Prussian law at the request of Frederick. The Corpus Juris Fredericiani, however, is not adopted.

1773. **Death.** Hutcheson.

1148. **England.** Lords Lovat and Derwentwater are executed for their share in the rebellion. [1747

1149. **France.** Negotiations for peace that have been opened at Breda during the winter are broken off, owing to the determination of Maria Theresa to continue the war.

1150. **Holland.** The French invade Holland. The Orange Party revives, and William, grand-nephew of William III., is made hereditary Stadtholder. Saxe defeats Cumberland at Lauffeld (July), and Bergen-op-Zoom is stormed (Sept.).

1151. **Italy.** Austria besieges Genoa, which receives aid from France, but is forced to raise the siege, as Sardinia refuses assistance.

Negotiations are recommenced; but Maria Theresa refuses to create a principality for Don Philip in Italy, having already given part of Lombardy to Sardinia.

1152. **Asia.** On the death of Nadir, his Cavalry-General, Ahmed Shah Durani, seizes the throne, and founds modern Afghanistan, extending from Herat to Peshawar, and from Cashmere to Scinde.

1153. **France.** Marshal Saxe lays siege to Maestricht, and a Russian army enters Germany. Before, however, any fighting occurs, England, France and Holland, failing to persuade Maria Theresa to terminate the war, sign preliminaries of peace at Aix-la-Chapelle (April), and force Europe to sign a peace (Oct.). The war of the Austrian Succession ends, and Maria Theresa is recognised. [1748

France evacuates the frontier fortresses, which are restored to the Dutch, and undertakes to exclude the Pretender. The war leaves her without acquisitions and without prestige.

1154. **Germany.** The title of Prussia to Silesia is recognised.

Francis is acknowledged Emperor.

1155. **Italy.** Don Philip receives Parma and Piacenza; the King of Sardinia recovers Savoy, Nice, and the portions of Lombardy ceded by the Treaty of Worms.

1156. **America.** England surrenders Cape Breton.

The Ohio Company is chartered by the English crown, and annoys the French settlers.

1157. **Asia.** An English fleet fails to take Pondicherry, which is defended by Dupleix.

The Treaty of Aix-la-Chapelle transfers Madras to England.

Ahmed Shah invades the Punjab.

1158. **France.** Machault, a friend of the Opposition, attempts to tax the clergy at one-twentieth of their revenues, but is forced to withdraw. [1749

1159. **Spain.** Ferdinand retires from the Family Compact, and devotes himself, in company with Ensenada, to domestic reform. A navy is created, the fiscal system is reformed, mining is developed, and the Inquisition deprived of its power.

1774. **Eng. Lit.** Johnson and Lauder conspire to prove Milton a plagiarist. [1747

1775. **French Lit.** Nivelle de la Chaussée's La Gouvernante, a type of the Comédie Larmoyante.

1776. **Italian Lit.** The Magliabecchian Library in Florence is opened.

1777. **Russian Lit.** Sumarokov's Hovev founds Russian drama on French models.

1778. **Science.** Bradley finds the nutation of the Earth's axis, in a cycle of 18 years, to be due to the Moon. His results are verified by Simpson and others.

Maupertuis enunciates the principle of least action.

1779. **History.** Florez' Christian Spain.

1780. **Law.** Burlamaqui's Principes du Droit Naturel, written from the standpoint of rational utilitarianism.

1781. **Deaths.** Lesage, Vauvenargues.

1782. **Eng. Ch.** Middleton's Free Inquiry concerning the Miraculous Powers of the Christian Church introduces the historic method. [1748

Hume's Essay on Miracles introduces the test of probability.

John and Charles Wesley's Hymns.

1783. **Italian Ch.** Liguori's Moral Theology refounds equiprobabilism.

1784. **Eng. Lit.** Richardson's Clarissa Harlowe.

Smollett's Roderick Random.

1785. **German Lit.** Klopstock's Messias.

1786. **Italian Lit.** Goldoni begins his comedies.

1787. **Science.** De Maillet insists on the explanation of the earth by the forces now in operation, and suggests the transformation of species.

Euler's Analysis Infinitorum, an introduction to pure analytical mathematics.

1788. **Politics.** Montesquieu's Esprit des Lois discusses the connection of laws with the natural and historical characteristics of a people, and declares, as against Hobbes, that justice precedes the rise of states, positive laws merely supplementing natural laws. Forms of Government vary with the character of the country and people, England possessing the best, owing to the separation of powers.

1789. **Archaeology.** The excavation of Pompeii is begun.

1790. **Social.** Paul invents a wool-carding machine.

1791. **Deaths.** Giannone, Halley.

1792. **Eng. Ch.** The Calvinists under Whitfield desert Wesley. Whitfield becomes chaplain to Lady Huntingdon. [1749

1793. **Eng. Lit.** Fielding's Tom Jones.

Johnson's Vanity of Human Wishes.

1794. **French Lit.** On the death of Mme Tencin, Mme Geoffrin's salon becomes pre-eminent, and is frequented by D'Alembert, Diderot, Marmontel, Morellet, and others, who also meet at the houses of

1160. **Austria.** On his return from Aix-la-Chapelle, Kaunitz receives a seat in the Cabinet and becomes chief adviser. The Empress requests all her councillors for their ideas on the situation. Kaunitz urges the recovery of Silesia, points out the uselessness of the English alliance and the insufficiency of Russia and Saxony as allies, and recommends an alliance with France. Despite the opposition of the Emperor and the other councillors, his policy is approved by the Empress.

Maria Theresa separates the judiciary from the legislative and executive functions.

1161. **England.** England joins the Austro-Russian alliance (of 1746), though refusing to recognise the articles directed against Prussia. Saxony signs unconditionally. England remonstrates against the efforts of Maria Theresa to restore the commerce of the Netherlands. [1750

The Asiento is abolished, Spain paying England an indemnity.

1162. **Austria.** Kaunitz is sent as envoy to Versailles to carry out his scheme of a French alliance against Prussia. He wins over Mme de Pompadour, but fails to convert the King, who is at this time under the influence of the Prince de Conti.

1163. **Portugal.** Joseph I. succeeds his father, John V., and leaves the government to Pombal, who becomes supreme.

1164. **America.** Spain and Portugal agree to exchange their colonies of Paraguay and San Sacramento. The Jesuits disapprove the transfer, persuade the Indians of Paraguay to resist, and stir up a war of six years.

Disputes take place between England and France in relation to the boundary between Canada and Nova Scotia.

1165. **Asia.** France and England support different candidates for the throne of Arcot. The French candidate is victorious, and appoints Dupleix Governor of the Carnatic.

1166. **England.** Frederick, Prince of Wales, dies. [1751

The Calendar is assimilated to that of the Continent, at the instance of Chesterfield, by moving the date 11 days forward.

1167. **Sweden.** Adolphus of Holstein-Gottorp becomes king, and the elder Bernstorff his chief minister.

1168. **Asia.** Dupleix, regardless of the Peace of 1748, threatens Madras. Clive, a clerk at Madras, who arrived in India 1744, volunteers as a soldier and is sent to seize Arcot. He takes it, and holds it against an attack by French sepoys.

1169. **America.** The English surveyors, Mason and Dixon, determine the boundaries of Pennsylvania, Delaware and Maryland, and continue the line west till their proceedings are stopped by the Indians.

Holbach, Helvétius, Mme d'Épinay, and, in a less degree, of Mme du Deffand.

1795. **German Lit.** Kleist's Spring.

1796. **Science.** Buffon's Histoire Naturelle, a large part of the detail of which is furnished by Daubenton and Lacépède.

1797. **Philosophy.** Hartley's Observations on Man maintain that simple sensations, solely by the law of contiguity, synchronous and successive, become thought, emotion, voluntary and involuntary action.

Diderot is imprisoned for expressing the doctrine of relativity in his Lettre sur les Aveugles.

1798. **German Ch.** Frederick issues a privilege for the Jews. [1750

1799. **Italian Ch.** Liguori's Glories of Mary.

1800. **Eng. Lit.** Mrs Montagu begins parties of 'blue-stockings' and is imitated by Mrs Chapman, Hannah More, Elizabeth Carter, Mrs Thrale.

1801. **Literature.** Voltaire visits Berlin, and quarrels with Maupertuis.

1802. **Science.** Euler revives the undulatory theory of light.

1803. **Art.** Baumgarten founds modern Aesthetics, and assumes the existence of a special psychological organ.

1804. **History.** Turgot's Progrès Successif de l'Esprit Humain, a discourse given at the Sorbonne, maintains that progress follows laws of development.

The Benedictines compile L'Art de vérifier les Dates.

Frederick the Great's Mémoires à l'Histoire de Brandenburg.

1805. **Politics.** Rousseau maintains that Science and Art have been detrimental to morals.

1806. **Deaths.** Bach, Muratori, Saxe.

1807. **Eng. Ch.** Byrom's poem on Enthusiasm. [1751

Antinomian excesses occur among the Moravians in England, and are sternly rebuked by Wesley and Whitfield.

1808. **German Ch.** Wetstein's enlarged edition of the New Testament contains variants and commentaries from classics and Rabbinical works.

1809. **Eng. Lit.** Fielding's Amelia.

Gray's Elegy.

1810. **French Lit.** The first two volumes of the Encyclopédie appear, edited by Diderot and D'Alembert (who writes an Introduction), aided by Voltaire, Turgot, Marmontel, Duclos, Daubenton, etc.

1811. **Art.** The Worcester Porcelain Company is formed.

Strange begins to work at line engraving.

1812. **Philology.** Harris' Hermes, a philosophical inquiry concerning universal grammar.

1813. **Economics.** Hume distinguishes wealth from money, of which a nation may possess too much, and condemns the majority of restrictions on commerce.

1814. **Deaths.** D'Aguesseau, Bolingbroke.

1170. **Scotland.** The estates forfeited by the rebellion of 1745 are bestowed on the Crown, the revenue being employed for the improvement of the Highlands. [1752

1171. **France.** De Broglie is sent to Poland to counteract the influence of Russia and Austria, and to work for the election of Conti.

1172. **Austria.** Spain allies with Austria by the Treaty of Aranjuez, guaranteeing each other's European possessions. The alliance is joined by Sardinia, Naples and Parma.

1173. **America.** The Trustees of Georgia surrender their charter to the Crown.

1174. **Asia.** Trichinopoly surrenders to Clive.

1175. **Africa.** The Portuguese recognise the Imam of Muscat and declare their limits to be Cape Delgado and Delagoa Bay.

1176. **England.** The Levant Company, the last of the old trading associations, is dissolved. [1753

1177. **France.** The King intervenes on the side of the Archbishop of Paris, and exiles the Parliament of Paris, which has forbidden the clergy to withhold the sacraments, and ordered the seizure of the Archbishop's possessions. The provincial Parliaments support the Parliament of Paris.

1178. **Germany.** Frederick learns the secret articles of the Austro-Russian Treaty of 1746; but war is prevented by England's refusal to aid Russia. France informs England that she will defend Prussia, if attacked, in accordance with the Treaty of 1741.

1179. **Austria.** Kaunitz leaves Paris and becomes chief minister, persuaded of the impossibility, at the present moment, of the French alliance.

Maria Theresa resolves to introduce uniform legislation for all her dominions.

1180. **America.** Duquesne, Governor of Canada, claiming the Mississippi and the St Lawrence and the country west of the Alleghanies, seizes Fort Duquesne, in the valley of the Ohio, and arrests traders of the Ohio Company. Virginia, in whose dominions lie the Company's lands, loudly protests.

1181. **England.** Pelham dies, and is succeeded by his brother, Newcastle, who attempts to induce Fox to lead the Commons. [1754

1182. **France.** Failing to obtain recognition for the Court which he substitutes for the Parliament, the King recalls that body, forbids the refusal of the sacraments, and exiles the Archbishop.

1183. **Spain.** Ensenada, who has attempted to drag Spain into the war of France and England, falls. Wall, an Irishman, late Spanish Ambassador in London, becomes first minister.

1815. **French Ch.** A Parisian Curé refuses the sacraments to persons suspected of Jansenism, and is supported by the Archbishop of Paris. [1752

1816. **German Ch.** Amort's Theologia Moralis et Scholastica, an ethical text-book on anti-probabilist lines.

1817. **Science.** Franklin draws lightning to his conductor, thus proving it to be electricity.

Clairaut explains the motion of the moon's apse.

1818. **Philosophy.** Samuel Johnson, an American disciple of Berkeley, publishes his Elements of Philosophy.

1819. **Politics.** Achenwall's European Constitutions, a statistical survey.

1820. **History.** Voltaire's Siècle de Louis XIV.

1821. **Deaths.** Alberoni, Bengel, Butler, Réaumur.

1822. **Eng. Ch.** Bishop Lowth's Lectures on the Sacred Poetry of the Jews apply the ordinary standards of literary criticism, and call attention to parallelism. [1753

1823. **French Ch.** Astruc, Professor of Medicine at Paris, publishes his Conjectures sur les Mémoires originaux de Moses, in which he detects two distinct conceptions,—the Elohistic and Jehovistic, thus explaining the contradictions and repetitions of Genesis.

1824. **Spanish Ch.** Frederick and Ensenada arrange a Concordat, by which the Pope acknowledges the king's right of patronage to nearly all the benefices of Spain, and control over the introduction of Bulls.

1825. **Eng. Lit.** Sir Hans Sloane bequeathes his collections to the nation. From these, the Harleian MSS., and the Cottonian library, the British Museum is formed. The royal library, chiefly formed by Prince Henry, son of James I., is presented, 1757.

1826. **French Lit.** Grimm's Correspondance Littéraire begins.

1827. **Art.** After three years' study in Italy, Reynolds begins to paint portraits in London.

A royal porcelain manufactory is established at Sèvres.

1828. **German Lit.** Lessing publishes two volumes of epigrams, fables, literary criticisms and translations.

1829. **Social.** Lord Hardwick's Marriage Act necessitates the services of an Anglican clergyman for all but Jews and Quakers.

1830. **Deaths.** Berkeley, Labourdonnais.

1831. **Eng. Ch.** Bolingbroke's Philosophical works, written from a deistic standpoint, are published by Mallet. [1754

Fletcher becomes Rector of Madeley, in Shropshire.

1832. **German Ch.** Reimarus' Chief Truths of Natural Religion, pronounced by Kant the best proof of the existence of God.

1833. **Science.** Black discovers 'fixed air,' i.e. carbonic acid gas, by heating limestone.

1184. **America.** Fighting begins, and Washington, who is sent to Ohio with the Virginia militia, is defeated. Newcastle sends Braddock, accompanied by Washington, to capture Fort Duquesne.

Hawke is ordered to seize French shipping, though war is not declared.

By direction of the British Board of Trade and Plantations, a Conference meets at Albany, and is persuaded by Franklin to draw up a plan of union of all the colonies under a President appointed by the Crown. A grand council of delegates, elected by the colonial assemblies, in numbers proportional to the taxation of the colony, is to possess the right of legislation, subject to the veto of the President and the approval of the Crown. Connecticut objects to the veto and refuses to sign, and the Albany plan is rejected by the colonies and the Crown. The Congress, nevertheless, greatly contributes to the growth of a sense of unity among the colonies.

1185. **Asia.** Dupleix is recalled, in order to conciliate England. His conquests are sacrificed and peace is made.

1186. **England.** Pitt, Legge, and Grenville are dismissed for opposing subsidies which are promised to Russia and Hesse for the protection of Hanover in the war which appears imminent. Henry Fox becomes the leader of the Commons. [1755

Thurot and French troops land in the Isle of Man.

1187. **France.** Kaunitz renews his offers to France, through Stahremberg, and Mme de Pompadour entrusts the negotiations to Abbé Bernis. When France refuses to desert Frederick, Kaunitz suggests German neutrality.

1188. **Italy.** Paoli ejects the Genoese, who have re-entered Corsica on the abdication of King Theodore, and becomes Dictator for 14 years.

1189. **Germany.** Elizabeth is asked and promises to defend Hanover if attacked. Austria refuses to strengthen her garrisons against a possible French invasion of the Low Countries, and the alliance with England comes to an end.

1190. **America.** Braddock falls into an ambush and is defeated and killed (July). Washington saves part of the Virginian militia. French ships are captured by Boscawen, and war becomes inevitable.

An attack is made on Crown Point, and forts are built at Ticonderoga and on Lake George.

1191. **France.** The King curtails the jurisdiction of Parliament in ecclesiastical cases. [1756

1192. **Germany.** England allies with Prussia, by the Treaty of Westminster, to oppose attacks in Germany (Jan.). This leads to the Treaty of Versailles, between France and Austria, by which the latter is to remain neutral in the Franco-English war, and to conclude a defensive

1834. **Philosophy.** Jonathan Edwards' Freedom of the Will.
Martinez Paschalis, a Portuguese Jew, teaches mysticism in South France, and founds an order, of which St Martin is the most prominent member.
1835. **Politics.** Rousseau's Origine de l'Inégalité declares inequality inconsistent with Natural Law, and vehemently denounces the existing social order.
1836. **History.** Hume's History of England, vol. I.
Voltaire's Essai sur les Mœurs.
1837. **Deaths.** Fielding, Holberg, Wolff.

1838. **Eng. Ch.** Hervey's Dialogues between Theron and Aspasia are attacked by Wesley and revive the Calvinistic controversy. [1755
1839. **French Ch.** Benedict XIV. advises the concession of the sacraments to the Jansenists, if not 'notoriously' refractory.
1840. **American Ch.** Mayhew publishes his sermons, the first Unitarian volume appearing in America.
1841. **Eng. Lit.** Johnson completes his Dictionary of the English Language, and writes a sarcastic letter to Lord Chesterfield.
1842. **Russian Lit.** Lomonosof attempts to reorganise the Academy, the stronghold of German influences.
1843. **Art.** Winckelmann's Thoughts on the Imitation of the Ancients demands a return to Greek art.
Soufflot designs the Panthéon, Paris.
1844. **Science.** Kant's Theory of the Heavens suggests the nebular hypothesis.
1845. **Philosophy.** Hutcheson's Moral Philosophy argues for a special moral sense and approves of what tends to the general happiness, though we are virtuous from pure benevolence.
1846. **Politics.** Brissot's Recherches sur la Propriété and Morellet's Code de la Nature become text-books of communism.
1847. **History.** Mosheim writes the first impartial survey of Church History, but treats the Church as a state.
1848. **Economics.** Cantillon's Nature du Commerce anticipates the Physiocrats.
The first Chair of Economics is created for Genovesi.
1849. **Social.** A destructive earthquake occurs at Lisbon.
1850. **Deaths.** Maffei, Montesquieu, St Simon, Bishop Wilson.

1851. **Eng. Ch.** Wesley's Twelve Reasons against a separation from the Church attempt to counteract a growing tendency among a certain section of his followers. [1756
Alban Butler's Lives of the Fathers, Martyrs and other principal Saints.
1852. **Eng. Lit.** Amory's John Buncle.

alliance, while, by secret articles, the two countries are to aid each other if attacked by an ally of England (May). Russia, indignant at England's alliance with Frederick, offers to join Austria, and promises to obtain the dismemberment of Prussia. Frederick learns of the treaties, and commences the 'Seven Years War' by advancing into Saxony (Aug.), though Augustus is not a member of the league. He takes Dresden, compels 18,000 Saxons to join the Prussian army, and publishes the correspondence relating to the plots for dismemberment of Prussia. A drawn battle is fought with the Austrians at Lobositz (Oct.).

1193. **England.** England declares war on France (May). A French fleet and army assails Port Mahon, in Minorca. Byng sets out to relieve it, but withdraws without serious fighting, and Port Mahon is taken.

Fox and Newcastle resign. Pitt becomes Secretary of State under the Duke of Devonshire, sends away the foreign troops brought over to protect England from invasion, reorganises the militia, and raises regiments in the Highlands.

1194. **Holland.** The Dutch resolve to remain neutral in the war.

1195. **America.** Montcalm takes Oswego and builds forts in Illinois.

1196. **Asia.** Surajah Dowlah takes Calcutta and thrusts 146 English into a small room, the 'Black Hole,' whence only 23 issue alive on the following day.

1197. **France.** The King is attacked by Damiens (Jan.), and Mme de Pompadour, in fear, dismisses D'Argenson and promotes [1757
Bernis, who, with Belleisle, henceforth directs French policy. The King is induced to sign the Second Treaty of Versailles with Austria to dismember Prussia, the Netherlands, excepting Ostend, to go to Don Philip (May).

1198. **Germany.** The Diet authorises the Emperor to defend Austria and Bohemia.

Russia adopts the defensive Treaty of Versailles (Jan.), and, a month later, makes an offensive alliance with Austria against Prussia, to recover Silesia and Glatz.

Frederick defeats Charles of Lorraine at Prague, but is routed by Daun at Kolin (June), and expelled from Bohemia. Cumberland is defeated at Hastenbeek by the French (July), and capitulates at Closter-Seven, surrendering Hanover and Brunswick (Sept.). A Russian army, at the same moment, defeats the Prussians at Grossjägerndorf (Aug.), but withdraws; and Sweden attacks Pomerania. In this critical situation, Frederick routs the French at Rossbach (Nov.); the Swedes are expelled; Pitt becomes supreme in England, and disavows the terms of Closter-Seven; and finally, Frederick routs Charles of Lorraine at Leuthen, and recovers Silesia (Dec.).

1199. **America.** Montcalm captures Fort William Henry.

1853. **German Lit.** Gessner's Idylls.

Frederick's battles are celebrated in war-songs by Gleim, Kleist, Ramler, and Abbt.

Zimmermann publishes the first sketch of his Essay on Solitude.

1854. **Russian Lit.** A Russian theatre is erected at St Petersburg, and Von Visin developes the national comedy.

1855. **Art.** Burke's Treatise on the Sublime and Beautiful, the first aesthetic treatise produced in England, sharply contrasts the two qualities, declaring beauty to consist in smallness, smoothness, brightness and softness of colour, variety of outline, delicacy suggesting fragility.

1856. **Science.** Aepinus experiments on tourmaline, which exhibits positive and negative poles on the application of heat.

1857. **Economics.** Mirabeau's Ami des Hommes discusses the improvement of agriculture.

1858. **Law.** Mansfield becomes Lord Chief Justice and developes mercantile law.

By the 'Rule of 1756,' the Powers agree that a neutral cannot exercise in war a trade forbidden in time of peace.

1859. **Death.** Cassini.

1860. **Eng. Ch.** Hume's Natural History of Religion introduces the comparative method, and declares polytheism the original form of belief. [1757

1861. **French Ch.** In consequence of Damien's attack on the king, Busenbaum's Ethics are burnt on the ground that they countenance tyrannicide.

1862. **German Ch.** Gellert's Hymns.

1863. **Portuguese Ch.** Pombal dismisses the king's confessor, a Jesuit, forbids the Jesuits to appear at Court or engage in trade, and denounces the Order to the Pope in the name of the king. The Pope appoints a friend of Pombal, Cardinal Saldanha, Visitor and Reformer of the Order.

1864. **Russian Ch.** The Skopzi (or Mutilated) form a sect, which grows rapidly.

1865. **Eng. Lit.** Gray's Pindaric Odes.

John Brown's Estimate of the Manners and Principles of the Times declares that England is in every respect degenerating.

Horace Walpole sets up a press at Strawberry Hill.

1866. **French Lit.** Diderot's Fils Naturel reforms the theatre by reviving naturalism. Beaumarchais introduces the reforms into comedy.

The Encyclopédie is forbidden by Parliament to proceed, but is again authorised, 1765.

1867. **Italian Lit.** Carlo Gozzi attacks Goldoni for introducing French models, and parodies the new style.

1868. **Science.** Haller's Elementa Physiologiae rejects epigenesis and adopts 'evolution,' or the pre-existence of organs in the germ.

Dollond constructs achromatic lenses.

1200. **Asia.** Clive marches to Bengal to avenge the Black Hole, takes Chandernagore, defeats Surajah Dowlah at Plassey, and retakes Calcutta (June). Surajah's chief officer is made Nawab of Bengal, over which English influence becomes supreme.

Ahmed Shah overruns the Punjab, which, on his retirement, 1758, is occupied by the Mahrattas.

1201. **England.** Pitt presents a new army to Ferdinand of Brunswick, who rids Hanover, Westphalia and Hesse of the French. The Prussian alliance is confirmed, each promising not to make peace alone (April). Pitt harasses the French coast. [1758

1202. **France.** Bernis counsels peace, but is overruled. He transfers the Foreign Ministry to Choiseul, French ambassador at Vienna, who insists on a modification of the alliance.

1203. **Germany.** Frederick defeats the Russian army at Zorndorf (Aug.), but is shortly repulsed by the Austrians at Hochkirch (Oct.).

1204. **Portugal.** The Marquis of Tavora and his wife, Malagrida, a Jesuit, and others, angered by Pombal's monopoly of power, plot a revolution, and wound the King (Sept.). They are, however, taken and executed, 1759.

1205. **America.** The greater part of Cape Breton is taken, and the way is opened into Canada. Abercrombie is repulsed from Ticonderoga; but Fort Duquesne is captured and renamed Pittsburg.

1206. **Asia.** Lally Tollendal attacks Madras.

Clive compels the Dutch by land and sea to capitulate at Chinsurah.

The Chinese invade and conquer Eastern Turkestan.

1207. **Ireland.** Flood enters Parliament and leads the Opposition. He urges the shortening of Parliaments, and the reduction of the pension list. [1759

A rumour of contemplated union leads to fierce riots in Dublin.

1208. **Germany.** Ferdinand of Brunswick defeats Choiseul's plan of invading Hanover at Minden, though Lord Sackville refuses to lead the cavalry to action (Aug.).

Frederick is defeated by the Russians and Austrians at Kunersdorf (Aug.), but the Russians retire. Saxony, however, is lost, and 12,000 men are forced to capitulate to Daun, at Maxen.

1209. **France.** Choiseul's second plan of a direct invasion of England is defeated by Boscawen's naval victory at Lagos over the Toulon fleet (Aug.), and by Hawke's destruction of the Brest fleet off Quiberon (Nov.).

1869. **Philosophy.** Price's Review of the Principal Questions of Morals declares that right and wrong are perceived by Reason, i.e. intuitively, and imposed on the will as a law.

1870. **Philology.** Ruhnken becomes assistant Professor to Hemsterhuys at Leyden.

1871. **Deaths.** D'Argenson, Fontenelle, Hartley.

1872. **Church Hist.** The last thorough revision of the Index is made. [1758

1873. **French Lit.** Voltaire's Candide satirises the fashionable optimism.

Rousseau's Letter to D'Alembert, vehemently condemning the Stage, marks his severance from the party of the Philosophes.

1874. **Spanish Lit.** José de Isla's Fray Gerundio satirises the preaching of the monks.

1875. **Art.** Roubiliac's Shakespere (British Museum).

1876. **Science.** Halley's comet returns.

Boscovitch's Philosophia Naturalis explains a theory of centres of force.

1877. **Philosophy.** Condillac's residence in Parma introduces sensationalism into Italy, where it is developed by Gioja and Romagnosi.

Helvétius' De l'Esprit (burned by the hangman, and condemned by the Pope and the Sorbonne) declares mind the sum-total of ideas arising from impressions, the character of which is chiefly determined by the educational and political system of the country. Happiness is self-love, and public ethics should be founded on utility.

1878. **Economics.** Quesnai's Tableau Économique pronounces government a necessary evil, existing in order to fulfil contracts, advocates freedom of exchange and competition, declares that increase of raw materials is alone productive, and recommends a direct land tax. His ideas are developed and popularised by the elder Mirabeau, Gournay, Dupont de Nemours, Mercier de la Rivière, Turgot, who form the so-called Physiocratic school. Adam Smith makes the acquaintance of Quesnai and Turgot, and becomes deeply influenced by their ideas.

1879. **Deaths.** Jonathan Edwards, Allan Ramsay.

1880. **German Ch.** Hamann's Socratic Memories vindicate Christianity against the Aufklärung. [1759

1881. **Portuguese Ch.** The Jesuits are expelled by the king and Pombal, and their estates sequestrated. The Viceroys of India and Brazil also receive orders to expel them.

1882. **Eng. Lit.** Johnson's Rasselas.

Goldsmith's The Bee, and, later, The Citizen of the World, aid Johnson in the revival of the Essay.

1883. **French Lit.** D'Alembert retires from the control of the Encyclopédie.

1884. **German Lit.** Nicolai begins his Letters, the organ of the Aufklärung.

1210. **America.** Choiseul fails to detach Pitt from the war; but Pitt and Frederick suggest an European Conference, which is regarded as a sign of weakness, and rejected.

Fort Niagara and Ticonderoga are taken; and Quebec is won by Wolfe, who, with Montcalm, is slain in the battle (Sept.).

1211. **Asia.** Lally fails to take Madras.

1212. **England.** The new king, George III., begins to work for peace as a means for overthrowing Pitt. [1760

The extension of the Militia Bill to Scotland is opposed by the Ministry. Its rejection leads to the creation of the Poker Club in Edinburgh.

1213. **Germany.** Austria is forced to make a new treaty with Russia, allowing her permanent possession of East Prussia (March). This greatly irritates France and the Baltic Powers.

Frederick loses a detachment near Landshut, but defeats Laudon at Liegnitz (Aug.). Berlin, however, is occupied by Russians and Austrians. Frederick defeats Daun in a fierce attack on Torgau (Nov.), the last pitched battle of the war.

Ferdinand of Brunswick defends Westphalia and Hanover against the French.

1214. **Austria.** Maria Theresa institutes a Council of State to watch over the whole administration, and gradually withdraws administrative power from the provincial diets. She protects the peasants, taxes the landowners, and substitutes central magistrates for the local courts.

1215. **America.** Montreal surrenders to Amherst, and Canada becomes wholly English.

1216. **Asia.** Sir Eyre Coote defeats Lally at Wandewash (Jan.), and the French power in India collapses. Lally is shut up in Pondicherry.

1217. **France.** Turgot becomes Intendant of the Limousin, reduces the *taille*, commutes the *corvée*, allows substitutes for service in the militia, frees the peasantry from the duty of collecting the taxes, and introduces the potato. [1761

Negotiations for peace break down, and Choiseul persuades Spain to make a new Family Compact, which guarantees the possessions of all Bourbon Powers, and by which Spain is to declare war against England unless peace is concluded by May, 1762 (Aug.).

1218. **England.** Pitt suspects the alliance between France and Spain, and proposes to attack the Spanish Indies. He is however, dismissed, and succeeded by Bute, who stands for peace (Oct.).

1885. **Science.** Wolff's Theoria Generationis defends epigenesis.

Smeaton designs the Eddystone Lighthouse.

1886. **Art.** Diderot begins his criticism of the Salon.

1887. **Philosophy.** Adam Smith's Theory of Moral Sentiments attributes emotions to the sympathy felt by an impartial spectator.

1888. **History.** The Annual Register is planned and largely written by Burke.

1889. **Politics.** F. C. Moser's Master and Servant sketches a political state, in which all is done for, nothing by, the People.

1890. **Law.** Hübner's Seizure of Neutral Vessels supports neutrality, but warns neutrals to avoid blockaded places.

1891. **Deaths.** Handel, Maupertuis.

1892. **Eng. Ch.** Wesley's lay-preachers take out licenses as dissenting teachers and administer the sacraments. Charles Wesley is shocked, and Grimshaw disowns the Methodists. [1760

Pitt asks and obtains from the Theological Faculties of the Sorbonne, Louvain, and other Universities, a declaration that the Pope has no civil authority in England, that he cannot absolve from the Oath of Allegiance, and that faith must be kept with heretics.

1893. **French Ch.** Diderot's La Religieuse fiercely attacks monastic life.

1894. **German Ch.** Semler explains his doctrine of accommodation.

1895. **Eng. Lit.** Sterne's Tristram Shandy.

Ossian's poems are published by Macpherson.

1896. **French Lit.** Rousseau's La Nouvelle Héloise introduces sentiment and a sense of the picturesque, and founds the romantic school in modern literature.

1897. **Science.** Brisson's Ornithologie.

Black discovers latent heat.

1898. **Art.** Horace Walpole begins to build his house at Strawberry Hill in Gothic style.

1899. **Social.** Roebuck erects blast furnaces working entirely with coal.

A flying shuttle is used in the cotton trade.

The Abbé de l'Épée founds an Institute for the education of the deaf and dumb.

1900. **Deaths.** Antoine Court, Zinzendorf.

1901. **Scotch Ch.** Gillespie is expelled for his opposition to patronage, and forms the 'Presbytery of Relief.' [1761

1902. **Science.** Morgagni collects particulars of diseases, post mortems, etc.

Avenbrugger adopts percussion of the chest for the recognition of diseases.

Bergmann proves that fixed air is an acid, and works at the chemical affinity of a number of substances.

Canton demonstrates the compressibility of water.

1903. **Art.** Greuze's first great picture, L'Accordée de Village.

Gainsborough first exhibits in London, and founds English landscape.

1219. **Germany.** No important battles are fought; but the Austrians and Russians winter in Silesia.

1220. **America.** Otis argues against the introduction of writs of assistance (i.e. warrants to the Customs officers to seize any goods suspected to be smuggled), on the ground that Parliament cannot legalise tyranny.

1221. **West Indies.** Dominica is taken by England from France.

1222. **Asia.** The Mahrattas are defeated by the Afghans under Ahmed Shah at Panipat. The Confederacy is broken up into five dynasties, the Peshwar at Poonah, Sindhia at Gwalior, Holkar at Indore, the Gaikwar at Baroda, and Bhonslar at Nagpur. The Moghul Emperor becomes virtually dependent on the Mahrattas.

Coote captures Pondicherry, which is restored, 1763.

1223. **Ireland.** The Whiteboys appear and attack tithe proctors. [1762

1224. **Spain.** Bute declares war with Spain (Jan.). England, aided by Portugal, defeats the Spanish invasion of Portugal, and takes Havannah and Manila.

1225. **Germany.** Bute refuses to continue subsidies to Prussia, which, however, is saved by the death of Elizabeth of Russia and the accession of Peter (Jan.), who deserts the Austrians and makes an offensive and defensive alliance with Prussia (May). The Swedes are forced to follow suit. The new Tsar, however, alienates all classes, and is deposed (July), and is murdered by his wife Catherine and the Orloffs. The Russian troops are recalled; but the alliance with Austria is not renewed. Frederick recovers part of Silesia, and Prince Henry compels the Diet at Ratisbon to declare neutrality, and a truce is arranged for Silesia and Saxony. Preliminaries are arranged between England, France and Spain (Nov.).

1226. **England.** The King dismisses all who oppose the peace.

1227. **America.** France cedes to Spain Louisiana and New Orleans.

1228. **West Indies.** Martinique, St Vincent, and Grenada are taken from the French.

1229. **England.** Bute, unpopular as a Scotchman and as a rival [1763
to Pitt, resigns (April). Most of the Whigs rally round Rockingham; others follow Bedford, others Grenville, Pitt's brother-in-law. The King summons Grenville, who has supported Bute, and who associates with himself the Bedford Whigs.

Wilkes attacks the King's speech in the North Briton, No. 45, and a general warrant is issued for its authors and printers. Wilkes is arrested, but is discharged by Pratt (Lord Camden) as a member of Parliament. Pratt declares general warrants illegal. The Commons, nevertheless, deny his privilege, and vote the North Briton a libel

1904. **Philosophy.** Robinet's De la Nature attacks optimism and pessimism and finds the beauty and truth of the world in the balance of truth and error, pleasure and pain. A first cause, though we know nothing of it, must be taken for granted.

1905. **Politics.** Wallace's Prospects of Mankind declares a large population an obstacle to Communism.

1906. **Social.** Protests against the slave-trade are raised in England by the Quakers and in France by the Amis des Noirs.

The Duke of Bridgewater employs Brindley to make a canal from his coal-mine to Manchester, a distance of 7 miles, through tunnels and over aqueducts.

1907. **Deaths.** Hoadley, Law, Richardson.

1908. **Eng. Ch.** Warburton attacks Wesley and 'Enthusiasm' in his Doctrine of Grace. [1762

1909. **French Ch.** Jean Calas, a Protestant, is broken on the wheel at Toulouse on the charge of murdering his son, a convert to Catholicism.

La Valette, a Jesuit trader, loses ships on which he has borrowed, and the deficit is ordered to be made up by the whole Order in France. At the instigation of Choiseul and Mme de Pompadour, the king deserts the Society, which is supported only by the Archbishop of Paris, and forbids teaching and the enlistment of recruits, and orders the sale of their property.

Voltaire publishes the Abbé Meslier's Testament, a document at once deistic and communistic.

1910. **Russian Ch.** Platon, afterwards Metropolitan of Moscow, compiles a Catechism. He rapidly gains an unrivalled reputation as a preacher.

1911. **French Lit.** Diderot's Neveu de Rameau.

1912. **Swiss Lit.** The Helvetic Society, half political, half literary, is formed, containing Gessner, Lavater, Balthasar, Iselin, and others of both races.

1913. **Science.** Bonnet and Spallanzani find that the limbs of the lower animals, when cut off, grow again, and suggest that these organs become more complicated till they reach man.

1914. **Art.** Gluck's Orfeo interprets the words, improves the recitative, and does not break the music up into airs.

Tiepolo is invited to paint in Spain.

1915. **Politics.** Rousseau's Contrat Social imagines a sovereign power to which every man gives up his individual rights. The surrender, however, is only apparent, being made not to an individual but to the community. Neither the legislature nor the executive are sovereign, the community retaining supreme power. Representatives are merely delegates, and the ideal state is small enough for the sovereign people to meet together in person.

1916. **Geography.** Carsten Niebuhr visits Arabia and Persia.

1917. **Deaths.** Bradley, Marivaux.

(Nov.), and the Lords attack Wilkes for his Essay on Woman (unpublished). Wilkes, however, obtains damages for imprisonment.

The Peace of Paris is signed by England, Spain, France, and Portugal (Feb.). France restores Minorca to England.

1230. **Spain.** Cuba, Manila and the Philippines are restored by England, which receives Florida, while France cedes Louisiana.

1231. **America.** France surrenders all her possessions in North America, except the islands of Saint-Pierre and Miguelon, as fishing-stations, reserving the right to fish off Newfoundland. The French Canadians are guaranteed their religion.

The Mississippi is fixed as the Western boundary of the English colonies.

Pontiac plots to expel the English, seeing that, with the defeat of France, the English will be supreme. He is encouraged by French traders, but his revolt is suppressed after great difficulties, 1766.

The King annuls a Virginian law that clergy may claim part of their salary in money when tobacco is below the usual price, and forbids the repeal or modification of any law till his pleasure is known. Patrick Henry, a Virginian advocate, declares that the King has become a 'tyrant,' and forfeited all right to his subjects' obedience.

1232. **West Indies.** France regains Guadeloupe, Martinique and St Lucia; England retains Grenada, Tobago, Dominica and St Vincent.

1233. **Africa.** Goree is restored to France, and Senegal becomes English.

1234. **Asia.** All conquests since 1749 are restored; but the French possessions are not to be fortified or garrisoned.

1235. **Germany.** Austrian and Prussian ambassadors meet at Hubertusberg, a castle of Augustus of Saxony, and restore the status before the war. Frederick evacuates Saxony, Maria Theresa restores Glatz, and Frederick promises to support Joseph's candidature as the King of Rome (Feb.).

1236. **England.** Wilkes is expelled by the House of Commons and condemned by the King's Bench, flies to France, and is outlawed. Riots take place in his favour. [1764

Grenville imposes customs duties on the colonies, and gives notice of the Stamp Act, in order to raise money for the support of an army sent over after the conspiracy of Pontiac.

1237. **America.** Samuel Adams draws up instructions to the Boston representatives in the General Court, denying the right of Parliament to execute Grenville's Stamp Act.

1238. **France.** Mme de Pompadour dies, but Choiseul remains supreme.

1239. **Poland.** On the death of Augustus III., 1763, Stanislas Poniatowski, the protégé of Catherine and Frederick, becomes king, despite the resistance of a Nationalist party and the jealousy of France and Austria, who support the Saxon dynasty. Russia and Prussia agree to guarantee the constitutions of Poland and Sweden, to control the election to the Polish throne, and to protect the Dissenters.

1918. **Eng. Ch.** Venn's Complete Duty of Man. [1763

1919. **German Ch.** Febronius (Nicolas von Hontheim), Suffragan Bishop of Trèves, in his De Statu Ecclesiae, urges the supremacy of General Councils, and episcopal independence. The work is condemned by the Pope, 1764, and is attacked by Ballerini and Mamachi. The author recants, 1778, though without changing his opinions.

1920. **Eng. Lit.** Boswell meets Dr Johnson.

1921. **Italian Lit.** Parini's Il Giorno, a social satire.

1922. **Art.** The Madeleine, Paris, is built after classical models.

1923. **Politics.** Mably's Entretiens de Phocion, strongly influenced by Plato's communism.

1924. **Education.** Frederick the Great institutes village schools in Prussia.

1925. **History.** The Almanach de Gotha is published.

1926. **Social.** Almack opens his gaming-house in London, which, later, becomes Brooks'.

1927. **Deaths.** Carteret, Dupleix, Abbé Prévost.

1928. **French Ch.** The Jesuit Order is suppressed. Clement XIII., in a Bull, confirms the Order and denies the charges against it. [1764

Voltaire's Dictionnaire Philosophique.

1929. **Bohemian Ch.** Spangenberg reforms the constitution of the Moravians, and suppresses the extravagances of the brotherhood.

1930. **Portuguese Ch.** Malagrida is burnt by Pombal as a heretic. Communication between Portugal and the Papacy is broken off for two years. Pombal in consequence works for the suppression of the Jesuits.

1931. **Eng. Lit.** Dr Johnson founds the Literary Club.

Walpole's Castle of Otranto founds the romantic school of fiction in England.

Goldsmith's Traveller, and the Deserted Village (1770), the last successful poems in the French or classical style.

1932. **French Lit.** Mlle de Lespinasse and Mme Necker open Salons in Paris.

1933. **Archaeology.** Winckelmann's History of the Art of Antiquity introduces the conception of development into the study of Greek sculpture.

The Dilettanti Society send three members to Asia Minor and Greece, publish 'Ionian Antiquities,' and aid the publication of Stuart's Athenian Antiquities and Chandler's Travels.

1934. **Philosophy.** Reid's Inquiry into the Human Mind on the Principles of Common Sense attacks Hume and founds natural realism, declaring that we have direct knowledge of objects.

1935. **Education.** Rousseau's Émile first wholly renounces the renaissance ideal of 'Knowing,' partially rejected by Montaigne and Locke. Till the age of 12, the boy is to learn nothing, and then science, handwork, and the elements of natural religion.

1240. **Russia.** Catherine confiscates the ecclesiastical lands, giving the clergy a salary.

1241. **Asia.** Munro defeats the Nabob of Oudh at Buxar.

1242. **Africa.** France takes Réunion.

1243. **America.** Despite the protest of six colonies and of Benjamin Franklin, Grenville imposes a duty on stamps on legal documents, and cases under it may be tried without a jury. The Americans attack the officers who distribute the stamped papers. Patrick Henry carries a Resolution against the Stamp Act in the Virginia Convention, compares George III. to Caesar and Charles I., and denies the right of Parliament to legislate on the domestic concerns of the Colonies. Governor Hutchinson's house in Boston is burned, and Samuel Adams carries the Massachusetts Resolves declaring the right of the Colonials to tax themselves. Delegates from nine colonies meet at New York, on the suggestion of Samuel Adams, draw up memorials to King and Parliament, and adopt a Declaration of Rights and Liberties. Grenville is surprised by the opposition, and offers to raise the money in any other way. [1765

1244. **England.** The King dismisses Grenville and Bedford and appoints Rockingham, who is weak, owing to the opposition of the King and to his refusal to employ corruption.

The King shows the first symptoms of madness, and a Regency Bill is discussed.

The sovereignty of the Isle of Man is bought by the Government from the Athol family.

1245. **Austria.** Francis dies, and his son Joseph, chosen king of the Romans, 1764, becomes Emperor and joint-ruler, with his mother, of the Austrian states.

1246. **Hungary.** Maria Theresa, in gratitude for aid against Prussia, extends the area of self-government.

1247. **Italy.** The Archduke Leopold, the second son of the Emperor, begins to govern Tuscany, abolishes the Inquisition, and reforms the penal laws on the principles of Beccaria.

1248. **Asia.** Clive obtains from the Great Moghul the financial administration of Bengal, Behar and Orissa, and allies with Oudh and the Moghul Emperor.

1249. **America.** On pressure from Benjamin Franklin, the agent of Pennsylvania, Pitt, Burke and Camden, Rockingham repeals the Stamp Act, which has brought in no revenue (Feb.), but passes a Declaratory Act asserting the right of the English Parliament to bind the Colonies 'in all cases whatsoever.' [1766

1250. **England.** The King dismisses Rockingham and summons Pitt, now created Earl of Chatham, and Grafton (July). Chatham's health, however, shortly gives way.

1251. **France.** Stanislas Leczynski dies, and Lorraine falls to France.

1936. **Law.** Beccaria's Crimes and Punishments urges the humanisation of the penal law.

1937. **Death.** Hogarth.

1938. **French Ch.** Owing to the persistent championship of Voltaire, the Calas family is declared innocent. [1765

La Barre, a youth of 18, is tortured for irreverence to a procession bearing the Sacrament.

1939. **Dutch Ch.** The Jansenist Church of Utrecht names itself the Old Roman Catholic Church of the Netherlands, acknowledges the Pope as the visible head of the Church, and accepts the Tridentine decrees. The Pope declares the Council null.

1940. **Church Hist.** The celebration of the Sacred Heart, founded by Margaret Alacoque and encouraged by the Jesuits, is sanctioned by the Pope.

1941. **Eng. Lit.** Bishop Percy, aided by Shenstone, edits Reliques of Ancient Poetry, which contribute to the romantic revival.

Chatterton forges the Rowley Poems.

1942. **French Lit.** Sedaine's Philosophe sans le savoir.

1943. **German Lit.** Nicolai edits the Universal German Library.

1944. **Science.** Watt constructs a steam-engine, in which the piston is moved by the expansion of steam, aided by the model of Newcomen and by Black's work on latent heat.

1945. **Philosophy.** Tucker's Light of Nature connects the universal motive of pleasure, through the will of God, with the general good.

1946. **Politics.** D'Argenson advocates communal government and decentralisation, and attacks the feudal régime and restraints on commerce.

1947. **Law.** Blackstone's Commentaries on the Laws of England describe the legal theory of the Constitution, reject the state of nature as a historical fact, reduce the contract to an instinctive holding together, and state the necessity of a sovereign power.

1948. **Eng. Ch.** Blackburne's Confessional, published anonymously, denies that churches have the right to make any confessions of faith. [1766

1949. **French Ch.** The observance of the Articles of 1682 is reimposed.

1950. **Russian Ch.** Catherine permits liberty of worship, and allows Mohamedans to build mosques.

1951. **Eng. Lit.** Goldsmith's Vicar of Wakefield.

Henry Brooke's Fool of Quality.

1952. **German Lit.** Wieland's Comic Tales.

1953. **Science.** Cavendish discovers hydrogen, or 'inflammable air.'

1954. **Art.** Lessing's Laocoön contends that poetry and the plastic arts are each subject to definite conditions, and approves an ideal or universal type in sculpture.

1252. **Spain.** D'Aranda becomes chief minister and introduces secular education, the nomination of the Rota (the chief Ecclesiastical Court), supervision of monasteries and taxation of Church lands.

A revolt is caused by sumptuary laws and the domination of foreigners.

1253. **Poland.** Russia attempts to secure full civil rights for the Dissidents; but the strongly Catholic Diet resists and is dissolved. The Russian ambassador, Repnin, organises confederations of the Dissidents, which are joined by the 'Patriot' party, and force the Diet to promise equal rights and administrative reforms.

[1767

1254. **Ireland.** An Octennial Act is passed.

1255. **America.** Despite the opposition of Shelburne, Townshend imposes import duties on glass, lead, paper, tea, estimated at £40,000, which is to be spent in paying judges and governors in America. The revenue officers are attacked, and juries refuse to convict the offenders. Dickinson attacks the scheme in his Farmers' Letters.

Samuel Adams issues a circular letter urging concerted action, though disclaiming independence.

The legislative power of New York is suspended in consequence of its refusal to make provision for troops quartered in the colony.

1256. **Germany.** Frederick renews his alliance with Russia, promising to support the Polish Dissenters, to enter Poland if Austria enters, and to support Catherine in the event of a war with Turkey.

1257. **Russia.** Catherine appoints a Commission, the first Assembly since Peter the Great, to draft a new code.

1258. **Denmark.** Catherine of Russia resigns Holstein-Gottorp and Schleswig to Denmark.

1259. **Asia.** Clive leaves India, and chaos ensues until the arrival of Warren Hastings.

[1768

1260. **England.** Chatham formally resigns office.

In the General Election, Wilkes is returned for Middlesex. An attempt is made to prevent him taking his seat, and riots break out.

A Secretary for the Colonies, or 'American Department,' is created, though the Board of Trade and Plantations still continues.

1261. **America.** The new Board of Commissioners at Boston seizes the 'Liberty,' which attempts to avoid payment of customs. A riot ensues, and a Convention of delegates from the towns of Massachusetts meets. Hutchinson asks for two regiments to be sent to Boston.

1262. **France.** France purchases Corsica from Genoa, which is unable to suppress the revolt of Paoli.

1263. **Germany.** Maria Theresa formally renounces all claim to Silesia.

1264. **Italy.** The Pope, as feudal superior, confiscates Parma, the weakest of the enemies of the Jesuits. Don Ferdinand, who has ruled since 1765, is supported by his minister Du Tillot, and the insult to the

1955. **Politics.** Ferguson's Essay on Civil Society ascribes progress in large measure to war and the well-being of states to activity in the acquisition and defence of liberty, and praises the military states at the expense of the commercial.

1956. **Economics.** Turgot's Réflexions sur la Formation et la Distribution des Richesses, a physiocratic treatise.

1957. **Geography.** Bougainville commences his voyage round the world.

1958. **Deaths.** Astruc, Elizabeth Farnese, Gottsched.

1959. **French Ch.** Oberlin becomes minister in Steinthal, Alsace. [1767

1960. **Spanish Ch.** Charles and Aranda banish the Jesuits, whom they suspect of provoking a rising in Madrid against a new tax. They are also expelled from the Sicilies and Parma.

1961. **German Lit.** Lessing's Minna von Barnhelm.

Lessing's Hamburg Dramaturgy attempts to establish a national theatre independent of French models and inspired by Shakespere.

Lavater's Swiss Songs.

1962. **Science.** Sprengel discovers the fertilisation of plants by insects.

Spallanzani attacks the theory of spontaneous generation.

1963. **Art.** Allan Ramsay becomes portrait painter to George III.

1964. **Philology.** Heyne, editor of Virgil, with Ernesti and Gesner, founds German classical scholarship.

1965. **Economics.** Steuart's Political Economy, the last and most complete statement of moderate mercantilism.

1966. **Geography.** Maskelyne, Astronomer-Royal, publishes the Nautical Almanack, which he conducts for 40 years.

1967. **Eng. Ch.** Oswald's Appeal to Common Sense founds, with Beattie and Soane Jenyns, the 'Common Sense School' of English apologists. [1768

Lady Huntingdon founds a seminary at Trevecca, of which Fletcher of Madeley becomes President.

Abraham Booth, a Particular Baptist, publishes his Reign of Grace.

1968. **Swiss Ch.** Felix Balthasar's Freedom of the Confederates in Religious Matters attacks Ultramontanism and the Jesuits.

1969. **Eng. Lit.** Sterne's Sentimental Journey.

1970. **Art.** The Royal Academy is founded by Reynolds, who becomes first President and delivers Discourses on Art.

1971. **History.** Schröckh's Church History, with Spittler, Planck and Henke, forms the pragmatist school, mostly indifferent to dogma, and attributing everything to individuals.

1972. **Geography.** Cook accompanies a party sent by the Royal Society to Tahiti to watch the Transit of Venus. He surveys the smaller Pacific islands, sails round New Zealand, visits the east coast of

Bourbons gives Pombal the opportunity of combining the states against the Jesuits. France seizes Avignon, and the King of Naples invades the Papal States.

1265. **Poland.** The opponents of toleration form the Confederacy of Bar and attempt to kidnap the King. Civil war follows, and Stanislas is supported by Russian arms.

Kaunitz discusses the partition of Poland in a memoir to Joseph.

1266. **Turkey.** Turkey declares war against Russia.

1267. **England.** Wilkes is expelled, but is re-elected. The House again expels him, and incapacitates him from sitting during the existing Parliament. A new election is held, and though Wilkes is at the head of the poll, the House declares his opponent, Colonel Luttrell, to be elected. Grenville, Rockingham and Chatham point out that only an Act could deprive the electors of the right of choosing whom they will. Wilkes is imprisoned, but the mob takes his part. [1769

Throughout the year the King and the Ministry are attacked in the Letters of Junius, probably Sir Philip Francis.

1268. **America.** Parliament urges the King to bring colonists charged with treason to England for trial, as authorised by an Act of Henry VIII. The Virginia Assembly therefore passes 'Resolves,' protesting against sending for trial outside the colony, and repeating that it alone can tax itself, and that the colonies, singly and collectively, may petition for redress of grievances. The Assembly is dissolved, but the burgesses agree not to use nor import goods taxed by Parliament. The policy of non-importation is adopted by the other colonies.

1269. **France.** France expels Paoli from Corsica.

1270. **Germany.** Russia and Prussia renew their alliance for eleven years. Catherine guarantees the succession of Anspach and Baireuth, and Prussia the constitution of Sweden of 1720, and undertakes to enter Pomerania if it is attacked.

Frederick meets Joseph, whom he wishes to detach from France, and offers a Polish partition.

1271. **Russia.** Russia defeats the Turks, and occupies Moldavia and Bucharest.

Russia allies with Denmark to guarantee the Swedish Constitution of 1720.

1272. **Africa.** Portugal loses its last foothold in Morocco.

1273. **England.** Grafton resigns and Lord North becomes Prime Minister. [1770

Grenville secures the hearing of election petitions by a Committee of 13 instead of by the House.

The printers and publishers of Junius' Letters are tried and acquitted. Lord Mansfield declares that a jury cannot decide whether the publication is libellous, but only whether it has been published.

Wilkes is elected Alderman and Sheriff of London.

Australia, names Botany Bay, and claims possession of New South Wales for the English Crown.

Pallas journeys through Russia and Siberia, as a naturalist on the expedition sent to observe the Transit of Venus, 1769.

1973. **Deaths.** Assemanni, Reimarus, Sterne.

1974. **Eng. Ch.** Price's Dissertations, written from the standpoint of optimistic Deism. [1769

1975. **German Ch.** The Coblenz Articles, or list of grievances against the Pope, are drawn up by the Archbishops of Mainz, Cologne and Trier, under the direction of Febronius, and presented to Maria Theresa, who takes no notice of them.

Mendelssohn publishes an Epistle to Lavater, who has urged him to desert Judaism.

1976. **Church Hist.** Spain, France and Naples demand the abolition of the Order of Jesuits; but Clement XIII. dies, and Ganganelli, a man without strong views, is chosen.

1977. **French Lit.** Ducis adapts Hamlet and other plays of Shakespere for the stage. Voltaire renews his protest against idolatry, and is echoed by Marmontel and La Harpe. Diderot and Grimm, however, eulogise Shakespere, who is henceforth widely studied in France.

1978. **Art.** Wedgwood opens potteries at Etruria in Staffordshire and copies Greek designs. Flaxman helps to design and model reliefs.

1979. **Science.** Boulton and Watt become partners.

1980. **Philosophy.** Bonnet's Palingénésie upholds the belief in the resurrection of the body.

1981. **Philology.** Ihre's Glossarium Suio-Gothicum.

Wood's Essay on the Original Genius of Homer asserts that the art of writing was unknown to Homer.

1982. **History.** Robertson's History of the Emperor Charles V.

1983. **Geography.** Bruce attempts to penetrate to the sources of the Nile from Massowah.

1984. **Social.** Arkwright patents a spinning roller worked by water-power.

1985. **Death.** Tersteegen.

1986. **Eng. Ch.** Wesley denounces Calvinism and Antinomianism at the Conference. [1770

The orthodox members of the General Baptists separate under the name of the General Baptists' New Communion. The Old Communion gradually merges with Unitarians.

1987. **American Ch.** John Murray, a Wesleyan, crosses to America and introduces Universalism, which he has learned from James Relly, an Unitarian Minister, in England.

1988. **Eng. Lit.** Chatterton comes to London and commits suicide.

1989. **German Lit.** Claudius' Wandsbeck Messenger.

1990. **Danish Lit.** Ewald's Rolf Krage, the first original Danish tragedy.

1274. **Spain.** At Choiseul's instigation, Spain sends a force to the Falkland Isles, which are claimed by England, and expels the English. England clamours for war; but Choiseul falls, and Charles is forced to surrender the islands. Aranda falls, and is succeeded by Campomanes.

1275. **Germany.** Joseph and Frederick meet to concert steps against the Russian advance towards the Austrian border.

1276. **Denmark.** Struensee becomes supreme in Denmark, supported by the Queen, and introduces freedom of religion and the press, improves education and the law, and reorganises the army.

1277. **America.** North repeals all duties but 3*d.* a pound on tea, retained as an assertion of the right to tax. Some soldiers in Boston fire on the crowd, and the 'Boston Massacre' ends in the withdrawal of the troops.

1278. **England.** The Ministry receives support from the Grenville and Bedford Whigs, and from Grafton and Wedderburn, who is made Solicitor-General. [1771

Freedom of reporting is secured by the Chatham and Rockingham sections and the influence of Wilkes. Henceforth publication of debates, though still a breach of privilege, is rarely interrupted.

1279. **France.** The Parliaments are attacked by Maupeou, and refuse to try cases. Maupeou abolishes the Parliaments and creates a new court.

1280. **Germany.** Baden-Baden falls to Charles Frederick, Margrave of Baden, a model ruler of the Aufklärung type, who introduces physiocratic ideas into Germany.

1281. **Poland.** Prince Henry of Prussia is sent to St Petersburg to discuss partition. Negotiations drag on, and Maria Theresa's objections are overruled by Joseph and Kaunitz

---

1282. **England.** The Royal Marriage Act forbids the descendants of George II. to marry without the consent of the sovereign, unless they are 25 and have given one year's notice to the Privy Council and the marriage has not been opposed by Parliament. [1772

1283. **America.** Adams organises Local Committees of Correspondence, for the discussion of the rights of colonists.

The Gaspee, a small vessel of war used for enforcing the Navigation Acts, is captured and burnt. A Commission of Inquiry is sent out, but the authors are not surrendered for trial.

1284. **Poland.** The first Treaty of Partition is signed at St Petersburg. Russia obtains White Russia, the territory beyond the Dnieper; Austria the county of Zips, which she incorporates in Hungary, and part of Galicia; Prussia renounces Danzig and Thorn, but obtains West Prussia, ceded to Poland by the Teutonic knights, 1466 (Aug.). Troops are sent to occupy the territories, and the consent of the Diet is extorted, 1773.

1991. **Art.** Gainsborough's 'The Blue Boy.'

Cosway, the miniaturist, exhibits at the Academy.

Chodowiecki, 'the Berlin Hogarth,' illustrates Minna v. Barnhelm, and many other works with scenes from bourgeois life.

1992. **Philosophy.** Holbach's Système de la Nature, borrowed in part from D'Alembert and Naigeon, is attacked by Voltaire, Frederick, and other Deists.

Beattie's Essay on Truth attacks Hume.

Kant writes De Mundi sensibilis et intelligibilis Forma et Principiis, after being 'awakened by Hume from his dogmatic slumber.'

1993. **Politics.** Burke's Thoughts on the present Discontents attack the influence of the king in politics.

1994. **Education.** Von Felbiger, of Silesia, organises elementary education in Maria Theresa's dominions.

1995. **Law.** Romagnosi's Origin of Penal Law aids the work of Beccaria.

1996. **Economics.** Galiani's Dialogues sur le Commerce des Blés attack the rigidity of the Physiocrats and recommend different policy for different circumstances.

1997. **Social.** Hargreaves patents the spinning-jenny, which works several spindles at once.

1998. **Deaths.** Tiepolo, Whitfield.

1999. **Eng. Ch.** Blackburne issues Proposals for a Petition to Parliament against subscription. A petition from the clergy is [1771
drawn up at the Feathers Tavern, but it is rejected by 217 to 71. Lindsey, Jebb and other clergy leave the Church and become Unitarians, and Lindsey founds a congregation in London, 1774. Priestley joins the Unitarians, 1782.

In face of a fierce attack on the Minutes of Conference, Wesley disavows justification by works, but publishes Fletcher's Checks to Antinomianism. The Calvinist case is stated by Toplady and Berridge.

2000. **German Ch.** Semler's Free Investigation of the Canon.

2001. **Eng. Lit.** Smollett's Humphry Clinker.

Mackenzie's Man of Feeling.

2002. **Art.** Sulzer's Theory of the Fine Arts declares that beauty consists in perfection, and that our pleasure in it rests on the feeling of heightened intellectual activity.

2003. **Science.** Hewson establishes the essential character of the process of coagulation of the blood and the forms of the red corpuscles.

2004. **Philology.** Anquetil du Perron translates the Zend Avesta.

Forcellini's Lexicon Latinum.

2005. **History.** Raynal's Histoire des Indes, a romantic picture of uncivilized life.

2006. **Deaths.** Gray, Helvétius, Smollett.

2007. **German Ch.** Albrecht v. Haller's Chief Truths of Revelation, and Euler's Letters to a German Princess, defend [1772
Christianity.

1285. **Sweden.** Gustavus, by a bloodless *coup d'état,* revokes the Constitution of 1720, becomes absolute, and ends the faction of Hats and Caps. By the new Constitution the King appoints the Senators and summons the Diet at will, which only discusses what he chooses to lay before them. He abolishes torture, allows a free press, and reforms the currency, the army and the navy.

1286. **Denmark.** The King is forced to sign the arrest of the Queen and Struensee, who is executed.

1287. **Turkey.** A truce is arranged and a Congress meets; but the Russian terms are not accepted, and war breaks out afresh.

1288. **Asia.** Warren Hastings is sent out as Governor of Bengal, restores order, and organises the administration on English principles.

1289. **America.** Lord North sends ships laden with tea to Boston. Hutchinson refuses to send them away, and young men rush on board and fling the tea overboard. [1773

1290. **Ireland.** Flood obtains the recall of the hated Lord Townshend, and joins the administration of Lord Harcourt.

1291. **France.** A legacy from his patron to Beaumarchais is disputed by the heir, who loses the case and appeals. Beaumarchais bribes the wife of Goezman, the judge appointed to report, who nevertheless pronounces against him, and is therefore exposed by Beaumarchais in a Mémoire, which damages the prestige of Maupeou's Parliament.

Avignon is restored to the Papacy on the suppression of the Jesuits.

1292. **Denmark.** The disputes with the line of Holstein-Gottorp are ended by the cession of Oldenburg to the younger line in exchange for their share of Holstein, which is now entirely incorporated in the Danish monarchy.

1293. **Russia.** Pougatcheff pretends to be Peter III., revolts, and is joined by the Cossacks of the Don. The rebellion checks Russian advance in Turkey.

1294. **Asia.** Lord North's Regulating Act establishes a Supreme Court under Elijah Impey, makes the Governor of Bengal, Warren Hastings, Governor-General of India, and appoints a Council of four to aid and control him. The election of the Governor-General is given to the Directors.

1295. **England.** Clive's mind is affected by the charges against him during the discussions on the Regulating Act, and he commits suicide. [1774

Wilkes is re-elected for Middlesex and allowed to take his seat, and is also elected Lord Mayor.

1296. **America.** The petition of Massachusetts for the removal of its governor is rejected by the Privy Council, and Franklin is insulted. The port of Boston is closed, the Assembly of Massachusetts is dissolved by Gage, the charter is annulled, troops are quartered, and public meetings are forbidden without the leave of the governor. Massachusetts calls a Congress, attended by all the Colonies but Georgia, and

2008. **Eng. Lit.** The Morning Post is founded.

2009. **German Lit.** Wieland settles in Weimar as tutor to Karl August.

2010. **Science.** Romé de l'Isle's Essai de Crystallographie proves that the angles in each class of minerals are constant.

Rutherford describes nitrogen.

2011. **Philology.** Herder declares language to have had a natural origin, and to be the necessary expression of man's inner life.

2012. **Law.** Mansfield declares, in the case of Somerset, that slavery cannot exist in England.

2013. **Geography.** Cook sets out to explore the Southern Continent, of which rumours had reached Dampier, and discovers New Caledonia.

2014. **Agriculture.** Coke begins to farm at Holkham, Norfolk, and introduces bones, oil-cake, and stall-feeding.

2015. **Death.** Swedenborg.

2016. **Church Hist.** The Society of Jesus is abolished by the Bull Dominus ac Redemptor. The Order continues to exist in Russia and Prussia. [1773

2017. **Eng. Lit.** Goldsmith's She Stoops to Conquer.

Johnson and Boswell visit Scotland.

Steevens revises Dr Johnson's edition of Shakespere. Malone appends his investigations into the order of the plays.

2018. **German Lit.** Goethe's Götz von Berlichingen begins the Sturm und Drang period.

Bürger's Lenore.

2019. **Science.** The brothers Montgolfier raise balloons by hot air.

2020. **Philology.** Lord Monboddo's Origin of Language anticipates Bopp.

2021. **Law.** John Erskine's Institutes of the Law of Scotland.

2022. **Social.** Export of corn from England on a large scale ceases. Foreign corn is admitted at 6*d.* when the price is 48*s.*, at 2*s.* 3*d.* between 44*s.* and 48*s.*, and at 24*s.* 3*d.* when under 44*s.* Exportation is forbidden above 44*s.*, and 5*s.* bounty is given below that price.

Pombal decrees the freedom of the grandsons of slaves in Portugal, and of all born subsequent to this declaration.

2023. **Death.** Chesterfield.

2024. **Irish Ch.** Catholics are allowed to take a simple oath of allegiance to the king. [1774

2025. **German Ch.** Lessing publishes fragments of Reimarus, which are attacked by Pastor Goeze of Hamburg and defended by Lessing.

Isenbiehl refers Isaiah's reference to the Virgin-born Emmanuel to past history.

2026. **American Ch.** Anna Lee, a Shaker, settles in New York State with 30 companions, who possess in common, remain unmarried and cherish millenarian ideas.

by Samuel and John Adams, Washington, Patrick Henry, Dickinson, Jay, Peyton Randolph. Jefferson draws up a Summary View of the Rights of British America, denying the legislative supremacy of Parliament. A moderate Declaration of Rights is issued, and the American Association is formed to organise a non-importation agreement, boycotting individuals who refuse to join. Burke speaks on American taxation.

The Quebec Act secures the legal establishment of Catholicism and the restoration of French civil law.

1297. **France.** Maurepas becomes Premier, Turgot Controller-General, Vergennes Foreign Secretary, and Malesherbes Controller of the Household. Maurepas recalls the Parliaments, against the wish of Turgot.

1298. **Turkey.** Romanzov wins a decisive victory, and the peace of Kutchuks Kainardji ends the war with Russia. The Tartars of the Crimea are declared independent of Turkey and are brought under Russian influence; Russia sends an ambassador to Constantinople, surrenders the conquered provinces except Azov, obtains privileges for the Christians, and promises for the better government of the Principalities, free navigation in Turkish waters, and a footing in the Crimea. To compensate, Austria obtains part of the old territory of Transylvania, a link with her recent acquisitions from Poland.

Aided by Russian influence in the Levant, Greek commerce makes great progress.

1299. **Asia.** To combat the Mahrattas, Hastings allies with Oudh and lends troops to the Nawab to aid in seizing Rohilcund from the Rohillas.

1300. **Scotland.** Dundas becomes Lord Advocate and rules Scotland till 1803, stubbornly resisting the cry for Borough and Parliamentary reform. [1775

1301. **America.** Chatham and Burke propose schemes of conciliation for the colonists, which are rejected, and new repressive measures are passed. A small British force sent to seize stores at Concord scatters some American volunteers at Lexington (April), and, on its return, is attacked. Boston is besieged, and Bunker's Hill is held against two British attacks, but captured in the third. An offer of Lord North before the battle to abandon the claim to tax any colony which will provide for its own defence and government now arrives, and is rejected. A second Congress, attended by all the Colonies, is held at Philadelphia, and sends an Olive Branch Petition for repeal of the obnoxious laws, which is rejected in England. An army is raised, and Washington is made General.

Franklin drafts the first plan of federal union.

1302. **France.** Turgot establishes free trade in corn within the country, and, with Malesherbes, who becomes Minister of the Interior, is hotly attacked by the nobles and clergy. Maurepas begins to intrigue against his colleagues.

The Comte de Saint-Germain reorganises the army, and Sartine increases the navy.

2027. **Polish Ch.** The Jesuits are expelled.

2028. **Eng. Lit.** Chesterfield's Letters to his Son.

Warton's History of English Poetry.

2029. **German Lit.** Goethe's Sorrows of Werther introduces the sentimentalism of Rousseau.

Justus Moser's Patriotic Phantasies attack the ideas of Rousseau and the Aufklärung.

2030. **Science.** Priestley discovers oxygen (discovered independently by Scheele in Sweden, 1775) and calls it dephlogisticated air.

Maskelyne, Astronomer Royal, aided by Hutton, estimates the density of the earth, measured from Mount Schiehallion (Loch Tay), to be $4\frac{1}{2}$ times that of water.

Desmarest's Essay on Volcanoes declares basalt volcanic.

2031. **Art.** Paris is divided into Gluckists and Piccinists.

2032. **Education.** Basedow applies Rousseau's methods in his Philanthropinum at Dessau, which points the way to the creation of Realschulen. J. H. Campe becomes Director, 1776.

2033. **Philosophy.** Dom Deschamps, a Benedictine, dies, leaving a treatise, in manuscript, which anticipates the ideas of Hegel.

2034. **Politics.** Cartwright's American Independence the Glory and Interest of Great Britain.

2035. **Deaths.** Clive, Goldsmith, Quesnai.

2036. **French Ch.** St Martin, who has been introduced to [1775
mysticism by the Portuguese Jew, Martinez Paschalis, and by the study of the writings of Böhme, publishes his mystical work, Des Erreurs et de la Vérité.

2037. **German Ch.** Griesbach's Greek Testament, the first really critical edition, based on that of the Elzevirs.

2038. **Eng. Lit.** Sheridan's Rivals, and The Duenna.

2039. **French Lit.** Beaumarchais' Barbier de Seville.

2040. **German Lit.** Goethe settles in Weimar, as the friend of Karl August, and obtains the post of Court preacher for Herder.

2041. **Italian Lit.** Alfieri's first play, Cleopatra.

2042. **Polish Lit.** Krasicki satirises the State and the monks.

2043. **Science.** Werner begins to lecture at the Saxon School of Mines at Freiburg, explaining the crust of the earth by the action of water, establishing geological succession, and classifying minerals.

Fabricius, a pupil of Linnaeus, classifies insects in his Systema Entomologiae.

Kant's Anthropology anticipates the idea of the evolution of man from animals.

2044. **Politics.** Burke's speech on the conciliation of America.

Delolme's Treatise on the English Constitution.

Thomas Spence, a schoolmaster, and Ogilvie, Professor at Aberdeen, advocate the nationalization of the land.

Necker's Législation et le Commerce des Grains attacks Turgot.

1303. **Austria.** Turkey is compelled to cede Bukovina.

1304. **Spain.** D'Aranda falls, owing to an unsuccessful campaign against the Moors, and Florida Blanca becomes chief minister.

1305. **Asia.** To support Francis Nuncomar forges evidence of peculation by Hastings, but is hung by the Supreme Court.

1306. **England.** Cartwright and Stanhope begin to agitate for Parliamentary reform. Wilkes' motion, however, is lost in the Commons without a division. [1776

The Whigs cease to attend Parliament, in protest against the war.

1307. **America.** A colonial invasion of Canada is repulsed (March). Gage's successor, Howe, is forced by Washington to evacuate Boston (March). Failing to obtain soldiers in England, George III. hires German mercenaries.

On the suggestion of Virginia, Congress votes a Declaration of Independence, written by Jefferson, revised by Franklin and John Adams, and defended and carried by Adams (July 4).

Howe occupies New York and Rhode Island (Sept.), but Washington drives in outposts on the Delaware and in New Jersey. The troops, however, desert in great numbers, and Congress flees to Baltimore. Washington ends the year's campaign by capturing the German camp.

Lee of Virginia proposes Articles of Confederation; and new State Constitutions are drawn up.

Silas Deane is sent to Paris to beg for alliance, and obtains a sum of money.

1308. **France.** Turgot abolishes the Corvée and the Jurandes, or privileged corporations, alters the Gabelle, and reduces the expenses of the royal household. The King is induced to hold a *lit de justice*, but is won over by the party of reaction, and Turgot and Malesherbes are dismissed, owing to the Queen and Máurepas. Necker becomes Comptroller-General. The Corvée, the Jurandes and the customs on corn are restored.

1309. **Italy.** Tanucci falls, and is succeeded by Sir John Acton.

1310. **America.** Franklin arrives in Paris to seek help for the colonies. His mission is aided by Vergennes and Beaumarchais, and Lafayette and other volunteers join Washington. [1777

The Colonials win at Princeton and recover New Jersey; but Howe defeats Washington at Brandywine (Sept.), and occupies Philadelphia. Burgoyne, however, emissary from Canada to join Clinton, is forced to capitulate at Saratoga (Oct.). Conway plots to supersede Washington by Gates. Washington winters in Valley Forge, Pennsylvania, where troops suffer from want of food and clothing, but where they are drilled by Sterben, a German veteran.

The Articles of Confederation replace the King of England by Congress, to which little power is given.

1311. **Portugal.** Joseph dies and Pombal is dismissed. By the Treaty

Boncerf's Inconvénients des Droits Féodaux shows that the lords would be better by commutation of rights, and adds that if they oppose, the king can enforce it.

2045. **Eng. Ch.** Kennicott points out the untrustworthiness of the Textus Receptus. [1776

2046. **German Ch.** Weishaupt founds the Illuminati in Bavaria. The members, though Deist, Rousseauist, and believers in perfectibility, are neither Antinomian nor revolutionary, but are suppressed by the Bavarian Government, 1786.

2047. **Italian Lit.** Ganganelli's Letters are published, perhaps with interpolations.

2048. **Politics.** Bentham's Fragment on Government attacks Blackstone's *à priori* theories of law and contract.

Tom Paine's Common Sense encourages the American colonies to revolt, and shows why reunion, even if possible, is undesirable.

2049. **History.** The first volume of Gibbon's Decline and Fall of the Roman Empire appears. The chapters relating to Christianity are hotly attacked.

2050. **Economics.** Adam Smith's Wealth of Nations, influenced by the writings of Hume and the physiocrats, attacks the theory and practice of Mercantilism, discusses the canons of taxation, recommends the division of labour, and asserts that rent, wages and profits are the elements of price.

2051. **Geography.** Cook sets out on his third voyage, to attempt the North West Passage from the Asiatic side, discovers the Sandwich Islands, but is turned back by the ice-fields, and is killed by the natives at Hawaii, 1779.

2052. **Social.** Parliament passes a resolution against the Slave Trade.

2053. **Death.** Hume.

2054. **Eng. Ch.** Priestley's Disquisitions on Matter and Spirit, influenced by Hartley and Boscovitch, declare the soul material. [1777
At the same time his Doctrine of Philosophical Necessity attacks the belief in the freedom of the will.

Blair's Sermons.

2055. **German Ch.** Sailer, a mystical and conciliatory Catholic, begins to teach at Ingoldstadt.

2056. **Eng. Lit.** Sheridan's School for Scandal.

Clara Reeve's Old English Baron.

2057. **Science.** Coulomb invents the torsion balance.

Lavater's Physiognomy.

2058. **Economics.** James Anderson's Nature of the Corn Laws explains the true theory of rent. His work, however, probably remains unknown to Malthus and West.

2059. **Social.** A Tailors' Co-operative Workshop is formed at Birmingham to employ men on strike.

of San Ildefonso, Spain and Portugal settle their disputes in South America.

1312. **Switzerland.** The Cantons, in fear of Austria, ally with Louis XVI.

1313. **Ireland.** Grattan obtains a Relief Bill for the Catholics, and a few commercial concessions. [1778

1314. **America.** France openly allies with the Colonies, undertaking to fight till their independence is recognised (Feb.), and sends a fleet to New York. Lord North hereupon declares war against France.

The English evacuate Philadelphia (June), but reach New York, owing to the treason of Lee. The campaign in the south, suspended since 1776, is resumed, and Savannah is taken.

Jefferson proposes that all slaves born henceforward be free.

Nootka Sound is discovered.

1315. **Germany.** In consequence of the death of the Elector of Bavaria, the younger House of Wittelsbach becomes extinct, and the Electorate ends. The heir, by the original partition of 1310, the childless Charles Theodore, Elector Palatine, is led by Joseph to recognise old claims on Lower Bavaria and part of the Upper Palatinate. Austrian troops occupy the ceded districts. Frederick the Great negotiates with Charles Theodore's heir, the Duke of Zweibrücken, and encourages him to protest. Frederick and Joseph join their armies; but, owing to the protests of Russia and the timidity of Maria Theresa, nothing but skirmishing on the Bohemian frontier takes place.

1316. **Spain.** A treaty of perpetual alliance is concluded with Portugal.

1317. **Africa.** Spain acquires Fernando Po, in the Gulf of Guinea.

1318. **America.** The English invade South Carolina without resistance. [1779

1319. **West Indies.** The French fleet takes St Vincent and Grenada.

1320. **Ireland.** Nearly all the troops being withdrawn for the war, Protestant volunteers come forward, in full sympathy with the 'Patriots,' who are led by Flood and Grattan, and, on the re-assembling of Parliament, demand free trade. Lord North concedes free export of woollens and free trade with the Colonies.

Dissenters are admitted to civil and military office.

1321. **France.** Necker suppresses sinecures, and orders a report on tolls.

1322. **Spain.** War is declared against England, and French and Spanish fleets besiege Gibraltar and sail up the Channel unchallenged.

1323. **Germany.** Maria Theresa writes to Frederick, and a Congress takes place at Teschen, with French and Russian mediation. The war of the Bavarian Succession is terminated, Joseph obtaining the Jura district, and the rights of the Duke of Zweibrücken being confirmed. Austria agrees to the future union of the margravates of Anspach and Baireuth with the Prussian monarchy.

Howard's State of the Prisons announces the result of his travels and investigations. Certain of his recommendations are embodied in an Act, 1778.

2060. **Death.** Haller.

2061. **Eng. Ch.** Sir George Savile obtains privileges for Catholics in reference to the holding of land and to education. [1778

2062. **French Ch.** The Commission des Réguliers, instituted by the King to reform the regulars, inspires an edict which regulates the admission and establishes a minimum number in monastic houses. As a result of the edict, nine congregations disappear. The Commission is abolished 1784.

2063. **Eng. Lit.** Fanny Burney's Evelina.

2064. **French Lit.** Voltaire visits Paris and meets with a remarkable reception.

2065. **German Lit.** Herder's collection of national songs leads to the study of folk-lore.

2066. **Science.** Benjamin Thompson (later Count Rumford) commences experiments on heat by friction.

Lavoisier explodes phlogiston, proving that in burning a gas is taken up out of the air. This discovery is accepted by Black, but rejected by Priestley.

2067. **Geography.** Rennell's chart of banks and currents founds oceanography.

2068. **Social.** Mesmer, who has discovered Animal Magnetism, visits Paris. A committee, of which Franklin and Bailly are members, examine him and denounce him as an impostor.

2069. **Deaths.** Chatham, Linnaeus, Rousseau, Voltaire.

2070. **Eng. Ch.** Dissenting Ministers and schoolmasters are relieved from subscription. [1779

Cowper and Newton's Olney Hymns.

2071. **Scotch Ch.** A riot takes place in Glasgow against the Catholics. Bishop Hay writes to King George and begs for protection.

2072. **German Ch.** Princess Galitzin settles in Münster and gathers round her most of the distinguished Catholics of Germany.

2073. **Eng. Lit.** Dr Johnson's Lives of the Poets.

2074. **German Lit.** Lessing's Nathan the Wise (a portrait suggested by the character of Mendelssohn) contributes to the spread of ideas of toleration.

Campe's Robinson the Younger.

2075. **Science.** Ingenhousz investigates the power possessed by vegetables to purify or poison the air, and experiments on the nutrition of plants.

2076. **Art.** Gillray and Rowlandson commence English caricature and satire.

2077. **Philosophy.** Hume's Dialogues on Natural Religion reject Deism.

1324. **Africa.** England takes French possessions in Senegal and Goree.

1325. **Asia.** The First Mahratta war is caused by the intervention of France and England in a disputed succession of the Peshwa.

1326. **England.** After a petition from Yorkshire and public meetings throughout the country, Burke introduces a Bill for Economical Reform, to abolish sinecures. [1780

Dunning carries a resolution that 'the influence of the crown has increased, is increasing, and ought to be diminished.'

On the same day that the Duke of Richmond proposes manhood suffrage and annual Parliaments, a mob, led by Lord George Gordon, President of the Protestant Association, founded 1778, marches to Westminster with a petition to repeal Savile's Act of 1778, and sacks the Chapels of the Catholic Ambassadors, burns Newgate, and for six days ravages London.

1327. **America.** Clinton takes Charlestown, Cornwallis defeats Gates in South Carolina, and Virginia is attacked. Greene, however, begins to drive the English out of the Carolinas and Georgia.

Benedict Arnold, one of Washington's ablest lieutenants, plots to betray the American forts on the Hudson. Major André, the British agent, is caught and hung ; but Arnold escapes.

1328. **Ireland.** Grattan and the Irish Volunteers demand Home Rule, subject only to the King. Free Trade is granted.

1329. **France.** Necker abolishes the farming of taxes, and creates a provincial assembly for the Province of Berry, to which the duties of the intendants are to pass.

1330. **Holland.** England learns that the Pensionary of Amsterdam had projected a treaty with the Colonies, 1778, and sent supplies, and therefore declares war.

1331. **Spain.** Rodney defeats the Spanish fleet off Cape St Vincent, and relieves Gibraltar.

1332. **Austria.** Joseph determines to transfer the Austrian territories of independent Bishoprics to native sees. The small states resolve on a league, and appeal to Prussia to support it. Frederick attempts to obtain the support of Russia, which, however, plunges into a Turkish war. Joseph meets Catherine, and further alienates her from Prussia.

Joseph abolishes serfdom in Bohemia, Hungary and the Southern provinces, and, later, in Austria proper.

1333. **Russia.** To prevent English ships searching neutral vessels for enemies' goods and seizing neutral vessels trading with their enemies' ports, Catherine declares that neutral vessels carrying enemies' goods may trade with belligerents in non-contraband articles. This declaration is confirmed by France, Spain, Austria, Prussia and the Northern Powers, which form the 'Armed Neutrality.'

1334. **Asia.** Hyder Ali overruns the Carnatic.

1335. **England.** The Secretary of State for the Colonies and the Council of Trade and Plantations are abolished. [1781

2078. **Geography.** Rennell's Bengal Atlas.
2079. **Social.** Crompton invents a spinning-machine known as the 'mule.'
2080. **Death.** Garrick.

2081. **Eng. Ch.** Raikes founds Sunday Schools at Gloucester. [1780 The Sunday School Union is founded 1785.

The Bampton Lectureship in Christian Apologetics is endowed and the first Sermons are delivered.

Martin Madan, an Anglican clergyman, advocates polygamy as sanctioned by Mosaic law.

2082. **German Ch.** Lessing's Education of the Human Race describes the religions of the world as steps in an evolution not yet completed.

2083. **German Lit.** Wieland's Oberon.

Frederick the Great's De la Littérature française praises Gellert and Gesner, and is criticised by Justus Moser.

2084. **Bohemian Lit.** The Czech language is expelled from the schools, and a great patriotic revival begins, to which Dobrowsky's Commentaries on Bohemian Literature contribute.

2085. **Art.** Erard manufactures his first piano.

2086. **Science.** John Brown's Elementa Medicinae teaches that most diseases arise from debility, not from strength, and attacks the lowering treatment.

Lagrange explains the libration of the moon.

2087. **Law.** Bentham's Principles of Morals and Legislation are printed, but are not published till 1789.

Filangieri's Science of Legislation pleads for the reform of procedure.

2088. **Politics.** Cartwright founds the Society for Constitutional information, from which the Corresponding Society springs.

2089. **History.** Johannes Müller's History of Switzerland.

2090. **Social.** The twelfth Earl of Derby founds the 'Derby' race.

2091. **Deaths.** Blackstone, Condillac, Maria Theresa.

2092. **Eng. Ch.** Lady Huntingdon, who has built a chapel in [1781 Spa Fields, is compelled to register it under the Toleration Act, and becomes recognised as a Dissenter. She is, in consequence, deserted by Venn, Berridge, Romaine and other clergy.

2093. **German Ch.** Planck's History of Protestant Dogma.

2094. **Austrian Ch.** The Emperor grants Toleration to Protestants and members of the Greek Church, though the practice of their worship remains limited, and opens offices to all.

700 out of the 2000 monasteries in the dominions of the Emperor are dissolved, and Bulls are excluded until they receive the Emperor's approval, a German Bible and German hymns are to be used, and no money to be sent to Rome. Six new bishoprics are created by the Emperor. The Pope comes to Vienna to protest, but effects nothing, 1782.

1336. **America.** Cornwallis routs Greene in North Carolina, but is forced, by lack of numbers, to withdraw to Virginia. He fortifies Yorktown, on the shores of the Chesapeake, but is blockaded by De Grasse's West Indian fleet and by an American army, and capitulates (Oct.). De Grasse seizes several of the West Indies.

1337. **France.** Necker publishes his 'Compte rendu' in order to retain the confidence of the moneyed classes, but is dismissed (May). The period of reform ends, and the feudal reaction increases. Roturiers are excluded from military command.

1338. **Netherlands.** The Emperor obtains the surrender of the Barrier towns.

1339. **Austria.** Joseph and Catherine form a close alliance, Joseph allowing Catherine a free hand in Turkey, on the tacit understanding that Russia will help him in Germany.

1340. **Asia.** Hastings demands money from the Rajah of Benares for the war, and, on his refusal, deposes him. He next demands money from the Nawab of Oudh, and helps him to secure his father's treasure, retained by his mother and grandmother.

Eyre Coote defeats Hyder Ali, with whom a French fleet under Suffren co-operates.

1341. **Africa.** The Kaffirs, who have been slowly drifting south, first come into conflict with the Boers.

England sends a fleet to seize the Cape; but Suffren interposes, and a French regiment garrisons Cape Town till the Peace.

1342. **England.** North resigns (March), and Rockingham returns with Fox and Shelburne, the leader of the Chatham Whigs. [1782
Burke's Bill, which has been thrown out, 1781, is modified and passed. Government contractors are excluded from the House, and pensions are reduced. Rockingham dies (July), and Shelburne, with Pitt as Chancellor of the Exchequer and leader of the House, becomes Premier. Pitt's motion to consider the state of representation is lost. The proceedings against Wilkes are expunged from the Journals.

1343. **Ireland.** Grattan and the Protestants pass resolutions for independence and free trade, and repeal of anti-Catholic laws, and Fox carries the repeal of the Act of 1720. 'Grattan's Parliament,' however, is chosen by Protestants alone, and has no control over the executive.

1344. **Spain.** Minorca is taken from England by Spain, after a long siege.

1345. **West Indies.** Rodney defeats De Grasse, and saves the English West Indies (April).

1346. **America.** The Preliminaries of Peace, arranged by Franklin, John Adams, and Jay, are signed (Nov.), and acquiesced in by America.

1347. **Asia.** Hyder Ali dies, and his son, Tippoo, makes peace.

2095. **Eng. Lit.** The Clarendon Press is founded at Oxford.
2096. **French Lit.** Rousseau's Confessions.
2097. **German Lit.** Voss' Translation of the Odyssey aids the classical revival.

Schiller's Robbers, his first romantic play, is followed by Fiesco, 1783, and Kabala u. Liebe, 1784.

2098. **Science.** William Herschel discovers Uranus.

Lavoisier declares that nothing in nature is lost and nothing created.

Monge's paper on the curves of curvature.

2099. **Art.** Hiller founds the Gewandhaus concerts at Leipzig.

Houdon sculptures a statue of Voltaire (Paris).

2100. **Philosophy.** Kant's Critique of Pure Reason declares knowledge to arise jointly from impressions and from the forms or moulds of the mind which receives them, and discusses the arguments for the existence of God. His teaching is spread by Reinhold, Fichte, and Schiller, and criticised by Nicolai, Schulze, and Herder.

2101. **Education.** Pestalozzi, who has received a number of children in his house at Neuhof near Bern, unfolds his theories of education in his Leonard and Gertrude.

Warren Hastings founds a Mohammedan College at Calcutta.

2102. **Deaths.** Lessing, Turgot.

2103. **Eng. Ch.** Priestley's Corruptions of the Christian Church is attacked by Horsley, but imitated by Gilbert Wakefield and others. [1782

Charles Simeon is ordained curate of Trinity Church, Cambridge, and introduces the evangelical movement into the University.

2104. **German Ch.** Herder's Spirit of Hebrew Poetry applies the conception of evolution, and shows that the Psalms were the work of many hands.

2105. **Church Hist.** Bartolotti projects an union with the Eastern Church, suggesting that the Filioque shall be declared a 'theological truth,' not a dogma, and that the primacy of Rome should be recognised as in primitive times.

2106. **Eng. Lit.** Mrs Siddons, engaged by Sheridan for Drury Lane theatre, makes her début, and acts henceforward with her brother J. P. Kemble.

Fanny Burney's Cecilia.

2107. **Italian Lit.** Tiraboschi's History of Italian Literature.

2108. **Science.** Herschel catalogues the double stars, and discovers that the solar system is moving towards the constellation of Hercules.

2109. **Social.** Gilbert's Act allows parishes or unions to nominate Guardians, who are obliged to find work. Wages are supplemented from the rates, and out-door relief for the able-bodied becomes common.

2110. **Deaths.** D'Anville, Lord Kames, Metastasio, Pombal, Tanucci.

1348. **England.** Shelburne is deserted by his colleagues, and replaced by a coalition of Fox and North, with Portland as nominal Premier (April). [1783

Fox introduces an India Bill, framed by Burke, and transferring the government from the Board to seven Commissioners appointed by the Parliament for four years and after by the Crown. The Bill is rejected in the Lords, and the ministry falls (Dec.). Pitt becomes Premier, with a large majority against him in the Commons. His resolution for reform obtains 149 votes.

1349. **America.** A treaty is signed at Paris (Sept.), and the independence of the United States is acknowledged. Their boundaries are declared to be the Mississippi, the Floridas, and Canada.

The Colonials promise mercy to loyalists, undertake to pay private debts to British creditors at the outset of the war, and obtain a share in the fisheries off Newfoundland.

1350. **France.** By the Treaty of Versailles with France and Spain, the latter retains Minorca and receives back Florida ; France may fortify Dunkirk, forbidden by the Treaty of Utrecht, and recovers her islands in the Antilles, and Senegal and Goree in Africa.

Calonne becomes finance minister, and, by disguising the state of the finances, obtains loans.

1351. **Holland.** England obtains right of traffic with the Dutch East Indies.

1352. **Russia.** Russia annexes the Crimea and Kuban, and reaches the Black Sea.

1353. **Bohemia.** Joseph enforces the German language, suppresses the permanent Committee of the Diet, and transfers its authority to the central government, leaving the Estates the right to vote the taxes. These measures lead to the growth of a nationalist movement.

1354. **Asia.** Agha Mohammed, a Persian chief, invades Georgia, and sacks Tiflis. Russia intervenes, and takes Baku.

1355. **England.** Pitt appeals to the country, and obtains a large majority (May). His first budget reduces the duties on tea and spirits. [1784

In consequence of Fox's exclusion after the Westminster election, the poll is reduced from forty to fifteen days.

1356. **Scotland.** The Disarming Act is repealed.

1357. **Netherlands.** Joseph demands free navigation of the Scheldt, and revives old claims in Maestricht. The Dutch resist and are joined by Prussia and Sweden.

1358. **Denmark.** Bernstorff becomes supreme, and abolishes serfdom, improves education, encourages commerce, and allows liberty of the press.

1359. **Hungary.** Joseph outrages national sentiment by removing the crown of Hungary to Vienna and making German the official language. On the other hand he suppresses the feudal courts and taxes the landowners.

A rebellion breaks out in Transylvania.

2111. **German Ch.** Eichhorn's Introduction to the Old Testament first exhaustively investigates the sources and contents of the writings, most of which he attributes to several hands. [1783

2112. **Austrian Ch.** The Emperor makes marriage a civil contract, and allows divorce. In 1784 he reserves a veto on the ordinances of the Bishops, whom he proposes to appoint without the confirmation of the Pope. He also suppresses the diocesan seminaries, and institutes schools, the teachers of which he appoints.

2113. **American Ch.** The Mennonites settle in America.

2114. **Church Hist.** Moses Mendelssohn's Jerusalem pleads for the emancipation of the Jews.

2115. **Eng. Lit.** Crabbe's The Village.

Blair's Lectures on Rhetoric.

2116. **Science.** Hunter founds a museum in Leicester Square for Comparative Anatomy.

2117. **Philosophy.** Kant's Prolegomena to any possible Metaphysic replies to attacks on the Critique of Pure Reason.

2118. **Social.** Karl Friedrich of Baden abolishes serfdom.

2119. **Deaths.** D'Alembert, Euler.

2120. **Eng. Ch.** Wesley leaves the government of his societies to a Conference of 100 preachers in his Deed of Declaration, on condition that they accept his notes on the New Testament (based on Bengel), and his sermons. He also secretly ordains Coke and Ashbury 'superintendents' in America, and two elders retire from the movement in disgust. [1784

2121. **Scotch Ch.** At the instigation of Bishop Skinner, the Scotch Bishops consecrate Seabury Bishop of Connecticut. This departure calls attention to the Scotch Church, and earns the gratitude of the English Church, which cannot conveniently consecrate owing to the war.

2122. **Eng. Lit.** Beckford's Caliph Vathek.

2123. **French Lit.** Beaumarchais' Figaro.

Bernardin de St Pierre's Études de la Nature.

2124. **Swedish Lit.** Gustavus III. founds an Academy of Arts and Sciences.

2125. **Science.** Atwood's Machine exhibits and verifies the accelerative action of gravity.

Cavendish explodes oxygen and hydrogen into water.

Cullen's Practice of Physic displaces Boerhaave and the pathologists, who trace diseases to the vitiation of the fluids of the body, but attributes too much to the solids of the body.

Laplace explains the long inequality of Jupiter and Saturn pulling one another, but ultimately reoccupying their old position.

Hauy's Crystallographie discovers the law of symmetry and the law of the alteration of axes.

2126. **Art.** David's Vow of the Horatii, and Brutus, found the classic reaction in France.

Bewick's Engravings to his Select Fables revive wood-engraving.

1360. **Asia.** Pitt passes an India Bill, establishing a Board of Control, composed of Ministers and Privy Councillors, which revises despatches, and can, if necessary, issue orders without the consent of the Directors. Except for the Governor-General and the highest officers, patronage remains with the Directors. The authority of the Governor-General over the Governors of Madras and Bombay is increased.

1361. **America.** Slavery is partially abolished in Connecticut.

1362. **England.** Pitt's third attempt at Parliamentary Reform, voting one million pounds to buy up and disfranchise 72 nomination seats, giving the seats to London and the Counties, is rejected, and he never makes another attempt. [1785

John Adams arrives in London as ambassador of the United States, and is coldly received.

1363. **Ireland.** Pitt's proposals for a commercial union, complete free trade, and a contribution to the navy, are thrown out by the English manufacturers. His modified proposals are rejected at Dublin.

1364. **France.** Cardinal Rohan is falsely informed that the Queen wishes for a valuable diamond necklace. When the jeweller demands the first instalment of payment, the fraud is exposed, but the Court loses prestige.

1365. **Germany.** The Emperor attempts to induce Charles Theodore to exchange Bavaria for the Austrian Netherlands except Luxemburg and Namur. The Duke appeals for help to Frederick, who forms the Fürstenbund with Saxony and Hanover, joined by the Archbishop of Mainz and many princes, and defeats the scheme (July).

Joseph makes a treaty with the Dutch by French mediation. His sovereignty is recognised over part of the Scheldt, and he sells his claims to Maestricht and the part of the Scheldt outside his dominions.

1366. **Asia.** Hastings, finding himself unsupported by Pitt, resigns, and returns to England.

1367. **England.** Pitt abrogates the Methuen Treaty, and concludes a commercial treaty with Vergennes, by which duties between France and England are largely decreased. [1786

Pitt creates a sinking fund, by which one million pounds, raised every year by extra taxes, is to accumulate for the payment of the National Debt. The scheme is dropped, 1807.

A Committee of Council for Trade is formed.

1368. **France.** Calonne informs the King of the state of affairs, and proposes sweeping reforms on the lines of Turgot and Necker, such as the revival of provincial assemblies, a land-tax without exemptions, free trade in corn, abolition of the corvée and tolls. The King agrees to summon the Notables in 1787.

1369. **Austria.** The Emperor promulgates a new code of laws.

1370. **Holland.** The 'Patriot' Party deprives the stadtholder, William V., of the command of the army.

2127. **Philosophy.** Herder's Ideas for a Philosophy of History hints the development of men from animals, and animals from plants.
2128. **History.** Kant's Ideas of an Universal History approves the notion of perfectibility, and regards the human race as exemplifying streams of tendency.
2129. **Philology.** The Royal Asiatic Society is founded, its first President being Sir William Jones.
2130. **Geography.** The Ordnance Survey of England is commenced.
2131. **Deaths.** Diderot, Johnson.

2132. **Austrian Ch.** Joseph II. abolishes all secret societies except the Freemasons, whose numbers, in consequence, increase very rapidly. [1785
2133. **American Ch.** Madison's Religious Freedom Act removes all religious tests in Virginia.
2134. **Eng. Lit.** Cowper's The Task.
2135. **German Lit.** Schiller's Don Carlos.

Baron Munchausen's Marvellous Travels and Campaigns in Russia, probably written by Raspe.

2136. **Science.** Watt enters into partnership with Boulton and constructs a double-acting steam-engine.
2137. **Philosophy.** Kant's Groundwork of the Metaphysic of Ethics declares the Good Will the only virtue.

Paley's Moral Philosophy, a system of theological utilitarianism.

Jacobi's Letters on Spinoza to Moses Mendelssohn defend the conception of 'Glaube' or belief.

Joseph Balsamo, Count Cagliostro, settles at Strassburg, where he is patronised by Cardinal Rohan, and founds a lodge of Egyptian masonry.

2138. **Social.** Cartwright patents a 'power-loom,' which weaves by machinery and is improved by Johnson, Radcliffe, and Horrocks.
2139. **Deaths.** Choiseul, Mably.

2140. **Eng. Ch.** Bishop Wilson's Sacra Privata. [1786
2141. **German Ch.** The Bishops of Mainz, Cologne and Trier, and the Archbishop of Salzburg, fearing the Nunciature established in Munich, 1785, draw up the Punctation of Ems, which contests Papal autocracy and urges the abolition of nuncios. The scheme, though supported by the Emperor, is opposed by the majority of the bishops.
2142. **Italian Ch.** Ricci, Bishop of Pistoja, holds a diocesan synod, which adopts the Gallican Articles of 1682 and the doctrines of Quesnel, which have been spread in Italy by Tamburini and others. The Pope orders him to wait till a Council of Tuscan bishops meets at Florence. In this Council, Ricci is outvoted. Leopold breaks with Rome, but on leaving Tuscany, 1790, deserts Ricci, who submits.
2143. **Eng. Lit.** Burns' Poems.
2144. **Dutch Lit.** Bilderdyck's Elias founds the romantic revival.

Danish Lit. Baggesen's Comic Tales.

1371. **Asia.** Pitt obtains permission for the new Governor-General, Cornwallis, to overrule his Council.

Penang is ceded to England by its Rajah.

1372. **America.** An insurrection breaks out in Massachusetts under Shays, who attempts to prevent the collection of debts. The weakness of the Union is revealed, and Virginia proposes a convention to form a stronger constitution.

[1787

1373. **England.** Beaufoy's motion for the repeal of the Test and Corporation Acts is lost.

1374. **France.** The Notables meet (only 7 out of 144 belonging to the Tiers État), and reject the proposals of Calonne, who is succeeded by Loménie de Brienne (Feb.). The Notables are dissolved, but the Parliament of Paris protests against Brienne's measures, demands the convocation of the States-General, and is banished (Aug.). A few weeks later it is recalled, and the King declares the States-General shall meet 1792.

1375. **Holland.** England and Prussia interfere on behalf of the Prince of Orange, who has been driven out. The Prince is restored, and Amsterdam surrenders.

1376. **Netherlands.** The Emperor declares the Netherlands a province of the Austrian Monarchy, but is forced by opposition, led by Van der Noot, to revoke the Union.

1377. **Russia.** Catherine visits the Crimea, the poverty of which is partially concealed by Potemkin. She forms a defensive alliance with the Emperor, and forces Turkey to declare war.

1378. **America.** A Convention meets at Philadelphia, Rhode Island alone being unrepresented. Washington presides, and among the delegates are Franklin, Madison, Edmund Randolph, Mason, Dickinson, Gouverneur Morris, Sherman, Rufus King, Hamilton and the Pinckneys. A Constitution is formed, providing for a President chosen by electors, a Senate composed of two representatives of each state, a House of Representatives chosen according to population, and a Supreme Court. The question of slavery is postponed.

The Ordinance of 1787 creates five states out of the territory N.W. of the Ohio, and provides for the creation of others, guarantees equal rights and freedom of religion, and forbids slavery.

1379. **Africa.** England obtains Sierra Leone for the settlement of liberated slaves.

[1788

1380. **England.** The King loses his reason, and Pitt and Fox agree that the Prince of Wales shall be Regent. Fox declares that he possesses a right to the post, and therefore ought not to be subjected to restrictions.

Pitt consents to an impeachment of Warren Hastings, which is chiefly conducted by Burke and Sheridan. After four years, Hastings is acquitted.

2145. **Science.** Herschel's first catalogue of Nebulae.
Chladni founds Acoustics by his experiments on vibrations.
Goethe discovers the intermaxillary bone.

2146. **Art.** Mozart's Figaro.

2147. **Law.** Bentham writes fragmentary essays on International Law, one of which sketches a plan of a league for universal peace.

2148. **Philology.** Sir William Jones declares Sanskrit to be related to European languages.

2149. **Geography.** John Perthes founds a Geographical Institute at Gotha.

2150. **Social.** Clarkson's Essay on the Slavery and Commerce of the Human Species denounces the traffic in slaves.

2151. **Deaths.** Frederick the Great, Mendelssohn.

2152. **Eng. Ch.** Porteus becomes Archbishop of Canterbury and leads the Evangelical revival within the Church, aided by Hannah More, Cowper, Milner, Scott, Simeon, Wilberforce, and the Clapham sect. [1787

A selection from Wesley's Sermons is published.

2153. **French Ch.** The Edict of Versailles grants religious freedom and legal civil status to Protestants.

2154. **German Lit.** Goethe's Iphigenie reveals the influence of his journey to Italy.

2155. **Science.** Laplace explains the secular acceleration of the moon's mean motion.

2156. **Art.** Mozart's Jupiter Symphony.
Talma's début.
Canova's monument to Clement XIV. is finished.
Blake illustrates his poems.

2157. **Politics.** John Adams' Defence of the Constitution of Government of the United States of America answers Turgot's Letter to Price, which blames the Americans for adopting checks and balances like England.

2158. **Economics.** Bentham's Defence of Usury.

2159. **Philology.** Catherine II. orders the composition of an Imperial Dictionary, in which 285 words are translated into 51 European and 149 Asiatic languages.

2160. **Social.** A public Committee for the abolition of Slave Trade is formed in England, nine out of the original twelve members being Quakers. Granville Sharp and Clarkson are added 1788.

2161. **Deaths.** Boscovich, Galiani, Gluck, Liguori, Lowth, Wahab.

2162. **Scotch Ch.** The Pretender dies, and the Episcopal clergy can henceforth conscientiously recognize George III.; but Skinner's plea for the repeal of the persecuting laws is defeated by Thurlow. [1788

2163. **German Ch.** Wöllner, Minister of Religion in Prussia, revives the censorship and imposes penalties for heresy in the clergy; but the edict is repealed by Frederick William III., 1797.

1381. **France.** Brienne fails to overcome the opposition of Parliament, announces a national bankruptcy, and is dismissed (Aug.). Necker is recalled, and the States-General are summoned for May 1, 1789, with a double representation of the Tiers État.

1382. **Germany.** Hertzberg induces England and Holland to join Prussia in a Triple Alliance to maintain the peace of Europe, more especially to defend Turkey against Joseph and Catherine.

1383. **Spain.** With the accession of the new king, Charles IV., the reformers lose power, which is grasped by the Queen, Marie Louise, and her favourite Godoy.

1384. **Russia.** Austria and Russia invade Turkey. Suvoroff repulses an attack on the Crimea, and Oczakov is taken by Potemkin; but Joseph is repulsed from Belgrad.

Gustavus of Sweden declares war against Russia, and invades Finland. His fleet, however, is defeated, Sweden is invaded by the Danes, and he is persuaded by the Triple Alliance to retire.

1385. **Turkey.** Ali, an Albanian in the service of the Sultan, seizes the town of Janina and obtains the Pashaliks of Janina, Arta, and Acarnania. He subsequently drives the Suliots out of Epirus, and rules south-west Macedonia and Thessaly.

1386. **America.** The Constitution is accepted by all the States except Rhode Island and North Carolina, despite the strenuous opposition of Patrick Henry, Samuel Adams, Lee, Mason, Clinton and others, who fear that the liberty of individual States is threatened by the powers granted to the Federal Government.

1387. **Australia.** Captain Philip lands convicts at Botany Bay, but, finding it unsuitable, moves to Sydney. Coal is found and sheep are introduced, and New South Wales is colonised.

1388. **England.** Pitt moves that the Prince be Regent, without power to create peers or to grant pensions or places. The King, however, recovers. [1789

Erskine successfully defends Stockdale, who is charged with libelling the Commons by publishing a defence of Warren Hastings.

The Revolution Society, founded to commemorate the Revolution of 1688, meets in London and congratulates the French National Assembly on the fall of the Bastille.

1389. **France.** The States-General meet (May 5). The deputies of the Tiers État declare themselves the National Assembly (June 17), and, meeting in the Tennis Court at Versailles, swear to establish a Constitution (June 20). They are joined by the other Estates; but Necker is dismissed and troops are collected round Paris. The Bastille is therefore stormed (July 14); Necker is recalled; Artois, Polignac and other nobles fly to Italy; Bailly becomes Mayor, and Lafayette commander of a newly-raised National Guard. Feudal privileges, serfdom, corvées, guilds, seigneurial jurisdictions, are abolished (Aug. 4), and a declaration of the Rights of Man is published. The Assembly decides that

2164. **American Ch.** The Presbyterians revise the Westminster Catechism, and introduce the principles of religious liberty and the equality of all Churches before the law.

2165. **Church Hist.** Abbé Grégoire's Rebirth of the Jews pleads for their emancipation.

2166. **Eng. Lit.** Walter, a bookseller, founds the Times.

2167. **French Lit.** Bernardin de St Pierre's Paul et Virginie.

2168. **German Lit.** Goethe's Egmont.

2169. **Science.** Lagrange's Mécanique Analytique deduces the whole of mechanics from the law of virtual work by the aid of the Calculus of Variations.

2170. **Philosophy.** Kant's Critique of Practical Reason declares God, Freedom, and Immortality moral postulates.

Cabanis' Rapports du Physique et du Moral restates the theories of Condillac.

2171. **Philology.** Porson's Letters to Travis prove the spuriousness of the text relating to the three heavenly witnesses, 1 John v. 7.

2172. **Geography.** Banks and Rennell form the African Association.

2173. **Social.** Clarkson publishes evidence relating to the slave-trade, and wins over Wilberforce. The Committee on Trade and Plantations hold an inquiry, and a Bill to improve the sanitation of the slave-vessels is introduced, but mutilated by the peers.

2174. **Deaths.** Buffon, Charles III., Filangieri, Gainsborough, Hamann.

2175. **French Ch.** Mirabeau carries a motion that the property of the Church belongs to the nation. [1789

2176. **German Ch.** The three ecclesiastical Electors submit, and recognize the right of the Pope to send Nuncios. Pius refutes the Articles of Ems.

2177. **American Ch.** Carroll becomes the first Catholic Bishop in America, which has hitherto been under the Vicar Apostolic of London. A Jesuit College is established at Georgetown. At this time there are about 30,000 Catholics, mostly in Maryland and Pennsylvania.

2178. **Church Hist.** In his communication to the German Church the Pope surrenders the authenticity of the Isidorian Decretals.

2179. **Eng. Lit.** Blake's Songs of Innocence.

White's Natural History of Selborne.

Bowles, a forerunner of the romantic movement, publishes Sonnets which influence Coleridge.

2180. **French Lit.** Barthélemy's Voyage du jeune Anacharsis en Grèce presents the first real living picture of Greek life, and contributes to the growth of classical and republican ideas.

Joseph Chénier's drama, Charles IX.

The Journal des Débats is founded.

2181. **German Lit.** Kotzebue's drama, Hatred and Remorse.

2182. **Science.** Galvani accidentally discovers the 'Galvanic fluid' in a frog's leg and assumes that the electricity exists in the frog. Volta hears of the discovery and declares that the electricity is not in the frog but is produced by metals, acted on by the moisture of the flesh.

there shall be only one Chamber in the new Legislature, and that the King's veto shall be merely suspensive. Owing in part to the plots of Orléans, who covets the throne, a large band of women marches to Versailles and compels the return of the Court to Paris (Oct. 6). Lamarck conveys a message from Mirabeau, urging the King to escape. Members of the Assembly are forbidden to accept office, as Mirabeau is believed to be striving to enter the Ministry (Nov.). Political clubs spring up, and the second emigration of nobles takes place. The provinces with their institutions are abolished, and France is divided into 80 departments with districts and cantons.

1390. **Netherlands.** Joseph revokes the Constitution of Hainault and Brabant, which therefore rises in revolt under Van der Noot. The Prince Bishop is expelled from Liége, but is restored by Prussia.

1391. **Sweden.** Gustavus makes the monarchy absolute.

1392. **Turkey.** Austria and Russia renew the alliance of 1781 for another eight years. Suvoroff and Potemkin win victories, and Loudon takes Belgrad and Passarowitz.

1393. **America.** Washington becomes President of the United States, John Adams Vice-President, Jefferson Secretary of State, Hamilton Secretary of the Treasury, and Jay Chief Justice.

The first Tariff Act is introduced, and the City of Washington laid out.

Tammany is founded as a benevolent society, but shortly becomes a political organisation.

Spain attacks England at Nootka Sound, in Vancouver Island, but in the following year retires, owing to the refusal of France to aid, and offers indemnity.

1394. **England.** Fox declares his sympathy with and Burke his detestation of the French Revolution. [1790

Motions for Parliamentary reform and the repeal of tests are withdrawn without a division.

1395. **France.** Mirabeau becomes the secret agent of the Crown (May), for which he composes a series of Notes. He fails to win the confidence of Lafayette or Necker, who retire (Sept.).

In the discussion as to the duty of France under the Family Compact to aid Spain in her quarrel with England in regard to Nootka Sound, the Assembly proposes to take the right of declaring war from the King. Mirabeau obtains a compromise, requiring the consent of the King and the Assembly. Louis is henceforth described as King of the French, and a civil list is allowed him in place of his domains.

1396. **Germany.** By a treaty with Prussia, Poland agrees to cede Thorn and Danzig in exchange for the retrocession of Austrian Galicia (March); but the new Emperor, Leopold, makes the Treaty of Reichenbach, Frederick William of Prussia withdrawing from his patronage of the Belgian rebels and his engagements with Sweden, Poland and

Jussieu's Genera Plantarum founds the 'natural system' of classification of plants, i.e., by all observable points, and sketches the characters of 'Families, or Natural Orders.'

Herschel constructs a reflector 40 feet long.

Lavoisier's Traité élémentaire de Chimie contains a new chemical nomenclature and a list of elements. Fourcroy, Guyton de Morveau, Berthollet, assist in establishing the system.

2183. **Philology.** Sir William Jones translates the Sakuntala of Kalidasa.

Reiske's Historical Annotations on Abulfeda.

2184. **Politics.** Sièyes' pamphlet, Qu'est-ce que le Tiers État? maintains the right of the bourgeois to a share in the government of the country.

Price preaches a sermon on the Love of Our Country before the Revolution Society, which sends congratulations to the National Assembly of France.

The fall of the Bastille is welcomed in Germany by Klopstock, Stolberg, Kant, Fichte, Schiller, J. Müller, and other distinguished thinkers.

Bentham's Principles of Morals and Legislation develope the principle of Utility, borrowed from Priestley.

Malouet's Considérations sur le Gouvernement qui convient à la France recommends limited monarchy.

The Declaration of the Rights of Man, based on Sièyes' Exposition des Droits de l'Homme, declares men born free and equal in regard to rights; that the object of political association is the defence of the Natural Rights of Man, liberty, property, personal safety and resistance to oppression. All citizens are eligible to all posts according to capacity; nobody may be molested for expressing his opinions, even religious, unless he disturbs public order.

2185. **Law.** Martens' Précis du Droit des Gens Moderne, the first systematic positive and historic treatment of International Law.

2186. **Death.** Holbach.

[1790

2187. **Eng. Ch.** Paley's Horae Paulinae.

2188. **French Ch.** Church property is confiscated, and monasteries abolished. The Constitution Civile du Clergé abolishes the Concordat of 1516, and reduces the Bishops to one for each department. The Bishops are to be chosen by the Parliamentary electors and instituted by the Metropolitan; the clergy by the electors to communal offices. The Pope's confirmation is dispensed with. The clergy are to take the oath to the Constitution Civile. After long hesitation, the King sanctions the law. Protestants become eligible for office and receive back the property confiscated by Louis XIV.

2189. **German Ch.** At the Imperial Election, the Gravamina against the Roman Church are discussed.

2190. **Church Hist.** The Jews are declared free in France and receive civic rights.

Turkey. The treaty marks the failure of the plan to make Prussia the arbiter of Europe, and Hertzberg is dismissed.

1397. **Netherlands.** A Republic is proclaimed, but the Democrats, or Vonckists, are driven from the country by the party of Van der Noot. Leopold, who succeeds his brother as Emperor, offers to restore the old Constitution. The offer is rejected; but the country is reoccupied without a blow. The project of exchanging the Netherlands for Bavaria is formally renounced.

1398. **Hungary.** The Emperor refuses to grant semi-independence, and marches to Pesth. The Magyars submit and Leopold restores the old Constitution; but a strong Nationalist movement remains, which is fostered by Kazinczy, who edits the first Magyar literary magazine.

1399. **Poland.** Stanislas is won over by the Reformers and grants a Constitution, drawn up by Kollontai, establishing responsible government, making the crown hereditary in the house of Saxony after the death of Stanislas, abolishing the liberum veto, allowing religious toleration and taxing the nobility. The Constitution is acknowledged by Prussia and Austria, but not by Russia.

1400. **Russia.** Peace is made with Sweden by the Treaty of Verela.

1401. **Turkey.** Suvoroff takes Ismail.

1402. **America.** Hamilton reports on the Finances, and carries the full payment of the 'foreign' and 'domestic' debt, and part of the State debts.

The first Anti-Slavery petitions are presented; but no settlement is reached.

1403. **Asia.** Lord Cornwallis enters on the second Mysore War, defeats Tippoo at Seringapatam, 1791, and compels him to cede half his territory, 1792.

1404. **England.** Anti-Jacobin riots take place at Birmingham, and Priestley's house is destroyed. [1791

Burke publicly renounces Fox's friendship.

1405. **Ireland.** Mitford's Bill removes certain Catholic disabilities.

The United Irishmen are formed at Belfast by Wolfe Tone, a Presbyterian, to widen the franchise and open Parliament and office to all.

1406. **France.** Mirabeau is chosen President of the Assembly, but dies (April). The royal family fly from Paris, but are arrested at Varennes (June). The Jacobins and Orleanists clamour for a republic, and Lafayette loses his influence by firing on the mob. The new Constitution is completed and accepted by the King. Ministers are to be responsible to the Legislative Chamber, which is to be elected by almost universal suffrage. The King's veto only holds good for six months. The country is divided into 80 Departments, with elected Councils, and the Parliaments are replaced by judges locally elected, with a Court of Appeal in Paris. The Constituent Assembly dissolves itself (Sept. 30). The Legislative Assembly, from which members of the Constituent are excluded, meets (Oct. 1). Lafayette ceases to command the National

2191. **German Lit.** Goethe's Tasso.
2192. **Russian Lit.** Derzhavin, the Homer of Catherine, writes an Ode on the taking of Ismail by Suvoroff.
2193. **Science.** Goethe's Metamorphosis of Plants shews the fundamental unity of floral and foliar parts. All organs are modifications of the leaf, and all plants modifications of a common type. The discovery receives little notice until taught by De Candolle.
2194. **Art.** Alison's Essay on Taste declares that beauty is not a quality of things but a product of the association of ideas.

Albrechtsberger's Guide to Composition.
2195. **Philosophy.** Kant's Critique of Judgment recognises a third department of philosophy, namely the Faculty of Pleasure and Pain (in addition to the Faculty of Knowledge and the Will). The *à priori* principles of the æsthetic consciousness are that beauty gives a disinterested pleasure and a pleasure felt by all, and must therefore be regarded as the outcome of universal reason and as transcending the subjective and phenomenal.
2196. **Politics.** Burke's Reflections on the French Revolution divides the English nation into two parties, and creates an unparalleled excitement throughout Europe. The work vehemently denounces the attack on the Church and the Monarchy and the abstract doctrines of the Rights of Man, and foretells the breakdown of the constitutional compromise and the rise of absolutism. Burke, however, judges the Revolution as a purely political phenomenon, and shews himself altogether blind to the existence of the social and economic problems that underlie it.
2197. **Law.** Hufeland's Text-book of Naturrecht, influenced by Kant.
2198. **Geography.** Vancouver explores the N.W. coast of America.
2199. **Social.** Raditschef, influenced by Raynal and other French writers, pleads for the emancipation of the serfs in his Journey from St Petersburg to Moscow.

Cartwright invents a wool-combing machine.

Kelly applies water as the motor-power for machinery in spinning.

The guillotine is brought into use.

Count Rumford arrests all the beggars in Munich simultaneously.
2200. **Deaths.** Cullen, Febronius, Franklin, Howard, Adam Smith.

[1791

2201. **Eng. Ch.** Robert Hall becomes pastor of a Baptist congregation at Cambridge for 15 years and preaches his most brilliant sermons.
2202. **French Ch.** Volney's Ruines des Empires compares the historic results of the chief religions of the world, to the disadvantage of Christianity.
2203. **American Ch.** The Sulpicians found the first Catholic seminary in the United States.
2204. **Eng. Lit.** Boswell's Life of Johnson.

Mrs Inchbald's A Simple Story.

Guard. Louis vetoes decrees for the return of the emigrants under pain of confiscation and death, and for the taking the oath to the Constitution Civile by the clergy; but the Assembly declares that they are not laws, and that the veto is therefore null.

The Comte d'Artois and other French nobles settle at Coblenz (July). The Emperor calls on the Powers to rescue Louis XVI., and persuades the King of Prussia to join him in issuing the Declaration of Pilnitz for joint action against France, if Europe will cooperate. Pitt refuses to join, and, when Louis accepts the Constitution, Leopold declares that the need for a coalition has ceased. The Girondins, however, urge war, and the King is forced to inform the Emperor and the Archbishop of Trier that if the military force of the emigrants is not disbanded within a month, he will attack (Dec.). The Elector orders the cessation of the military preparations, but the emigrants refuse to obey. The Emperor expresses his desire for peace, but declares that he will regard an attack on Trier as a *casus belli*; and Gustavus of Sweden offers to lead a crusade.

France decrees the annexation of Avignon and the Venaissin.

1407. **Germany.** The principalities of Anspach and Bayreuth fall to Prussia in accordance with the Gera Bond, 1598.

1408. **Turkey.** In defiance of the Treaty of Reichenbach, the Sultan is forced to cede the district of Orsowa and part of Croatia to Austria by the Treaty of Sistowa. Odessa is founded, the commerce of which is almost monopolised by the Greeks.

Pitt considers but dismisses the idea of supporting Turkey against Russia.

1409. **America.** The first ten Amendments to the Constitution are added, securing the separation of Church and State, free press and petition, trial by jury, etc., and declaring that powers not expressly delegated to the Federal Government are reserved to the States.

Hamilton imposes an excise on whisky, and founds a National Bank. These extensions of federal power are opposed by Jefferson.

The provinces of Upper and Lower Canada are separated, and receive representative institutions.

1410. **West Indies.** A Negro insurrection takes place in the French part of San Domingo, and the Commissioner of the French Republic declares the natives free, 1793.

1411. **Africa.** Spain is finally expelled from Oran.

1412. **England.** Fox's Libel Bill allows juries to decide what constitutes a libel. [1792

The Society of the Friends of the People is formed to promote Parliamentary Reform.

Tom Paine is tried, and defended by Erskine.

Pitt refuses to accept Grey's motion for Parliamentary Reform as unseasonable, and a Proclamation against seditious writings is issued.

1413. **France.** Three French armies are collected on the frontier. The Emperor therefore makes an offensive and defensive alliance with

Wordsworth visits France, and is carried away by enthusiasm for the Revolution, the influence of which also appears in the early works of Southey and Coleridge.

2205. **German Lit.** Goethe becomes Director of the theatre at Weimar till 1817.

2206. **Science.** Herschel ceases to believe that all nebulae consist of stars.

Rennie sets up in business in London as an engineer, and builds bridges, canals, harbours, breakwaters and lighthouses.

2207. **Art.** Haydn composes his six first Grand Symphonies for a series of concerts in London.

2208. **Politics.** Mackintosh, in his Vindiciae Gallicae, Tom Paine, in his Rights of Man, and many others, reply to Burke's attack on the French Revolution.

Burke writes his Appeal from the New to the Old Whigs, and his Letter to a Member of the National Assembly, in the latter of which he first advocates the intervention of the Great Powers in the affairs of France.

W. v. Humboldt's Attempt to determine the Limits of the Functions of the State protests against the principle that the securing of the moral well-being of the community lies within the sphere of State action.

2209. **History.** Martens' Recueil des principaux Traités, 1671—1791.

2210. **Social.** Bentham presents his scheme of a Panopticon prison (i.e. a building every part of which is made visible from a single point by reflectors) to the Government; though empowered to proceed, nothing further is done.

2211. **Deaths.** Mirabeau, Mozart, Potemkin, Semler, Wesley.

2212. **Scotch Ch.** The penal laws against the Scotch episcopalians are rescinded, partly owing to the influence of Horsley. [1792
Some disabling clauses, however, are inserted by Thurlow.

2213. **French Ch.** A law by which priests may be banished on the petition of 20 citizens is rejected by the King. After Aug. 10, the non-jurors are given 14 days to leave. The religious orders are dissolved, and civil marriage and divorce are introduced.

2214. **German Ch.** Fichte's Critique of all Revelation, the ideas of which he declares to be a development from the philosophy of Kant, rejects doctrinal Christianity.

2215. **American Ch.** The first Swedenborgian Church is founded at Baltimore.

2216. **Eng. Lit.** The Libel Act is passed, and is strongly attacked by Robert Hall and others.

Hannah More's Village Politics, designed to prevent the spread of revolutionary principles.

Bage and Holcroft write didactic novels with a revolutionary tendency.

2217. **American Lit.** Cobbett's Journal, Peter Porcupine, attacks the American Republic.

Prussia, and declares that the security of Europe demands order in France. The Girondins take office and force the King to declare war against the Emperor (April 20). In an attack on Belgium a panic occurs. The cry of treachery is raised, 20,000 volunteers from the departments are collected, and a camp of 80,000 men outside Paris is decreed. The King vetoes the latter measure, dismisses the ministry, and appoints Feuillants, but fails to support them. The contingent from Marseilles for the volunteers' camp arrives singing the Marseillaise. When war is declared against Prussia (July 8), Brunswick threatens Paris with destruction if the royal family is harmed. The mob demand the deposition of the King and Danton takes control of Paris. The Swiss guards are massacred (Aug. 10), the King is shut up in the Temple, and a National Convention is summoned to revise the Constitution. Lord Gower, the English ambassador, is at this moment recalled. The capture of Longwy and Verdun by the Prussians (Sept. 2) is followed by the September massacres of nobles and others. The Convention meets, declares France a Republic, and inaugurates a new Calendar. The tide of success at this point turns. Dumouriez holds Valmy against the Prussians, and Savoy and Nice are annexed. Custine invades the Rhine Provinces, and takes Spires, Worms and Mainz, the Princes fleeing without a blow. Dumouriez defeats the Austrians at Jemappes (Nov.), enters Belgium, and opens the Scheldt. These victories impel the Assembly to offer aid to all nations revolting against their governments (Nov.).

The Jacobins become powerful and demand the King's death (Nov.). Louis' correspondence with Mirabeau is discovered, and serves as a basis for the trial.

The last remains of the feudal régime are abolished.

The Colonies are granted representation in Parliament.

1414. **Sweden.** Gustavus III. is assassinated.

1415. **Poland.** Catherine invades Poland and is joined by the Patriots, who form the Confederation of Targowicz, and demand the restoration of the old Constitution. The Poles, led by Kosciuzko, are defeated, Stanislas is terrified, and the new Constitution is abolished by Russia. Catherine begins to negotiate with Austria and Prussia for a partition.

1416. **Spain.** Godoy becomes supreme.

1417. **Turkey.** The Peace of Jassy is made with Russia, which obtains Oczakov. The Dniester is fixed as the boundary.

1418. **England.** Pitt issues Exchequer Bills. [1793

Grenville's Alien Act empowers to remove suspected foreigners, and a Treasonable Correspondence Act is passed. Muir and other republican propagandists are heavily punished.

1419. **Ireland.** Alarmed by the United Irishmen, Pitt frees the Catholics from some penalties, and allows them to vote.

1420. **France.** The King is executed (Jan. 21), and France declares war against England and Holland. The coalition is joined by Spain, Portugal and Tuscany. Dumouriez is defeated at Neerwinden, and

2218. **Science.** Pinel becomes physician at the asylum of Bicêtre, discards the theory of possession, dispenses, where possible, with physical restraint, and introduces humane treatment of the insane. In the same year Tuke applies similar principles in the asylum at York.

2219. **Art.** Raphael Morghen settles in Florence, and engraves Leonardo's Last Supper, and other works.

2220. **Philosophy.** Dugald Stewart's Philosophy of the Human Mind popularises, without adding to, the ideas of Reid.

Schulze's Aenesidemus or the fundamental Principles of the Elementary Philosophy of Reinhold, declares it a contradiction to say that categories apply only to phenomena and that things in themselves are causes of impressions, and asserts that criticism ought logically to deny the possibility of things in themselves.

2221. **Numismatics.** Eckhel's Doctrina Nummorum Veterum.

2222. **Social.** Kelly invents the self-acting mule, which is improved by Roberts.

Mary Wolstonecraft's Rights of Woman declares the chief end of marriage to be intellectual companionship, contends for greater freedom of divorce, and recommends state education.

The King of Denmark first forbids the buying, selling or transport of slaves.

2223. **Death.** Reynolds.

2224. **Eng. Ch.** Elkanah Winchester, an American Unitarian, founds South Place Chapel, London. [1793

2225. **Scotch Ch.** Privileges are conceded to the Scotch Catholics.

2226. **French Ch.** Hébert's Père Duchesne advocates atheism, and with the aid of the Cordeliers Club, Chaumette, Anacharsis Clootz and others, forces the Convention to abolish the Catholic faith and to threaten non-juring priests with death. On Nov. 10th they celebrate the Feast of Reason in the Church of St Eustache.

2227. **Italian Lit.** Monti's Bassvilliana, an epic, attacks the French Revolution.

2228. **Science.** Sprengel's Secret of Nature Displayed explains the fertilisation of plants by insects which carry pollen-dust from flower to flower. In certain cases pollen-dust is carried by the wind.

Chappe constructs the aërial telegraph.

2229. **Art.** The Louvre is transformed into a national museum of art.

2230. **Philosophy.** Kant's Religion within the Limits of Reason declares the religious life of the individual independent of the truth or falsehood of historical Christianity.

The Décade Philosophique, a review of science and philosophy at home and abroad, is published as the organ of the Idéologues, Say, Ginguéné, Condorcet, Siéyes, Roederer, Volney, Saint-Lambert, Cabanis, Garat.

Condorcet's Tableau du Progrès de l'Esprit Humain surveys the

deserts to the Austrians (March). The Committee of Public Safety is formed, the Reign of Terror begins, the Revolutionary Tribunal commences. The Girondins fall, and Marat is murdered by Charlotte Corday in revenge for their death. Robespierre, St Just, Billaud, Collot, Barère, and Couthon become supreme. Toulon, Lyons and La Vendée rise against the Government. The English troops, under the Duke of York, are repulsed near Dunkirk (Sept.), the Austrians are defeated at Wattignies, and Austrians and Prussians are driven back to the Rhine (Oct.). Lyons surrenders, the Vendeans are suppressed, and Toulon is captured by Bonaparte (Dec.).

Equal division of real property is introduced.

1421. **Poland.** Russia and Prussia secretly sign the second Partition, (Jan.). Frederick William occupies the stipulated districts, Danzig, Thorn, with the provinces of Great Poland, Posen, Kalisch, and Gnesen. Russia takes the remainder of Lithuania, and Volhynia and Podolia, and obtains free entrance for her troops, the conduct of wars and the confirmation of treaties made with foreign powers. At Vienna, Thugut, the new minister, refuses to accept the treaty.

1422. **America.** The first Fugitive Slave Act is passed, but proves inoperative in the North.

Washington issues a proclamation of Neutrality on the outbreak of the great war, despite the treaty with France of 1778. In defiance of this, Genet, the French agent, fits out privateers, but, at the request of Washington, is recalled.

1423. **Asia.** Bengal is assessed for land-tax by the order of Lord Cornwallis, and the Permanent Settlement comes into operation.

Lord Macartney is sent to China to obtain commercial privileges for the East India Company, but fails.

1424. **England.** The Habeas Corpus Act is suspended. The Whig party splits into two parts, and Portland, Grenville and Windham enter the Cabinet. Fox and Grey remain with only a handful of supporters. Horne Tooke, Hardy and Thelwall are acquitted of treason. [1794

1425. **Ireland.** Pitt is persuaded by his new Whig allies to pursue a policy of conciliation, and selects Fitzwilliam, who, however, is forbidden to expel any officials for misconduct. Fitzwilliam gathers that Pitt authorises a complete change of system and justice to the Catholics.

Curran begins to take part in the great State Trials.

1426. **France.** Jourdan defeats the allies at Fleurus (June), and drives them out of the Netherlands. Pichegru enters Holland. York is beaten at Bois-le-Duc.

Howe defeats a French fleet near the mouth of the Channel (June), but the victory has no decisive results. Hoche defeats a body of Émigrés at Quiberon Bay (July).

Robespierre crushes Hébert, Chaumette, and Clootz (March), and Danton and Camille Desmoulins (April). Carrier at Nantes and Lebon

intellectual development of mankind, and foretells perfectibility and a greatly increased longevity.

2231. **Politics.** Godwin's Political Justice, the only attempt by an Englishman during the 18th century at a system based on French Communism, exerts a wide influence, especially over young men. Its principles are continued by Charles Hall and others.

Spence edits a Journal, entitled Pigs' Meat, in which he contends for land nationalisation.

Mallet du Pan's Considérations sur la Révolution Française.

Gentz translates and edits Burke's Reflections on the French Revolution.

Anacharsis Clootz proposes that the Convention shall decree the creation of an universal republic.

2232. **Education.** The French Assembly decides on a free and compulsory elementary education from 6 to 8; but education ceases to be free or compulsory 1795.

2233. **Philology.** Porson becomes Professor of Greek at Cambridge, and edits Euripides and Aeschylus. With Gaisford, Elmsley, Dobree, Blomfield, Monk, he revives English classical scholarship.

2234. **Agriculture.** An Agricultural Board, suggested by Lord Kames, is founded, with Sir John Sinclair as President, and Arthur Young as Secretary. The Board collects statistics and advocates enclosures and the cultivation of potatoes.

2235. **Social.** Eli Whitney invents a cotton gin, which increases the pace of cleaning cotton three hundredfold, and facilitates the export of cotton from the Southern states of the American Union.

England becomes dependent on foreign corn.

Slavery is abolished in French possessions.

2236. **Deaths.** Mansfield, Robertson, Gilbert White.

2237. **Eng. Ch.** Paley's Evidences of Christianity assume the existence of a Personal God, and infer the probability of a revelation, the reality of which he proves chiefly by miracles. Though admitting, like Butler, that the evidence is not complete, he considers it sufficient, and declares the discrepancies of the N.T. to be in no way inconsistent with its general inspiration. [1794

Paine's Age of Reason attacks Christianity and the Old Testament from a Deistic standpoint, declaring the conduct attributed to Jehovah inconsistent with moral ideas.

Stonyhurst College is founded.

2238. **French Ch.** Robespierre carries a decree formally recognizing the existence of a Supreme Being and immortality (May). In June he presides over the Feast of the Supreme Being.

2239. **Eng. Lit.** Godwin's Caleb Williams.

Gifford's Baviad and Maeviad satirise the affectation and sham romanticism of the Della Cruscans.

Mrs Radcliffe's Mysteries of Udolpho.

at Arras supervise the revolution in the provinces. Robespierre carries a law by which deputies may be tried by an order of the Committee of Public Safety, and no proof of guilt is required. The deputies are frightened, and Robespierre is arrested, with Couthon and St Just, and executed (July 28). The Moderates and Dantonists, Sièyes, Tallien, Barras, Boissy d'Anglas, seize power and crush Billaud, Collot, Barère, Tinville, and Carrier, abolish the Commune of Paris, close the Jacobin Club, amnesty the Vendéans, and recall the Girondins, expelled from the Assembly in 1793.

Paoli appeals to the English fleet to aid him to expel the French. The island is taken, and Paoli retires into private life, but England withdraws, 1796.

1427. **Poland.** Kosciuzko leads a revolt against the Russians, who are expelled from Warsaw. A Prussian army in vain besieges the capital; but Suvoroff arrives, defeats and captures Kosciuzko, and takes the city.

1428. **America.** Exasperated by the retention of posts in the North-west, the capture of neutral vessels carrying provisions to French ports, and the search of American vessels for British seamen, Congress lays an embargo on British shipping in American ports for 30 days. To avoid war Jay is sent to England to negotiate a treaty. England promises to evacuate the posts, to appoint commissioners to settle the debts and the North-west Boundary dispute, but yields nothing in regard to neutral trade and impressment. The 12th article of the treaty opens the British West Indies to American vessels under 70 tons, provided the United States do not export molasses, sugar, coffee, cocoa, and cotton.

1429. **West Indies.** An English invasion of Hayti leads to the emancipation of the slaves. Toussaint L'Ouverture drives out the British.

Guadeloupe, Martinique and Santa Lucia are taken by England from France. Guadeloupe is recaptured.

1430. **Africa.** England takes the Seychelles from France.

1431. **England.** A Treason Act declares writing or speaking against the King's authority treason, and stirring up hatred against the King's person and the Constitution a misdemeanour; and a Sedition Act forbids political meetings unless advertised beforehand, and permits two justices to disperse them if they consider them dangerous. [1795

1432. **Ireland.** Fitzwilliam arrives, but at once dismisses two notorious jobbers. The Irish Chancellor, FitzGibbon, and the victims complain to the King. Fitzwilliam is promptly recalled, and Pitt sends Lord Camden and begins to contemplate a Union. Orange lodges are organised by Protestants, and the United Irishmen take up the cause of the Catholics.

1433. **France.** The Dauphin dies in the Temple.

Bread riots take place in Paris, and a revolt of the Sections is suppressed by Napoleon (Oct.). La Vendée and the Chouans of Brittany negotiate with England, which sends ships to Quiberon; but the expedition fails.

2240. **French Lit.** André Chénier's Poésies, the highest point of the classical influence in French poetry.

Xavier de Maistre's Voyage autour de ma Chambre.

2241. **German Lit.** Schiller edits the Horen, to which Goethe, Herder, Jacobi, Gleim, the Humboldts, Fichte and the Schlegels contribute.

Fichte's Vocation of a Scholar.

2242. **Spanish Lit.** Jovellanos' comedy, El Delincuente honorado.

2243. **Art.** Flaxman returns to England from seven years' residence in Italy.

2244. **Science.** Legendre's Éléments de Géométrie, widely adopted as a substitute for Euclid.

Darwin's Zoonomia declares species are evolved from each other, not separately created.

John Hunter's Treatise on the Blood, Inflammation, and Gunshot Wounds.

2245. **Philosophy.** Fichte's Science of Knowledge adopts the transcendental method of Kant, but shews that self-consciousness, the ultimate ground of reality, is not to be regarded as individual. He fails, however, to connect the development of reason with history and nature or to advance beyond a position of ethical solipsism.

2246. **Politics.** Fichte's Rectification of Public Opinion concerning the French Revolution fully accepts Rousseau's theory of Contract, which he translates into the terms of Kantian ethics.

2247. **Philology.** Hermann begins to lecture on classical literature at Leipzig.

2248. **Education.** The École Normale, for the training of teachers, and the École Polytechnique for instruction in science are founded at Paris.

2249. **Law.** The Prussian Landrecht, a system of State Socialism, chiefly prepared by Carmer, becomes law.

2250. **Deaths.** Beccaria, Camden, Chénier, Condorcet, Gibbon, Goldoni, W. Jones, Kaunitz, Lavoisier, Justus Moser, Tiraboschi.

2251. **Eng. Ch.** Stapleton, late Rector of St Omer, brings the students of St Omer and Douai to England and founds St Edmund's Hall, Ware. [1795

2252. **Irish Ch.** The Government found the College of Maynooth to prevent priests going to Paris for education and bringing back revolutionary ideas.

2253. **American Ch.** Ballou, an Universalist, maintains that punishment is confined to this life and borne by the sinner, and in no way by Christ.

2254. **Eng. Lit.** Lewis' The Monk carries on the romanticism of Mrs Radcliffe and Horace Walpole.

Wordsworth and Coleridge meet.

2255. **French Lit.** Mme. Roland's Memoirs.

As a substitute for the Academies, abolished 1793, the Institute is founded by Lakanal, Daunou and Carnot, and consists of three

A Constitution is drawn up, creating a Council of Ancients and a Council of 500, in both cases one-third to be replaced yearly, and a Directory of five, chosen by the Ancients from a list drawn up by the 500, one to retire each year. The executive and legislative power are thus separated. Two-thirds of the new Assembly are to be chosen from the present Convention. Carnot, Lareveillère-Lepeaux, Rewbell, Letourneur, and Barras are chosen Directors.

Prussia makes peace at Basle with France, which cedes the conquered districts on the right bank of the Rhine. Prussia promises to cede her possessions on the left bank in return for ecclesiastical estates to be secularised in Germany. A line of demarcation secures the neutrality of Northern Germany. Peace is also made with Sweden and some German States.

After the Treaty of Basle, England and Austria renew their alliance. France is driven across the Rhine, Pichegru attempting to turn traitor.

1434. **Spain.** Spain concludes peace with France, ceding Spanish St Domingo.

1435. **Holland.** Pichegru overruns Holland, captures the Dutch fleet in the Texel, and establishes a Batavian republic. The British evacuate Holland.

1436. **Italy.** Tuscany makes peace with France. The Austrians are defeated by Schérer at Loano.

1437. **Poland.** The third partition is arranged, and Stanislas abdicates. Russia takes East Poland, and Austria West Galicia. The remainder, with Warsaw, is assigned to Prussia. Austria and Russia secretly sign a declaration by which Austria is to assist Russia, in any war with Turkey, to take the Danubian principalities, and to be compensated by acquisitions in France or Venice. The Duke of Courland is compelled to abdicate, and his duchy becomes a Russian province.

1438. **America.** Jay's treaty is hotly attacked, but is ratified, the Federalists, however, being much weakened.

A treaty between the United States and Spain determines the southern boundary, and secures free navigation of the Mississippi.

The French retake Santa Lucia.

1439. **Africa.** War being declared against the Dutch, the Cape of Good Hope is captured by England.

1440. **Asia.** Agha Mohammed defeats and exterminates the Zend line and becomes ruler of all Persia, and founds the Kajar dynasty. In 1796 he seizes Khorasan.

[1796

1441. **England.** Lord Malmesbury is sent to Paris to negotiate a peace, asking France to withdraw from the Austrian Netherlands and from Italy. The Directory promptly refuses (Oct.).

1442. **Ireland.** Wolfe Tone is sent to France by the United Irishmen to urge the Directory to invade Ireland and establish a Republic. Hoche sails from Brest with 20,000, but the fleet is dispersed and only a few vessels reach Bantry Bay, whence they are driven by a storm.

divisions, the Natural Sciences, the Moral and Political Sciences, and the Arts.

2256. **German Lit.** Goethe's Wilhelm Meister. The Confessions of a Beautiful Soul are modelled on the personality of his early friend, F. v. Klettenberg.

2257. **Art.** Carstens exhibits his collected pictures in Rome, copied from the antique.

Schiller's Letters on Aesthetic Culture, modelled on the teaching of Kant, declares a sense-impulse and a form-impulse to exist in us, which, working together, give rise to a play-impulse (spiel-trieb), the object of which is living shape, or beauty.

2258. **Science.** Geoffrey Saint-Hilaire suspects that all species are variants on a primordial form of life. Goethe reaches a similar conviction about the same time.

Hutton's Theory of the Earth founds Uniformitarianism, and recognizes the activity of heat. His ideas are developed in Playfair's Illustrations of the Huttonian Theory, 1802, and extended by the experiments of Sir James Hall, but are attacked by Jameson, a rigid Wernerian.

2259. **Politics.** Kant's Perpetual Peace hopes for peace by a world republic with a central Diet. A somewhat similar scheme is put forward by Görres, 1797.

2260. **Philology.** Wolf's Prolegomena to Homer declares part of the poems by the Homeridae, composed without writing, and therefore much changed. The work opens the modern period of classical scholarship. His view is worked out by Lachmann and Hermann.

2261. **Education.** Lakanal persuades the Convention to create 100 'Écoles Centrales' for higher education.

2262. **Geography.** Mungo Park undertakes a journey in West Africa.

2263. **History.** Dupuis' Origine de tous les Cultes, a mythological analysis of the Gospel and one of the earliest studies in comparative religion.

2264. **Social.** Some Berkshire Justices of the Peace meet at Speenhamland, declaring their conviction of the necessity of making an allowance out of the rates to every poor family in proportion to its numbers. The 'Speenhamland Act of Parliament' becomes very widely adopted, and the allowance system goes far to demoralise the working classes.

2265. **Death.** Boswell.

2266. **Eng. Ch.** Watson's Apology for Christianity, a reply to Paine's Age of Reason, defends the morality of the Old Testament, but admits the existence of errors and contradictions in reference to matters of fact. [1796

2267. **French Ch.** Lareveillère-Lepeaux inaugurates the Theophilanthropy movement, a creed natural, primitive and universal, and destined to unite all sects and form an Institut Moral. It is practised by 10 churches in Paris, till forbidden by Napoleon, 1802.

1443. **France.** Brittany and La Vendée are pacified by Hoche.

Baboeuf's conspiracy, aided by Sylvain Maréchal and Buonarotti, to restore the constitution of 1793 and destroy the government, is detected. Baboeuf is executed.

Prussia agrees to the cession of the left bank of the Rhine to France, in return for ecclesiastical territories on the right bank, which it hopes to secularise.

1444. **Germany.** Jourdan and Moreau enter Germany, but are forced to re-cross the Rhine.

1445. **Italy.** Bonaparte receives the command of the Italian army, defeats the Austrians and Sardinians at Montenotte and Dego, compels the King of Sardinia to withdraw from the Coalition and to cede Savoy and Nice. He then enters Milan, expels the Austrians from Lombardy, and besieges Mantua, beating off Austria's relieving armies at Castiglione, Bassano, and later at Arcola.

1446. **Spain.** At the instance of Godoy, Spain concludes the Treaty of San Ildefonso with the Directory, fearing English preponderance at sea (Aug.), and declares war (Oct.). The English withdraw from Corsica.

1447. **Portugal.** A secret treaty is made by France and Spain to partition Portugal, which therefore begs England for aid. Troops are sent and an invasion is prevented.

1448. **America.** John Adams defeats Jefferson in the Presidential election by three votes, and retains Washington's Hamiltonian advisers, who intrigue against him.

1449. **West Indies.** England takes Santa Lucia, St Vincent and Grenada.

1450. **Asia.** England takes Ceylon.

1451. **England.** The Bank of England suspends cash payments. [1797

Admiral Jervis defeats the Spanish fleet off Cape St Vincent, Nelson disobeying orders and dashing in (Feb.). Admiral Duncan is sent to blockade the Dutch in the Texel, while Lord Bridport, at Spithead, is to watch the French. The sailors at Spithead mutiny for better pay and treatment (April), and Howe is authorised by the Admiralty to promise them justice. The sailors at the Nore also mutiny, and demand to vote on the management of the ships in battle, and are joined by mutineers in the fleet off the Texel (May). The mutiny is suppressed, and the leaders hanged (June). Duncan defeats the Dutch fleet off Camperdown.

1452. **Germany.** Frederick William III. becomes King of Prussia, and determines to remain neutral in the struggle with France.

1453. **France.** The anti-republican directors, Carnot and Barthélemy, are expelled by Augereau, at the bidding of Bonaparte and the other Directors (Sept.). The elections are annulled in 49 departments, and the Directors are given absolute power.

2268. **Eng. Lit.** Burke's Letter to a Noble Lord replies to the Duke of Bedford's attack on the grant of a pension from the Crown.

Ireland's Shakspere forgeries impose on Sheridan and Kemble, but are exposed by Malone.

2269. **German Lit.** Brockhaus issues the first edition of his Conversationslexikon, or Cyclopædia.

Iffland becomes Director of the National Theatre at Berlin.

2270. **Art.** Goya's Los Capriccios, satirising the Government, society and religion, are seized by the Inquisition.

2271. **Science.** Laplace's Exposition du Système du Monde enunciates the Nebular Hypothesis, probably in ignorance of the work of Kant.

Jenner inoculates a boy with cow-pox as a preservative against small-pox.

2272. **Politics.** De Bonald's Pouvoir Politique et Religieux dans la Société Civile bases absolutism on traditionalism, and initiates the speculative reaction in France.

Joseph de Maistre's Considérations sur la France advocate a royalist restoration and denounce the French Revolution as an attack on religion and society.

Kant's Metaphysical Foundations of the Theory of Right founds the State on the principle of contract, and opposes absolutism and extreme centralisation.

Fichte's Naturrecht, influenced by Kant, contends that the State exists only to carry out the law.

Burke's Letters on a Regicide Peace subjects the different periods and parties of the Revolution to indiscriminate abuse.

2273. **Law.** Cambacérès issues a Projet de Code Civil, the basis of Napoleon's Code. With Merlin de Douay he is commissioned to revise all existing laws in France, and publishes the Code Français, 1797.

2274. **Deaths.** Burns, Catherine of Russia, Raynal, Reid.

2275. **Eng. Ch.** Wilberforce's Practical View of the prevailing religious System exercises great influence among Evangelicals. [1797

The Methodist New Connexion leave the Wesleyans owing to a dispute in regard to the position of the laity and the relation to the Church of England.

2276. **Eng. Lit.** Gifford, Canning, Hookham Frere and other conservatives edit the Anti-Jacobin.

The works of Kotzebue invade the London stage, but are parodied by Canning and Frere in The Rovers.

2277. **French Lit.** Chateaubriand's Essai sur les Révolutions attacks the theory of perfectibility.

2278. **German Lit.** Goethe's Hermann und Dorothea.

Augustus Schlegel and Tieck's translation of Shakspere.

Wackenroder's Outpourings of a Monk quickens the reaction to romanticism, and the study of mediæval art.

Holderlin's Hyperion.

1454. **Italy.** Napoleon defeats a fourth relieving army at Rivoli (Jan.), takes Mantua (Feb.), and crosses the Alps to invade Austria. Venice rises behind him, and, fearing to be cut off, he signs the Preliminaries of Leoben, by which Austria cedes the Netherlands and part of Lombardy to France, and recognises the Cisalpine Republic to be formed. Austria is to be indemnified at the expense of Venice (April).

Napoleon at once declares war on Venice, abolishes the Constitution, occupies the Ionian Islands (which are taken by Turkey, 1799). The Cisalpine Republic is proclaimed, consisting of Milan, Modena, Ferrara, Bologna and the Romagna, and Genoa is transformed into the Ligurian Republic.

The Pope surrenders Avignon and the Romagna.

Hoche advances into Germany, and Mainz is taken.

1455. **Austria.** The Peace of Campo Formia is signed (Oct.). Austria cedes Belgium to France, and receives Venetia, as far as the Adige, with Istria and Dalmatia. France retains the Ionian Islands. By secret articles, Austria promises to cede the left bank of the Rhine from Basle to Andernach, including Mainz, to France, the princes who suffer by the cession to receive indemnification in Germany. France is to help Austria obtain Salzburg and part of Bavaria. A Congress meets at Rastadt to arrange peace with the Empire.

1456. **America.** The American Minister in Paris is expelled, and a Commission sent to preserve peace is also ejected.

1457. **West Indies.** England takes Trinidad from Spain.

1458. **England.** A tax of 10 per cent. is imposed on incomes over £200. [1798

Fox's name is struck off the list of Privy Councillors, and Fox and his friends temporarily withdraw from Parliament.

1459. **Ireland.** The United Irishmen prepare an insurrection; but the plot is betrayed, and Lord Edward Fitzgerald is arrested. The peasants rise in Wexford and massacre the Protestants, but are defeated at Vinegar Hill, near Wexford, by Lake (June). 1,100 French troops land (Aug.), but are forced to surrender (Sept.). Lord Cornwallis succeeds Camden as Lord Lieutenant, and attempts to suppress the cruelty. Wolfe Tone is taken and commits suicide.

1460. **France.** Jourdain introduces conscription.

1461. **Africa.** The Directory urges Bonaparte to attack England; but he prefers to go to Egypt, as a starting-point for the creation of an Eastern Empire and an attack on the English in India, with the aid of Tippoo. He seizes Malta from the Knights of St John, lands in Egypt, and defeats the Mamelukes at the Battle of the Pyramids (July). Nelson follows and annihilates the French fleet in Aboukir Bay (Aug. 1). Turkey declares war on France.

1462. **Italy.** Joseph Bonaparte, the French envoy in Rome, provokes riots, and a French general is shot. Berthier seizes Rome; and the Pope, who refuses to surrender the temporal power, is removed to Valence,

Gentz' Open Letter to Frederick William III. King of Prussia, on his accession, pleads for freedom of the Press.

2279. **Art.** Haydn's The Creation.

Girtin exhibits in the Royal Academy and founds modern water-colour.

Cherubini's Medea.

Thorwaldsen settles in Rome, and becomes profoundly influenced by the spirit of Greek sculpture.

2280. **Science.** Lagrange's Théorie des Fonctions analytiques rejects the use of infinitesimals, and founds the differential calculus on a study of algebraic forms.

Olbers' method of reckoning the path of a comet.

De Saussure's Recherches Chimiques sur la Végétation investigates vegetable physiology.

Bewick's British Birds.

The Philosophical Magazine is instituted.

2281. **Philosophy.** Schelling's Philosophy of Nature, a system of Objective Idealism, in which the individual is lost in the whole, separates him from Fichte. Though discarding exact science, Schelling's teaching increases the general interest for science, and being applied by Oken, Krause, Solger, Novalis, Steffens, Schubert, remains dominant for a generation.

Kant's Metaphysic of Morals declares the good-will the only goodness, the categorical imperative of duty an ultimate fact, and points out the duties involved in membership of a community of rational beings.

Villers introduces Kant's philosophy into France.

2282. **Education.** Dr Bell, after teaching, as Army Chaplain in Madras, the orphans of soldiers, returns to England, publishes a Report on his method, that of pupil teachers, and institutes schools of his own.

2283. **Deaths.** Burke, Hutton, Horace Walpole, Wilkes.

2284. **Scotch Ch.** The Evangelical leaders, Robert and James Haldane, invite Rowland Hill to make a preaching tour in Scotland. [1798

2285. **Eng. Lit.** The Lyrical Ballads, by Wordsworth and Coleridge (including the Ancient Mariner), give an immense impetus to the romantic movement in England.

Coleridge visits Germany, and studies German philosophy and literature.

Joanna Baillie's Plays on the Passions.

Landor's Gebir.

Pitt's Newspaper Act forbids the export or import of papers, and demands the registration of proprietors.

2286. **German Lit.** The Allgemeine Zeitung is founded at Augsburg.

The Schlegels edit the Athenæum, and attack the dry, unmystical rationalism of Nicolai and the Aufklärung. The romantic movement is aided by Richter, Tieck, Brentano, Arnim, Novalis.

2287. **Italian Lit.** Foscolo's Jacopo Ortis, an Italian Werther.

where he dies, 1799. A Roman Republic is proclaimed, and the King of Naples, who marches on the city, is defeated.

1463. **Switzerland.** Intrigues are provoked in the Vaud. Bern intervenes, and France declares war. Bern is taken, the old Constitution abolished, and the Helvetic Republic set up under the control of a Directory of five. Geneva is united to France, and Switzerland is forced to form an alliance.

1464. **Spain.** Godoy is forced to resign, and the reforming party for the moment obtains power.

England recaptures Minorca without a blow.

1465. **Holland.** The Dutch East India Company is dissolved, its possessions passing to the Government.

1466. **Turkey.** Rhegas, the author of Greek patriotic songs, is executed by the Turks.

1467. **America.** The 'Alien and Sedition' Acts are aimed at the Republicans, many of whom are foreigners and sympathisers with France. Naturalisation is deferred from 5 to 14 years, and dangerous aliens may be expelled. The Sedition Act imposes fine and imprisonment on all who attack or defame the Government. They are opposed by Gallatin and Jefferson, who help to draw up the Kentucky Resolutions, hinting that the compact of the States is not irrevocable.

British Honduras is finally conquered from Spain.

1468. **England.** Pitt forms the second coalition with Austria and Russia, Portugal, Naples and Turkey (June). The Duke of York leads an expedition to Holland, but capitulates at Alkmaar (Oct.). [1799

1469. **Italy.** The King of Naples is expelled by the French, and the Parthenopean Republic is formed (Jan.). The King of Sardinia and the Duke of Tuscany are deposed. Schérer, however, is routed in North Italy (April), Suvorof takes Milan, the Cisalpine Republic collapses, Joubert is routed by Suvorof at Novi (Aug.), Rome is surrendered (Sept.), the King of Naples is restored with the aid of Nelson, and Italy is for the time lost to France.

The Society of the Carbonari is formed in the kingdom of Naples.

1470. **Austria.** To settle the affairs of Germany, Austrian diplomatists attend the Congress of Rastadt. The French representatives are murdered on their journey home, and Bernadotte, the French ambassador at Vienna, is insulted. The Directory declares war (March). Jourdain is defeated by the Archduke Charles, and driven back across the Rhine; but Masséna defeats the Russians at Zurich (Sept.), Suvorof arriving from Italy too late to aid.

1471. **Africa.** Bonaparte learns that a Turkish army is coming to attack him, and sets out to meet it. He is baffled by the resistance of the Turkish garrison of Acre, aided in its defence by Sir Sidney Smith (March—May). He withdraws to Egypt, and suppresses the Mamelukes, who had risen. Hearing of events in France, he leaves Kléber in command, and hurries back.

2288. **American Lit.** Brockden Brown's first novel, Wieland.

2289. **Science.** While engaged in the boring of cannon, Count Rumford discovers that heat is generated by friction, and is not a thing, 'caloric.' He also melts ice by friction.

Cavendish estimates the density of the earth at 5½ times that of water.

A fall of meteorites in India leads to their study by Pictet, Biot, Berzelius and others.

Legendre's Science des Nombres contains the law of quadratic reciprocity between any two odd primes, and other theorems.

Lacépède's Histoire des Poissons.

Kant's Anthropology hints at the evolution of Man from a lower animal stage.

2290. **Philosophy.** Fichte is expelled from Jena, nominally for atheism, but chiefly owing to his Jacobinism.

Fichte's System of Morals according to the Principles of the Science of Knowledge, declares obedience to the standard set by conscience, without regard to external authority or advantage, the only good.

2291. **Politics.** Malthus' Essay on Population, suggested by Godwin's optimism, by his father's liking for Rousseau, and by Pitt's Allowance System. He contends that population increases in geometrical and food in arithmetical progression, but that population is checked by misery and vice.

2292. **Law.** Thibaut's Theory of Law asserts that history without philosophy cannot explain law.

2293. **Education.** Lancaster, a Quaker, unaware of Dr Bell's experiment, begins to teach in Southwark on the Monitor system.

2294. **Geography.** Bass proves that Tasmania is separate from Australia, thus completing the coast map.

2295. **Deaths.** Galvani, John Hunter.

[1799

2296. **Eng. Ch.** The Church Missionary Society is resolved on by Venn, Wilberforce, Granville Sharp, Mason, and is established 1801, with Thomas Scott as Secretary. The Society first devotes its attention to Sierra Leone, Thornton's colony for freed American slaves.

2297. **German Ch.** Schleiermacher's Discourses on Religion, strongly influenced by the Moravian Brethren and by Spinoza, lay stress on inward feeling and the sense of personal dependence on God.

2298. **Eng. Lit.** Campbell's first poems, the Pleasures of Hope.

2299. **French Lit.** Laharpe's Cours de Littérature first offers a review of the entire development of literature from the classical standpoint.

2300. **German Lit.** Schiller's Wallenstein and Song of the Bell.

Frederick Schlegel's Lucinde applies romanticism to married life, and, though defended by Schleiermacher, is hotly attacked.

2301. **Science.** Laplace's Mécanique Céleste (1799—1825) states and applies methods for calculating the motions and determining the figures of the planets, and resolving tidal problems, and adds a number of astronomical tables.

1472. **France.** Bonaparte lands at Fréjus (Oct.), and is warmly greeted. He agrees with Sièyes, now a Director, to overthrow the Directory on 18th Brumaire (Nov. 9). The members of the Lower House are expelled, and the recalcitrant Directors arrested. Bonaparte becomes First Consul, with two colleagues, Talleyrand becomes Foreign Minister, and Fouché becomes Minister of Police. Prefectures and sub-prefectures are created, and the present system of administrative centralisation is introduced. Taxes are fairly levied and collected.

Bonaparte's offer of peace to the Emperor and George III. is rejected.

1473. **Germany.** Montgelas becomes supreme in Bavaria, and introduces Josephine ideas.

1474. **America.** Further Kentucky resolutions recommend the nullification of all unauthorised acts by the States.

1475. **Asia.** Seringapatam, Tippoo's capital, is stormed, and Tippoo slain (May). His territories are divided between England and the Nizam. About the same time, the Carnatic and the Principality of Tanjore are placed under British administration, and the Presidency of Madras obtains approximately its present form.

[1800

1476. **England.** Malta is taken, after a long siege (Sept.).

Russia, Sweden, and Denmark agree to resist the English search of neutrals, and are soon joined by Prussia.

1477. **Ireland.** Despite the opposition of Grattan and the Nationalists, the Union is carried, Pitt having agreed to compensate owners of seats with £15,000 each and distributed peerages. Ireland is to return 100 members, and 28 peers are elected to sit in the House of Lords for life, with four Bishops. Free-Trade is established with England.

1478. **France.** The revolt in La Vendée comes to an end, and many émigrés are allowed to return.

The Bank of France is founded.

1479. **Italy.** Genoa is forced to surrender; but Masséna holds Melas at bay till Napoleon, with an army collected at Dijon, crosses the Alps and takes the Austrian army in the flank at Marengo (June 14).

1480. **Austria.** Moreau crosses the Rhine and drives the Austrians back to Ulm, but is forbidden by Napoleon to advance. On the arrival of the news of the battle of Marengo, Moreau takes Munich and concludes an armistice. Austria, however, refuses to make peace apart from England, and the Archduke Joseph is routed by Moreau at Hohenlinden (Dec.), after which another armistice is concluded.

1481. **Spain.** Godoy regains power and makes the Treaty of San Ildefonso, by which Spain restores Louisiana, and Napoleon secretly promises Tuscany and the title of King to the Duke of Parma, son-in-law of Charles IV.

1482. **America.** An American Commission is received by Napoleon, who declares the treaty of 1778 no longer binding, but refuses to pay for property seized before his accession.

Alexander Humboldt sets out on his five years' voyage of discovery in America.

The Royal Institution is founded by Rumford, Banks becoming its first president. Davy is chosen by Rumford as first lecturer.

2302. **Science.** Davy rubs two pieces of ice together in the vacuum of an air-pump, the temperature being kept below freezing-point, and finds that they melt, thus confirming Rumford's opinion in regard to the nature of heat.

2303. **Philosophy.** Herder's Metakritik hotly attacks the Critical Philosophy of Kant and Fichte, chiefly on the ground of danger to religion.

2304. **Politics.** Mackintosh's Lectures on the Law of Nature and Nations attack Godwin, and reveal a modification of his earlier opinions under the influence of Burke.

2305. **Education.** Fellenberg founds a school and farm at Hofwyl, near Bern, to some extent on Pestalozzi's lines.

2306. **Philology.** The French find a stone at the Rosetta mouth of the Nile, which is taken with other spoil by the English, containing inscriptions in Greek, Coptic, and Hieroglyphics.

2307. **Deaths.** Aranda, Beaumarchais, Black, Marmontel, Lord Monboddo, Parini, Spallanzani, Washington.

2308. **Eng. Ch.** Geddes, a Catholic, declares that the Pentateuch was not written by Moses, but by several hands, and not earlier than the time of David. [1800

2309. **German Ch.** Schleiermacher's Monologues emphasise the element of freedom and personality in the religious life.

Count Stolberg becomes a Catholic, largely owing to the influence of Princess Gallitzin. His conversion is bitterly attacked by Voss, but is followed by that of F. Schlegel, Overbeck, and Werner.

2310. **American Ch.** Otterbein and Boehm found the United Brethren in Christ.

2311. **Eng. Lit.** Wordsworth prefixes a manifesto of romanticism to the second edition of the Lyrical Ballads.

Maria Edgeworth's Castle Rackrent.

2312. **French Lit.** Mme de Staël's De la Littérature relates literature to the manners, laws, and religion of the time.

Delille publishes his poems, and with Ducis, Lemercier and Lebrun leads the pseudo-classicists or Racinists.

2313. **Science.** The Voltaic pile or battery is completed. Two metals plus moisture produce a supply of electricity which is increased by adding acid to water.

Herschel discovers that there are infra-red solar rays.

The Royal College of Surgeons is founded.

2314. **Philosophy.** Fichte's Vocation of Man preaches the religion of duty.

2315. **Philology.** Panduro's Lenguas de las Naciones Conocidas describes 300 tongues.

Jefferson is elected President, despite the intrigues of Hamilton and Burr, and the Federalist party wanes. Madison becomes Secretary, Gallatin Treasurer, and John Marshall Chief Justice.

1483. **Africa.** Kléber defeats the Turkish and Mameluke troops at Heliopolis, but is shortly assassinated.

1484. **England.** Pitt proposes a measure for the relief of Catholics, but resigns on finding the King and nation refuse to endow the Irish Catholic priests or to admit Catholics to office or Parliament. Addington succeeds, with Pitt's support, and Eldon becomes Lord Chancellor. The King becomes insane for a short time, and on his recovery Pitt promises never to again bring forward Emancipation. [1801

The Northern Confederation is treated as a declaration of war. The Danish and Swedish West India Islands are seized. A fleet is sent to break up the confederacy, and Nelson bombards Copenhagen and forces Denmark to leave the League (April). The Tsar Paul is murdered, and his successor, Alexander, makes a treaty admitting the right of search.

The ruling in Horne Tooke's case establishes that clergy of the Church of England may not sit in Parliament.

1485. **France.** The Emperor asks for peace, which is signed at Lunéville (Feb.). France extends her border to the Rhine. Austria retains Venice, Tuscany is given to the son of the Duke of Parma, and Ferdinand is allowed to retain Naples, on promising to exclude English ships. The Cisalpine and Ligurian Republics are restored.

Napoleon establishes special tribunals in which the majority is nominated by himself. The Tribunate opposes this step, and its recalcitrant members are expelled. Taking advantage of an attempt on his life by a few Chouans, Napoleon exiles 130 Jacobins.

1486. **Holland.** The Batavian Republic is organised.

1487. **Portugal.** Napoleon makes impossible demands, and Portugal declares war on Spain, but is defeated and sues for peace at Badajos, ceding half Guiana to France, and undertaking to shut its ports against England.

1488. **Russia.** The Tsar of Georgia, despite his former professions of allegiance to Persia, resigns his crown to Russia. His subjects resist, and Persia joins in the war. Persia recognises the cession of Georgia, 1813.

The Tsar Paul, an enthusiastic admirer of Napoleon, is assassinated, and is succeeded by Alexander, a man of strong liberal sympathies, which are encouraged by Adam Czartoryski. Speranski becomes State Secretary, and strives for reform.

1489. **West Indies.** Toussaint, once a slave, appointed to command the army, 1797, is made President of Hayti for life, proclaims the independence of the island, and expels the French. Napoleon re-establishes slavery, and sends a large fleet and army.

Hervas, a Spanish Jesuit, compiles a Catalogue of Languages, anticipating the recognition of the Malay and Polynesian family of speech, and the relationship of Greek and Sanskrit.

2316. **Politics.** Fichte's Exclusive Commercial State sketches a community which has no external commercial relations, in which all must work, and where wages and prices are fixed.

2317. **Social.** The Combination Act forbids associations, which in consequence become secret.

2318. **Death.** Cowper.

2319. **Eng. Ch.** Marsh's dissertation on the origin of the Synoptics is hotly attacked. [1801

2320. **French Ch.** A Concordat is made with the Papacy, the details of which are arranged by Talleyrand and Consalvi. Catholicism is recognised as the religion of the nation. The State guarantees salaries and chooses the bishops, whom the Pope confirms. The clergy are chosen by the bishops but confirmed by the State. A few bishops refuse to recognise the Concordat and form La Petite Église, which lasts over half a century. Père Delpuits forms the Congregation.

2321. **American Ch.** The Episcopal Church adopts the 39 Articles.

2322. **Eng. Lit.** Southey's Thalaba introduces orientalism.

2323. **French Lit.** Chateaubriand's Atala inaugurates the Catholic revival.

2324. **Art.** The French expedition to Egypt leads to the study of Egyptian art.

Boieldieu's Caliphe de Bagdad.

2325. **Science.** Young confirms Huyghens' emission theory, discovers the 'interference of light,' and declares the original colours to be red, yellow, and blue, but later asserts that red, green, and violet are the originals.

Lamarck's Organisation of Living Bodies explains the development of an animal in response to new needs, and asserts that such developments become hereditary.

Berthollet's Lois de l'Affinité investigates salts.

Bichat's Anatomie Générale appliquée à la Physiologie et à la Médecine, influenced by the Vitalist school, reduces the structure of living beings to simple tissues, the character of the disease varying with the tissues attacked.

Gauss's Disquisitiones Arithmeticæ introduce a new notation and methods of analysis, and discuss the theory of numbers.

Piazzi discovers a planet, Ceres, revolving between Mars and Jupiter. Olbers discovers another, Pallas, at nearly the same distance from the sun as Ceres.

2326. **Philosophy.** Destutt de Tracy's Élémens d'Idéologie develope the ideas of Condillac.

Schelling and Hegel found the Critical Journal of Philosophy for the discussion of the philosophy of Identity.

1490. **America.** Napoleon obtains an extension of French Guiana from Portugal.

1491. **Africa.** Abercromby lands in Egypt, and defeats the French outside Alexandria (Aug.). The French army agrees to evacuate the country, and Egypt is restored to the Porte.

1492. **England.** By the Treaty of Amiens, England abandons her colonial conquests except Ceylon and Trinidad, surrenders Malta to the Knights, restores Minorca to Spain, and drops the royal title of France (March). [1802

Napoleon agrees to evacuate the Sicilies and the Papal States, Portugal, and Egypt.

Napoleon vainly demands restrictions on the English press and the dismissal of French persons obnoxious to him.

1493. **France.** Napoleon organises a plébiscite, which confers on him the Consulate for life, with power to nominate his successor. The Tribunate is reduced to impotence, and the Senate is allowed to meet only by his summons.

Napoleon institutes the Legion of Honour.

1494. **Italy.** Piedmont, Parma, Piacenza and Elba are annexed to France (Aug.—Oct.), and Napoleon is nominated President of the Italian republics. His deputy, Melzi, introduces many reforms and governs with conspicuous success.

1495. **Austria.** Gentz enters the Austrian service and writes a series of pamphlets exhorting to war against France and the Revolution.

1496. **Russia.** Alexander creates eight ministers.

1497. **West Indies.** Moreau's army is sent to San Domingo. Toussaint is kidnapped and sent to France as a prisoner. Next year, however, an insurrection takes place, and the French retire.

1498. **Asia.** By the Treaty of Bassein, the Peshwa surrenders his independence to the East India Company, in return for help against Holkar. Sindhia and the Rajah of Nagpur join Holkar against the English.

1499. **England.** Fearing French designs on Egypt, England refuses to give up Malta, and demands the evacuation of Holland and Switzerland. Napoleon is angered by the attacks of Peltier, and insults Whitworth, the English envoy (March). England declares war (May). Napoleon seizes 10,000 English travellers, occupies Hanover, despite the Treaty of Basle, and leads an army to Boulogne. [1803

1500. **Ireland.** Encouraged by France, Emmett revolts in Dublin, but is arrested and executed.

1501. **Germany.** The redistribution agreed on at the Treaty of Lunéville takes place. The ecclesiastical states are secularised, nominally to compensate the princes who suffer by the cession of the left bank of the Rhine to France; but the princes who profit most are those of Prussia, Bavaria, Baden, Würtemburg and Hanover. Forty-four cities of the Empire are suppressed, Hamburg, Lubeck, Bremen, Frankfurt,

2327. **Law.** Anselm Feuerbach's German Criminal Law dominates theory and practice for half a century.

2328. **Social.** The first Census is taken in England.

The first General Enclosure Act passes.

2329. **Deaths.** Lavater, Rivarol, Suvorof.

2330. **Eng. Ch.** Paley's Natural Theology developes the argument from design. [1802

Bishop Milner's End of Religious Controversy, a defence of Catholicism.

2331. **French Ch.** The Concordat is promulgated, and with it the Organic Articles which have not been discussed by the Pope. No bull nor legate may enter France and no synod be held without the consent of the Government; the Articles of 1682 must be accepted, and the Council of State constitutes the court of appeal in case of abuses. The Protestant clergy are recognised and paid.

Chateaubriand's Génie du Christianisme defends Catholicism from the emotional and the æsthetic standpoint.

2332. **Asiatic Ch.** England first interferes with religion in India by forbidding the sacrifice of children at a festival.

2333. **Eng. Lit.** The Edinburgh Review is founded to support Whig principles by Sydney Smith, Brougham, Horner and Jeffrey, the latter being appointed Editor.

Cobbett edits the Political Register.

2334. **Science.** Treviranus declares that all creatures are modified by circumstances, and that one species transforms into another.

Wedgwood finds that he can take a photograph, but cannot prevent it fading away.

Herschel discovers that some double stars revolve round one another.

Wollaston observes seven dark lines in the Solar Spectrum.

The tug 'Charlotte Dundas' is tried on the Forth and Clyde canal.

2335. **Philosophy.** Schelling's Æsthetic declares that each living unit, in developing its life, carries out the type of the species to which it belongs.

2336. **Law.** Bentham's Civil and Penal Legislation.

Noah Webster's Rights of Neutrals.

2337. **Education.** Dorpat University, which has ceased to exist since the wars of Peter the Great, is restored.

2338. **Philology.** Porson edits the Hecuba.

2339. **Social.** Telford constructs roads in Scotland. Macadam introduces angular granite fragments, 1815.

The first Factory Act is passed by Sir Robert Peel to protect apprentices in the cotton trade.

2340. **Death.** Bichat.

Augsburg, Nuremberg alone remaining. The College of Electors is increased from 8 to 10; the Electorates of Trier and Cologne are suppressed, and new ones are created for Baden, Würtemburg, Salzburg and Hesse-Cassel. Mainz alone remains an ecclesiastical Electorate. In the Chamber of Princes, the votes are reduced from 100 to 82, of which the Protestants form a majority. The power of the Emperor in the Diet almost disappears.

1502. **Italy.** The French enter Naples.

1503. **Spain.** Spain agrees to pay monthly subsidies to France, and is allowed to remain neutral.

1504. **Switzerland.** The Federalists and Centralists quarrel, the Helvetic Constitution falls, and a French army enters the country. By the Act of Mediation, the federal power is weakened, and the cantonal rights restored. Feudalism, however, is not revived. Six new cantons are added (Vaud, Aargau, Thurgau, Ticino, St Gall, and the Grisons). Napoleon is recognised as Mediator. He retains Geneva as part of France, and establishes the independent republic of the Valais.

1505. **Austria.** The Emperor obtains the secularised possessions of the bishoprics of Trent and Brixen; but Salzburg and the Breisgau are given to the Dukes of Tuscany and Modena, in compensation for the loss of their Italian principalities.

1506. **America.** Napoleon sells Louisiana, the territory between the Mississippi and the Rocky Mountains, for £3,000,000. The Federalists oppose the ratification, as not contemplated by the Constitution, and propose the secession of the Federalist states.

British Guiana is finally taken from the Dutch.

1507. **West Indies.** England takes Tobago and St Lucia from France.

1508. **Africa.** The Cape of Good Hope is restored to the Dutch, but is recaptured, 1806.

1509. **Asia.** Arthur Wellesley defeats Sindhia, the Mahratta chief, at Assaye (Sept.), and Lake crushes him at Laswaree, and captures Delhi. Sindhia and the Rajah of Berar submit, and surrender territory.

[1804

1510. **England.** Addington resigns, and Pitt returns to power.

1511. **France.** A plot against Napoleon, arranged by Cadoudal, a Chouan, Pichegru, and the Count of Artois, with the sympathy of Moreau, is discovered (Feb.). Napoleon seizes the Duke of Enghien near Strassburg, though not privy to the plot, and has him shot at Vincennes. Pichegru and Cadoudal are executed, and Moreau banished for life to America. Napoleon takes advantage of the plot to make himself Emperor, Carnot alone of the Tribunate protesting (May).

1512. **Spain.** France compels Spain to declare war against England.

1513. **Austria.** Francis assumes the title of Francis I., Emperor of Austria.

1514. **Portugal.** Napoleon allows Portugal to buy neutrality.

2341. **Irish Ch.** Castlereagh increases the Regium Donum to Presbyterians. [1803

2342. **Eng. Lit.** John Murray sets up a publishing business in London.

2343. **French Lit.** The Institute is reorganised by Napoleon, the Académie des Sciences Morales et Politiques being suppressed.

2344. **German Lit.** Tieck's collection of Minnelieder stimulates the study of old German Literature.

Henrietta Herz loses her money, and the place of her salon in Berlin is taken by that of Rahel Levin.

2345. **Greek Lit.** Korais' Present Condition of Civilisation in Greece calls attention to the country.

2346. **Science.** Poisson's Traité de Mécanique.

Carnot's Géometrie de Position.

2347. **Art.** Beethoven's Fidelio.

Crome gathers the artists of Norwich, Stark, Vincent, B. Crome, and others, into a society, and organises an annual exhibition.

2348. **Philosophy.** Maine de Biran's Mémoires sur l'Habitude initiates the reaction against materialism.

2349. **Politics.** The second edition of Malthus' Principles of Population adds moral restraint to the list of checks.

2350. **Economics.** Say's Traité d' Économie Politique systematises the ideas of Adam Smith.

2351. **Social.** Johnson invents a dressing-machine.

2352. **Deaths.** Samuel Adams, Alfieri, Campomanes, Herder.

2353. **Eng. Ch.** The British and Foreign Bible Society is founded. [1804

2354. **Scotch Ch.** The Synod of Lawrencekirk signs the 39 Articles.

2355. **French Ch.** Napoleon dissolves the congregation of Fathers of the Faith, restores the laws against perpetual vows, forbids the formation of associations without his approval, and demands the presentation of the statutes of existing Orders for the inspection of the Council of State.

2356. **French Lit.** Senancour's Obermann.

2357. **Eng. Lit.** William Blackwood sets up a publisher's business in Edinburgh.

2358. **German Lit.** Jean Paul Richter's Flegeljahre greatly influences the Romantics.

2359. **Art.** The Water Colour Society is founded by seceders from the Royal Academy.

2360. **Science.** The first engine to draw carriages is constructed.

Poinsot's Éléments de Statique.

Jomini's Grandes Operations Militaires.

2361. **Philosophy.** Krause's Plan of a System of Philosophy explains a theory of the All not as God but in God, i.e., panentheism.

1515. **Russia.** Alexander demands the evacuation of Hanover and Naples, breaks off diplomatic relations with France, in consequence of the death of Enghien, and makes a preliminary agreement with Austria.

1516. **America.** The Twelfth Amendment is carried, by which the electors vote for the President and Vice-President in separate ballots.

1517. **Australasia.** Hobart is founded as the capital of Tasmania, and the inhabitants of Norfolk Island are transferred to it.

1518. **Asia.** Holkar annihilates an English force in the Makundra Pass, but is defeated in the following year.

1519. **England.** A motion by Grenville and Fox to consider Catholic disabilities is rejected. [1805

Dundas, Lord Melville, is impeached for peculation.

1520. **Austria.** A third coalition against France is formed by England and Russia, and joined by Austria and Sweden (April). Prussia remains neutral.

The defeat of a French and Spanish fleet in the Bay of Biscay, by Calder (July), leads Napoleon to transfer his army from Boulogne to the Danube. He compels Mack to capitulate at Ulm (Oct.), enters Vienna (Nov.), and defeats the Russians and Austrians at Austerlitz (Dec. 2). Francis signs the Treaty of Pressburg, abandoning Venetia, Istria, Dalmatia, and Cattaro to the Italian kingdom, the Vorarlberg and the Tyrol to Bavaria, and Outer Austria to Baden and Würtemberg. The rulers of Bavaria and Würtemberg receive the title of king, and, with Baden, are declared independent of the Emperor.

1521. **France.** On the day after Mack's capitulation, Nelson destroys the French and Spanish fleets at Trafalgar (Oct. 21), but is himself killed.

1522. **Italy.** Napoleon crowns himself King of Italy (May), joins Parma and Piacenza to the Italian kingdom, annexes Genoa, and grants Lucca to his sister Eliza. Eugène Beauharnais is appointed viceroy.

1523. **Germany.** Prussia, which had allied with Austria (Nov.), is compelled by Napoleon, after the battle of Austerlitz, to cede Neuchatel and the remainder of Cleves to France, and Anspach to Bavaria. Prussia receives Hanover provisionally, and promises to exclude English vessels from the North Sea harbours.

1524. **America.** Pitt prohibits American trade to the West Indies; vessels are seized, and war is in all but name declared.

1525. **West Indies.** The French and Spanish fleets fail to take Dominica.

1526. **England.** Pitt dies (Jan.), and the Ministry of All the Talents is formed under Grenville. [1806

1527. **Italy.** Ferdinand is ejected by a French army, and Joseph Bonaparte becomes King of Naples, the English fleet holding Sicily for Ferdinand (March).

1528. **Austria.** Francis is compelled to abandon the title of Holy Roman Emperor. The Holy Roman Empire comes to an end.

Brown's Relation of Cause and Effect declares the relation to be one of antecedence and sequence, but admits an intuitive belief in the permanence and universality of the causal connection.

2362. **Economics.** Lauderdale's Nature and Origin of Public Wealth attacks Smith's account of value, and condemns the importance attached to saving.

2363. **Law.** The Code Civil, inspired by Bentham's Theory of Legislation, begun by the Constituent and Convention, is issued. Compiled chiefly by Tronchet, Portalis, Cambacérès, and, to some degree, by Napoleon himself, from Roman law, royal ordinances, customs, the teaching of the great French jurists, and the legislation of the Revolutionary period, the Code is rapidly adopted by many countries in Europe and America.

2364. **Deaths.** Alexander Hamilton, Kant, Necker, Priestley.

2365. **Eng. Lit.** Scott's Lay of the Last Minstrel. [1805

Cary translates Dante's Inferno.

2366. **Church Hist.** The Pope is allowed by Napoleon to return to Italy; but on being crowned, Napoleon refuses to respect the Concordat concluded with the Cisalpine Republic 1803, and occupies Ancona on the Pope's refusal to divorce his brother Jerome.

2367. **French Lit.** Chateaubriand's René may be said to inaugurate the period of romanticism in French literature.

2368. **Danish Lit.** Öhlenschläger meets Steffens, fresh from the influence of Schelling, burns his old verses, and founds romanticism by his tragedy of Hakon Jarl.

2369. **Art.** David's Coronation of Napoleon.

Paganini begins his violin tours.

Pye, 'the father of landscape engraving,' begins to engrave for Turner.

2370. **Science.** Monge's Application de l'Algèbre à la Géométrie helps to create modern synthetic geometry.

Alexander Humboldt and Bonpland's Essai sur la Géographie des Plantes.

2371. **Philology.** Colebrooke's Essay on the Vedas, the first critical examination to which they are subjected, introduces the period of the scientific study of oriental literatures and religions.

2372. **Numismatics.** Lord Liverpool's Coins of the Realm.

2373. **Law.** Zachariæ's Key to Law attempts to found on the rules of grammar and logic a system of interpretation applicable to all systems of law.

2374. **Deaths.** Greuze, Schiller.

2375. **French Ch.** Napoleon convokes a Sanhedrim, to which [1806 he puts questions relative to military service and other duties of citizenship, and establishes a consistorial organisation for the Jews of France. The State commences to pay the Rabbis, 1831.

1529. **Germany.** Napoleon unites Bavaria, Würtemburg, Mainz, Baden and eight lesser principalities, into the Confederation of the Rhine, under his patronage and control, with Dalberg as Prince-Primate (July). In the next three years, 16 other members join. The German Knights are abolished, and their territories annexed to the larger states. Serfdom and other feudal abuses are suppressed.

Napoleon forms Berg (taken from Bavaria) and Cleves into the Grand Duchy of Berg, which he gives to his brother-in-law Murat.

Prussia is compelled by Napoleon to definitely accept Hanover, in consequence of which England declares war (April). Napoleon next offers to restore Hanover to England, and war is therefore declared by Prussia (Oct.). A new coalition is formed by England, Prussia, Russia and Saxony; but the Prussian armies under Hohenlohe and Brunswick are destroyed at Jena and Auerstadt (Oct. 14), and Berlin is occupied. Hesse-Cassel and Brunswick are formed into the kingdom of Westphalia. Saxony enters the Confederation of the Rhine, promises 20,000 men to Napoleon, and obtains the royal title.

The Berlin Decrees close all European ports under Napoleon's influence against English commerce. All British ports are declared in a state of blockade, and all goods coming from England or her colonies are to be destroyed.

1530. **Holland.** The Grand Pensionary Schimmelpenninck is deposed, and Louis Bonaparte and Hortense Beauharnais are crowned King and Queen.

1531. **Denmark.** Holstein is taken.

1532. **Turkey.** The Servians revolt under Kara George, owing to the refusal of the Sultan to garrison the forts with native troops.

France conquers the republic of Ragusa.

1533. **America.** Miranda fails to raise a revolt in Venezuela.

Popham takes Buenos Ayres, but is quickly expelled by the Spaniards and censured. A further expedition is sent to attack Chili.

1534. **Asia.** Ranjit Singh, ruler of the Sikhs, makes a treaty with the English, and peace is maintained till his death, 1839.

1535. **England.** The first series of Orders in Council is issued (Jan.). [1807

The King expels Grenville for not promising never to propose concessions to the Catholics. Portland succeeds, with Canning as Foreign Secretary.

Cardinal Henry of York, the last male in the direct line of the Stuarts, dies.

1536. **Germany.** Scharnhorst reforms the Prussian Army, and Stein's Emancipating Edict, based on the report of a commission appointed by Hardenberg, declares serfs free after 1810, establishes free trade in land, and opens all occupations to all classes.

1537. **France.** Frederick William renews the struggle with Russian aid, but is defeated at Eylau (Feb. 8). By the Treaty of Bartenstein, Russia, Prussia and Sweden agree to carry on the war till a satisfactory

2376. **German Ch.** De Wette's Contributions to an Introduction to the Old Testament declares Deuteronomy to be a late priestly summary of law, and Chronicles a late priestly recast of early history. The other books of the Old Testament are successively investigated, and the legendary character of most of the miraculous narratives is asserted.

Stolberg's Church History, a Catholic counterpart to the work of Milner, presents an apologia for the Catholic Church.

2377. **Asiatic Ch.** Buchanan, a Bengal chaplain, urges an Ecclesiastical Establishment for India. The plan is supported by Lord Teignmouth and other Evangelicals in England, but is attacked by most Anglo-Indians.

2378. **Eng. Lit.** Mrs Hutchinson's Memoirs of the Great Civil War are published.

2379. **German Lit.** Arnim's and Brentano's The Boy's Wonder-horn, a collection of popular songs, begins the second or mediaevalist generation of romantics.

Arndt's Spirit of the Age attacks Napoleon and the French influence, and attempts to create the spirit of nationality.

2380. **Science.** Latreille's Genera Crustaceorum et Insectorum.

Davy discovers potassium and sodium by electrolysis.

Poisson discusses the question of the stability of the planetary orbits.

2381. **Art.** Bell's Anatomy and Philosophy of Expression as connected with the Fine Arts investigates the relations between feeling and muscular movements, and recommends the artist to keep close to reality instead of seeking ideals in his own mind.

2382. **Philology.** Adelung's Mithridates, a history of languages and dialects.

2383. **History.** Lysons' Magna Britannia.

2384. **Education.** Herbart, who has had practical experience of teaching, introduces Psychology into the theory of Education, emphasises 'apperception,' or the combination of perception with memory, and points out how education should make for moral ends.

2385. **Social.** Hauy founds an Institute for teaching the blind by means of touch.

2386. **Deaths.** Fox, Princess Gallitzin.

2387. **Eng. Ch.** Wilberforce, Thornton, Sir James Stephen, Lord Teignmouth, Granville Sharp and other Evangelicals gather round John Venn, Rector of Clapham, and form the Clapham Sect. [1807

2388. **German Ch.** Schleiermacher maintains that the First Epistle to Timothy was not written by Paul.

2389. **American Ch.** The first Conference is held of the Evangelical Association, founded by Jacob Albright.

2390. **Asiatic Ch.** The organisation of Thugs, a society for the commission of murders, becomes known.

arrangement is made (April). The Russians and Prussians, however, are defeated at Friedland (June 14), and Napoleon and the Tsar meet at Tilsit, where a treaty is signed (July). Napoleon forms West Prussia into a kingdom, Westphalia, for his brother Jerome, and grants Prussian Poland as the 'Grand Duchy of Warsaw' to the King of Saxony. East Frisia is given to Holland. The Confederation of the Rhine is to include all German States but Austria and Prussia. Prussia is forced to support French garrisons. Russia cedes the Ionian Islands and part of Dalmatia, and, by secret clauses, accepts the blockade and is to be allowed to conquer Finland from Sweden and is allowed to try and obtain Moldavia and Wallachia from Turkey. Russia declares war on England (Nov.), which retaliates by a second series of Orders in Council, declaring all ports of France and her allies in a state of blockade, and vessels prize unless they touch at a British port (Nov.). To this Napoleon replies by the Milan Decree, declaring all neutral vessels liable to seizure if they touch at a British port (Dec.).

The Tribunate is suppressed.

1538. **Denmark.** Canning learns that Napoleon is about to seize the Danish fleet, and use it against England. He therefore bombards Copenhagen, seizes the fleet, and takes Heligoland (Sept.).

1539. **Portugal.** Napoleon agrees with Spain to partition Portugal, which alone refuses the Continental System. Junot invades Portugal, and occupies Lisbon, the royal family, on the advice of England, escaping to Brazil (Nov.).

1540. **America.** Burr, who has planned an Empire in Texas or Mexico, is tried for treason, but acquitted by Marshall.

The American frigate, Chesapeake, is fired on and boarded by an English ship. Jefferson therefore lays an embargo on all vessels in American ports. Napoleon retaliates by the Bayonne Decree, 1808.

Whitelocke fails to recover Buenos Ayres.

1541. **Africa.** Sierra Leone and Gambia are organised as English Crown Colonies.

1542. **France.** Napoleon and Alexander meet at Erfurt (Oct.), and Napoleon confirms the promise of Moldavia and Wallachia. [1808
Alexander promises aid against Austria, in the event of war. After the conference, Napoleon hurries off to Spain.

1543. **Italy.** French troops occupy Rome, the Pope having refused to recognise the King of Naples and the French bishops, and to close his ports to England.

1544. **Russia.** Speranski, a Liberal, becomes supreme.

Russia invades Finland, at this time a possession of Sweden. An English army is sent to Stockholm, but achieves nothing.

1545. **Spain.** A mob rises against Godoy, and Charles abdicates in favour of his son, Ferdinand VII., but quickly withdraws his abdication. Father and son appeal to Napoleon, who forces both to abdicate. Napoleon appoints his brother Joseph king, and sends Murat to succeed him at Naples. A French army, however, under Dupont, is forced to

2391. **Eng. Lit.** Wordsworth's Ode on the Intimations of Immortality.
Moore's Irish Melodies.
Charles and Mary Lamb's Tales from Shakespeare.
Crabbe's Parish Register.

2392. **French Lit.** Mme de Stael's Corinne.

2393. **German Lit.** Hagen edits the first correct text of the Nibelungen Lied.

2394. **Art.** Prud'hon's Justice and Vengeance Pursuing Crime.
Turner's Liber Studiorum.
Méhul's Joseph.

2395. **Science.** Fulton builds a steamboat, the Clermont, in which he sails up the Hudson.

Sommering constructs an electric telegraph by means of the Voltaic pile.

2396. **Philosophy.** Fries' New Critique of Reason developes the ideas of Kant, and insists on psychology as the basis of all metaphysics.

Hegel's Phenomenology of Spirit finally parts from Schelling by vindicating the power of consciousness and reflection to rise to the absolute standpoint. The conditions through which the individual and humanity pass before they arrive at absolute knowledge are traced by means of a dialectic, borrowed in part from Fichte.

2397. **History.** Wilken's History of the Crusades.
Sismondi's History of the Italian Republics in the Middle Age.

2398. **Social.** The slave trade is forbidden in English dominions, largely owing to the Clapham Sect, aided by Brougham, Wilberforce, Clarkson, Zachary Macaulay.

2399. **Death.** Paoli.

2400. **German Ch.** Sulpiz Boisserée begins to agitate for the completion of Cologne Cathedral, and excites interest in mediaeval art. [1808

2401. **Spanish Ch.** Napoleon abolishes the Inquisition, suppresses most of the monasteries and forces the clergy to profess Gallican principles.

2402. **Italian Ch.** Napoleon abolishes the Inquisition.

2403. **Eng. Lit.** The Quarterly Review is founded by Scott, Lockhart, Gifford, Southey and other Tories, in order to counteract the Whiggism of the Edinburgh Review.

Leigh Hunt edits the Examiner, an organ of the Opposition, and is imprisoned for a 'libel' on the Prince Regent, 1811.

Scott's Marmion.

Sidney Smith's Peter Plymley's Letters attack the disabilities imposed on Catholics, and exert a very wide influence throughout the country.

Lamb's Specimens of the English Dramatists first interpret the Elizabethans.

Crabb Robinson is sent by the 'Times' to the Peninsular Campaign as Special Correspondent.

2404. **German Lit.** Goethe's Faust, part I.

capitulate at Baylen (July). Joseph flies from Madrid, and the army retreats behind the Ebro. Napoleon enters Spain, and retakes Madrid (Dec.). Sir John Moore, who has advanced towards Burgos to aid the Spaniards, learns that Napoleon has joined Soult and is marching against him, and in consequence retreats.

1546. **Portugal.** On the news of the rising in Spain, the Portuguese revolt and appeal to England for aid. Wellesley is sent to Portugal, and defeats Junot at Vimiera (Aug. 21), but is superseded. By the Convention of Cintra, Junot is allowed to return with his army to France.

1547. **Germany.** Stein reorganises the Prussian municipalities.

Napoleon is compelled by the Spanish war to recall his army of occupation, and therefore forces Prussia to dismiss Stein, to limit its army to 42,000, and to promise 16,000 men in the event of a war with Austria (Sept.).

The Tugendbund is instituted, but, despite its undertaking to avoid politics, is disapproved by Stein, and dissolved 1809.

1548. **America.** The importation of slaves into the United States is prohibited.

1549. **England.** Burdett's motion for reform (the first since 1797), is lost. [1809

Castlereagh forms a coalition with Austria (April), and sends an expedition to take Antwerp. Flushing is taken, but disputes arise, and fever ravages the army left in the Isle of Walcheren. Canning, Castlereagh and Portland resign, and Perceval becomes Prime Minister.

1550. **Italy.** Napoleon annexes the Papal States. The Pope refuses to recognise the annexation, excommunicates its author, and is imprisoned in Savona.

1551. **Austria.** Napoleon is recalled from Spain by the news that Austria has declared war on Bavaria, and that the Tyrolese peasants, under Hofer, have risen (May). Russia declares war against Austria. Napoleon fails to cross the Danube at Aspern (May), but crosses by night on rafts and defeats the Austrians at Wagram (July 5—6). The Treaty of Vienna gives Napoleon the Illyrian Provinces, cedes the Tyrol and Salzburg to Bavaria, West Galicia and Cracow to the Duchy of Warsaw, East Galicia to Russia and Bohemia, and the possessions in Lusatia to Saxony (Oct.).

Stadion and the Archduke Charles retire, and Metternich becomes Chancellor.

1552. **Portugal.** Soult overtakes Moore's army, for which the transports have not arrived, at Corunna, but is defeated (Jan. 16). Moore is killed, but his army is safely removed.

Wellesley is restored to command, and defeats Soult at Oporto and Victor at Talavera (July). The Spanish army, however, gives no aid, and Wellesley is obliged to fall back.

2405. **Science.** Malus discovers the polarisation of light by reflection.

Dalton explains the law of constant, definite and multiple proportions, and weighs the elements. The atomic theory is accepted by French chemists, but is rejected by Davy.

Cuvier and Brongniart publish their investigations on the basin of the Seine, and found stratigraphical geology.

Gay-Lussac discovers the laws of the combinations of gases by volume.

Wilson's American Ornithology.

2406. **Philosophy.** James Mill makes the acquaintance of Bentham, of whom he becomes an interpreter.

2407. **Politics.** Fourier's Théorie des Quatre Mouvements advocates the removal of restraints and the creation of communities or Phalanges.

Fichte's Addresses to the German Nation lay stress on Education, and broach the idea of national unity under Prussian headship.

2408. **Education.** The Royal Lancastrian Institution for promoting the education of the Poor, afterwards the British and Foreign School Society, is formed.

Napoleon institutes the University of France.

2409. **Philology.** F. Schlegel's Language and Wisdom of the Indians suggests the relationship of Sanskrit with European languages.

2410. **Law.** Eichhorn's History of German Law and Institutions.

2411. **Social.** Romilly agitates for the reduction of the list of capital offences.

2412. **Deaths.** Florida Blanca, Porson.

2413. **French Ch.** The Pope refuses institution to Napoleon's bishops. [1809

2414. **Italian Ch.** The French Concordat is extended to Italy.

2415. **German Ch.** Tschokke's Hours of Meditation revive Evangelicalism in Germany.

2416. **American Ch.** Elizabeth Seton (converted to Catholicism during a tour in Italy, 1804) founds the Sisters of Charity of St Joseph.

2417. **Eng. Lit.** Byron's English Bards and Scotch Reviewers replies to an attack in the Edinburgh Review on his Hours of Idleness.

Coleridge writes The Friend.

Hannah More's Cœlebs in Search of a Wife, a treatise on the education of young women.

Campbell's Gertrude of Wyoming.

2418. **French Lit.** Chateaubriand's Les Martyrs marks the beginning of the historical novel.

2419. **German Lit.** Goethe's Elective Affinities.

August Schlegel's Lectures on Dramatic Art and Literature introduce modern principles of literary criticism.

2420. **Russian Lit.** Kriloff's Fables.

2421. **American Lit.** Washington Irving's Knickerbocker's History of New York.

1553. **Sweden.** Finland and part of West Bothnia are surrendered to Russia, Finland being guaranteed a separate Diet and army. Charles recognises Bernadotte as his heir.

1554. **Russia.** Russia begins a war for the conquest of Wallachia and Moldavia (April), and gains several victories.

1555. **America.** The embargo is removed, except in regard to France and England, from which countries no goods are to be imported.

An attempted revolt in Mexico is suppressed.

1556. **West Indies.** England takes Martinique and Guadeloupe.

1557. **England.** Grattan's motion for the relief of Catholics is rejected. [1810

Burdett is sent to the Tower by the House of Commons for contempt, and riots take place.

The King loses his reason, which he never recovers.

Nathan Meyer Rothschild, of Frankfurt, assists the English Government with a loan, and founds the world-wide influence of his house.

1558. **France.** Napoleon, who has divorced Josephine, 1809, marries Marie Louise, daughter of the Emperor of Austria. 13 out of 26 Cardinals in Paris absent themselves from the religious ceremony.

Napoleon annexes the Valais.

1559. **Holland.** Louis Bonaparte resigns, refusing to ruin the country by enforcing the Continental System, and Holland is incorporated with France, on the ground that it is 'the alluvial deposit of French rivers.'

1560. **Germany.** The coast of North Germany, including Hamburg and most of the Hanse Towns and the Duchy of Oldenburg, is annexed, and the Elbe and Weser are closed against England.

Hardenberg founds a National Bank, secularises Church lands, and reforms taxation.

1561. **Austria.** Hofer is captured and shot at Mantua.

1562. **Spain.** The French troops overrun the Peninsula; but the attempt to capture Cadiz, whither the Cortes are summoned, fails.

1563. **Portugal.** Masséna captures Ciudad Rodrigo (July), but is defeated by Wellington at Busaco (Sept.). Wellington entrenches himself for the winter behind lines at Torres Vedras, extending from the Tagus to the sea, which Masséna does not attempt to force.

By the mediation of Russia, the Treaty of Paris is concluded with France.

1564. **Sweden.** Sweden joins the Continental System, and obtains the restoration of Swedish Pomerania (Jan.). In the autumn, Sweden declares war against England.

1565. **Russia.** Angered by the ejection of his kinsman, the Duke of Oldenburg, by the cession of Galicia to the Duchy of Warsaw, and by the Austrian marriage, Alexander deserts the Continental System.

2422. **Science.** Gauss' Theoria Motus Corporum Caelestium improves practical astronomy, and introduces the principle of curvilinear triangulation.

Maclure's Geological Survey of the United States.

Carnot's Défense des Places Fortes.

2423. **Philosophy.** Oken's Text-book of the Philosophy of Nature declares the classes of animals a representation of the sense-organs, and must be arranged in accordance with them.

2424. **Politics.** Adam Müller's Art of Politics, influenced by Burke, violently attacks the ideas of the French Revolution, declares the State organic, and exalts the position of the executive.

De Maistre's Principe Générateur des Constitutions Politiques declares that all political institutions are divine. The rights of the ruler and aristocracy have no known author; those of the people are concessions from the other classes. No nation therefore can obtain liberty if it does not possess it.

2425. **Economics.** Ricardo denounces the over-issue of paper-money in his High Price of Bullion.

2426. **Social.** Restrictions on the English cloth trade are removed, as the manufacture is now carried on chiefly under the factory system and trade-marks have become a guarantee.

2427. **Death.** Johannes v. Müller.

2428. **Eng. Ch.** Bishop Milner's Elucidation of the Veto opposes the claim of the Government to exercise a veto on the appointment of Catholic Bishops, a claim approved of by Butler and other Catholics. [1810

2429. **German Ch.** Paulus offers natural explanations of the miracles.

2430. **Swiss Ch.** The members of Zinzendorf's circle in Geneva form a Société des Amis and begin a revival of Protestantism. César Malan, Frédéric Monod and Haldane join the movement and preach Justification by Faith. The revivalists are attacked by the Calvinist clergy, and the Church of Le Témoignage is founded 1820.

2431. **American Ch.** The 'Cumberland Presbytery' leaves the Presbyterian Church, owing to its rejection of the Calvinist view of reprobation.

2432. **French Lit.** Mme de Stael's L'Allemagne introduces the knowledge of German philosophy and literature.

2433. **German Lit.** Perthes edits the Vaterländisches Museum, to which almost every distinguished writer and thinker in Germany contributes.

2434. **Swedish Lit.** Atterboom founds the Phosphorus to introduce romanticism and combat foreign influences.

2435. **Russian Lit.** Jukovski introduces romanticism in his ballad Ludmila.

2436. **Art.** Overbeck settles in Rome, is joined by Cornelius, Schadow and Veit, and later by Schnorr, Fuhrich and Steinle, and revives Catholic art. The painters are named 'Nazarenes.'

On the suggestion of Speranski, the Council of State is reformed, and is divided into the three departments of Legislation, Finance and Church and Civil Administration, which examine ministerial projects of laws. Speranski begins to be fiercely attacked, and falls, 1812.

1566. **America.** Napoleon's Rambouillet decree orders the sale of all American vessels that have been seized for violating the French decrees. Madison now declares that if England or France revoke its decrees, the United States will prohibit trade with the other. The French decrees are accordingly revoked, and a non-importation act is enforced against England.

Harrison crushes Tecumseh's confederation of tribes on the Tippecanoe River.

Mexico, Argentina, Chili and Upper Peru refuse to acknowledge Joseph Bonaparte.

Miranda proclaims a Republic in Venezuela and New Granada or Columbia. He aims at a federation of the South American Colonies, but jealousies arise, and he capitulates, 1812, and dies in prison.

1567. **Africa.** England takes Mauritius and the Île de Bourbon.

[1811

1568. **England.** The Prince of Wales becomes Regent by a Bill modelled on that of 1788.

1569. **France.** A son is born to Napoleon, and receives the title of King of Rome.

1570. **Spain.** Wellington defeats Masséna at Fuentes d'Onoro and takes Almeida. Beresford defeats Soult, who is hastening to the relief of Badajos, at Albuera (May 16), but fails to take Badajos.

1571. **Italy.** Lord William Bentinck, British Envoy Extraordinary and Commander, rules Sicily.

1572. **Sweden.** The Continental System ceases to be strictly observed.

1573. **Germany.** Prussia negotiates with Napoleon for a reduction of her contribution and the removal of the restriction of her army to 42,000 men.

Hardenberg creates peasant proprietorship in Prussia, giving the peasants absolute possession of two-thirds of their holdings, the remaining third passing to the lord as compensation. Representative assemblies come into existence for a few years.

1574. **Austria.** After fifty years preparation, the Civil Code comes into force throughout the Empire, except in Hungary.

1575. **Russia.** Karamsin's Memoir on Old and New Russia protests against any deviation from the traditional autocratic system.

1576. **Turkey.** The Russians take Belgrade; and a Turkish army which crosses the Danube is made captive.

1577. **America.** Paraguay declares its independence of Spain.

An engagement takes place between an American and a British ship.

2437. **Science.** Davy discovers that chlorine is a simple body.

Robert Brown applies the natural system of the Jussieus to his specimens collected in Van Diemen's Land and New Holland.

Goethe's Theory of Colours asserts that yellow is light seen through a thickened medium, blue is darkness seen through an illuminated medium.

Berzelius investigates the proportions and weights of atoms.

Gall and Spurzheim declare psychology a branch of biology, and assign definite functions to definite organs of the brain. The doctrines of phrenology are attacked by Flourens, Majendie, Wagner and other physiologists.

Hahnemann's Organon of Therapeutics founds Homoeopathy.

2438. **Philosophy.** Royer-Collard becomes Professor of Philosophy at the Sorbonne, and introduces the ideas of Reid into France.

2439. **Politics.** Stahl's Philosophy of Law from a historical standpoint makes the State the picture of the absolute life or God.

2440. **Philology.** Creuzer's Symbolism of the Ancients pronounces classical myths to be borrowed from Egypt and India.

Sylvestre de Sacy's Arabic Grammar.

2441. **Education.** Berlin University is founded on the plans of Wolf, Fichte, Schleiermacher and Wilhelm v. Humboldt.

W. v. Humboldt, Prussian Minister of Education, introduces a matriculation before entering the university and an examination of candidates for teaching, and undertakes a reform of the Gymnasien, which is continued by Schulze.

2442. **Geography.** Maltebrun's Géographie Universelle.

2443. **Deaths.** Cavendish, Queen Louisa of Prussia.

[1811

2444. **Eng. Ch.** The Welsh Calvinistic Methodists leave the Church.

2445. **French Ch.** Napoleon calls a Council in Paris to sanction a project for the institution of Bishops. Most of the members, yielding to intimidation or promises, approve the project, subject to the Pope's approval. The Pope approves, with a few trifling restrictions; but Napoleon refuses the Papal brief and dissolves the Council.

2446. **American Ch.** Hobart becomes Bishop of New York, and strengthens the Episcopal Church by his loyalty to the Republic.

2447. **Eng. Lit.** Jane Austen's Sense and Sensibility.

Coleridge's Lectures on Shakespeare and Hazlitt's Characters of Shakespeare introduce the aesthetic study of the dramas.

2448. **Norwegian Lit.** Christiania University is founded, and stimulates the growth of a national literature.

2449. **German Lit.** Goethe's autobiographical Truth and Poetry.

Fouqué's Undine.

1578. **Africa.** Mehemet Ali, Pasha of Egypt, destroys the Mamelukes.

1579. **Asia.** Lord Minto takes Java, of which Stamford Raffles becomes Governor.

1580. **England.** Grattan carries the second reading of a Bill for Catholic relief; but admission to Parliament is lost in Committee. [1812

Perceval is murdered, and Liverpool becomes Prime Minister, with Castlereagh Foreign Secretary, Sidmouth Home Secretary, Palmerston Secretary at War, and Peel Secretary for Ireland.

1581. **Germany.** Prussia promises aid in a Russian war and a passage for French troops through her territories, and joins the Continental System (Feb.). Scharnhorst, Gneisenau and other nationalists resign in disgust.

1582. **Sweden.** Bernadotte secretly allies with Russia, promising to effect a diversion in North Germany, with Russian aid, and renouncing his claim to Finland in return for an indemnity and a promise of Norway (April). The alliance is joined by England (July).

1583. **Russia.** Stratford Canning persuades Turkey to make the Treaty of Bucharest, by which Russia gains part of Bessarabia and Moldavia, and becomes free for the French war (May).

Napoleon re-establishes the Polish kingdom, despite the stipulation of the Treaty of Tilsit, and the Poles warmly espouse his cause. He crosses the Niemen with an army of nearly 500,000 men, including contingents from all countries subject to him (June 24), storms Smolensk (Aug.), drives back the Russians at Borodino (Sept. 7) and enters Moscow (Sept. 14), which is deserted and set on fire by Rostopchin, its governor. Owing to the climate, the lack of provisions and the shrinkage of his army, Napoleon sets out on his return (Oct. 19) with only 100,000 men, and wins a fierce battle at Jaroslavetz (Oct. 24). The frost begins (Nov. 6), and 20,000 cross the Beresina under heavy fire (Nov. 27). At this point the retreat becomes a rout, and Napoleon hurries back to Paris on news of the plot of Malet. The survivors cross the Niemen (Dec. 13), about 250,000 having perished in the campaign.

General Yorck, the commander of the Prussian contingent in French service, concludes the Convention of Tauroggen with Russia, by which he undertakes to remain neutral (Dec. 30).

1584. **Turkey.** The Treaty of Bucharest leaves Turkey free to invade Servia, which, after nine years struggle for independence, is subdued. A second revolt breaks out under Milosch Obrenovitch, 1815.

1585. **Spain.** Wellington storms Ciudad Rodrigo (Jan.), and Badajos, which bar his entry into Spain (April), routs Marmont at Salamanca (July 22), and enters Madrid. The French armies, however, leave the south and compel Wellington, who fails to take Burgos, to retire to Portugal.

The Cortes issue a constitution, framed on French models, with a single assembly and limited monarchy, free press, abolition of feudal rights, and confiscation of Church lands. Catholicism, however, is proclaimed the only true religion.

2450. **Science.** Bell distinguishes sensory and motor nerves.

Avogadro founds the mechanical theory of gases, proving that equal volumes of gases under the same conditions of temperature and pressure contain the same number of molecules.

Arago discovers that double refraction is possessed by the smallest plates of a crystal.

Oppel first satisfactorily classifies reptiles.

Chevreul investigates oils, soap and other fatty bodies.

Leslie investigates heat-rays, but finds no affinity between radiant heat and light.

2451. **Art.** Thorwaldsen sculptures the Procession of Alexander the Great, commissioned by Napoleon for the Quirinal.

2452. **Philology.** Boeckh, a pupil of Wolf, becomes Professor of Classical Philology at Berlin.

Rask, a Dane, compiles an Icelandic Grammar.

2453. **Education.** The National Society for educating the Poor in the Principles of the Established Church is founded by Joshua Watson, Marsh, Archbishop Sutton, and other churchmen.

2454. **History.** Niebuhr's History of Rome.

2455. **Economics.** The Bullion Committee of the Commons vainly urge the resumption of cash payments.

2456. **Social.** Believing that mechanical inventions diminish opportunities of employment and reduce wages, many working men, who are nicknamed Luddites, destroy machinery in the Yorkshire towns.

2457. **Deaths.** Karl Friedrich of Baden, Kleist.

2458. **Eng. Ch.** The Act of William III. against Non-Trinitarians, and the Conventicle and Five-Mile Acts are repealed. [1812

2459. **Russian Ch.** The Tsar founds a Bible Society, which, however, is suppressed by his successor.

2460. **Eng. Lit.** Byron's Childe Harold, Cantos 1—2.

James and Horace Smith's Rejected Addresses.

Landor's Count Julian.

2461. **German Lit.** Grimm's Fairy Tales.

2462. **Science.** Laplace's Théorie Analytique des Probabilités.

John Herschel, Peacock and Babbage introduce the analytical methods in use on the Continent.

Cuvier's Recherches sur les Ossements Fossiles des Quadrupèdes founds palaeontology.

Henry Bell's steam-boat, the Cornet, plies on the Clyde.

2463. **Philosophy.** Hegel's Logic unfolds the logical genesis of the Absolute, which is conceived as a spiritual and self-conscious principle, by means of a dialectic.

2464. **Philology.** Gesenius' Hebrew and Chaldaic Dictionary.

1586. **Hungary.** The Diet is dissolved, the Emperor promising to call it again within three years.

1587. **America.** Louisiana is admitted to the Union as a slave state.

Exasperated by the Orders in Council and by the search for deserters, the United States declare war against England. American privateers do considerable damage; but an attack on Canada is repulsed.

[1813

1588. **Spain.** Wellington routs Joseph at Vittoria (June 21), and Soult at the battle of the Pyrenees, storms St Sebastian and takes Pampeluna.

1589. **Germany.** The King of Prussia annuls the Convention of Tauroggen and condemns Yorck. On his own responsibility, Stein summons a Diet at Königsberg (Feb.), which decrees a levy in arms of the whole population against France. The King, finding his hand forced, makes the Treaty of Kalisch with the Tsar, who promises to restore Prussia to her position before the battle of Jena (Feb.). Frederick William declares war (March), but Napoleon, with an army of young recruits, defeats the Russians and Prussians at Lutzen and Bautzen (May), and is joined by troops from Denmark and Saxony. He makes an armistice, hoping to win over Austria. Metternich, however, agrees with Prussia, by the secret Treaty of Reichenbach, to mediate, and, if rebuffed, to declare war against France (June). His demands are refused, and, on receiving a large English subsidy, he declares war (Aug.). Oudinot is defeated by Bernadotte and Macdonald by Blucher, and, after Napoleon's victory at Dresden (Aug.), Vandamme capitulates to Russia at Culm, and Ney is crushed by Bernadotte (Sept.). By the Treaty of Töplitz, Austria and Prussia confirm their alliance and agree to recognise the rulers of S. and W. Germany. Bavaria joins the allies, who rout Napoleon at Leipsic (Oct. 16—19), where the Saxon troops desert. The French are driven across the Rhine, and the Confederation of the Rhine dissolves. From the camp at Frankfort, terms are offered to Napoleon, leaving him the left bank of the Rhine, but are refused (Dec.). Stein induces the Tsar to break off negotiations, and the Austrian armies enter France through Switzerland.

1590. **Italy.** On the news of the battle of Leipzic, Italy rises and Eugéne Beauharnais is defeated by the Austrians (Oct.).

1591. **Holland.** On the news of the battle of Leipsic, the French are expelled, and the son of the former Stadtholder is restored as William I.

1592. **Denmark.** Denmark is forced to abandon the French alliance, and Norway is ceded to Sweden. Heligoland is ceded to England.

1593. **Switzerland.** The Constitution of 1803 is abolished.

1594. **Montenegro.** British and Montenegrin forces take Cattaro from the French; but Russia agrees with Austria to take and keep it.

1595. **Russia.** By the Peace of Gulistan, Persia cedes Shirvan and Russia gains access to the Caspian.

1596. **America.** The English are defeated on Lake Erie.

1597. **Asia.** Trade with India is opened to all, the East India Company still retaining the monopoly of the Chinese trade.

2465. **Archaeology.** Leake's Researches in Greece.
2466. **Agriculture.** Thaer's Rational Agriculture.
2467. **Social.** Grillion's Club is founded in London.

2468. **French Ch.** Realising the absolute necessity of terminating his feud with the Pope, Napoleon has him conveyed from Italy, and resorts to intimidation. A Concordat is made at Fontainebleau, providing that the Pope shall give Napoleon the nomination of bishops in France and Italy and that the Metropolitan shall institute if the Pope does not do so within six months of nomination. After signing the document, Pius consults with Consalvi and Pacca, who persuade him to withdraw his concessions. [1813

2469. **German Ch.** Röhr's Letters and Wegscheider's Institutes of Rationalism assert that reason, the supreme authority in matters of religion, possesses the right to reject all doctrines which are repugnant to it, which go beyond natural religion, or which have no moral end.

2470. **Asiatic Ch.** The new Charter of the East India Company provides for a Bishop for India, and allows the introduction of missionaries.

2471. **Eng. Lit.** Southey's Life of Nelson.

Shelley's Queen Mab.

2472. **German Lit.** Körner, Arndt, Uhland and Jahn compose patriotic songs.

2473. **Science.** Brewster distinguishes single and double axis crystals.

Gay-Lussac's Memoir on Iodine.

De Candolle's Théorie de la Botanique retains Jussieu's divisions of acotyledons, monocotyledons and dicotyledons.

2474. **Art.** The Philharmonic Society is founded in London.

Bishop's opera, The Miller and his Men, containing When the Wind Blows, and other songs.

2475. **Philosophy.** Herbart's Introduction to Philosophy leads a reaction against the pantheism of Fichte and Schelling, to some extent on the lines of Leibnitz.

2476. **Politics.** Benjamin Constant's De l'Esprit de Conquête et de l'Usurpation vigorously attacks Napoleon.

2477. **Anthropology.** Pritchard's Physical History of Man founds anthropology in England, and contends for the primitive unity of the species. He discusses peoples in regard to language, bodily form and civilisation.

2478. **Social.** Elizabeth Fry begins to visit the prisons.

Insolvent debtors are released from prison.

The Apprenticeship and Wages Act of 1563 is repealed.

2479. **Deaths.** Körner, Lagrange, Scharnhorst, Wieland.

1598. **England.** Lord Cochrane is accused of defrauding the Stock Exchange by inventing a rumour of the death of Napoleon. [1814

1599. **France.** Negotiations begin at the Congress of Chatillon (Feb.); but Napoleon wins a few trifling successes, and refuses the boundaries of 1792, which are offered by the Allies. Castlereagh joins the Allies (March), and Schwarzenburg and Blucher fight their way to Paris. Napoleon abdicates (April 6), and is allowed to retire to Elba. At the same moment Wellington defeats Soult at Toulouse. Louis XVIII. becomes King, and is forced by Alexander to grant a Charter of representative government.

Louis concludes the first Treaty of Paris (May 30). The frontier of 1790 is increased, France obtaining Avignon, the Venaissin, and part of Savoy, and regaining all her Colonies except Mauritius, St Lucia, and Tobago. England retains Malta, the Cape of Good Hope, and the Île de France. Belgium is to be united to Holland, and Germany to form a Confederacy. Secret clauses resolve that German Princes are to be compensated on the left bank of the Rhine. Sardinia is to receive Genoa, and Austria, Lombardy and Venice. Details are to be arranged at a Congress which meets at Vienna (Nov. 1), and is attended by Metternich, Talleyrand, Hardenberg, Nesselrode, Castlereagh and Wellington.

1600. **Spain.** Ferdinand returns to Madrid (May), and at first promises to respect the Constitution of 1812, but soon dissolves the Cortes, and restores the nobles' exemptions.

1601. **Italy.** Murat joins the Allies (Jan.). Beauharnais defeats the Austrians (Feb.), but Genoa is taken by the English (April). The Pope returns to Rome, and Victor Emanuel is restored to his dominions.

1602. **Sweden.** By the Peace of Kiel, Norway is transferred from Denmark to Sweden, which cedes Swedish Pomerania and Rugen to Denmark (Jan.). Charles XIII. accepts the Constitution and declares Norway independent and indivisible (Nov.).

1603. **America.** The English troops burn the public buildings of Washington; but their invasion *viâ* Lake Champlain is repulsed. A large army is sent to take New Orleans. In the summer, the American commissioners, Clay, Quincy Adams and Gallatin, are sent to Ghent, and sign a treaty, the indirect cause of war being removed by the fall of Napoleon (Dec.). Meanwhile the New England States, where the war is strongly disapproved, meet in convention at Hartford, and propose States Rights Amendments to the Constitution.

Argentina forces Monte Video to desert Spain.

Francia becomes Dictator of Paraguay.

1604. **Asia.** By the Treaty of Teheran, England promises to aid Persia if attacked, and Persia to attack Afghanistan if the latter invades India.

2480. **Eng. Ch.** The Wesleyan Missionary Society is organised. A great outburst of missionary activity takes place at the same time in Holland, Switzerland and Germany. [1814

Joanna Southcote, the prophetess, who declares she is the woman spoken of in Revelation, dies, leaving followers, the New Israelites, who found a chapel in London.

Routh's Reliquiae Sacrae collect literary fragments of the early Christian Church.

2481. **Scotch Ch.** Chalmers becomes minister at Glasgow.

2482. **Italian Ch.** The Inquisition is restored.

2483. **Spanish Ch.** Ferdinand restores the Inquisition, and renews the Index.

William Mark, Consul at Malaga, introduces Protestantism, which is extended by Borrow and Rule.

2484. **Russian Ch.** Mme de Krudener begins to preach, and gains influence over the Tzar.

2485. **Church Hist.** The Order of Jesuits (already revived in Russia and Naples) and the Index are restored by the Pope, and Bible Societies, which are founded in Prussia and Russia, are condemned.

2486. **Asiatic Ch.** The first English Bishopric in India is established at Calcutta.

2487. **Eng. Lit.** Walter Scott's Waverley (anonymously published) commences the series of Waverley Novels.

Wordsworth's Excursion.

Walter begins to print the 'Times' with steam.

Edmund Kean makes his début as Shylock.

2488. **German Lit.** Görres' German Mercury demands the left bank of the Rhine, and earns for its author the title of the Fifth Great Power against Napoleon.

Chamisso's Peter Schlemihl.

Rückert's Poems.

2489. **Science.** Wells explains the phenomenon of dew.

Fraunhofer discovers 576 black lines in a ray of sunlight, but fails to explain them.

Orfila's Toxicologie creates the science of poisons.

2490. **Art.** David Cox writes a treatise on landscape-painting, and with Prout, de Wint, Creswick and Bonington, continues the work of Constable.

2491. **Philology.** Young begins to decipher the Rosetta Stone.

Abel Rémusat translates the Chinese romance, The Two Cousins, and studies Japanese Literature.

2492. **Politics.** Benjamin Constant's Esquisse de Constitution recommends the constitutional government of England and influences the composition of the Charter.

Niebuhr's Prussia's Right to Saxony supports the annexation on the ground of nationality.

Chateaubriand's Bonaparte et les Bourbons bitterly attacks the former and recommends the restoration of the latter.

1605. **England.** A secret treaty is made with Austria and France to counteract the ambitions of Russia and Prussia. [1815

1606. **France.** Napoleon escapes from Elba, and lands in France (March). Russia, Austria, Prussia, and England at once ally to resist him. Ney is sent against him, but joins him, and Louis XVIII. escapes to Belgium. He enters Paris (March 21), and issues the Acte Additionnel, drawn up by Constant. His offer to accept the Treaty of Paris is refused, and he marches north. Sending Ney to keep the English in check at Quatre Bras, he defeats the Prussians at Ligny and detaches Grouchy to keep them from joining Wellington (June 16). Napoleon attacks Wellington at Waterloo. Wellington's troops repulse every attack until the Prussians arrive, and then charge (June 18). The Allies enter Paris, Napoleon abdicates, and is removed to St Helena, and Louis is restored. By the Second Peace of Paris, France is to pay 30 millions and maintain a garrison for five years, to cede the portion of Savoy retained in 1814 to the King of Sardinia, and small districts to Belgium, Prussia, and Switzerland, and to restore the works of art removed during the wars. Richelieu succeeds Talleyrand, Ney is shot (Dec. 7), and the White Terror breaks out in Marseilles, Nîmes, Toulouse, and other parts of the South.

1607. **Italy.** On the landing of Napoleon in France, Murat attacks the Papal States, but is defeated by Austrian troops. Ferdinand IV. returns, and Murat, who attempts to raise an insurrection, is captured and shot (Oct.). Ferdinand secretly agrees with Metternich not to introduce constitutional liberty, and suppresses the Parliament granted to Sicily in 1813.

Consalvi obtains the restoration of the Marches and the Legations to the Papacy, and, aided by Capaccini, begins to reorganise the Papal States.

Genoa is annexed to the Sardinian Kingdom. Austria receives Lombardy and Venetia. The Dukes of Modena and Tuscany are restored. Marie Louise, Napoleon's wife, receives Parma and Piacenza, with succession to the rightful heir, who receives for the time the duchy of Lucca.

1608. **Germany.** A Staaten-bund is formed, consisting of 39 States, each sending representatives to the Diet at Frankfort, presided over by Austria. The Diet may order federal execution against recalcitrant States, each of which, however, is to have an assembly. Prussia receives the Rhineland, part of Saxony (Lusatia), the provinces of Posen and Thorn, and Swedish Pomerania and Rugen. Bavaria obtains Anspach and Bayreuth. Hanover becomes a Kingdom and gains East Friesland and Hildesheim.

Frederick William promises a Constitution to Prussia.

1609. **Austria.** Trieste, Istria, Dalmatia, Ragusa, Carniola, Croatia, South Tyrol and part of Southern Galicia are restored to the Emperor.

1610. **Sweden.** Sweden is confirmed in the possession of Norway. Denmark loses Swedish Pomerania, and receives the Duchy of Lauenburg.

1611. **Holland.** Belgium is united to Holland under William Frederick

2493. **Law.** Savigny's work, The Claim on our Age of Legislation and a Science of Law, declares law part of the organic life of a nation.

Thibaut urges the necessity of a national code for Germany.

2494. **Social.** Sweden and Holland abolish the Slave Trade in their dominions. On his return from Elba Napoleon follows their example. The Congress of Vienna refuses Castlereagh's proposal for a Council of Ambassadors charged with the duty of expediting the close of the traffic, and contents itself with a formal condemnation. Spain and Portugal alone continue the commerce (the latter only on the south of the line), alleging in their defence that their colonies are not so well supplied with slaves as those of England when prohibition was carried.

2495. **Death.** Fichte.

2496. **German Ch.** Wessenberg, Vicar-General of the diocese of Constance, urges the Vienna Congress to found a German national Church under a German primate. [1815

Each state makes its own Concordat with the Pope.

2497. **French Lit.** Béranger's first collection of songs.

Benjamin Constant's Adolphe, a romance based on his relations with Mme de Staël.

2498. **American Lit.** Bryant's Thanatopsis.

2499. **Literature.** Beowulf is found and published by Thorkelin.

2500. **Art.** Schubert composes music to Goethe's ballad, the Erlking.

2501. **Science.** William Smith completes his stratigraphical map of England and Wales, after 25 years' surveying.

Leslie investigates radiant heat.

Dupuytren becomes chief surgeon of the Hôtel-Dieu at Paris and improves diagnosis.

Fresnel's Memoir on the Diffraction of Light independently reaches Young's discovery of the principle of interference. Arago adopts the undulatory theory, which now becomes generally accepted.

Von Buch visits the Canary Isles, which he attributes to volcanic action.

2502. **Philosophy.** Cousin becomes Professor of Philosophy at the Sorbonne, and aids Royer-Collard in the revival of idealism.

2503. **Economics.** Malthus and West independently state the true doctrine of rent, already outlined by Anderson, 1779, namely, that rent is equal to the excess of the price of the produce of land over the cost of production, the price of the entire supply being regulated by the cost of production on the worst land.

of Nassau. Luxemburg becomes a member of the Bund, and is given to the King of the Netherlands in return for a renunciation of his Nassau lands. The town is made a Bund fortress.

1612. **Switzerland.** The Congress of Vienna adds Geneva, Valais, and Neuchâtel (the latter with reservation of Prussia's sovereign rights), and guarantees neutrality.

1613. **Poland.** The Grand Duchy of Warsaw is formed into the Kingdom of Poland in union with Russia, but with responsible government, a national army, flag, and budget, a free press, and the official use of the native language. Cracow is made a free state.

1614. **Russia.** Under the influence of Madame de Krudener, the Tsar forms the Holy Alliance with Austria and Prussia for the application of Christian principles to politics (Aug.).

1615. **Greece.** The Ionian Islands become an independent republic under English protection, Sir Thomas Maitland being appointed High Commissioner.

1616. **America.** Before the news of the Treaty of Ghent arrives, Jackson routs the English at New Orleans.

Brazil becomes a kingdom under the Prince Regent of Portugal.

1617. **West Indies.** France retains Guadeloupe and Martinique.

1618. **Africa.** England occupies and garrisons Ascension Island.

Réunion is restored to France.

1619. **England.** The income-tax is abolished, and silver is demonetised. [1816

1620. **France.** After a violent conflict between the Government and the Ultra-royalists, an Amnesty Bill is carried by Richelieu. The Chamber demands other reactionary measures, but, by the advice of Decazes, is dissolved by the King, who, on his own authority introduces direct representation. A moderate majority is returned, and the ministry of Richelieu receives support from the party of Doctrinaires, led by Royer-Collard, De Serre, Camille Jordan and De Broglie. The new dynasty, however, is attacked in the Chamber and the Press by the Left, led by Benjamin Constant, Lafayette, Manuel and Laffitte, by the Bonapartists Fouché and Béranger, and by Courier. The Government continues to be attacked by the Ultra-royalists, of whom Villèle becomes the leader.

1621. **Germany.** Saxe-Weimar obtains a Constitution; and its example is shortly followed by Hanover, Bavaria, Baden.

1622. **Austria.** By the Treaty of Munich, Salzburg and the Circle of the Inn are restored to Austria.

1623. **America.** A Tariff Act is passed which imposes heavy duties on cotton, woollens, salt and iron, and introduces the minimum principle.

A second United States Bank is chartered for 20 years.

Chief Justice Marshall pronounces a series of decisions in favour of the United States, and diminishes State Rights.

The provinces of La Plata proclaim their independence as the Argentine Republic.

2504. **Social.** The Apothecaries' Act forbids medical practice without a qualification.

The importation of wheat into England is forbidden until the price reaches 80*s.* Bounties on corn cease, and export is allowed.

2505. **Death.** Rumford.

2506. **Eng. Ch.** A motion for the relief of Catholics is rejected by the Lords. [1816

2507. **Eng. Lit.** Jane Austen's Emma.

Scott's Old Mortality.

Cobbett's Political Register, the first cheap periodical, is published at 2*d.*

Byron's Childe Harold, Canto III.

Coleridge's Christabel is published.

Peacock's Headlong Hall satirises the romanticists.

2508. **French Lit.** The King revives the French Academy, and the Academies of Science, Art, and Belles-Lettres.

2509. **Art.** Parliament purchases the Elgin Marbles.

Rossini's Barber of Seville.

2510. **Science.** Brewster invents a Kaleidoscope.

2511. **Politics.** Owen's New View of Society sketches a communistic association, and declares character the product of circumstances.

Haller's Restoration of Political Science attacks the contract theory and supports autocracy, aristocracy and ultramontanism.

2512. **Philology.** Bopp's System of Conjugation proves the common origin of grammatical forms.

2513. **Education.** Froebel organises a community at Keilhau in Thuringia.

Polytechnic schools for Applied Science, borrowed from French models, are established in Germany.

2514. **Law.** Niebuhr finds the Commentaries of Gaius at Verona.

2515. **History.** Karamsin's History of Russia.

2516. **Social.** Unusual distress is caused by a bad season, and riots occur at Spa Fields and elsewhere. A stream of emigrants begins to leave England for America and the colonies.

2517. **Death.** Sheridan.

1624. **Africa.** Lord Exmouth bombards Algiers and releases many Christian slaves. The Dey is forced to abolish Christian slavery.

The Gambia colony is formed, chiefly by settlers forced to leave Senegal when restored to France.

1625. **Asia.** Lord Amherst is sent on a mission to Pekin, but refuses to 'kow-tow,' and in consequence returns without obtaining an audience of the Emperor.

The war between the East India Company and Nepal, a tributary state of China, caused by a frontier outrage, is terminated, and an English Resident is placed at the capital.

Java is restored by England to the Dutch.

[1817

1626. **England.** The Regent is attacked and the Blanketeers march from Manchester, but are dispersed. The Habeas Corpus Act is suspended, and the Sidmouth Circular to the Lords Lieutenant authorises the arrest of libellers.

The Princess Charlotte, only child of the Regent, married in 1816 to Prince Leopold of Saxe-Coburg, dies. In consequence, the Dukes of Cambridge, Clarence, and Kent marry, 1818.

The Military and Naval Officers' Oath Bill opens all ranks in the army and navy to Catholics.

1627. **Ireland.** The two Exchequers are united, the Irish Debt is joined to the National Debt, and equal taxes are levied on articles in both countries. Exemptions and abatements may be granted whenever necessary.

1628. **France.** The partial renovation of the Chamber still further weakens the Ultra-royalists. Part of the troops are recalled, and the Tsar diminishes the indemnity. Financial credit is restored and arrangements for a loan are made.

1629. **Germany.** The Grand Duchy of Weimar, where alone a constitution has been granted, becomes the centre of liberal propaganda. The celebration of the third centenary of Luther's protest and the battle of Leipsig by German students at the Wartburg, and the burning of the writings of Haller, Schmalz, and other reactionaries, frightens the Powers. The Duke of Weimar is forced to curtail the liberties of his subjects.

1630. **Turkey.** Milosh, who has murdered his rival, Kara George, is declared hereditary prince of Servia. Turkish troops continue to garrison the fortresses, and the Sultan receives tribute. The quarrel between the families, however, continues through the century.

1631. **Russia.** A Secret Society is founded to obtain constitutional government. Among its members are many republicans.

1632. **America.** The United States send Commissioners to establish commercial relations with the revolted colonies of Spain.

The Portuguese of Brazil conquer Montevideo.

Bolivar, after several repulses, defeats the Spanish troops and becomes the head of the Government of Venezuela.

2518. **Eng. Ch.** By the efforts of Joshua Watson, the Church Building Society is founded, few churches having been erected since the reign of Queen Anne. Application for assistance is made to Lord Liverpool, who persuades Parliament to grant one million pounds for the purpose, and appoints a Commission to superintend its distribution. [1817

2519. **French Ch.** Lamennais' Essay on Indifference attacks individualism and scepticism.

A new Concordat abolishes that of 1801 and restores the instrument of 1516, but is attacked by Frayssinous and is never adopted.

2520. **German Ch.** At the wish of King Frederick William, the Lutheran and Reformed Churches unite in the Evangelical Union to commemorate 1517. The Union spreads from Prussia to Würtemburg, Baden, Anhalt, Nassau, and the Rhine Provinces.

An ultramontane Concordat is made by Bavaria with Rome, on the fall of Montgelas.

2521. **Spanish Ch.** Llorente, late Secretary of the Inquisition, publishes a History of the Spanish Inquisition.

2522. **African Ch.** Robert Moffat begins mission work in South Africa.

2523. **Eng. Lit.** Blackwood's Magazine is founded, edited by Christopher North (Wilson), who contributes his Noctes Ambrosianae.

Mary Shelley's Frankenstein.

Moore's Lalla Rookh.

2524. **Science.** Cuvier's Régne Animal classifies animals as vertebrata, mollusca, articulata and radiata.

2525. **Art.** Chantrey's Sleeping Children. (Lichfield.)

2526. **Philosophy.** Schubert lectures at Munich on magic and magnetism, and carries romanticism into philosophy.

2527. **Philology.** Boeckh's Domestic Economy of the Athenians.

Ottfried Müller's Hellenic Races.

2528. **Politics.** Ballanche explains his theory of Palingenesis, i.e., a return through trials to the state before the fall.

2529. **Economics.** Ricardo's Political Economy and Taxation explains the theory of rent, and states that wages tend to the level of subsistence. His system is popularised by James and John Mill, Malthus, McCulloch, Torrens, and Harriet Martineau.

2530. **Geography.** Ritter's Geography in relation to Nature and History founds comparative geography.

2531. **Deaths.** Jane Austen, Dalberg, Kosciusko, Mme de Staël, Werner.

1633. **England.** The Habeas Corpus Act is restored, and is not again suspended. [1818

Romilly and Brougham fail to repeal the Septennial Act.

1634. **Russia.** Alexander addresses the Polish Diet in a very liberal strain, and announces his intention of extending representative institutions to Russia. A few weeks later, however, he is thought to have received information of the existence of numerous anti-dynastic secret societies. At any rate he abandons his liberalism at this moment, and adopts the views of Metternich, and inspires an alarmist pamphlet by Stourdza, a Moldavian.

1635. **France.** The Ultra-royalist reaction having almost spent itself, the Tsar summons the Powers to a Congress to meet at Aix-la-Chapelle, and decrees the evacuation of France, though five years' occupation had been originally contemplated. Louis agrees with the Powers to act together for peace, and in any disturbance to concert measures at a Congress. A tacit understanding to combine against liberal movements is arrived at. England is prevented by Canning from joining the Concert.

1636. **Germany.** Under the influence of Wilhelm v. Humboldt, the King of Prussia determines to grant a Constitution; but Metternich advises the creation of provincial Diets.

The King of Bavaria grants a Constitution.

List conceives the idea of the Zollverein, or Customs Union, and Prussia abolishes duties on transit through its territories.

1637. **Sweden.** Bernadotte becomes King of Sweden.

1638. **America.** Jackson, while pursuing some Indians in the Seminole war, crosses the border of Florida and seizes two Spanish towns.

England and the United States agree to occupy Oregon jointly for ten years. The Northern boundary is fixed; the question of fisheries is settled; and England gives up her rights to the navigation of the Mississippi.

Chili proclaims her independence, and San Martin defeats a Spanish army.

1639. **Asia.** The Pindaries are suppressed by the Marquis of Hastings; the Peshwas are extinguished and their dominions annexed; the Rajah of Nagpur is put under British guardianship, and the Rajputana States place themselves under British protection.

1640. **England.** Burdett's motion for annual Parliaments, the ballot, and universal suffrage is lost. [1819

A Manchester reform meeting is broken up by the military at the Peterloo massacre (Aug.). The Six Acts, carried against strong opposition, forbid training to arms, take steps against libels, empower Justices of the Peace to search for and seize arms, impose a newspaper stamp on pamphlets, prevent meetings of more than 50 without six days' notice to the Justice of the Peace, and forbid the attendance of all but freeholders or residents, and deprive defendants in cases of misdemeanour of the right of traversing.

2532. **French Ch.** Vianey becomes Curé d'Ars. [1818

2533. **German Ch.** Representatives of several West and South German states meet at Frankfurt and revive the ideas of Febronius; but the nationalist movement is combated by Niebuhr, the Prussian envoy at Rome.

2534. **Eng. Lit.** The Quarterly Review (probably Gifford) and Blackwood's Magazine roughly attack Keats' Endymion. Shelley protests.

Shelley's Revolt of Islam.

Scott's Heart of Midlothian.

Susan Ferrier's novel, Marriage.

2535. **French Lit.** Mme de Staël's Considérations sur la Révolution Française eulogise Necker, and discriminate the lasting benefits from the temporary extravagances.

2536. **German Lit.** Grillparzer's Sappho.

2537. **Art.** Landseer's Fighting Dogs getting Wind, his first great success.

2538. **Science.** De Candolle's Prodromus Systematis Naturalis describes 80,000 species.

Bessel's Fundamenta Astronomiæ contain reduced places of stars observed by Bradley.

Encke's comet is discovered, revolving round the sun in 3½ years.

2539. **Education.** The king of Prussia founds a University at Bonn.

2540. **History.** Hallam's History of the Middle Ages.

Mill's History of British India.

2541. **Geography.** Sir John Ross is sent to find the North Pole.

2542. **Social.** An agricultural pauper colony is planted at Fredericksoord in Holland.

2543. **Deaths.** Monge, Thugut.

2544. **Irish Ch.** Doyle becomes Bishop of Kildare and Leighlin. [1819

2545. **French Ch.** De Maistre's Du Pape contends for infallibility and for the temporal power, not only as an ecclesiastical right, but as a political and social precaution.

2546. **German Ch.** Hermes' Philosophical Introduction to Christian Theology asserts that the belief of reason precedes and strengthens the belief of revelation.

2547. **American Ch.** Channing, a minister at Boston, preaches a sermon, which becomes the manifesto of Unitarianism. The Unitarian body is joined chiefly by Congregationalists.

2548. **Eng. Lit.** Keats' Odes to a Nightingale and to a Grecian Urn.

Shelley's Prometheus Unbound, the Cenci, and Ode to the West Wind.

Scott's Bride of Lammermoor.

Byron's Don Juan.

Richard Carlile is imprisoned for seven years for publishing free-thinking and republican works.

Peel effects the resumption of cash payments by the Bank of England.

1641. **France.** The election of the Abbé Grégoire as a Deputy is regarded by the King as an attack on the throne, and frightens Decazes into a less liberal policy.

1642. **Germany.** Sand, a student, murders Kotzebue, a Russian agent, who is thought to have caused the Tsar's apostasy from liberalism, and has written against the German universities (March). Metternich therefore calls a meeting of ministers at Carlsbad, and recommends the muzzling of the press, the control of the teaching of the universities by Government officials, and a commission to sit at Mainz to investigate the conspiracy. The Carlsbad resolutions are framed, and are adopted by the Diet. Metternich's proposal to suspend the constitutions of the minor States is defeated by the Tsar's influence. The proposed Russian constitution is given up, and W. v. Humboldt and other Liberals withdraw from the service of the State. Görres' Germany and the Revolution passionately denounces the breaking of their promises by the Governments.

1643. **Russia.** Araktcheief forms the first military colonies.

1644. **Turkey.** Ali Pasha, of Jannina, obtains Parga, the last of the Venetian possessions, and reaches the highest point of his power.

1645. **America.** A treaty is concluded with the King of Spain (who is in need of money), giving up his claim to West Florida (occupied by the United States since 1810) and ceding East Florida. The United States surrender their claim to Texas.

Missouri's petition to be admitted as a slave state is discussed, but no decision is reached. Maine, joined to Massachusetts since 1676, also petitions for admission.

Bolivar defeats the Spaniards, forms the Republic of Columbia from the unión of New Granada and Venezuela, and becomes its first President.

1646. **Asia.** Speranski becomes Governor-General of Siberia.

Singapore is occupied by Sir Stamford Raffles.

1647. **England.** Thistlewood's conspiracy to kill the ministers is detected. [1820

The new King attempts to dissolve his marriage on charges of misconduct; but the project is resisted by public opinion, led by Brougham and Denman, and abandoned.

Russell's Bill for disfranchising four rotten boroughs passes the Commons and is rejected in the Lords.

London merchants petition for Free Trade.

1648. **France.** The Duke of Berry, son of the Count of Artois, is murdered; but his widow gives birth to a son, afterwards the Comte de Chambord. A strong royalist reaction sets in and Decazes resigns.

1649. **Spain.** The army declares for the Constitution of 1812. The King is forced to yield, and appoints Liberals to office (Feb.), but

2549. **Literature.** Mai becomes Librarian of the Vatican, and discovers Cicero's De Republica, which he publishes, 1822.

2550. **Science.** The first steamboat crosses the Atlantic.

Mitscherlich discovers isomorphism, i.e., that an equal number of atoms in compounds of the same class can replace each other in the compound without altering its crystalline form.

Oersted discovers electro-magnetism. Ampère repeats the experiments and reaches the laws of electro-dynamical action.

Dulong and Petit discover the connexion between the specific heats and the atomic weights of the elements.

Laennec invents auscultation.

2551. **Art.** Weber's Der Freischütz.

Turner ceases to be imitative and produces Childe Harold's Pilgrimage, Ulysses deriding Polyphemus, etc.

Géricault's Raft of the Medusa initiates the romantic reaction.

2552. **Philology.** H. H. Wilson's Sanskrit Dictionary.

Grimm's German Grammar reaches Bopp's results independently, and states the law of Lautverschiebung, or permutation of consonants, already guessed by Rask.

2553. **Philosophy.** Schopenhauer's World as Will and Representation declares the will to live the root of evil, and maintains that extinction should be the goal of endeavour.

2554. **Law.** Kluber publishes a system of positive international law.

2555. **Economics.** Sismondi's Nouveaux Principes d'Économie Politique lay greater stress on well-being than on wealth.

2556. **Geography.** Parry accompanies Ross on an unsuccessful expedition in search of the North Pole. In the following year, he traces a considerable portion of the North-West passage.

2557. **Deaths.** Blucher, Watt.

2558. **Eng. Ch.** Darby, an Anglican clergyman, leaves the Church and founds a community at Plymouth, teaching a rigid Calvinism and the priesthood of all believers. Some years later, he goes to reside in Switzerland, which becomes the headquarters of the Plymouth Brethren. [1820

2559. **Scotch Ch.** Erskine's first book, Revealed Religion, adopts Coleridge's method of discussing theology. McLeod Campbell, minister of Row, shares Erskine's ideas, and is expelled from the Kirk.

2560. **German Ch.** Bretschneider contests the authorship of St John's Gospel and Epistles.

2561. **American Ch.** John England becomes Bishop of Charlestown, and increases the influence and prestige of Catholicism by his administration and his writings.

appeals for aid to the Holy Alliance. The Cortes abolish the monasteries and Inquisition, and secure freedom of the press and meeting (July).

1650. **Portugal.** Owing to the rising in Spain, a revolt takes place and a constitution is introduced. The King returns from Brazil.

1651. **Italy.** The Carbonari revolt in Naples, and the army under Pepe demands the Spanish Constitution of 1812. The King forms a Liberal ministry and swears to the Constitution, but informs the Emperor of Austria that he has acted under restraint. Sicily also demands independence.

1652. **Germany.** On news of the revolutions in Southern Europe, Metternich convenes a Congress at Troppau (Oct.), (transferred to Laybach, Dec.). Austria is authorised to intervene in Italy. Castlereagh protests against united action, contemplated in the Circular of Troppau.

The Diet adopts the Supplementary Act of Vienna, by which the Federation obtains power to interfere to maintain order in the weaker states.

Würtemberg receives a Constitution.

1653. **America.** Maine and Missouri are admitted as states; but slavery is forbidden in the Louisiana purchase, north of Arkansas. The Missouri Compromise postpones the struggle over the extension of slavery for a generation.

Iturbide marches on Mexico and establishes a Regency.

1654. **Africa.** About 3,000 emigrants are sent to Cape Colony.

The Washington Colonisation Society founds Liberia for the repatriation of negroes.

Mehemet Ali conquers the Sudan and Kordofan.

1655. **England.** Grampound is disfranchised by Lord John Russell, and the two seats are given to Yorkshire. [1821

1656. **France.** Richelieu, failing to keep pace with the royalist reaction, resigns, and Villèle forms the first homogeneous Ministry of the Right. The Congregation becomes a formidable organ of the reaction.

1657. **Italy.** Ferdinand is allowed to go to meet the sovereigns at Laybach. An Austrian army is dispatched to Naples, and defeats Pepe. Death, imprisonment, or exile are meted out to the Constitutionalists. Sicily is also reduced.

While the Austrian troops are absent a revolt breaks out in Piedmont. Victor Emanuel abdicates in favour of his brother, Charles Felix, who is absent in Modena, the administration being given to Charles Albert, of Carignano, who proclaims the Spanish Constitution. Charles Felix declares these measures void, and Austrian troops suppress the revolt.

1658. **Greece.** A revolt, prepared chiefly by the Hetairia Philike, and to some extent by literary influences and Russian intrigues, begins in Moldavia, led by Hypsilanti, in the expectation, perhaps fostered by

2562. **Eng. Lit.** Keats' Eve of St Agnes.
De Quincey's Confessions of an Opium-Eater.
2563. **French Lit.** Lamartine's Méditations, the first poem of romanticism.
2564. **American Lit.** Washington Irving's Sketch-book.
2565. **Russian Lit.** Pushkin's first poems, deeply influenced by Byron.
2566. **Art.** The Vénus de Milo is found (Louvre).
2567. **Philosophy.** Brown's Lectures on the Philosophy of Mind introduce the idea of a 'muscular sense,' and reduce most of Reid's first principles to secondary products.
2568. **Philology.** Abel Rémusat's Langues Tartares.
2569. **Politics.** Grote's pamphlet on Radical Reform and James Mill's article on Government in the Encyclopædia Britannica advocate a low suffrage, and reveal the hostility of the new radicals to the current Whig philosophy.
Zacharia, Steffens, Rotteck, and Troxler publish works in support of constitutionalism. Ancillon defends autocracy.
2570. **Law.** Romagnosi's Science of Law declares civil society the offspring not of an arbitrary contract but of reason, and maintains that right is not created by law.
2571. **Deaths.** Banks, Grattan, Young.

2572. **German Ch.** Schleiermacher's Christian Belief declares that Christianity is accepted on the strength of internal experience, and is therefore independent of miracles or history. [1821
Niebuhr, on behalf of Prussia, concludes a Concordat highly favourable to the Roman Church.
2573. **Eng. Lit.** Shelley's Adonais.
Galt's Annals of the Parish.
2574. **German Lit.** Platen's Lyrics.
Wilhelm Müller's Songs of the Greeks.
2575. **American Lit.** Fennimore Cooper's novel, The Spy.
2576. **Bohemian Lit.** Kollar's Daughter of Slava, a series of sonnets on love and Bohemian nationality.
2577. **Science.** Faraday discovers electro-magnetic rotation.
Sabine commences pendulum measurements in order to ascertain the shape of the earth.
Seebeck discovers thermo-electricity.
2578. **Philosophy.** De Maistre's Soirées de St Pétersbourg attempt to vindicate the existence of evil.
2579. **Philology.** Champollion's L'Écriture hiératique.
W. Humboldt's Essay on the Basques and their Language.
2580. **Politics.** Hegel's Philosophy of Right advocates constitutional

Capodistrias, Foreign Minister of Russia, of Russian support. The revolt is, however, disowned by the Tsar, and the Turks are victorious at Dragatschan (June). At this moment, the Morea and Central Greece rise, and are joined by Ali Pasha of Jannina.

1659. **America.** Brazil declares itself independent, and Don Pedro, eldest son of John VI., is elected Emperor.

Chilians and Argentines enter Lima, the capital of Peru and the stronghold of Spanish power. The Viceroy flies, and independence is proclaimed. Guatemala, Costa Rica, La Plata, Uruguay, Venezuela also declare their independence.

The Republic of San Domingo is formed.

1660. **England.** Castlereagh commits suicide, and Canning, despite the opposition of the King, becomes Foreign Secretary. [1822

Canning's Bill to admit Catholic peers to the House of Lords passes the Commons.

1661. **Spain.** The Powers meet at Verona, where Wellington represents England, to discuss the revolutions in Greece and Spain, in which civil war again breaks out, and demand a modification of the Spanish Constitution and the restoration of the authority of the King. In the event of refusal, France is authorised to use compulsion. A proposal is made to suppress the revolt of the Spanish colonies.

1662. **Greece.** The independence of Greece is proclaimed, and a national Convention drawn up a Constitution. Ali Pasha is defeated and slain by the Turks (Feb.), and the inhabitants of Chios are massacred. The invasion of the Morea, however, is repulsed, Missolonghi is unsuccessfully besieged, and Admiral Canaris burns part of the Turkish fleet.

1663. **Turkey.** The Phanariot rule in the Danubian Principalities is ended by the Greek revolt, and Roumanian nobles are appointed Hospodars by the Porte.

1664. **America.** San Martin, the Dictator of Peru, falls.

Iturbide becomes Emperor of Mexico; but he is deserted by his supporters and abdicates, 1823. The United States recognise the revolted colonies.

1665. **Russia.** War with Turkey is averted by the influence of Metternich, and Capodistrias resigns his position.

1666. **England.** 17,000 Freeholders of Yorkshire demand reform. [1823

Nugent's Bill to admit Catholics to the franchise and to certain officers passes the Commons.

1667. **Ireland.** The Catholic Association is formed by O'Connell and Sheil, to support the movement for Emancipation.

1668. **Spain.** A French army, under the Duke of Angoulême, invades Spain, and enters Madrid after slight resistance (May). Ferdinand, who has been deposed (June), is restored, revokes everything done since 1820, and inflicts savage penalties on the Constitutionalists.

monarchy as a historical growth, and declares the State the realisation of the absolute spirit.

Görres' Europe and the Revolution depicts Europe as a prey to alternate fits of despotism and revolution.

2581. **History.** The École des Chartes is founded in Paris for the study of historical documents.

2582. **Deaths.** Keats, Joseph de Maistre, Napoleon.

2583. **Eng. Ch.** Edward Irving begins to preach in London. [1822

2584. **German Ch.** Walther's Ecclesiastical Law, an ultramontane text-book.

Tschirner's Protestantism and Catholicism blends evangelicalism and rationalism and anticipates the theological revolution.

2585. **Eng. Lit.** Lamb's Essays of Elia.

Rogers' Italy.

2586. **French Lit.** De Vigny's poems.

2587. **German Lit.** Heine's first poems.

2588. **Russian Lit.** Griboiedof's The Misfortune of being too Clever, a satirical play.

2589. **Science.** Fourier's Théorie analytique de la Chaleur explains the propagation of heat, but assumes that the conductivity of a substance for heat is constant for all temperatures.

Flourens' Système Nerveux dans les Animaux vertèbres.

Poncelet's Propriétés projectives des Figures establishes the chief properties of conics and quadrics by means of projection.

Oken founds the German Association for Science, which is extended by Alexander Humboldt, 1828.

2590. **Art.** Liszt's début as a pianist at Vienna.

2591. **Philosophy.** Baader's Fermenta Cognitionis, deeply influenced by Böhme, attempts a theosophic system in which the kingdoms of Grace and Nature run parallel.

Grote elaborates and publishes Bentham's Analysis of the Influence of Natural Religion, a vigorous attack on theism.

2592. **Philology.** Colebrooke founds the Royal Asiatic Society.

2593. **Education.** Spilleke widens the curriculum of the Real-Schule, and leads it to look beyond purely commercial ideals.

2594. **Politics.** Charles Comte's Traité de Législation continues and corrects the work of Montesquieu.

2595. **Deaths.** Canova, Hardenberg, William Herschel, Shelley.

2596. **French Ch.** Lanjuinais, a Jansenist, attacks the Jesuits. [1823

2597. **Science.** Arago discovers rotatory magnetism.

Faraday liquefies chlorine and other gases.

2598. **Art.** Ingres' La Source (Paris).

Schubert's music to Rosamund.

Spohr's oratorio Jessonda.

1669. **Portugal.** John abrogates the Constitution, but orders the preparation of one on the English model. The Queen, however, and Don Miguel, the younger son of the King, prefer absolutism, and lead a revolt against the King, which is suppressed.

1670. **America.** The King of Spain begs the aid of the Holy Alliance to reduce the South American Republics. Canning suggests to Rush, the American envoy in London, a joint declaration against the expected move of Europe, and informs France that if the Holy Alliance attacks the Republics, England will recognise them. Monroe's Message, composed by John Quincy Adams, declares that 'the American continents are henceforth not to be considered as subjects for future colonisation by any European Power.' The Monroe Doctrine becomes an established principle of American policy.

Morales capitulates, and Columbia becomes independent.

1671. **Australia.** New South Wales obtains a Constitution.

1672. **Asia.** Ahmed Khan returns from a pilgrimage to Mecca, and introduces Wahabism among the Mohamedans of India. He establishes a camp on the Punjab frontier, and attacks the Sikhs.

1673. **France.** A new organ of the Opposition, the Globe newspaper, is founded by Thiers and Mignet, and supported by Sainte-Beuve, Ampère, Lerminier, Jouffroy, Rémusat, Duvergier de Hauranne. [1824

Artois succeeds, and restores the Jesuits and their rights of education, revives the laws of sacrilege, compensates the Emigrants, and threatens the principle of equal division.

1674. **America.** The United States and Russia agree on a line which neither is to cross, and open the Pacific to fishing and navigation by both.

Duties are raised from 25 per cent. to 37 per cent.

The Spanish, who have won back the greater part of Peru, are finally routed by Bolivar. The country becomes the independent republic of Bolivia, and Bolivar becomes President.

Canning recognises the independence of the South American Republics, thus carrying into execution one of the latest plans of Castlereagh.

1675. **Greece.** A proposal of the Czar to divide Greece into three Principalities, tributary to the Sultan and garrisoned by the Turks, but autonomous, is not adopted. Ibrahim Pasha is sent by Mehemet, at the request of the Sultan, to take Crete, and overruns the Peloponnesus. The Turkish fleet, however, is destroyed at Mitylene. Byron, who has come to aid the struggle for independence, dies at Missolonghi.

1676. **Africa.** The English are defeated in Ashantee.

1677. **Asia.** The East India Company takes Rangoon.

England restores Sumatra to Holland, and receives Malacca.

2599. **Philology.** Klaproth's Asia Polyglotta.
2600. **History.** Thiers' History of the French Revolution.
2601. **Education.** Jacotot's Enseignement Universel asserts that all children possess equal intelligence, and that the task of the teacher is rather to stimulate than to instruct.

Birkbeck founds the first Mechanics' Institute.
2602. **Geography.** An English expedition discovers Lake Chad.
2603. **Social.** Owing to the efforts of Romilly and Mackintosh, Peel abolishes the death penalty on 100 crimes.

Huskisson carries his Reciprocity of Duties Bill, largely modifying the Navigation Acts.

Owen plants communistic settlements in America, which, however, quickly fail.

The Oxford Union Society is founded.
2604. **Death.** Ricardo.

2605. **Eng. Ch.** The Catholic English and Irish bishops declare that the Popes possess no civil authority. [1824
2606. **French Ch.** Lamennais visits Rome, is warmly greeted by the Pope, and on his return attacks Gallicanism, and advocates theocracy and the political supremacy of the Pope. He is prosecuted for his Religion considérée dans ses Rapports avec l'Ordre Politique et Civile, and defended by Berryer.
2607. **Eng. Lit.** Landor's Imaginary Conversations.
2608. **Italian Lit.** Leopardi's Canzoni.
2609. **Science.** Liebig establishes a chemical laboratory at Giessen.

Von Buch's geological map of Germany.

Carnot's Puissance motrice du Feu attempts to determine mathematically the power of a steam-engine. In later writings he grasps the law of the conservation of energy.

Bessel introduces 'Bessel's Functions' into pure mathematics.
2610. **Art.** The National Gallery is founded in London, with Angerstein's collection as a nucleus.
2611. **Philology.** Boeckh begins the Corpus Inscriptionum Graecarum.
2612. **Philosophy.** Herbart's Psychology as a Science rejects the theory of the mind as an aggregate of faculties. Ideas become associated in groups, the strong recalling the weak.

The Westminster Review is founded, Bentham being the proprietor and Bowring editor. In the first number James Mill attacks the Edinburgh Review. Similar Radical principles are championed by Fonblanque in the Examiner.
2613. **History.** Ranke's Latin and Teutonic Nations, 1494—1519, with an appendix on the sources, inaugurates the critical period of historiography.

Clinton's Fasti Hellenici.
2614. **Social.** Hume and Huskisson repeal the Combination Laws.
2615. **Deaths.** Byron, Consalvi, Joubert, Wolf.

1678. **Ireland.** The Catholic Association is suppressed for three years; but the work is continued without the name. [1825

Emancipation resolutions are carried by Burdett in the Commons.

Bishop Doyle is examined by Parliament on the creed of Catholics, and his evidence greatly contributes to remove the objections against Emancipation.

1679. **Netherlands.** A movement for independence begins.

1680. **Germany.** Bavaria and Würtemberg make a commercial treaty, which becomes the nucleus of the Zollverein.

1681. **Hungary.** In consequence of the rising discontent the Diet is allowed to meet every three years. Szechenyi speaks in Hungarian and founds a Hungarian Academy of Sciences. The demand for the use of the Magyar language excites the resentment of the Slav races.

1682. **Russia.** Nicholas succeeds, after putting down a dangerous revolt in the army, and declares against Western methods and ideas. The Slavophil party, led by Aksakov and Koshelev, rapidly grows.

1683. **Greece.** Ibrahim besieges Missolonghi, and the Greeks place themselves under the protection of England.

1684. **Turkey.** Stratford Canning, first cousin of George Canning, becomes ambassador at Constantinople.

1685. **America.** With Monroe's resignation, the 'era of good feeling' ends. In the presidential election, Jackson, the victor of New Orleans, obtains most votes; but Clay's supporters vote for Quincy Adams, who is consequently elected. Jackson's friends raise the cry of a corrupt bargain.

A Congress of South and Central American States is summoned by Bolivar to Panama. Columbia, Peru, Mexico, and Central America ally; but Bolivar's scheme of a federal army and navy is not adopted.

Adams desires to send to take part in the Congress in order to obtain recognition of the Monroe Doctrine. But Congress delays its sanction till the Congress is over.

The inhabitants of the 'Banda Oriental' (Montevideo, etc.) revolt against Brazil and found the Republic of Uruguay.

England makes commercial treaties with Columbia and Mexico.

1686. **Australia.** Tasmania becomes a separate colony.

1687. **Portugal.** The King dies, and his son, Pedro, Emperor of Brazil, issues a charter, and, being debarred by the Constitution, gives the inheritance to his daughter, Maria. Miguel opposes her, and [1826

2616. **Eng. Ch.** Thirlwall translates Schleiermacher's Essay on Luke, and adds a preface, in part composed by Hare, on German theology. Hugh James Rose preaches a course of sermons at Cambridge, denouncing the Protestantism of Germany as anti-Christian. [1825

Whately's Peculiarities of the Christian Religion founds the Broad Church treatment of theology.

The Earl of Bridgewater endows a lectureship on Natural Science as a branch of Christian evidence, which is held by Chalmers, Whewell, Bell, and others.

Coleridge's Aids to Reflection base religion on spiritual apprehension, not on 'Evidences.'

W. J. Fox, Minister at South Place Chapel, founds the British and Foreign Unitarian Association.

2617. **American Ch.** Joe Smith, a farmer, publishes the Book of Mormon, which he declares to be a translation from tablets written by the remnants of the ten tribes who migrated to America.

2618. **Eng. Lit.** Lord Braybrooke edits Pepys' Diary.

Macaulay's Essay on Milton in the Edinburgh Review.

Scott is involved in the ruin of his publishers.

2619. **Italian Lit.** Manzoni's The Betrothed founds the romantic school.

Vieusseux edits the Antologia, a review to which Tommaseo, Mamiani, Romagnosi, and other reformers contribute.

2620. **Spanish Lit.** Heredia's Poems mark the birth of Spanish-American literature.

2621. **Swedish Lit.** Tegner's Frithiofs Saga.

2622. **Russian Lit.** Pushkin's Boris Godounoff founds the historical drama.

2623. **Science.** Stephenson's railway from Stockton to Darlington is opened.

Poulett Scrope's Considerations on Volcanoes.

Legendre's Traité des Fonctions Elliptiques.

W. E. and E. H. Weber's Wave Theory.

2624. **Art.** Cornelius frescoes the Ludwigskirche at Munich, and with Kaulbach revives fresco painting.

2625. **Anthropology.** Flint tools and bones of extinct animals are found in Kent's Cavern, Torquay.

2626. **History.** Neander's History of the Christian Church.

2627. **Economics.** Dunoyer's La Liberté du Travail, an extreme presentation of laissez-faire.

2628. **Education.** The University of London is founded by Brougham, Joseph Hume, and others, including a number of Dissenters.

2629. **Social.** All combinations except for the purpose of fixing wages are declared illegal.

2630. **Deaths.** David, Courier, Richter, St Simon.

2631. **Eng. Ch.** Rose preaches at Cambridge on the duties of the clergy, and founds the conception of modern High Churchmanship. [1826

Spain equips an expedition, and Canning therefore sends English troops to her aid.

1688. **Greece.** Missolonghi falls after a year's siege. Canning makes a secret convention with the Tsar, to whom Wellington is sent, to obtain autonomy for Greece. Both Powers disclaim the intention of seeking any territorial or commercial advantages. France joins, but Austria and Prussia oppose intervention. The Holy Alliance is virtually dissolved by the action of Nicholas.

1689. **Turkey.** The Janissaries mutiny and are massacred. This occurrence leaves the Sultan without an army, and compels him to accept the whole of the Tsar's demands. The Convention of Ackermann confirms the Treaty of Bucharest. Russia is to occupy the fortresses on the East coast of the Black Sea, Russian ships to have the right of entering all Turkish waters, and Servia to elect its prince and manage its internal affairs. The princes of Moldavia and Wallachia are to be elected by the nobles for seven years, the Sultan not to refuse confirmation nor depose without consent of the Tsar. The princes are also enjoined to pay attention to Russian representations.

Russia declares war against Persia.

1690. **Asia.** The East India Company takes Assam.

[1827

1691. **England.** Lord Liverpool resigns; Canning becomes Prime Minister, and gives office to Palmerston and a few other Whigs. Wellington, Peel and Eldon refuse to serve with him (April), and withdraw. Canning dies four months later, and is succeeded by Goderich.

1692. **France.** The National Guards are broken up for demanding the charter and a free press. Villèle creates 76 new Peers and dissolves the Chambers; but the candidates of the Government are routed, and Villèle is forced to resign.

1693. **Portugal.** Miguel becomes Regent.

1694. **Greece.** A treaty is made by England, France, and Russia, pledging themselves to offer mediation and to demand an armistice, Greece to become autonomous. Secret articles declare that if the Sultan refuses mediation, the Powers shall themselves take steps to obtain an armistice, if possible without recourse to arms (July).

Ibrahim takes the Acropolis, and receives large reinforcements. The Sultan, encouraged by Metternich, refuses the mediation of the Powers. Lord Cochrane becomes Admiral of the Greek fleet, and Richard Church General of the land forces. The allied fleets, commanded by Codrington, call on Ibrahim to cease hostilities, and enter the harbour of Navarino to enforce submission; the Turkish fleet fires, and, after a sharp battle, is destroyed (Oct.). Ibrahim is recalled. The battle is described by Wellington as an untoward event, and, on the death of Canning, his

2632. **French Ch.** Montlosier, a Gallican, attacks the Jesuits, the Congregation, and the non-observance of the Articles of 1682.

2633. **American Ch.** Hicks, a Quaker, denies the divinity of Christ, and leaves the Society with many others.

2634. **Eng. Lit.** Disraeli's Vivian Grey and Bulwer's Pelham introduce the 'dandy school.'

2635. **French Lit.** De Vigny's Cinq-Mars.

2636. **German Lit.** Heine's Pictures of Travel.

Hauff's Lichtenstein.

Lachmann edits the Nibelungenlied texts.

2637. **Art.** Schadow's arrival ushers in the golden age of the Dusseldorf school of painting.

2638. **Science.** Élie de Beaumont and Dufrénoy construct a geological map of France.

Nobili's galvanometer proves the existence of an electric current in animals.

Dutrochet studies the respiration of plants.

Ohm's Law asserts that the electromotive force, divided by the resistance, equals the strength of the current.

Tiedemann and Gmelin study digestion.

Raffles founds the Zoological Society and Gardens in London.

2639. **Economics.** Rau, Hermann and Nebenius develope the ideas of Adam Smith and the 'classic' Political Economy. Van Thunen's Isolated State investigates the problems connected with the market and wages.

2640. **Politics.** Saint Simon's Nouveau Christianisme outlines a social system afterwards adopted by his pupil Comte.

2641. **Law.** Kent's Commentaries on American Law.

2642. **History.** The Monumenta Germaniæ Historica, planned by Stein and edited by Pertz, begin to appear.

2643. **Deaths.** Adams, Heber, Jefferson, Oberlin, Raffles.

2644. **Eng. Ch.** Keble's Christian Year. [1827

Heber's Hymns.

2645. **German Ch.** Hengstenberg's Kirchenzeitung revives Lutheran orthodoxy.

2646. **Eng. Lit.** The brothers Hare issue Guesses at Truth.

2647. **French Lit.** Victor Hugo's Preface to his drama Cromwell explains the romantic movement.

Stendhal's Racine et Shakspere maintains that all new works are romantic, and become classic with age.

2648. **Italian Lit.** Leopardi publishes his Moral Works.

2649. **Danish Lit.** Heiberg edits the Copenhagen Flying Post.

2650. **American Lit.** Dana's The Buccaneer.

2651. **Science.** Von Baer's Origin of the Ovum founds scientific Embryology, and shews that all ova are at first identical. His work is continued by Rudolph Wagner.

Green states his theorem concerning 'the potential,' of which he

policy is reversed, and Russia is left to continue the combat single-handed. The annihilation of the Turkish fleet, however, completely alters the conditions of the struggle.

1695. **Africa.** Waghorn organises transport between Cairo and Suez.

1696. **Asia.** A disputed succession leads to British intervention in Bhurtpore.

[1828

1697. **England.** Goderich resigns (Jan.), and Wellington and Peel take office, leaving Emancipation an open question. Huskisson, Palmerston, Lamb, and other Canningites resign, the ministry becoming purely Tory.

Russell carries the Repeal of the Corporation and Test Acts, admitting Nonconformists to Parliament, though retaining the declaration against Transubstantiation.

1698. **Ireland.** The Catholic Association is revived, and O'Connell is elected for Clare. His election is regarded as rendering Emancipation inevitable.

1699. **France.** Martignac forms a moderate ministry, which, however, is distrusted by the King, and receives no support from the Liberals.

1700. **Portugal.** Miguel seizes the crown and revokes the Constitution.

1701. **Russia.** The two years' war with Persia ends, Russia obtaining part of Armenia and forbidding Persia to possess armed ships on the Caspian.

1702. **Greece.** Capodistrias is appointed president of Greece for seven years, and is informed that Greece must remain tributary to the Sultan.

A French army is sent to expel Ibrahim from the Morea, and Capodistrias clears the country north of the Gulf of Corinth.

1703. **Turkey.** The Sultan summons the Mohamedan world to an attack on Russia, and expels the Christian residents in Constantinople. The Tsar declares war (April), and takes Varna, Kars, and Erzerum. The failure to take Silistria, however, encourages Metternich to another attempt to form a coalition against Russia.

1704. **America.** The 'Tariff of Abominations' imposes high duties on raw materials and on manufactured goods. In an Exposition and Protest, drawn up by Calhoun, South Carolina suggests a convention to declare the Act null and void. Webster foretells a Southern Confederacy.

Jackson is elected President, representing a nationalist democracy, and Calhoun Vice-President. Van Buren is chosen Secretary of State.

1705. **Africa.** The African Company being dissolved, 1821, the Government grants the Gold Coast to London merchants, who create the Gold Coast Protectorate.

---

proves the chief properties, and applies the results to electricity and magnetism. Gauss arrives independently at the same results, 1839.

2652. **Art.** Strauss 'Kettenbrücke' waltzes.

2653. **History.** Hallam's Constitutional History of England.

2654. **Education.** A Society for the Diffusion of Useful Knowledge is founded by Brougham and his friends.

2655. **Philology.** W. Humboldt's Letter to Rémusat on grammatical forms.

2656. **Deaths.** Beethoven, William Blake, Foscolo, Fresnel, La Place, Pestalozzi, Volta.

2657. **Eng. Ch.** Pusey replies to Rose's attack on German theology. [1828

Milman's History of the Jews is hotly attacked.

2658. **German Ch.** Ullmann founds the journal, Theologische Studien, as an organ of the disciples of Schleiermacher.

Gunther's Introduction to Speculative Theology is accused of denying Christianity.

2659. **Eng. Lit.** The Athenæum newspaper is founded.

Carlyle's Essay on Goethe calls attention to German Literature, hitherto studied only by William Taylor, Coleridge, and Crabb Robinson.

2660. **French Lit.** Villemain lectures at the Sorbonne on literature.

2661. **Science.** Wöhler produces urea, an organic compound, from an inorganic substance, ammonium cyanite, thus founding organic chemistry.

Abel discusses the higher transcendents of multiple periodicity, and founds the study of elliptic functions.

Cuvier's Histoire naturelle des Poissons.

Brongniart's Histoire des Végétaux Fossiles.

2662. **Art.** Sontag and Malibran make their début.

Ainmüller becomes director of the new painted glass manufactory in Munich, and works with transmitted light.

2663. **Philosophy.** Herbart's General Metaphysics asserts that the unit of being is the monad, the states of which are ideas and their relations, and which possesses no power of self-development.

Combe's Constitution of Man popularises phrenology and the idea of the connexion between mind and body.

2664. **Philology.** Noah Webster's English Dictionary.

2665. **History.** Guizot lectures at the Sorbonne.

Napier's History of the Peninsular War.

2666. **Law.** Jacob Grimm's Legal Antiquities.

2667. **Politics.** Coleridge's Constitution of Church and State maintains that the National Church should embrace the whole 'spiritual power' of the nation.

Bazard and Enfantin explain and develope the teaching of St Simon.

2668. **Social.** A sliding scale duty on corn is adopted, 36/8 when the price is 50/, decreasing as it rises and increasing as it falls.

1706. **England.** Wellington and Peel propose Catholic Emancipation, and overcome the King's resistance. [1829

Hume's motion for a Committee to consider the repeal of the Corn Laws obtains 12 votes.

1707. **Ireland.** O'Connell is re-elected for Clare, and begins to agitate for repeal. The Catholic Association is suppressed.

1708. **France.** Martignac is dismissed, and Polignac forms an ultra-royalist ministry. Lafayette leads an agitation against the Government.

1709. **Germany.** Prussia joins the Zollverein.

1710. **Spain.** The King marries for a fourth time, and issues a pragmatic sanction, abolishing the Salic Law. The King's brother, Don Carlos, protests. A daughter, Isabella, is born, and is recognised by the King as his heiress.

1711. **Portugal.** Chartists and Constitutionalists revolt against Miguel and declare for Maria.

1712. **Greece.** Russia, England, and France decide on the complete independence of Greece, and resolve to place a prince of one of the lesser royal houses on the throne.

1713. **Turkey.** The Russians cross the Balkans, take Silistria, and threaten Adrianople, where a treaty is signed. The Sultan recognises the independence of Greece. Russia resigns her conquests, except some islands at the mouth of the Danube and a strip of territory in Asia Minor. The Sultan is to pay a large indemnity. Moldavia and Wallachia become virtually independent, paying a fixed sum annually to the Porte, which withdraws its garrisons. The Hospodars are to be appointed for life. The navigation of the Danube becomes free, and vessels of neutral powers may pass through the Dardanelles. Polignac and Charles X. propose a partition of the Ottoman Empire, and a rearrangement of Europe.

1714. **America.** Jackson expels a large number of officials and substitutes his own friends and supporters, thus inaugurating the Spoils system. He neglects his official ministers for a group of personal friends, known as the Kitchen Cabinet.

1715. **Australasia.** Captain Stirling founds Western Australia.

Gibbon Wakefield's Letter from Sydney lays down the principles afterwards elaborated in his Art of Colonisation, urging the cessation of free grants of land, the regulation of the volume of emigration according to the needs of the colony, the maintenance of proportion in the sexes, and the systematic survey of territory.

1716. **England.** The Birmingham Political Union leads the cry for reform, but Wellington declares that the constitution admits of no improvement. He is defeated, and resigns (Nov.). Grey forms a ministry, including Russell, Althorp, Melbourne, Brougham, and Palmerston, and stipulates that reform shall be a Cabinet measure. [1830

1717. **France.** The Liberals form a majority in the new Parliament, led by Royer-Collard and Guizot, and carry votes of want of confidence.

2669. **German Ch.** Nitzsch's System of Christian Doctrine, an orthodox Lutheran presentation deeply influenced by Schleiermacher. [1829

2670. **American Ch.** The first Catholic Provincial Council is held.

2671. **Asiatic Ch.** Suttee is forbidden in India.

2672. **French Lit.** Sainte-Beuve's Joseph Delorme, Hugo's Orientales, Mérimée's Charles IX., and Dumas' Henri III. et sa Cour, apply the principles of romanticism.

2673. **Polish Lit.** Mickiewicz' Conrad Wallenrod, a poem on the struggles of the Poles against the Teutonic Knights.

2674. **Norwegian Lit.** Wergeland's Poems introduce romanticism.

2675. **Science.** Jacobi's Theory of Elliptic Functions.

Gauss enunciates the principle of least constraint.

Lobatchewsky continues the study of metageometry inaugurated by Gauss, and declares that the Euclidean axiom of parallels cannot be deduced from the others. The same result is reached independently by Bolyai, 1832.

Graham's Law states that the diffusion rate of gases is inversely as the square root of their density.

Nicol lays the foundation of microscopical petrology by improving the optical methods of investigation of rocks.

The Liverpool and Manchester railway is opened, Stephenson's engine moving 35 miles an hour.

2676. **Art.** Chopin's début as a pianist.

Rossini's William Tell.

Solger's Aesthetics, influenced by Schelling and Herbart, represent beauty as an immediate revelation of God.

2677. **Philosophy.** James Mill's Analysis of the Human Mind developes Hartley's doctrine of association.

Hamilton's article on the Philosophy of the Conditioned, in the Edinburgh Review, criticises the opinions of Cousin.

2678. **Philology.** Lobeck's Aglaophamus replies to Creuzer and declares that the Mysteries possessed no important esoteric knowledge.

Dobrovsky's Grammar of the Czech Language.

2679. **Education.** Thomas Arnold becomes Head Master of Rugby.

2680. **Social.** The first Temperance societies are founded in England.

Peel creates a new police for London.

Lady Blessington and Count D'Orsay open their salon in London.

2681. **Deaths.** Abel, Davy, F. Schlegel, Young.

2682. **Eng. Ch.** Mary Campbell of Rosneath begins to speak with tongues, and cases shortly occur in Irving's congregation in London. [1830

2683. **French Ch.** The Congregation is broken up, the bishops cease to sit in the House of Peers, and the new Government proclaims that Catholicism is no longer the State religion.

Lamennais founds a journal L'Avenir, aided by Montalembert, Lacordaire, Gerbet, Salinis, Rohrbacher, and advocates a free press and

The Chamber is dissolved, but its successor proves even more hostile. The King therefore issues Ordinances, dissolving the Chamber, suppressing the Liberal papers, and raising the property qualification (July 25). The Revolution of the 'Three Days' (July 27—9) takes place, and the King dismisses Polignac and withdraws the Ordinances. Meanwhile a provisional government is formed by Lafayette, Lafitte, and Casimir-Périer, who, with Thiers, invite Louis Philippe to become Lieutenant-General till the meeting of the Chamber. Orléans assures Charles of his fidelity; but the King and the Dauphin resign in favour of the Duke of Bordeaux, and ask Orléans to be Regent. A rumour spreads that Charles meditates an attack on Paris, and a mob marches to Rambouillet. Charles flies to England, and Orléans becomes King. A new Charter is issued. The press is freed, hereditary peerage is abolished, direct election is restored, the franchise is lowered, and the King is forbidden to suspend laws, to appoint extraordinary tribunals, or to employ foreign troops. The new ministry includes Lafitte, Casimir-Périer, Guizot, and De Broglie.

1718. **Belgium.** Relying on French support the Belgians rise against the King, and the Dutch troops are expelled. The provisional government proclaims independence, and summons a congress, which confirms the declaration and pronounces for a monarchy. A conference of the great Powers, to whom the King appeals, meets in London, and, largely owing to the influence of Palmerston, recognises the claims of Belgium to independence. Louis Philippe promises not to accept the crown, nor to allow the formation of a republic.

1719. **Germany.** The Duke of Brunswick is expelled (Sept.), and risings occur in Rhenish Prussia, Saxony, Hanover, and Hesse-Cassel. Saxony grants a Constitution, and concessions are made in several of the smaller principalities. The Young Germany movement revives.

1720. **Switzerland.** The oligarchy in certain of the large towns is overthrown, and constitutional reforms are introduced.

1721. **Poland.** Owing to breaches of the constitution since 1819, and to the activity of secret societies, a rising takes place at Warsaw, the Russians are massacred, and Adam Czartoryski becomes head of the provisional government. Terms are proposed to Nicholas, but are refused.

1722. **Greece.** A Conference in London defines the frontier of Greece. A constitution is granted, and the crown is offered to Leopold of Saxe-Coburg, who refuses it.

1723. **Turkey.** Milosch is confirmed as Prince of Servia, under the obligation to pay tribute to the Sultan and to maintain a Turkish garrison in Belgrade.

1724. **America.** In a debate on the disposal of public lands, Daniel Webster replies to Hayne's vindication of State Rights, and declares that the Constitution is not a compact, but an instrument formed by the 'People of the United States.'

After several attempts to throw off the authority of Bolivar, Columbia breaks up into New Granada (Columbia), Venezuela, and Ecuador, and Bolivar withdraws from public life and dies.

education, and cessation of the subsidy for the clergy. Montalembert and Lacordaire open a school, which is quickly suppressed.

2684. **German Ch.** Gerlach denounces Gesenius and Wegscheider of Halle as non-Christians.

2685. **Asiatic Ch.** Rammohun Roy founds the first Brahmo Somaj, or Theistic Church, in Calcutta.

2686. **Italian Ch.** Rosmini founds the Institute of Charity.

2687. **Eng. Lit.** Carleton's Traits and Stories of the Irish Peasantry.

2688. **French Lit.** Victor Hugo's Hernani is acted, and Gautier, his disciple, publishes his first poems.

Mérimée's Colomba.

Thiers founds a review, the National, and is shortly succeeded in the editorship by Armand Carrel.

2689. **German Lit.** Anastasius Grün's (Auersperg) The Last Knight.

2690. **Science.** Robert Brown studies structural and physiological botany.

Lyell's Principles of Geology continue the work of Hutton and enforce the doctrine of Uniformitarianism.

Audubon's Birds of America.

G. St Hilaire and Cuvier discuss the evolution or creation of animal types.

Vaughan Thompson discovers that barnacles are degenerate Crustacea, and studies the group Polyzoa.

2691. **Art.** Rauch begins his 20 years' work on the statue of Frederick the Great, Berlin.

King Ludwig of Bavaria commissions Klenze to build the Walhalla, on the model of the Parthenon, near Regensburg, and fills it with the busts of distinguished Germans. During the same period, Schinkel designs the Museum at Berlin in Classical style.

Auber's Fra Diavolo.

2692. **Philosophy.** Comte's Philosophie Positive declares that Thought has passed through a theological and a metaphysical stage, and has now entered a positive or scientific stage, in which the sciences are related and classified, and a sociology, or science of society, is reached.

Rosmini's Origin of Ideas introduces Kantianism into Italy.

Mackintosh's Dissertation on Ethical Philosophy supports Intuitionism, but adopts the Benthamite view of utility as a test of rightness.

2693. **Philology.** Nitzsch leads a reaction against Wolf and declares Homer to have founded the Epopee, i.e., to have blended old songs into an epic. Grote adopts this view, but adds that Homer's work, the 'Achilleid,' has been developed into an Iliad.

Freytag's Arabic Lexicon.

2694. **Politics.** Stahl's Philosophy of Law from a Historical Standpoint sketches the Christian state and attacks the conception of Naturrecht as involving too much human freedom.

Jouffroy defends the conception of Droit Naturel.

2695. **Law.** Speranski codifies the Russian law.

2696. **Education.** King's College, London, is founded for members of the Established Church.

1725. **Africa.** French troops land in Algiers to avenge an insult to their ambassador, and take Algiers. Constant fighting follows with Abdul Kader in East Algeria.

1726. **Asia.** Mysore is taken under British administration.

[1831

1727. **England.** Russell introduces a Reform Bill, to abolish 60 boroughs, and to deprive 46 others of one member, the seats being given to the counties and the great towns, eight to Scotland and five to Ireland. In the counties the franchise is given to £10 copyholders and £50 leaseholders, and in the boroughs to £10 householders (March). The second reading is carried by one, and on an amendment in committee against the reduction of members for England and Wales it is withdrawn and Parliament is dissolved. A great Whig majority returns, and the Bill, slightly amended, is passed, with the addition of the Chandos amendment, giving the franchise in counties to £50 tenants at will, but is rejected by the Lords. Riots break out at Bristol and in London, and the Bill is again introduced (Dec.).

Joseph Hume advocates the representation of the colonies.

1728. **Belgium.** The London Conference determines that Holland shall return to the boundaries of 1790, with the addition of Luxemburg, and that Belgium shall pay half the Dutch debt. These terms are rejected by Belgium, which elects Leopold of Saxe-Coburg, the English candidate. The great Powers grant Belgium more favourable terms, which, however, are rejected by the Dutch, who invade Belgium, but retire on the appearance of a French army and an English fleet. The London Conference draws up a third plan, dividing Luxemburg, and increasing Belgium's contribution to the debt. Belgium accepts these terms, and is recognised by all the Powers but Russia. Its neutrality is guaranteed by the Powers.

1729. **Italy.** A revolution breaks out in Modena, in the Papal States, where Louis Napoleon joins the insurgents, and in Parma. The rulers, however, are restored by the Austrian troops.

The direct male line of Savoy ends with the death of Charles Felix, and the crown passes to Charles Albert. Mazzini urges the new King to fulfil the promise of his youth.

1730. **Poland.** Nicholas is deposed, and a Russian army enters Poland (Feb.), and after meeting with a heroic resistance at Grochow and Ostrolenka takes Warsaw and Cracow. Many thousand Poles are sent to Siberia.

1731. **Denmark.** Frederick VI. creates legislative chambers in each province, to discuss new ordinances and approve taxes.

1732. **Greece.** Capodistrias is assassinated.

1733. **America.** The Liberator newspaper is established by Lloyd Garrison in Boston, urging immediate abolition of slavery without compensation.

2697. **Geography.** The African Association becomes the Geographical Society.

The Brothers Lander, sent out by the English Government, trace the Niger from Busa to the sea.

Sturt traces the course of the Murray.

2698. **Social.** Cholera first appears in Europe.

2699. **Death.** Fourier.

2700. **Scotch Ch.** McLeod Campbell is deposed from the ministry for his views on the universality of the Atonement. [1831

2701. **American Ch.** William Miller founds the Adventists.

2702. **Eng. Lit.** Peacock's Crotchet Castle.

2703. **French Lit.** Victor Hugo's Notre Dame.

Stendhal's Rouge et Noir.

Buloz founds the Revue des Deux Mondes.

2704. **German Lit.** Heine settles in Paris.

2705. **Russian Lit.** Pushkin's Eugène Oniéguine.

2706. **Science.** Murchison and Sedgwick begin to study strata, and differentiate the oldest fossiliferous formations as Cambrian, Silurian, and Devonian, thus completing palæozoic stratigraphy. Till this time nothing is known of the succession lower than the Old Red Sandstone.

Melloni constructs the thermo-multiplier for measuring invisible heat rays.

Faraday obtains electric currents from magnetism.

The British Association for Science is founded.

2707. **Art.** Bellini's La Somnambula.

Delaroche's Princes in the Tower founds the historic school of French painting (Louvre).

The works of the Barbizon School, Rousseau, Corot, Diaz, Dupré, Daubigny, are exhibited in the Salon.

David D'Angers' sculptures in the Pantheon and Baryé's first sculptures of animals are exhibited.

2708. **Philosophy.** Hegel dies, and his work is continued by Gabler, Ganz, Hinrichs, Michelet, Daub, Marheineke, Vatke, Rosenkranz. It is criticised in the sphere of logic by Weisse, Beneke, Stahl, Trendelenburg, I. H. Fichte; in theology by Strauss, Feuerbach, Fechner, Bruno Bauer.

2709. **Philology.** Lachmann's edition of the New Testament first throws aside the Textus Receptus.

2710. **Anthropology.** Pritchard's Eastern Origin of the Celtic Nations declares the Celts allied by language with the Slav, German, and Pelasgian stocks.

2711. **Education.** Stanley founds a school system in Ireland, and a grant of £30,000 is made.

Physical science and modern languages are adopted in the curriculum of the Jesuits.

2712. **History.** Böhmer collects and edits the Regesta of the mediæval Emperors from Conrad to Henry VII.

1734. **Asia.** Mehemet Ali invades Syria as a stepping-stone to Constantinople, and Acre is besieged by Ibrahim.

1735. **Australia.** Lord Ripon issues regulations imposing a minimum price on unoccupied lands, i.e. belonging to the Crown.

[1832

1736. **England.** The Reform Bill passes the Commons (March), and the Lords pass the second reading. An amendment to postpone the discussion of the disfranchising clauses is inserted by Lyndhurst. The Ministry asks the King to create 50 new Peers, and, on his refusal, resigns. Wellington offers to take office and introduce a partial reform Bill, but Peel refuses to join him. Grey returns, the King promises to create Peers, if necessary, and Wellington persuades his friends to allow the passage of the Bill (June). Fifty-six boroughs are abolished, and 30 lose one member. Sixty-five seats are given to the counties, two to 22 towns, and one to 21. The qualification proposed in 1831 is retained.

1737. **France.** Legitimists rise in La Vendée and republicans in Paris, but are suppressed, and the Duchesse de Berry is arrested. The death of the Duke of Reichstadt also strengthens the throne.

1738. **Belgium.** The Dutch King rejects the proposals of the London Conference. A French army takes Antwerp, and an English fleet blockades the Dutch coast. Leopold marries the daughter of Louis Philippe.

1739. **Germany.** The Diet forbids popular assemblies and festivals, and promises military aid to any sovereign threatened by revolution.

1740. **Italy.** A new revolt breaks out in the Romagna, and Austrian troops again intervene (Jan.). To appease the outcry against letting Austria occupy the Romagna, Louis Philippe seizes Ancona.

1741. **Switzerland.** The Siebener-Concordat is formed by the Protestant and liberal Cantons, and the Sarner Bund by the conservative and Catholic Cantons.

1742. **Poland.** Poland is declared a Russian province, with a separate administration, and Alexander's constitution is cancelled.

1743. **Hungary.** Szechenyi compels the nobles to contribute to the building of a bridge to unite Buda and Pesth.

1744. **Portugal.** Pedro, late Emperor of Brazil, lands in Portugal to support his daughter against Miguel, who is defeated.

1745. **Greece.** Otto of Bavaria accepts the Greek crown.

1746. **Turkey.** Samos becomes a principality, guaranteed by France, England and Russia, under the sovereignty of Turkey.

The Sultan declares war against Mehemet Ali, who has defeated the Pasha of Acre, but is himself defeated.

1747. **America.** Clay carries a new tariff, returning substantially to the rates of 1824. South Carolina, led by Calhoun, declares the Acts of 1828 and 1832 null and void, and forbids the payment of duties.

2713. **Economics.** Richard Jones shews that Ricardo's theory does not apply to peasant rents.

2714. **Social.** An experiment in communal farming is made at Ralahine in Ireland; but the land is shortly seized by the creditors of the landlord.

2715. **Deaths.** Bilderdyck, Gneisenau, Robert Hall, Hegel, Hermes, Krause, Niebuhr, Stein.

2716. **Eng. Ch.** Palmer's Origines Liturgicae prepares the way for the Oxford Movement; and Rose founds the British Magazine for the defence of High Church principles. [1832

Hampden's Bampton Lectures contend that our theology is inherited from scholasticism, and that 'an atmosphere of mist' parts us from primitive truth.

Dr Arnold's essay on Church Reform advocates the inclusion of Dissenters in the Church.

2717. **French Ch.** Lamennais' ideas are condemned in the bull, Mirari Vos. Montalembert and Lacordaire submit, but Lamennais revolts.

2718. **German Ch.** Möhler's Symbology insists on the impossibility of reunion, attacks the theory of justification by faith and asserts that Protestantism, though born of a real need, has degenerated. He is answered by Baur, Nitzsch and Marheineke.

The Gustavus Adolphus Society is founded to combat Catholicism; but the strict Lutherans hold aloof.

2719. **Church Hist.** Gregory XVI., enraged by the new Belgian Constitution, issues an Encyclical condemning freedom of conscience and of the press.

2720. **Eng. Lit.** Tennyson publishes the Lotos-Eaters, Oenone, the Palace of Art, the Dream of Fair Women and other poems.

2721. **French Lit.** Georges Sand's Indiana, her first great novel.

2722. **German Lit.** Goethe's Faust, part 2.

2723. **Italian Lit.** Silvio Pellico's My Imprisonment.

2724. **Norwegian Lit.** Welhaven attacks Wergeland from a conservative standpoint, and satirises the extravagances of romanticism.

2725. **Science.** Gauss anticipates the theory of equivalence of heat.

Gauss measures the earth's magnetic force.

Joseph Henry discovers electrical self-induction.

Steiner's Mutual Dependence of Geometrical Figures founds synthetic geometry.

Marshall Hall discovers the 'reflex action' of some nerve centres simultaneously with J. v. Müller.

De la Bêche obtains funds from the Board of Ordnance to colour Ordnance maps geologically.

2726. **Art.** Grisi's début in Paris.

Philippon, Henri Monnier and Gavarni found French caricature.

2727. **Philosophy.** Hegel's Philosophy of Religion is printed.

2728. **Law.** Austin's Province of Jurisprudence Determined reaches a

Jackson issues a nullification proclamation, condemning the doctrine of states' rights, and orders a fleet and troops to Charleston, and obtains the Force Bill from Congress. The nullification ordinances are in consequence suspended.

England occupies the Falkland Islands.

1748. **England.** Resolutions condemning the Corn Laws are [1833 rejected in the Commons.

Grote's motion for the ballot is rejected.

A Judicial Committee of the Privy Council is formed.

1749. **Ireland.** Stanley carries a Bill for trials in disturbed districts by court-martial, on the ground of systematic intimidation of juries.

Ten Bishoprics are suppressed, and their revenues are applied to make up church cess, which is abolished.

1750. **Belgium.** A preliminary treaty terminates hostilities.

1751. **Germany.** The Tsar, the Emperor of Austria and the Crown-Prince of Prussia form the League of Münchengrätz to guarantee each other's rights in Poland and to counteract the liberalising tendencies of England and France.

The King of Hanover grants a Constitution.

A rising at Frankfort (April) is followed by the introduction of an Austro-Prussian garrison, and new laws against the press and Universities.

The Zollverein is adopted by all the German states.

1752. **Spain.** Ferdinand leaves the crown to his daughter Isabella, aged three, and Christina acts as Regent. The Regency is recognised by England and France. Don Carlos at once claims, and is supported by the Basques and by the Church. Christina is therefore forced to gain the liberals by signing the Estatuto Real, establishing two chambers chosen by indirect election. French and English volunteer 'legions' are formed to support Christina.

1753. **Portugal.** Saldanha defeats the Miguelites by land, and Charles Napier destroys Miguel's fleet.

1754. **Turkey.** Mehemet Ali is compelled by Russian intervention to cease hostilities, but by the Peace of Kutaya receives the government of Syria and Egypt (April). The Sultan in return signs the Treaty of Unkiar Skelessi with Russia, which promises aid when required, secretly binding himself to close the Dardanelles to foreign war-ships when the Tsar is at war (July).

1755. **America.** Disliking the Bank, which is managed by his opponents, Jackson removes all Government deposits to local banks.

1756. **Asia.** The dominion of the East India Company is confirmed for 20 years; but its monopoly of the Chinese trade is abolished. A legal member is added to the Governor's Council, and a penal code is drafted under the direction of Macaulay.

---

pure science of positive law and classifies institutions irrespective of their origin and justification.

2729. **Social.** Capital punishment for forgery, coining, horse-stealing, sheep-stealing, and sacrilege is abolished.

2730. **Deaths.** Bentham, Champollion, Cuvier, Gentz, Goethe, Krause, Mackintosh, Scott.

2731. **Eng. Ch.** Keble's Assize Sermon on National Apostasy denounces the suppression of Irish bishoprics, and is afterwards declared by Newman to have inaugurated the Oxford Movement. A conference takes place at Rose's house at Hadleigh, and the Tracts for the Times begin to appear. Newman becomes Vicar of St Mary's. [1833

The Congregational Union adopts a confession and discipline.

Nonconformists are allowed to celebrate marriages in their chapels, and Quakers to substitute an affirmation for an oath.

2732. **French Ch.** The Abbé Bautain's Philosophie du Christianisme, declaring that reason cannot reveal God, is condemned by Rome. Traditionalism is taught by Ubaghs in Belgium, Donoso Cortes in Spain, and Ventura in Italy.

2733. **Church Hist.** The Church of Greece declares itself independent.

2734. **Eng. Lit.** Carlyle's Sartor Resartus appears in Fraser's Magazine.

2735. **French Lit.** The Académie des Sciences Morales et Politiques is revived.

Janin becomes theatrical critic of the Journal des Débats.

2736. **Swedish Lit.** Runeberg's The Elk-hunters, an epic.

2737. **Science.** Faraday discovers the law of electro-chemical equivalents.

Weber and Gauss construct an electric telegraph.

2738. **Art.** Rude's Neapolitan Fisher Boy.

Ivanof paints the Appearance of the Messiah among the People.

2739. **Philology.** Bopp's Comparative Grammar first fully reveals the relationship of the different Indo-European languages.

Gesenius' Lexicon Hebraicum.

Pott's Studies in the Indo-Germanic Languages bases etymology on phonology.

2740. **Law.** Edward Livingston's Code of Criminal Law and Procedure.

2741. **Education.** Guizot establishes schools in every French Commune.

The first government grant is made to English schools.

2742. **Social.** By the efforts of Fowell Buxton, Zachary Macaulay, Wilberforce and others, slavery is abolished throughout the British Empire by 20 millions being granted in compensation.

Children under nine are excluded from cotton mills, and Inspectors are appointed.

A National Trades' Union is organised by Owen and Fielden, who urge a general strike for 8 hours. The money, however, is lost in several small strikes, and the association collapses, 1834.

2743. **Deaths.** Legendre, Rammohun Roy, Wilberforce.

1757. **England.** Stanley, Graham and Lord Ripon resign on a proposal to appropriate further revenues of the Irish Church (May). Lord Grey, finding himself in growing discord with his party, also resigns, and Melbourne forms a Cabinet. But when Lord Althorp, leader of the Commons, becomes Earl Spencer by his father's death (Nov.), the King seizes the opportunity to dismiss the Ministry. Peel, who is staying in Rome, is appointed Prime Minister, and, in an address to his constituents at Tamworth, declares for moderate reform. [1834

Palmerston forms a Quadruple Alliance with France, Spain and Portugal, to prevent the defeat of constitutionalism in Spain and Portugal.

Six Dorsetshire labourers are sentenced to seven years' transportation for administering an oath.

1758. **Ireland.** O'Connell's motion for the repeal of the Union is defeated by 523 to 38.

1759. **Italy.** Mazzini founds Young Europe, and an Italian, a German and a Polish section are organised. He also organises a raid into Savoy from Geneva.

1760. **Spain.** The Carlist war begins, and the Queen receives promise of support from England and France. The Basque provinces, in their desire to escape centralisation, support Don Carlos.

1761. **Portugal.** By the Treaty of Evoramente, Maria is recognised, and Miguel undertakes to quit Portugal and renounce his claim in consideration of a pension.

1762. **Switzerland.** The Confederate Assembly dissolves the Sarner Bund.

1763. **Hungary.** The Diet of Transylvania, which has not been summoned since 1811, attacks the Court and is dissolved, and Wesselenyi, the leader of the opposition, is exiled.

1764. **Australasia.** A South Australian Association is formed by Buller, Grote, Molesworth, Torrens, to carry out the ideas of Gibbon Wakefield. The first emigrants settle, 1836.

1765. **England.** Though the Conservatives gain in the election, Peel finds himself in a minority in the new Parliament, and the Whigs make the 'Lichfield House Compact' with O'Connell. Peel is outvoted and resigns, after four months of office, and Melbourne succeeds, with Russell as leader of the House (April). [1835

By the Municipal Corporations Bill, the Mayor and Corporation are to be elected by the ratepayers. London is excepted from the operation of the bill, the investigation of its history and circumstances being incomplete.

1766. **France.** Fieschi attempts the King's life, and the 'Laws of September' to gag the press and control political trials are passed.

1767. **Germany.** The Diet forbids the publication of the works of Heine and Börne and of other writers of the Young Germany school.

2744. **Eng. Ch.** The Lords defeat the admission of nonconformists to University degrees. [1834

2745. **Scotch Ch.** Chalmers carries a Veto Act in the General Assembly, giving the people the veto on an unacceptable candidate. The Court of Session and House of Lords support the right of patrons and rejected presentees in the Auchterarder case.

2746. **Portuguese Ch.** The monasteries are suppressed.

2747. **Eng. Lit.** Henry Taylor's drama, Philip van Artevelde.

2748. **French Lit.** Balzac's Père Goriot.

Lamennais' Paroles d'un Croyant, a theistic and socialistic rhapsody.

2749. **Russian Lit.** Bielinski begins his criticisms of Russian literature.

2750. **Polish Lit.** Mickiewicz' poem, Thaddeus, sketches Polish Life.

2751. **Science.** John Herschel reaches the Cape of Good Hope and commences his four years' survey of the southern heavens.

Dumas discovers the Law of Substitution.

Faraday discovers electric self-induction.

Milne-Edwards' Histoire Naturelle des Crustacés.

Duméril's Histoire Naturelle des Reptiles.

Ehrenberg investigates the growth of coral reefs.

Schwann discovers the envelope of the nerve-fibres ('Schwann's sheath'), and studies muscular contractility.

Hamilton enunciates a principle for obtaining the equations of motion in dynamics.

2752. **Art.** Meissonier's Chess Party.

Schumann's Symphonic Studies.

2753. **Philology.** Csoma Körösi's Tibetan Dictionary and Grammar.

2754. **History.** Bancroft's History of the United States.

2755. **Social.** The New Poor Law, framed on the Report of Senior, Blomfield, and Sumner, forbids out-door relief.

2756. **Deaths.** Coleridge, Lafayette, Lamb, Malthus, Schleiermacher.

2757. **Eng. Ch.** Wiseman returns to England, and lectures on the beliefs and system of Catholicism. The Dublin Review appears and the Catholic revival begins. [1835

A proposal to abolish subscription at matriculation is defeated by the High Churchmen. Pusey joins the movement and contributes a Tract on Baptism.

Blanco White becomes a Unitarian.

2758. **French Ch.** Lacordaire preaches at Notre Dame.

2759. **German Ch.** Vatke's Biblical Theology declares the Levitical law post-exilic, an assertion later adopted by Graf. Reuss reaches a similar conclusion about the same time.

Strauss' Life of Jesus attacks the miracles and places the Gospels in the second century.

2760. **Italian Ch.** Perrone's Praelectiones Theologicae.

1768. **Spain.** Zumalacarregui, the ablest Carlist leader, dies; but the Carlists win a number of victories, and the cause of the Queen is weakened by the dissensions between the Moderados and Progresistas.

1769. **Austria.** Ferdinand I. succeeds, but Metternich retains power.

Gaj advocates 'Illyrism,' a movement to unite the Illyrian states; but the scheme is opposed by Hungarians and Servians.

1770. **America.** Jackson compels France to pay indemnity for damage to American commerce since 1803.

War breaks out with the Seminole Indians.

1771. **Australasia.** The Port Phillip Association founds Victoria.

1772. **Africa.** The Sultan reasserts his authority in Tripoli.

[1836

1773. **England.** The division lists are published by the House of Commons.

Tithe in kind is commuted into a rent-charge, to vary with the price of corn.

1774. **Ireland.** The Orange Lodges, which have increased in numbers and activity, owing to the success of the Catholics, are dissolved.

The Irish Tithe Bill is resisted by the Lords and abandoned by the Government.

1775. **France.** Louis Napoleon, son of Napoleon's brother, Louis, King of Holland, tries to stir up a rising among the troops at Strasburg, but fails, and is sent to America.

Thiers becomes Premier, but fails to obtain the approval of the King for his proposal to support the Spanish constitutionalists, and resigns.

1776. **Spain.** The Progresistas compel Christina to re-establish the Constitution of 1812. Espartero takes command, and defeats the Carlists with the aid of an English fleet and troops.

1777. **Portugal.** The Queen confirms the Constitution of 1822, and the adherents of Miguel are finally suppressed.

1778. **Switzerland.** In consequence of an attack on the life of Louis Philippe, Thiers, supported by Austria, compels Switzerland to expel all political refugees.

1779. **Italy.** Lambruschini, the leader of the reactionaries, becomes Papal secretary.

1780. **Bohemia.** The publication of Palacky's History of the Bohemians first acquaints the Czechs with their past, and more than anything else contributes to revive the spirit of Bohemian nationality. It is aided by Safarik's Slavic Antiquities.

1781. **Russia.** Tchadaieff's Philosophical Letters attack the government and the country for their resistance to western ideas, and ridicule Aksakov and other Slavophils.

1782. **America.** Petitions against Slavery are presented to Congress, and 'gag resolutions' are passed, forbidding their consideration. Adams protests, presents a petition and defends himself against the proposal of censure.

2761. **Eng. Lit.** Browning's Paracelsus.
Walker's humorous periodical, the Original.
2762. **French Lit.** Jasmin's Gascon poems, Papillotos.
2763. **German Lit.** Grimm's German Mythology.
Bettina v. Arnim publishes Goethe's Correspondence with a Child.
2764. **Danish Lit.** Hans Andersen's first Fairy Tales.
2765. **Finnish Lit.** The Kalevala is collected and published.
2766. **Science.** Hooker institutes a botanical laboratory at Kew.
2767. **Art.** Donizetti's Lucia di Lammermoor.
2768. **Philosophy.** Quetelet's La Physique Sociale.
2769. **Philology.** W. Humboldt investigates the Kawi language of Java.
2770. **Politics.** De Tocqueville's Democracy in America.
Cobden's pamphlets, England, Ireland and America, and Russia advocate free trade and non-intervention.
2771. **Education.** The introduction of Western culture and the use and study of the English language into India is determined.
University College, London, is allowed to grant degrees.
2772. **History.** Thirlwall's History of Greece.
2773. **Deaths.** Cobbett, W. v. Humboldt.

2774. **Eng. Ch.** Newman's Prophetical Office of the Church defines the theory of the Oxford movement. [1836
Tithe-Commutation is effected.
The Ecclesiastical Commissioners are incorporated.
Hampden is appointed Regius Professor of Theology at Oxford, but is fiercely attacked by the High Churchmen and censured by the University.
The Presbyterian Church of England establishes a Synod.
2775. **German Ch.** Görres' Christian Mysticism.
Fliedner institutes deaconesses in the Lutheran Church.
2776. **Italian Ch.** The Jesuits control the College of the Propaganda.
2777. **Eng. Lit.** Dickens' Sketches by Boz, and Pickwick.
2778. **French Lit.** De Musset's Confession d'un Enfant du Siècle.
Émile de Girardin edits La Presse.
Lamartine's Jocelyn.
2779. **German Lit.** Rückert's Wisdom of the Brahmans.
2780. **Russian Lit.** Gogol's The Revisor attacks official corruption.
2781. **Hungarian Lit.** Josika writes his first novel, Abafi.
2782. **American Lit.** Emerson's lecture on Nature founds Transcendentalism.
2783. **Science.** Struve's Investigations of double and composite stars.
2784. **Art.** Meyerbeer's The Huguenots.
Glinka's opera, Life for the Tsar.
2785. **Philology.** Burnouf deciphers inscriptions at Ecbatana.
Diez' Grammar of the Romance Languages.

Emigrants from the Southern States overturn the constitution of Texas as part of the Mexican republic, adopt a new constitution, and, under Houston, proclaim independence from Mexico. The Texans desire to be admitted as a slave state; but Jackson and Van Buren refuse.

1783. **Australasia.** South Australia receives a government, and Adelaide becomes the capital.

1784. **Africa.** Owing to inadequate compensation for the abolition of slavery and for the damage done by Kaffir inroads, and to their exclusion from political privileges, a large number of Boers 'trek' from Cape Colony and settle in Natal. After desperate fighting, they break the power of the Zulus, depose their King, Dingan, and set up another King, Panda.

1785. **England.** Victoria, daughter of the Duke of Kent, becomes Queen. In the interval between her accession and her marriage, she is guided chiefly by Lord Melbourne and by Baron Stockmar, a close friend of her uncle, King Leopold. [1837

The Working Men's Association is formed, and a Charter of six points is adopted, demanding manhood suffrage, the ballot, annual Parliaments, payment of members, abolition of property qualification, equal electoral districts.

Grote proposes the ballot.

1786. **Germany.** On the death of William IV. of England, Hanover passes to his brother, the Duke of Cumberland, who ascends the throne as Ernest I., abolishes the Constitution of 1833, and dismisses Jacob and Wilhelm Grimm, Dahlmann, Gervinus, Ewald, Weber, and other Göttingen professors who protest.

1787. **Spain.** Don Carlos is decisively defeated.

The Constituent Cortes draw up a Constitution of two Chambers, but allowing the sovereign greater power than that conferred by the Constitution of 1812.

1788. **Russia.** Vitkievitch is sent as the first Russian agent to Afghanistan.

1789. **America.** Wendell Phillips joins Garrison in his crusade against slavery. The first abolitionist martyr, Lovejoy, an editor, is murdered. Anti-slavery opinion begins to grow rapidly in New England.

In Canada complaints are made of misgovernment in both French and English provinces, and a rebellion breaks out under Papineau.

The National Debt being paid off, Jackson lends the surplus revenue to the States without interest, his policy provoking a mania for speculation.

1790. **Asia.** Despite the protests of England, the Shah of Persia, under Russian influence, invades Afghanistan as an ancient possession of Persia, and besieges Herat. After 10 months the Persians withdraw, on the threat of English intervention. Lord Auckland in alarm sends Burnes to urge Dost Mohammed to ally with England. Burnes

2786. **History.** Mignet edits the negotiations relative to the Spanish Succession.

Palacky's History of Bohemia.

2787. **Politics.** A Communist League is founded in Paris.

2788. **Law.** Wheaton's International Law developes the idea of neutrality.

2789. **Education.** London University becomes a purely examining body, the teaching being carried on by University College.

2790. **Deaths.** A. M. Ampère, Armand Carrel, Godwin, Jussieu, James Mill, Sieyès.

2791. **French Ch.** Ravignan preaches at Notre-Dame. [1837

2792. **German Ch.** The Archbishop of Cologne is imprisoned by the King of Prussia for rejecting his predecessor's compromise on mixed marriages; the Archbishop of Gnesen and Posen and others are similarly treated. An Ultramontanist party is in consequence formed, led by Görres in Munich. On the accession of Frederick William IV., 1840, the laws cease to be enforced.

Rothe's Beginnings of the Christian Church declares that Christ did not found a Church, and that the function of the Church is to create the ideal State in which it will be merged.

2793. **Swiss Ch.** Vinet becomes Professor of Practical Theology at Lausanne, and advocates the entire separation of Church and State.

2794. **Danish Ch.** Grundtvig's Songs for the Danish Church.

2795. **American Ch.** The Presbyterians split into Old School and New School, the latter being charged with Arminianism.

2796. **Church Hist.** Hodgson discovers Northern Buddhist literature in Nepal.

2797. **Eng. Lit.** Lockhart's Life of Scott.

Barham commences to write the Ingoldsby Legends.

2798. **German Lit.** Eckermann publishes his Conversations with Goethe.

2799. **Russian Lit.** Lermontof's Elegy on Pushkin's death.

2800. **Flemish Lit.** Conscience's Flemish novel, the Year of Miracles.

2801. **Literature.** Pitman invents a system of shorthand.

2802. **Science.** Agassiz proves a glacial period.

Dana's System of Mineralogy.

Schwann attacks the theory of spontaneous generation.

Mohrs' paper, On the Nature of Heat, first enunciates the theory of the conservation of energy.

Cooke and Wheatstone improve the electric telegraph, which is perfected by Morse, whose instrument and alphabet are rapidly adopted.

Gould's Birds of Europe.

2803. **Art.** Cruikshank illustrates Oliver Twist.

2804. **Philology.** Lepsius' Hieroglyphic Alphabet.

Grotefend deciphers cuneiform inscriptions of Persia.

promises him aid in his domestic quarrels; but Auckland refuses to ratify this agreement.

A British ambassador is allowed to reside at Canton.

1791. **Australasia.** The New Zealand Association is established, of which Gibbon Wakefield becomes managing director.

1792. **Africa.** Constantine is taken by the French, and a peace is made with Abdelkader; but war breaks out again, 1839.

1793. **England.** Villiers' first motion to consider the Corn Laws is rejected by 300 to 95. An Anti-Corn Law League is formed in Manchester by Cobden and Bright. [1838

1794. **Ireland.** Drummond, the Chief Secretary, announces that property has its duties as well as its rights. A Poor Law is passed to save evicted tenants from starvation; and a Tithe Act levies tithe on the landowner instead of on the tenant, the appropriation clause having been dropped to disarm the Lords.

1795. **France.** At the demand of France, Switzerland expels Louis Napoleon, who settles in England.

1796. **Italy.** The Austrians evacuate the Papal States (but retain Ferrara), and the French withdraw from Ancona.

1797. **America.** The rebellion is suppressed. Lord Durham is appointed Governor General of Canada, and on his arrival transports rebels to Bermuda, and threatens them with death if they return. He is in consequence recalled; but his advice, contained in a report drawn up chiefly by Charles Buller on the lines of Gibbon Wakefield, is taken, the two colonies are united, and the legislature receives control over the executive.

France declares war on Mexico, and captures Vera Cruz. Peace is restored, 1839.

1798. **Asia.** Dost Mohammed receives a Russian mission at Cabul, and England declares war.

1799. **Africa.** Mehemet Ali refuses to pay tribute to the Sultan, and claims the hereditary Governorship of Egypt and Syria.

1800. **England.** Spring-Rice announces a deficit without proposing a remedy, and the majority falls to five. Melbourne resigns, and Peel, who forms a government, demands the removal of the relatives of the late government among the ladies of the Queen's bedchamber. The Queen refuses, Peel declines office, and Melbourne returns. [1839

Meetings are held in support of the Charter, and a national convention of delegates from the great towns, led by Fergus O'Connor and

2805. **Education.** Froebel institutes his first Kindergarten.
Horace Mann reforms Education in Massachusetts.
2806. **History.** Ranke's History of the Popes.
Carlyle's History of the French Revolution.
Prescott's Ferdinand and Isabella.
Spruner's Historico-Geographical Atlas.
2807. **Anthropology.** Zeuss' The Germans and the Neighbour Races.
2808. **Deaths.** Colebrooke, Leopardi, Pushkin.

2809. **Eng. Ch.** Newman's Lectures on Justification. [1838
Froude's Remains, edited by Newman and Keble, condemn the Reformation. Newman is joined by W. G. Ward.
2810. **French Ch.** Lacordaire revives the Dominican Order in France.
2811. **Eng. Lit.** The Sterling Club is formed, of which Carlyle, Mill, Thirlwall, Wilberforce, Trollope, Trench, Hare, Maurice, are members.
2812. **French Lit.** Rachel's début revives the French classical drama.
2813. **Science.** Schleiden's Cellular Theory of Plants.
Bessel measures the distance of a fixed star (61 Cygni).
Miller founds geometrical crystallography on a true basis.
The London and Birmingham Railway, the work of Robert Stephenson, is opened.
The Sirius and the Great Western cross the Atlantic.
2814. **Art.** Jenny Lind's début.
Menzel illustrates Kugler's Life of Frederick the Great.
2815. **Philosophy.** The Hallische Jahrbücher, edited by Ruge, champions Hegelianism, but in 1841 turns to radical politics, supported by Blum, Herwegh, Marx, Freiligrath, Gutzkow, Börne.
2816. **Philology.** Julius Mohl translates the Shah-Nameh of Firdusi.
2817. **Politics.** Lieber's Political Ethics.
2818. **Economics.** Cournot applies mathematics to economics.
2819. **History.** Ranke edits the Year-books of mediaeval Germany.
Arnold's History of Rome.
2820. **Geography.** Eyre explores Australia from East to West.
2821. **Social.** Father Mathew undertakes a Temperance crusade in Ireland.
Chadwick obtains a Sanitary Commission in Whitechapel.
2822. **Deaths.** Möhler, Talleyrand, Sylvestre de Sacy.

2823. **Eng. Ch.** Newman studies Monophysitism, and is 'hit' by Wiseman's article in the Dublin Review on the Donatists. [1839
2824. **German Ch.** Dorner's History of the Doctrine of the Person of Christ.
Julius Müller's Christian Doctrine of Sin defends the ideas of personality and liberty in God and man against pantheism and determinism.
2825. **Russian Ch.** Philaret, Metropolitan of Moscow, composes a

Ernest Jones, draws up a petition to Parliament, which, however, refuses to consider it.

1801. **France.** Les Saisons, a secret Socialist Society, organises a revolt in Paris, but is put down.

1802. **Spain.** Espartero compels the Basques and the North to recognise Christina. Don Carlos resigns his claim to his son. The Regent attempts to rule with the Moderados, who are supported by France. England, however, supports the Progresistas.

1803. **Belgium.** Holland accepts the proposals of 1831.

1804. **Russia.** An expedition under Perofski, sent to attack Khiva and to prevent the East India Company gaining influence in Central Asia, fails.

1805. **Turkey.** The Sultan determines to prevent Mehemet Ali from becoming completely independent, and declares war on Egypt. Ibrahim routs the Turks at Nisib (June). Sultan Mahmoud dies a few days later, and is succeeded by his son, Abdul Mezid. On this the Turkish admiral, who has orders to attack the Syrian coast, sails to Alexandria and surrenders his fleet to Mehemet Ali, who plans to supplant the Sultan. France encourages Mehemet; but Palmerston resolves to maintain the power of Turkey.

Reshid Pasha persuades the new Sultan, Abdul Mezid, to issue a scheme of reforms, but fails to obtain support in their execution, and a reaction sets in.

1806. **America.** The Confederation of Central America is dissolved. The Republic of Honduras is proclaimed.

1807. **Asia.** A British army enters Afghanistan, deposes Dost Mohammed, and places Shah Soojah on the throne.

The English in Canton are forced to surrender their opium and to leave China (May). War breaks out, and Hong Kong is taken.

Aden is annexed by England.

1808. **Africa.** A French settlement is founded on the Congo coast.

1809. **England.** The Queen marries Albert of Saxe-Coburg-Gotha. [1840

1810. **Ireland.** The Irish Municipal Act is passed.

O'Connell renews the repeal agitation.

1811. **France.** Louis Napoleon lands at Boulogne and tries to excite an insurrection (Aug.), but is captured (Oct.), and condemned to lifelong imprisonment at Ham, whence he escapes to England, 1846.

Thiers fails to persuade the King to actively support Mehemet Ali against the Coalition, and falls. Guizot becomes supreme.

The remains of Napoleon are brought from St Helena and buried in the Church of the Invalides at Paris.

Guizot mentions the plan of a Spanish marriage for one of the King's sons, in conversation with Palmerston.

1812. **Spain.** Christina is forced to retire to France.

Catechism, which is authorised by the Holy Synod and used in the schools and churches.

The two million Uniates are declared by a Ukase incorporated with the Greek Church. A few Uniate Churches continue to exist in Galicia, South Hungary and Transylvania.

2826. **Swiss Ch.** Strauss is appointed Professor at Zurich, but is expelled.

2827. **Eng. Lit.** Lever's Harry Lorrequer.

2828. **American Lit.** The Lowell Lectures are instituted at Boston.

Longfellow's Hyperion.

2829. **Italian Lit.** Carcano's novel, Angiola Maria.

2830. **Portuguese Lit.** Almeida-Garrett's works found the romantic school.

2831. **Polish Lit.** Krasewski's poem, The World and the Poet.

2832. **Science.** Leverrier studies the relations of the planets.

Daguerre invents a process of photography, which is improved by Talbot by introducing a negative.

Schwann studies the structure of the elementary textures, and shews that the same cellular structure exists in the simpler plants and animals.

Ehrenberg points out the share of the remains of minute organisms in chalk and other formations.

Agassiz' Fresh-water Fishes of Europe.

Purkinje founds the first physiological institute at Breslau and applies the microscope.

2833. **Art.** Wiertz' picture of Patroclus (Brussels).

Turner's Fighting Téméraire.

2834. **Philosophy.** Gioberti's Introduction to the study of Philosophy tends towards Hegelianism.

2835. **Philology.** Madvig edits Cicero's De Finibus.

2836. **Education.** Russell founds the Committee of Council, and introduces a system of inspection and report. A Vice-President is appointed 1856.

2837. **Death.** Speranski.

2838. **Eng. Ch.** Palmer visits the Russian Church to discuss reunion. [1840

2839. **Scotch Ch.** Thomas Guthrie begins to preach in Edinburgh.

2840. **American Ch.** Emerson addresses the Divinity School at Cambridge, Massachusetts, from a frankly rationalistic standpoint.

2841. **Church Hist.** The Jews are accused of human sacrifice in Rhodes and Damascus. Montefiore goes to the East, and obtains from the Sultan a firman dismissing the charges, and declaring the equality of Jews before the law.

2842. **French Lit.** Maurice de Guérin's Le Centaur.

Sainte-Beuve's Histoire de Port Royal.

2843. **German Lit.** Geibel's Poems.

2844. **American Lit.** Margaret Fuller and Emerson edit the Dial, the

1813. **Turkey.** Palmerston persuades Prussia and Austria to conclude the Treaty of London, shortly joined by Russia, to compel Mehemet Ali to restore Syria and Crete (July). An English fleet is sent, and is joined by Turkish and Austrian ships; Ibrahim is defeated in Syria, and Beyrout and Acre are bombarded. Mehemet receives Egypt as a hereditary possession, paying tribute to the Sultan.

1814. **America.** To cope with the financial crisis, Van Buren makes large vaults in the chief cities, where government funds are to be received and paid out. In the presidential election, Harrison, the Whig candidate, is successful, but dies a month after his installation, and is succeeded by the Vice-President Tyler, an extreme Democrat of the Calhoun school.

Lopez succeeds to supreme power in Paraguay.

1815. **Australasia.** The Treaty of Waitangi is concluded with the Maoris, who cede their sovereignty, i.e. their political rights, to the Queen. Their lands are guaranteed, but pre-emption is claimed by the Government.

The transportation of convicts to New South Wales ceases.

1816. **Asia.** An English fleet blockades Canton, and takes Chusan, after which a truce is concluded.

Dost Mohammed surrenders, and leaves the country.

[1841

1817. **England.** To make up the deficit, a fixed duty of 8*s.* a quarter on corn and a sugar duty are proposed. Peel carries a vote of want of confidence by one. Melbourne resigns, Peel obtains a very large majority, and includes Stanley, Graham, and Ripon in his Ministry. The question of the Queen's household is compromised.

Delane becomes editor of the Times, in which Henry Reeve now begins to write the leading articles on foreign policy.

1818. **Germany.** Jacoby's Four Questions Answered claims the grant of the constitution promised to Prussia.

1819. **Switzerland.** The monasteries are abolished in Aargau, and Lucerne answers by admitting the Jesuits and giving them the control of education.

1820. **Spain.** Espartero is appointed Regent during the minority of Isabella.

1821. **Hungary.** Kossuth and Deak supplant Szechenyi in the leadership of the nationalist party, and Kossuth, who has been imprisoned by Metternich and is now released, founds a political daily paper.

1822. **Turkey.** Mehemet Ali restores the Turkish fleet, and his position in Egypt is recognised. The Powers, including France, sign a convention by which the Dardanelles are closed to all ships of war, Russia thus sacrificing her rights under the treaty of Unkiar Skelessi. The Sultan is placed under the protection of Europe.

Canning again becomes British Ambassador at Constantinople.

organ of the American Transcendentalists, aided by Freeman Clarke, Channing, Theodore Parker, Thoreau, Ripley.

2845. **Science.** Biot's researches on the polarisation of light.

Liebig's Chemistry in application to Agriculture and Physiology.

Reichert, aided by Kölliker and Virchow, proves all organs to be derived from the multiplication and combination of cells.

Forbes' British Star-fishes.

Hugh Miller's Old Red Sandstone.

2846. **Art.** Clara Wieck marries Schumann and performs his works.

Barry designs the Houses of Parliament, aided by Pugin, the greatest work of the Gothic revival in England.

2847. **Archaeology.** Fellows discovers Xanthus and other Lycian cities.

2848. **Philosophy.** Trendelenburg's Logical Investigations attack Hegel.

2849. **Politics.** Proudhon's Qu'est-ce que la Propriété declares that government will become unnecessary when the causes of ill-doing are removed.

2850. **Social.** Rowland Hill introduces the penny post.

2851. **Deaths.** Olbers, Paganini, Poisson.

2852. **Eng. Ch.** Tait and three other Oxford tutors issue a Protest against Tract 90, in which Newman explains the 39 Articles in a Catholic sense. Newman is censured by the Hebdomadal Board, and the Bishop of Oxford persuades him to bring the Tracts to a close. Newman is deeply affected by the agreement, negotiated by Bunsen, for Prussia and England jointly to institute a bishopric at Jerusalem. [1841

Miall founds and edits The Nonconformist.

2853. **Italian Ch.** Don Bosco founds the Oratory of St Francis de Sales for work among boys.

2854. **American Ch.** Theodore Parker preaches on Transient and Permanent Elements in Christianity.

2855. **African Ch.** Livingstone begins missionary work in S. Africa.

2856. **Australasian Ch.** Selwyn becomes first Bishop of New Zealand.

2857. **Church Hist.** Cureton publishes the Syriac version of three of Ignatius' Epistles.

2858. **Eng. Lit.** Mark Lemon edits Punch, which Leech illustrates and to which Gilbert à Beckett, Douglas Jerrold and Thackeray contribute.

2859. **French Lit.** Mérimée's Colomba.

2860. **German Lit.** Herwegh's Poems.

Hebbel's Judith.

Hackländer's Pictures from the Life of Soldiers.

2861. **Dutch Lit.** Paludan-Müller's Adam Homo.

2862. **Italian Lit.** D'Azeglio's Niccolo de Lapi.

1823. **America.** Negotiations begin concerning the frontier line between Venezuela and British Guiana.

Horace Greely begins to edit the New York Tribune.

1824. **Australasia.** New Zealand becomes a separate colony.

1825. **Asia.** A treaty made by the Chinese Commissioner, ceding Hong Kong, is disavowed by the Emperor, and the war continues.

An insurrection at Cabul takes place, and Burnes and others are murdered. The officers agree to withdraw the army.

1826. **Africa.** The Great Powers agree to allow mutual right of search in order to suppress the slave trade.

A treaty of commerce is made between England and Abyssinia, and a consul is shortly appointed.

[1842

1827. **England.** Peel reimposes Pitt's income-tax for three years, and lowers a number of duties. In regard to corn, he carries a sliding scale duty of 20*s.* when the price of corn is 51*s.*, decreasing to 1*s.* at 73*s*.

A great Chartist petition is drawn up; but a motion to hear counsel in its support is lost.

1828. **Ireland.** The Young Ireland movement, working on parallel lines to that of O'Connell, is begun by Davis and Gavan Duffy, who edit the Nation, and attempt to revive the interest of the people in their history and literature.

1829. **France.** The dynasty is weakened by the death of the Duke of Orleans, leaving two infant sons, the Comte de Paris, and the Duc de Chartres.

1830. **Servia.** The son of Milosch Obrenovitch is expelled, and a Karageorgevitch is chosen.

1831. **America.** Lord Ashburton and Daniel Webster, the Secretary of State, arrange the frontier between Canada and Maine by the Ashburton Treaty. Both agree by the Treaty of Washington to watch the African coast in order to stop the slave trade, and to surrender the right of search.

1832. **Australasia.** The Tahiti Isles, for a long time the scene of English missionary effort, become a French Protectorate.

Partial representation is introduced in N. S. Wales and South Australia.

1833. **Asia.** The English retreat begins, almost all the troops being treacherously slain in the Khyber Pass (Jan.). Pollock is sent to reoccupy Cabul, and dismantles the fortifications; but he is forced to recognise Dost Mohammed, and Afghanistan is evacuated. Sir Charles Napier is sent by Lord Ellenborough to annex Scinde.

The opium war ends with the Treaty of Nankin. Canton, Shanghai, and three other ports are opened to English trade; Hong Kong is ceded; an indemnity is paid; a tariff is framed; and official intercourse on a basis of equality is provided for.

2863. **Spanish Lit.** Espronceda's El Diablo Mundo.
2864. **American Lit.** Longfellow's Ballads.
2865. **Science.** Cauchy's researches on determinants.

Stas studies the atomic weights of a number of elements, and declares that there are no simple relations between them.

James Forbes declares glaciers viscous bodies.

Rokitansky's Handbook of Pathological Anatomy.

2866. **Archaeology.** J. L. Stephens explores the dead cities of the Mayas of Yucatan, and studies their calculiform writing.

2867. **Philosophy.** Vatke's Free Will in relation to Sin and Grace attempts to combine Hegel and Schleiermacher.

Feuerbach's Essence of Christianity maintains that Christianity is the creation of human hopes and fears.

2868. **Politics.** Cabet's Voyage en Icarie, a scheme of communism.

Louis Blanc recommends national workshops.

2869. **Economics.** List insists that absolute free trade conflicts with the National Idea.

2870. **Geography.** Livingstone discovers Lake Ngami.

Sir James Ross finds the great Southern continent.

2871. **Education.** Degrees are granted to women in America.
2872. **Deaths.** Baader, Chantrey, Decandolle, Lermontof.

2873. **Eng. Ch.** Isaac Williams is defeated in a contest for the Chair of Poetry at Oxford vacated by Keble. [1842

2874. **French Ch.** Veuillot becomes editor of the Univers, which he makes the organ of Ultramontanism.

2875. **Spanish Ch.** Balmes' Protestantism and Catholicism, a survey of their respective contributions to civilisation.

2876. **Swedish Lit.** Frederika Bremer's novel, The Neighbours.

2877. **Church Hist.** The Refutation of all Heresies of Hippolytus is found at Mount Athos.

2878. **Eng. Lit.** Macaulay's Lays of Ancient Rome.

Tennyson's Poems, chiefly lyrical.

2879. **French Lit.** Scribe's Verre d'Eau.
2880. **Russian Lit.** Gogol's Dead Souls.
2881. **American Lit.** Brook Farm, near Boston, is taken by Ripley and the Transcendentalists for the purpose of a common life.

2882. **Science.** Mayer reaches the mechanical theory of heat without experiments.

Steenstrup's Alternation of Generations shows that many species are represented by two distinct types.

Dr Braid, a Manchester surgeon, studies 'Hypnotism.'

Murchison establishes the Permian system.

Schleiden proves that the plant embryo and all vegetable tissues spring from a nucleated cell.

Darwin investigates the origin of coral reefs.

1834. **Africa.** Morocco enters the war between France and Abd-el-Kader.

The Sultan annexes Tripoli and Barca.

The Dutch settlers in Natal are expelled by an English expedition to Durban, and the greater number trek into the Orange Free State and the Transvaal, where they engage in desperate struggles with the Matabele. Natal is declared a crown colony, 1844.

[1843

1835. **England.** Fergus O'Connor explains his land scheme.

1836. **Ireland.** O'Connell's proposed meeting at Clontarf, near Dublin, is forbidden by the Government, which is anxious to avoid bloodshed. O'Connell thereupon dissuades his followers from attending, but is arrested for sedition.

Peel passes an amended Arms Act, forbidding the possession of arms except by special license.

1837. **France.** Louis Blanc founds La Réforme, the organ of the Radical-Socialist party, and agitates for Parliamentary reform. He is supported by Ledru-Rollin and Arago.

The Entente Cordiale, established by Aberdeen and Guizot, and resting on their mutual confidence, is ratified by the visit of the Queen and Prince Consort to Louis Philippe at Eu. The King assures the Queen that they are not contemplating a marriage of one of his sons with Isabella of Spain.

1838. **Spain.** Espartero becomes unpopular, and is forced by Narvaez to fly to England. Christina is recalled, Isabella is declared of age, and the Moderados, under Narvaez, supported by French influence, become supreme.

1839. **Switzerland.** The seven Catholic Cantons make the Sonderbund, to prevent the suppression of religious houses and to oppose the revision of the federal constitution.

1840. **Hungary.** The Magyars attempt to exclude all languages but their own from official use, and fighting between Slavs and Magyars occurs in Croatia.

1841. **Greece.** Otho is compelled by a revolt to dismiss his Bavarian counsellors and to grant a constitution. The country, however, continues to suffer from brigandage and bankruptcy.

1842. **Africa.** The Gambia is separated from Sierra Leone; and the Gold Coast is taken over by the Crown.

France establishes a port on the Gold Coast as a base for French traders.

[1844

1843. **England.** Peel's Bank Charter Act separates the department which issues notes from that which carries on ordinary banking business, limits the issue of notes to the amount of bullion in

2883. **Law.** Richter's Catholic and Lutheran Church Law in Germany.

2884. **Social.** A Royal Commission on Mines first reveals the evils of women's and of children's labours, which is forbidden by a bill introduced by Ashley.

Godin founds a Familistère at Guise.

2885. **Deaths.** Thomas Arnold, Bell, Channing, Espronceda, Gesenius, Stendhal.

2886. **Eng. Ch.** Newman resigns his position at St Mary's. [1843

Pusey is forbidden to preach for two years owing to his sermon on the Eucharist.

2887. **Scotch Ch.** Four hundred and seventy-four clergy leave the established Church, led by Chalmers, Guthrie and Hugh Miller, on account of lay patronage being made legal by the Auchterarder case. A sustentation fund is rapidly raised.

2888. **French Ch.** Forbin-Janson founds l'Œuvre de la Sainte-Enfance.

2889. **German Ch.** Beck revives Evangelicalism at Tübingen.

2890. **Italian Ch.** Gioberti's Primacy of the Italians declares Italy morally and intellectually pre-eminent among nations.

2891. **American Ch.** Joseph Smith authorises polygamy for the Mormons.

2892. **Eng. Lit.** Carlyle's Past and Present.

2893. **French Lit.** Hugo's Les Burgraves marks the decline of the romantic school, and Ponsard's Lucrèce revives classicism.

2894. **German Lit.** Gutzkow's Tassel and Sword.

2895. **Polish Lit.** Kraszewski's social novel, The Magic Lamp.

2896. **Science.** Logan, of the Canada Survey, detects pre-Cambrian formations, which he calls Laurentian.

Henson constructs an Aerostat.

Quenstedt classifies the Jurassic rocks of Swabia.

2897. **Art.** Balfe's Bohemian Girl.

Designs for the decoration of the Houses of Parliament are submitted by Watts, Maclise and Madox Brown.

Ruskin's Modern Painters, vol. I.

2898. **Philosophy.** Mill's Logic discusses the theory and method of inductions, and maintains that the conception of Causation is purely empirical. The concluding Book applies the methods of Physical Science to moral and political problems.

2899. **History.** Ewald's History of the Jews.

2900. **Economics.** Roscher founds the Historical School.

2901. **Agriculture.** Lawes and Gilbert practise scientific agriculture.

2902. **Death.** Southey.

2903. **Eng. Ch.** Ward's Ideal of a Christian Church is condemned by the Hebdomadal Board at Oxford. [1844

Miall and other Nonconformists found the Liberation Society.

2904. **German Ch.** Ronge and Czerski denounce the exhibition of the

the Bank, plus 14 millions, plus two-thirds the amount issued by any bank that ceases to exist, and restricts the issue of provincial banks.

Mazzini's letters are opened by the English Government, in order to discover whether he is plotting against the despotic governments of Italy.

1844. **Ireland.** O'Connell is tried and sentenced to a fine and a year's imprisonment; but the sentence is reversed by the Lords on a technical error.

1845. **Denmark.** Holstein declares Schleswig and Holstein independent, indivisible, and governed by the rule of male descent.

1846. **Germany.** Weavers' riots break out in Silesia, where the economic distress is very grave.

1847. **Russia.** On his visit to England, Nicholas proposes to Lord Aberdeen to act together in the event of a disruption of Turkey.

1848. **America.** Tyler, a slave-holder, and Calhoun, the Secretary of State, secretly negociate the annexation of Texas. The Senate reject it; but in the presidential election, Polk, who stands for annexation, defeats Clay and a Liberty Party candidate.

1849. **West Indies.** The Republic of San Domingo is founded.

1850. **Africa.** The Emperor of Morocco invades Algeria, and a large French expedition is sent out. Tangier and Mogador are bombarded, and the Emperor is forced to make the Treaty of Tangier.

1851. **England.** Peel abolishes or diminishes many duties on imports, and removes all duties on exports. A letter written by Russell from Edinburgh declares for complete abolition; but Peel fails to persuade his Cabinet to take the step, is bitterly attacked by Disraeli and Bentinck, and resigns (Dec.). Russell fails to form a ministry, and Peel returns to power. [1845

1852. **Ireland.** Catholics are permitted to hold property in their own name.

Peel raises the grant to Maynooth College. Though he approves the step, Gladstone resigns his office on the ground that the grant conflicts with the views expressed in his published works.

The Devon Commission, appointed 1844, to inquire into the grievances of tenants, condemns the system of Leinster, Munster, and Connaught, but praises the Ulster custom of tenant-right. Peel therefore introduces a Bill extending compensation to tenants, which is rejected by the Lords.

The potato crop is destroyed by disease.

1853. **Italy.** Disturbances break out in the Romagna; and France garrisons Ferrara, in accordance with her rights under the Treaty of Vienna.

1854. **Spain.** The Moderados frame a reactionary Constitution, and abolish the right of the Cortes to assemble unsummoned.

1855. **America.** Texas is admitted to the Union as a slave state.

Holy Coat of Trèves, and found a German Catholic Church; but Ronge loses his belief in the divinity of Christ, and Czerski withdraws, and the movement collapses.

The Pope condemns the rationalistic teaching of Hermes.

2905. **American Ch.** John Thomas founds the Christadelphians.

2906. **Eng. Lit.** Kinglake's Eothen.

Stanley's Life of Dr Arnold.

Disraeli's Coningsby.

2907. **French Lit.** Dumas' Monte Cristo.

2908. **Science.** Chambers' Vestiges of the Natural History of Creation asserts that all forms of life have an impulse to rise and to modify according to environment.

2909. **Art.** Joachim makes his début.

2910. **Philosophy.** Stirner's The Individual and his Property propounds a system of ultra-individualism in morals, economics and politics.

2911. **Philology.** Castren studies North Asiatic philology and ethnology.

2912. **History.** Waitz' Constitutional History of Germany.

2913. **Law.** Heffter's International Law of the Present.

2914. **Economics.** Mill's Unsettled Questions of Political Economy discuss the theory of international trade.

2915. **Social.** The Rochdale Pioneers found a Cooperative Store.

2916. **Deaths.** Dalton, Thorwaldsen.

[1845

2917. **Eng. Ch.** Ward is condemned and degraded by Convocation and joins the Roman Church (Sept.). Newman follows, explaining his step in his Development of Christian Doctrine. After the secession, Pusey, Marriott and Mozley lead the Anglo-Catholic party. Pusey founds the first sisterhood.

Wilberforce becomes Bishop of Oxford.

2918. **German Ch.** Rothe's Theological Ethics leads the reaction against the rigidity of the Hengstenberg school, and asserts that the consciousness of God is equally immediate with the consciousness of the Ego, that religion lies in morality, and that the Church, when its work is done, becomes merged in the moral community, the State.

2919. **Hungarian Lit.** Eötvös' novel, The Village Notary.

2920. **Danish Lit.** Hertz' lyrical drama, King René's Daughter.

2921. **American Lit.** Hawthorne's Mosses from an old Manse.

2922. **Science.** Lord Rosse constructs a large reflector at Parsonstown.

Adams computes the orbit of an unknown planet, which would explain the irregularities observed in the motion of Uranus.

Humboldt's Cosmos, a survey of the world.

Faraday discovers the connection of electro-magnetism and light.

Armstrong invents the hydraulic crane.

Neumann states the mathematical laws of magneto-electric induction.

Reichenbach's researches on Magnetism and Vital Force.

Cayley states the theory of Invariants.

1856. **Australasia.** The first Maori war breaks out, owing to the breach of the Treaty of Waitangi. Sir George Grey arrives, declares that the treaty remains intact, and suppresses the revolt.

1857. **Asia.** The Sikhs invade British territory, and are defeated in two fierce battles at Ferozeshah and Moodkee (Dec.).

1858. **Africa.** A massacre of Christian converts takes place in Madagascar. A joint French and English expedition is sent, but fails to effect a landing, and the island is closed to European commerce for some years.

[1846

1859. **England.** Peel carries a Bill for the gradual abolition of the corn duty, which is to sink to 1*s.* a quarter after 1849.

Disraeli and the Protectionist conservatives join Russell in rejecting a Coercion Bill for Ireland, Peel resigns (June), and Russell forms a ministry.

1860. **Ireland.** The potato crop again fails, and, despite the sale of Indian corn and the institution of relief works, the area and intensity of the famine increase.

1861. **Italy.** Pius IX. becomes Pope, amnesties political offenders, and appoints a Council of State. Metternich occupies the city of Ferrara, contrary to the Treaty of Vienna. Pius protests, and prepares for armed resistance.

Leopold of Tuscany and the Duke of Lucca are forced to grant administrative reforms; but the latter sells his duchy to Tuscany and retires into private life.

1862. **Spain.** Louis Philippe, on the advice of Guizot, chooses Francis, Duke of Cadiz, her cousin, who is unlikely to have children, as husband for the Queen of Spain, and marries her only sister to the Duke of Montpensier, his own son, on the same day, despite his express promise to Queen Victoria to wait till Isabella had an heir. Though he asserts that Palmerston, who succeeds Aberdeen, was intriguing against Montpensier, his conduct arouses great resentment in England, abruptly terminates the Entente Cordiale, and weakens the position of the Orleanist dynasty.

1863. **Portugal.** The followers of Miguel again revolt, but are suppressed with the aid of an English fleet.

1864. **Denmark.** Christian VIII. declares the whole Danish State indivisible and heritable by females as well as males. This decree excludes the Duke of Augustenburg and disappoints the Duchies, which aspire to become a separate province under a German prince.

1865. **Poland.** A revolt of the peasants in Galicia takes place, and the republic of Cracow is annexed by Austria, in violation of the Treaty of Vienna.

1866. **America.** On a proposal to buy land from Mexico, Wilmot carries a proviso that slavery shall be forbidden in any territory thus acquired. Owing, however, to opposition in the Senate, an Appropriation Bill is passed without the slavery proviso.

2923. **Art.** Viollet le Duc begins the restoration of Notre-Dame at Paris, and revives Gothic art.

Day's Treatise on Harmony.

2924. **Archaeology.** Layard explores Nineveh.

2925. **History.** Carlyle's Letters and Speeches of Cromwell.

Thiers' History of the Consulate and Empire.

2926. **Economics.** Bastiat's Sophismes Économiques defends laissez-faire.

2927. **Education.** Peel founds Queen's Colleges in Ireland for unsectarian education for the laity.

2928. **Agriculture.** The General Enclosure Act is passed.

2929. **Geography.** Abbé Huc enters Thibet, and reaches Lhassa.

2930. **Deaths.** Jackson, A. W. Schlegel, Sydney Smith.

2931. **Eng. Ch.** The Evangelical Alliance is formed to oppose Romanism, Puseyism and rationalism. Many Americans, French and Germans join, and several conferences take place abroad. [1846

Holyoake founds the National Secular Society.

2932. **French Ch.** The Virgin is believed to appear at La Salette.

2933. **German Ch.** Baur places the Gospels in the second century and declares that the original gospel was an Ebionite Gospel of the Hebrews, which 'Matthew' combined with some more liberal document; Luke was a Pauline protest against Judaism, but was later supplemented by Ebionite or Jewish hands; Mark was an adapter of Matthew and Luke; and Paul expanded a Jewish Messiah into an universal teacher.

2934. **Italian Ch.** Rosmini's Wounds of the Church complains that the clergy lack education, that clergy and people may not choose their bishops, etc.

Gioberti's Modern Jesuit replies to Curci's attack on his Primacy of the Italians.

2935. **Eng. Lit.** Browning marries Elizabeth Barrett.

The Daily News, the first cheap daily paper, begins to appear.

2936. **German Lit.** Freiligrath's revolutionary cycle of songs, Ça ira.

2937. **Italian Lit.** D'Azeglio attacks the Papacy and the revolutionists, and urges the princes to adopt a national policy.

2938. **Hungarian Lit.** Maurus Jokai's first novel.

2939. **Russian Lit.** Grigorovich's The Village.

2940. **Science.** Independently of Adams, Leverrier infers a planet beyond Uranus, and Galle of Berlin, whom he asks to verify it, finds it close to the place indicated. The planet receives the name of Neptune.

Weber's Determination of Electro-dynamic forces explains the laws of action of electric currents and of the resistance of conductors.

2941. **Art.** Mendelssohn produces the Elijah at Birmingham.

Berlioz' Faust.

2942. **Philology.** Rawlinson's work on the Persian cuneiform inscriptions at Behistan opens up Assyrian history.

War with Mexico arises over the question of the boundaries of Texas.

To propitiate the North, Polk claims Oregon, and arranges with England to fix the boundary at the 49th parallel.

1867. **Asia.** The Sikhs are defeated at Aliwal (Jan.), and their entrenched camp is stormed (Feb.). By the Treaty of Lahore, England obtains territory beyond the Sutlej. Henry Lawrence is appointed British Resident.

1868. **England.** Short service of 10 or 12 years is introduced, with option of joining for 21 years. [1847

Rothschild is elected for the City of London, the first Jewish member of Parliament.

1869. **Ireland.** A large emigration takes place, which, with the famine, reduces the population by three millions.

1870. **France.** The extension of the franchise is demanded by Odilon Barrot, Lamartine, Ledru-Rollin, Garnier-Pagès, and by the Socialists Louis Blanc, Blanqui, and Marrast.

1871. **Germany.** The King of Prussia is forced to call a Landtag; but he declares that he will never grant a constitution, and dissolves the Diet.

1872. **Belgium.** The Liberals, Rogier and Frère-Orban, take office.

1873. **Italy.** Marie Louise of Parma dies, Parma passes to Lucca, and Modena receives part of Tuscany. Riots ensue, and the Austrians occupy the town of Ferrara.

Charles Albert introduces liberal reforms in Piedmont, and Cavour edits the Risorgimento.

1874. **Switzerland.** War breaks out, the Sonderbund is routed and dissolved, and the Jesuits are expelled.

1875. **Portugal.** England, France and Spain end the civil war.

1876. **Hungary.** Szechenyi approves proposals for reform made by Vienna; but Deak, Eötvös, and Kossuth demand more far-reaching changes.

1877. **America.** Gold is discovered in California.

1878. **Africa.** Abd-el-Kader surrenders conditionally.

British Kaffraria is created.

1879. **Asia.** Sattara is annexed to British India by Lord Ellenborough, though Bartle Frere has recognised a new Rajah, and in violation of the treaty of 1819.

2943. **Philosophy.** Hamilton's edition of Reid expounds the theory of relativity.

Theodor Waitz' Foundation of Psychology continues the teaching of Herbart.

2944. **Geography.** The Hakluyt Society is founded.

2945. **History.** Grote's History of Greece.

Herculano's History of Portugal.

2946. **Deaths.** Bessel, List, Tegner.

2947. **Eng. Ch.** Lord John Russell's appointment of Hampden to the Bishopric of Hereford raises a storm of protest. [1847

F. W. Robertson becomes incumbent of Trinity Chapel, Brighton.

2948. **Scotch Ch.** The United Presbyterian Church is formed from the union of the Secession Church of 1733 and the Relief Church of 1752.

2949. **German Ch.** Hundeshagen's Vital Questions for German Protestantism discusses its relation to the political and intellectual questions of the time.

Baur's History of Dogma teaches that dogmas develope logically, and that movements are greater than individuals.

2950. **American Ch.** Salt Lake City is founded by the Mormons, led by Young. Their colony is made a Territory, 1850, and silver is found in Utah, 1870.

Ward Beecher becomes minister of a Congregational church in Brooklyn.

2951. **Asiatic Ch.** The Pope revives the Patriarchate of Jerusalem.

2952. **Eng. Lit.** Charlotte Brontë's Jane Eyre.

Bohn's Libraries begin to appear.

2953. **American Lit.** Emerson's Poems.

2954. **Italian Lit.** Salvini, a pupil of Modena, begins to act.

2955. **Russian Lit.** Herzen's Who is to Blame? advocates a modification of the marriage laws.

2956. **Science.** Simpson uses chloroform as an anaesthetic in operations.

William Thomson introduces the modern method of treating electro-magnetism, i.e., illustrates electro-magnetic forces by the distortions of an elastic solid.

Joule lectures on the Mechanical Equivalent of Heat, which he discovers independently of Mayer, and which is at once adopted by William Thomson. Helmholtz reads an essay on the Conservation of Energy before the Physical Society of Berlin, without being aware of the work of Mayer.

Von Staudt and Steiner create modern synthetic geometry, a system without reference to number or magnitude.

Herschel publishes his Observations made at the Cape.

2957. **Art.** Kaulbach's six studies of the History of Man (Berlin).

Vischer's Aesthetic elaborates the ideas of Hegel, and declares that beauty results from the union of the real and the ideal, i.e. through the partial departure of each individual from the type.

2958. **Philology.** Lassen's Indian Antiquity.

1880. **England.** Fergus O'Connor summons a Chartist meeting [1848 to carry a monster petition to Parliament. About 25,000 meet, but are stopped by special constables, and Chartism as an organised political movement comes to an end.

1881. **Ireland.** Russell carries the Encumbered Estate Act.

A Treason Felony Act punishes seditious writing and speaking. Smith O'Brien attacks a police station, is captured and transported, and Mitchell, editor of the United Irishman, is convicted.

1882. **France.** A proposed Reform banquet is prohibited, and riots ensue. Guizot resigns (Feb. 22), and Thiers, who is invited to form a ministry, insists on electoral reform. The King abdicates to his grandson and escapes to England. A republic is proclaimed, and a provisional government is formed by Lamartine, Arago, Ledru-Rollin, Garnier-Pagès and Crémieux. Lamartine announces to foreign states that France is peaceful. Louis Blanc is made president of a commission for the 'organisation of labour,' and erects national workshops. A national assembly, elected by universal suffrage, appoints an executive, from which the Socialists are excluded. An attack on the Chamber is repulsed, and the Socialist leaders are imprisoned or fly. Unmarried workmen of 18 to 25 are ordered to enter the army, and all others are to leave the capital (June 22). The decree is resisted, Cavaignac is appointed Dictator, and four days of fierce conflict follow. On the suppression of the revolt, the workshops are abolished. A Constitution is formed with a single Chamber, and a President elected by manhood suffrage for four years. Louis Napoleon receives 5½ million votes against 1½ million cast for Cavaignac.

1883. **Italy.** Sicily obtains a Constitution, but establishes a provisional government (Jan.), and deposes the King (April). Piedmont, Naples, and Tuscany also obtain Constitutions. On the news from Paris, the Pope forms a ministry under Antonelli. On the news of a revolution in Vienna, Milan and other Lombard towns revolt; the Duke of Parma is expelled, and Venice proclaims a republic under Manin. Charles Albert declares war against Austria (March 25), and marches against Radetzky. Lombardy is annexed to Piedmont, Venice declares herself incorporated with them, and Tuscany, the Pope and Naples send troops. The Pope and Ferdinand, however, quickly recall their armies, and the latter overthrows the Neapolitan and Sicilian Constitutions. Charles Albert is defeated by Radetzky at Custozza (July), Milan is recaptured, Charles Albert signs an armistice, withdrawing to Piedmont, and Radetzky turns to the siege of Venice.

In Rome the ministers resign, finding that the Pope does not assent to their measures, and Rossi forms a new ministry, but is murdered. The Pope flees to Gaeta, and declares everything done in his absence void (Nov.). A Constituent Assembly, in which Mazzini and Garibaldi sit, decides that the Pope has forfeited his temporal power. The Duke of Tuscany also flees, and a republic is proclaimed under Guerrazzi.

1884. **Germany.** The King of Prussia promises a free press, a Landtag and the formation of a closer German federation (March 9). The populace demands also the dismissal of the soldiers; and, after a fierce fight

2959. **History.** Lamartine's Histoire des Girondins.
2960. **Anthropology.** Boucher de Perthes publishes an account of the stone weapons found by him in the gravel-pits at Abbeville.
2961. **Economics.** Haxthausen visits Russia, at the request of Nicholas, and describes its land system.
2962. **Geography.** Franklin, sent by the British Government to discover a North-West passage, 1845, is lost.
2963. **History.** Ferrari's Philosophie de l'Histoire points out the difficulties in any theory of teleology.
2964. **Social.** Marx and Engels issue a Communist Manifesto, urging the proletariat of all countries to unite.

The Ten Hours' Bill for women and children of 13 to 18 is carried.

Father Kolping institutes clubs for Catholic working-men in Cologne; at his death, 1865, over 400 exist in the Rhine country.
2965. **Deaths.** Chalmers, O'Connell, Vinet.

2966. **Eng. Ch.** Robert Wilberforce's Doctrine of the Incarnation. [1848

Froude's Nemesis of Faith illustrates the reaction from the Oxford movement, and leads to the resignation of his Fellowship at Oxford.
2967. **French Ch.** Many liberal Catholics enter the National Assembly and help Napoleon to the Presidency. Falloux, Minister of Education, introduces a bill, with the approval of Thiers, by which Catholics may be educated at primary and secondary Catholic schools, but can only obtain degrees at the University. The compromise is accepted by Montalembert but fiercely attacked by Veuillot.

Frederick Monod founds the Église Libre in Paris, seceding from the National Church, the Synod refusing to acknowledge the divinity of Christ. Adolphe Monod remains; and the Church soon becomes more orthodox.
2968. **German Ch.** The Pius Verein is founded at Mainz to advocate clerical direction of education, and independence of State control.

A meeting of Bishops held at Würzburg resolves to work for the abrogation of the sovereign's placet, for the full independence of ecclesiastical legislation, administration and jurisdiction and the control of education. Many of the desires expressed at Würzburg are fulfilled by Concordats concluded in the following years with the states of Southern Germany.
2969. **American Ch.** Members of the Fox family, in New York State, become mediums and profess to hold communication with the departed. Andrew Jackson Davis publishes Nature's Divine Revelation, alleged to be dictated in a clairvoyant trance. Spiritualism spreads rapidly throughout the States, and is introduced into England by Home, 1855.
2970. **Italian Ch.** Ventura recommends the surrender of the Temporal Power.
2971. **African Ch.** Gray becomes Bishop of Cape Town.
2972. **Eng. Lit.** The Bacon-Shakspere controversy is begun by Hart's scepticism as to Shakspere. The authorship of Bacon is suggested by

in Berlin, the King orders the troops to withdraw, dismisses the ministry, and amnesties political prisoners. A National Assembly meets, the almost republican Left led by Waldeck and Jacoby, the Left Centre by Rodbertus and Schulze-Delitzsch, the Centre by Unruh, and the Right by Bismarck (May). The Assembly, however, is dissolved (Dec.), and a new Constitution is issued, with two Chambers chosen by indirect election.

Baden grants a liberal Constitution (March), and is followed by Bavaria, where Louis abdicates, and by Saxony and Hanover.

The Liberal leaders meet at Heidelberg (March), and invite past and present members of constitutional assemblies to a Vorparlament, which meets at Frankfort, and decrees a federal Parliament with a single head and two Chambers. The Parliament opens at Frankfort, with Gagern as President (May). Blum contends for a federal republic; Dahlmann, Gervinus, Arndt, Jacob Grimm demand a constitutional Empire under the King of Prussia. The Assembly discusses and publishes the Fundamental Rights of the German People.

1885. **Denmark.** Christian dies, and Frederick VII. issues a liberal Constitution. When the news of the German revolution arrives, Schleswig and Holstein demand admission to the Bund, and a joint Constitution on the German model. A provisional government is formed under the Duke of Augustenburg. Frederick sends an army against the Duchies, which obtain help from Prussia.

1886. **Austria.** The populace of Vienna demand the fall of Metternich, who escapes to England (March). The Emperor promises a Constitution, and appoints Deak, Batthyany and Kossuth ministers for Hungary. They abolish feudalism, introduce responsible government, and extend the franchise. Jellacic tells the Croatians that if Hungary becomes independent, she will oppress them. They therefore induce the Emperor to make Jellacic Governor-General. The Magyars repulse Jellacic's troops, and Kossuth organises a riot in Vienna to prevent the departure of reinforcements. Ferdinand flees (May), but Jellacic marches to Vienna and saves the dynasty. A Constituent Assembly meets, and the Emperor returns. Jellacic and Windischgrätz open the campaign against the Hungarians. Another insurrection breaks out in Vienna, and the Emperor again flees (Oct.). The capital is retaken, Schwarzenberg forms a reactionary ministry, and the Emperor abdicates in favour of his nephew, Francis Joseph.

1887. **Bohemia.** The Czechs meet at Prague, and demand autonomy (March); but the meeting is broken up and the city surrenders to Windischgrätz (June). A Slavonic Congress is held at Prague, under the presidency of Palacky.

1888. **Poland.** Prussia and Austria crush revolts in Warsaw and Cracow.

1889. **Holland.** Thorbecke obtains a liberal Constitution.

1890. **Switzerland.** A National Council and a Council of Estates, with a federal executive appointed by them, and a federal court are created.

Neufchâtel throws off allegiance to the King of Prussia.

1891. **America.** Mexico relinquishes Texas, New Mexico, California, Nevada, Utah, Arizona, and parts of Colorado and Wyoming.

1892. **Africa.** The Orange Free State is conquered at Boomplatz.

Miss W. H. Smith, 1856, and reasserted by Nathaniel Holmes, an American lawyer, 1866, and by the Bacon Society in London, 1885.

Thackeray's Vanity Fair is completed.

Thackeray's Book of Snobs.

Mrs Gaskell's Mary Barton, one of the earliest studies of the life of the poor.

Aytoun's Lays of the Scottish Cavaliers.

Matthew Arnold's first poems.

2973. **French Lit.** Murger's Scènes de la Vie de Bohème.

2974. **German Lit.** Hoffmann founds and edits the Kladderadatsch, a comic journal.

2975. **Spanish Lit.** Juan Valera's Pepita Jimenez marks the renaissance of the novel.

2976. **American Lit.** Lowell's Biglow Papers.

2977. **Science.** Du Bois Reymond's Animal Electricity.

William Thomson establishes the absolute thermodynamic scale of temperature.

2978. **Art.** Holman Hunt, Millais, and Rossetti found a brotherhood. In the Academy of 1849, Millais exhibits Ferdinand and Isabella. The Germ is started in 1850, but ceases after the appearance of four numbers. The new school is encouraged by Ford Madox Brown and eulogised by Ruskin.

Watts' Paolo and Francesca.

Niels Gade returns from Leipsig and fosters Norwegian music.

2979. **Archaeology.** Dennis' Cities of Etruria.

2980. **History.** Macaulay's History of England from the accession of James II. defends the Whig theory of government and depicts William III. as a hero.

2981. **Economics.** Mill's Principles of Political Economy present a systematic exposition of Ricardo's ideas, but draw a marked distinction between production, the laws of which are based on unalterable natural facts, and distribution, the methods of which may readily be changed. In subsequent editions, Mill verges steadily towards socialism.

2982. **Philology.** Ritschl's edition of Plautus.

Grimm's History of the German Language.

2983. **Geography.** Krapf and Rebmann discover the mountains Kenia and Kilimanjaro.

2984. **Social.** Cabet founds Icaria, a communistic settlement in America.

The Public Health Act is passed, the first sanitary measure on the Statute Book.

Slavery is abolished in French colonies.

Caird's High Farming the best Substitute for Protection.

Maurice, Ludlow, and other Christian Socialists attempt to found a Cooperative movement.

2985. **Deaths.** Berzelius, Balmes, Bielinsky, Chateaubriand, Görres, Hermann, G. Stephenson.

1893. **England.** The Navigation Laws are repealed. [1849

1894. **Italy.** Charles Albert is crushed by Radetzky at Novara, and abdicates to his son, Victor Emanuel (March). A revolt in Lombardy is suppressed by Haynau. The *status quo* before the war is restored, and Victor Emanuel pays an indemnity. Venice is forced to capitulate, and Sicily is reduced by Ferdinand.

A Republic is proclaimed in Rome, and Mazzini assumes control. Oudinot, sent by the French Government to the Pope's aid, lands at Civita Vecchia (April), and takes Rome after a long siege (July).

1895. **Germany.** The hereditary headship is refused by Prussia, and the Austrians withdraw from the Assembly. Frederick William forms the Dreikönigsbund with Hanover and Saxony, and is joined by 24 minor states. Austria, however, induces Prussia to join in a Commission at Frankfort for interim management of the Confederation. Hanover breaks away, and Saxony shows her desire to do so.

Prussia suppresses revolts in Saxony, Baden, and the Palatinate.

1896. **Denmark.** The Bund sends 45,000 men to aid the Duchies; but a Danish victory at Fredericia leads to a truce, by which Schleswig is to receive a Danish government and the German troops are to be withdrawn. The Duchies are forced to accept these terms.

1897. **Austria.** A Constitution is granted, 'by the Grace of the Emperor.'

1898. **Hungary.** Independence is proclaimed, and Kossuth becomes head of the Provisional Government (April). Bem and Görgei repulse Austria, which appeals to Russia. The Hungarians are defeated at Temesvar, Kossuth resigns, and Görgei capitulates at Vilagos (Aug.). Batthyany is shot, and Szechenyi, Kossuth and Bem take refuge in Turkey, which, supported by England and France, refuses to surrender them. Hungary is deprived of all constitutional rights.

1899. **Turkey.** A revolution in Wallachia and Moldavia is suppressed, and Russia and Turkey jointly nominate the princes for seven years.

1900. **America.** Taylor secretly urges the settlers in California to apply for admission to the Union as a free state. Texas claims a larger part of New Mexico.

1901. **Africa.** Cape Colony forbids convicts to land.

1902. **Asia.** A second Sikh war breaks out, and the whole of the Punjab is annexed, and governed by Henry and John Lawrence.

1903. **England.** The Queen sends a memorandum to Palmerston, demanding to be kept acquainted with the business of the Foreign Office. [1850

Palmerston defends his policy in the Don Pacifico debate.

1904. **Ireland.** A Tenant Right League is formed.

1905. **France.** The Parti de l'Ordre, headed by Thiers, Broglie, Molé,

2986. **Eng. Ch.** Faber founds the Oratory in London. [1849

F. W. Newman's treatise on The Soul, written from the standpoint of theism.

Danish Ch. Martensen's Christian Dogmatics offers a philosophical explanation of each separate Christian tenet.

2987. **French Ch.** Dupanloup is induced by Falloux to accept the Bishopric of Orleans.

2988. **German Ch.** Canon Hirscher's Condition of the Church, an outspoken criticism of Jesuit influence and of the centralising policy of the Church, is put on the Index and provokes many replies.

2989. **Italian Ch.** The Pope issues an Encyclical to the Italian Bishops condemning socialism and communism.

2990. **Church Hist.** The Pope issues an Encyclical inviting the expression of opinion as to the advisability of a definition of the Immaculate Conception.

2991. **Eng. Lit.** Kingsley's Alton Locke calls attention to social problems and points towards Christian Socialism.

2992. **French Lit.** Chateaubriand's Mémoires d'Outre-Tombe, a defence of his public life.

Scribe's Adrienne Lecouvreur.

Sainte-Beuve contributes Causeries du Lundi to the Constitutionnel, which react against the rigid methods of Nisard and develope purely literary criticism to its utmost extent.

2993. **Spanish Lit.** Fernan Caballero's first novel, La Gaviota (The Sea-Gull).

Ticknor's History of Spanish Literature.

2994. **Science.** Fizeau experimentally determines the velocity of light. The construction of the Menai Bridge is undertaken.

2995. **Art.** Ruskin's Seven Lamps of Architecture.

2996. **Archaeology.** Lepsius' Monuments of Egypt and Ethiopia presents a report of an expedition organised by Bunsen and paid for by the Prussian Government.

2997. **Philology.** Tischendorf's edition of the New Testament, strongly influenced by Lachmann.

Max Müller translates the Rig-Veda.

2998. **History.** Kemble produces the first trustworthy account of the political and social institutions of the Anglo-Saxons.

2999. **Social.** Raiffeisen institutes cooperative loan banks in Germany. In the following year, Schulze-Delitzsch founds credit associations for the working-classes. Both movements spread rapidly through the country.

3000. **Deaths.** Chopin, Marheineke, Mehemet Ali.

3001. **Eng. Ch.** The Pope appoints Catholic Bishops to English Sees, and a fierce storm of indignation is aroused. [1850

Gorham, presented to a living by the Lord Chancellor, is refused by the Bishop of Exeter in consequence of denying the regenerative power of Baptism. The Bishop is upheld by the Court of Arches, but overruled by the Privy Council. As a result of this decision, Manning, Aubrey de Vere, and others join the Roman Church.

and Montalembert, restricts the franchise, and compels the authors of articles in the press to sign them.

1906. **Italy.** The Pope returns to Rome, abandons all his reforms, and makes Antonelli Secretary of State. A French garrison remains.

1907. **Germany.** The King of Prussia grants a new Constitution.

Beust forms a scheme of a Middle Germany, and Saxony, Bavaria and Wurtemberg ally.

A Parliament of the German Union meets at Erfurt, to form a Confederation in opposition to Austria (March). In reply, Austria summons the old Bundestag to Frankfort (May). A rupture is brought within sight by an insurrection in Hesse-Cassel (Sept.). By Russian mediation, however, Prussia subordinates herself to Austria by the Convention of Olmütz, by which she recognises the Frankfort Diet (Nov.). The two powers now unite in the pacification of Hesse-Cassel.

1908. **Denmark.** Prussia and Denmark agree that Schleswig shall be governed by Denmark, and Holstein by an administrator.

1909. **Greece.** Palmerston blockades the Piraeus and seizes Greek shipping to obtain redress for an assault on Don Pacifico, a Portuguese Jew, born in Gibraltar. The Greek government concedes his demands. France and Russia, the sponsors of Greek independence, are deeply annoyed, and peace is momentarily endangered by the action of the English Minister.

1910. **America.** Clay carries a series of Acts known as the Compromise of 1850. California is admitted as a free state; the slave trade is forbidden in the District of Columbia; Utah and New Mexico become territories without restriction as to slavery; Texas surrenders her claims to New Mexico; a severe fugitive slave law is passed. The slave law is largely nullified by sympathisers in the North and by the 'Underground Railroad.'

1911. **Africa.** England buys the Danish forts on the Gold Coast.

1912. **Asia.** The Tai-ping rebellion breaks out under Hung, a Chinese schoolmaster, who promulgates a religious system tinctured with Christianity. He takes Nanking and Shanghai, proclaims himself Emperor, and vainly attacks Peking.

1913. **Australasia.** Victoria is separated from N. S. Wales, with Melbourne as capital.

The Australian Government Act grants representative government to South Australia, Tasmania and Victoria.

[1851

1914. **England.** Locke King carries a motion for assimilating the county to the borough franchise, and Russell resigns. Stanley fails to form a ministry, and Russell returns. Palmerston is dismissed for expressing his approval of the *coup d'état* to the French ambassador, without consulting the Cabinet or the Queen.

Pusey adapts Catholic books of devotion, is censured by Bishop Wilberforce, and refrains from preaching for two years.

3002. **German Ch.** The King of Prussia hands over the almost unfettered management of the Evangelical Churches to a Church Council.

3003. **Italian Ch.** The Civilta Cattolica is founded and edited by Curci, and becomes the organ of the Jesuits and the Curia.

The Siccardi laws abolish the jurisdiction of the Church in Victor Emmanuel's dominions over heresy and sacrilege.

3004. **Asiatic Ch.** The Bab, who has come forth as a religious leader in Persia, and attacked polygamy and the formalism of the Koran, is shot. Many of his followers are executed or tortured; but their numbers grow rapidly.

3005. **Eng. Lit.** Tennyson's In Memoriam.

Mrs Browning's Sonnets from the Portuguese.

Dickens' David Copperfield.

Reynolds' Newspaper is founded.

3006. **American Lit.** Hawthorne's Scarlet Letter.

3007. **Norwegian Lit.** Ibsen's first play, Catalina.

3008. **Science.** Remak studies the embryology of the chick and frog.

Foucault finds that the velocity of light in water is less than in air. His discovery finally discredits the emission theory of light.

Melloni investigates radiant heat, and proves that heat rays vary no less than visible rays.

Clausius founds the kinetic theory of gases.

3009. **Art.** Liszt produces Wagner's Lohengrin at Weimar.

3010. **Archaeology.** Mariette discovers the Serapeum.

3011. **Philology.** Lachmann's edition of Lucretius.

3012. **Economics.** Marlo's (Winkelblech) System of Economics advocates Protection and the reorganisation of industry by the State and by Guilds.

3013. **History.** Laurent's Études sur l'Histoire de l'Humanité present the first picture of political development in connexion with the history of ideas.

3014. **Education.** A University Commission is appointed at Oxford, and urges the abolition of subscription, and the opening of fellowships and scholarships to all.

Ewart's Act inaugurates Free Libraries.

3015. **Geography.** Galton explores Damaraland.

3016. **Social.** Titus Salt founds Saltaire works.

3017. **Deaths.** Balzac, Calhoun, Oehlenschläger, Lenau, Neander, Peel, Louis Philippe, Wordsworth.

[1851

3018. **Eng. Ch.** Greg's Creed of Christendom.

Newman lectures on the Present Position of Catholics.

The Ecclesiastical Titles Bill is introduced and carried against the opposition of Gladstone and the Peelites.

3019. **Eng. Lit.** Carlyle's Life of Sterling.

Molesworth moves to cease civil and military expenditure on the colonies and to grant self-government.

1915. **France.** Changarnier is dismissed because his regiments had not cried Vive l'Empereur (Jan.). Petitions, organised by Napoleon's agents in the provinces, demand the revision of the Constitution. The *coup d'état* is carried out (Dec. 2). During the night, Cavaignac, Changarnier, Lamoricière, Thiers, Victor Hugo and others are imprisoned, the Assembly is dissolved, and a new ministry is formed, including Morny and Rouher. Napoleon issues an Appeal to the People, proposing the election of an executive for ten years, and a Constitution modelled on that of Brumaire. 250 deputies who meet and propose a protest are arrested. Revolts take place, and are suppressed with bloodshed. The plébiscite declares in favour of a new constitution by a majority in the proportion of twelve to one (Dec. 20).

1916. **Germany.** Prussia sends a representative (Bismarck) to the Frankfurt Diet, and the return to the Confederation of 1815 becomes complete. Legislative decisions of the Diet need the confirmation of the States Chambers; executive resolutions become operative at once. The Fundamental Rights decreed by the Parliament of Frankfurt are repudiated.

1917. **Austria.** The Constitution of 1849 is abolished.

1918. **Denmark.** Austrian troops occupy Holstein.

1919. **Montenegro.** The ecclesiastical and political functions of the Prince are separated, and he is permitted to marry.

1920. **Australasia.** Hargraves discovers gold in New South Wales.

The importation of convicts, except to West Australia, ceases.

1921. **West Indies.** Cuba declares its independence of Spain; but the revolt is quickly suppressed.

1922. **England.** Palmerston carries an amendment to a Militia Bill, and Russell resigns. Derby and Disraeli form a ministry (Feb.). Derby declares protection shall be settled by the elections, and Disraeli frankly approves free trade. The elections leave Derby in a minority. Villiers moves that the repeal of the Corn Laws was 'wise, just, and beneficial.' Palmerston softens the motion, which is accepted by all but fifty-three, and the Conservative party is thus freed from the burden of protection. Disraeli's budget is defeated, Derby resigns, and Lord Aberdeen forms a ministry of Whigs and Peelites, with Gladstone, Palmerston, Russell, Clarendon, Sidney Herbert, and Granville. [1852

A Bribery Act enjoins enquiry into corrupt practices.

1923. **Ireland.** Owing to the Tenant League, fifty tenant-right advocates are returned. When, however, Sadler and Keogh join Aberdeen, the League falls to pieces.

1924. **France.** Napoleon banishes his opponents, and confiscates the appanages of the House of Orleans. The new Constitution is formally

Borrow's Lavengro.

Macready retires from the stage, and Charles Kean and Phelps take his place.

3020. **French Lit.** Barbey d'Aurevilley's Une vieille Maîtresse anticipates the naturalistic school.

3021. **German Lit.** Bodenstedt's Songs of Mirza Schaffy.

3022. **American Lit.** Longfellow's Golden Legend.

3023. **Greek Lit.** Rangabé's Marriage of Kutrulis revives Aristophanic drama.

3024. **Science.** The first submarine telegraph is laid from Dover to Calais.

Schwabe proves the periodicity of sun spots.

Hofmeister proves that phanerogams and cryptogams possess many common features.

William Thomson independently proves the law of thermodynamics discovered by Clausius.

Perkin discovers aniline purple and creates the industry of coal-tar colours.

Ruhmkorff constructs a coil which produces sparks in air two inches in length.

3025. **Art.** Wagner's Opera and Drama attacks the work of Meyerbeer, and explains his theory of the relation of words and music.

Ruskin's Stones of Venice.

Verdi's opera, Rigoletto.

Tenniel begins to draw for Punch.

3026. **Politics.** Spencer's Social Statics, an attempt at Sociology.

3027. **Education.** Owens, a Manchester merchant, founds a college in his native town.

3028. **History.** Solovief's History of Russia.

3029. **Anthropology.** Schoolcraft's Indian Tribes of the United States.

3030. **Social.** The sale of intoxicants is prohibited in the State of Maine, by the efforts of Neal Dow.

An Exhibition is held in Hyde Park, at the suggestion of the Prince Consort.

3031. **Deaths.** Karl Jacobi, Lachmann, Oersted.

3032. **Eng. Ch.** Owing to the efforts of Bishop Wilberforce and Lord Redesdale, and on the assurance of Phillimore that no legal bar exists, Convocation recommences. [1852

3033. **French Ch.** The Oratory is revived by Perraud and five other priests.

Gaume's treatise on Holy Water alienates the moderate Catholics.

3034. **German Ch.** The Eisenach biennial conference is instituted, consisting of representatives of the Protestants in each state. Several of its suggestions are adopted by the legislatures. By its direction, a revision of Luther's Bible is made.

3035. **Spanish Ch.** The Pope accepts some of the changes of 1836.

issued (Jan.). In the autumn Napoleon makes a grand tour through the provinces, and on his return arranges a plébiscite by which he is chosen hereditary Emperor.

1925. **Germany.** Hesse-Cassel obtains a Constitution.

1926. **Italy.** Cavour becomes Premier in Piedmont, succeeding D'Azeglio.

1927. **Denmark.** Holstein is delivered to the Danes with the vague condition of 'respecting the rights of the duchies.' The Treaty of London, signed by the five great Powers and Sweden, guarantees the unity of the monarchy, and promises the succession of the monarchy and the duchies to Christian of Glücksburg. It is recognised by Austria and Prussia, Hanover, Saxony, and Würtemberg, though not by the Bund.

1928. **Turkey.** Napoleon obtains the right of free entry to the Holy Sepulchre for Latin Christians, hitherto contested by Greek monks, and thereby alienates Russia.

Montenegro and Herzegovina revolt.

1929. **Australasia.** A federal constitution is granted to New Zealand, at the instance of Sir George Grey.

1930. **Africa.** The independence of the Transvaal is recognised by the Sand River Convention.

1931. **Asia.** The second war in Burmah breaks out, and Pegu, or the valley of the Irawaddy, is annexed.

1932. **England.** Gladstone's Budget abolishes the duty on soap, [1853 reduces 133 taxes, imposes a succession duty, and suggests the gradual abolition of the income-tax.

1933. **France.** Napoleon marries Eugénie de Montijo.

1934. **Italy.** Mazzini instigates an unsuccessful insurrection at Milan.

1935. **Turkey.** The Tsar proposes to Sir Hamilton Seymour, the English ambassador, that if the Turk, 'the sick man,' dies, England shall take Crete and Egypt, the Sultan's European states become independent under Russian protection, and Constantinople be temporarily occupied by Russia. England, however, disclaims any desire to partition the Turkish Empire. The Tsar orders the Sultan to recognise him by treaty as official protector of his Christian subjects. Encouraged by assurances of help from Stratford de Redcliffe, the Sultan refuses the demand. Nicholas occupies Moldavia and Wallachia (June), and Turkey declares war (Oct.). Austria and Prussia refuse to employ coercion; but England and France promise their aid if Russia refuses reasonable terms (Nov.). The Russian fleet destroys the Turkish fleet at Sinope (Nov.). The English and French fleets enter the Black Sea, and the Russian ships retire to Sebastopol harbour (Dec.).

3036. **American Ch.** The first Plenary Council of the Roman Church is held at Baltimore.
3037 **Asiatic Ch.** The Shah of Persia is attacked by the Babis, who are in consequence cruelly persecuted.
3038. **Church Hist.** Richard Burton visits Medinah and Mecca.
3039. **Eng. Lit.** Thackeray's Esmond.
3040. **American Lit.** Mrs Stow's Uncle Tom's Cabin.
3041. **French Lit.** Dumas' La Dame aux Camélias (an adaptation of the novel published 1848) introduces realism into the theatre, the romantic drama having become as unreal as the classical. The reaction is strengthened by the influence of Émile Augier.
3042. **German Lit.** Freytag's comedy, The Journalists.
3043. **Russian Lit.** Turgenief's Sketches of a Hunter.
3044. **Science.** Spencer first uses and explains the word 'Evolution.'
Stokes discovers the change in the refrangibility of light.
William Thomson discovers the law of the dissipation of energy.
Hamilton publishes his lectures on Quaternions.
Sabine, Wolf, and Gautier announce the coincidence of the terrestrial-magnetic and sun-spot periods.
3045. **Art.** Méryon's Etchings of Paris.
3046. **Philosophy.** Gury's Theologia Moralis developes Jesuit casuistry.
3047. **Philology.** Mommsen's Inscriptiones Regni Neapolitani.
3048. **Law.** Ihering's Spirit of Roman Law.
3049. **History.** Delisle enters the Manuscript department of the Bibliothèque Impériale, and issues a series of palaeographical and bibliographical studies.
3050. **Geography.** Maclure achieves the North-West Passage.
Barth explores Lake Chad and Hausa-land, and studies the languages of the central Soudan.
3051. **Deaths.** Burnouf, Clay, Froebel, Gioberti, Gogol, Turner, Webster, Wellington.

3052. **Eng. Ch.** Archdeacon Denison publishes two sermons in favour of the Real Presence and is condemned by an Ecclesiastical Court, but acquitted by the Privy Council. [1853
Maurice is ejected from the Professorship of Theology at King's College, London, for questioning eternal punishment.
Spurgeon begins to preach in London.
3053. **German Ch.** Hupfeld points out the three sources of Genesis.
3054. **Dutch Ch.** The Pope creates a Catholic hierarchy.
3055. **American Ch.** Muhlenberg draws up a Memorial calling on the Episcopal Church to widen its activity.
3056. **Eng. Lit.** Kingsley's Hypatia.
3057. **French Lit.** Leconte de Lisle's Poèmes Antiques found the school of the Parnassiens or devotees of form.
Gautier's Émaux et Camées.
3058. **Science.** Hugo v. Mohl discovers protoplasm in plants.
Joseph Hooper's Flora of New Zealand.

1936. **Greece.** On the outbreak of the war, the Greeks attempt to seize Thessaly and Epirus, but are easily repulsed.

1937. **America.** The Treaty of Messilla cedes extensive territory to the United States, and reduces Mexico to its present limits.

The Central American Federation of Guatemala, Salvador, Honduras, Nicaragua, Costa Rica is dissolved.

1938. **Africa.** Cape Colony obtains representative institutions.

1939. **Australasia.** France takes possession of New Caledonia.

1940. **Asia.** An India Bill continues the powers of the Company till Parliament decides otherwise ; but the Court of Direction is to contain six nominees of the Crown, and the Civil Service is thrown open to competition.

England annexes Nagpur.

The first railway in India is opened.

Salar Jung becomes Prime Minister of Hyderabad.

Commodore Perry, of the U.S.A. navy, signs a treaty with the Shogun, opening Japan to American trade.

1941. **England.** Russell introduces a Reform Bill, which is withdrawn owing to the war. [1854

A Corrupt Practices Act makes necessary the publication of accounts after elections, and forbids payments except through authorised agents.

The Prince Consort is charged with unconstitutional interference.

1942. **France.** The Crédit Foncier, established 1852 to provide landowners and communes with cheap loans, becomes a state institution.

1943. **Spain.** O'Donnell revolts, and the Moderado *régime* of eleven years is ended. Christina leaves the country, and a constituent Cortes resolves to keep Queen Isabella on the throne. Espartero becomes Prime Minister. Castelar becomes famous as an orator.

1944. **Greece.** English and French troops land at the Piraeus, and compel Greece to abandon the Russian alliance.

1945. **Russia.** England and France send an Ultimatum to the Tsar (Feb.), and declare war (March). The Russians are forced to withdraw from Moldavia and Wallachia, owing to threats of intervention from Prussia and Austria (July), the latter of which occupies the Principalities. The English and French fleets are sent to the Baltic, but effect nothing. The French and English armies land in the Crimea under St Arnaud and Raglan (later, Canrobert and Simpson), defeat the Russians at Alma (Sept. 20), and blockade Sebastopol, which is defended by Todleben. A Russian attempt to cut off the communication between the English base at Balaclava and Sebastopol leads to the charge of the Light Brigade (Oct. 25). The Russians are beaten back at Inkermann (Nov. 5); but winter inflicts terrible sufferings on the invading armies.

1946. **America.** Douglas moves the organisation of the Louisiana

Claude Bernard studies the liver.
Brunel constructs Saltash Bridge.
3059. **Art.** Steinway begins to manufacture pianos.
Brunn's History of Greek Sculpture.
3060. **Archaeology.** Visconti superintends the excavations at Ostia.
Brugsch organises an expedition to Egypt.
3061. **Philosophy.** Kleutgen attacks the position of Gunther and Hermes, and stimulates the study of scholasticism.
Gratry's Connaissance de Dieu.
3062. **Philology.** Zeuss' Grammatica Celtica.
Böthlingk and Roth's Sanskrit Dictionary.
3063. **Education.** Thring becomes Head Master of Uppingham.
3064. **Anthropology.** Keller finds remains of the Lake dwellings at a depression of Lake Zurich.
3065. **History.** Mommsen's Roman History.
Sybel's History of the French Revolution.
3066. **Economics.** Rodbertus' Letters to v. Kirchmann predict and approve a slow progress towards socialism.
3067. **Social.** The Mayor of Mulhausen founds a society of working men, who gradually become possessors of their own houses.
Haussmann rebuilds large portions of Paris.
3068. **Deaths.** Arago, Von Buch, Diepenbrock, F. W. Robertson.

3069. **German Ch.** The New Lutherans, led by Stahl, Delitzsch, Vilmar, Kliefoth, attack pietism and individualism. [1854
Schweizer's History of the Central Dogmas of Protestantism.
Herzog edits an Encyclopaedia of Protestant Theology.
A Jewish seminary is instituted at Breslau.
3070. **Italian Ch.** The immaculate conception of the Virgin, the definition of which is prepared by Passaglia and Perrone, is declared an article of faith.
3071. **Danish Ch.** Kierkegaard attacks and Martensen defends Christianity.
3072. **Eng. Lit.** Coventry Patmore's Angel in the House.
Kingsley's Westward Ho.
Sydney Dobell's Balder founds the so-called Spasmodic School, of which Alexander Smith and Bailey are members.
3073. **French Lit.** The journal Le Figaro is founded.
3074. **German Lit.** Hermann Lingg's Poems.
3075. **Swiss Lit.** Gottfried Keller's Der Grune Heinrich.
3076. **Science.** Murchison's Siluria, based on travels since 1827.
Henry Smith studies the theory of numbers.
Helmholtz explains the conservation of the sun's heat by shrinkage.
Riemann's Hypotheses of Geometry conceive space as a particular case of a manifold.
Hansen infers from the lunar theory the necessity of reducing Encke's estimate of the sun's distance.

purchase north of the line of the Missouri Compromise and west of Missouri and Iowa as the Territory of Nebraska, asserting that the Missouri Compromise was nullified by the Compromise of 1850. A Bill passes, creating Kansas and Nebraska Territories, in the expectation that Kansas will become a slave and Nebraska a free state, and declares the Missouri Compromise superseded by that of 1850. Some opponents of the Kansas Nebraska Bill issue an Appeal of the Independent Democrats. Men of both parties settle in Kansas, and civil war ensues. The opponents of the Nebraska Bill assume the name of Republicans.

1947. **Africa.** De Lesseps plans the construction of a canal at Suez.

Faidherbe extends the French colony of Senegal.

The independence of the Orange Free State is acknowledged by the Bloemfontein Convention.

1948. **Asia.** Muravieff, Governor of Eastern Siberia, seizes the Amur.

1949. **England.** Russell resigns on notice of Roebuck's motion for enquiry into the conduct of the war. The motion is carried, and Aberdeen resigns. Russell and Derby fail to form governments, and Palmerston is chosen. The Peelites soon resign, and are succeeded by Russell and Cornewall Lewis. [1855

1950. **Italy.** Cavour joins the anti-Russian alliance (Jan.), and sends Sardinian troops to the Crimea under La Marmora.

1951. **Russia.** Nicolas dies, and is succeeded by his son, Alexander II. (March).

A Conference takes place at Vienna, which Russell attends; but Russia refuses to agree to limit her Black Sea fleet. After the unsuccessful storming of the Malakoff Tower by the French, and of the Redan by the English (June), a Russian attack is repulsed by the French and Italians on the Tchernaya (Aug.). The French storm the Malakoff, and the city is evacuated (Sept. 11). General Williams surrenders Kars, after a long defence (Nov.). The English and French fleets in the Baltic bombard Helsingfors. Proposals are made to Russia through Austria (Dec.).

1952. **Germany.** The King of Hanover is compelled by the Diet to abolish the constitution.

1953. **Denmark.** Frederick VII. issues a 'Common Constitution,' though allowing the Duchies separate provincial Estates. Several members of the Duchies, however, protest, and the Bund declares that Denmark has broken the federal law. The King therefore revokes the constitution in regard to Holstein and Lauenburg.

1954. **Australasia.** Responsible government is introduced into all colonies except Western Australia.

3077. **Philosophy.** Kuno Fischer's History of Modern Philosophy.
Renouvier's Essais de Critique, deeply influenced by Kant, attempt a general analysis of consciousness.
Ferrier's Institutes of Metaphysics, a geometrical demonstration of Idealism.
3078. **Education.** A Catholic University is founded in Dublin, of which Newman becomes Rector.
Maurice, Hughes, and Ludlow found a Working Men's College, in Great Ormond Street, London.
The Hebdomadal Board of Oxford is replaced by an Elective Council.
3079. **Philology.** Cobet's Variae Lectiones.
3080. **Politics.** Colins' La Science Sociale founds Belgian socialism.
3081. **Archaeology.** Beulé discovers the Propylaea of the Acropolis.
3082. **History.** Milman's History of Latin Christianity.
3083. **Geography.** Burton and Speke explore Somaliland.
3084. **Social.** The English usury laws are repealed.
3085. **Deaths.** Beneke, Lamennais, Mai, Ohm, Schelling.

3086. **Eng. Ch.** Jowett edits the Epistles of St Paul. [1855
The Society of the Holy Cross is founded.
3087. **Austrian Ch.** Catholic Bishops may issue ordinances without the approval of the civil power, decree penalties, and supervise education, marriage, and the press.
3088. **Italian Ch.** The Sardinian Monastic law abolishes all Orders but those employed in preaching, education and the care of the sick.
3089. **Church Hist.** The Pope condemns Traditionalism.
3090. **Eng. Lit.** Thackeray's The Newcomes.
The Saturday Review is founded.
3091. **French Lit.** Gérard de Nerval's Sonnets and Le Rêve et la Vie form the starting-point of the Symbolist movement.
Augier's Le Gendre de M. Poirier.
3092. **American Lit.** Whitman's Leaves of Grass.
3093. **German Lit.** Scheffel's Ekkehard.
Freytag's Soll und Haben.
3094. **Science.** Maury's Physical Geography of the Sea.
3095. **Art.** Courbet introduces realism into French Art.
Adelaide Ristori acts in Paris.
Manns becomes musical director of the Crystal Palace.
3096. **Philosophy.** Buchner's Force and Matter expounds materialism.
Bain's Senses and the Intellect explains associationist psychology.
Herbert Spencer's Principles of Psychology builds on biological evolution.
3097. **Philology.** Renan's Histoire Générale des Langues Sémitiques.
3098. **History.** Giesebrecht's History of the Mediaeval Empire.
Droysen's History of Prussian Policy.
Hefele's History of the Councils.
Lewis attacks the credibility of early Roman History.
3099. **Deaths.** Charlotte Brontë, Gauss, Kierkegaard, Rosmini.

1955. **England.** A Committee of the Lords report against the creation of life peers in the case of Sir James Parke, created Baron Wensleydale. [1856

1956. **Turkey.** Peace is signed at Paris (March). The fortifications of Sebastopol are destroyed, and Russia promises not to re-fortify it; no war ships are to enter the Black Sea; the Danube is to be free to navigation; the Principalities are restored to their former position; Russia restores Kars to Turkey, and cedes part of Bessarabia to Moldavia. The Sultan undertakes to confirm the privileges of his Christian subjects, but the Powers are not to use this as a pretext for interfering with his domestic government. The Russian protectorate over the Eastern Christians is abolished. The Porte is admitted to all the advantages of Public Law, and to the Concert. Two weeks after the treaty, France, England and Austria guarantee the independence and integrity of Turkey.

In gratitude for Servia's neutrality in the war, the Powers agree that it shall remain under Turkish suzerainty, while its rights and privileges are guaranteed by the Powers. The Porte receives tribute, and retains the border fortresses, but cannot invade the country without the consent of the Powers.

Privateering is forbidden; a neutral flag covers an enemy's goods, except contraband of war; neutral goods, except contraband of war, are not liable to capture under an enemy's flag; blockades, to be binding, must be effective.

1957. **America.** The Whigs and the Know-Nothings disappear, and the Republicans and Democrats are left face to face. Sumner is assaulted in the Senate by a slave-owner.

1958. **Asia.** Oudh is annexed, on the ground of misrule.

Some Chinese seize the Arrow in search of suspected pirates. Canton is therefore bombarded by the English fleet.

Persia sends an expedition against Herat, and England declares war. Troops are despatched from India.

1959. **England.** Cobden carries a motion condemning the policy of the Government in reference to the seizure of the Arrow (March). Palmerston appeals to the country, Bright, Cobden, and Milner Gibson lose their seats, and Palmerston secures a large majority. [1857

A commercial panic occurs, the Bank Charter is suspended, and the Bank Charter Indemnity Act is carried.

1960. **Germany.** The King of Prussia becomes insane, and his brother William becomes Regent. Moltke becomes Head of the Staff.

1961. **Italy.** Mazzini attempts to raise an insurrection in Genoa.

Maximilian, brother of the Emperor, becomes Viceroy of Lombardy and Venetia.

1962. **Switzerland.** Prussia renounces her claims in Neuchâtel.

3100. **Eng. Ch.** McLeod Campbell applies the ideas of Erskine of Linlathen to the Atonement. [1856

3101. **Irish Ch.** Miall proposes the disestablishment of the Irish Church.

3102. **German Ch.** The Catholic, an Ultramontane journal, directed by Ketteler of Mainz, and the Stimmen aus Maria Laach, a Jesuit organ, oppose the Munich School of Döllinger and Frohschammer.

Bunsen's Signs of the Time, a series of letters on liberty of conscience and the rights of the Christian Church.

3103. **Eng. Lit.** Charles Reade's Never too late to Mend.

3104. **Science.** Helmholtz' Physiological Optics works out Young's colour-theory, and declares red, green and violet the three primitives.

Bessemer invents a process for obtaining a new and cheaper steel for rails. Siemens manufactures more ductile steel for boiler plating.

Oppel applies Quenstedt's classification of the Jurassic to other countries, and founds detailed stratigraphy by the recognition of life zones.

3105. **Art.** Rubinstein's début as a pianist.

Holman Hunt's Scape Goat.

Böcklin's Pan.

3106. **Philosophy.** Lotze's Microcosmus supplements Weisse's idealistic monism with Herbart's pluralistic realism, and builds metaphysics on ethics. The change of monads does not result from an inner law but from real interaction. The seemingly transient is the immanent working within itself of one all-embracing Being.

3107. **Philology.** Goldstücker's Sanskrit Dictionary.

3108. **History.** Motley's Rise of the Dutch Republic.

De Tocqueville's Ancien Régime.

Le Blant's Inscriptions Chrétiennes de la Gaule.

3109. **Geography.** Burton and Speke are sent by the Geographical Society to discover the great Lakes, of which rumours abound. Burton discovers Tanganyika and Speke the Victoria Nyanza.

Livingstone journeys from the Cape to Angola, and thence to the East Coast exploring the Zambesi from source to mouth.

3110. **Anthropology.** A skull discovered in Neanderthal represents a type lower than those found in the Quaternary deposits.

3111. **Deaths.** Hamilton, Heine, Lobatschewsky, Adolphe Monod, Schumann.

3112. **Eng. Ch.** The first great ritual judgments are given. [1857

The ecclesiastical Courts are deprived of their testamentary jurisdiction and control over the law of marriage.

3113. **Scotch Ch.** Dr Lee introduces written prayer and a richer ritual into the Established Church; but the 'Innovations' are hotly attacked.

3114. **Irish Ch.** Father Burke, a Dominican, begins a series of missions.

3115. **German Ch.** Gunther's works are condemned for dualism.

Ritschl's Growth of the Early Church combats the Tübingen school.

1963. **Russia.** Herzen demands reforms in The Bell.

1964. **America.** In the case of Dred Scott, Chief Justice Taney declares that slaves are property and that Congress cannot legislate against property, and that the Missouri Compromise is therefore void. This decision is taken to mean that Congress cannot exclude slavery from Territories.

A financial crash occurs, and the Walker tariff is modified to rates lower than at any time since 1816.

1965. **Asia.** Owing to Lord Dalhousie's policy of annexation, and to a belief that the new cartridges are greased with cow's fat, a mutiny breaks out at Meerut and Delhi, and spreads through Oudh, the North-West Provinces, and Lower Bengal (March). The descendant of the Great Moghul is proclaimed Emperor. Sir John Lawrence, Governor of the Punjab, disarms the Sepoys in the Punjab by the aid of the Sikhs, and sends troops to besiege Delhi. Salar Jung keeps the Mohammedan state of Hyderabad loyal. Sir Henry Lawrence holds out in the Residency at Lucknow. At Cawnpore about a thousand English are besieged by Nana Sahib, and allowed to depart. On reaching the boats they are shot, only four surviving (June 26). Delhi is taken (Sept. 20), but Nicholson is killed in the assault. Havelock and Outram save Lucknow (Sept. 26), which is finally relieved by Sir Colin Campbell (Nov. 17).

England allies with France against China, and sends Lord Elgin as Envoy. The Chinese fleet is destroyed, and Canton is captured.

Before any decisive contest occurs in Persia, a treaty is signed by England and Persia at Paris. Herat is to be evacuated, and slavery to be suppressed in the Persian Gulf.

Ignatieff, a Russian envoy, is sent on a mission of military, political, and geographical reconnaissance to the Khanates of Khiva and Bokhara.

England occupies Perim.

1966. **Africa.** Algeria is finally conquered by France.

[1858

1967. **England.** On Orsini's attempt to murder Napoleon, Palmerston is induced by the Emperor to introduce a Conspiracy to Murder Bill, which, in consequence of boastful French talk, is defeated. Palmerston resigns, and Derby becomes Prime Minister.

Jews are admitted to Parliament.

Property qualification for members of Parliament is abolished.

1968. **France.** Orsini, a Carbonaro, plots to murder Napoleon (Jan.). Jules Favre gains notoriety by defending him, enters Parliament, and becomes one of the leaders of the opposition. Napoleon is frightened, and meets Cavour at Plombières (July), promising to help Victor Emanuel to expel Austria from Italy. Victor Emanuel is to have Lombardy and Venetia, and Napoleon to take Savoy and Nice.

1969. **Switzerland.** A society known as Helvetia is formed by Fazy of Geneva to resist reaction and Ultramontanism.

1970. **Montenegro.** Owing to boundary disputes, a Turkish army

3116. **Eng. Lit.** George Eliot's Scenes from Clerical Life.
Hughes' Tom Brown's School Days.
Miss Mulock's John Halifax Gentleman.

3117. **French Lit.** Flaubert's Madame Bovary.
Baudelaire's Fleurs du Mal.

3118. **Science.** Joule perfects the kinetic theory of gases.
Clerk Maxwell proves Saturn's Rings to be meteoric.
Pasteur proves the vitalistic theory of fermentation against Liebig, who believes the process to be purely chemical.
Clausius explains electrolysis by dissociation.

3119. **Art.** Rossetti frescoes the Oxford Union, aided by William Morris and Burne-Jones.
Schwind frescoes the Wartburg with scenes from the history of the Landgraves.
The National Portrait Gallery is founded.

3120. **Archaeology.** Charles Newton discovers the tomb of Mausolus at Halicarnassus.

3121. **Philosophy.** Taine's Philosophes Classiques attacks Cousin and the eclectic Idealists.
On the death of Comte, Lafitte became the leader of the Positivist movement. Comte's ideas are spread in England by Congreve, Frederic Harrison, Bridges, Beesly, Cotter Morison and others.

3122. **Philology.** Fürst's Hebrew and Chaldee Dictionary.

3123. **History.** Buckle's History of Civilisation traces progress to the advance in physical science.
The Calendar of English State Papers and the Rolls series of Chronicles begin to appear.

3124. **Law.** Gneist's Modern English Constitutional Law.

3125. **Education.** The Universities of Calcutta, Bombay and Madras are founded.
Mary Carpenter, who has set up a Reformatory at Kingswood, 1852, obtains the Industrial Schools Act.

3126. **Deaths.** Béranger, Cauchy, Comte, De Musset, Rauch, Reschid Pasha, Manin.

3127. **Eng. Ch.** W. G. Ward rehabilitates the Dublin Review to oppose the Rambler, (later the Home and Foreign Review) which under Simpson and Acton represents the liberal Catholic movement. [1858
Mansel's Bampton Lectures, based on Hamilton's philosophy, argue from the impotence of Reason to the necessity of Faith.

3128. **French Ch.** The Virgin is believed to appear at Lourdes.

3129. **Russian Ch.** The Stundists, who approximate to Lutheran doctrine and reject ceremonial, form a sect.

3130. **American Ch.** Hecker founds the Order of St Paul, aiming at a reconciliation of Catholicism with American civilisation.

3131. **Church Hist.** A Christian servant baptises the child of Mortara,

invades Montenegro, and is annihilated. The boundaries are fixed by the Great Powers.

1971. **Turkey.** The Great Powers arrange that Moldavia and Wallachia shall be ruled by separate princes, chosen by the assemblies, and shall pay tribute to the Sultan. Both choose the same prince, Alexander Cusa, and are allowed to form one state as Roumania.

1972. **Russia.** Alexander emancipates the serfs on the royal domain.

1973. **America.** Lincoln debates with Douglas, and declares that the *status quo* cannot last. Seward confirms the existence of an 'irrepressible conflict.'

1974. **Asia.** The Mutiny is finally suppressed by Colin Campbell and Sir Hugh Rose. The East India Company is abolished, and India is transferred to the Crown, and governed by a Viceroy and a Secretary of State, with 15 advisers.

Lord Elgin forces China to sign the Treaty of Tientsin, opening China to European commerce, establishing diplomatic relations, and obtaining recognition of equality between foreigners and natives and freedom for missionaries.

After the murder of some missionaries, the French fleet captures Saigon.

By the Treaty of Aigun, China recognises the dominion of Russia over the whole of Siberia.

A massacre of Christians takes place at Jeddah, which is therefore bombarded by an English ship. The Sultan is forced to grant reparation.

Treaties for amity and unrestricted commerce with England, France, Russia, and the United States are signed by Japan, and Yokohama and Nagasaki are opened to trade.

1975. **Africa.** The Grondwet of the South African Republic provides for a President, elected for five years by burghers over sixteen, and a Volksraad.

1976. **England.** Disraeli announces franchise proposals, but is defeated, and Palmerston returns to power with Russell and Gladstone. Cobden refuses the Presidency of the Board of Trade. [1859

Volunteer rifle corps are formed.

1977. **Ireland.** The Phoenix Club, under O'Donovan Rossa and Stephens, forms the nucleus of Fenianism.

1978. **Italy.** At the New Year's Day reception, Napoleon regrets his relations with Austria, and begins to mobilise. His cousin, Prince Napoleon, marries a daughter of the King of Sardinia. Austria refuses to allow Sardinia to be represented at a congress to settle the affairs of Italy, and demands disarmament within three days (April 23). Cavour refuses, and Napoleon also declares war (May 3). The Austrians march on Turin, but are defeated by Victor Emanuel, who has been joined by Napoleon, at Magenta and Solferino (June). Tuscany, Parma, Modena, and Bologna are deserted by their rulers. Napoleon, fearing a strong Italy, dreading a quarrel with the Pope, and learning the hostility of

her Jewish employer, believing him to be dying. The boy recovers and is carried off to be educated as a Christian. His parents demand his restoration, which is refused by the Pope.

3132. **Eng. Lit.** Tennyson's Idylls of the King.

The Spectator is bought by R. H. Hutton and Townsend.

3133. **American Lit.** Holmes' Autocrat of the Breakfast Table.

3134. **French Lit.** Feuillet's Roman d'un jeune Homme pauvre.

3135. **Norwegian Lit.** Björnson's Arne.

3136. **Science.** Donati's Comet appears.

Helmholtz enunciates his Vortex Motion theory.

Wallace's paper on Natural Selection, based on study in the Malay Archipelago, and a paper by Darwin, both reaching the theory of Evolution, are simultaneously communicated to the Linnaean Society.

Sorby's Microscopical Structure of Crystals.

William Thomson invents a mirror galvanometer, which detects very small electric currents.

3137. **Art.** Titiens begins to sing in London.

Alfred Stevens designs the Wellington monument in St Paul's.

Frith's The Derby Day.

3138. **Philosophy.** Vacherot's La Métaphysique et la Science, asserting that as the individual is the real the ideal cannot be real, is attacked by Caro, Janet and Ravaisson.

3139. **Philology.** Renier's Inscriptions Romaines de l'Algérie.

Oppert detects 'Accadian,' a Scythic idiom among the cuneiform alphabets.

3140. **Education.** The Oxford and Cambridge Local Examinations are instituted.

The government of Cambridge University is taken from the Caput.

3141. **History.** Carlyle's Frederick the Great.

Villari's Life of Savonarola.

3142. **Deaths.** Robert Brown, Johannes Müller, Robert Owen.

3143. **Eng. Lit.** George Eliot's Adam Bede. [1859

George Meredith's Ordeal of Richard Feverel.

Fitzgerald translates the Rubaiyat of Omar Khayyam.

3144. **French Lit.** Hugo's Légendes des Siècles.

Erckmann and Chatrian begin to collaborate.

3145. **Russian Lit.** Gontcharof's Oblomof, a realistic novel.

3146. **Science.** Zirkel investigates the lavas of the Eifel district.

Kirchhoff and Bunsen discover that the dark lines of the solar spectrum arise from the presence in the solar atmosphere of substances which in a flame produce bright lines. Kirchhoff concludes that sodium, iron, magnesium, copper, zinc, barium and nickel exist in the sun.

Darwin publishes the Origin of Species by Natural Selection. The

Germany, suddenly makes an armistice at Villa Franca (July 11), Sardinia to receive Lombardy, Italy to be federated under the Pope, and Austria to retain Venetia and the Quadrilateral. Cavour resigns in disgust. Victor Emanuel, however, makes Napoleon promise not to allow any forcible restoration of the refugee rulers. The terms of Villa Franca are confirmed at Zurich (Nov.). The Italian states are to be under the honorary presidency of the Pope; the sovereigns of Tuscany and Modena to be reinstated; the revolted Legations to return to the Pope. Modena, Parma and Tuscany, and the Legations, however, declare in favour of annexation to Sardinia.

1979. **Germany.** The German National Union is formed by Bennigsen to substitute a strong executive and a national Parliament for the Bund. The Union dissolves, 1867.

1980. **Russia.** Shamil, a Circassian chief, surrenders to Russia.

1981. **Servia.** The Karageorgevitch dynasty replaces the Obrenovitch.

1982. **America.** John Brown appears at Harper's Ferry, Virginia, with 19 followers, and seizes the arsenal, but is captured and executed.

1983. **Australasia.** Queensland is separated from N. S. Wales, with Brisbane as capital.

1984. **Africa.** Spain attacks Morocco.

The Senussi, ruler of the Mohammedan sect in the Libyan desert, dies, and is succeeded by the present ruler, who prepares for the holy war from his capital at Jerabub.

Sir George Grey suggests the federation of British and Dutch South Africa.

1985. **England.** A Bill abolishing the paper duty is rejected by the Lords. Palmerston therefore carries resolutions to render a similar occurrence impossible. [1860

Cobden, supported by Gladstone, arranges a commercial treaty with Napoleon, the duties between France and England being greatly reduced.

1986. **Italy.** Cavour returns to power. Tuscany, Parma, Modena, and Romagna declare for Sardinia by a plébiscite, and are annexed. Napoleon obtains Savoy and Nice.

Garibaldi sails with 1,000 volunteers to Sicily (May), where the ground is prepared by Crispi, and in two months subdues it. Francis II., of Naples, promises a Constitution; but Garibaldi crosses and enters Naples (Sept.). Victor Emanuel joins Garibaldi, takes Capua, besieges Gaeta, and enters Naples. Cavour annexes Umbria and the two Sicilies. Garibaldi acknowledges the authority of Victor Emanuel, and retires to Caprera.

The Pope fights for the Legations, and Lamoricière is routed by Cialdini at Castel Fidardo (Sept.), and is compelled to surrender at Ancona. The Papal States, with the exception of the Patrimonium Petri, are annexed.

1987. **France.** Napoleon allows criticism of the speech from the Throne and the Budget.

theory is embraced by Lyell, Hooker, Huxley, Haeckel, and others, but is attacked by Owen.

Gegenbaur's Comparative Anatomy.

Darwin's two chapters on geology in the Origin of Species point out the imperfection of the geological record and the vast time that has elapsed between the formations.

Huxley's Oceanic Hydrozoa.

3147. **Art.** Millet's Angélus.

Busch begins his sketches for the Fliegende Blätter, and is joined by Oberländer.

Gounod's Faust.

3148. **Politics.** Lazarus' Psychology of Peoples.

J. S. Mill's On Liberty pleads for individualism.

Hare contends that all candidates who obtain a minimum number of votes should be elected members of parliament.

3149. **Economics.** Carey's Principles of Social Science assume a rational system of beneficent laws, point out that land owes a large part of its value to man, and strongly advocate protection.

3150. **History.** Sybel edits a Historical Review.

Maximilian of Bavaria creates the Historical Commission under the direction of Ranke.

3151. **Education.** A curriculum is framed by the Prussian Government for boys in the Realschulen destined to callings for which University studies are not needed. The study of Latin, however, is retained.

The Duke of Newcastle's Commission reveals the inadequate provision for elementary education that exists in England.

3152. **Philology.** Tischendorf discovers the Sinaitic MSS. of the New Testament.

Max Müller's Lectures on the Science of Language.

3153. **Geography.** Livingstone discovers Lake Nyasa.

3154. **Deaths.** Aksakov, Austin, David Cox, De Tocqueville, Hallam, Alexander Humboldt, Edward Irving, Macaulay, Metternich, Karl Ritter.

3155. **Eng. Ch.** A series of Essays and Reviews, by Temple, [1860
Jowett, Mark Pattison, Baden Powell and others are condemned in Convocation, though defended by Stanley, and are praised in the Positivist organ, the Westminster Review.

At the meeting of the British Association at Oxford, Wilberforce attacks and Huxley defends the theory of Evolution.

The English Church Union is founded to organise the High Church movement.

Bradlaugh founds and edits The National Reformer.

Norman Macleod edits Good Words.

3156. **Italian Ch.** Dupanloup's Letter to La Guerronière replies to

1988. **Sweden.** Norway protests against the Governor-General, and asserts its right to suppress the post. The King refuses to recognise the claim.

1989. **America.** In the Presidential election, the Northern Democrats split off on the demand to recognise slavery as morally right and to urge Congress to assume its protection in the territories. Abraham Lincoln is therefore elected. South Carolina summons a Convention, which dissolves its union.

1990. **Australasia.** The Second Maori War breaks out.

1991. **Asia.** The Chinese treacherously attack the English squadron; Parkes, the English ambassador, is imprisoned; the French Minister is insulted. France and England join their forces, Pekin is captured, and the Summer Palace burnt. The Treaty of Pekin confirms that of Tientsin, and imposes a large indemnity. Christianity is to be tolerated, and the tariff is revised.

The Druses attack and massacre the Maronites, and the Christians at Damascus are massacred by Mohammedans. Order is restored by a French army.

1992. **Africa.** Morocco is forced by Spain to surrender territory, and to transfer the control of customs in default of payment of the indemnity.

1993. **England.** The abolition of the Paper Duty is combined with the financial scheme of the Government and passes the Lords. [1861

The Prince Consort dies.

1994. **Italy.** The surrender of Gaeta terminates the resistance of Ferdinand (Feb.). The first Italian Parliament meets at Turin (Feb. 18), and Victor Emanuel is greeted as King of Italy. At this moment, Cavour dies.

1995. **Germany.** William I. becomes King of Prussia, and a conflict over the reorganisation of the army breaks out. The Fortschritts-Partei is formed by Waldeck, Virchow and Karl Twesten, and demands economy and ministerial responsibility.

1996. **Austria.** Schmerling becomes the head of a centralising cabinet, and the Council is changed into a central Parliament. Bohemia refuses to send deputies.

1997. **Hungary.** The old constitution is restored to Hungary; but the Diet is dissolved for demanding full autonomy.

1998. **Russia.** Alexander frees the peasants, who become owners of part of their land by loans from the State. Immediately after the issue of the Edict, Milutin, its principal author, falls from power.

1999. **America.** Mississippi, Florida, Alabama, Georgia, Louisiana, and Texas secede (Jan.). A Convention of the Southern States meets at Montgomery, adopts a provisional constitution for the Confederate

Napoleon's pamphlet, and advocates the maintenance of the temporal power.

3157. **Asiatic Ch.** Russia builds a monastery and a house for pilgrims at Jerusalem.

3158. **French Lit.** Labiche's comedy, Le Voyage de M. Perrichon.

Coquelin makes his début at the Comédie française.

3159. **German Lit.** Spielhagen's Problematic Natures.

Fritz Reuter begins a series of stories of peasant life, called Olle Kamellen, written in Platt Deutsch.

3160. **Russian Lit.** Tolstoi's War and Peace.

Ostrowski's The Storm and Pisemski's Bitter Fate introduce realism.

3161. **Science.** Sir John Brown invents armour-plating for ships.

3162. **Art.** Macfarren's Rudiments of Harmony.

3163. **Philosophy.** Fechner's Psycho-Physics applies Weber's law of the relation between stimulus and change of sensation.

3164. **Philology.** Oppert's Assyrian Grammar.

Gabelentz' Melanesian Languages.

3165. **Politics.** Mill's Treatise on Representative Government.

3166. **History.** Montalembert's Moines de l'Occident.

3167. **Law.** Bruns' Fontes Juris Romani Antiqui.

3168. **Geography.** Speke and Grant discover the Victoria Nyanza lake to be the main source of the Nile.

3169. **Deaths.** Aberdeen, Arndt, Baur, Bunsen, Dalhousie, Heiberg, Lobeck, Szechenyi, Theodore Parker, Schopenhauer.

[1861

3170. **Eng. Ch.** 'Essays and Reviews' are attacked by Wilberforce in the Quarterly Review, and by Thomson, Mansel, Ellicott, Harold Browne and others. Wilson and Williams are suspended by the Court of Arches, but are acquitted by the Privy Council. Convocation formally condemns the book.

The first Church Congress is held at Cambridge.

3171. **German Ch.** Döllinger's The Church and the Churches first reveals his hostility to curialism.

3172. **Italian Ch.** Prota-Giurleo, a Dominican, attempts to form a National Church, demanding the election of the priest by the parish and of the Bishop by clergy and people, the abolition of celibacy, the circulation of the Bible, prayers in the vernacular, Communion in both kinds The movement, however, does not spread beyond the South.

Passaglia's work on The Temporal Power is put on the Index.

3173. **Church Hist.** Patteson becomes Bishop of Melanesia, but is murdered, 1871.

3174. **Asiatic Ch.** Chunder Sen joins the Brahmo movement, and works for education, the abolition of caste, and the raising of the position of women.

3175. **Eng. Lit.** George Eliot's Silas Marner.

States of America, and chooses Jefferson Davis President, and A. H. Stephens Vice-President (Feb.). Fort Sumter, in Charleston harbour, is fired on and reduced (April). Virginia, North Carolina, Tennessee, and Arkansas join the secessionists. Delaware, Maryland, and Kentucky, and, in 1862, Missouri join the North. Lincoln calls for 75,000 volunteers, and proclaims a blockade. The army of the North is driven back at Bull Run, in North Virginia (July). New volunteers are therefore called out, and McLellan is put in command.

Mason and Slidell, sent by the Confederates to seek the friendship of England and France, are taken from the English ship Trent, by an American man-of-war. Captain Wilkes is congratulated by Congress. Palmerston and Russell demand the surrender of the agents in a despatch, the wording of which is modified by the Prince Consort. Adams, the American ambassador, strongly urges submission.

Seward advises a foreign war in order to rally the South.

After eight years' civil war in Mexico, Juarez, the leader of the advanced Liberals, enters the capital. He confiscates Church property, and decides to suspend payment to foreigners for two years. England, France and Spain therefore claim compensation for the losses of their subjects, and send a joint expedition.

2000. **West Indies.** San Domingo is annexed to Spain.

2001. **Africa.** The ruler of Lagos cedes it to England.

2002. **England.** The Alabama is allowed to leave the Mersey under pretence of a trial trip, but in reality ordered by the Confederates. After doing immense damage to the North, it is sunk, 1864. [1862

2003. **France.** Napoleon obtains Mentone and Roquebrune.

2004. **Italy.** Garibaldi plans to attack Rome, but is taken prisoner by Victor Emanuel's troops at Aspromonte.

2005. **Germany.** The Prussian Parliament attacks the military policy of the King and Roon, and is dissolved. A still larger Progressive opposition is returned, and the King prepares to abdicate, but is dissuaded by Bismarck, who becomes chief minister. The Lower House refuses the military credits, and Bismarck governs without a budget, and speaks of the necessity of 'blood and iron.'

2006. **Greece.** King Otho is expelled, and the crown is offered to the Duke of Edinburgh. The ruling houses having agreed not to accept the crown, England chooses George, second son of the King of Denmark. Representative institutions are established.

2007. **America.** Juarez promises, but fails, to pay the arrear of debt and an indemnity. England and Spain withdraw; but Napoleon, who dreams of a Latin Empire, renews the attack.

Mason and Slidell are surrendered by the United States. Admiral Farragut takes New Orleans, and obtains control of the lower Mississippi

3176. **French Lit.** Eugénie de Guérin's Journals.
3177. **Art.** Garnier designs the Opera-house at Paris.
Patti makes her début.
William Morris begins work as a decorator and designer.
Harpignies begins to exhibit his landscapes.
3178. **Science.** Pasteur finds anaerobic life.
3179. **Education.** Lowe determines the scale of Government grants.
Spencer's Education, Moral, Intellectual, Physical, contends that scientific, rather than literary culture, is best adapted for gaining a livelihood and performing the duties of a citizen.
3180. **Philology.** Dahl's Dictionary of the Russian Language.
Schleicher's Comparative Grammar of the Indo-European Languages summarises all work done since Bopp and Grimm, and makes each language stand out clearly from a common background.
3181. **Economics.** Walras urges that the State should appropriate rent.
3182. **History.** Dahn's Kings of the Germans.
3183. **Law.** Maine's Ancient Law examines the ideas on which ancient civilisation rested.
3184. **Anthropology.** Bachofen studies the position of women in primitive times.
3185. **Social.** The American Civil War stops the supply of cotton, and leads to widespread distress in Lancashire.
3186. **Deaths.** Mrs Browning, Clough, Czartoryski, Lacordaire, Savigny, Stahl.

3187. **Eng. Ch.** Colenso's The Pentateuch asserts that the Bible contains 'unhistorical' parts. He is urged by English Bishops to resign, but refuses, and Gray, Bishop of Capetown, deposes him. The Privy Council declares that Gray possesses no jurisdiction, and the Bishop therefore excommunicates him. [1862
The Confraternity of the Blessed Sacrament is founded to teach the doctrine of the Real Presence.
Father Ignatius (Rev. Joseph Lyne) attempts to revive monasticism, and founds Llanthony Abbey.
3188. **German Ch.** Froschammer's works are placed on the Index.
Hase's Handbook of Polemic against the Roman Church.
3189. **Church Hist.** With the approval of Convocation and of the American Episcopalians an attempt is made to unite the Anglican and Greek Churches.
The Pope canonises the Japanese martyrs.
3190. **Eng. Lit.** Henry Kingsley's Ravenshoe.
George Meredith's Poems and Ballads.
3191. **French Lit.** Victor Hugo's Les Misérables.
3192. **American Lit.** Whittier's Snow Bound.
3193. **Italian Lit.** Witte's translation of and commentary on Dante.
3194. **Art.** Gilbert Scott designs the Albert Memorial, Kensington Gardens.
Israels' The Shipwrecked Man, and The Cradle.

(April). At the same moment, Grant drives the Southerners back at Shiloh. The Merrimac destroys some Northern frigates, but is worsted by the Monitor. The Alabama leaves the Mersey, despite the repeated protests of Adams. Lee and 'Stonewall' Jackson defend Richmond, and repulse the Federals at Bull Run (Aug.). Lee invades the North, and fights a drawn battle with McLellan at the Antietam (Aug.), then withdraws and repulses an attack on Fredericksburg (Dec.). In Tennessee, Sheridan repels a fierce Southern onslaught at Stone River.

Congress issues paper money as legal tender; the premium on gold reaches 200 p.c.; and prices and rents rise, followed at a distance by wages.

Congress abolishes slavery in Territories without compensation.

2008. **Africa.** France purchases Obok, opposite Aden, and obtains a foothold on the Guinea Coast.

2009. **Asia.** The Treaty of Saigon closes the war of France and Annam, which cedes parts of Cochin China. The remainder is annexed, 1867.

Hart becomes Inspector of maritime customs in China.

[1863

2010. **England.** The Times accuses Cobden and Bright of preaching spoliation. Cobden retaliates by addressing Delane by name.

2011. **France.** Thiers returns to public life, and forms an opposition.

Napoleon invites the nations to a Peace Congress; but Russell refuses on behalf of Great Britain.

2012. **Germany.** Austria proposes a meeting of princes at Frankfort to reorganise the Bund by creating a Directory of five princes, with the Emperor as hereditary president. Bismarck persuades the King of Prussia to refuse to attend, and the scheme lapses.

Parliament demands the dismissal of Bismarck, and is prorogued, and the press is muzzled. The Crown Prince disapproves the unconstitutional policy of the King and Bismarck.

2013. **Denmark.** Schleswig is incorporated with Denmark (March), but Holstein receives independent rights. Frederick dies, and Christian IX. succeeds, and is at once ordered by the Bund to separate the Duchies from Denmark (Oct.). The Bund sends an army (Dec.), and Frederick of Augustenburg, for whom the Holstein Diet declares, is proclaimed Duke of Schleswig-Holstein (Dec.).

2014. **Greece.** The Ionian Islands are united to Greece.

2015. **Russia.** Katkof edits the Moscow Gazette, which obtains immense influence, and leads the reaction against liberalism.

2016. **Poland.** Poland revolts against conscription, and carries on guerilla warfare for two years. Prussia offers to assist Russia, which defies the remonstrance of the remaining Powers. The insurrection is ruthlessly suppressed by Muravieff.

3195. **Archaeology.** Newton describes the Mausoleum of Halicarnassus.

3196. **Science.** Pasteur disproves spontaneous generations. The theory is revived by Bastian, 1876, and again refuted by Pasteur.

Andrews proves the existence of a critical point in gases.

The Bonn catalogue, enumerating the stars visible in the Northern Hemisphere, is completed by Argelander, a pupil of Bessel.

Ramsay suggests that certain lake-basins were scooped out by glaciers.

Darwin's Fertilisation of Orchids by Insects.

3197. **Philosophy.** Spencer's First Principles pronounces the nature of things unknowable, and declares the persistence of force the key of the physical universe.

Mill's Utilitarianism expands the teaching of Bentham and his father.

3198. **Philology.** Bleek's Comparative Grammar of the South African Languages.

3199. **History.** Potthast's Bibliotheca Historica Medii Aevi.

Friedländer's History of the Civilisation of the later Roman Empire.

3200. **Economics.** Lassalle's Working-Class Programme recommends a system of State Socialism, cooperative production to be begun immediately by State aid.

3201. **Education.** A college is founded in each American State for scientific and technical studies on an equality with classics.

3202. **Geography.** Gifford Palgrave journeys through Arabia.

3203. **Deaths.** Biot, Buckle, Nesselrode, Uhland.

3204. **French Ch.** Renan's Vie de Jésus. [1863

3205. **German Ch.** At a Congress of Catholic scholars, held at Munich, Döllinger, Reinkens, Schulte and others assume an Old Catholic position.

A Protestant Union is founded by Bluntschli, Rothe, Ewald, Hitzig, Schenkel, Hilgenfeld, who desire a federation into a National Church, the concession of further power to the laity, and disapprove subscription to creeds.

3206. **Danish Ch.** Strife breaks out between Grundtvig and Martensen.

3207. **Church Hist.** At a Catholic Congress at Malines, Montalembert demands toleration and the separation of Church and State.

3208. **Eng. Lit.** George Eliot's Romola.

3209. **French Lit.** Le Petit Journal, a halfpenny paper, is founded.

3210. **Russian Lit.** Tchernichevsky attacks current ideas on marriage.

Nekrasof's Frost the Red-nose.

3211. **Science.** Helmholtz' Sensations of Tone.

Huxley's Man's Place in Nature interprets Darwin's ideas.

Huxley demonstrates the separation of Reptiles and Batrachians.

3212. **Art.** The Salon des Refusés is founded, in which Manet and other Impressionists exhibit.

Whistler's Symphony in White.

2017. **America.** Lincoln issues a proclamation abolishing slavery (Jan.).

Grant captures Vicksburg, and controls the Mississippi from source to mouth (July). Meanwhile Lee wins at Chancellorsville (April), and again invades the North, but is repulsed at Gettysburg.

Two rams, constructed by Messrs Laird for the Confederate States, are stopped at the moment of completion by Russell.

The creation of national banks is authorised on the deposit of bonds of one-third of their capital with the Government, which issues bank notes redeemable in green-backs to ninety per cent. of the value of the bonds.

The French capture Puebla, and the crown of Mexico is offered to Maximilian, brother of the Emperor of Austria.

2018. **Asia.** A French protectorate is proclaimed over Cambodia.

Gordon suppresses the revolt of the Taipings.

The French, English, and American fleets attack Japan.

2019. **Italy.** Napoleon agrees to withdraw the French garrison from Rome within two years, on condition that Victor Emanuel undertakes to defend the Papal States. [1864

2020. **Denmark.** Austrian and Prussian armies enter the Duchies, and the lines of Düppel are carried by the Prussians under Prince Frederick Charles. An armistice is made, and Russell presides over negotiations in London. Prussia and Austria secede from the London protocol, according to which Christian was to succeed to the entire monarchy. The Bund desire the severance of the Duchies under the Duke of Augustenburg. Austria and Prussia are prepared to allow the personal union with a separate constitution. England proposes the division of Schleswig into a German and a Danish half; but the boundary cannot be fixed. The war is renewed, Jutland is overrun, the Danish fleet is defeated by the Austrian admiral, Tegethoff, Christian is forced to sign the Treaty of Vienna, ceding the Duchies and Lauenburg to Austria and Prussia to make their own arrangements (Oct.). Holstein is evacuated, and the two Powers establish a common government in Schleswig.

2021. **Russia.** Zemstvos, or elective provincial governments, are instituted.

2022. **Poland.** On the advice of Milutin, the peasants are made absolute owners of the land they occupy, in order to separate their interests from those of the nobles, and to bind them to the crown.

2023. **America.** Sherman marches through Georgia and captures Savannah, and Thomas destroys a Southern army at Nashville (Dec.).

Grant meets Lee in the Wilderness, near Chancellorsville, and fighting lasts a month. Though Grant loses most heavily, his ranks are refilled.

3213. **History.** Gardiner's History of England in the 17th century.
Kinglake's History of the Crimea.

3214. **Philology.** Lane's Arabic Lexicon.
Littré's Dictionary of the French Language.

3215. **Education.** Robert College is founded at Constantinople.

3216. **Law.** Harcourt discusses 'recognition' in Historicus' Letters to the Times.

3217. **Anthropology.** Lyell's Antiquity of Man.

3218. **Deaths.** Jacob Grimm, Lyndhurst, Steiner, Thackeray, Whately.

3219. **Eng. Ch.** Newman's project for a Catholic college at Oxford is defeated by Manning and withdrawn. [1864

In answer to an attack by Kingsley, Newman writes his Apologia pro Vita Sua.

3220. **Scotch Ch.** Ministers episcopally ordained in Scotland are allowed to hold benefices in the English Church.

3221. **Polish Ch.** Catholic monasteries are dissolved, the bishopric of Chelm is united with the Russian Church, and the control of Catholic affairs is given to the Minister of Worship.

3222. **Church Hist.** The Pope issues a Syllabus, condemning 80 errors. It is defended by Dupanloup and turned to extreme anti-liberalism by Veuillot. From this moment, infallibility is widely discussed.

3223. **Eng. Lit.** Swinburne's Atalanta in Calydon.

3224. **Science.** Croll explains the glaciations of the earth by variations in the eccentricity of its orbit.

Clausius' Mechanical Theory of Heat predicts a more uniform distribution of heat and a diminution of local movements, and discusses the kinetic theory of gases.

Huggins proves certain nebulae to be gaseous.

Bertrand's treatise on the Differential and Integral Calculus.

3225. **Art.** Du Maurier begins to draw for Punch.
Nilsson makes her début.

3226. **Archaeology.** Rossi's work in the Roman Catacombs.

3227. **Philology.** The Monumentum Ancyranum, relating to Augustus, is found.

Munro edits and translates Lucretius.

3228. **Philosophy.** Vera and Spaventa introduce Hegelianism into Italy.

Lange's History of Materialism introduces Neo-Kantianism.

3229. **History.** Fustel de Coulanges' La Cité Antique.

3230. **Law.** The Geneva Convention, accepted by all civilised countries, prescribes immunity for the 'Red Cross' League, and equality of treatment for the wounded in warfare on land.

3231. **Geography.** Samuel Baker discovers the Albert Nyanza lake.

3232. **Anthropology.** Mortillet and Quatrefages maintain the existence of man in Tertiary times.

Lincoln is re-elected President by an enormous majority, defeating McLellan, the candidate of the Northern Democrats, who are opposed to the further prosecution of the war.

Francisco Lopez, the dictator of Paraguay, invades Brazil, which allies with Uruguay and Argentina. Paraguay is invaded and defeated.

Maximilian accepts the Mexican crown.

2024. **England.** At the General Election, Gladstone loses his seat at Oxford. Palmerston dies, and Russell becomes Prime Minister. [1865

2025. **Italy.** Florence becomes the capital.

2026. **Austria.** To allay discontent, Austria re-establishes provincial diets, revoking the centralised Constitution of 1861.

A Convention is made at Gastein (Aug.), by which both Powers are to retain the sovereignty of both Duchies in common, but Austria is to provisionally administer Holstein and Prussia Schleswig, while Prussia buys the duchy of Lauenburg, and controls the port of Kiel. Austria accepts this arrangement unwillingly. Prussia begins negotiations with Italy, and Bismarck visits Napoleon at Biarritz in order to obtain his consent to the union of Italy and Prussia against Austria.

2027. **Hungary.** Transylvania is united to Hungary.

2028. **Sweden.** Representation by orders is replaced by direct representation.

2029. **America.** Congress passes the Thirteenth Amendment abolishing slavery, and sends it to the State legislatures for adoption.

Sherman enters Columbia, capital of South Carolina, Richmond is taken by Sheridan, and Grant forces Lee to capitulate at Appomattox (April 9). Lincoln is murdered (April 14).

Juarez revolts against Maximilian, and the United States demand the recall of the French troops.

Chile joins Peru in war against Spain.

2030. **West Indies.** The negroes revolt in Jamaica, in part owing to labour regulations, and are severely repressed by Governor Eyre, who is recalled and prosecuted. Jamaica is made a Crown Colony; but the elective element is partially restored, 1884.

2031. **Australasia.** Convicts cease to be sent to Western Australia.

2032. **Asia.** Tashkent and its territory are annexed by Russia.

2033. **Africa.** Brand becomes President of the Orange Free State.

3233. **Social.** The International Association of Working Men is founded, and is shortly joined by Bakunin, an Anarchist.

Le Play's Réforme Sociale advocates the paternal relation of the employer to employed and of the State to the weak, and exhorts the Church to aid the workers.

Octavia Hill begins to reform low class tenements.

3234. **Deaths.** Hawthorne, Landor, Lassalle.

3235. **Eng. Ch.** General Booth begins work in East London.

The Church Association is founded to oppose ritualism. [1865

Manning succeeds Wiseman as Archbishop of Westminster.

Lightfoot's Commentary on Galatians.

Pusey's Eirenicon declares the Papal supremacy, Mariolatry, the veneration of saints and sacred pictures, the chief obstacles to reunion.

Seeley's Ecce Homo.

3236. **Eng. Lit.** Matthew Arnold's Essays in Criticism.

Ruskin's Sesame and Lilies.

Lewis Carroll's (Dodgson's) Alice in Wonderland.

The Fortnightly Review is founded and edited by G. H. Lewes, who is succeeded by John Morley, 1869.

T. W. Robertson's play, Society, is acted by Mrs Bancroft.

3237. **Italian Lit.** Carducci's Hymn to Satan.

3238. **German Lit.** A German Shakspere Society is founded by Bodenstedt, Delius, Elze, Leo and others, and a new translation is undertaken by Bodenstedt, Freiligrath and Heyse.

3239. **American Lit.** Artemus Ward (C. F. Brown) His Book.

3240. **Science.** Lister introduces antiseptic surgery in Glasgow Infirmary, excluding the bacteria of the air by germecide spray.

Ludwig investigates the pressure of the blood.

Kekule explains the structure of benzene and the aromatic compounds, and predicts the number of isomeric compounds producible from benzene and its derivations.

Pasteur discovers remedies for the diseases of silkworms.

Plücker invents Line Geometry.

3241. **Art.** Wagner's Tristan and Isolde.

Ford Madox Brown's picture, Work.

3242. **Philosophy.** Stirling's Secret of Hegel.

Mill attacks the philosophy of Hamilton.

Green's Spiritual Philosophy explains the teaching of Coleridge.

3243. **Philology.** Dillmann's Ethiopic Lexicon.

3244. **History.** Dexter's History of Congregationalism.

Gaston Paris' Histoire Poétique de Charlemagne.

3245. **Education.** Duruy creates secondary education in France.

Ziller's Doctrine of Instruction developes the ideas of Herbart, and adds the theory of 'concentration,' according to which the teacher must group the more abstract and difficult subjects round the simple and concrete.

3246. **Anthropology.** Lubbock's Pre-historic Times, Tylor's Early

2034. **England.** Gladstone introduces a Reform Bill, which is attacked by Lowe. Russell resigns, and Derby succeeds. An agitation for reform begins, and a meeting forces an entry into Hyde Park. [1866

2035. **Germany.** Austria encourages Holstein to demand Frederick as its ruler. Bismarck complains of 'anarchy' in Holstein, and allies with Victor Emanuel (April). Prussia is accused of violating the Convention of Gastein, and the Bund is asked to mobilise. Bismarck proposes to divide the Bund into a northern federation under Prussia, and a southern under Bavaria, Austria being excluded. The Estates meet in Holstein, which Manteuffel at once occupies, and the Bund resolves to mobilise. Prussia secedes from the Bund. Beust, of Saxony, who wishes a Central German Association, declares for Austria. War is declared against Saxony, Hanover and Hesse-Cassel. Hesse-Cassel and Saxony are occupied without resistance, and the Hanoverian army, after a battle at Langensalza, capitulates. The Austrians are routed at Königgrätz (July 3); the Bavarians and the Federals are defeated separately, and Prussia signs peace with Würtemberg and Bavaria (Aug. 23). By the Peace of Prague (Aug. 23), Austria retires from the Bund, renounces claims to the Duchies, and cedes Venetia, which is to pass to Victor Emanuel. Prussia restores Saxony, which enters the North-German Confederation, promises to transfer Northern Schleswig to Denmark if the inhabitants wish, and annexes Hanover and Hesse-Cassel, with Frankfort and Nassau. The King is dissuaded by Bismarck from annexing Bohemia. By secret treaties, Bavaria, Würtemberg, and Baden agree, in the event of a foreign war, to place their troops under Prussia. After the war, the Prussian National Liberals desert the Fortschritts-Partei, and support Bismarck.

2036. **Italy.** On the outbreak of war, Austria offers Venetia to Victor Emanuel, who, however, adheres to Prussia. The Italians are defeated at Custozza (June), and their fleet is almost destroyed off Lissa in the Adriatic (July).

2037. **France.** After the war, Napoleon demands Rhenish Bavaria and Rhenish Hesse as a reward of non-intervention; but Prussia refuses.

2038. **Austria.** Beust resigns his post in Saxony, and becomes Foreign Minister and Chancellor.

2039. **Spain.** Isabella appoints a ministry under Narvaez; O'Donnell, Prim, and Serrano flee, and the Cortes are dissolved.

2040. **Greece.** Crete revolts, and proclaims its union to Greece; but war between Turkey and Greece is prevented by the Powers, and the revolt is suppressed.

2041. **Turkey.** Alexander of Roumania is deposed, and Charles of Hohenzollern-Sigmaringen is elected Prince by a plébiscite. The suzerainty of the Sultan is reduced to a shadow.

2042. **America.** The President, Andrew Johnson, comes into conflict with Congress over the Freedman's Bureau, the education of negroes, and the Civil Rights Bill protecting the negroes, and giving jurisdiction

History of Mankind, and McLennan's Primitive Marriage reconstruct primitive society.

3247. **Social.** The Commons Preservation Society is founded by Shaw Lefevre and Fawcett.

Jevons' The Coal Question foretells the exhaustion of the coal-beds of England within a century.

3248. **Deaths.** Cobden, Encke, Rowan Hamilton, Hurter, Wiseman.

3249. **Eng. Ch.** At the instance of Manning, the Pope condemns a Society of Anglicans and Catholics for reunion. [1866

The National Secular Society is founded.

3250. **German Ch.** Graf repeats Vatke's hypothesis that the priestly legislation of the Jews was incorporated after the Exile.

3251. **Italian Ch.** Monasteries and benefices without the cure of souls are suppressed in Piedmontese dominions, present possessors retaining their establishments for life.

3252. **Eng. Lit.** Bancroft, Hare, Irving, and Wyndham appear on the London stage.

3253. **Norwegian Lit.** Ibsen's drama, Brand.

3254. **Russian Lit.** Dostoiefsky's Crime and Punishment.

3255. **Science.** Haeckel's General Morphology.

Kovalevsky's study of the development of Ascidians and of Amphioxus shews the necessity of extending Schwann's cellular theory to animal embryology.

Owen's Anatomy of Vertebrates collects a mass of valuable information, but suggests a valueless classification.

Delaunay explains outstanding lunar acceleration by lengthening of the day through tidal friction.

Schiaparelli identifies the orbit of the Perseid shower of meteors with that of a comet.

The Atlantic Cable is laid under the direction of William Thomson.

3256. **Art.** Ambroise Thomas' Mignon.

Street, a pupil of Gilbert Scott, is chosen to build the new Law Courts in London.

Rossetti's Beata Beatrix.

3257. **Archaeology.** Rougé's Researches on Early Egyptian History.

Captain Wilson first systematically surveys the environs of Jerusalem, and excavations begin under the direction of the Egypt Exploration Fund.

3258. **Philosophy.** Villari's Positive Philosophy and the Historic Method introduces positivism into Italy, which is adopted by Ardigo, Mantegazza and Ferri.

3259. **History.** Bryce's Holy Roman Empire.

3260. **Economics.** The Cobden Club is founded by T. B. Potter, who became its first Secretary.

3261. **Geography.** Rohlfs journeys from Morocco across the Niger, to the Gulf of Guinea, and later explores the Libyan desert.

Yule's Cathay and the Way thither.

in the cases arising out of it to the Federal Courts alone. The latter is incorporated in the fourteenth Amendment, 'all persons are citizens of the United States, and of the states where they reside,' thus cancelling the Dred Scott decision.

Fenians invade Canada from the United States.

2043. **Asia.** Yakub Beg rebels against China in Kashgar.

2044. **England.** Disraeli introduces a Reform Bill, in consequence of which Lords Cranborne and Carnarvon resign. The bill is made still more democratic by Gladstone in Committee. In boroughs, the franchise is granted to householders and to lodgers who pay £10 rent and have resided for one year; in the counties, to inhabitants of houses at £12 rental. Lord Cairns obtains minority representation for three-cornered constituencies. [1867

2045. **Ireland.** A Fenian rising is attempted, but easily suppressed. In Manchester some Fenian prisoners are rescued from a prison van, and in the struggle a policeman is shot. Three of the rescuers are hanged. A wall of Clerkenwell prison is blown up (Dec.).

2046. **France.** Napoleon grants the right of interpellation.

Napoleon desires to buy Luxemburg from Holland, which is willing to sell. Prussia, however, objects. The fortress is demolished, and the Grand Duchy is made hereditary in the Nassau Family, its neutrality being guaranteed by Europe.

Napoleon visits the Emperor of Austria at Salzburg, and Bismarck makes known his treaties with the South German States.

2047. **Germany.** The North German Federation is established. The executive power is given to the Prussian King, the hereditary president and general, aided by a Federal Council, presided over by a Chancellor chosen by Prussia; the legislative is vested in a Reichstag chosen by manhood suffrage. Military service is organised throughout the Federation on the Prussian model, and made compulsory at 17. Bismarck is made Chancellor.

2048. **Austria.** The forms of Parliamentary Government are adopted. The Upper House is composed of the royal house, bishops, hereditary and life peers; the Lower House is chosen by four classes, landowners, rural communes, cities, chambers of commerce.

2049. **Hungary.** On the advice of Beust, and with the aid of Deak, responsible government is granted to Hungary. An 'Ausgleich' arranges the quota of the national debt, the tariff, etc. for 10 years. The Emperor is crowned King of Hungary. The common affairs of Austria and Hungary are settled by the Delegations, chosen by the two Houses, re-elected annually and meeting alternately in Pesth and Vienna. Foreign and military affairs and finance are controlled by joint ministers.

2050. **Italy.** Rattazzi secretly encourages Garibaldi to attack Rome. Napoleon therefore sends a new garrison, which, with the Papal army, routs Garibaldi at Mentana (Nov.).

3262. **Anthropology.** Remains discovered in America are thought by some to prove the existence of man in Tertiary times.

3263. **Social.** The Gothenburg system (State control of the sale of spirits) is introduced in Sweden.

A Wholesale Society is founded at Manchester for wholesale buying and distribution to cooperative stores.

Luzzatti establishes People's Banks in Milan, whence they spread throughout Italy.

3264. **Deaths.** Weisse, Whewell.

3265. **Eng. Ch.** The first pan-Anglican Synod meets, under the presidency of Archbishop Tait. A letter is sent to the Greek Church, and Bishop Colenso's case is discussed. [1867

Mackonochie, Incumbent of St Albans', Holborn, is prosecuted for ritualism.

Bishop Forbes of Brechin explains the 39 Articles in a Catholic sense.

3266. **Italian Ch.** The Pope celebrates the 18th centenary of the death of SS. Peter and Paul in presence of 500 Bishops, and announces his intention to hold an Oecumenical Council. An agitation for the proclamation of infallibility is organised by the Jesuits.

3267. **Church Hist.** Emanuel Deutsch's Essay on the Talmud.

3268. **American Ch.** Laurence Oliphant joins the communistic society established by Thomas Lake Harris at Brockton.

3269. **French Lit.** Sarcey becomes dramatic critic of the Temps.

3270. **American Lit.** Whittier's Maud Müller.

3271. **Australian Lit.** Gordon's Sea Spray and Smoke Drift.

3272. **Science.** Siemens invents a process for producing steel.

Maudsley's Physiology and Pathology of Mind.

3273. **Art.** Sterndale Bennett's Woman of Samaria.

The Paris Exhibition introduces Japanese art to notice, and members of the Impressionist School are influenced by it.

Strauss' 'Blue Danube' waltz.

3274. **Education.** Mill's Rectorial Address at St Andrews insists on the importance of an education at once literary and scientific.

'Essays on a Liberal Education' and Pattison's Suggestions on Academic Organization urge the reform of English education.

Professor James Stuart organises a movement for University Extension.

3275. **Philosophy.** Drobisch's Moral Statistics and the Freedom of the Human Will continues the work of Quetelet.

3276. **History.** Freeman's History of the Norman Conquest.

Schwegler's History of Rome.

Sickel edits the Acta Karolinorum.

3277. **Politics.** Bagehot's English Constitution.

3278. **Economics.** Marx' Capital declares value to arise from labour, which receives but a small share of the product, the surplus being seized by the owners of capital.

3279. **Social.** Baron v. Schorlemer-Alst founds the Westphalian

2051. **America.** Napoleon recalls his troops from Mexico, Maximilian is taken and shot, and Juarez becomes President.

The Dominion of Canada is joined by Nova Scotia and New Brunswick. A Governor-General is appointed by the Crown, and a federal Parliament meets at Ottawa. The North-Western Territory, Manitoba, Prince Edward Island, and British Columbia quickly join.

The Reconstruction Act is passed over the President's veto. The States which had passed ordinances of secession are formed into military districts. A Convention is to frame a State Constitution, and to elect a legislature, which will ratify the Fourteenth Amendment.

Alaska is bought by the United States from Russia.

2052. **England.** Derby resigns, owing to ill-health, and is succeeded by Disraeli. Gladstone carries a resolution for the disestablishment of the English Church in Ireland, obtains a Liberal majority at the General Election, and becomes Prime Minister. [1868

Compulsory church-rates are abolished.

Election petitions are transferred to the judges.

Cardwell, the War Minister, introduces short service.

2053. **France.** Rochefort attacks the Government in La Lanterne.

Gambetta defends a paper prosecuted for collecting money for a victim of 1851, and is acclaimed the coming leader. Ollivier and Émile de Girardin attempt to make a Liberal Imperialism.

2054. **Spain.** Narvaez dies, Prim and Serrano revolt, and Isabella flees to France. The Cortes draw up a popular Constitution.

2055. **Austria.** Bohemia and Moravia demand the same rights as Hungary.

2056. **Russia.** Poland is incorporated with Russia administratively.

2057. **Turkey.** The 'Young Turkey' party creates a new literature, but does not advocate the adoption of European ideas.

2058. **America.** Congress passes the Tenure of Office Act over Johnson's veto, making the consent of the Senate necessary to the dismissal of officials. Despite this, the President removes Stanton, Lincoln's War Secretary. Stanton appeals to the House, which impeaches the President for disregarding the law; but the impeachment is lost in the Senate. Grant is elected President.

To defend the negroes against the Ku-Klux and other secret societies, Congress passes the Force Laws, and entrusts the execution of justice to the Federal Courts.

2059. **Africa.** An expedition under Napier rescues English prisoners of King Theodore of Abysinnia.

Basutoland becomes British, and is annexed to Cape Colony, 1871.

2060. **Asia.** The Emir of Bokhara cedes to Russia the Khanate of Samarcand, and Bokhara itself becomes a dependent State.

Farmers' Union, consisting only of professing Christians and of landowners, for mutual assistance and to encourage agriculture. The Union obtains considerable power and agitates for high protective duties.

A Factory Inspection Act is passed.

3280. **Deaths.** Böckh, Bopp, Cousin, Faraday, Ingres, Poncelet, Rothe.

3281. **Eng. Ch.** Altar lights are condemned by the Privy Council. [1868

Compulsory Church rates are abolished by Gladstone.

3282. **Austrian Ch.** Civil marriage is restored and the schools freed from clerical control. The Concordat itself is abolished 1870, in consequence of the Vatican decrees.

3283. **African Ch.** Lavigerie founds the Pères Blancs for missionary and educational work.

3284. **Eng. Lit.** Browning's Ring and the Book.

William Morris' Earthly Paradise.

Quaritch issues his first General Catalogue of Books.

3285. **Danish Lit.** Brandes begins his work as a critic.

3286. **Belgian Lit.** De Coster's Légende d'Uylenspiegel.

3287. **Science.** Haeckel's History of Creation.

Darwin's Variation of Plants and Animals under Domestication.

Ångstrom constructs a map of the normal solar spectrum. The prominences seen round the sun at an eclipse are found to be gaseous, and Janssen and Lockyer deduce a spectroscopic method of observing them in daylight.

3288. **Art.** Wagner's The Mastersingers.

Boito's Mefistofele.

3289. **Philosophy.** Ravaisson's Philosophie en France au 19ème Siècle upholds idealism.

Huxley's Physical Basis of Life.

3290. **History.** Quinet attacks the Terror as the enemy of the Revolution and the Jacobins as absolutists.

3291. **Geography.** Schweinfurth explores the While Nile and Bahr el Ghazal, and discovers the sources of the Ubanghi.

Nachtigal enters the Sahara Desert from Tripoli, explores Lake Chad and Wadai and returns through Egypt.

3292. **Politics.** Alexander Stephens' War between the States (of North America) defends the action of the South.

3293. **Social.** Bodelschwingh founds Bethel, near Bielefeld, for epileptics.

Cardinal Mermillod founds Catholic Socialism in Switzerland, his work being extended by Decurtins.

Bakunin spreads his ideas in Italy and founds a number of branches of the International Association, which is also introduced into Spain.

3294. **Deaths.** Berryer, Brougham, Milman.

2061. **Ireland.** The Anglican Church is disestablished, and is henceforth governed by a synod of clergy and laity; the Maynooth grant and the Regium Donum to the Presbyterians are commuted; endowments since 1660 are reserved to the Church; the clergy and officials are secured their life interest; the remaining funds are to be applied for the relief of unavoidable suffering. [1869

2062. **France.** At a general election, Napoleon loses ground in the towns, above all in Paris and Lyons. The Chamber receives the initiative of legislation equally with the Emperor. The Ministers, though still responsible only to the Emperor, may be accused by the Senate. Rouher resigns.

2063. **Germany.** Prussia secures control of the South German fortresses.

2064. **Spain.** A Constituent Assembly declares Serrano Regent. The King of Portugal, Don Carlos, Alfonso, the youthful son of Isabella, Montpensier, and the Duke of Aosta are suggested for the throne.

2065. **America.** The United States reject the settlement of the Alabama claims made by Clarendon and Reverdy Johnson, their ambassador.

The Fifteenth Amendment is passed, forbidding the withholding of the franchise from race and colour by States or the Federal Government.

Macdonald becomes Premier of Canada, and introduces Protection as part of his 'National Programme.'

The Hudson's Bay Company sells its territories to the British Government, which incorporates them with Canada. The Company, however, retain its trading rights.

2066. **Africa.** The opening of the Suez Canal renders Egypt of great importance to England.

2067. **Asia.** After civil war, the Mikado undertakes the government at Tokio, the Daimios surrender their privileges, and Japan throws off the feudal system.

Hunter executes a statistical survey of the Indian Empire.

2068. **England.** Civil Service posts are thrown open to competition. [1870

The Commander-in-chief is placed under the control of the Secretary for War.

2069. **Ireland.** Landlords are obliged to compensate their tenants for improvements and on ejection except for non-payment of rent. Tenants desiring to buy land from their landlords, if willing to sell, may receive loans of two-thirds the amount from the Government.

The Home Government Association is founded to work for an Irish Parliament to regulate all internal affairs.

2070. **Belgium.** Neutrality is secured by a treaty between England, France and Prussia.

3295. **French Ch.** Père Hyacinthe leaves the Carmelites and breaks with Rome, and establishes an Old Catholic congregation at Geneva. [1869

3296. **German Ch.** Biedermann's Christian Dogmatic, influenced by Hegel, excludes supernaturalism.

3297. **Spanish Ch.** The Protestant Churches hold their first Synod.

3298. **Church Hist.** The Vatican Council meets, (Dec.). Manning advocates a definition of Infallibility; but Newman, Dupanloup, Maret and Ketteler declare the Council inopportune. 'The Pope and the Council,' by Janus (written by the Munich professors) vigorously attacks the project.

3299. **Eng. Lit.** R. S. Hawker's Cornish Ballads.

3300. **Norwegian Lit.** Ibsen's Young Men's League, the first modern Norwegian comedy.

3301. **Science.** Mendeleeff, Lothar Meyer and Newlands develope the law that the properties of the elements are a periodic function of their atomic weights, which leads to the discovery of scandium, gallium, etc.

3302. **Art.** Carolus Duran's Dame au Gant, his first masterpiece.

Alma Tadema's The Pyrrhic Dance, with the works of Leighton and Poynter, forms the English Classic School.

Defregger begins his series of pictures of Hofer's rising of 1809.

Boehm's statue of the Queen, his first important work.

3303. **Philosophy.** Hartmann's Philosophy of the Unconscious developes the ideas of Schopenhauer.

The Metaphysical Society is founded in London by James Knowles, and joined by Tennyson, Argyll, W. G. Ward, Manning, Huxley, Sidgwick, Martineau, and others.

3304. **Philology.** Benfey's History of Oriental Philology.

3305. **Law.** Hinschius' Ecclesiastical Law in Germany.

The Revue de Droit international is founded, edited by Rolin Jacquemyns.

3306. **Politics.** Matthew Arnold's Culture and Anarchy.

3307. **Economics.** Thornton's work on Labour explodes the wage-fund theory. A final defence is attempted by Cairnes, 1874.

3308. **History.** Kuenen's Religion of Israel.

J. E. B. Mayor declares the De Situ Britanniae, attributed to Richard of Cirencester, to be a forgery of the 18th century.

3309. **Social.** Mill's Subjection of Women pleads for emancipation on social and political as well as on moral grounds.

Women's suffrage is introduced in Wyoming.

3310. **Deaths.** Derby, Lamartine, Purkinje, Sainte-Beuve.

3311. **Eng. Ch.** Newman's Grammar of Assent maintains the existence of an 'illative sense.' [1870

The Revisers of the New Testament are chosen by Convocation and begin their work. The selection of Vance Smith, an Unitarian, and his admission to Communion is strongly condemned.

2071. **France.** Ollivier forms a Liberal Ministry, and a new Constitution is submitted to a plébiscite. Seven million approve and one and a half million disapprove. A fierce anti-dynastic outbreak occurs when Pierre Bonaparte, son of Lucien, shoots a man who brings him a challenge.

Leopold of Hohenzollern-Sigmaringen, the candidate of General Prim, accepts the Spanish throne, with the approval of King William. Napoleon complains, and Leopold withdraws (July 12). Benedetti demands of the King at Ems an assurance that he will never allow Leopold to accept, but is refused (July 13). Bismarck garbles the Emperor's telegram, describing his intercourse with Benedetti, and Napoleon declares war (July 17), believing that Bavaria will join him, and perhaps hoping for Austrian aid. Bismarck publishes Napoleon's propositions for seizing Belgium. The armies meet at Saarbrück (Aug. 2). The Crown Prince defeats Macmahon's army at Weissemburg and Wörth, and Frossard is repulsed at Spicheren. On the evacuation of Alsace, the main army concentrates round Metz. Bazaine is routed at Gravelotte (Aug. 18), and shuts himself up in Metz. Frederick Charles is left to watch Metz, and the Crown Prince marches on Paris. Macmahon marches from Chalons to relieve Metz. The French are routed at Sedan (Sept. 1), and the Emperor and his army capitulate (Sept. 2). The Empire falls, and the Empress flees to England, and a government of national defence is formed by Gambetta, Jules Favre, Arago, Trochu, Crèmieux, Jules Simon, and Rochefort. The Senate is abolished, and the Corps Législatif is dissolved. Thiers is sent to seek the mediation of the sovereigns of Europe. Paris is invested (Sept. 20). Strassburg capitulates (Sept. 28), and Bazaine capitulates in Metz with 150,000 (Sept. 23). Gambetta escapes from Paris in a balloon to Tours, and organises the army of the Loire, which advances to relieve Paris, but is broken up by Frederick Charles. The provisional government moves to Bordeaux (Dec.).

2072. **Germany.** The South German States enter the North German Confederation (Nov.), and the Reichstag offers the title of Emperor to the King of Prussia. William replies that the offer must come from the princes (Dec.).

2073. **Italy.** On the outbreak of war, the French troops are recalled from Civita Vecchia, and Italian troops occupy Rome after a short bombardment (Sept. 20). The Law of Guarantees establishes the inviolability of the Pope and his servants, concedes postal and telegraphic intercourse, and free diplomatic activity, and offers a civil list. The latter is declined, and the rest ignored.

2074. **Russia.** Gortschakoff, at Bismarck's secret instigation, repudiates the clauses of the Treaty of 1856, forbidding a Russian fleet and arsenal in the Black Sea.

2075. **Spain.** Isabella abdicates in favour of her son Alfonso, and the Duke of Aosta, son of Victor Emanuel, is chosen King.

2076. **America.** The Red River revolt of Indian half-breeds in Manitoba is suppressed by Wolseley.

2077. **Africa.** Diamonds are found on the western border of the Orange

Bishop Wordsworth discovers an Act of Henry VIII., allowing Suffragans, who are speedily appointed.

Voysey is prosecuted for publishing the Sling and the Stone, and is ejected from the Anglican Church. He founds a Theist congregation.

Frazer becomes Bishop of Manchester.

Keble College, Oxford, is founded.

3312. **Russian Ch.** Lord Radstock visits St Petersburg on an evangelical Mission.

3313. **Church Hist.** Despite the opposition of Dupanloup, Darboy, Maret, Hefele, Ketteler, Strossmayer, Kenrick and other German, French and American bishops, and of Döllinger and Montalembert, the Vatican Council declares Papal *ex cathedra* definitions of faith and morals infallible, by 533 to 2 (July 18). The decrees are accepted by the Bishops who had disapproved them; but Catholic professors and scholars record a dissent at Nuremberg (Aug.).

3314. **German Ch.** Ritschl's Theory of Justification and Atonement discards natural theology and metaphysics and attempts to build on the work and words of Christ as believed by the early Christian community. The moral element is put in the foremost place, and the problems of inspiration, sin and the pre-existence of the Son are not discussed.

3315. **Eng. Lit.** Rossetti's Poems.

Disraeli's Lothair.

3316. **German Lit.** Anzengruber's Pastor of Kirchfeld.

3317. **American Lit.** Lowell's My Study Windows.

3318. **Norwegian Lit.** Jonas Lie begins his Sea Stories.

3319. **Science.** Galton's Hereditary Genius.

Smokeless powder is invented.

3320. **Art.** Baudry paints the Paris Opera House.

Fortuny's La Vicaria.

Wagner's Essay on Beethoven estimates the significance of Beethoven and discusses the metaphysic of music from the standpoint of Schopenhauer.

3321. **Education.** Syed Ahmed Khan founds a Mohammedan College at Aligarh.

Jowett becomes Master of Balliol College, Oxford.

Forster's Bill creates Board Schools, where there are no Voluntary schools, for elementary education. The Birmingham League, led by Dixon and Chamberlain, oppose the religious settlement. In Committee, Cowper-Temple's amendment is accepted, forbidding denominational teaching in rate-aided schools. In Scotland, the religious teaching is settled by local ballot.

3322. **Philosophy.** Crookes' Spiritualism and Science records his experiments with mediums.

John Grote's examination of the Utilitarian Philosophy.

3323. **History.** Mommsen's Staatsrecht, a study of the government and officers of the Roman state.

3324. **Geography.** Nordenskiold explores the interior of Greenland.

Free State. The land is taken by England, nominally on behalf of a Griqua chief, and Kimberley is founded. Some years later, President Brand obtains a solatium of £90,000.

[1871

2078. **England.** The Lords postpone a clause in an army regulation bill for the abolition of the purchase of commissions in the army, and Gladstone advises the Queen to cancel the Royal warrant legalising purchase

The Local Government Board is created.

2079. **France.** The army of the North, under Faidherbe, is defeated at Saint-Quentin, the second army of the Loire, under Chanzy, is destroyed at Le Mans, and the army of the East, under Bourbaki, is driven into Switzerland. An armistice is arranged for three weeks, except at Belfort and in the Jura. Paris capitulates (Jan. 28). An Assembly meets at Bordeaux (Feb. 12) and elects Thiers as head of the executive. Thiers and Jules Favre arrange preliminaries (Feb. 26), which are confirmed by the Treaty of Frankfort (May). France cedes Alsace, except Belfort (which surrenders Feb. 18), and most of Lorraine, including Metz. The indemnity is fixed at 200 millions, to be paid in three years, the German army to be withdrawn as instalments are paid.

Though the Republicans are in a minority in the Constitutional Assembly, a Republic is proclaimed, the Comte de Chambord refusing to renounce the white flag.

The Commune breaks out in Paris (March 18), led by Felix Pyat and Louise Michel, and is put down by the national troops under Macmahon (May), after the death of Archbishop Darboy and other hostages and the destruction of the Tuileries and the Hôtel de Ville.

Jules Guesde founds the Socialist movement, which is developed by Brousse, Allemane, and Blanqui.

2080. **Germany.** The King of Prussia is acknowledged German Emperor. A Federal Constitution is adopted. The Reichstag is elected for three years, and chosen by universal suffrage. The Bundesrath consists of delegates from the Governments (Prussia sending 17), each state voting solid. Changes in the Constitution, the army and taxation can be vetoed by 14 members. A Court of Appeal decides questions of imperial law, and an imperial court judges of political offences. Popular government is introduced everywhere except in Mecklenburg.

2081. **Italy.** The seat of Government is transferred to Rome.

2082. **Austria.** The Emperor appoints a Federalist Ministry under Hohenwart, who negotiates the concession to Bohemia of full self-government, except in foreign affairs, war, and trade. German opposition becomes so fierce that the Emperor withdraws his promises, and Hohenwart resigns.

Beust, who is considered anti-Prussian, is dismissed.

2083. **Russia.** At a Conference held in London, at the suggestion of Bismarck, the action of Russia in reference to the Black Sea clauses is confirmed.

3325. **Social.** Infanticide is forbidden in India.
Women become eligible as members of School Boards.
3326. **Deaths.** Clarendon, Dickens, Dumas, Farragut, Herzen, Lee, Mérimée, Montalembert, Prévost-Paradol, Villemain.

[1871

3327. **Eng. Ch.** Miall's motion for disestablishment obtains 96 votes.
3328. **French Ch.** Macall begins mission work in Paris.
3329. **German Ch.** The Archbishop of Munich orders Döllinger to accept the Decrees. He refuses 'as a Christian, a theologian, a historian, and a citizen,' and is excommunicated. The first Congress of Old Catholics is held at Munich. 500 delegates attend, and Schulte presides, supported by Döllinger, Reinkens, Friedrich, Huber, Maassen.
The Catholic members of the Prussian Landtag petition the Emperor to restore the temporal power of the Pope. The Bundesrath and the Reichstag pass the Kanzel-paragraph, restraining priests from abusing their pastoral functions for political purposes. To oppose this legislation, Windhorst founds the Centre Party.
Political and civil equality is granted to the Jews.
3330. **Italian Ch.** The Law of Guarantees declares the Pope's person inviolable, accords the honours of a sovereign prince, allows the possession of the Vatican and other palaces, and grants an annuity, which he rejects.
3331. **French Lit.** Zola's Rougon-Macquart series.
3332. **German Lit.** Rosegger's Stories from the Steiermark.
3333. **Science.** Darwin's Descent of Man.
The Mont Cenis tunnel is opened.
3334. **Art.** The first Impressionist exhibition in France is held, containing works of Manet, Monet, Pissaro, Degas, Renoir.
3335. **Philology.** B. Delbruck's Researches in Syntax.
3336. **Geography.** Livingstone discovers the Upper Congo.
3337. **Education.** Miss Clough opens a house at Cambridge for girls, which later becomes Newnham College.
The religious test is abolished in English Universities.
3338. **Economics.** Jevons' Theory of Political Economy applies mathematical methods, and introduces the conception of 'Final Utility
3339. **Politics.** Ruskin's Fors Clavigera.
3340. **History.** Maine's Early Institutions investigates early Irish society.
3341. **Social.** Trade Unions are legalised.
Moufang, a pupil of Ketteler, in standing for the Reichstag, issues an address which becomes the programme of the party of Catholic Socialists.
Adolph Wagner's The Social Question founds Protestant Socialism in Germany, and urges the State to mitigate the pressure on the workers.

2084. **America.** By the Treaty of Washington, England and the United States agree to submit the Alabama claim to arbitration.

The corrupt governors of New York, known as the Tweed Ring, are exposed and fall; but Tammany rapidly regains its influence.

The last of the seceding States re-enter the union, and are restored to their full rights.

Silver is demonetised.

2085. **Africa.** Holland cedes her settlements on the Gold Coast to England.

2086. **England.** The Ballot is introduced.

[1872

A Court of Arbitration, sitting at Geneva, awards the United States three millions damages for the Alabama; Cockburn, the British representative, dissents, England having renounced her claim to compensation for the Fenian attack on Canada. The money, however, is paid.

A Commercial Treaty with France modifies that of 1860, of which Thiers, a strict Protectionist, disapproves.

A motion to extend county franchise is lost, but is frequently re-introduced by Sir George Trevelyan.

Sir Charles Dilke declares himself a republican, and Fawcett claims the right to discuss the form of government.

2087. **France.** The Orleans princes accept compensation for the confiscation of their estates. This step is widely regarded as a renunciation of their claims.

2088. **Germany.** Bismarck remodels the local government of Prussia, destroying the absolute control of local affairs by the nobility.

The Emperors of Russia and Austria visit Berlin, and a Dreikaiserbündniss is tacitly established with a view to maintain the *status quo,* to act in harmony on the Eastern Question, and to oppose revolutionary aims.

2089. **America.** The German Emperor is called upon to arbitrate between England and the United States in reference to the ownership of St Juan Island, and assigns it to the latter.

Owing to the corruption of Grant's administration, Carl Schurz and other 'Liberal Republicans' nominate Greeley for the Presidency; but Grant is again returned.

2090. **Africa.** Responsible Government is obtained for Cape Colony, chiefly owing to the efforts of Sir John Molteno, who becomes the first Premier.

Bruce fails to carry a Liquor Bill, by which licenses would lapse after 10 years, and the increase of public-houses is forbidden.

3342. **Deaths.** Babbage, Grillparzer, Grote, Herschel, Murchison.

3343. **Eng. Ch.** Stanley and Tait recommend the omission of the Athanasian Creed, but are defeated by Pusey, Liddon, and Wilberforce. [1872

Matthew Arnold's Literature and Dogma.

3344. **French Ch.** Père Hyacinthe attempts to found a national Church.

The General Assembly of the Protestants, the first since 1659, meets. The Liberals, led by Coquerel, protest against the adoption of any creed.

3345. **German Ch.** Döllinger lectures on Reunion at Munich, and the Old Catholics meet at Cologne.

The Prussian Government reduces clerical influence in schools. The Bishops meet at Fulda and protest, and the Pope excommunicates the authors of the law. Bismarck declares that he 'will never go to Canossa,' and the Jesuits are banished. Civil marriage is declared necessary; and the clergy are forced to swear allegiance before appointment.

Strauss' The Old and the New Faith answers the question, Are we still Christians? in the negative.

3346. **Church Hist.** George Smith discovers in Assyrian tablets the sources of certain of the narratives in Genesis.

3347. **Eng. Lit.** Calverley's Fly Leaves.

3348. **French Lit.** Daudet's Tartarin de Tarascon.

Sardou's Rabagas, a satire on Gambetta.

3349. **Science.** The Challenger sets out to study ocean depths.

Zittel's Handbook of Palaeontology.

Darwin's Expression of the Emotions.

Edison perfects duplex telegraphy.

3350. **Art.** Fred Walker's Harbour of Refuge.

Briton Rivière's Daniel.

3351. **History.** Brunner's Origin of Compurgation.

3352. **Economics.** The 'Katheder-Sozialisten,' who merge economics in sociology and desire an extension of State action, meet at Eisenach. The new departure is fiercely attacked by Treitschke, and defended by Schmoller.

3353. **Politics.** Spencer's Study of Sociology.

3354. **Law.** Lorimer's Institutes of Law attacks the Positive school.

Arthur Orton claims the Tichborne estates.

3355. **Social.** Bakunin is expelled from the International Association.

Joseph Arch founds the Agricultural Union, and agitates for the extension of the franchise.

3356. **Deaths.** Feuerbach, Gautier, Horace Greeley, Grundtvig, Juarez, Maurice, Mazzini, Seward, Trendelenburg.

2091. **England.** Gladstone resigns on the defeat of his Irish University Bill; but Disraeli refuses office. [1873

The National Liberal Federation is founded, and Schnadhorst becomes Secretary.

Selborne, Cairns and Coleridge obtain the reform of the Courts. The Supreme Court is divided into the High Court (including Queen's Bench, Chancery, Probate, Divorce and Admiralty), and the Court of Appeal.

2092. **France.** Thiers is overturned, and Macmahon is nominated President for seven years.

The last instalment of the indemnity is paid, and France is evacuated by the German troops.

Chambord comes to Paris, is urged to make a coup, hesitates, and flies. A deputation is sent to offer him the crown; but he finally refuses to renounce the use of the white flag. The Comte de Paris acknowledges the claim of the childless Comte de Chambord, whom he visits at Frohsdorf. He regards himself as next heir, as the representative of hereditary, not parliamentary, monarchy.

Bazaine is tried by a court under the Duc d'Aumale, and condemned to life-long imprisonment.

Conscription is introduced for all who attain the age of 20, with few exceptions.

Napoleon dies at Chislehurst, leaving an only son 17 years of age.

2093. **Spain.** A Socialist insurrection breaks out in Spain, and the Secret Society of La Mano Negra is organised.

King Amadeus resigns, a Republic is proclaimed, and Castelar becomes Dictator. The Carlists revolt in the North, and the Federalists and Communists in the South.

2094. **Austria.** Croatia obtains internal self-government, its representatives at Buda-Pesth only taking part in business which affects the Hungarian monarchy as a whole.

2095. **Denmark.** The Lower House claims to control ministers.

2096. **Africa.** By the Treaty of Zanzibar, the export of slaves is forbidden, and the markets for imported slaves are closed.

The Khedive is allowed by the Sultan to make treaties and maintain an army.

2097. **Asia.** Kaufmann conquers Khiva, the Khan declaring himself a vassal, and ceding part of his territory.

The Kotow by foreign ambassadors at Pekin lapses.

A revolt breaks out in a province of Sumatra.

2098. **England.** Gladstone dissolves Parliament, and proposes to abolish the income tax; but Disraeli returns to power with the first clear Conservative majority since 1841. [1874

Northcote establishes a Sinking Fund, which is not suspended till 1885.

2099. **Ireland.** Isaac Butt's motion for Home Rule secures 61 votes.

2100. **Germany.** Count Arnim, late ambassador in Paris, is arrested

3357. **Eng. Ch.** Moody and Sankey inaugurate the Great Mission. [1873

3358. **German Ch.** Prussia passes the May Laws relating to the education of the clergy, jurisdiction in Church cases, excommunication, the appointment and dismissal of ministers.

With the approval of the Prussian Government, Reinkens is consecrated Bishop of the Old Catholics by the Jansenist Bishop of Deventer.

3359. **Swiss Ch.** Herzog is consecrated Bishop of the Old Catholic Church. Mermillod is appointed Apostolic Vicar, but is not recognised by the Confederation.

3360. **Eng. Lit.** Pater's Essays on the Renaissance.

3361. **German Lit.** Paul Heyse's Children of the World.

3362. **Science.** Charcot begins his pathological observations and experiments at the Salpetrière Hospital, Paris.

Clerk Maxwell's Electricity and Magnetism asserts that light and electro-magnetic phenomena have their seat in the same medium, and are identical in nature.

Plateau eliminates the action of gravity on liquid masses.

Rosenbusch's Physiography of Minerals.

Scholes invents the Remington type-writing machine.

3363. **Art.** Repin introduces realism into Russian painting.

Brahms' Requiem.

3364. **Archaeology.** Schliemann commences excavations at Troy.

3365. **Philosophy.** Lewes' Problems of Life and Mind.

Mill's Autobiography.

Sigwart's Logic.

3366. **Politics.** Sir James Stephen's Liberty, Equality, Fraternity, attacks Mill's individualism.

Bagehot's Physics and Politics discuss the phenomena of early society in the light of scientific conceptions.

Lilienfeld's Sociology of the Future attempts the anatomy of society from a biological standpoint.

3367. **Economics.** Bagehot's Lombard Street explains the banking system.

3368. **Anthropology.** Spencer edits a Descriptive Sociology.

3369. **Geography.** Payer and Weyprecht discover Franz Josef land.

3370. **Agriculture.** A period of depression begins in England.

3371. **Deaths.** Landseer, Liebig, Livingstone, Lytton, Manzoni, J. S. Mill, Napoleon, Sedgwick, Wilberforce.

3372. **Eng. Ch.** An anonymous author attacks Christian orthodoxy in Supernatural Religion. Lightfoot points out errors in his use of the Fathers, and the author replies. [1874

Tait's and Disraeli's Public Worship Regulation Act ('to put down ritualism') is in vain opposed by Salisbury and Gladstone. Lord Westbury is chosen judge.

Gladstone's pamphlets on Vaticanism declare the acceptance of the

and prosecuted, ostensibly for embezzling official documents, in reality because he attacks the French Republic.

The Conservatives plot with the Empress Augusta to replace Bismarck by Count Arnim.

The Lassalleans and Marxians unite at the Congress of Gotha.

2101. **Denmark.** Iceland obtains from Denmark self-government and a legislature, after a long contest, largely by the influence of Sigurdsson.

2102. **Spain.** The Cortes are dissolved by the army, Castelar resigns, Serrano assumes the Presidency, but is overthrown by Martinez Campos, by whom Alfonso, son of Isabella, is proclaimed King (Dec.).

2103. **Switzerland.** The Constitution is revised and becomes more centralised. The Federal Council (the Executive) is elected by the Federal Assembly. The President, who is no more than the Chairman, is elected for one year. The Federal Government controls the army, ecclesiastical matters, education, commercial laws, social reform. A Referendum is allowed, if demanded by 30,000 voters or by eight cantons. The Federal Tribunal, the only Federal Court, receives greater power.

2104. **Russia.** Conscription is made compulsory on reaching the age of 21.

2105. **Australasia.** The Fiji Islands are surrendered by the chiefs to England.

2106. **Africa.** The war with Ashanti, in defence of the Gold Coast Settlements, ends with the capture of Coomassie.

Darfur is conquered by Egypt.

2107. **Asia.** Annam accepts French protection, and submits its foreign policy to France, thus breaking off its shadowy vassalage to China.

2108. **England.** Gladstone retires, and Hartington leads the Liberal party. [1875

Disraeli buys four millions worth of shares in the Suez Canal from the Khedive.

Strangers may only be excluded from the debates by a vote of a majority of the House.

2109. **France.** A new Constitution is constructed, chiefly by the influence of Gambetta, consisting of a President chosen for 7 years by both Houses, a Chamber of Deputies chosen for 4 years by universal suffrage by Scrutin d'Arrondissement, and a Senate to be elected for 9 years by an electoral body in each department, one-third being renewed every three years, and 75 chosen by the Senate for life.

Owing to measures for the reorganisation of the army, a war scare arises in Germany, and an article appears in the Berlin 'Post,' entitled War in Sight. England and Russia intervene, and the crisis terminates.

2110. **Hungary.** The Deak party breaks up, and the Left accepts the compact of 1867. Tisza, its leader, becomes Premier, with the aid of Deak's followers, and remains in power till 1890.

2111. **Greece.** The people compel the King to dismiss his Ministry, which has acted unconstitutionally.

decrees of 1870 inconsistent with civil allegiance. Newman's Letter to the Duke of Norfolk rebuts the charge.

3373. **Scotch Ch.** Lay patronage is given to male communicants.

3374. **German Ch.** The Old Catholics permit the use of the vernacular, recognize the marriage of priests, consent to drop the Filioque, and abolish compulsory confession.

Civil marriage is made compulsory in Prussia, and ecclesiastics who have disobeyed the May Laws may be banished. At the General Election 100 members are returned to the Centre.

3375. **Austrian Ch.** The May Laws are substituted for the Concordat of 1855.

3376. **Italian Ch.** Curci urges the recognition of the new kingdom.

3377. **Science.** Observations of the Transit of Venus fail to establish the distance of the Earth from the Sun.

Allport's Contributions to the Petrography of England.

3378. **Art.** Strauss' Fliedermaus.

3379. **Philosophy.** T. H. Green's Introduction to Hume criticises Empiricism.

Mill's Three Essays on Religion admit an intelligent mind with limited power.

Sidgwick's Methods of Ethics, a Utilitarian treatise.

Wundt's Physiological Psychology presents psychology as an experimental science.

3380. **History.** Green's Short History of England.

Stubbs' Constitutional History of England.

Reeve edits Greville's Memoirs.

3381. **Politics.** Auberon Herbert begins to teach Voluntaryism.

3382. **Education.** Bonghi becomes Italian Minister of Education.

3383. **Philology.** Corssen declares Etruscan an Italic dialect.

3384. **Anthropology.** Pitt-Rivers exhibits his collections illustrative of savage life.

3385. **Deaths.** Guizot, Michelet, Strauss, Sumner, Tischendorf.

[1875

3386. **Eng. Ch.** Dale's Treatise on the Atonement.

3387. **German Ch.** The Pope declares recent anti-Catholic legislation invalid. The Government refuses payment to clergy who will not promise to obey the laws, and 8 of the 12 Prussian bishoprics and 1,400 curacies become vacant.

3388. **Church Hist.** The Worship of the Sacred Heart is instituted.

Laveleye's L'Avenir des Peuples Catholiques attacks the political and intellectual influence of Catholicism.

3389. **Eng. Lit.** The 9th edition of the Encyclopaedia Britannica is edited by Baynes and Robertson Smith.

3390. **French Lit.** Réjane makes her début.

3391. **German Lit.** Julius Wolff's Ratcatcher of Hamelin.

3392. **Science.** Darwin's Insectivorous Plants.

Galton introduces the conception of the stirp.

3393. **Art.** Bizet's Carmen.

The Hermes of Praxiteles is found at Olympia.

2112. **Turkey.** A revolt breaks out in Bosnia and Herzegovina. England refuses to join in a memorandum to the Porte; but the Austrian minister, Andrassy, draws up a note, enumerating the concessions that the Sultan ought to make (Dec.).

2113. **Australasia.** Provincial Governments in New Zealand are abolished, and the Government centralised.

2114. **Africa.** Disraeli's Circular on fugitive slaves orders English ships in the neighbourhood to refuse an asylum to slaves and to surrender them at a port, but is withdrawn in consequence of the indignation it excites.

Lord Carnarvon sends Froude to South Africa to recommend federation.

President Macmahon pronounces on the English and Portuguese claims in Delagoa Bay in favour of the latter.

De Brazza makes his first expedition in the Congo country, and persuades many tribes to accept French direction.

Roustan becomes French Consul-General at Tunis.

2115. **Asia.** The Gaikwar of Baroda is deposed for attempting to poison the British Resident, and a nominated child of the family succeeds.

Russia annexes the Khanate of Khokand.

2116. **England.** The Appellate Jurisdiction Act restores the jurisdiction of the House of Lords and the Judicial Committee [1876 of the Privy Council. The Court of Appeal becomes intermediate. The House of Lords as a Court of Appeal consists of the Law Lords, the Chancellor, four Lords of Appeal in Ordinary.

2117. **Italy.** An equilibrium in the Budget is obtained. Minghetti's Ministry, however, is defeated, and the Right loses power. Depretis succeeds with an immense majority, and the group system developes. The constant ministerial changes gravely diminish the prestige of Parliamentary institutions.

2118. **Spain.** The Carlist war is ended, and a new Constitution is introduced.

2119. **Turkey.** The Andrassy note is accepted by the Sultan and the Powers; but the insurgents demand guarantees, and the Berlin Memorandum threatens coercion unless the concessions are made within two months. Beaconsfield refuses to approve.

Servia and Montenegro declare war on the Sultan. At the same moment, a revolt in Bulgaria is suppressed with inhuman cruelties. Intense indignation is excited in England by the details in the report of Baring and the pamphlet of Gladstone. An army of Russian volunteers, under Tchernaieff, joins the Servians, who are defeated; but the Montenegrins win several victories. Abdul-Hamid becomes Sultan,

3394. **Philosophy.** Theosophical propaganda is begun by Col. Olcott, Mme Blavatsky, and Sinnett.

3395. **History.** Taine's Origines de la France Contemporaine hotly attacks the Jacobin tradition.

Fustel de Coulanges' Institutions politiques de l'ancienne France.

The Dictionary of German Biography is commenced.

3396. **Geography.** Stanley circumnavigates Victoria Nyanza and Tanganyika, and traces the Congo to the Atlantic.

Nares reaches 83° 20′ 26″, a limit surpassed by a few miles by the Greely expedition of 1882–4.

Nordenskiold makes the North-East passage.

3397. **Agriculture.** The Agricultural Holdings Act arranges for compensation for unexhausted improvements.

3398. **Social.** Plimsoll carries the Merchants' Shipping Bill.

The Friendly Societies are brought under the law.

The Universal Postal Union is instituted.

3399. **Deaths.** Hans Andersen, Corot, Ewald, Finlay, Kaulbach, Kingsley, Lyell, Millet, Pertz, Quinet, Thirlwall.

3400. **Eng. Ch.** The Order of Corporate Union is instituted. [1876

3401. **American Ch.** Savage, a Unitarian Minister in Boston, attempts to blend evolution with a theistic element.

Mrs Eddy founds the Christian Scientists.

Adler founds a Society for Ethical Culture in New York.

3402. **Church Hist.** Thiele's History of Religion to the Spread of the Universal Religions presents the first connected and comparative account of early religious ideas.

3403. **German Lit.** Dahn's novel, A Struggle round Rome.

3404. **Danish Lit.** Jacobsen's Fru Marie Grubbe introduces realism.

3405. **Portuguese Lit.** João de Deus' Flores de Campo.

3406. **Science.** Bell invents a telephone. Its defects as a transmitter are remedied by Edison and Hughes, 1877–8.

Lembroso's The Criminal founds comparative criminology.

3407. **Art.** Leighton's Daphnephoria.

Bouguereau's La Vierge Consolatrice.

Puvis de Chavannes, Bonnat and Laurens fresco the Pantheon.

Wagner's Ring of the Nibelungs is performed at Bayreuth.

Édouard and Jean de Reszke make their début.

Richter begins to conduct orchestral concerts in England.

3408. **Philosophy.** Avenarius' Philosophy as the Thought of the World.

Mainländer and Hellenbach advocate celibacy and suicide.

3409. **Philology.** Strack edits the Prophetarum posteriorum Codex Babylonicus Petropolitanus.

3410. **Education.** A Commission appointed to revise the Statutes of the colleges of Oxford University reduces clerical fellowships, and abolishes clerical headships except in Christ Church and Pembroke. Its work is bitterly attacked by Burgon.

and a Turkish army enters Servia, but is brought to a halt by the Russian ultimatum.

A truce of six months is arranged, and ambassadors of the Powers meet at Constantinople.

2120. **America.** After a vigorous struggle for the Presidency, Hayes defeats Tilden, a Democrat. Hayes removes the soldiers who uphold federal authority in the South and leaves the whites to regain power.

The publication of the Mulligan Letters, written by Blaine, 1869, when Speaker, destroys a great part of his prestige and power.

Diaz defeats Tejada, the President, and becomes supreme in Mexico.

2121. **Africa.** The Khedive Ismail being 100 millions in debt, Goschen is sent to Egypt, and the Dual Control of France and England is established.

2122. **Asia.** England takes Socotra.

2123. **England.** Obstruction is practised by the Irish members, Biggar and Parnell, during the debate on South Africa. [1877

2124. **France.** Macmahon dismisses Jules Simon (May 16), and appoints De Broglie President of the Council. 363 members protest, the Chamber is dissolved, a large republican majority is returned, and De Broglie resigns.

2125. **Russia.** Skobeleff declares that an invasion of India with 50,000 men would be free from all risk.

2126. **Turkey.** The conference at Constantinople fails, the Sultan refusing to allow the powers a voice in the election of provincial governors. Montenegro remains in arms. Russian troops cross the Danube and clear and hold the Shipka Pass (July 17). Charles of Roumania signs a convention with Russia, promising active co-operation. The Sultan deposes him, and Roumania proclaims her independence, and joins the Russians before Plevna. Osman Pasha repulses an attack on Plevna (Sept.), which, however, capitulates (Dec.). In Asia Minor, Kars is stormed (Nov.).

2127. **Africa.** Bartle Frere is made High Commissioner of South Africa, and instructed to work of federation. Lord Carnarvon's Permissive Bill is, however, rejected by all the governments of South Africa.

The South African Republic is annexed by Sir Theophilus Shepstone, during a recess of the Volksraad, on the ground that it is bankrupt and in danger from Basutos and Zulus. Three-fourths of the burghers send a deputation to England to protest.

2128. **Asia.** A great famine occurs in India.

The Queen is proclaimed Empress of India at Delhi.

Yakub Beg's rebellion is suppressed.

A rebellion breaks out in Satsuma, but is suppressed, after heavy fighting, by the Japanese government.

3411. **Economics.** Cliffe Leslie attacks the ideas of Ricardo.
3412. **Geography.** Reclus' Géographie Universelle.
3413. **Anthropology.** Spencer's Principles of Sociology explain the "ghost-theory" of religion, asserting that a second or invisible self, inferred from shadows, sleep, and dreams, has led to ancestor-worship.
3414. **Social.** Brockway founds Elmira Reformatory.
3415. **Deaths.** Antonelli, Deak, Lassen, Harriet Martineau, Paludan-Müller, George Sand.

3416. **Eng. Ch.** The Methodist Conference admits the laity. [1877
Farrar's Eternal Hope is answered by Pusey's What is of Faith concerning Everlasting Punishment?
3417. **French Ch.** A Protestant Institute is established in Paris.
3418. **Eng. Lit.** James Knowles edits the Nineteenth Century, a monthly magazine.
Mallock's New Republic.
3419. **Italian Lit.** Carducci's Odi Barbare imitate classical metres and introduce exotic forms.
3420. **American Lit.** Henry James' The American.
3421. **Russian Lit.** Tolstoi's Anna Karenina.
3422. **Norwegian Lit.** Ibsen's Pillars of Society.
3423. **Science.** Pictet and Caillet liquefy the 'permanent gases' by pressure and low temperature.
Hall discovers the satellites of Mars.
Schiaparelli discovers 'canals' in Mars.
Miss Ormerod publishes her first annual report on injurious farm insects.
Van't Hoff suggests a tri-dimensional theory of atomic space-relations.
Lord Rayleigh's Treatise on Sound.
3424. **Art.** Grant Allen's Physiological Aesthetics denies the existence of anything intrinsic in objects which calls forth aesthetic pleasure. The beautiful is that which affords the maximum of stimulation and the minimum of fatigue or waste.
Saint-Saens' Samson and Dalila.
Prout's Instrumentation.
3425. **Education.** Elementary Education is made compulsory in Italy between the ages of six and nine.
3426. **History.** Ficker's Contributions to the Study of Documents.
3427. **Geography.** Richthofen's China.
Stanley traces the Congo to its mouth.
3428. **Social.** Todt's Socialism and Christian Society aids the foundation of a Protestant Socialist movement in Germany, of which Stöcker, a Court Chaplain, becomes the leader.
Archbishop Pecci issues liberal Pastorals on the Social Question.
3429. **Deaths.** Courbet, Cournot, Ketteler, Lanfrey, Leverrier, Palacky, Ritschl, Thiers, Tholuck.

2129. **Germany.** Attempts are made to assassinate the Emperor, and severe laws against the Socialists are passed. [1878

2130. **Italy.** The Irredentist agitation (to obtain Trieste and other districts where Italian is spoken) grows.

2131. **Turkey.** Believing that the Russians are marching to Constantinople, Disraeli sends the English fleet through the Dardanelles (Feb.). Carnarvon and Derby resign, and Salisbury becomes Foreign Secretary. Credits of six millions are obtained, the Reserves are called out, and Indian troops summoned to Malta.

Russia and Turkey sign the Treaty of San Stefano (March). Roumania, Servia, and Montenegro are to be independent and to receive territory; an autonomous but tributary Bulgaria reaches from the Black Sea to the Aegean; Batum, Erzerum and Kars pass to Russia, which receives the strip of Bessarabia lost 1856, and part of Armenia. England demands an European Congress. Russia agrees to the discussion only of the Articles concerning the general interests of Europe. The deadlock is removed by Schouvaloff, who prepares a list of questions to be discussed. Beaconsfield and Salisbury represent England at the Berlin Congress, Waddington France, Schouvaloff and Gortchakoff Russia, Andrassy Austria. By the Treaty of Berlin, Bulgaria north of the Balkans is to become an autonomous state, paying tribute to the Sultan; the south is to become Eastern Roumelia, to have administrative autonomy, and to be ruled by a Christian prince, nominated by the Sultan and approved by the Powers. Russia regains the strip of Bessarabia, and obtains Kars and Batum. The Protectorate over Bosnia and Herzegovina is given to Austria; the Danube is neutralised, and the fortresses on its banks are to be razed. Russia resigns Erzerum. Roumania is recognised as a sovereign state, and Montenegro and Servia are declared independent.

The Sultan undertakes to grant reforms, under the superintendence of the Powers, and complete political equality.

By the Convention of Cyprus, made by England and Turkey shortly before the Congress, England guarantees the remaining Turkish possessions in Asia Minor, the Sultan handing over Cyprus and promising reforms.

2132. **Greece.** The Powers recommend the Sultan to grant Thessaly and part of Epirus to Greece.

2133. **Austria.** Austria reduces Bosnia and Herzegovina.

2134. **Russia.** General Trepoff is murdered by Vera Sassoulitch.

2135. **America.** The purchase of not less than two millions silver bullion monthly for coinage into silver dollars at 16 to 1 is adopted.

2136. **Australasia.** The United States, Germany and England make commercial treaties with the King of Samoa.

2137. **Africa.** The report on the Zulu boundary question submitted to arbitration, 1877, is issued. The ultimate award is left to Bartle Frere, who adds a number of demands.

English sovereignty is proclaimed over Walfisch Bay.

2138. **Asia.** The Ameer receives a party of Russian officers, but refuses to receive an English mission. An ultimatum is disregarded, and Roberts is ordered to invade Afghanistan.

3430. **Eng. Ch.** The Hibbert Lectures on Comparative Religion are opened by Max Müller. Subsequent courses are delivered by Renan, Rhys Davids, Renouf, D'Alviella, Kuenen, Rhys, Hatch, Pfleiderer. [1878

3431. **Scotch Ch.** Leo XIII. restores the Catholic hierarchy, a measure recommended by Wiseman and promised by Pius IX.

Rainy advocates Disestablishment in his Church and State.

Robertson Smith is tried for heresy. After his condemnation, he delivers popular lectures on the Old Testament in the Jewish Church, and on the Prophets.

3432. **Spanish Ch.** The Spanish Protestants petition the Anglican Church for a Bishop.

3433. **American Ch.** Colonel Ingersoll begins to speak and write against Christian dogma.

3434. **Church Hist.** Leo XIII. succeeds Pius, and appoints liberal Ministers; but Rampolla, an ultramontane, is soon forced on him by the Jesuits.

3435. **Eng. Lit.** Ellen Terry joins Irving's company.

3436. **French Lit.** Sully-Prudhomme's La Justice.

3437. **German Lit.** Fontane's Before the Storm, a story of the War of Liberation.

3438. **Science.** Marsh discovers gigantic fossil forms in America.

Lockyer explains his theory of the compound nature of the chemical elements.

The Eddystone Lighthouse, built 1759, is taken down and replaced by a new structure.

Electric lighting is introduced.

Lapworth's Life Zones in the lower palaeozoic rocks of Scotland.

Van't Hoff applies the Avogadrian rule to solutions.

David Hughes discovers the microphone, which is used as a transmitter to the telephone.

3439. **Art.** Millais' Yeoman of the Guard.

3440. **Philosophy.** Wundt institutes a Laboratory at Leipzig for psychophysical research.

Hartmann's Phenomenology of the Ethical Consciousness traces the steps in the development of the moral idea.

3441. **History.** Lecky's History of England in the 18th century.

Wellhausen's History of Israel blends the currents starting from Vatke, Ewald and Reuss.

Oncken edits an Universal History, to which Stade, Dahn, Hertzberg, Philippson, Droysen, Brückner, Stern and others contribute.

3442. **Social.** The Pope issues an encyclical against Socialism, changing his attitude in part owing to attempts on the Emperor William and King Humbert.

3443. **Deaths.** Claude Bernard, Bryant, Dupanloup, Fazy, Gutzkow, Gilbert Scott, Secchi, E. H. Weber.

2139. **England.** Gladstone attacks Beaconsfield in his Midlothian Campaign. [1879
2140. **Ireland.** Davitt forms the Land League.
2141. **France.** The Prince Imperial is killed in South Africa.
Grévy succeeds Macmahon, who resigns.
2142. **Germany.** Russia's resentment being aroused by the part played by Germany in the Treaty of 1878, Bismarck concludes a defensive alliance with Austria.
Bismarck imposes protective duties.
The Supreme Court is fixed at Leipzig.
Alsace-Lorraine is declared a Reichsland, or Territory, a Statthalter is appointed, and the assembly is allowed to originate legislation.
2143. **Austria.** Taafe forms a composite Cabinet.
2144. **America.** The resumption of payment in gold is made.
Chile quarrels with Peru and Bolivia over nitrate deposits, cripples the Peruvian navy, and captures Peru's chief ports.
Lesseps begins to plan the Panama Canal.
2145. **Africa.** Ismail is deposed by the Sultan, and Tewfik succeeds.
Cetewayo neglects Bartle Frere's ultimatum, and Lord Chelmsford enters Zululand. A division is almost annihilated at Isandlhwana, but the Zulus are checked by the defence of Rorke's Drift, and crushed at Ulundi.
The French extend their power in Senegambia, on the Upper Niger, and on the Guinea coast.
Stanley is sent out by Belgium to found the Congo Free State.
2146. **Australasia.** England acquires the right of most favoured nation in Tonga.
2147. **Asia.** The Ameer of Afghanistan dies, and the Treaty of Gandamak is signed with Yakub Khan, the new Ameer. The English envoy Cavagnari, however, is murdered, Afghanistan is again invaded, and Cabul captured.
Warburton is appointed Political Officer in the Khyber. By winning the confidence of the Afridis, he reduces the Pass to perfect order.

2148. **England.** The Liberals win the General Election. Beaconsfield resigns, Hartington fails to form a Ministry, and [1880 Gladstone becomes Premier. Bradlaugh claims to make an affirmation, and, failing that, to take the oath. Randolph Churchill, Gorst, and Drummond Wolff form the so-called 'Fourth Party,' acting independently of Stafford Northcote.
2149. **Ireland.** Forster's Compensation for Disturbance clause in a relief Bill is rejected by the Lords. The Land League organises an agitation against eviction and rent.
Parnell becomes Sessional Chairman of the Home Rule party.
2150. **France.** Rochefort and the exiles are allowed to return.

3444. **French Ch.** Jules Ferry's education bill forbids members of unauthorised communities to teach. The clause is resisted in the Senate by Jules Simon and postponed. [1879

Ribet's La Mystique Divine.

3445. **German Ch.** Dorner's System of Christian Doctrine, a Lutheran exposition.

Treitschke calls attention to the growth of Jewish influence, and an anti-semitic crusade is initiated by Stöcker; but the movement is discouraged by the Court.

3446. **American Ch.** Phillips Brooks delivers the Bohlen Lectures on the Influence of Jesus.

3447. **Church Hist.** Max Müller edits a translation of the Sacred Books of the East, beginning with the Upanishads.

The Pope recommends Catholic schools to study Aquinas.

3448. **Eng. Lit.** Edwin Arnold's Light of Asia.

3449. **French Lit.** Zola's L'Assommoir.

3450. **Swedish Lit.** Strindberg's Red Room introduces naturalism.

3451. **Norwegian Lit.** Ibsen's Doll's House.

3452. **Science.** Fouqué and Lévy's Microscopical Study of the Igneous Rocks of France.

Crookes infers an ultra-gaseous state of matter from studying the passage of the electric discharge through highly rarefied gases.

Hansen studies fermentation.

3453. **Art.** Bastien-Lepage's Joan of Arc.

Grove's Dictionary of Music.

3454. **Philology.** Whitney's Sanskrit Grammar.

3455. **Philosophy.** Spencer's Data of Ethics traces the evolution of conduct, and sets up the test of social efficiency.

Balfour's Defence of Philosophic Doubt asserts the uncertainty of knowledge.

Huxley depicts Hume as the embodiment of the scientific spirit.

3456. **History.** Janssen's History of the German People during the Reformation, a powerful Ultramontane presentation.

Treitschke's History of Germany in the 19th century.

3457. **Economics.** Giffen's Essays in Finance.

3458. **Social.** Canon Blackley proposes a scheme of Old Age Pensions.

3459. **Deaths.** Clifford, Espartero, Garrison, Lord Lawrence, Delane, Roon.

3460. **Eng. Ch.** The Burials Bill allows Christian Dissenters to hold services in the churchyard of the parish. [1880

Cheyne edits the Book of Isaiah.

3461. **French Ch.** Grévy overrides the Senate's opposition to Ferry's bill. The Jesuits are dissolved, military chaplains are abolished, and candidates for the ministry are compelled to serve in the army for a year.

3462. **Belgian Ch.** In consequence of the School Law of 1879, diplomatic relations with the Papacy are broken off.

3463. **German Ch.** Finding the National Liberals growing restive,

2151. **Germany.** Most and Hasselmann, Anarchists, are expelled from the Social Democratic party.

2152. **Russia.** France alienates Russia by refusing the extradition of Hartmann, who had been concerned in the Moscow attempt on the Tsar's life.

Loris Melikoff is given dictatorial power to deal with Nihilists, but makes concessions.

2153. **Montenegro.** Dulcigno is transferred to Montenegro by pressure from the Powers, at the instance of Gladstone.

2154. **Asia.** Abdurrahman becomes Ameer of Afghanistan. An English force is defeated at Maiwand by Ayub Khan, son of Shere Ali (Dec.), and Roberts marches rapidly to Candahar.

2155. **Africa.** A petition for the reversal of the annexation of the Transvaal is refused by Gladstone's Government, on the ground that many English have settled there. The burghers therefore declare independence under Kruger, Pretorius and Joubert (Dec.), and the British garrisons are surrounded.

2156. **Australasia.** A conference at Melbourne discusses federation.

France annexes the Tahiti Isles.

[1881

2157. **Ireland.** A Land Bill enables a tenant to sell his interest, the purchaser acquiring all the seller's rights, and to apply to a land court to fix a rent for 15 years. The landlord may object to a new tenant, and has rights of pre-emption and of resumption. The Duke of Argyll disapproves of the Bill, and leaves the ministry. Parnell is arrested (Oct.). The No Rent Manifesto is published, and the Land League is suppressed as an illegal and criminal association.

2158. **France.** Ferry resigns on an attack on his Tunis policy, and Gambetta forms a ministry from which all distinguished men, except Paul Bert, hold aloof.

2159. **Italy.** An Electoral Reform Bill enfranchises men of 21, of property or education, and adopts Scrutin de Liste. Minority representation is granted to districts returning five members.

2160. **Russia.** The Tsar is murdered, having that day signed an Ukase calling a consultative Assembly of Notables.

Alexander III. begins to tamper with the privileges of Finland and the Baltic Provinces.

2161. **Greece.** The Powers compel Turkey to cede to Greece the greater part of Thessaly and the command of the Gulf of Arta.

2162. **Bulgaria.** Alexander suspends the constitution and makes a Russian general his premier.

2163. **America.** President Garfield is murdered.

2164. **Africa.** Negotiations are opened with the Boers; but Colley is defeated at Laing's Nek (Jan.), and Majuba Hill (Feb.), where he is killed. Sir Evelyn Wood declares that he has the Transvaal at his

Bismarck conciliates the Centre by making the application of the May Laws discretionary.

3464. **Eng. Lit.** Shorthouse's John Inglesant.

Thompson's City of Dreadful Night.

3465. **French Lit.** Zola's Le Roman Expérimental explains 'naturalism.'

3466. **American Lit.** Mark Twain's A Tramp Abroad.

3467. **Literature.** Burton's translation of Camoens.

3468. **Science.** Francis Balfour's Comparative Embryology.

3469. **Art.** Verdi's Aida.

Cologne Cathedral is finished.

Pearson designs Truro Cathedral, which is opened, 1887.

Hans Thoma's portrait of himself (Dresden).

3470. **Archaeology.** The Gigantomachia is discovered at Pergamus.

3471. **Philosophy.** John Caird's Philosophy of Religion.

3472. **Education.** High Schools are instituted for girls in England.

3473. **History.** Hodgkin's Italy and her Invaders.

3474. **Economics.** Bagehot points out that Ricardo's economics rest on assumptions only true within very narrow limits.

3475. **Law.** Holland's Jurisprudence.

3476. **Social.** Bertillon measures criminals for purposes of detection.

An Employers' Liability Bill compensates for accidents due to the negligence of employer or foreman.

The Ground Game Act secures farmers' crops against hares and rabbits.

Fawcett introduces Parcels' Post, and improves Savings-banks.

3477. **Deaths.** George Eliot, Flaubert, Stratford de Redcliffe, Ricasoli.

3478. **Eng. Ch.** The Revised Version of the New Testament appears. [1881

Westcott and Hort edit the Greek Testament.

3479. **French Ch.** Ferry expels the unauthorised Congregations.

3480. **Italian Ch.** Campello becomes a Protestant.

Anti-papal manifestations occur on the occasion of the removal of the remains of Pius IX.

3481. **Russian Ch.** Pobyedonostseff becomes the Procurator of the Holy Synod and furiously persecutes the Jews.

3482. **French Lit.** Perfect freedom is granted to the press.

Pailleron's Le Monde où l'on s'ennuie.

Sarah Bernhardt leaves the Comédie Française.

3483. **German Lit.** Wildenbruch's Carolingians revives the historical drama.

3484. **Norwegian Lit.** Ibsen's Ghosts.

3485. **Roumanian Lit.** Carmen Sylva's (The Queen of Roumania) Roumanian Poems.

3486. **Science.** Pasteur attenuates anthrax virus by vaccine.

Langley invents the Bolometer.

George Darwin investigates tidal friction.

3487. **Art.** Liebermann's Orphanage in Amsterdam.

Munckaczy's Christ before Pilate.

Perrot and Chipiez' L'Art dans l'Antiquité.

mercy; but the negotiations are resumed, and the Convention of Pretoria restores self-government to the Transvaal, except in regard to relations with foreign countries and native races, and establishes a British Resident.

Under pretence of chastising a border tribe, the French enter Tunis, and compel the Bey to invest France with a virtual protectorate.

Mahomet Achmet of Dongola proclaims himself the Mahdi, and raises the Sudan against the Khedive.

2165. **Asia.** Skobeleff takes the Turkoman stronghold of Geok Tepe, and orders a wholesale massacre.

[1882

2166. **England.** Randolph Churchill explains his ideas of Tory democracy, and wins a steadily increasing influence in the provinces. The Primrose League is founded.

A Channel Tunnel is discussed, but disapproved by the military authorities.

2167. **Ireland.** The 'Kilmainham Treaty' is arranged by which Parnell is released on promising to put down outrage. Forster resigns, and Lord F. Cavendish becomes Chief Secretary, but on his arrival is murdered with Burke, the Permanent Secretary, in Phoenix Park. The Prevention of Crimes Bill is therefore passed.

2168. **France.** Gambetta's ministry falls, after 10 weeks' power.

2169. **Italy.** In consequence of the French policy in Tunis, Italy enters the Triple Alliance.

2170. **Austria.** An insurrection in Dalmatia, Bosnia, and Herzegovina, aided by Panslavist agitators, is suppressed.

Anti-Semite riots begin.

2171. **Russia.** Gortschakoff and Ignatieff, leaders of the anti-German party, are dismissed, and Giers becomes Foreign Secretary.

2172. **Greece.** Tricoupis attempts to create a fleet, army, roads, railways and harbours, but reduces the country to bankruptcy.

2173. **America.** Chinese immigration is suspended for 10 years.

The Panama Canal is begun.

2174. **Africa.** Arabi leads a movement against foreign influences in Egypt. The English fleet arrives, and, on the murder of some Europeans, bombards Alexandria. The English army is landed, and Wolseley defeats Arabi at Tel-el-Kebir. Arabi is banished for life to Ceylon, and 12,000 men are left to restore order.

Italy takes possession of Assab Bay, in the Red Sea, extends her coast possessions North and South, and founds the colony of Eritrea.

The German Colonial Society is founded.

De Brazza founds Brazzaville and Franceville near the Congo, and obtains a protectorate of the surrounding territory for France.

2175. **Asia.** The cotton duties in India are abolished.

3488. **Archaeology.** Flinders Petrie begins to excavate in Egypt.
3489. **Economics.** Henry George's Progress and Poverty urges the substitution of a single tax on rent for existing taxes.
3490. **History.** Ranke's History of the World.
The Vatican archives are thrown open to students.
3491. **Social.** The German Emperor sends a message to the Reichstag, indicating a programme of social reform.
Alfred Russell Wallace founds a Land Nationalisation Society, and urges the purchase of existing rights and the revival of the yeomanry class. Hyndman, Morris and Bax found the Social Democratic Federation.
The Married Women's Property Act gives the wife complete control of her property.
3492. **Deaths.** Beaconsfield, Bluntschli, Carlyle, Dostoievsky, Littré, Lotze, Mariette, Schleiden, Dean Stanley.

3493. **American Ch.** Dr Clark, a Congregationalist, founds the Society of Christian Endeavour. [1882
Ward Beecher declares himself an Unitarian.
3494. **Church Hist.** Blunt's Future of Islam.
Lyall's Asiatic Studies.
3495. **Eng. Lit.** Walter Besant's All Sorts and Conditions of Men.
Froude's Life of Carlyle.
3496. **French Lit.** Mallarmé's L'Après Midi d'un Faune.
3497. **American Lit.** Howells' A Modern Instance.
3498. **Science.** Koch's paper on the Aetiology of Tuberculosis.
3499. **Art.** Gounod's The Redemption.
Wagner's Ring of the Nibelungs is performed in London.
Oscar Wilde's Lectures on the Decorative Arts explain the aims of the Aesthetic movement.
3500. **Philosophy.** Leslie Stephen's Science of Ethics sets up a standard of social efficiency.
Frey, a Positivist, and Fiske introduce Spencer's philosophy into the United States, and attempt to combine the Unknowable and Humanity.
3501. **Econômics.** Jevons' State in relation to Trade repudiates laissez faire.
3502. **Law.** Martens' Consular Law in the East.
3503. **History.** Sénart's Légende de Buddha denies the existence of a historical personality.
3504. **Education.** Elementary education in France is made compulsory.
3505. **Social.** Pastor Bodelschwingh establishes a Labour Colony near Bielefeld.
Rudolph Meyer and Vogelsang found Catholic Socialism in Austria.
3506. **Deaths.** Auerbach, Louis Blanc, Darwin, Emerson, Gambetta, Garibaldi, T. H. Green, Jevons, Le Play, Longfellow, Pusey, Rossetti, Schwann, Skobeleff, W. G. Ward, Wöhler.

2176. **France.** Ferry returns to power. [1883
Chambord dies without leaving or naming an heir.

2177. **Bulgaria.** Alexander restores the Constitution, and the Russian ministers resign. A Russian plot to kidnap the Prince is discovered.

2178. **Turkey.** Bismarck notifies his desire that nothing further should be done by the Powers for the assistance of the Christian subjects of the Sultan.

Prussian officers are employed to drill the Turkish troops.

2179. **America.** A Civil Service Act introduces competitive examination.

2180. **Australasia.** A Federal Council is created to legislate on fisheries, intercolonial legal process, the influx of criminals, etc. The Council possesses no executive power, and New South Wales and New Zealand hold aloof.

The request of Queensland, which needs cheap labour, to be allowed to annex New Guinea is refused by England.

2181. **Africa.** A French war with Madagascar begins.

France occupies Obok.

The Khedive abolishes the joint control, and appoints an English financial adviser. A Legislative Council and General Assembly are created, but possess little power.

The Dervishes destroy Hicks' Egyptian army in Kordofan.

2182. **Asia.** A French Protectorate is declared over Annam and Tonkin, with commercial privileges and the administration of the customs.

The Ilbert Bill, to extend the jurisdiction of the rural Criminal Courts over Europeans, excites the violent protests of Anglo-Indians, and a compromise is made.

2183. **England.** A Franchise Bill is introduced with uniform household and lodger franchise for boroughs and counties. [1884
Cairns carries an amendment demanding the disclosure of the Government's redistribution scheme. The Bill is reintroduced in an autumn session, and a compromise effected, a Redistribution Bill being jointly drafted by the leaders of both parties.

An Imperial Federation League is formed.

2184. **France.** No more life senators are to be created.

2185. **Germany.** The Liberal Union joins the Fortschrittspartei and becomes the Freisinnige, led by Richter.

2186. **Norway.** After 12 years' struggle, the Left compels the King to accept a ministry resting on a majority. Democratic reforms are introduced; but the Sverdrup ministry proves clerical, and is deserted by the radicals under Björnson.

2187. **America.** Cleveland defeats Blaine (whose nomination splits the Republican vote), and lowers the tariff.

3507. **Russian Ch.** The Raskolniks are allowed to hold office. [1883
3508. **Church Hist.** The 'Didache' is published.
3509. **Eng. Lit.** Stevenson's Treasure Island.
Richard Jefferies' Story of My Heart.
Olive Schreiner's Story of an African Farm.
The Irish Literary Society is founded in London.
3510. **French Lit.** Bourget's Essais de Psychologie Contemporaine.
Amiel's Journal is published posthumously.
Gyp's (Comtesse de Martel) Autour du Mariage.
3511. **Norwegian Lit.** Garborg's Peasant Students.
Björnson's Beyond Human Endurance.
3512. **Science.** Maxim invents an automatic machine-gun.
Sachs' Physiology of Plants.
Weierstrass' Elliptic Functions.
3513. **Art.** Orchardson's Voltaire at the Duc de Sully's.
Morelli's Criticisms on Italian Painters.
3514. **Philosophy.** Green's Prolegomena to Ethics restates and developes the central positions of Kant's teaching.
3515. **Philology.** Brugsch's Inscriptiones Aegyptiacae.
Skeat's English Dictionary.
3516. **History.** Reusch's History of the Index of Forbidden Books.
Seeley's Expansion of England.
Seebohm's English Village Community attacks the Mark theory.
3517. **Politics.** Lester Ward's Dynamic Sociology.
3518. **Economics.** Karl Menger attacks the extreme historical school.
Sidgwick's Political Economy modifies the Ricardian system.
3519. **Law.** Stephen's History of Criminal Law in England.
3520. **Agriculture.** An Agricultural Holdings Bill secures compensation to tenants at the end of their tenancies, without power to the parties to contract out of the Act.
3521. **Social.** The 'Fabyans' leave the Social Democratic Federation.
3522. **Deaths.** Conscience, Gortschakoff, J. R. Green, Salar Jung, Manet, Marx, Sabine, Siemens, Turgeneff, Veuillot, Wagner.

3523. **French Ch.** The Pope exhorts the Bishops not to show hostility to the Republic. [1884
3524. **African Ch.** Hannington becomes Bishop of Eastern Equatorial Africa, but is murdered 1885.
3525. **Science.** Ray Lankester founds the Marine Biological Association.
Owen's British Fossil Reptiles.
G. W. Hill determines the inequalities of the moon's motion, due to the non-spherical nature of the earth.
Flower becomes Director of the Natural History Museum.
3526. **Art.** Dvorak's Stabat Mater.
Mackenzie's Rose of Sharon.

2188. **Africa.** The Convention of London is signed with the Transvaal. The Resident is withdrawn; the assertion of Suzerainty is dropped; Great Britain retains the right to veto treaties concluded by the South African Republic with foreign powers.

Basutoland is placed under the English Crown.

Native courts are established in Egypt with native and foreign judges. Baring returns as Consul-General. Gordon is sent to withdraw the European residents from the Sudan, and reaches Khartoum, where he is cut off by the Dervishes (March). A relief expedition under Wolseley is sent out (Aug.).

Bismarck calls a Conference at Berlin for the discussion of African affairs. Germany establishes a Protectorate over Togoland, the Cameroons, and South-West Africa, north of the Orange River.

England establishes a Protectorate over Somaliland by accord with Italy.

2189. **Asia.** France annexes Tonkin, and seizes two towns in Annam.

France occupies Grand Bassam and Porto Novo.

Russia annexes Merv.

[1885

2190. **England.** The Redistribution Bill merges boroughs under 15,000 in county districts, allows one member to towns under 50,000, and two to towns under 165,000. Except for these and the City of London, one member districts are universal. 160 seats are extinguished.

Gladstone's Government falls on an amendment to the Budget (June). Salisbury becomes Premier. 335 Liberals are returned, 249 Conservatives, 86 Irish Home Rulers (Nov.). Gladstone is now believed to accept the principle of Home Rule.

Chamberlain's 'unauthorised programme' demands 'ransom' from the rich, e.g. free education, improved dwellings at fair rents, a land bill, allotments, free libraries, abolition of indirect taxes, the restoration of commons, disestablishment, graduated taxation and burdens on landowners.

2191. **France.** The Scrutin de Liste is introduced.

Ferry falls in consequence of a repulse at Hanoi.

2192. **Bulgaria.** Eastern Roumelia throws off the Turkish yoke, joins Bulgaria, and is accepted by Prince Alexander. Servia invades Bulgaria and is repulsed.

2193. **Africa.** Stewart, with an advance guard, defeats a Dervish force at Abu Klea (Jan. 14). Khartoum is taken and Gordon killed (Jan. 26). Two days later Wilson sights Khartoum, but retires. The Sudan is evacuated, and the Mahdi becomes supreme, but dies a few months later, and is succeeded by the Kalifa.

The Berlin Congress recognises the Congo Free State, and declares the Congo open.

A British Protectorate is proclaimed over North Bechuanaland, and South Bechuanaland becomes a Crown Colony.

3527. **Philology.** Christ's edition of the Iliad tries to reconcile Wolf and Nitzsch by asserting that Homer composed independent lays, but with a general idea.

Murray edits an English Dictionary.

3528. **Politics.** Spencer's The Man versus the State champions extreme individualism.

3529. **History.** Duchesne edits the Liber Pontificalis.

Justin Winsor edits a History of America.

3530. **Anthropology.** Andrew Lang's Custom and Myth attacks the philological treatment of myths, and seeks their explanation in folklore.

3531. **Social.** A Royal Commission on the Housing of the Working Classes is appointed, under Sir Charles Dilke.

Bismarck declares in favour of the right to labour for the able-bodied, support for the infirm, and pensions for old age.

3532. **Deaths.** Dorner, J. B. Dumas, Fawcett, Bartle Frere, Lasker, Lepsius, Martensen, Mignet, Pattison, Wendell Phillips, Todleben.

3533. **Eng. Ch.** Drummond's Natural Law in the Spiritual World assumes that the spiritual and natural belong to the same world-order. [1885

3534. **German Ch.** Beyschlag's Life of Jesus denies the personal pre-existence of the Logos.

3535. **Russian Ch.** Tolstoi's My Religion declares non-resistance the central point of Christ's teaching, and urges a literal fulfilment of His precepts.

3536. **American Ch.** The Mormons split into a polygamic and monogamic section.

3537. **Eng. Lit.** Pater's Marius the Epicurean.

Leslie Stephen edits a Dictionary of National Biography, with the assistance of Sidney Lee, who succeeds him as editor.

3538. **French Lit.** Vogüé's Le Roman Russe attacks French realism.

Verlaine's Jadis et Naguère.

Bourget's Cruelle Énigme.

3539. **German Lit.** 'Jung Deutschland,' a collection of lyrics, mainly by new poets, appears.

3540. **Art.** Sullivan composes music for Gilbert's The Mikado.

Onslow Ford's statue of Folly is bought by the Chantrey Bequest.

3541. **Science.** Pasteur cures a boy of hydrophobia. The efficacy of the treatment is contested; but persons bitten by mad dogs are sent from all parts to Paris.

De Bary's Lectures on Bacteria.

Neumayr recognises climatic zones in the Jurassic rocks of Europe, and constructs a map showing the divisions of land and sea during the Jurassic age.

3542. **Philosophy.** Royce's Religious Aspects of Philosophy.

3543. **Philology.** Fleischer's Arabic Philology.

Carl Abel's Philological Essays.

3544. **History.** Denifle's Mediaeval Universities.

England proclaims a Protectorate over the Niger Coast and River, and charters the Royal Niger Company.

Germany gains territory in the interior of the Zanzibar Protectorate.

Italy occupies Massowah.

2194. **America.** Cable's The Silent South calls attention to the treatment of negroes.

The Saskatchewan rebellion is crushed.

2195. **Asia.** Disputes arise as to whether Penjdeh is within the Afghan Boundary. Russia suddenly ejects the Afghans from Penjdeh (March). Gladstone asks for 11 millions, but a compromise is made allowing Russia the road and the Afghans the command of the pass.

English troops invade Upper Burmah and annex it.

France makes peace with China, which withdraws its claims and recognises the Protectorate over Annam and the possession of Tonkin.

2196. **Australasia.** A British Protectorate is declared over the south of New Guinea in consequence of the annexation of the north by Germany.

[1886

2197. **England.** The Government is beaten on an Amendment to the Address on Allotments and resigns, and is replaced by a Ministry under Gladstone, who introduces a Home Rule Bill and a Land Purchase Bill (April). The Home Rule Bill is defeated on second reading by 341 to 311, 93 Liberals, including Bright, Chamberlain, Courtney, Goschen, Hartington and James, voting in the majority (June 7). Gladstone appeals to the country and is defeated. Hartington refuses to form a Ministry, and Salisbury becomes Premier. Randolph Churchill, the leader of the House, shortly resigns, differing on questions of public expenditure (Dec.).

2198. **France.** Boulanger becomes Minister of War.

Freycinet expels the members of the ruling families.

2199. **Germany.** King Ludwig of Bavaria commits suicide.

2200. **Russia.** Russia repudiates the clause of the Berlin Treaty making Batoum a free port, and fortifies it.

2201. **Bulgaria.** Austria threatens to join Servia, and Alexander therefore makes peace. He is kidnapped by Russian agents, but restored by Stambuloff; but he is so unnerved by a letter from the Tsar disapproving his return that he abdicates.

2202. **America.** The Canadian Pacific Railway is finished.

2203. **Australasia.** England and Germany agree on limits for acquisition in the Western Pacific. The German possession of Kaiser Wilhelm's Land, on the N.E. of New Guinea, is recognised and a line is drawn from the S.E. of New Guinea, through the Solomon Islands, then N.E. to the Marshall group. S. and E. of this Germany may acquire nothing. Samoa and Tonga are excluded.

2204. **Africa.** An Anglo-German Agreement defines the Sultanate of Zanzibar and the spheres of influence of the two powers on the coast.

Gold is discovered on the Witwatersrand.

3545. **Economics.** Cohn's Foundation of Political Economy, influenced by, but often diverging from, the Katheder-Sozialisten.

3546. **Politics.** Maine's Popular Government unfavourably contrasts the English with the American Constitution, on the ground that the former offers no sufficient obstacle to precipitate legislation.

Kropotkin's Paroles d'un Révolté explain Philosophical Anarchism, which is also supported by Élisée Reclus and Jean Grave.

3547. **Education.** Rein becomes Professor of Pedagogy at Jena, and applies Herbart's ideas. He draws up an eight years' course, beginning with Grimm's Fairy Tales and the Old Testament.

3548. **Anthropology.** Ratzel's History of Mankind.

3549. **Geography.** Ney Elias explores the Pamirs, Chitral and Gilghit.

3550. **Social.** The Pope excommunicates the Knights of Labour, but is persuaded by Gibbons to withdraw his censure.

3551. **Deaths.** Grant, Victor Hugo, Lord Houghton, Milne-Edwards, Lord Shaftesbury, Scholten.

3552. **American Ch.** The Bishops of the Episcopal Church issue a Declaration concerning Unity. [1886

3553. **Asiatic Ch.** Archbishop Benson founds a mission to aid the Assyrian Christians.

3554. **French Lit.** D'Aumale bequeaths Chantilly to the Institute.

Lemaître's Les Contemporains introduce impressionist criticism.

3555. **Eng. Lit.** Rider Haggard's King Solomon's Mines.

3556. **German Lit.** Sudermann's Frau Sorge.

3557. **Asiatic Lit.** Chatterji's novel, Chrishna.

3558. **Literature.** Naville edits the Book of the Dead, from the oldest text.

3559. **Science.** Moissan isolates fluorine.

Krafft-Ebing's Psychopathia Sexualis.

Milne studies earthquakes.

The Severn Tunnel is opened.

3560. **Art.** Max Klinger's Judgment of Paris.

3561. **Philosophy.** Nietzsche's Beyond Good and Evil.

James Ward's article on Psychology.

3562. **Philology.** Brugmann's Comparative Grammar of Indo-German Languages.

Blunt's Ideas about India advocates the restoration of native states under English control, and the reduction of expenditure.

3563. **History.** Lea's History of the Inquisition in the Middle Ages.

Harnack's History of Dogma.

Weizsäcker's Apostolic Age.

The English Historical Review is founded, edited by Creighton, and subsequently by Gardiner.

3564. **Politics.** Dicey's Law of the Constitution.

Carnegie's Triumphant Democracy.

3565. **Anthropology.** Two skeletons of low type are found in a cave near Namur, with the bones of extinct animals.

3566. **Social.** The Avelings undertake a Socialist crusade in America.

The British East Africa Company is formed, and Lugard occupies Uganda, 1890.

France obtains a virtual protectorate over Madagascar, and a footing at Diego Suarez Bay, and declares a protectorate over the Comoro Islands.

2205. **Asia.** A French Protectorate is declared over Annam.

The Siberian railway to Vladivostock is begun.

2206. **England.** Goschen becomes Chancellor of the Exchequer and W. H. Smith leader of the House. A Round Table Conference on Home Rule is held by Chamberlain, Trevelyan, Harcourt, Morley, and Herschell, and Trevelyan rejoins the Liberals. [1887

The Jubilee of the Queen's accession is celebrated.

A Colonial Conference is held, and the idea of federation advances.

A revival of Fair Trade agitation takes place, and Howard Vincent obtains the condemnation of free imports at the convention of Conservative Associations at Oxford.

The Independent Labour Party is formed.

2207. **Ireland.** Balfour becomes Chief Secretary, and the Crimes Bill is carried by the closure. At the trial of O'Brien at Michelstown, the police kill one man and fatally wound two.

A Land Bill facilitates purchase, and the Land Court may stay evictions and order payments by instalments. Judicial rents fixed before 1886 are readjusted with reference to the price of produce.

The Plan of Campaign is announced on Lord Clanricarde's estate.

2208. **France.** Corruption is traced to Wilson, son-in-law of President Grévy, who is in consequence forced to resign, and is succeeded by Carnot.

2209. **Germany.** The Kiel canal is begun.

Cancer is suspected in the Crown Prince, and an operation is proposed. Morell Mackenzie is called in and opposes it.

The Septennate is renewed and the Army increased by 40,000.

2210. **Italy.** Crispi succeeds Depretis as Prime Minister.

2211. **Bulgaria.** Ferdinand of Coburg is induced to accept the crown, but is not recognised by Germany or Russia. Stambuloff becomes Prime Minister.

2212. **Russia.** The Tsar accuses Germany of secretly encouraging the Prince of Bulgaria while publicly disclaiming him ; but Bismarck proves the letters on which the Tsar relies to be forgeries.

2213. **Africa.** Drummond Wolff's mission to Constantinople to arrange for England's withdrawal from Egypt fails on account of French protests against the article permitting conditional re-entry.

French Senegambia is extended to the Upper Niger.

2214. **Asia.** The Quetta district becomes British Beluchistan.

The Social Democrats at this time separate from the Anarchists, owing to the violence of Most's paper, Freiheit.

3567. **Deaths.** Beust, Forster, Kraszewski, Liszt, Madvig, Minghetti, Ranke, Waitz.

3568. **Eng. Ch.** Spurgeon enters on the 'Down Grade Crusade' against the new ideas of the Baptist Union, from which he retires. He issues, in conjunction with 30 ministers, a circular on verbal inspiration, 1891. [1887

Cotter Morison's Service of Man asserts that morality was worst while the sway of Christianity was greatest, and looks to the spirit of social service to reform the world.

3569. **German Ch.** The Kulturkampf is terminated, and the Pope urges the Centre to vote for the Septennate.

3570. **Italian Ch.** Tosti, Abbot of Monte Cassino, negotiates with Crispi for a *modus vivendi*, with the Papal approval. The opposition from the Curia, however, is so great that the Pope orders Tosti to discontinue his mission.

3571. **Eng. Lit.** Birkbeck Hill's edition of Boswell's Life of Johnson.

Barrie's Auld Licht Idylls.

3572. **French Lit.** The Théâtre Libre in Paris is opened for the performance of the naturalistic plays of Henri Becque and his disciples.

3573. **Norwegian Lit.** Vogt and Krag reintroduce verse, which had been repudiated, 1874.

3574. **Russian Lit.** Tolstoi's Dominion of Darkness.

3575. **Science.** The first congress of criminal anthropologists is held at Rome, under the presidency of Lombroso.

Burdon Sanderson's Physiology of Nerve.

Hubrecht draws up a report on the Nemertea collected on the voyage of the Challenger.

3576. **Art.** Paderewski, a pupil of Leschetiszky, gives pianoforte recitals in Vienna.

Cowen's Ruth.

3577. **Education.** Fräulein Lange begins to work for the opening of the teaching profession to women.

3578. **Philosophy.** Rauwenhoff's Philosophy of Religion.

3579. **Law.** Maitland edits 'Bracton's Note-book.'

3580. **History.** Sorel's Europe et la Révolution française.

Kingsford's History of Canada.

Renan's Histoire du Peuple d'Israel.

Knapp's Emancipation of the Prussian Peasantry founds a school of social history.

3581. **Geography.** Stanley goes to find Emin Pasha. Starting up the Congo, he crosses the Bantu Borderland and discovers the Albert Edward Nyanza.

3582. **Numismatics.** Head's Historia Nummorum.

3583. **Social.** Facilities for obtaining allotments are granted.

3584. **Deaths.** Ward Beecher, Fechner, Richard Jefferies, Katkof, Kirchhoff, Jenny Lind, Stafford Northcote.

2215. **England.** Goschen reduces the interest on part of the National Debt to $2\frac{3}{4}$, to fall in 1903 to $2\frac{1}{2}$. [1888

Parnell brings an action against the Times for publishing letters approving of the Phoenix Park murders. A special Commission is appointed (Sept.).

County Councils are created, elected for three years by household suffrage. Lord Rosebery becomes Chairman of the London County Council.

2216. **Germany.** William I. dies (March 9), and his son Frederick III. dies (June 15). William II. becomes Emperor.

The attitude of the Russian press becomes so alarming that Bismarck publishes the text of the Austro-German defensive alliance.

2217. **Africa.** The Dervishes are defeated near Suakin.

The British Central Africa Company begins operations.

Lobengula, king of the Matabele, promises not to treat with foreign nations without English approval.

Rhodes amalgamates the Kimberley Diamond Companies.

2218. **Australasia.** An Imperial Defence Act provides for a force of seven men-of-war for 10 years, at the cost of the colonies.

Queensland promises to share in the expenses of British New Guinea.

The New Hebrides question is settled, France and England withdrawing their territorial claims and creating a joint Naval Commission to protect life and property.

2219. **America.** A Treaty is made in relation to the fisheries of the N.W. coast, but is vetoed by the Senate.

2220. **England.** Pigott confesses to forging the Parnell letters. [1889

$21\frac{1}{2}$ millions are voted for 70 additional ships.

2221. **France.** Boulanger is denounced as a plotter by the Minister of the Interior, Constans, and flies, and is sentenced by the Senate to perpetual imprisonment. In the general election, the Comte de Paris urges Monarchists to vote for the Boulangists, who obtain, however, but few seats. The scrutin d'arrondissement is hurriedly restored.

The Panama Canal Company becomes bankrupt.

2222. **Germany.** Geffcken is prosecuted for treason for publishing the Crown Prince's Diary during the Franco-German war.

2223. **Austria.** The Emperor's only son commits suicide.

2224. **Servia.** King Milan abdicates in favour of his son, Alexander, but retains a share of power.

2225. **America.** A Republic is declared in Brazil.

2226. **Africa.** A Charter is given to the British South Africa Company, formed by Rhodes and Beit.

British Central Africa is declared under British protection, and the flag is hoisted on Lakes Tanganyika and Nyasa.

France and England agree on boundaries on the Guinea Coast and Senegambia.

3585. **Eng. Ch.** Lux Mundi, a collection of essays edited by Gore, defines the position of the new Oxford movement. [1888

Martineau's Study of Religion, a theistic treatise.

3586. **Church Hist.** The Pope issues an Encyclical on Human Liberty.

3587. **Eng. Lit.** Mrs Humphry Ward's Robert Elsmere.

Kipling's Plain Tales from the Hills.

William Morris's Dream of John Ball.

3588. **French Lit.** Anatole France's La Vie Littéraire begins.

3589. **Australian Lit.** Rolf Boldrewood's (T. A. Browne) Robbery under Arms.

3590. **Science.** The Lick Observatory begins work.

The Pasteur Institute is established in Paris, under Duclaux and Roux.

Hertz verifies the hypothesis of Faraday and Clerk Maxwell by detecting the presence of electro-magnetic waves arising from Leyden jar or coil sparks.

Teall's British Petrography.

3591. **Archaeology.** The University of Pennsylvania equip an expedition for the excavation of Nippur.

3592. **History.** Zahn's History of the Canon of the New Testament.

H. C. Lea's History of the Inquisition.

3593. **Geography.** Nansen crosses Greenland.

3594. **Agriculture.** A Board of Agriculture is instituted.

3595. **Social.** Bellamy's Looking Backward, a Socialist Utopia.

3596. **Deaths.** Matthew Arnold, Guyau, Maine.

3597. **Eng. Ch.** Mansfield Congregational College, Oxford, is founded. [1889

3598. **Italian Ch.** A statue is erected to Bruno in Rome, on the spot on which he was burned.

3599. **Russian Ch.** Tolstoi's What to do.

3600. **American Ch.** A Catholic University in Washington is inaugurated.

3601. **Church Hist.** Stead's Papacy, a Prophecy, declares the Papacy will head the Socialist movement and will become Anglo-Saxon, and will then once more dominate the world.

3602. **German Lit.** Liliencron's first Poems.

3603. **Norwegian Lit.** Björnson recommences prose fiction with In God's Way.

3604. **Science.** Weismann's Essays on Heredity attempt to prove that acquired aptitudes and characteristics are not directly transmitted.

Schiaparelli discovers the synchronous rotation and revolution of Mercury.

Eiffel builds the Eiffel Tower, Paris, 984 feet high.

3605. **Art.** Stuck's Warder of Paradise.

3606. **Philosophy.** Nietzsche becomes insane.

3607. **Philology.** Henry Nettleship's Contributions to Latin Lexicography.

Lagarde's Formation of Nouns in Aramaic, Arabic, and Hebrew.

Salisbury remonstrates against the establishment by Portugal of a new province on both banks of the Zambesi, barring advance into the interior.

A French expedition forces Dahomey to respect the protectorate over Porto-Novo and to cease from incursions.

King John of Abyssinia is defeated and slain by the Dervishes, and Menelek succeeds.

By the treaty of Uchali, as interpreted by Italy, Abyssinia becomes an Italian protectorate.

Italy establishes her influence over the whole Somali coast from Cape Guardafui.

The Brussels Conference takes further steps to suppress the slave trade, and regulates the sale of guns and liquor to the native.

2227. **Asia.** Japan obtains constitutional government.

2228. **Australasia.** England, Germany, and the United States create a Supreme Court and a municipal council in Samoa under a president representing the Powers.

2229. **England.** In consequence of the case of O'Shea v. Parnell, Gladstone advises the latter to resign his position. The Irish Nationalists, with the exception of Redmond and a few others, renounce his leadership and elect Justin McCarthy Chairman of the party. [1890

2230. **Germany.** Bismarck is succeeded by Caprivi as Chancellor.

Heligoland is handed over to Germany by England.

The Anti-Socialist law of 1878 is repealed.

2231. **Austria.** The Young Czechs defeat a proposal for separate administration of the German and Czech portions of Bohemia. The Old Czechs, who have accepted the plan under protest, are routed at the general election.

2232. **Spain.** Sagasta introduces universal suffrage.

2233. **Holland.** The King of the Netherlands dies, leaving a daughter, Wilhelmina, and Luxemburg becomes an independent neutral state under the Duke of Nassau.

2234. **America.** Sherman's Silver Bill is carried, authorising the purchase of 42 million ounces of silver bullion monthly, and the issue of Treasury notes in payment.

McKinley's Tariff offers reciprocity where it favours home manufactures.

France and England delimit the fisheries of Newfoundland.

2235. **Australasia.** At the suggestion of Sir Henry Parkes a Conference is held at Melbourne to discuss Federation.

Full self-government is conceded to Western Australia.

2236. **Africa.** Germany surrenders the region north of the British East Africa Company, and acknowledges the British Protectorate over

W. D. Whitney edits the Century Dictionary.

3608. **Education.** An International Catholic University is founded in Fribourg.

The Welsh Intermediate Education Act carries out Sir Hugh Owen's schemes for secondary education.

3609. **History.** Mas Latrie's Trésor de Chronologie.

Bresslau's Handbook to the Study of Original Documents.

3610. **Politics.** Bryce's American Commonwealth, a study of political institutions and ideas.

3611. **Social.** The London Dockers' strike is led by Burns, Mann, and Champion. Manning, Sidney Buxton and the Lord Mayor form a Committee of Conciliation, and the men obtain an advance from 5*d.* to 6*d.* an hour, and a minimum employment of four hours.

The London County Council suggests, but fails to carry, the principle of Betterment.

Crispi transfers ecclesiastical endowments in Italy to a poor fund, administered by local boards.

3612. **Deaths.** Anzengruber, Augier, Bright, Browning, Jefferson Davis, Lightfoot, Ritschl, Scherer.

3613. **French Ch.** Père Didon's Vie de Jésus. [1890

3614. **Eng. Ch.** On the instigation of the Church Association, the Bishop of Lincoln is prosecuted for ritualistic practices in the Archbishop's Court. The Judgment decides against the Bishop in reference to mixing water with wine, the hiding of the Manual Act, and the signing the Cross in the Absolution and the Benediction, and is received with general satisfaction.

3615. **Russian Ch.** The crisis of the persecution of the Jews occurs, and protests are sent from England. Baron Hirsch attempts to organise Jewish colonies in Argentina.

3616. **Church Hist.** Lenormant, Bartolo, and other Catholic scholars who have accepted some of the results of modern criticism are silenced.

3617. **Eng. Lit.** Stead edits the Review of Reviews.

3618. **French Lit.** Villiers de l'Isle-Adam's Axël, a Symbolist drama.

3619. **American Lit.** John Hay's Poems.

3620. **Russian Lit.** Tolstoi's Kreutzer Sonata.

3621. **Science.** Sophus Lie invents a method of analysis by groups.

Poincaré's Électricité et Optique.

The Forth Bridge is opened, its central spans being 115 feet longer than that of Brooklyn.

3622. **Art.** Puvis de Chavannes leads a secession of artists from the Salon in the Champs Elysées, and exhibits in the Champ de Mars.

3623. **Philology.** Fick's Comparative Grammar of the Indo-Germanic Languages, aided by Whitley Stokes and Bezzenberger.

Hatzfeldt and Darmesteter's Dictionnaire de la Langue Française.

3624. **Philosophy.** Egidy's Serious Thoughts.

3625. **Economics.** Marshall's Principles of Economics.

Zanzibar. England recognizes German rights over the coast to Mozambique, and German influence in the Hinterland up to Lake Tanganyika and the Congo State. England may extend her southern provinces towards the Zambesi. A further agreement revises the boundaries in the Niger regions and divides the German Protectorate of Togo and the Gold Coast Colony.

A Convention with Portugal gives England the control of the Lower Zambesi and the right to colonise the central territory up to the Congo State.

An Anglo-French Convention recognises British control over Sokoto and the Lower Niger, and recognises the French sphere of influence between Lake Chad, the Niger, and Algeria. France recognises a British Protectorate over Zanzibar and Pemba, and England recognises a French Protectorate over Madagascar.

The French destroy the Empire of Ahmadou, and take Timbuctoo.

Bechuanaland is placed under the Governor of British Bechuanaland.

The Chartered Company enters Mashonaland.

Rhodes becomes Prime Minister of Cape Colony.

In consequence of the enormous influx to the mines the period of naturalisation in the South African Republic is raised from 5 to 14 years.

Uganda is occupied by Captain Lugard on behalf of the East African Company.

2237. **England.** The Newcastle Programme is drawn up, advocating Home Rule, Local Veto, the Disestablishment of the [1891
Church in Wales, Parish Councils, Reform of the House of Lords, Registration Reform.

2238. **France.** Boulanger commits suicide.

Méline introduces rigid protection.

Cardinal Lavigerie announces his adhesion to the Republic.

2239. **Germany.** The Emperor concludes reciprocity treaties with Austria, Italy, Russia and other countries.

2240. **Norway.** Norway demands an independent foreign policy.

2241. **Russia.** A French loan is floated and a French fleet is enthusiastically welcomed at Cronstadt.

2242. **Switzerland.** On the demand of 50,000 citizens, any project must be submitted to the people.

2243. **America.** Baron Hirsch settles Russian Jews in Argentina.

2244. **Australasia.** Ballance (succeeded by Seddon) forms a radical-socialist ministry in New Zealand. A progressive tax is laid on land and income, life senators are abolished, female suffrage is introduced, and labour is protected.

A Convention in Sydney draws up a Federal Constitution; but the scheme receives little support from the politicians.

3626. **Politics.** Tarde's Lois de l'Imitation declares imitation the chief factor in sociological development.

Dilke's Problems of Greater Britain.

3627. **History.** Mahan's Influence of Sea Power, 1660–1783, followed by works on the French war and the life of Nelson, found the philosophy of naval history.

Sybel's Founding of the German Empire.

3628. **Education.** Free Elementary Education is established in England.

3629. **Anthropology.** Frazer's Golden Bough, a study of Greek mythology.

3630. **Social.** An International Congress on Labour is held at Berlin.

Booth's In Darkest England and the Way Out outlines a scheme of social reform, including Farm Colonies and Emigration. A farm is taken at Hadleigh, Essex.

Pastor Naumann's Social Programme of the Protestant Church, an address to an Evangelical Congress at Berlin, revives Protestant Socialism.

The Housing of the Working-Classes Act is passed, by which residents may initiate inquiry, and destroy bad property, and public authorities may compulsorily buy land and erect houses.

The first May-Day Celebration of Labour is held.

Baring's Bank fails, owing to the failure of South American securities.

Braille invents a method of writing for the blind.

3631. **Deaths.** Andrassy, Burton, Church, Delitzsch, Döllinger, Hase, Gottfried Keller, Liddon, Newman, Schliemann.

3632. **Eng. Lit.** John Oliver Hobbes' (Mrs Craigie) Some Emotions and a Moral. [1891

3633. **Eng. Ch.** Driver's Introduction to the Old Testament.

Church's History of the Oxford Movement.

3634. **Italian Ch.** Rudini attempts to persuade the Pope to recognise the Law of Guarantees; but the Pope demands full independence.

3635. **French Lit.** Sardou's Thermidor.

Talleyrand's Memoirs are published by the Duc De Broglie, but are declared spurious by Aulard and others.

3636. **Literature.** Eleonora Duse makes her début at Vienna and Berlin.

3637. **Science.** Harvard University founds an Observatory at Arequipa in Peru.

3638. **Philosophy.** Oliver Lodge calls the attention of the British Association to the need for scientific investigation of occultism.

3639. **Education.** An attempt to render Greek optional at Cambridge is defeated.

3640. **History.** Bilbassoff's Catharine II. of Russia.

Krumbacher's History of Byzantine Literature.

Firth edits the Clarke Papers.

2245. **Africa.** The British South Africa Company receives the territory under British influence north of the Zambesi, except Nyasaland, which is declared an English Protectorate under an Imperial Commissioner.

England obtains pre-emption of the Portuguese sphere of influence. An Anglo-Portuguese Convention agrees on boundaries north and south of the Zambesi, which is opened to all.

England permits Italy to occupy Kassala.

The first of a series of French expeditions is undertaken against Samory, who is captured 1898.

The British East Africa Company announces its intention of evacuating Uganda.

2246. **England.** Hartington becomes the Duke of Devonshire, and Chamberlain leads the Liberal Unionists in the Commons. [1892

A Liberal majority of 40 is returned, and Gladstone becomes Prime Minister for the fourth time.

2247. **France.** The Panama scandals are revealed.

The Pope orders French Catholics to accept the Republic.

2248. **Germany.** A Bill providing for the religious education of children in Prussia by the clergy is hotly attacked and withdrawn.

The Duke of Cumberland, late King of Hanover, makes his submission, and the Guelf fund is restored to him.

2249. **Portugal.** The payment of interest on two-thirds of the debt is suspended.

2250. **Norway.** A conflict breaks out over the appointment of Consuls, which the Chamber declares a purely Norwegian matter. The King declares that all changes must be jointly made by the two countries.

2251. **Russia.** On the death of Giers, Lobanof succeeds and pursues a strongly Slavophil policy in the Balkans, Servia, Montenegro, and Bulgaria.

Witte becomes Minister of Finance.

A party is formed in Russian Poland to demand the revival of Poland as a democratic and Socialist republic.

2252. **Asia.** The Indian Councils Bill permits election to the Viceregal and Provincial Councils.

2253. **America.** Cleveland becomes President of the United States for the second time.

2254. **Africa.** Abbas, a youth of 18, succeeds his father Tewfik as Khedive, but shews himself far less friendly to English influences, and the nationalist party raises its head.

Round's Introduction of Knight Service into England shews that the military obligation of the tenant-in-chief was settled by the King, irrespective of the size of his holding.

3641. **Politics.** Goldwin Smith's Canadian Question advocates the union of Canada with the United States.

3642. **Art.** Richmond decorates the interior of St Paul's Cathedral.

Sullivan's Ivanhoe is produced at the new English Opera House.

3643. **Economics.** Böhm-Bawerk's Positive Theory of Capital.

3644. **Geography.** Peary crosses Greenland to the North.

3645. **Anthropology.** Westermarck's History of Marriage.

3646. **Social.** The Pope's Encyclical on Labour condemns Socialism and strikes, and advocates the revival of gilds.

A comprehensive Public Health Act is passed.

3647. **Deaths.** George Bancroft, Bradlaugh, Grévy, Granville, Kinglake, Kuenen, Lagarde, Lowell, Sir John Macdonald, Meissonier, Moltke, Parnell, Reuss, Windhorst.

3648. **Eng. Ch.** A conference is held at Grindelwald, to discuss the reunion of the Established Church and Nonconformist bodies. [1892

3649. **Church Hist.** Mrs Lewis discovers the Old Syriac version of the Gospels in St Catherine's monastery, on Mount Sinai.

3650. **Eng. Lit.** Kipling's Barrack-Room Ballads.

Lord de Tabley's Poems.

Zangwill's Children of the Ghetto.

Hardy's Tess.

Austin Dobson's 18th Century Vignettes.

3651. **French Lit.** Zola's La Débâcle.

3652. **German Lit.** Sudermann's The Home (Magda).

3653. **Belgian Lit.** Maeterlinck's Pelléas et Mélisande.

3654. **Science.** Romanes' Darwin and after Darwin.

Haffkine begins to study Asiatic cholera.

Horsley and other scientists defend vivisection.

3655. **Art.** Parry's Job.

3656. **Philology.** Darmesteter edits the Zend-Avesta.

3657. **Philosophy.** Simmel's Science of Ethics maintains that the moral system resulting from the struggle of forces expresses only the tendency of the majority.

3658. **Politics.** Faguet's Politiques et Moralistes français du 19ème Siècle.

3659. **Education.** A Herbart Club is founded in America.

3660. **Social.** The Pioneer Club for Ladies is founded in London.

A Commission on English Labour is appointed.

Malabari obtains the raising of the age of marriage for girls in India to 12.

3661. **Deaths.** Adams, Freeman, Ihering, Lavigerie, Lipsius, Manning, Owen, Renan, Spurgeon, Taine, Tennyson, Whitman, Whittier.

2255. **England.** The second Home Rule Bill retains the Irish members at Westminster and makes no reference to the land. [1893 In Committee, 'in and out' is changed to 'always in.' The third reading passes by 34 votes, but the Bill is rejected by the Lords by 419 to 41.

2256. **France.** A Russian squadron is welcomed at Toulon.

2257. **Germany.** A Military Bill increases the army and shortens the period of service to two years.

The Socialists obtain two million votes at the elections.

2258. **Italy.** Giolitti falls in consequence of Bank scandals, and Crispi forms his second Ministry.

2259. **Spain.** Castelar retires from public life, but advises his followers to join the Liberal party.

2260. **Belgium.** Plural voting is allowed for wealth and education, and to fathers of families, but no one is entitled to more than three votes. The exercise of the vote is rendered obligatory.

2261. **Greece.** The payment of the debt is suspended.

2262. **America.** Cleveland revokes the compulsory purchase of silver.

The Behring Sea Arbitration is held at Paris. The United States are ordered to pay compensation, and new regulations are introduced.

The World's Fair is held at Chicago.

A Republic is proclaimed in Hawaii, and is recognised by the United States.

2263. **Australia.** A great financial depression occurs.

2264. **Asia.** Lanessan, Governor of Indo-China, attacks Siam, which vainly appeals to England for aid. Siam is forced to accept an ultimatum, ceding 50,000 square miles and commercial privileges, and paying a heavy fine. At the same time the frontier dispute with England is settled.

The Indian Mints are closed to the free coinage of silver, as a preliminary to the establishment of a gold standard. The value of the rupee is fixed at 1*s.* 4*d.*

2265. **Africa.** Dahomey becomes a French Protectorate.

The British East Africa Company evacuates Uganda. Gerald Portal is sent to report, and strongly reprobates evacuation and recommends the construction of a railway.

Kruger is for the third time elected President of the South African Republic; but General Joubert, the candidate of the Progressives, obtains almost as many votes.

Natal obtains complete self-government.

A conflict breaks out between the Matabele and the Chartered Company, which takes Bulawayo after some fighting. Lobengula flies and Bulawayo becomes the capital of Rhodesia. Lobengula dies and the military system of the Matabele is broken up.

The Khedive dismisses his ministers and appoints anti-English advisers, but is forced to dismiss his new premier.

3662. **German Ch.** Gizycki and Förster found an Ethical Movement. [1893
3663. **American Ch.** Briggs, a Presbyterian, is suspended for heterodoxy.
3664. **Russian Ch.** The Stundists are persecuted and banished.
3665. **Church Hist.** Michaud edits the Revue Internationale de Théologie, chiefly for the purpose of discussing and promoting reunion.
3666. **Eng. Lit.** Ellis and Yeats edit Blake's mystical works.
Le Gallienne's Religion of a Literary Man.
Pinero's Second Mrs Tanqueray.
Davidson's Fleet Street Eclogues.
3667. **French Lit.** Hérédia's Les Trophées.
Sardou's Mme Sans-Gêne.
3668. **Science.** Zirkel's Handbook of Petrography.
3669. **Art.** Tschaikowsky's 'Pathetic' Symphony.
Furtwängler's Masterpieces of Greek Sculpture.
F. C. Gould begins to draw for the Westminster Gazette.
3670. **Philosophy.** Huxley's Romanes Lecture declares the ethical process contrary to the cosmic process.
Bradley's Appearance and Reality.
Fouillée's Psychologie des Idées-Forces.
3671. **History.** Lavisse and Rambaud edit a General History.
Harnack's History of Christian Literature before Eusebius.
Vinogradoff proves Folkland was not *ager publicus*.
3672. **Politics.** Giddings' Sociology lays stress on kinship.
Pearson's National Life and Character declares the white races limited in powers of adaptability, and therefore of colonisation, and that the pressure from the yellow and black races may possibly prove irresistible.
3673. **Geography.** Nansen starts in the Fram for the arctic regions. Leaving the vessel, he reaches 86° 14′ N. latitude, in longitude 95′ E., 200 miles nearer the Pole than any previous explorer. On his return he further explores Franz Josef Land.
3674. **Agriculture.** Lord Winchelsea forms an Agricultural Union.
3675. **Social.** Stead's If Christ came to Chicago.
Women's Franchise is adopted in New Zealand.
Wages Boards are instituted in Victoria, with power to fix a minimum rate of wages in certain trades.
A Royal Commission reports that the London Water Companies cannot long provide the required supply. The County Council subsequently resolve to purchase the undertakings at their then value and seek an additional supply in Wales, but are prevented by Parliament.
3676. **Deaths.** Blaine, Ford Madox Brown, Ferry, Gounod, Jowett, Macmahon, Tschaikowsky, Tyndall.

2266. **England.** Parish Councils are created.

The Lords insert 'contracting out' in the Employers' [1894 Liability Bill. Gladstone withdraws the Bill and in his last speech in Parliament deplores the action of the Upper Chamber.

Harcourt imposes sliding-scale death-duties.

2267. **Scotland.** A Standing Committee is appointed for the consideration of purely Scotch measures.

2268. **Ireland.** The Lords reject an Evicted Tenants' Bill.

Lord Rosebery declares Home Rule impossible till the 'predominant partner' is converted.

Plunkett founds the Agricultural Organisation Society.

2269. **France.** Carnot is murdered, and Casimir-Périer becomes President.

Dreyfus is arrested as a spy.

2270. **Germany.** A commercial treaty is made with Russia which proves very unpopular with the farmers and leads to the fall of Caprivi, who is succeeded as Chancellor by Hohenlohe.

2271. **Italy.** In consequence partly of economic misery and partly of socialist agitation, riots occur in Sicily.

Crispi and other ministers are discovered to have received money from the Banca Romana.

2272. **Spain.** Certain of Castelar's followers are admitted into the Council of Regency.

2273. **Belgium.** The Socialists gain a number of seats, the Liberals are routed, and the Ultramontanes become supreme.

2274. **Bulgaria.** Prince Boris is baptized in the Greek Church, and Stambuloff is dismissed, Ferdinand hoping thereby to conciliate Russia.

2275. **America.** Cleveland repeals the McKinley Tariff.

2276. **Africa.** Rhodes' Glen Grey Act breaks up the system of native communal ownership and compels natives who do not hold land to work during part of the year.

A British Protectorate is announced over Uganda, and a railway is begun 1896.

A boundary is agreed on between the French and Belgian Congo.

Swaziland is placed under the protection of the Transvaal.

Italy takes Kassala from the Dervishes.

2277. **Asia.** A revolt in Korea causes the King to ask China for aid. Japan also sends troops, and proposes a joint administration. China replies that Japan must evacuate before negotiation. Japan refuses, and informs China that she will regard the further despatch of troops as a casus belli, and orders Korea to dismiss the Chinese troops. Korea proposes simultaneous evacuation. Japan demands delay, seizes the King, and attacks the Chinese (July 25). War is declared (Aug.) and Port Arthur is captured by the Japanese.

Massacres occur at Sasun in Armenia. The Powers interpose, and are invited to assist in an enquiry.

3677. **Eng. Ch.** Lord Halifax and the Abbé Portal, a French priest, discuss reunion. Portal visits the Pope, who approves the project, and Rampolla writes a semi-official letter of encouragement. Duchesne at the same moment declares his conviction of the validity of Anglican orders. Halifax introduces Portal to Archbishop Benson, who, however, declines to commit himself. [1894

Illingworth's Bampton Lectures on Personality.

3678. **Spanish Ch.** Plunket, Archbishop of Dublin, consecrates Cabrera Bishop of the Spanish Protestants.

3679. **Austrian Ch.** The Hungarian Ministry establishes compulsory civil marriage and freedom of worship.

3680. **American Ch.** Hecker's Life is published, with a preface by Archbishop Ireland, and is translated into French, with a letter of approval from Cardinal Gibbons; but an attack on Hecker's memory and the American Cardinals receives the Vatican imprimatur.

3681. **Church Hist.** The Gospel according to St Peter is discovered in an Egyptian tomb.

The Armenian Patriarch visits Rome to discuss reunion. A programme is agreed on, and an Encyclical to the Churches of the East is issued; but the Armenian massacres stop further negotiations. The Pope's proposals are rejected by the Greek Patriarch, Anthimus.

3682. **Education.** A Circular is issued by the London School Board, proposing direct dogmatic teaching.

3683. **Eng. Lit.** Kipling's Jungle-Book.

Mrs Steel's The Potter's Thumb.

George Moore's Esther Waters.

Du Maurier's Trilby.

John Watson's (Ian Maclaren) Beside the bonny Briar Bush.

3684. **French Lit.** Zola begins his 'Trois Villes,' Lourdes, Rome, Paris.

3685. **Russian Lit.** Anton Tchekhoff's In the Twilight, a collection of stories.

3686. **Science.** Dewar liquefies oxygen.

Maxim invents a flying-machine of 8,000 lbs., with two engines of 300 horse-power.

Roux discovers that the serum of the blood of a horse mitigates diphtheria.

3687. **Art.** Humperdinck's Hansel and Gretel.

Aubrey Beardsley becomes Art Editor of the Yellow-Book.

Schack bequeaths his pictures to the German Emperor, who allows them to remain in Munich.

3688. **Philosophy.** Meinong and Ehrenfels discuss the subjective elements in value.

3689. **Politics.** Kidd's Social Evolution attempts to apply biology to sociology, and declares reason the selfish element, and religion—which is by its nature non-rational—the unselfish and progressive element in human societies.

3690. **History.** Flint's History of the Philosophy of History in France.

Sidney and Beatrice Webb's History of Trade Unionism.

2278. **Ireland.** In view of the expiry of the judicial term of 15 years, Morley introduces a Land Bill to amend that of 1881, exempting all tenants' improvements from rent, removing obstacles to certain tenants coming into the fair-rent court, and abolishing the right of pre-emption. [1895

2279. **England.** Rosebery's Government falls on a vote in reference to the supply of cordite, and the Conservatives obtain a majority of 150.

2280. **France.** Bourgeois forms a homogeneous Radical Ministry.

2281. **Germany.** The Baltic Canal is opened.

2282. **Austria.** Lüger, an Anti-Semite, becomes Burgomaster of Vienna.

2283. **Bulgaria.** Stambuloff is murdered.

2284. **Greece.** Tricoupis falls, and retires from public life.

2285. **America.** Cleveland claims that English interference with the boundary between British Guiana and Venezuela is forbidden by the Monroe doctrine, and recommends resistance by the United States 'by every means in its power' to any attempt to appropriate land which an American Commission declares to belong to Venezuela (Dec. 17).

2286. **Africa.** Disputes arise between the Transvaal and Great Britain in reference to commandeering and to the closing of the Drifts over the Orange River. An ultimatum in regard to the latter causes the Transvaal to give way. The Transvaal National Union issues a manifesto setting forth the grievances of the Outlanders.

Khama visits London to protest against the absorption of Bechuanaland in Cape Colony. A narrow strip is given to the Chartered Company for the railway to Matabeleland.

Dr Jameson, the Administrator of the Chartered Company's territories, invades the Transvaal from Bechuanaland (Dec. 29).

England recaptures the Eastern Sudan.

Sir Edward Grey announces that French occupation of the Upper Nile would be regarded as an unfriendly act.

An ultimatum to the King of Ashanti from the Governor of the Gold Coast demands the fulfilment of treaty obligations.

2287. **Australia.** New South Wales rejects a Federal Constitution.

2288. **Asia.** The Rosebery Cabinet decide to evacuate Chitral. Lord Elgin, the Viceroy, protests, and the Salisbury Government retains it. Robertson, the British political agent at Gilgit, is invested in Chitral. Two relieving forces are sent, one of which suffers severely in the Malakand Pass.

The Japanese capture Wei-hai-wei and other strongholds. China makes peace, pays an indemnity, cedes Formosa and the Liao-Tung peninsula, and opens new treaty ports (April). Russia, France and Germany protest against the cession of mainland, and Japan surrenders the peninsula and Port Arthur in return for an increase of the indemnity. Korea proclaims itself independent.

Russia and England delimit the Pamirs.

A massacre of Armenians in Constantinople begins (Sept.).

Pollock and Maitland's History of English Law.

3691. **Social.** Compulsory Arbitration is adopted in New Zealand.

The Trade Union Congress adopts Socialist resolutions.

Lord Salisbury introduces, but fails to carry, a bill for the exclusion of destitute aliens.

3692. **Deaths.** Brugsch, Carriere, Helmholtz, Hertz, O. W. Holmes, Kossuth, De Lesseps, Comte de Paris, Stevenson.

3693. **Eng. Ch.** Lord Halifax visits the Pope, who issues an Apostolic Letter, Ad Anglos, in which, however, he shews no recognition of the English Church. [1895

The Revue Anglo-Romaine is founded to work for reunion.

A Catholic Cathedral at Westminster is commenced.

3694. **American Ch.** The Protestant majority in Manitoba refuses to continue to support separate Catholic Schools. In the following year, an attempt is made to arrange for religious instruction on the basis of facilities for Catholic and Protestant teaching according to numbers. In 1897 the Pope advises the acceptance of a compromise.

3695. **Eng. Lit.** W. B. Yeats' Poems.

3696. **Literature.** Brandes' Study of Shakspere.

3697. **Science.** Ramsay and Rayleigh discover argon in the atmosphere.

3698. **Art.** Kraus' History of Christian Art.

3699. **Philosophy.** Balfour's Foundations of Belief criticises naturalism, asserting that the dicta of physical science rest on assumptions, and vindicates the claim of authority to be the guide of life.

Nordau detects tokens of degeneration in the popular interest in Wagner, Zola, Tolstoi, Ibsen, and other dominant intellectual forces of the time.

3700. **History.** Seeley's Growth of British Policy from Elizabeth to William III.

3701. **Education.** The French Universities become once more partially independent of the Minister of Education.

3702. **Politics.** Durkheim explains historical progress by economics, particularly by the division of labour.

3703. **Anthropology.** A skull, a femur, and two teeth are discovered in tertiary strata, Java. Their possessor is named by Dubois, the discoverer, Pithecanthropus Erectus.

3704. **Deaths.** Bonghi, Cayley, Randolph Churchill, Dumas, Freytag, De Giers, Huxley, Karl Ludwig, Pasteur, Sybel.

2289. **England.** Rosebery resigns the leadership of the Liberal Party in consequence of his views on the Armenian question (Oct.). [1896

G. W. E. Russell founds the Liberal Forward movement.

Chamberlain proposes a Colonial Zollverein.

The Rating Bill relieves the occupier of agricultural land for five years of half the rate payable on buildings and other hereditaments.

2290. **Ireland.** A Land Bill, partly based on Morley's Bill of 1895, facilitates purchase and further extends the rights of tenants in regard to improvements.

A Committee on Irish Finance reports that Ireland is overcharged.

2291. **France.** The Tsar visits Paris.

The Chamber approves but the Departments condemn the plan of a Progressive Income-tax. Bourgeois resigns and Méline forms a ministry.

2292. **Germany.** Bismarck reveals that a treaty, unknown to Austria, existed with Russia 1887–90.

2293. **Austria.** The artisan classes are enfranchised.

2294. **Turkey.** Christians are massacred at Canea; but a proposal by the Powers to blockade Crete is rejected by England.

The National Bank in Constantinople is attacked by Armenians, and a new massacre takes place.

2295. **America.** Bryan is nominated by the Democratic Convention and the Populists on a policy of free coinage of silver at 16 to 1. McKinley, the Republican candidate, obtains 271 votes, Bryan 176.

Laurier, a Liberal, becomes Premier of Canada.

Nicaragua, Salvador and Honduras form the Republic of Central America, for foreign relations.

2296. **Australasia.** Tasmania adopts the Hare system of election.

2297. **Africa.** Jameson is stopped by a Boer force near Dornkop and surrenders. The leaders of the Reform movement are imprisoned. The Emperor William congratulates President Kruger, and Rhodes resigns the Cape Premiership. A Committee of the Cape Assembly report that Rhodes engineered the Raid. The Transvaal sends large orders to Europe for guns and ammunition, and hastens the construction of forts at Pretoria and Johannesburg.

A rising takes place in Matabeleland.

Sir Richard Martin is sent to report on the administration of the Chartered Company, against which he draws a severe indictment.

Kitchener fights his way from Wady Halfa to Dongola. Forces are brought from India at India's expense.

Coomassie is entered without fighting, and Prempeh is captured.

An Italian army is almost annihilated at Adowa, and the Protectorate over Abyssinia is withdrawn.

Madagascar is annexed to France, and the commercial treaties of other nations are annulled. General Gallieni becomes governor.

Asia. England and France arrange their frontiers in Siam.

A revolt breaks out in the Philippines.

3705. **Eng. Ch.** Acting on the report of a Commission, of which Gasquet is understood to be the moving spirit, the Pope condemns Anglican orders. Gladstone publishes a letter on the decision. The Revue Anglo-Romaine is suppressed, and the attempted rapprochement comes to an end. [1896

Purcell's Life of Manning is hotly attacked by many Catholics as a misrepresentation.

3706. **Eng. Lit.** Mrs Steel's On the Face of the Waters, a tale of the Indian Mutiny.

Stephen Phillips' Christ in Hades.

Watson's Purple East, and Year of Shame.

Wheatley prints an almost complete edition of Pepys' Diary.

3707. **French Lit.** Barrès' Les Déracinés.

3708. **Italian Lit.** Scartazzini's Enciclopedia Dantesca.

3709. **Science.** Lowell discusses the 'Canals' of Mars.

Langley constructs a flying machine which rises 90 feet and flies half a mile.

Boltzmann's Kinetic Theory of Gases.

Röntgen, Professor at Wurzburg, accidentally discovers the X-rays, to which many substances, opaque to ordinary rays, are transparent.

3710. **Art.** Leighton's Clytie.

The Kelmscott Chaucer, with designs by William Morris and Burne-Jones, is issued.

3711. **Philosophy.** Sabatier's Philosophy of Religion.

MacTaggart's Studies in the Hegelian Dialectic defends the Logic against the criticisms of Trendelenburg, Seth, and other writers.

Stout's Analytic Psychology.

3712. **History.** Lea's History of Auricular Confession and Indulgences.

Renouvier's Philosophie Analytique de l'Histoire surveys the development of morals, religion, philosophy and science.

3713. **Politics.** Lecky's Democracy and Liberty criticises democratic ideas and practice in a hostile spirit.

Godkin's Problems and Unforeseen Tendencies of Modern Democracy.

3714. **Law.** The German Civil Code, the result of 30 years' labour, is adopted, marking the decisive victory of German over Roman Law.

3715. **Geography.** Jackson explores Franz Josef Land, and discovers it is merely a group of islands.

Sven Hedin crosses the Takla Makau desert.

Sir Martin Conway crosses Spitzbergen from east to west.

3716. **Education.** The Universities of Prussia admit women to the lectures.

A Bill is introduced, largely based on the Church of England Memorial, 1895, creating new Educational Authorities, increasing the grant to all Voluntary Schools, limiting the School Board rate, and providing facilities for denominational teaching. Owing in part, however, to criticisms by Unionist members, the Bill is withdrawn.

3717. **Deaths.** Challemel-Lacour, Curtius, Du Bois Reymond, Frère-Orban, Leighton, Lobanof, Millais, William Morris, Parkes, Treitschke, Tricoupis.

2298. **England.** The Diamond Jubilee is celebrated. [1897

England denounces the treaties with Belgium and Germany which prevent preference being given by Canada to Great Britain.

2299. **France.** A Franco-Russian Alliance is proclaimed (Aug.).

Scheurer-Kestner demands the revision of the condemnation of Dreyfus and declares Esterhazy the author of the bordereau.

2300. **Spain.** Canovas is murdered and Sagasta becomes Premier.

Weyler is recalled from Cuba, and autonomy is promised.

2301. **Austria.** Badeni's decree that future candidates for the civil service in Bohemia and Moravia must know Czech is fiercely opposed by the Germans.

2302. **Hungary.** The Kossuthists oppose the renewal of the Ausgleich.

2303. **Greece.** The Cretan insurgents proclaim union with Greece, and Prince George and Colonel Vassus are sent to Crete. The Powers occupy Canea and promise autonomy, if the Greek force retire, and, on refusal, shell the insurgents. Strong feeling is aroused in England and Gladstone publishes a pamphlet. Armies now gather on the frontier of Thessaly and Epirus. The Powers declare that the aggressor shall not benefit. After a raid by the Hetairists Turkey declares war (April 7). 100 Members of the English Parliament send a telegram of sympathy to Greece.

Edhem Pasha invades Thessaly, and Greece speedily begs the Powers to intervene (May 8). The Turkish frontier is pushed further south, and Turkish troops remain in Thessaly till an indemnity is paid.

2304. **America.** Gold is discovered at Klondyke.

The Venezuela Arbitration Treaty is signed, but the General Arbitration Treaty is rejected by the Senate.

Hawaii is annexed by the United States.

2305. **Africa.** The Boer Republics make a defensive treaty.

A Committee of Inquiry into the Jameson raid is held at Westminster. Rhodes admits that he prepared an insurrection and an incursion, and confesses he had not informed the Chartered Company or the High Commissioner, but denies that he knew of the actual Raid. Colonel Frank Rhodes declares that the plot in Johannesburg cost £250,000. Schreiner, late Attorney-General of Cape Colony, testifies to the disastrous effect of the Raid on race feeling. The Committee strongly condemns Rhodes; but Chamberlain refuses to dismiss him from the Privy Council, and declares that he has done nothing inconsistent with the character of a man of honour.

The Transvaal Alien Immigration Bill is repealed on Chamberlain's protest that it violates the Convention of 1884.

The English Administrator in Zanzibar is instructed not to recognize slavery or restore slaves to their masters.

The Soudanese troops in Uganda mutiny.

Owing to the massacre of a British expedition sent to protest against human sacrifices, Benin is occupied.

The Egyptian army takes Berber, and Italy hands over Kassala.

3718. **French Ch.** Père Olivier declares the burning of the Paris Charity Bazaar a mark of God's wrath against those who reject the teaching of the Church. [1897

3719. **Russian Ch.** The Doukobortsi are persecuted for refusing to undergo military service.

3720. **Church Hist.** The 'Logia' are found on the site of Oxyrhynchus, and contain a Pantheist reference.

The first Zionist Congress is held at Basle, under the direction of Herzl and Nordau, to promote the resettlement at the Holy Land. The rich Jews, with few exceptions, hold aloof from the movement.

3721. **Eng. Lit.** The Browning Letters are published.

Forbes Robertson presents Hamlet at the Lyceum.

3722. **German Lit.** Sudermann's Johannes.

3723. **Italian Lit.** D'Annunzio's Triumph of Death.

3724. **Science.** Richard improves Lippmann's discovery of colour photography.

Geikie's Ancient Volcanoes of Great Britain.

Suess' Form of the Earth.

Ramsay discovers Helium.

Moissan and Dewar liquefy fluorine.

3725. **Art.** Byam Shaw exhibits 'Love's Baubles' and 'The Comforter.'

Lady Wallace presents to the nation the pictures inherited by her husband from the Marquis of Hertford.

The Tate Gallery is founded in London.

Stanford's Requiem.

3726. **Anthropology.** Max Müller's Contributions to the Science of Mythology are attacked by Andrew Lang on the ground of the undue importance attached to the evidence of language.

3727. **Philology.** Bacchylides' poems are found.

3728. **History.** Maitland's Domesday Book and Beyond rejects the theory of a servile origin of the village, and declares the manor merely the unit of assessment.

Roberts' 41 Years in India.

Crozier's History of Intellectual Development.

3729. **Economics.** Sidney and Beatrice Webb's Industrial Democracy explains the theory and structure of Trade Unions, and recommends the State organization of labour.

3730. **Politics.** John Morley's Romanes Lecture on Macchiavelli protests against the divorce of ethics from politics.

Bloch's Future of War maintains that war between the nations of Europe is impossible except at the price of national suicide.

3731. **Education.** The proposal to grant degrees to women at Cambridge is rejected by a large majority.

Lord Salisbury's Government abolishes the 17*s.* 6*d.* limit, and grants an average of 5*s.* extra to the children of Voluntary Schools.

Sadler reports on the state of elementary education in foreign countries.

3732. **Geography.** Andrée attempts to reach the North Pole in a balloon, but is not heard of again.

2306. **Asia.** The plague breaks out at Poona, and two English Plague Commissioners are murdered.

India suffers from a terrible famine, for the relief of which £500,000 is collected in England.

In revenge for the murder of German missionaries, Germany obtains Kiao-Chau from China on a lease of 99 years.

The Afridis attack the English posts in the Khyber. Tirah is occupied, and on the approach of winter Lockhart informs the tribes that he will return in the spring.

The King of Korea proclaims himself Emperor. A Russo-Japanese Convention pledges the signatories to maintain order, while leaving the Emperor free.

[1898

2307. **Ireland.** County and District Councils are created.

2308. **France.** Zola writes his letter 'J'accuse' to the President, and is condemned for asserting that Esterhazy was acquitted 'by order.' On the discovery of Henry's forgeries, Brisson, who has succeeded Méline, sends the case to the Court of Cassation, but falls in consequence and is succeeded by Dupuy. Delcassé remains Foreign Minister.

2309. **Italy.** Partially in consequence of the rise in the price of bread, riots break out in Milan and other towns.

A commercial treaty is concluded with France.

Crispi is censured by the Chamber for his conduct in reference to the Neapolitan bank.

2310. **Germany.** The Emperor visits the Holy Land.

2311. **Austria.** The Empress is murdered at Geneva.

2312. **Holland.** Queen Wilhelmina comes of age.

2313. **Greece.** The loan is negotiated and Thessaly is evacuated.

Prince George of Greece is appointed Governor of Crete.

2314. **Russia.** The Tsar invites the Powers to cooperate with him in the reduction of armaments (Aug. 24).

2315. **America.** The cry for intervention in Cuba is strengthened by the destruction of the Maine in Havana harbour (Feb. 15). An ultimatum orders Spain to relinquish her authority in Cuba and to withdraw her forces (April 19), but no reply is received. A Spanish fleet is destroyed at Manila by Dewey (May 1); and Sampson destroys the chief Spanish fleet as it tries to escape from Santiago (July 3). The town surrenders (July 13), and Spain asks terms (July 26). Cuba is to become a Protectorate, and the future of the Philippines is to be settled at a Conference. Peace is signed at Paris (Dec. 10), the United States obtaining Cuba and Porto Rico and paying £4,000,000 for the Philippines, which, however, require to be conquered.

2316. **Africa.** Schreiner forms a ministry in Cape Colony resting principally on Dutch votes. £30,000 a year is offered towards the expenses of the Imperial navy.

Mary Kingsley's Travels in W. Africa.

Zurbriggen, a Swiss guide employed by Fitzgerald, ascends Aconcagua in the Andes.

3733. **Social.** Lord Penrhyn and his quarrymen disagree.

A strike for an Eight Hours' day begins among the Engineers in London and spreads through the country.

A Bill to compensate for accidents in dangerous trades and on buildings over 30 feet high is carried, despite the protest of extreme Conservatives. Either party may contract out with the approval of the registrar-general of Friendly Societies. The Act is extended to include agricultural labourers, 1900.

The Commission on Agricultural Depression presents its final report, recording a slight improvement in the situation.

Charles Booth completes his study of the London Poor.

3734. **Deaths.** D'Aumale, Brahms, Canovas, Daudet, Drummond, Henry George, Hutton, Sachs, Vacherot, Weierstrass.

3735. **Eng. Ch.** The Benefices Act forbids the public sale of advowsons and increases the power of bishops. In the discussion, the question of ritualism is raised. Samuel Smith, John Kensit, Harcourt's Letters to the Times, and Walsh's Secret History of the Oxford Movement attack the ritualist party. [1898

3736. **Asiatic Ch.** The German Emperor receives the plot of ground at Jerusalem known as La Dormition de la Vierge, and presents it to the German Catholics.

3737. **Eng. Lit.** Watts-Dunton's Aylwin.

Elizabeth and her German Garden.

Sidney Lee's Life of Shakspere.

The Ashburnham Library is sold.

3738. **French Lit.** Rostand's Cyrano de Bergerac.

Huysmans' La Cathédrale marks his entry into the Symbolist movement.

3739. **Belgian Lit.** Maeterlinck's Wisdom and Destiny.

3740. **Science.** Crookes' address to the British Association discusses the exhaustion of corn, and calls attention to psychic phenomena.

Hans Gadow's Classification of the Vertebrata.

Dewar liquefies and solidifies hydrogen.

Bastian lectures on Aphasia.

Ramsay and Travers discover Neon and Metargon, constituents of air.

3741. **Art.** Rodin's statue of Balzac.

Sargent's portrait of Asher Wertheimer.

3742. **Philosophy.** Shadworth Hodgson's Metaphysic of Experience attacks the conception of Cause, which must ever remain unexplained, and substitutes that of Real Condition, which simply expresses the empirical fact of causal relation between existents without assumptions as to the nature of the relation.

3743. **Philology.** Frazer's edition of Pausanias.

3744. **Politics.** Pobyedonostseff's Reflections criticise liberalism in

England and Germany obtain the reversion of Portugal's African possessions, Delagoa Bay to fall to England.

An Anglo-French Agreement on the Niger is concluded.

Kruger is elected President of the Transvaal for the fourth time, by an enormous majority.

The Sirdar defeats a Dervish force at the Atbara (March), and annihilates the Dervish army outside Omdurman (Sept. 2).

A Dervish steamer brings news of a white force at Fashoda (Sept. 7). The Sirdar proceeds thither and finds Marchand, who has been sent by the Governor of the Ubanghi Provinces, with a few French officers (Sept. 21). Marchand refuses to leave. England holds to Grey's declaration in 1895, and the French Government yields (Nov. 4).

2317. **Asia.** Russia occupies Port Arthur and Talienwan. England protests, but herself obtains the lease of Wei-hai-Wei. The Dowager Empress of China seizes power and executes the leaders of the Reform party, and shortly after refuses Italy's demand for Sammun Bay. An anti-foreign society, known as the Boxers, is instituted to resist European aggression and to prevent the spread of Christianity.

2318. **England.** Campbell-Bannerman becomes Liberal leader in the Commons. [1899

Borough Councils are created for London.

Country clergy receive half the rates on tithe rent-charge.

2319. **France.** Faure dies and is succeeded by Loubet.

The Court of Cassation unanimously annuls the first trial of Dreyfus and orders re-trial (June). Dupuy is succeeded by Waldeck-Rousseau as Premier. The second trial of Dreyfus begins at Rennes (Aug. 7). Freystätter reveals the illegality of the former trial, and Germany again officially denies any relations with Dreyfus, who is, nevertheless, condemned by 5 to 2, with extenuating circumstances, but pardoned by the President.

Déroulède and a number of Orleanist plotters are tried for treason and are banished, and Gallifet restores discipline in the army.

2320. **Austria.** Clary revokes Badeni's language ordinances.

2321. **Russia.** The Conference of Peace meets at the Hague (May—June), extends the Geneva Convention to naval warfare, condemns explosive bullets and asphyxiating gas, and authorises a permanent Court of Arbitration, planned by Pauncefote, Martens, and the American delegates.

The privileges of Finland are curtailed.

2322. **Spain.** Spain sells her last Pacific possessions to Germany.

2323. **Australasia.** The Federal Constitution is modified by a Conference of Premiers to conciliate New South Wales, and is approved by a referendum.

England withdraws from Samoa, and receives the Tonga Islands and Savage Island.

politics and religion, and defend the principle of authority as applied in the institutions of Russia.

3745. **Education.** The London University Bill creates a teaching University.

3746. **History.** Bodley's France declares that Cabinet Government is unsuited to the French genius and traditions, and that the equilibrium of the country is owing to the centralised administration established by Napoleon.

Bismarck's Reflections and Memoirs, and Busch's Memoirs of Bismarck are published. The latter are widely denounced as unfair representations.

3747. **Geography.** Sven Hedin describes his travels across Central Asia, 1894–7.

3748. **Social.** A pension of 7*s.* a week is granted in New Zealand to all reaching the age of 65 who have less than 10*s.* a week and have not been convicted of crime.

Penny postage is extended to South Africa and India.

Vaccination ceases to be imposed on the 'conscientious objector'; but less decrease occurs than was anticipated.

The Engineers' strike ends in failure (Jan.).

A strike against the sliding-scale and for higher wages takes place among the coal-miners in South Wales. A rise of 5 p.c. is secured.

A Committee on Old Age Pensions, presided over by Lord Rothschild, declares that it can neither accept any of the 100 schemes suggested to it nor frame one itself.

3749. **Deaths.** Bismarck, Puvis de Chavannes, Gladstone, Sir George Grey.

3750. **Eng. Ch.** The Protestant agitation continues, and the Archbishops pronounce an 'opinion' against incense and processional lights, leaving it to each bishop, however, to determine whether or no to enforce it. Lord Halifax declares the judgment 'one of the greatest misfortunes that have fallen on the Church since the Oxford movement'; but Dean Hole and others resign their membership of the English Church Union. [1899

3751. **Irish Ch.** Balfour issues a manifesto in favour of a Catholic University, but obtains no support from the other members of Lord Salisbury's Government.

3752. **American Ch.** The Pope addresses a letter to Cardinal Gibbons, condemning the 'Americanism' of Hecker.

Sheldon's didactic tale, In His Steps, obtains an unprecedented circulation.

3753. **Eng. Lit.** Stevenson's Letters are published.

Gosse's Life of Donne.

3754. **American Lit.** F. P. Dunne's Mr Dooley in Peace and War.

3755. **Russian Lit.** Gorski's novel, Thomas Gordeyev.

3756. **Norwegian Lit.** A national Norwegian theatre is opened.

3757. **Science.** Sclater's Geography of Mammals.

2324. **Asia.** Gold is made legal tender in India.

2325. **America.** An attempt to settle the Alaska boundary fails.

The Arbitrators on the boundary of British Guiana and Venezuela award England the Schomburgh line, with two small exceptions.

2326. **Africa.** The Crown buys the dominions of the Niger Company.

England and France agree as to the division of North Africa.

The Khalifa is killed by Wingate on the White Nile (Nov.).

Rhodes arranges with Germany for a telegraph and railways in South East Africa.

A petition, professing to be signed by 21,000 Johannesburg Outlanders, is forwarded to the English Government (March), and a fruitless conference is held at Bloemfontein, Kruger refusing to grant a 5 years' franchise. Milner's despatch of May 4 on the grievances is now published. A 7 years' franchise is enacted by the Transvaal, and England suggests a joint Commission on the new law. Before replying, the Transvaal offers more than Milner has asked, on condition that the present occasion should not be regarded as a precedent for future interference. This condition is refused, and the offer is withdrawn. The invitation to a joint Commission is now accepted; but the English Government declares it is too late. England proposes a 5 years' franchise,—one quarter of the Raad to represent the gold-fields,—equality of languages in the Raad, and a vote for the President. These proposals, conveyed in a despatch which reasserts the suzerainty claim, are rejected. The English Cabinet reply that they will formulate new proposals (Sept. 22). On Oct. 7, however, the order for the mobilisation of an Army Corps is given, the Reserves are called out, and Parliament is summoned. Kruger hereupon demands the withdrawal of troops on the frontier, and the recall of the reinforcements and of the troops now at sea (Oct. 9). The demands are refused, and the Boers enter Natal, and besiege Mafeking and Kimberley. The Boers are defeated at Glencoe (Oct. 17), and Elandslaagte (Oct. 21); but 900 men are cut off at Nicholson's Nek (Oct. 30), and Ladysmith is surrounded (Nov. 1). Methuen sets out to relieve Kimberley, and wins at Belmont, Graspan, and Modder River (Nov.), but is defeated at Magersfontein (Dec. 12). Gatacre is repulsed in a night attack in the north of Cape Colony (Dec. 10), and Buller's Ladysmith relief column fails to cross the Tugela at Colenso (Dec. 15). In consequence of the week of disaster, Lord Roberts is appointed Commander-in-Chief, and Lord Kitchener is summoned from Egypt as Chief of the Staff, the difficulties involved in the campaign in Natal rendering it impossible for Buller adequately to supervise the operations in other parts.

Canada and the Australasian colonies send volunteers to the war, and a quickened sense of the unity of the Empire begins to prevail.

Marconi experiments in wireless telegraphy.

The malarial mosquito is discovered.

J. J. Thomson developes the theory that matter can exist of less mass than the atom of hydrogen.

The Geological Survey in the N. W. Highlands establishes the base of the stratigraphical series.

3758. **Art.** Thorneycroft's statue of Cromwell is placed outside Westminster Hall.

3759. **Philosophy.** Ward's Gifford Lectures criticise naturalism and the system of Herbert Spencer.

3760. **History.** Maitland proves that the supremacy of Canon Law in England before the Reformation was virtually uncontested.

3761. **Politics.** Bosanquet's Philosophical Theory of the State explains its organic nature, and claims permanent value for the teaching of Rousseau and Hegel.

Benoist's Crise de l'État Moderne advocates representation not of numbers but of interests and professions.

3762. **Economics.** Bernstein criticises Marxian Socialism from an evolutionary standpoint, which is adopted by several of the leaders of the Social Democratic Party in Germany.

3763. **Education.** Robson's Bill raises the age of Half-Timers from 11 to 12, carrying out a promise made by the English representative at the Berlin Labour Conference, 1890.

A Board of Education is created, consisting of a President and of the Lord President of Council, the Secretaries of State, etc., possibly aided by a Consultative Committee, uniting the Education with the Science and Art Department.

3764. **Social.** An International Women's Congress is held in London.

Bills for enforcing automatic couplings and for checking the practice of Secret Commissions are withdrawn.

A Bill is passed to facilitate the purchase of houses by workmen.

A Federation of Trade Unions for fighting purposes is organised; but many Unions stand aloof.

A Committee of the Commons, presided over by Chaplin, recommends a scheme for a pension of 5*s.* to 7*s.* a week at 65 years of age, if the candidate is of good character, does not possess more than 10*s.* a week, and has made an attempt to save.

The Licensing Commission issues a Majority and Minority Report. The latter, drawn up by Lord Peel, the Chairman, recommends that a seven years' notice shall be substituted for money compensation, which shall only be granted if the license be extinguished before the expiry of the notice.

3765. **Deaths.** Rosa Bonheur, Büchner, Bunsen, Castelar, Cherbuliez, Herschell, Nubar Pasha, Pailleron, Weiszäcker.

APPENDIX A.

BIBLIOGRAPHY.

Works of Reference.

Bibliographies. Stein's *Bibliographie Générale.* Sonnenschein's *Best Books.* Langlois' *Bibliographie Historique.* Adams' *Historical Literature.* Hurst's *Literature of Theology.* Muhlbrecht's *Litteratur d. Staatswissenschaften.*

Encyclopaedias, etc. *Encyclopaedia Britannica.* Brockhaus' *Conversations-Lexicon.* Herbst's *Encyclopädie d. Neueren Geschichte.* Larned's *History for ready reference.* Haydn's *Dictionary of Dates.* Ersch u. Gruber's *Künste u. Wissenschaften.* Conrad's *Staatswissenschaften.* Palgrave's *Dictionary of Political Economy.* Poggendorf's *Exacte Wissenschaften.* Wetzer und Welte's *Katholisches Kirchenlexikon.* Herzog's *Protestantische Theologie u. Kirche* (abridged and translated by Schaff). Franck's *Dictionnaire des Sciences Philosophiques.* Vapereau's *Dictionnaire des Contemporains.* Réclus' *Géographie Universelle.* Mulhall's *Dictionary of Statistics.* Keltie's *Statesman's Year-book.*

General Political History.

Universal. Lavisse et Rambaud, *Hist. Générale*, 4—12. Weiss' *Weltgesch.*, 6—22. Kaemmel's *Weltgesch.*, 2—10. Dreyss' *Chronologie Universelle*, 2. Stokvis' *Chronologie Universelle*, 3. George's *Genealogical Tables.* Grote's *Stammtafeln.*

General European. Morse Stephens' *Modern European History.* Lodge's *Modern Europe. Periods of European History.* Philippson's *Neuere Gesch.*, 3. Flathe's *Neueste Gesch.*, 3. Hassall's *European History.* Lorenz' *Genealogisches Handbuch.* Bourgeois' *Politique Extérieure*, 2. Freeman's *Historical Geography.* Perthes' *Geschichtsatlas.*

Periods. Ruge's *Zeitalter d. Entdeckungen.* Häusser's *Period of the Reformation.* Dreysen's *Gegenreformation.* Philippson's *West Europa im Zeitalter v. Philip*, 2, *Elizabeth u. Heinrich*, 4. Winter's *Dreissigjähriger Krieg.* Philippson's *Ludwig*, 14. Noorden's *Spanischer Erbfolgekrieg*, 3. Arneth's *Prinz Eugen*, 3. Oncken's *Friedrich d. Grosse*, 2. Ranke's *Ursprung d. Revolutionären Kriege.* Fyffe's *Modern Europe.* Rose's *Revolutionary and Napoleonic Era.* Oncken's *Revolution, Kaiserreich u. Befreiungskriege*, 2. Seignobos' *Europe*, 1814—96, 2. Debidour's *La Diplomatie*, 1814—78, 2. Stern's *Europa seit* 1815, 2. Flathe's *Restauration u. Revolution*, 1815—51. Maurice's *The Year* 1848. Bulle's *Zweites Kaiserreich u. Königreich Italiens.* Hamley's *Crimean War.* Duff's *European Politics* (published 1866). Oncken's *Wilhelm I*, 2. Schulthess' *Europ: Geschichtskalendar*, since 1869 (yearly). Marquardsen's

Handbücher d. öffentlichen Rechts d. Gegenwart. Lowell's *Constitutions of Continental Europe*, 2. Hamley's *Operations of War.* Leroy-Beaulieu's *Colonisation chez les peuples modernes.* Beer's *Welthandel im* 19ten *Jahrhundert*, 3.

General Culture.

A. *General.*

General Surveys. Laurent's *Études sur l'histoire de l'humanité*, 8—17. Renouvier's *Philosophie Analytique de l'Histoire*, 4. Henne-am-Rhyn's *Kulturgesch.*, 4. Cournot's *Marche des Idées*, 2.

Church History. Kurtz' *Church History*, 2—3. Schaff's *History of the Creeds.* Werner's *Apologetische Literatur*, 5. Dorner's *Person of Christ*, 4—5. Schweizer's *Protestantische Central-Dogmen*, 2. Ritschl's *Pietismus*, 3, and *Rechtfertigungslehre*, vol. 1. Wallace's *Anti-Trinitarian Biography*, 3. Rule's *The Inquisition.* Crétineau-Joly's *Les Jésuites*, 6. Reusch's *Index d. verbotenen Bücher*, 2. Meyer's *Die Propaganda*, 2. Kattenbusch's *Confessionskunde.* Pichler's *Kirkliche Trennung zwischen d. Orient u. d. Occident*, 2. Graetz' *Jews*, 4—5. Schulte's *Quellen d. Kanonischen Rechts*, 3. Döllinger's *The Church and the Churches.* Geffcken's *Church and State*, 2. Lecky's *Rationalism*, 2. White's *Warfare of Science and Theology*, 2.

Literature. Saintsbury's *Periods of European Literature.* Hallam's *Literature of Europe.* Prölss' *Neueres Drama*, 6.

Art. Carrière's *Kunst u. Culturentwickelung*, 5. Bosanquet's *Aesthetic.* Taine's *Philosophie de l'Art*, 2. Kugler's *Schools of Painting*, 4. Fergusson's *Modern Architecture.* Lubke's *Sculpture*, vol. 2. Rockstro's *Music.*

Moral Science. Fischer's *Neuere Philosophie*, 8. Höffding's *Modern Philosophy*, 2. Lange's *Materialism*, 3. Pfleiderer's *Philosophy of Religion since Spinoza*, 2. Jodl's *Ethik*, 2. Sidgwick's *History of Ethics.* Janet's *Philosophie Politique*, 2. Pollock's *Science of Politics.* Gierke's *Althusius.* Franck's *Publicistes*, 3. Ingram's *Political Economy.* Kautz' *Nationalökonomie*, 2.

Natural Science. Buckley's *Short History of Science.* Bury's *Astronomy.* Cajori's *Physics.* Mach's *Mechanics.* Sachs' *Botany.* Meyer's *Chemistry.* Hirsch's *Medizin.* Carus' *Zoologie.* Ball's *Mathematics* (abridged as 'Primer'). Cantor's *Vorlesungen über Math.* (to 1758), 2—3. Zittel's *Geologie.* Geikie's *Founders of Geology.* Kobell's *Mineralogie.* Peschel's *Erdkunde.* Du Bois Reymond's *Reden*, 2. Tyndall's *Fragments of Science*, 3.

Law. Walker's *Law of Nations.*

Education. Schmidt's *Pädagogik*, 3—4. Quick's *Educational Reformers.*

Philology. Müller's *Classische Philologie.* Pattison's *Essays*, vol. 2. Benfey's *Orientalische Philologie.*

B. *Periods.*

Beard's *Lectures on the Reformation.* Möller's *The Reformation.* Stöckl's *Philosophie d. Mittelalters*, vol. 3. Hefele's *Conciliengesch.*, 8—9 (Hergenrother). Maurenbrecher's *Katholische Reformation.* Drummond's *Erasmus*, 2. Seebohm's *Protestant Revolution.* Pastor's *Reunionsbestrebungen.* Prost's *Agrippa*, 2. Roth's *Vesalius.* Prowe's *Copernicus*, 2. (G.) Gothein's *Loyola.* Ward's *Counter-Reformation.* Philippson's *Contre-révolution religieuse.* Dejob's *L'influence du Concile de Trente.* Nisard's *Gladiateurs de la République d. Lettres*, 2. Pattison's *Casaubon.* Döllinger's *Bellarmin*, and *Moralstreitigkeiten in d. Kath. Kirche.* Sayous' *Littérature française à l'étranger*, 4. Muther's *Modern Painting*, 3. Nippold's *Neueste Kirchengesch.*, 4. Blennerhassett's *Mme de Stael*, 3. Janet's *Philosophie de la Révolution française.* Cheyne's *Founders of O. T. Criticism.* Nash's *History of N. T. Criticism.* Brandes' *Hauptströmungen d. Litteratur d. 19ten Jahrhundert*, 5. Barnard's *Pestalozzi.* Clerke's *Astronomy in 19th Century.* Pfleiderer's *Theology in 19th Century.* Tulloch's *Modern Theories of Philosophy and Religion.* Bunsen's *Life*, 2. Lubbock's 50 *years of Science.* Figuier's *Année Scientifique*, since 1857 (annually). Friedrich's *Vaticanisches Concil*, 3. Lavollée's *Classes Ouvrières en Europe*, 3. Barth's *Philosophie d. Geschichte*, vol. 1. Nitti's *Catholic Socialism.* D'Alviella's *Contemporary Religious Thought.* Greely's *Arctic Discoveries.*

England.

Politics.

General. Gardiner and Mullinger's *Introduction to English History. Dictionary of National Biography.* Law and Pulling's *Dictionary of English History.* Acland and Ransome's *English Political History.* Gardiner's *Student's History.* Green's *Short History*, and *English People*, 2—4. *Twelve English Statesmen.* Brosch's *England*, 5—10. Gneist's *Constitutional History.* Taswell-Langmead's *Constitutional History.* Hallam's *Constitutional History.* Dicey's *Privy Council.* Stephen's *Criminal Law*, 3. Clowes' *Royal Navy*, 6. Dowell's *Taxation*, 4. Sharpe's *London*, 3.

Periods. Busch's *English under the Tudors.* Stubbs' *Lectures on Henry VII. and Henry VIII.* Brewer's *Henry VIII.*, 2. Friedmann's *Anne Boleyn*, 2. Pollard's *Protector Somerset.* Ranke's *England principally in the 17th Century*, 6. Seeley's *Growth of British Policy* (1558—1702), 2. Winsor's *America*, vol. 3. Wiesener's *Jeunesse d'Elizabeth.* Fox-Bourne's *Sidney.* Hume's *Burleigh*, and *Elizabeth's Suitors.* Prothero's *Const. documents of Elizabeth and James I.* (Introduction). Spedding's *Bacon*, 7. Hume's *Raleigh.* Gardiner's *England*, 1603—54, 16. Figgis' *Divine Right of Kings.* Masson's *Milton*, 6. Hannay's *Blake.* Lister's *Clarendon*, 3. Warburton's *Rupert*, 3. Markham's *Fairfax.* Firth's *Cromwell.* Guizot's *Portraits Politiques*, and *Richard Cromwell*, 2. Airy's *The Restoration.* Mahan's *Sea*

Power, 1660—1789. Klopp's *Fall d. Hauses Stuart*, 14. Christie's *Shaftesbury*, 2. Foxcraft's *Halifax*, 2. Macaulay's *History of England.* Lecky's *England in 18th Century*, 7. Burton's *Anne*, 3. Wolseley's *Marlborough*, 2. Stebbing's *Peterborough.* Salomon's *Letztes Ministerium d. Königin Anna.* Ward's *England and Hanover.* Traill's *Central Government.* Coxe's *Walpole*, 3, and *Pelham*, 2. May's *Constitutional History*, 1760—1860, 3. Trevelyan's *Fox.* Fitzmaurice's *Shelburne*, 3. Rae's *Sheridan*, 2. Russell's *Life and Memorials of Fox*, 7. Stanhope's *Pitt*, 4. Mahan's *Sea Power and the Revolution*, 2, and *Life of Nelson.* Maxwell's *Wellington*, 2. Wilberforce's *Wilberforce*, 5. Walpole's *Perceval*, 2. Wallas' *Place.* Reid's *Sidney Smith.* Stapleton's *Canning*, 4. Smith's *Cobbett*, 2. Twiss' *Eldon*, 3. Walpole's *England*, 1815—61, 6, and *Lord John Russell*, 2. Lord John Russell's *Recollections.* Harris' *Radical Party.* Kebbel's *Tory Party.* Le Marchant's *Althorp.* Martin's *Lyndhurst.* Greville's *Journals*, 8. Bright's *England*, 1837—87. Irving's *Annals of the Reign*, 2. Parker's *Peel*, 3. Disraeli's *Bentinck.* Ashley's *Palmerston*, 2. Trevelyan's *Macaulay.* Mrs Grote's *Grote. Queen's Prime Ministers*, ed. Reid, 9. Martin's *The Prince Consort.* Morley's *Cobden.* Laughton's *Reeve*, 2. Martin's *Sherbrooke*, 2. Nash's *Westbury*, 2. Selborne's *Memoirs*, 4. Reid's *Forster.* Lang's *Iddesleigh.* Maxwell's *W. H. Smith*, 2. Bonner's *Bradlaugh*, vol. 2. Bagehot's *English Constitution.* Dicey's *Law and Custom of the Constitution.* Anson's *Crown and Parliament*, 2.

Church History.

General. Perry's *Church of England*, 2—3. Hook's *Archbishops of Canterbury*, 6—12. Hunt's *Religious Thought in England*, 3. Gillow's *English Catholics*, 4. *Diocesan Histories.*

Periods. Seebohm's *Oxford Reformers.* Demaus' *Tyndale*, and *Latimer.* Westcott's *English Bible.* Hutton's *More.* Bridget's *Fisher.* Maitland's *Essays on the Reformation.* Dixon's *Church of England*, 4. Gasquet's *Henry VIII. and the English Monasteries.* Hardwick's *The Articles.* Schickler's *Églises du réfuge en Angleterre*, 3. Bonet-Maury's *Origins of English Unitarianism.* Bellesheim's *Allen.* Simpson's *Campion.* Dexter's *Congregationalism.* Waddington's *Congregational History*, 2—5. *Leaders of Religion* (Andrewes, Donne, Laud, Fox, Howe). Walton's *Lives.* Coleridge's *Notes on English Divines*, 2. Weingarten's *Revolutionskirchen Englands.* Barclay's *Religious Societies of the Commonwealth.* Stoughton's *Religion in England*, 1640—1850, 8. Tulloch's *Rational Theology in the 17th Century*, 2. Elrington's *Ussher.* Brown's *Bunyan.* Overton's *Life in the English Church*, 1660—1714. Stoughton's *Penn.* Plumptre's *Ken*, 2. Lathbury's *Non-jurors.* Carrau's *Philosophie religieuse depuis Locke.* Abbey and Overton's *English Church in 18th Century*, 2 (abridged, 1). Stephen's *English Thought in the 18th Century*, vol. 1. Skeat's *Free Churches.* Rees' *Nonconformity in Wales.* Van Mildert's *Waterland.* Overton's *Law.* Watson's *Warburton.* Keble's

Bishop Wilson. Overton's *Wesley.* Tyerman's *Wesley*, 3, and *Whitfield*, 2. Amherst's *Catholic Emancipation*, 2. Overton's *English Church*, 1800—33. Churton's *Joshua Watson*, 2. Moule's *Simeon.* Stanley's *Arnold.* Ward's *Wiseman*, 2. Lock's *Keble.* Church's *Oxford Movement.* Liddon's *Pusey*, 4. Newman's *Apologia.* Ward's *W. G. Ward*, 2. Pattison's *Memoirs.* Mrs Oliphant's *Irving.* Burgon's *Twelve Good Men.* Stephens' *Hook.* Ullathorne's *Restoration of the Catholic Hierarchy. Archdeacon Denison's Life.* Kingsley's *Kingsley.* Maurice's *Maurice*, 2. Ashwell's *Wilberforce*, 3. Hodder's *Shaftesbury.* Brooke's *Robertson.* Purcell's *Manning*, 2. Prothero's *Stanley*, 2. Miall's *Miall.* Dale's *Dale.* Davidson's *Tait*, 2. Rawnsley's *Harvey Goodwin.* Kitchin's *Harold Browne.* Benson's *Benson*, 2. Barry's *English Church in other Lands.*

Literature.

General. Sharp's *Dictionary of English Authors. English Men of Letters*, ed. J. Morley, 39. Stopford Brooke's *English Literature.* Saintsbury's *English Literature.* Taine's *English Literature*, 2. Ward's *Dramatic Literature*, 3. Matthew Arnold's *Essays*, 3. Leslie Stephen's *Hours in a Library*, 3, and *Studies of a Biographer*, 2.

Periods. Morley's *English Writers*, 6—11. Courthope's *English Poetry*, vol. 2. Saintsbury's *Elizabethan Literature.* Lee's *Life of Shakspere.* Brandes' *Shakspere.* Jusserand's *English Novel in the time of Shakspere.* Swinburne's *Ben Jonson*, and *Chapman.* Gosse's *Donne*, 2; *Poets of James I*; and 17*th Century Studies.* Masson's *Milton*, 6. Garnett's *Age of Dryden.* Beljame's *Le Public et les hommes de lettres.* Gosse's 18*th Century Literature.* Raleigh's *English Novel.* Fox-Bourne's *English Newspapers*, 2. Dennis' *Age of Pope.* Craik's *Swift*, 2. Aitken's *Steele*, 2. Thackeray's *English Humourists.* Dobson's 18*th Century Vignettes*, 4. Texte's *Origins of Literary Cosmopolitanism.* Seccombe's *Age of Johnson.* Angellier's *Burns*, 2. Legouis' *Youth of Wordsworth.* Herford's *Age of Wordsworth.* Saintsbury's 19*th Century Literature.* Dowden's *Shelley.* Smiles' *Murray*, 2. Clayden's *Rogers*, 3. Bagehot's *Literary Essays*, 2. Pater's *Appreciations.* Froude's *Carlyle's Life in London*, 2. Mrs Gaskell's *Charlotte Brontë.* Forster's *Dickens*, 3. Merivale's *Thackeray.* Tennyson's *Tennyson.* Mrs Orr's *Browning.* Cross' *G. Eliot.* Reid's *Lord Houghton*, 2. Saintsbury's *Matthew Arnold.* Archer's *English Dramatists of To-day.* McCarthy's *Reminiscences*, 2.

Art, Science, Philosophy, etc.

General. Traill's *Social England*, 2—6.

Periods. Mullinger's *University of Cambridge* (to 1625), 2. Walpole's *Painting in England.* Woltmann's *Holbein.* Nichol's *Bacon.* Rémusat's *Philosophie* *depuis Bacon jusqu'à Locke*, 2. D'Arcy Power's *Harvey*. Edwards' *Founders of the British Museum*. Loftie's *Inigo Jones and Wren*. Robertson's *Hobbes*. Fitzmaurice's *Petty*. Weld's *Royal Society*, 2. Brewster's *Newton*, 2 (abridged, 1). Ball's *Mathematics at Cambridge*. Fox-Bourne's *Locke*, 2. Fraser's *Locke*. Lyon's *Idéalisme en Angleterre au* 18*ème siècle*. L. Stephen's *English Thought in* 18*th Century*, vol. 2. Fraser's *Berkeley*. Smiles' *Engineers*, 5. Dobson's *Hogarth*. Leslie and Taylor's *Reynolds*, 2. Seth's *Scottish Philosophy*. Kegan Paul's *Godwin*, 2. Rutt's *Priestley*, 2. Hasbach's *Adam Smith*. Bagehot's *Economic Studies*. Bonar's *Malthus*. Kent's *English Radicals*. Stephen's *Utilitarians*, 3. Gilchrist's *Blake*, 2. Bain's *James Mill*. *Century Science Series*, ed. Roscoe (Herschel, Rennell, Dalton, Davy, Faraday, Lyell, Darwin, Clerk Maxwell). Bence Jones' *Royal Institution*. Markham's *British Geography in the last* 100 *Years*. Watson's *Kant and his English Critics*. J. S. Mill's *Autobiography*. Bonner's *Bradlaugh*, vol. 1. Darwin's *Darwin*. Huxley's *Huxley*, 2. Collingwood's *Ruskin*, 2. Hobson's *Ruskin*. Mackail's *Morris*, 2. Parkin's *Thring*, 2. Abbott & Campbell's *Jowett*, 2. Clough's *Miss Clough*. Prothero's *Bradshaw*. Balfour's *Educational Systems of Great Britain*. Ward's *Reign of Queen Victoria*, 2.

Social History.

General. Cunningham and MacArthur's *Economic History*. Cunningham's *English Industry and Commerce*, 2. Rogers' *Agriculture and Prices*, 3—6, and *Six Centuries of Work and Wages*. Nicholls and Mackay's *The Poor Law*, 3. Hall's *The Customs*, 2.

Periods. Mrs Green's *Town Life in the* 15*th Century*, 2. Denton's 15*th Century*. Ashley's *Economic History*. Williamson's *Foreign Commerce under the Tudors*. Schanz's *Englische Handelspolitik*, 2. Hall's *Society in the Elizabethan Age*. Fox-Bourne's *English Merchants*, 2. Prothero's *Pioneers of English Farming*. Hewins' *Trade and Finance in the* 17*th Century*. Rogers' *First Nine Years of the Bank of England*. Ashton's *Social Life under Queen Anne*, 2. Sydney's *England in the* 18*th Century*, 2. Toynbee's *Industrial Revolution*. Schulze-Gavaernitz' *Social Peace*. Held's *Zwei Bücher d. Socialen Gesch. Englands*. Lloyd Jones' *Owen*. Holyoake's Co-operation, 2. Webb's *Trade Unionism*. Hobson's *Evolution of Modern Capitalism*. Levi's *British Commerce*. Mulhall's *Prices*, 1850—85. Giffen's *Essays in Finance*, 2. Webb's *Industrial Democracy*, 2. Shaw's *Municipalities*. Hobson's *Problems of Poverty*.

Scotland.

Politics.

General. Hume Brown's *Scotland*. Lang's *Scotland*. Burton's *Scotland*, 3—8, and '1688—1745,' 2.

Periods. Herkless' *Beaton*. Skelton's *Maitland*, 2. Philippson's *Marie Stuart*, 2. Hosack's *Mary Stuart*, 2. Napier's *Montrose*, 2. Mackay's *Stair*.

Morris' *Claverhouse*, 3. Story's *Carstairs*. Klopp's *Fall des Hauses Stuart*, 14. Mackinnon's *The Union*. Omond's *Lord Advocates*, 2. Lang's *The Young Pretender*.

Culture.

General. Bellesheim's *Catholic Church in Scotland*, 4. Luckock's *Church of Scotland*. Walker's *Three Centuries of Scotch Literature*, 2. Buckle's *Civilization*, vol. 3. Grant's *University of Edinburgh*, 2.

Periods. *Famous Scots Series* (Cameron, Fletcher of Saltoun, Ramsay, the Erskines, Thomson, Fergusson, Reid, Burns, Hogg, Campbell, Mungo Park, Hugh Miller, Guthrie, Simpson, Aytoun, Ferrier, Stevenson). Mackay's *Major*. Lorimer's *Patrick Hamilton*. Rogers' *Wishart*. McCrie's *Knox*, and *Melville*, 2. Hume Brown's *Knox*, 2, and *Buchanan*. Masson's *Drummond*. Aiton's *Henderson*. Graham's *Social Life in 18th Century*, 2. Burton's *Hume*, 2. Rae's *Adam Smith*. Hanna's *Chalmers*, 4. Lockhart's *Scott*. Cockburn's *Jeffrey*, 2. Lang's *Lockhart*, 2. Froude's *Carlyle's Early Life*, 2. Veitch's *Hamilton*. Mrs Oliphant's *Blackwood*, 3, and *Tulloch*. Story's *Lee*, 2, and *Robert Story*. McLeod's *Norman McLeod*. Cairns' *Dr John Brown*. Smith's *Henry Drummond*. Stoddart's *Blackie*.

Ireland.

Politics.

General. Morris' *Ireland*, 1494—1868. Ball's *Legislative Systems of Ireland*.

Periods. Bagwell's *Ireland under the Tudors*, 3. Gilbert's *Viceroys*. Gardiner's *England*, 1603—1654, 6. Taylor's *Owen Roe O'Neill*. Prendergast's *Cromwellian Settlement*, and *Ireland*, 1660—1688. Todhunter's *Sarsfield*. Lecky's *Ireland in the 18th Century*, 5. Wolfe Tone's *Autobiography*, ed. O'Brien, 2. Morris' *Ireland*, 1798—1898. McCarthy's *Ireland since the Union*. Fitzpatrick's *Doyle*, 2. Dunlop's *O'Connell*. O'Brien's *Drummond*. Duffy's *Davis*; *Young Ireland*; *Four Years of Irish History*; *League of North and South*. Sullivan's *New Ireland*. O'Brien's *Fifty Years' Concessions to Ireland*, 1831—81, 2; *Irish Wrongs and English Remedies*; *Irish Land Question*, 2; and *Parnell*, 2. Gladstone's *Aspects of the Irish Question*. Dicey's *Case against Home Rule*.

Culture.

Bellesheim's *Katholische Kirche in Irland*, 2—3. Ball's *Reformed Church in Ireland*. Reid's *Presbyterian Church in Ireland*, 2. Stubbs' *Trinity College, Dublin*.

British Colonies.

General. Lucas' *Historical Geography of the British Colonies*, 4. Woodward's *Expansion of the British Empire.* Lord's *England's Lost Possessions.* Dilke's *Problems of Greater Britain.* Parkin's *Imperial Federation.* Todd's *Parliamentary Government in the Colonies.*

Australasia. Rusden's *Australia*, 3, and *New Zealand*, 3. Jenks' *Australasian Colonies.* Garnett's *Gibbon Wakefield.* Reeves' *Long White Cloud.* Rees' *Sir G. Grey.* Parkes' *Fifty Years Making of Australian History*, 2. Turner and Sutherland's *Australian Literature.*

South Africa. Theal's *South Africa*, 5, and *Story of South Africa.* Rees' *Sir G. Grey.* Martineau's *Bartle Frere*, vol. 2. Molteno's *Molteno*, 2. Cox' *Colenso*, 2. Bryce's *Impressions of South Africa.* Fitzpatrick's *Transvaal from Within.* Hobson's *The War, its Causes and Effects.* Thomson's *Rhodesia.* Rhodes' *Speeches.*

Central Africa. Johnston's *British Central Africa.*

East and West Africa. Lucas' *Colonies*, 3—4.

Canada. Kingsford's *History of Canada*, 10. Bourinot's *Canada.* Parkman's *French and English*, 10. Pope's *Macdonald*, 2. G. Smith's *Canada and the Canadian Question.* Sulte's *Canadiens Français*, 8. *Canada, an Encyclopaedia*, ed. Hopkins, 5.

West Indies. Lucas' *Colonies*, vol. 2. Rodway's *Story of the West Indies.*

France.

Politics.

General. Monod's *Bibliographie de l'histoire de France.* Lalanne's *Dict. historique de la France.* Langlois et Stein's *Archives de l'histoire de France.* Henri Martin's *France*, 7—16. Kitchin's *France*, vols. 2—3. Flassan's *Diplomatie française*, 7. Ranke's *Französische Geschichte*, 6.

Periods. Cherrier's *Charles VIII*, 2. Maulde-la-Clavière's *Louis XII*, 3. Paris' *François I*, 2. Forneron's *Ducs de Guise*, 2. D'Aumale's *Princes de Condé*, 7. Marcks' *Coligny.* Atkinson's *L'Hôpital.* Baird's *Huguenots*, 4. Aguesse's *Protestantisme* (to 1592), 4. Poirson's *Henri IV*, 4. Willert's *Henry of Navarre.* Anquez' *Assemblées Protestantes*, and *Henri IV et Allemagne.* Weill's *Théories sur le pouvoir royal.* Labitte's *Démocratie chez les Prédicateurs de la Ligue.* Philippson's *Heinrich IV u. Philip III*, 3. Zeller's *Louis XIII*, 6. Lodge's *Richelieu.* D'Avenel's *Richelieu*, 4. Hanotaux' *Richelieu*, 2. Fagniez' *Père Joseph*, 2. Perkins' *Richelieu and Mazarin*, 2. Cousin's *Mme d'Hautefort*; *Mme de Chevreuse*; *Jeunesse de Mazarin*; *Mme de Longueville*, 2. Chéruel's *Minorité de Louis XIV*, 4, and *Ministère de Mazarin*, 3. Airy's *English Restoration and Louis XIV.* Gaillardin's *Louis XIV*, 5. Hassall's *Louis XIV.* Sargent's *Colbert.* Rousset's *Louvois*, 4. Legrelle's *Louis XIV* *et l'Espagne*, 4. Michaud's *Louis XIV et Innocent XI*, 4. Morel's *Louis XIV*, 1700—15, 3. Wiesener's *La Régence*, 3. Perkins' *The Regency*. Rocquain's *Esprit révolutionnaire avant la révolution*. Aubertin's *Esprit publique au* 18*ème siècle*. Perkins' *Louis XV*, 2. D'Haussonville's *Réunion de Lorraine à la France*, 4. De Broglie's *Frédéric II et Louis XV*, 1742—4; *Marie Thérése*, 1744—6; *Saxe et D'Argenson*; *La Paix d'Aix-la-Chapelle*; *Le Secret du Roi*, 1752—74; *L'Alliance Autrichienne*. Flammermont's *Maupeou et les Parlements*. Taine's *Ancien Régime*. Tocqueville's *Ancien Régime*. Foncin's *Ministère de Turgot*. Chérest's *Chute de l'Ancien Régime*, 3. Champion's *Les Cahiers de* 1789. Lichtenberger's *Socialisme dans la Révolution française*. Doniol's *Révolution et la Féodalité*. Debidour's *L'Église et l'État*, 1789—1870. Jervis' *Gallican Church and the Revolution*. Ricard's *Cardinal Maury*. Aulard's *Révolution française*. Sorel's *Révolution française*, 4. Sybel's *French Revolution*, 4. Taine's *La Révolution*, 3. Stern's *Mirabeau*, 2 (French Tr.). Willert's *Mirabeau*. Neton's *Sieyès*. Biré's *Légendes révolutionnaires*. Daudet's *L'Émigration*, 3. Blennerhassett's *Mme de Stael*, 3. Pierre's *Assemblées politiques*, 1789—1876, 2. Sciout's *Le Directoire*, 4. D'Haussonville's *L'Église Romaine et le Premier Empire*, 5. Taine's *Régime Moderne*, vol. 1. Masson's *Napoléon et sa Famille*, 4. Welschinger's *Enghien*; *La Censure*; *Divorce de Napoléon*; *Ney*. Vandal's *Napoléon et Alexandre III*, 3. Houssaye's 1814, and 1815, 3. Vieil-Castel's *La Restauration*, 20. Thureau-Dangin's *Parti Libéral sous la Restauration*. Barante's *Royer-Collard*, 2. Thureau-Dangin's *Monarchie de Juillet*, 8. Hillebrand's *Frankreich*, 1830—48, 2. D'Haussonville's *Politique Extérieure*, 1830—48, 2. Guizot's *Mémoires*, 8. Lacombe's *Berryer*, 3. Blanc's *Dix Ans*, 5. Pierre's *Révolution de* 1848, 2. Le Gorce's *Deuxième Empire*, 3. Daniel's *Année Politique* (since 1859). Ollivier's *L'Empire Libéral*, 3. Senior's *Conversations in France*, 6. Mazade's *Thiers*. Denis' *Histoire Contemporaine*, 3. Daudet's *Duc d'Aumale*. Sorel's *Histoire diplomatique de la Guerre*, 1870—1, 2. Hippeau's *Hist. diplomatique de la troisième république*. Zévort's *Troisième République*, 3. Simon's *Gouvernement de Thiers*, 2. Reinach's *Ministère de Gambetta*. Coubertin's *Third Republic*. Bodley's *France*, 2. Lowell's *Governments and Parties*, vol. 1. Rambaud's *La France Coloniale*.

Culture.

General. Rambaud's *Civilisation française*, 3. *Grands Écrivains Français*, ed. Jusserand. Julleville's *Littérature Française*, 3—8, and *Théâtre en France*. Faguet's *Littérature Française*, and *Études littéraires*, 4. Sainte-Beuve's *Lundis*, 28. Brunetière's *Études Critiques*, 6, and *Histoire de la Critique*. Egger's *Hellénisme en France*, 2. Rossel's *Relations littéraires avec l'Allemagne*. Paradol's *Moralistes français*. Guettée's *L'Église de France*, 8—12. Jervis' *Church in France till* 1789, 2. Félice's *French Protestants*. Flint's *Philosophy of History*, vol. 1. Lévy-Bruhl's *Philosophy in France*. Levasseur's *Classes Ouvrières*, 4. Compayré's *Doctrines d'Éducation en France*, 2. Kingsley's *French Art*.

Periods. Sainte-Beuve's *Poésie française au 16ème siècle.* Darmesteter et Hatzfeldt's *16ème siècle.* Mrs Pattison's *Renaissance in France*, 2. Gebhardt's *Rabelais.* Robinson's *Margaret of Navarre.* Desjardins' *Moralistes français au 16ème siècle.* Christie's *Dolet.* Lenient's *Satire en France au 16ème siècle*, 2. Bourciez' *La Cour de Henri II.* Waddington's *Ramus.* Jourdain's *L'Université de Paris.* Douarche's *L'Université de Paris et les Jésuites.* Owen's *Sceptics of the French Renaissance.* Lowndes' *Montaigne.* Baudrillart's *Bodin.* Haag's *La France Protestante*, 10. Hamon's *François de Sales*, 2. Damiron's *Philosophie en France au 17ème siècle*, 2. Puyol's *Richer*, 2. Perraud's *L'Oratoire.* Houssaye's *Bérulle*, 3. Sainte-Beuve's *Port Royal*, 7. Beard's *Port Royal*, 2. Cousin's *Jacqueline Pascal*; *La Société au 17ème siècle*, 2; *Mme de Sablé.* Perrens' *Libertins au 17ème siècle.* Maury's *Académie des Belles-Lettres.* Bertrand's *Académie des Sciences*, 1660—1793. Rébelliau's *Bossuet.* Crouslé's *Bossuet et Fénelon*, 2. De Broglie's *Mabillon*, 2, and *Montfauçon*, 2. Séché's *Derniers Jansénistes*, 1710—1870, 3. Damiron's *Philosophie en France au 18ème siècle*, 3. Coquerel's *Églises du désert*, 2. Lady Dilke's *French Painters, Architects and Sculptors of 18th Century*, 3. Desnoiresterres' *Voltaire*, 8. Morley's *Voltaire*; *Rousseau*, 2; *Diderot*, 2; *Miscellanies*, vol. 2. Lichtenberger's *Socialisme en France au 18ème siècle.* Lavergne's *Économistes français au 18ème siècle.* Higgs' *The Physiocrats.* Berthelot's *Lavoisier.* Loménie's *Beaumarchais*, 2. Jusserand's *Shakspere in France.* D'Haussonville's *Salon of Mme Necker*, 2. Goncourt's *Société pendant la Révolution*, 2. Debidour's *L'Église et l'État*, 1789—1870. Jervis' *Gallican Church and the Revolution.* D'Haussonville's *L'Église romaine et le Premier Empire*, 5. Girandeau's *Presse Périodique*, 1789—1887. Picavet's *Idéologues.* Sainte-Beuve's *Chateaubriand*, 2. Taine's *Régime Moderne*, vol. 2. Faguet's *Politiques et Moralistes*, 3. Ravaisson's *Philosophie en France au 19ème siècle.* Maury's *Réveil religieux*, 1810—50, 2. Foisset's *Lacordaire*, 2. Mrs Oliphant's *Montalembert*, 2. Booth's *St Simon.* Weill's *École Saint-Simonienne.* Littré's *Comte.* *Rapports sur les progrès des Sciences en France*, 1867 (Zoologie, Minéralogie, Physiologie, Géometrie, Géologie, Histoire, etc.). Lenient's *Comédie en France au 19ème siècle*, 2. Brunetière's *Poésie lyrique au 19ème siècle*, 2. Claretie's *Peintres et Sculpteurs contemporains*, 2. Lagrange's *Dupanloup* (Eng. Trans.), 2. Mrs Bishop's *Mrs Craven.* Ricard's *Lavigerie.* Frankland's *Pasteur.* Darmesteter's *Renan.* Bourget's *Psychologie Contemporaine*, 2. Symons' *Symbolist Movement.* Lemaître's *Les Contemporains*, 8.

Germany.

Politics.

General. Dahlmann-Waitz' *Deutsche Quellenkunde.* *Allgemeine Deutsche Biographie.* Kaemmel's *Deutsche Geschichte.* Droysen's *Preussische Politik*, 4—14. Bryce's *Holy Roman Empire.* Tuttle's *Prussia till* 1740. Janssen's *Deutsches Volk*, 2—5 (to 1618).

Periods. Ulmann's *Maximilian*, 2. Ranke's *Deutsche Gesch. im Zeitalter d. Reformation*, 6. (E. T. of vols. 1—3.) Baumgarten's *Karl V*, 3. Ritter's *Gegenreformation*, 2. Gardiner's *Thirty Years War*. Winter's *Dreissigjähriger Krieg*. Erdmannsdörffer's *Deutsche Gesch.* 1648—1740, 2. Lavisse's *Youth of Frederick the Great*, and *Frédéric avant l'avénement*. Tuttle's *Frederick II*, 2. Koser's *Friedrich II*. Schäfer's *Siebenjähriger Krieg*, 3. Schmoller's *Wirthschaftliche Politik Friedrichs*, and *Preussische Finanzpolitik*. Ranke's *Oesterreich und Preussen* 1748—63, and *Deutsche Mächte u. d. Fürstenbund*, 1780—90. Heigel's *Deutsche Geschichte seit* 1786. Treitzschke's *Deutsche Gesch. im* 19*ten Jahrhundert*, 5 (to 1848). Seeley's *Stein*, 3. Springer's *Dahlmann*, 2. Ernest of Coburg-Gotha's *Memoirs*, 4. Headlam's *Bismarck*. Busch's *Bismarck*, 3. Bismarck's *Memoirs*, 2. Sybel's *Begründung d. deutschen Reichs*, 7. Marcks' *Wilhelm I*. Friedjung's *Kampf um d. Vorherrschaft in Deutschland*, 1859—66, 2. Moltke's *War of* 1870—1, 2. Poschinger's *Friedrich III*. Lowe's *William II*. Russell's *German Socialism*. Lowell's *Governments and Parties*, 2.

Culture.

General. *The Munich Histories of the Sciences* (Protestant Theology (Eng. Trans.), Catholic Theology, Philosophy, Politics, Historiography, Jurisprudence, Political Economy, Classical Philology, Oriental Philology, Germanic Philology, Zoology, Geology, Mineralogy, Physics, Astronomy, Geography). Scherer's *Deutsche Sprache*, and *Deutsche Litteratur*. Goedeke's *Deutsche Dichtung*, 2—7. Paulsen's *Gelehrter Unterricht*, 2. *Deutsche Kunst*, ed. Janitschek, 5.

Periods. Janssen's *D. Volk*, vols. 1 and 6—8 (to 1618). Geiger's *Humanismus in Italien u. Deutschland*, and *Reuchlin*. Kampschulte's *Erfurter Humanistenkreis*, 2. Strauss' *Hutten* (Eng. Trans.). Köstlin's *Luther*, 2 (abridged trans.). Bezold's *D. Reformation*. Heath's *Anabaptists*. Thausing's *Dürer*, 2. Herford's *Literary Relations with England in* 16*th Century*. Droysen's *Gegenreformation*. Henke's *Calixtus*, 2. Hossbach's *Spener*, 2. Geiger's *Berlin*, 1688—1840, 2. Merz' *Leibnitz* (English). Pichler's *Leibnitz als Theologe*, 2. Lévy-Bruhl's *L'Allemagne depuis Leibnitz*. Biedermann's *Deutschland im* 18*ten Jahrhundert*, 4. Hettner's *Deutsche Litteratur*, 4. Andler's *Origines du Socialisme en Allemagne*. Justi's *Winckelmann*, vol. 1. (G.) Sime's *Lessing*, 2. Schmidt's *Lessing*, 2. Meyer's *Römisch-deutsche Frage*, 3. Nevinson's *Herder*. Haym's *Herder*, 2, and *Romantische Schule*. Mrs Jennings' *Rahel*. Minor's *Schiller*, 2. Grimm's *Goethe*, 2. Dilthey's *Schleiermacher*. Kant, Fichte, Hegel, in Blackwood's *Philosophical Classics*. Noack's *Schelling*, 2. Sepp's *Görres*. Janssen's *Stolberg*, 2. Prölss' *Junges Deutschland*. Wolff's *Deutsche Litteratur d. Gegenwart*. Bruhns' *Alexander v. Humboldt*, 2. (Eng. Trans.) Haym's *Wilhelm v. Humboldt*. Lichtenberger's *German Theology*. Witte's *Tholuck*, 2. Bachmann's *Hengstenberg*, 3. Hausrath's *Strauss*, 2. Acton's *German Schools of History* (Eng. Hist. Rev.

vol. 1). Ritschl's *Ritschl*, 2. Nippold's *Rothe*, 2. Friedrich's *Döllinger*, 3. Goyau's *L'Allemagne religieuse.* Schulte's *Altkatholicismus.* Dawson's *Germany*, 2. *Deutsche Universitäten*, ed. Lexis, 2.

Austria.

General. Wurzbach's *Biog. Lexicon Oest.* Leger's *Austro-Hungary.* Krones' *Oest. Gesch.* 5, and *Grundriss.* Vambéry's *Hungary.* Maurice's *Bohemia.* Palacky's *Böhmen*, 5—10.

Periods. E. Denis' *Fin de l'Indépendance de Bohême*, 2. Gindely's *Rudolph II*, 2; *Böhmische Brüder*, 2; and *Gegenreformation in Böhmen.* Hurter's *Ferdinand II*, 11. Walewski's *Leopold I*, 2. Gaedeke's *Oesterreich u. d. Spanische Erbfolgefrage*, 2. Arneth's *Maria Theresa*, 7. Bright's *Maria Theresa*, and *Joseph II.* Springer's *Oest. im* 19*ten Jahrhundert*, 2. Beer's *Orientalische Politik Oest.* Metternich's *Mémoires*, 8. Mazade's *Metternich.* Demelitsch's *Metternich's Auswärtige Politik*, 2. Arnold-Forster's *Deak.* Beust's *Memoirs*, 2. Lowell's *Governments and Parties*, vol. 2. Matlekovits' *Königreich Ungarns*, 2. Bourlier's *La Bohême Contemporaine.* Pypin's *Slavische Literatur*, 2. Lützow's *Bohemian Literature.* Reich's *Hungarian Literature.* Leger's *Études Slaves*, 6.

Spain.

Politics.

General. Lafuente's *Hist. de España*, 10—29. Armstrong and Hume's *Spain*, 1479—1788. Duro's *Armada Española*, 5.

Periods. Poole's *Moors in Spain.* De Nervo's *Isabelle la Catholique.* Baumgarten's *Karl V*, 3. Winsor's *America*, vol. 2. Hume's *Philip II.* Stirling-Maxwell's *Cloister Life of Charles V*, and *Don John*, vol. 1. Forneron's *Philippe II*, 4. Philippson's *Heinrich IV und Philip III*, 3. Canovas' *Reinado de Felipe IV.* Legrelle's *Louis XIV et l'Espagne*, 4. Parnell's *Spanish War of Succession.* Coxe's *Bourbons in Spain*, 5 (1700—88). Baudrillart's *Philippe V*, 3. Armstrong's *Elizabeth Farnese.* Danvila y Collado's *Reinado de Carlos III.* Hume's *Modern Spain.* Baumgarten's *Gesch. Spaniens seit* 1789, 3. Napier's *Peninsular War.* Hannay's *Castelar.*

Culture.

General. Lafuente's *Hist. Ecclesiastica de España*, 5—6. Lea's *Chapters from the Religious History of Spain.* Ticknor's *Spanish Literature*, 3. Fitzmaurice-Kelly's *Spanish Literature.* Menendez y Pelayo's *Heterodoxos*, 2—3, and *Ideas Estéticas en España*, 2—5. Stirling-Maxwell's *Artists of Spain*, 4. Colmeiro's *Economia Politica en España.*

Periods. Mariéjol's *L'Espagne sous Ferdinand et Isabelle.* Heidenheimer's *Petrus Martyr.* Hefele's *Ximenes* (Eng. Trans.). Wilkens' *Reformation in*

Spain. Grahame's *St Theresa*, 2. Fitzmaurice-Kelly's *Cervantes*. Morel-Fatio's *L'Espagne aux 16—17èmes siècles*, 2. Werner's *Suarez*, 2. Justi's *Velasquez* (Eng. Trans.). Valera's *Juicios Literarios*, and *Estudios Criticos*, 2.

Portugal.

Morse Stephen's *Portugal.* Schäfer's *Portugal*, 2—5 (to 1820). Whiteway's *Portuguese Power in India.* Smith's *Pombal*, 2. Michel's *Portugais en France, Français en Portugal.* Loiseau's *Littérature Portugaise.*

Italy.

Politics.

General. Muratori's *Annali d' Italia* (to 1749). Cantu's *Italiani*, 9—14. Reumont's *Toscana*, 2, and *Stadt Rom*, vol. 3. Ranke's *Popes*, 3. Brosch's *Kirchenstaat*, 2. Brown's *Venice.* Bent's *Genoa.* Carutti's *Storia diplomatica di Savoia*, 1494—1793, 4.

Periods. Reumont's *Lorenzo de Medici*, 2 (Eng. Trans.). Creighton's *Papacy*, 4—6. Pastor's *Popes*, from vol. 4. Pasolini's *Catherine Sforza.* Burd's *Prince* of Macchiavelli. Tommasini's *Machiavelli.* Villari's *Macchiavelli*, and *Savonarola* (Eng. Trans.). Brosch's *Julius II.* Nitti's *Politica di Leone X.* Höfler's *Adrian VI.* De Leva's *Carlo V in Italia*, 5. Sylvain's *Borromée*, 3. Hubner's *Sixtus the Fifth*, 2. Reumont's *Carafas of Maddaloni.* Zwiedineck-Sudenhorst's *Venedig's Politik während. d. Dreissigjährigen Krieges*, 2. Tivaroni's *Risorgimento*, 1735—1870, 9. Theiner's *Clement XIV*, 2. Colletta's *History of Naples*, 2. Helfert's *Carolina v. Neapel.* Ranke's *Consalvi* (in *Biographische Studien*). Reumont's *Cesare Balbo.* Bolton King's *Italy*, 1814—71, 2. Faldella's *Giovane Italia*, 2. Mazade's *Cavour.* Mazzini's *Works*, vols. 1 and 5. O'Clery's *Making of Italy*, 1856—70. Stillman's *Crispi.* Lowell's *Governments and Parties*, vol. 2.

Culture.

General. Garnett's *Italian Literature.* Ranke's *Popes*, 3. Reumont's *Tavole di Storia Toscana*, and *Beiträge z. Italienischen Gesch.*, 6. Cantu's *Eretici d' Italia*, 3. Crowe and Cavalcaselle's *Painting in Italy*, 5. Ferrari's *Scrittori politici d' Italia.*

Periods. Symonds' *Renaissance*, 7. Burckhardt's *The Renaissance.* Gregorovius' *City of Rome*, vol. 8. Pater's *Renaissance.* Villari's *Savonarola*, and *Macchiavelli* (Eng. Trans.). Owen's *Italian Sceptics.* Rodocanachi's *Renée de Ferrara.* Benrath's *Ochino* (Eng. Trans.). Reumont's *Vittoria Colonna.* Muntz' *Leonardo*, 2, and *Raphael* (Eng. Trans.). Symonds' *Michelangelo*, 2. Crowe and Cavalcaselle's *Titian*, 2. Solerti's *Tasso*, 3. Dejob's *Muret.* Waters' *Cardan.* Fiorentino's *Telesio*, 2. Berni's *Bruno.* Campbell's *Sarpi.*

Vernon Lee's *Italy in the Eighteenth Century.* Flint's *Vico.* .Justi's *Winckelmann*, vol. 2. Vernon Lee's *Countess of Albany.* Ferri's *Philosophie en Italie*, 2. Espinas' *Philosophie experimentale en Italie.* De Sanctis' *Leopardi.* Reumont's *Gino Capponi.* Massari's *Gioberti*, 2. Lockhart's *Rosmini*, 2. Hillebrand's *Italia*, 4.

Switzerland.

Politics.

Dändliker's *History of Switzerland.* Adams and Cunningham's *Swiss Confederation.* Roget's *Genève* (1476—1602), 9, and *Genève au temps de Calvin.* Lowell's *Governments and Parties*, vol. 2. Deploige's *The Referendum.*

Culture.

General. Secrétan's *Galerie Suisse*, 3. Rossel's *Histoire Littéraire de la Suisse romande*, 2. Gelpke's *Kirchengesch. d. Schweiz*, 2.

Periods. Stähelin's *Zwingli*, 2, and *Calvin*, 3. Pestalozzi's *Bullinger.* Buisson's *Castellion*, 2. Baum's *Beza*, 2. Mörikofer's *Evangelische Flüchtlinge*, and *Schweizerische Litteratur d. 18ten Jahrhunderts.* Maury's *Réveil religieux*, 1810—50, 2. Rambert's *Vinet.* Dawson's *Social Switzerland.*

Holland and Belgium.

Politics.

General. Pirenne's *Bibliographie de l'histoire de Belgique. Biographie Nationale de Belgique.* Wenzelburger's *Niederlande*, 2 (to 1648). Blok's *Dutch People.* Juste's *Belgique*, 3, and *États-Généraux des Pays-Bas*, 1465—1790, 2. Gachard's *Études sur les Pays-Bas*, 3.

Periods. Henne's *Charles Quint en Belgique*, 10. Rackfahl's *Margaret von Parma.* Putnam's *William the Silent*, 2. Harrison's *William the Silent.* Juste's *St Aldegonde.* Maxwell's *Don John*, vol. 2. Lettenhove's *Huguenots et les Gueux*, 6. Motley's *Dutch Republic*, 3; *United Netherlands*, 4; *Barneveldt*, 2. Lefévre-Pontalis' *John de Witt*, 2. Geddes' *De Witt*, vol. 1. Gachard's *Belgique au 18ème siècle.* Laborie's *Dominion française en Belgique*, 2. Gerlache's *Royaume d. Pays-Bas*, 1814—30, 3. Balan's *Belgique*, 1815—84. Juste's *Léopold I et II*, and *Fondateurs de la Monarchie Belge*, 22. Discaille's *Rogier*, 4. Destrées et Vandevelde's *Socialisme en Belgique.*

Culture.

General. Hellwald's *Niederländische Litteratur.* Pringsheim's *Wirthschaftliche Entwickelung d. Nied.* Müller's *Classische Philologie in d. Nied.* Heppe's *Pietismus in d. Nied.* Nippold's *Katholische Kirche in d. Nied.*

Periods. Altmeyer's *Précurseurs de la Réforme*, 2. Cano's *F. Junius.* Bernays' *Scaliger.* Neale's *Jansenist Church of Holland.* Hatin's *Gazettes de Hollande. Cinquante Ans de Liberté*, 1830—80, 4. Hamelius' *Le Mouvement Flamand.*

Denmark, Norway, Sweden.

General. Otté's *Scandinavian History*; *Denmark*; and *Iceland.* Boyesen's *Norway.* Dahlmann und Schäfer's *Dänemark*, 3—4. Geffroy's *États Scandinaves.* Geiger und Carlson's *Schweden*, 6 (to 1706). Maurer's *Island.* Schybergson's *Finland.*

Periods. Watson's *Gustavus Vasa.* Theiner's *Schweden's Stellung z. Heiligen Stuhl.* Fletcher's *Gustavus Adolphus.* Droysen's *Gustav Adolf*, 2. Bain's *Christina.* Bain's *Charles XII.* Wittich's *Struensee.* Bain's *Gustavus III*, 2. Schmidt's *Charles XIV.* Butler's *Reformation in Sweden.* Schweitzer's *Skandinavische Litteratur*, 3. Gosse's *Northern Studies.* Brandes' *Holberg*; *Kierkegaard*; *Menschen u. Werke*, and *Moderne Geister.* Weitermayer's *Denmark.*

Russia.

Politics.

General. Morfill's *Russia.* Rambaud's *Russia*, 2. Brückner u. Herrmann's *Russischer Staat*, 2—7 (to 1797). Kostomarof's *Russ. Gesch. in Biographien*, 2. Kleinschmidt's *G. d. Russischen Hohen Adels*, and *Russland*, 1598—1898. Richter's *Ostseeprovinzen*, 5. Schybergson's *Finland.* Krausse's *Russia in Asia*, 1558—1899. Howorth's *Mongols*, 2—3.

Periods. Schiemann's *Russland, Poland u. Livland bis ins* 17*te Jahrhundert.* Brückner's *Peter d. Grosse*, and *Europäisierung Russlands.* Waliszewski's *Peter the Great.* Bain's *Daughter of Peter the Great*, and *Pupils of Peter the Great.* Pingaud's *Les Français en Russie.* Blum's *Sievers.* Brückner's *Caterina II.* Bilbassoff's *Caterina II*, 2. Waliszewski's *Catherine II*, 2. Czartoryski's *Memoirs*, 2. Vandal's *Napoléon et Alexandre III*, 3. Bernhardi's *Russland*, 1815—30, 3. Pypin's *Russische Gesellschaft unter Alexander I.* Kinglake's *Crimean War*, 9. Schmeidler's *Alexander II.* Leroy-Beaulieu's *Milutin.* Liwof's *Katkof.* Kropotkin's *Memoirs*, 2. Eckardt's *Modern Russia.* Novikoff's *Skobeleff and the Slavonic Cause.* Lowe's *Alexander III.* Stepniak's *Russian Peasantry*, 2. Thompson's *Russian Politics.* Leroy-Beaulieu's *Empire of the Tsars*, 3.

Culture.

General. Walisewski's *Russian Lit.* Boissard's *L'Église de Russie*, 2. Dalton's *Evangelische Kirche in Russland*, 2. Stanley's *Eastern Church.* Leger's *Études Slaves*, 6.

Periods. Pierling's *La Russie et le Saint Siège.* Brückner's *Possoschkow.* Lescœur's *L'Église Catholique en Pologne et en Russie.* Ford's *Mme de Krudener.* De Vogüé's *Roman Russe.* Brandes' *Impressions of Russia.* Errera's *Jews in Russia.* Leroy-Beaulieu's *Empire of the Tsars,* vol. 3. Perris' *Tolstoi.*

Poland.

Politics.

General. Morfill's *Poland.* Schiemann's *Russland, Polen u. Livland bis ins 17te Jahrhundert,* 2.

Periods. Caro's *Polen,* vol. 5. Waliszewski's *Marysienka* (Trans.). Smitt's *Suvoroff u. Polens Untergang,* 2. Czartoryski's *Memoirs,* 2.

Culture.

Nitschmann's *Pölnische Litteratur.* Fischer's *Reformation in Poland,* 2. Dalton's *John a Lasco.* Eichhorn's *Hosius,* 2. Lescœur's *L'Église Catholique en Pologne,* 1772—1875, 2. Theiner's *L'Église Catholique en Pologne et en Russie.* Von der Brüggen's *Polen's Auflösung.* Brandes' *Polen.*

The Balkan States.

Miller's *The Balkans.* Laveleye's *Balkan Peninsula.* Dicey's *Bulgaria.* Beaman's *Stambuloff. Memoirs of Charles of Roumania.* Samuelson's *Roumania.* Gubernatis' *La Serbie.* Bérard's *La Macédoine,* and *L'Hellénisme Contemporain.*

Greece.

Finlay's *Greece,* 5—7. Mendelssohn's *Griechenland seit* 1453, 2. Laborde's *Athènes,* 2. Sergeaunt's *Greece in the* 19*th Century.* Gidel's *Litt. Grecque Moderne,* 2.

The Ottoman Empire.

Poole's *Turkey.* Zinkeisen's *Osmanisches Reich,* 2—7 (to 1812). Finlay's *Byzantine Empire,* 5—7. Posen's *Turkei,* 1826—56, 2. Poole's *Stratford Canning,* 2. Kinglake's *Crimea,* 9. Argyll's *Eastern Question,* 2. Bryce's *Transcaucasia.* Bérard's *La Politique du Sultan.* Davey's *Sultan and his Subjects,* 2.

North America.

Politics.

General. Channing and Hart's *Guide to American History.* Appleton's *American Biography.* Channing's *Student's History of U. S.* Winsor's *History of America,* 7. *American Commonwealths,* ed. Scudder. Bancroft's *Pacific States* (Works, vols. 15—35).

Periods. Winsor's *Columbus.* Palfrey's *New England to* 1760, 4. Fiske's *Virginia,* 2. Bence's *Economic History of Virginia in 17th Century,* 2. Maclay's *American Navy,* 2. Parton's *Franklin,* 3. *American Statesmen* (Franklin, Samuel Adams, Henry, Washington, John Adams, Hamilton, Morris, Jay, Marshall, Jefferson, Madison, Gallatin, Monroe, Quincy Adams, Randolph, Jackson, Van Buren, Clay, Webster, Calhoun, Benton, Cass, Lincoln, Seward, C. F. Adams, Stevens, Chase, Sumner). Winsor's *Handbook of the American Revolution.* Bancroft's *The Constitution,* 2. Story's *Commentaries,* ed. Cooley, 2. Holst's *Constitutional History,* 1750—1854, 5. Taussig's *The Tariff,* 1789—1888. Fiske's *Critical Period of American History.* Conway's *Tom Paine,* 2. Randall's *Jefferson,* 3. Flanders' *Chief Justices,* 2. Stanwood's *The Presidency.* Rives' *Madison,* 3. J. Q. Adams' *Diary,* 12. Reddaway's *Monroe Doctrine.* Benton's *Thirty Years View of Congress,* 1820—50, 3. Parton's *Jackson,* 3. Curtis' *Webster,* 2. Rhodes' *United States of America from* 1850, 4. Nicolay and Hay's *Lincoln,* 10. Morse's *Lincoln,* 2. Greely's *American Conflict,* 2. Stephens' *War between the States,* 2. Jefferson Davis' *Confederate Government,* 2. Pierce's *Sumner,* 4. Seward's *Memoirs.* Blaine's *Twenty Years in Congress,* 2. Sherman's *Recollections,* 2. Bigelow's *Tilden,* 2. Whittle's *Cleveland.* Maguire's *Irish in America.* Bryce's *American Commonwealth,* 2.

Culture.

General. *American Men of Letters Series.* Tyler's *American Literature,* 4. Wendell's *American Literature. American Church History Series.*

Periods. Baird's *Huguenot Emigration,* 3. Dexter's *Congregationalism,* and *As to Roger Williams.* Channing's *Channing,* 3. Swift's *Brook Farm.* Frothingham's *Theodore Parker,* and *Transcendentalism.* Adams' *Dana,* 2. Cabot's *Emerson,* 2. Holmes' *Motley.* Abbott's *Ward Beecher.* Nordhoff's *Communistic Societies.* Weeden's *Economic and Social History of New England.* Allen's *Phillips Brooks,* 2.

Central and South America.

Bancroft's *Central America,* 2, and *Mexico,* 6 (abridged, 1). Deberle's *Amérique du Sud.* Watson's *Spanish and Portuguese America,* 2. Levasseur's *Le Brésil.* Markham's *Peru.* Gothein's *Jesuitenstaat in Paraguay.* Coudreau's *La France Équinoxiale.* Child's *Spanish-American Republics.*

Asia.

Persia, China, Japan, etc.

Howorth's *Mongols,* 2—3. Curzon's *Persia,* 2. Markham's *Persia.* Curzon's *Russia in Central Asia.* Skrine and Ross' *Heart of Asia.* The Ameer's *Autobiography,* 2. Smyth's *Siam,* 2. Egerton's *Raffles.* St John's *Rajah Brooke.*

Murray's *Japan*. Douglas' *China*. Poole's *Parkes*, 2. Michie's *Alcock*, 2. Colquhoun's *China in Transformation*. Curzon's *Problems of the Far East*. Norman's *The Far East*. Krausse's *Russia in Asia*, 1558—1899. Krahmer's *Russland in Asien*, 4. Rambaud's *La France Coloniale*.

India.

Hunter's *The Indian Empire*, and *Imperial Gazetteer*, 14. *Rulers of India Series*, ed. Hunter. Whiteway's *Portuguese Power in India*. Hunter's *British India*, 2 (to 1708). Lyall's *Rise of British Dominion*. Frazer's *British India*. Malleson's *French in India*, 2. Hunter's *Indian Mussulmans*. Trotter's *India under Victoria*, 2. Kaye and Malleson's *The Mutiny*, 6. Hunter's *Mayo*, 2. B. Smith's *Lawrence*, 2. Roberts' *Forty-one Years in India*. Cotton's *India* (English Citizen Series). Ilbert's *Government of India*. Lee Warner's *Protected Princes*. Dutt's *Indian Famines*. Blunt's *Ideas about India*. Morison's *Imperial Rule in India*. Samuelson's *India Past and Present* (with bibliography by Hunter). Nash's *The Great Famine*. Warburton's 18 *Years in the Khyber*.

Culture.

Ferguson's *Indian Architecture*. Frazer's *Literary History of India*. Aston's *Japanese Literature*. Barth's *Religions of India*. Gobineau's *Religions de l'Asie Centrale*. Edkin's *Chinese Buddhism*. Famin's *Protectorat des Églises Chrétiennes*. Mestral's *Tableau de l'Église Chrétienne*. Venn's *Xavier*. Lyall's *Asiatic Studies*, 2. Max Müller's *Chips*, vol. 3, and *My Indian Friends*. D'Alviella's *Contemporary Religious Thought*. Blunt's *Future of Islam*.

Africa (*and see Africa, under English Colonies*).

General. Johnston's *Colonisation of Africa*. Keltie's *Partition of Africa*.

Egypt. Traill's *England, Egypt and the Sudan*. Milner's *England in Egypt*. Butler's *Gordon*. Wingate's *Mahdism and the Egyptian Sudan*.

North Africa. Rambaud's *La France Coloniale*. Poole's *Barbary Corsairs*. Meakin's *Moorish Empire*.

South Africa. Theal's *Portuguese in Africa*, and *South Africa*, 5.

APPENDIX B.

TABLES.

Kings and Queens of England.

1485	Henry VII.
1509	Henry VIII.
1547	Edward VI.
1553	Mary.
1558	Elizabeth.
1603	James I.
1625	Charles I.
1649	Interregnum.
1660	Charles II.
1685	James II.
1689	William and Mary
(1694	William III.)
1702	Anne.
1714	George I.
1727	George II.
1760	George III.
1820	George IV.
1830	William IV.
1837	Victoria.

Prime Ministers since Walpole.

1721	Walpole.
1742	Wilmington.
1743	Henry Pelham.
1754	Newcastle.
1756	Devonshire.
1757	Newcastle.
1762	Bute.
1763	Grenville.
1765	Rockingham.
1766	Chatham.
1767	Grafton.
1770	North.
1782	Rockingham.
	Shelburne
1783	Portland.
	Pitt.
1801	Addington.
1804	Pitt.
1806	Grenville.
1807	Portland.
1809	Perceval.
1812	Liverpool.
1827	Canning.
	Goderich.
1828	Wellington.
1830	Grey.
1834	Melbourne.
	Peel.
1835	Melbourne.
1841	Peel.
1846	Russell.
1852	Derby.
	Aberdeen.
1855	Palmerston.
1858	Derby.
1859	Palmerston.
1865	Russell.
1866	Derby.
1868	Disraeli.
	Gladstone.
1874	Disraeli.
1880	Gladstone.
1885	Salisbury.
1886	Gladstone.
	Salisbury.
1892	Gladstone.
1894	Rosebery.
1895	Salisbury.

Archbishops of Canterbury.

1486 Morton.
1501 Deane.
1503 Warham.
1533 Cranmer.
1556 Pole.
1559 Parker.
1576 Grindal.
1583 Whitgift.
1604 Bancroft.
1611 Abbot.
1633 Laud.
1660 Juxon.
1663 Sheldon.
1677 Sandcroft.
1691 Tillotson.
1695 Tenison.
1715 Wake.
1737 Potter.
1747 Herring.
1757 Hutton.
1758 Secker.
1768 Cornwallis.
1783 Moore.
1805 Manners Sutton.
1828 Howley.
1848 Sumner.
1862 Longley.
1868 Tait.
1882 Benson.
1896 Temple.

Kings of France.

The Valois Line.

1483 Charles VIII.
1498 Louis XII.
1515 Francis I.
1547 Henry II.
1559 Francis II.
1560 Charles IX.
1574 Henry III.

(Accession of *The Bourbon Line.*)

1589 Henry IV.
1610 Louis XIII.
1643 Louis XIV.
1715 Louis XV.
1774 Louis XVI.

The Republic, 1792–1799.

1792 The Convention.
1795 The Directory.

The Consulate, 1799–1804.

The First Empire.

1804 Napoleon I.

The Restoration, 1814–1848.

1814 Louis XVIII.
1824 Charles X.
1830 Louis Philippe.

The Republic of 1848.

The Second Empire.

1852 Napoleon III.

The Republic of 1870.

Presidents.

1871 Thiers.
1873 Macmahon.
1879 Grévy.
1887 Carnot.
1894 Casimir-Périer.
1895 Faure.
1899 Loubet.

Kings of Spain.

1479 Ferdinand and Isabella.
1504 Ferdinand, King of Spain.
1516 Charles I.
1556 Philip II.
1598 Philip III.
1621 Philip IV.
1665 Charles II.
1700 Philip V.
1746 Ferdinand VI.
1759 Charles III.
1788 Charles IV.
1808 Ferdinand VII.
Joseph Bonaparte
1813 Ferdinand VII.
1833 Isabella II.
1870 Amadeo I.
1873 Republic.
1874 Alfonso XII.
1885 Maria.
1886 Alfonso XIII.

Kings of Portugal.

1481 John II.
1495 Emmanuel.
1521 John III.
1557 Sebastian.
1578 Henry.
1580 Antony.
United to Spain, 1580–1640.
1640 John IV.
1656 Alfonso VI.
1683 Peter II.
1706 John V.
1750 Joseph Emmanuel.
1777 Maria I., Peter III. } jointly.
1786 Maria, alone.
1816 John.
1826 Maria II.
Dom Miguel, usurper, 1828–33
1853 Peter V.
1861 Luis I.
1889 Don Carlos.

The House of Savoy.

1482 Philibert II.
1504 Charles III.
1553 Emanuel Philibert.
1580 Charles Emanuel.
1630 Victor Amadeus I.
1637 Francis.
1638 Charles Emanuel II.
1675 Victor Amadeus II. (Receives title of King of Sicily, 1713; changed to Victor Amadeus I., King of Sardinia, 1720.)
1730 Charles Emanuel I.
1773 Victor Amadeus II.
1796 Charles Emanuel II.
1802 Victor Emanuel I.
1821 Charles Felix.
1831 Charles Albert.
1849 Victor Emanuel II.
1878 Humbert.
1900 Victor Emanuel III.

The Popes.

1492	Alexander VI. (Borgia).	1644	Innocent X. (Pamfili).
1503	Pius III. (Piccolomini).	1655	Alexander VII. (Chigi).
	Julius II. (Rovere).	1667	Clement IX. (Rospigliosi).
1513	Leo X. (Medici).	1670	Clement X. (Altieri).
1522	Adrian VI. (Boyers).	1676	Innocent XI. (Odescalchi).
1523	Clement VII. (Medici).	1689	Alexander VIII. (Ottoboni).
1534	Paul III. (Farnese).	1691	Innocent XII. (Pignatelli).
1550	Julius III. (Monte).	1700	Clement XI. (Albani).
1555	Marcellus II. (Cervini).	1721	Innocent XIII. (Conti).
	Paul IV. (Caraffa).	1724	Benedict XIII. (Orsini).
1559	Pius IV. (Medici).	1730	Clement XII. (Corsini).
1565	Pius V. (Ghislieri).	1740	Benedict XIV. (Lambertini).
1572	Gregory XIII. (Buoncompagni).	1758	Clement XIII. (Rezzonico).
1585	Sixtus V. (Peretti).	1769	Clement XIV. (Ganganelli).
1590	Urban VII. (Castagna).	1775	Pius VI. (Braschi).
	Gregory XIV. (Sfondrati).	1800	Pius VII. (Chiaramonti).
1591	Innocent IX. (Facchinetti).	1823	Leo XII. (Della Genga).
1592	Clement VIII. (Aldobrandini).	1829	Pius VIII. (Castiglioni).
1605	Leo XI. (Medici).	1831	Gregory XVI. (Capellari).
	Paul V. (Borghese).	1846	Pius IX. (Mastai-Ferretti).
1621	Gregory XV. (Ludovisi).		(End of the Temporal Power, 1870).
1623	Urban VIII. (Barberini).	1878	Leo XIII. (Pecci).

Grand Dukes of Tuscany.

1537 Cosmo de Medici. (Receives the Granducal title, 1569.)
1574 Francis.
1587 Ferdinand I.
1609 Cosmo II.
1621 Ferdinand II.
1670 Cosmo III.
1724 Giovanni Gastone.

(Accession of the Hapsburg-Lorraine line.)
1737 Francis.
1765 Leopold I.
1790 Ferdinand III.
1825 Leopold II.
1859–60 Ferdinand IV.
(Annexed to the Kingdom of Italy.)

The Bourbon Rulers of Naples and Sicily.

1735 Don Carlos (later Charles III. of Spain).
1759 Ferdinand IV. (Receives the royal title as Ferdinand I., 1815.)
1825 Francis I.
1830 Ferdinand II.
1859–60 Francis II.
(Annexed to the Kingdom of Italy.)

The Hapsburg Emperors.

1440 Frederick III.
1493 Maximilian I.
1520 Charles V.
1556 Ferdinand I.
1564 Maximilian II.
1576 Rudolf II.
1612 Matthias.
1619 Ferdinand II.
1637 Ferdinand III.
1658 Leopold I.
1705 Joseph I.
1711 Charles VI.
(Maria Theresa, 1740–80.)
1742 Charles VII. of Bavaria.
1745 Francis I.
1765 Joseph II.
1790 Leopold II.
1792 Francis II. (Francis assumes the title of *Emperor of Austria.*)
1806 Francis I.
1835 Ferdinand I.
1848 Francis Joseph.

Kings of Prussia.

1640 Frederick William, the Great Elector.
1688 Frederick I. (receives the royal title, 1701).
1713 Frederick William I.
1740 Frederick II. the Great.
1786 Frederick William II.
1797 Frederick William III.
1840 Frederick William IV.
1861 William I. (Emperor, 1871).
1888 Frederick III.
William II.

Kings of Bavaria.

1799 Maximilian I. (receives the royal title, 1805).
1825 Ludwig I.
1848 Maximilian II.
1864 Ludwig II.
1886 Otho.
(The Regent Leopold).

Kings of Saxony.

1763 Frederick Augustus I. (receives the royal title, 1806).
1827 Anthony.
1836 Frederick Augustus II.
1854 John.
1873 Albert.

Kings of Würtemberg.

1806 Frederick I.
1816 William I.
1864 Charles I.
1891 William II.

Electors and Kings of Hanover.

1679 Ernest Augustus (receives the Electoral title, 1692).
1698 George I.
1727 George II.
1760 George III. (receives the royal title, 1814).
1820 George IV.
1830 William IV.
1837 Ernest.
1851–66 George V.
(Annexed to Prussia).

Stadtholders and Kings of Holland.

1587 Maurice.
1625 Frederick Henry.
1647 William II.
1650 William III.
1702 William IV.
1751 William V.
1795 Batavian Republic.
1806 Louis Bonaparte.
1810 Annexed to France.
1814 William I. (receives the royal title).
1840 William II.
1849 William III.
1890 Wilhelmina.

Kings of Belgium.

1831 Leopold I.
1865 Leopold II.

Kings of Denmark.

1481 John.
1513 Christian II.
(Sweden becomes independent).
1523 Frederick I.
1533 Christian III.
1559 Frederick II.
1588 Christian IV.
1648 Frederick III.
1670 Christian V.
1699 Frederick IV.
1730 Christian VI.
1746 Frederick V.
1766 Christian VII.
1784 Frederick VI. (Regent).
(Norway is joined to Sweden, 1814.)
1839 Christian VIII.
1848 Frederick VII.
1863 Christian IX.

Kings of Sweden.

1483 John II.
1503 Protectors.
1520 Christian II.
1523 Gustavus I., Vasa.
1560 Eric XIV.
1569 John III.
1592 Sigismund III.
1604 Charles IX.
1611 Gustavus Adolphus.
1632 Christina.
1654 Charles X.
1660 Charles XI.
1697 Charles XII.
{1718 Ulrica Eleanora.
{1720 Frederick I.
1751 Adolphus Frederick.
1771 Gustavus III.
1792 Gustavus IV.
1809 Charles XIII.
1818 Charles XIV.
1844 Oscar I.
1859 Charles XV.
1872 Oscar II.

Kings of Poland.

1492 John Albert.
1501 Alexander.
1506 Sigismund I.
1548 Sigismund II.
(End of Jagellon Dynasty.)
1573 Henry of Valois.
1575 Stephen Bathori.
1587 Sigismund III.
1632 Wladislaus VII.
1648 John Casimir V.
1669 Michael.
1674 John Sobieski.
1697 Frederick Augustus I. Elector of Saxony.
(1704–9 Stanislaus Leszczynski.)
1734 Frederick Augustus II.
1764–95 Stanislas Poniatowski.
(Final partition of Poland).

Tsars of Russia.

1462 Ivan III.
1505 Basil.
1533 Ivan the Terrible.
1584 Feodor.
1598 Boris Godounoff.
1605 Interregnum.
(Accession of House of Romanov.)
1613 Michael Romanov.
1645 Alexis.
1676 Feodor Alexiévitch.
1682 Peter the Great.
1725 Catharine I.
1727 Peter II.
1730 Anna.
1740 Ivan VI. (dep.).
1741 Elizabeth.
1762 Peter III.
Catharine II.
1796 Paul.
1801 Alexander I.
1825 Nicholas I.
1855 Alexander II.
1881 Alexander III.
1894 Nicholas II.

Princes and Kings of the Balkan States.

Roumania (Wallachia and Moldavia united, 1861; independent, 1878).
1861 Alexander Couza.
1866 Charles of Hohenzollern-Sigmaringen (receives the royal title, 1881).

Servia (Independent, 1878).
1868 Milan (receives the royal title, 1881).
1889 Alexander.

Bulgaria (Independent, 1878).
1879 Alexander of Battenberg.
1887 Ferdinand of Coburg.

Montenegro (Independent, 1878).
1860 Nicholas.

Greece (Independent, 1829).
1832 Otho of Bavaria.
1863 George of Denmark.

Sultans of Turkey.

1481	Bajazet II.	1695	Mustapha II.
1512	Selim I.	1703	Achmet III.
1520	Solyman I.	1730	Mahmoud I.
1566	Selim II.	1754	Othman III.
1574	Amurath III.	1757	Mustapha III.
1595	Mohammed III.	1774	Abdul Hamid I.
1603	Achmet I.	1789	Selim III.
1617	Mustapha I.	1807	Mustapha IV.
1618	Othman II.	1808	Mahmoud II.
1623	Amurath IV.	1839	Abdul Mejid.
1640	Ibrahim.	1861	Abdul Aziz.
1649	Mohammed IV.	1876	Amurath V.
1687	Solyman II.		Abdul Hamid II.
1691	Achmet II.		

Pashas and Khedives of Egypt.

1805	Mehemet Ali.	1863	Ismail (receives Khedivial title, 1866).
1848	Abbas.	1879	Tewfik.
1854	Said.	1892	Abbas.

High Commissioners of South Africa.

1854	Grey.	1881	Robinson.
1861	Wodehouse.	1889	Loch.
1870	Barkly.	1895	Robinson.
1877	Bartle Frere.	1897	Milner.

Governors-General of Canada.

1867	Monck.	1888	Stanley.
1872	Dufferin.	1893	Aberdeen.
1878	Lorne.	1898	Minto.
1884	Lansdowne.		

Presidents of the United States.

1789 Washington.
1797 John Adams.
1801 Jefferson.
1809 Madison.
1817 Monroe.
1825 J. Q. Adams.
1829 Jackson.
1837 Van Buren.
1841 Harison.
(Tyler, 1841.)
1845 Polk.
1849 Taylor.
(Fillmore, 1850.)
1853 Pierce.
1857 Buchanan.
1861 Lincoln.
(Johnson, 1865).
1869 Grant.
1877 Hayes.
1881 Garfield.
(Arthur, 1881).
1885 Cleveland.
1889 Harrison.
1893 Cleveland.
1897 Mackinley.

India.

Moghul Emperors (to Aurungzebe).

1526 Baber.
1530 Hamaiun.
1556 Akbar.
1605 Jehangir.
1627 Jehan.
1658–1707 Aurungzebe.

Governors-General and Viceroys.

Governors-General.

1774 Warren Hastings.
1785 Cornwallis.
1793 Shore.
1798 Wellesley.
1805 Cornwallis.
1807 Minto.
1813 Hastings.
1823 Amherst.
1828 Bentinck.
1836 Auckland.
1842 Ellenborough.
1844 Hardinge.
1848 Dalhousie.
1856 Canning.

Viceroys.

1858 Canning.
1862 Elgin.
1864 Lawrence.
1869 Mayo.
1872 Northbrook.
1876 Lytton.
1880 Ripon.
1884 Dufferin.
1888 Lansdowne.
1893 Elgin.
1898 Curzon.

INDEX.

Note. The numbers in the Index denote the paragraph, not the page,—the upright figures referring to 'Politics,' the slanting figures to 'Culture.' In the case of a King or Minister who is repeatedly mentioned, the years over which his activity extends are given for the sake of brevity, the figures being connected by a hyphen, and printed in blacker type.

Nearly half the names mentioned in the text will be found in the Index. Where a man is known in history by more than one title, the most familiar is given, as Bolingbroke instead of St John, and Buckingham instead of Villiers. Pseudonyms are retained in the case of such writers as George Eliot (Marian Evans) and Georges Sand (Mme Dudevant).

The political history of the chief countries of Europe is not indexed, since it can be readily traced by turning over the pages of the text; but under Germany, Italy, Austria, Turkey, are given the chief Provinces or States of which they have been composed. The less important countries and subjects are indexed in full; the more important only till the time at which the entries become so frequent that no further clue is needed. Thus, Ireland is indexed till the Union, British India till the French War, Prussia till Frederick the Great, Russia till Peter the Great, Egypt till the Dual Control, Economics till Adam Smith, Politics till Hobbes, History till Ranke, English, French and German Literature till Spenser, Corneille, Lessing respectively. In certain cases, selected departments of a subject or of national history are given, as in Philosophy, English, French and German Church History, the United States, etc.

The Countries and States in Asia, Africa, America, Australasia are indexed under their respective Continents; the Sciences under Science; the Arts under Art.

D

E

G

N

S